W9-BZK-334

THE STATISTICAL IMAGINATION

Elementary Statistics
for the Social Sciences

SECOND EDITION

Ferris J. Ritchey
Department of Sociology
University of Alabama at Birmingham

Boston   Burr Ridge, IL   Dubuque, IA   New York
San Francisco   St. Louis   Bangkok   Bogotá   Caracas   Kuala Lumpur
Lisbon   London   Madrid   Mexico City   Milan   Montreal   New Delhi
Santiago   Seoul   Singapore   Sydney   Taipei   Toronto

*To Wanda, Daniel, Holly, Alan, Sarah, Kitty, Dorrance, and Agnes
for their love and encouragement.*

To Daniel O. Price and P. Neal Ritchey for their generous assistance.

In loving memory of Phillip Ritchey.

The **McGraw·Hill** Companies

Published by McGraw-Hill, an imprint of The McGraw-Hill Companies, Inc., 1221 Avenue of the Americas, New York, NY 10020. Copyright © 2008 by the McGraw-Hill Companies, Inc. All rights reserved. No part of this publication may be reproduced or distributed in any form or by any means, or stored in a database or retrieval system, without the prior written consent of The McGraw-Hill Companies, Inc., including, but not limited to, in any network or other electronic storage or transmission, or broadcast for distance learning.

This book is printed on acid-free paper.

3 4 5 6 7 8 9 0 QPF/QPF 0 9

ISBN: 978-0-07-294304-7
MHID: 0-07-294304-1

Editor in Chief: Emily Barrosse
Publisher: Frank Mortimer
Sponsoring Editor: Gina Boedeker
Senior Marketing Manager: Lori DeShazo
Development Editor: Robin Reed, Carlisle Publishing Services
Project Manager: Valerie Heffernan, Carlisle Publishing Services
Manuscript Editor: Susan M. Dolter
Designer: Marianna Kinigakis
Senior Production Supervisor: Rich DeVitto
Media Producer: Christie Ling

This book was set in 10/12 Times Roman by Carlisle Publishing Services and printed on 45# New Era Matte Plus by Quebecor World

Library of Congress Cataloging-in-Publication Data

Ritchey, Ferris Joseph.
    The statistical imagination : elementary statistics for the social sciences / Ferris J. Ritchey.—2nd ed.
      p. cm.
    Includes bibliographical references and index.
    ISBN 0-07-294304-1
     1. Social sciences—Statistical methods. 2. Statistics. I. Title.

HA29.R666 2006
519.5—dc22   2006046710

www.mhhe.com

BRIEF CONTENTS

CONTENTS

PREFACE

We all use statistical thinking—the calculation of likelihoods or probabilities—as we go about our daily lives. The simple decision about whether to carry an umbrella involves estimating the likelihood of rain. Probabilities come into play when one makes important life decisions such as whether to marry, take a job, invest in a stock, or change lanes in traffic. Even a moderate amount of statistical expertise in the workplace provides an employee with a competitive advantage. For students in scientific fields, statistical thinking is an essential ingredient for a clear understanding of the natural world, the social order, and human behavior. On a lighter note, statistical thinking underlies games of chance; just as gaming and gambling are fun, statistics is fun.

Unfortunately, students do not always appreciate how much fun a statistics course can be. Social science majors typically have a limited background in mathematics and resent being forced to take this required course. Some statistics texts disregard this fact by presenting complex formulas and thus cause unnecessary math anxiety. Other texts are "dumbed down" to reduce math anxiety, but usually by sacrificing basic statistical principles. This text attempts to teach the difficult concepts of statistics without sacrificing essential mathematics and calculations. However, it is designed to convince students that mathematics is only a tool for—not the essence of—learning statistics.

I learned that statistics can be taught thoroughly without overemphasizing mathematics when I had the great fortune of working as a graduate student assistant with Daniel O. Price, to whom this text is dedicated. His enthusiasm for the subject, along with his clear explanations of logical processes, caused me to fall in love with the subject matter. Like Dan, I have strived in over 25 years of teaching statistics to develop techniques to share this enthusiasm with students. In particular, I have targeted several conceptual hurdles with the idea of easing students past them. The course design of this text follows four basic principles:

- Statistics is not about mathematics. Instead, it is a learned way of thinking about things.
- Early assignments should be designed to build students' confidence.
- Mastery of the basic elements of statistical reasoning facilitates mastery of the more complex elements; therefore, the learning process is a cumulative one.
- Statistics is learned by doing. There will be many assignments, but the subject matter is inherently interesting and enjoyable. Have fun and have confidence that the work will pay off.

Let me describe these principles in a little more detail. The first is that statistics is not about mathematics per se but about proportional thinking: the visualization of a part to a whole. This view on reality I call *the statistical imagination*. This concept parallels C. Wright Mills's idea of the sociological imagination, which defines the relationship of the individual to the larger society. Similarly, the statistical imagination calls for viewing data in a number of larger contexts. First, observations of individual behavior are viewed within the context of the larger social structure. Second, conclusions about a large population of subjects based on a sample of those subjects are viewed as only one of many sets of conclusions, because a second sample will produce slightly different results. Third, interpretations of statistical data must take into account practical circumstances and cultural realities that provide the essential meaning of the numbers.

The second principle of this text is that the course design should allow students to succeed early on in building confidence and allaying fear of failure. Thus, in the very first pages of the text simple but essential statistical calculations of fractions, proportions, and percentages are introduced. These calculations are presented as ways to quantify proportional thinking, reinforcing the idea that mathematics is only a tool for—not the essence of—learning statistics. Moreover, statistical abstractions that appear as hurdles to many students (for example, the standard deviation, standardized scores, sampling error, and sampling distributions) are given plenty of attention. The importance of diligence in statistical work is emphasized to encourage students to develop a sense of competence.

The third principle is that for students to grasp the logic of inferential statistics and hypothesis testing successfully, the basic elements of the testing procedure must be well mastered. Part of this objective is achieved through text design. Lots of coverage is given to working with areas under a bell-shaped graphical curve called the normal distribution curve. Considerable time is allowed for actually producing sampling distributions: descriptions of the outcomes that occur when, say, 10 coins are repeatedly tossed or samples of beans are repeatedly drawn from a boxful. Through actual repeated sampling, students learn that the statistics of any single sample are only one set of many possible estimates for the larger group from which the sample came. This hands-on approach will demystify this concept, which is at the core of statistical reasoning. Students learn that sampling distributions are real, not abstract, conjectures. The text also presents the logic of hypothesis testing in six steps, one of which requires drawing sampling distribution curves. This attention to detail fosters proportional thinking. The other part of the objective of mastering basic ideas is that students must apply themselves and keep up with course material and assignments.

The fourth principle is related to the previous ones: Statistics is learned by doing. Each chapter has pencil-and-paper questions and exercises that encourage the proportional thinking that underlies statistical analysis. For classes using computers, *The Statistical Imagination* provides *SPSS for Windows* software. The text Web site provides chapter exercises, detailed illustrations on interpreting output, and a variety of data sets chosen to stimulate interest as well as expose students to real-world research.

TO THE INSTRUCTOR

This course is designed to cover basic elements of hypothesis testing in such a way that when inferential statistics are approached (Chapters 9 and beyond), the abstract concepts are easily achievable. The Instructor's Manual, Test Bank, and Solutions Manual (available on the Web site), provide details of the pointers listed below, along with lecture ideas, sample problems to present in class, multiple forms of assignments, quizzes, exams, and grading keys. Chapter exercises come in four sets.

While most instructors have developed their own effective techniques, I have found that the following pedagogical regimen maximizes students' success. This regimen has been class tested over 25 times, and it is based on the idea that assignments and quizzes are rehearsals for major exams. In my experience, major exams should be given "closed-book" (except for formulas and statistical tables). Open-book exams foster poor study habits. I alleviate the pressures of a closed-book exam, however, by providing students with ample opportunity to learn from mistakes on assignments.

- Require weekly assignments that are due on the class day after the completion of a lecture on a chapter's material.

- Return graded assignments at the next class and make assignment keys (from the Solutions Manual) available on reserve or on a Plexiglas-covered bulletin board. Since keys are to be made available, grading of assignments does not require extensive "red marking." (I have found that the availability of assignment keys does not compromise the next term's work. Moreover, exercises come in four sets for alternating terms.)

- At the next class or in lab, quiz students on that chapter's material. Collect the quizzes five minutes after the first completed quiz is turned in. Distribute clean copies of the quiz and present or have students present the answers immediately.

- Give two or three in-term exams as well as a final exam (all closed-book except for formulas and statistical tables).

In my experience, several topics in the course must be given sufficient attention when presented or much time will be lost later attempting to fill in gaps.

- To eliminate math anxiety, allow students to enjoy early success with assignments on proportions, frequency distributions, and graphing. Moreover, a thorough review of proportions and percentages facilitates instruction on probability theory, sampling distributions, p-values, type I and type II errors, and so on.

- To foster linear thinking and proportional thinking skills, take plenty of time to explain the standard deviation and standardized scores and have the students work many problems partitioning areas under the normal curve.

- Actually generate at least two sampling distributions in class. Thereafter, when the concept is addressed, students will fully understand what a sampling distribution is.

- Require students to produce the details of the six steps of statistical inference— especially drawing the sampling distribution curve in step 2—on every hypothesis test on assignments, quizzes, and exams. Repeating this procedure will bring all students along. Some will grasp the details immediately (Chapter 9). By Chapter 11, every student who is truly working hard will have grasped the logic. Thereafter, you will be able to cruise because the pedagogical aspects of the six steps will be second nature to the students. Thus, in later chapters on bivariate analysis, you may concentrate on conceptual issues related to hypothesis testing and research ideas.

SPECIAL FEATURES

- **Readability.** The text has been class tested many times.
- **Conceptual themes to spark interest.** The text is designed around several conceptual themes that make statistics an enjoyable endeavor. First, statistics is about proportional thinking, and mathematical calculations are simply tools to assist in this process. Second, when the statistical imagination is used, statistical estimates are interpreted in relation to the larger pictures of not only a population of subjects but also a "population" of ideas, values, normative forces, practical circumstances, and theories. Distinctions are made between statistical significance and practical/theoretical significance. Third, the text emphasizes the importance of precision, diligence, and professionalism in the conduct of research.
- **Targeting results to the proper audience.** Discussions are included on how to present results to both scientific and public audiences, along with examples of tabular presentation.
- **Overcoming conceptual hurdles.** Conceptual hurdles are identified, and many devices learned by the author through long years of instruction are employed to get students past them. Such devices include a thorough delineation of the standard deviation, extensive coverage of standardized scores and sampling distributions, and a clear explanation of degrees of freedom.
- **A separate chapter on sampling distributions.** Sampling distributions are presented and illustrated to provide the essential ingredient of proportional thinking.
- **Six steps of statistical inference.** The logical procedures of hypothesis testing are consistently presented as "the six steps of statistical inference." Every statistical test is illustrated within this framework. Illustrations are set off.
- **The four aspects of a relationship.** The interpretations of bivariate statistical tests follow four aspects of a relationship: existence, direction, strength, and practical applications.
- **Complete examples of each statistical procedure.** By adhering to the six steps of statistical inference and the four aspects of a relationship, complete examples in solution boxes keep students informed about what is expected on assignments and exams. Distinctions between "givens" and "calculations" facilitate problem solving.
- **Guidelines on choosing the proper statistical test.** Each hypothesis test is preceded by a box describing when to use a test (i.e., number of samples, level of measurements of variables, sample size). A cumulative decision-tree diagram at the end of each hypothesis-testing chapter further reinforces the test selection process.
- **Highlighting of important terms and formulas.** Concepts and formulas are boxed throughout for easy review, and each chapter has a chapter summary and summary of formulas. The index is thorough. Symbols and formulas are listed inside the book cover.

- **Conceptual diagrams.** To teach students to think proportionally, all hypothesis tests are presented with conceptual diagrams that distinguish populations and parameters from samples and statistics.

- **Varied chapter exercises.** Pencil-and-paper exercises present a good mix of practical, everyday life problems and scientific problems from a variety of social science and health journals. Exercises are ordered from simple to complex. Answers to selected exercises are provided in Appendix C.

- **Optional computer applications.** Whether or not a class is using computers, throughout the text the utility of computers is described. A free compact disk contains *SPSS for Windows* software. Varied data sets, such as the General Social Survey, an ecological data set extracted from U.S. Census population data and U.S. Department of Justice crime data, and surveys on homelessness and physicians' fears of malpractice litigation appear on the Web site with exercises.

- **Statistical follies and fallacies.** Each chapter presents common (and often comical) misinterpretations of statistics in everyday life and by the mass media and researchers.

- *The Statistical Imagination* **Web site.** In addition to data sets and extensive computer application exercises, the text Web site at www.mhhe.com/ritchey3 provides both student and instructor resources. For students, there are chapter outlines, self-evaluation quizzes, terminology flash cards, PowerPoint slides, glossaries, and links to data resources and statistical sites. In the secure professors' corner, there are printable and downloadable PDF files for a Test Bank, an Instructor's Manual, a Solutions Manual with complete keys to all four sets of chapter exercises, PowerPoint slides, and teaching resource links.

SECOND EDITION ENHANCEMENTS

- The addition of Appendix D—*Guide to SPSS for Windows*—is organized by chapter. This appendix provides flowcharts of point-and-click command sequences for each procedure and a brief description of output.

- A section titled "Chapter Extensions on *The Statistical Imagination* Web Site" appears at the end of each text chapter directing readers to the Web site. These extensions are available in easily downloadable and printable PDF files. Chapter extensions include: (1) first edition topics that are infrequently covered, such as gamma (Chapter 16 of the first edition); (2) newly added, slightly advanced concepts and procedures, such as calculation of statistical power; (3) introductions to partial and multiple correlation and *N*-Way ANOVA with interaction terms; and (4) methodological issues, such as validity and reliability of measurement scales. These additions facilitate use of the text in a first-level graduate course. Generally speaking, any material removed from the first edition, such as interval-like ordinal variables, is retained on the Web site.

- Chapter summaries appear near the end of each chapter.

- The number of available pencil-and-paper exercises is doubled. Four sets of parallel exercises accommodate instructors who teach many sections per year. (Supplements include a Solutions Manual with complete answers to all pencil-and-paper exercises.)

- Illustrations of procedures and many data tables are updated.

- For each statistical procedure, a complete example appears in "How to" and "Solution" boxes to provide students with guides for working chapter exercises.

- The approximately normal t-distribution is introduced later in Chapter 10 in conjunction with the small single-sample means test (t-test).

- The large single-sample means test for $n > 121$ using the test statistic Z and the normal curve table is introduced in Chapter 9 to facilitate instruction on the logic of hypothesis testing.

- In the six steps of statistical inference, several formatting changes simplify and shorten presentation: (1) *Statistical hypothesis* (Stat. *H*) is now consistently called *null hypothesis* (H_0) and a section in Chapter 9 thoroughly explains what *null* means. (2) In the Test Preparation and Six Steps, redundancies are eliminated.

- *The Statistical Imagination* Web site includes an Instructor's Manual that provides a turnkey method for effective instruction. The instructional techniques are based on the workshop "Successfully Teaching Statistics Without Watering Down," which has been conducted at many professional meetings by the author and Thomas A. Petee of Auburn University.

ACKNOWLEDGMENTS

Many family members were of special help to me in preparing this text. Thanks to Wanda for her love, help, and patience. Sarah and Kitty were especially helpful in editing early drafts, and Daniel assisted in mathematical formulations and computer applications. Gail provided advice on graphics. Lynn Harper Ritchey, a fellow sociologist, provided both encouragement and assistance.

I am especially appreciative of the help of two persons. First is Daniel O. Price, who was my mentor when I was a student at the University of Texas at Austin. Dan coauthored a statistics text with Margaret Hagood in the 1950s and taught Hubert M. Blalock, whose text *Social Statistics* (McGraw-Hill) was a mainstay for so many graduate students in the 1960s and 1970s. Many of the ideas and pedagogical devices of this text—the emphasis on reifying sampling distributions, the six steps of statistical inference, the four aspects of a relationship—I learned from Dan. In fact, he first suggested that I write a text as his coauthor. As it turned out, time passed and he retired before the project moved very far, but he has been helpful since. Second, special thanks to P. Neal Ritchey, my brother and fellow sociologist at the University of Cincinnati. When I encountered conceptual challenges, he was always there with the correct insights and answers. He suspended his very busy schedule to read, critique, and edit for me. I truly appreciate the advantages of having an older brother in the same field. My love and thanks go to Neal, who has guided me in so many endeavors over the years.

I extend heartfelt thanks to the following who were generous with their time and assistance: Jeffrey E. Hall, Brian P. Hinote, Jason Wasserman, and Mercy Mwaria, whose effects are viewable on the Web Site; Jackie Skeen, Charlotte Edwards, and LaShundra Wormsley-Dooley for help with assembly. I wish to thank Sean-Shong Hwang for helping me sort out ways to present topics. I also thank the following for constructive suggestions: Julie Locher, Akilah Dulin, Cullen Clark, Thomas Petee, Darlene Wright, Jennifer Moren-Cross, and Lynn Gerald. And thanks to William C. Cockerham, Mark LaGory, Patricia Drentea, Jeffrey Clair, Mike Wilson, Becky Trigg, Shelia Cotten, Ken Wilson, Kevin Fitzpatrick, Abdullah Khatri, Harry Hamilton, Gregory Sheinfeld, and Tennant S. McWilliams for their support, encouragement, and advice.

I wish to thank the following and several anonymous reviewers for their comprehensive and constructive suggestions:

Neil W. Henry, Virginia Commonwealth University,
Therese Seibert, Keene State College,
Surendar Yadava, University of Northern Iowa,
Jay Alperson, Palomar College,
Christopher Bradley, Indiana–Purdue University Fort Wayne,
Furjen Deng, Sam Houston State University,
Lisa Pellerin, Ball State University,
Robin Perrin, Pepperdine University, and
William Wells, Southern Illinois University.

Finally, I very much appreciate the guidance and cooperation of the wonderful people at McGraw-Hill, including my editor Sherith Pankratz and previous editors Sally Constable, Carolyn Meier, and Jill Gordon, and also Julie Abodeely, Kathy Shackleford, and Gina Boedecker. Thanks to Developmental Editors Robin Reed, Beth Baugh, and Production Editor Valerie Heffernan of Carlisle Publishing Services; Jill Rietema of SPSS; and others who helped bring this project to fruition.

1

The Statistical Imagination

Introduction

One day when Chicken Licken was scratching among the leaves, an acorn fell out of a tree and struck her on the tail. "Oh," said Chicken Licken, "the sky is falling! I am going to tell the King."

From *Tomie dePaola's Favorite Nursery Tales* by Tomie dePaola. Copyright © 1986 by Tomie dePaola. Used by permission of G. P. Putnam's Sons, a Division of Penguin Young Reader's Group, a member of Penguin Group (USA) Inc., 345 Hudson Street, New York, NY 10014. All rights reserved.

Chicken Licken did something everyone does from time to time: blow things out of proportion. Although this is a normal reaction for storybook animals and many human beings, statisticians must not react to situations too quickly and emotionally. A statistician must step back and dispassionately observe so that a clear sense of balance and proportion is maintained.

   The **field of statistics** is *a set of procedures for gathering, measuring, classifying, coding, computing, analyzing, and summarizing systematically acquired numerical information.* A course in statistics generally is perceived as one that involves lots of

1

formulas and calculations. Indeed, some mathematical operations are involved, but this is not the thrust of statistics, and computers typically handle that part anyway. Statistics is truly about learning a new way of seeing things—acquiring a vision of reality based on careful analysis of facts rather than emotional reactions to isolated experiences.

---

the field of statistics   A set of procedures for gathering, measuring, classifying, coding, computing, analyzing, and summarizing systematically acquired numerical information.

Not all pursuits require accurate, objective portrayals of reality.[1] Popular entertainment media—movies, television, romance novels, and so on—are by definition fiction and fantasy, with imaginary characters and events. They are designed to excite, humor, sadden, or inspire us. Similarly, product advertising enters the world between fact and fantasy, appealing not only to reason but also to emotions to convince us that a purchase will *feel* good. Political campaigns appeal to the emotions of pride, patriotism, fear, and hatred. While most candidates are dedicated public servants, not all politicians stick to facts, and they are not legally required to do so. Many politicians hire "spin doctors" to dress up their images.

The political arena provides a strong contrast to science, an endeavor specifically designed to produce a clearer understanding of nature. Science is practiced, to the greatest extent possible, independently of political or ideological influence. Statistical analysis is a vital part of the scientific method. There is a great difference between the objective statistics of independent scientific polls and the biased opinions of pollsters hired by ambitious politicians. While the goal of a political campaign staff is to bolster support, independent firms attempt to gauge public opinion. For example, to show that a congressional representative is ahead in the polls, the campaign staff may hire a polling firm that is willing to ask loaded questions and survey only voters who have donated money. Of course, such a poll will reveal strong support, but the staff may neglect to mention to the media that the sample was not representative of all voters. Such manipulation of numerical information calls to mind Mark Twain's saying: "There are liars, damned liars, and statisticians."

If a professional statistician conducted the same poll, the survey would not shade facts or include loaded questions. Instead, a statistician follows carefully controlled procedures and samples the entire population of voters. The results are presented as having a known range of error and a known degree of confidence, say, plus or minus 3 percentage points with 95 percent confidence. Statistics is about having a balanced perspective and using exacting precision in the gathering and presentation of information.

The major theme of this book is that the field of statistics is about obtaining an accurate sense of proportion in regard to reality. To acquire a sense of proportion is to see things objectively, to make fair judgments about events and behavior, to give the correct amount of attention to things that really matter and not be distracted by irrelevant events. A sense of proportion helps rein in subjective feelings, biases, and prejudices that can distort perceptions of reality. Learning to put things in the proper perspective requires imagination, and therein lies the potential for seeing statistical analysis as an interesting and enjoyable endeavor.

The Statistical Imagination

The intent of this text is to provide a new vision of reality based on statistical analysis. We will call this vision the statistical imagination. The social scientist C. Wright Mills (1959) defined the **sociological imagination** as *an awareness of the relationship of the individual to the wider society and to history.* The *sociological* imagination is the recognition that individual behavior is conducted in relation to larger social structures, that most actions by individuals involve conformity to *society's* rules and not personal initiative, and that right and wrong are defined within a cultural context. The sociological imagination involves seeing an isolated detail (a part) in relation to a larger picture (the whole), seeing the forest as well as the trees.

Similarly, the statistical imagination involves seeing a part in relation to a whole. The **statistical imagination** is *an appreciation of how usual or unusual an event, circumstance, or behavior is in relation to a larger set of similar events and an appreciation of an event's causes and consequences.*

---

the statistical imagination   An appreciation of how usual or unusual an event, circumstance, or behavior is in relation to a larger set of similar events and an appreciation of an event's causes and consequences.

To have the statistical imagination is to understand that most events are predictable (i.e., they have a probability of occurrence based on long-term trends and circumstances).[2] The statistical imagination is the ability to think through a problem and maintain a sense of proportion or balance when weighing evidence against preconceived notions. The statistical imagination involves recognizing highly unusual events for what they are and not overreacting to them.

To be statistically *un*imaginative is to blow things out of proportion, to think in a reactionary rather than proportional way. For example, in 1991 many people became upset over news that a highly troubled person had stooped to cannibalism, as in the notorious case of serial killer Jeffrey Dahmer. While this event understandably evoked rage, fear, and disgust, many saw it as a symbol of moral decline in America. Such a notion is reactionary. Cannibalism is just as rare now as it has ever been! The statistical imagination says: Look at this over the long run. Is it happening frequently? Do a lot of people engage in this behavior? Am I likely to become someone's lunch? In fact, the Jeffrey Dahmer incident was an isolated occurrence involving a single person out of 250 million people. Seeing this event in its proper proportion brings reason to arguments about the larger picture of cultural stability.

To acquire the statistical imagination is to open one's eyes to the broader picture of reality and overcome misunderstandings, prejudices, and narrowmindedness. For example, public health officials report that more than 40,000 people are killed in vehicle crashes every year. They puzzle over the fact that Americans do not see this major cause of death as a public health problem, one related to road safety and automobile design and therefore one to be solved by government policies. Instead, the public sees traffic fatalities as individual misfortunes or failures. We assume that traffic deaths result from bad luck (the victim got in the way of a careless driver), stupidity, recklessness or carelessness (the victim was speeding or dozed off), miserliness (too cheap to buy new tires), or immorality (the driver should not have been drinking). Why does the public fail to look past individual explanations? One reason is that traffic deaths and injuries infrequently strike any particular family and therefore appear to occur to "the other guy." As long as we are convinced that the victim brought it upon himself or herself, we are reassured that it will not happen to us. We, of course, would never drink and drive, and we speed only where it is safe to do so!

The statistical imagination, however, allows us to recognize the large-scale effects of this mode of transportation. We look at the broad picture of how traffic crashes affect the population as opposed to individuals. We compute total deaths and rates of deaths per million miles driven by using data covering many years. We determine which unsafe road conditions result in fatalities when individuals *are* careless or stupid. For example, it is well known that more deaths occur on two-lane roads than on four-lane or interstate highways. In fact, taking into account increases in automobiles and drivers (i.e., millions of miles driven), traffic death rates have dropped greatly since the interstate highway system was built in the 1950s and 1960s. By focusing on the group and examining circumstances in addition to individuals, we place traffic deaths in the larger context of public health. Only then do we begin to consider the safety value of other modes of travel, such as buses and subways.

Linking the Statistical Imagination to the Sociological Imagination

Statistical Norms and Social Norms

A balanced view requires more than careful mathematical calculation. For example, even if we are aware of the number of yearly automobile crash deaths, we may be "prejudiced" in favor of this private form of transportation. We may resist efforts to substitute mass transit systems because automobiles embody the strongly held American social value of individual freedom. We are willing to chance injury or death for freedom and convenience.

When human beings use their illustrious brains to compute proportions, percentages, and other statistics, they are simply struggling to obtain a measure of reality. A statistic, however, does not mean much by itself. A key principle of the statistical imagination is that statistical interpretations must take into account the circumstances of a phenomenon, including the social values of the society or some group within it. Social values may work to limit, or perhaps enlarge, the human response to a statistic. In this sense, any statistic is culturally bound or **normative**: *Its interpretation depends on the place, time, and culture in which it is observed.* A **social norm** is *a shared idea of the behavior that is appropriate or inappropriate in a given situation in a given culture.* In a word, a norm is a rule, and norms are peculiar to a particular society, a period of history, and the specific situation in which the action occurs. What is considered right or wrong, a lot or a little, depends on the place and the time. For example, being naked in the shower is normal; in fact, it would be peculiar to shower with one's clothes on. Being naked in the classroom, however, is deviant (or nonnormal) behavior.

When Is a Little a Lot?   Any single statistic is meaningless if we do not establish some basis of comparison—a statistical norm. A **statistical norm** is *an average rate of occurrence of a phenomenon.* Such an average may differ from one society to another or from one group to another because any statistical norm is influenced by social norms. To illustrate statistical norms and their relationship to social norms, let us compare some national infant mortality rates (IMRs), the number of children who die in the first year of life per 1,000 live births. Table 1–1 presents the IMRs of selected countries for the year 2003. In the United States the IMR was approximately seven deaths per 1,000 live births.

Was this U.S. rate high or low compared to the statistical norm? It was low compared to the world's statistical norm of 51.1, but Americans should not feel reassured by this. IMRs are closely tied to economic development; therefore, the U.S. rate is more appropriately compared to the statistical norms of cultures and economies like our own, such as the industrialized countries of Japan and Western Europe. As it turns out, our IMR is rather high compared with the IMRs of these countries, and U.S. public health officials are greatly concerned about this. Taken in context, a little is a lot. Any single infant death is significant to the victim's family, but public health officials in a poor country with a high IMR may not view this with alarm (any more than Americans view traffic deaths with alarm). For one thing, high IMR rates have endured for centuries, making a country's statistical norm appear stable. Second, cultural circumstances—poor sanitation and medical care and lack of economic resources—may greatly challenge efforts to reduce this rate. Third, other causes of death, such as acquired immunodeficiency syndrome (AIDS) may be so great that they make the IMR appear rather low or simply part of a larger problem. How public officials or a society as a whole interprets a statistic depends on the state of affairs at a given time. As this rudimentary analysis of the IMRs in Table 1–1 suggests, cultural circumstances influence the interpretation of statistical findings.

For some measurements, such as those for cognitive or behavioral performance, health status, and academic achievement, statistical norms are necessary even to make sense of a score. For example, with intelligent quotient tests (IQ tests), the scores are normed against the psychological research community's informed *judgment* about what constitutes *average intelligence.* Thus, IQ tests are often specifically designed with a statistical norm of 100, a number with which we are familiar and comfortable. A person of presumably average intelligence scores 100, while those scoring higher have an above-average IQ, and those scoring lower have a below-average IQ.

Statistical Ideals and Social Values

A discussion of infant mortality rates brings to mind another distinction that links statistics to social reality: that between statistical norms and statistical ideals. Whereas a statistical norm is an existing average, a **statistical ideal** is *a socially desired rate of occurrence of a phenomenon,* an optimum target rate. Statistical ideals often reflect

TABLE 1-1 | Infant mortality rates for selected nations in 2003

Nation	Infant Mortality Rate (deaths to children under 1 year of age per 1,000 live births)
Already Industrialized	
Japan	3.3
Iceland	3.5
Sweden	2.8
Germany	4.2
Canada	4.9
Great Britain	5.3
United States	6.8
Industrializing	
Mexico	22.5
People's Republic of China	25.3
India	59.6
Haiti	76.0
Ethiopia	103.2
Afghanistan	142.5
World	51.1

Source: U.S. Bureau of the Census, International Date Base. http://www.census.gov/ipc/www/idbnew.html.

social values—*shared ideas among the members of a society about the way things ought to be.* Values are a society's common notions of what a truly good society would hold dear. In the United States, for example, freedom, equality, achievement, material comfort, efficiency, and nationalism are highly valued (Williams 1970: 452–500). These social values are only ideals and are never realized in a pure sense. For example, individual freedom is highly valued, but pure freedom—every individual making his or her own rules—is anarchy. Values are like lighthouses on rocky shorelines. We use these lights as guides, but to reach them completely would be hazardous.

In response to social values, statistical ideals (target rates of occurrence) often are substituted for statistical norms. For example, the infant death rate in the United States (6.8 deaths per 1,000 live births) is a statistical fact, and this rate is higher than the norm for most *already industrialized* countries, such as Japan and Germany. Thus, U.S. public health officials may target the rates of these countries as a statistical ideal, a rate to shoot for. The public, however, may not be willing to accept the changes needed to bring this about, such as higher taxes and greater government involvement in health care. Debates over statistical ideals often reveal underlying conflicts and opinions on social values. Statistical ideals, then, are just that. They are greatly influenced and constrained by social values.

The meaning of any statistic sometimes depends merely on practical circumstances. For instance, biophysical-based statistical norms and ideals abound in competitive sports, reflecting the practical limitations of physics. For example, is four minutes a long time? It is a terribly long time to circle the track in an automobile race but a remarkably short time to run a mile. A professional basketball player with a free-throw percentage of 50 percent is taking a chance of losing a multimillion-dollar contract. However, a professional major league baseball player need hit the ball only about 33 percent of the time (a batting average of .333) to win the league's batting title and get a multimillion-dollar raise. Sometimes a little is a lot. The significance of a statistic depends on statistical norms (averages), statistical ideals (optimum target rates), and practical circumstances. The statistical imagination is employed to choose the appropriate statistical norms and ideals to which statistics and observations are compared.

The statistical imagination, with its awareness of the linkages between statistical measurements and social facts, requires a degree of skepticism—a critical and doubting attitude. Just as a statistician is skeptical of what is reported as fact by those with vested political or economic interests, skepticism must be applied to a statistician's work, especially scientific work.

Statistics and Science: Tools for Proportional Thinking

As has been noted, statistics is about observing and organizing systematically acquired numerical information. *Systematically acquired information that is organized by following the procedures of science and statistics* is called **data** (the plural of *datum*).

Statistics and the gathering of data are not casual activities; rather, they are enterprises that require maximum effort. Statistical analysis is about precision: following procedures and making precise measurements of and accurate predictions on how events in the world will occur. When statistical analysis is properly done, the analyst knows the limitations of reasoning and mathematical procedures and knows when predictions about events or behaviors are less than perfectly precise. Furthermore, a statistician can express the degree of confidence he or she has in a conclusion. In this regard, statistics is about controlling error. Statistical errors are not mistakes. Instead, **statistical error** refers to *known degrees of imprecision in the procedures used to gather and process information*. To control error is to be as precise as necessary to enhance confidence in the conclusions drawn from statistical findings.

---

statistical error   Known degrees of imprecision in the procedures used to gather and process information.

The statistical imagination requires not only a sense of balance in regard to reality, but also the diligence to keep track of details in order to minimize error.

Descriptive and Inferential Statistics

Data are gathered for different statistical purposes. One purpose of statistical analysis is to take a lot of data about a category of people or objects and summarize this information with a few accurate mathematical figures, tables, and/or charts. This first step in statistics is called descriptive statistics.

Descriptive statistics tell us *how many observations were recorded and how frequently each score or category of observations occurred in the data.* For example, data from 291 survey respondents may show that 40 percent are male and have an average age of 21 years, with the youngest being 19 and the oldest 51. Descriptive statistics are used by scientists as well as by pollsters, marketing analysts, urban planners, and those in many other occupations. These calculations inform the public about what products to purchase, which politicians to believe, what stocks to buy, what cars are the most reliable, at what age annual physical checkups are in order, and so on. Descriptive statistics also are computed by scientists as a first step in analyzing scientific research hypotheses, the task of inferential statistics.

A second purpose of statistical analysis is to draw conclusions about the mathematical relationships among characteristics of a group of people or objects. For example, we might investigate whether Americans who are better educated are less likely to believe that the devil exists. This type of analysis is called inferential statistics. **Inferential statistics** are computed to *show cause-and-effect relationships and to test hypotheses and scientific theories.* (To infer means *to draw conclusions about something.*) The bulk of this text deals with inferential statistics. Understanding the basic principles of science is essential to grasping inferential statistics; thus, we will review these principles.

What Is Science?

Science is *a systematic method of explaining empirical phenomena.* **Empirical** means *observable and measurable.* Phenomena (the plural form of the Latin word *phanomenon*) are facts, happenstances, events, circumstances, or, simply put, "things that exist naturally." Empirical phenomena, then, are things that can be observed and measured, such as natural conditions, processes, events, situations, objects, groups of people, behaviors, thoughts, beliefs, knowledge, opinions, emotions, and feelings.

Not everything is measurable and observable. For example, whether there is an afterlife is not readily observed, although over 70 percent of American adults assert a belief in it. Furthermore, many intangible things, such as emotions, feelings, and beliefs, must be measured indirectly. In the social sciences such indirect measurements include survey questionnaires that measure opinions, knowledge, attitudes, and even behavior. Physical scientists use indirect measures as well. For instance, physicists indirectly observe neutrinos, subatomic particles so tiny and fast that they typically pass through the earth without bumping into anything. (Millions are passing through you right now.) Occasionally a neutrino displaces a water molecule, releasing observable energy, and this effect can be measured. An important aspect of the expansion of science is finding new ways to accurately measure things that are not readily visible to the naked eye. Microscopes, computerized X-ray machines, and seismometers, as well as survey instruments, are the tools scientists use to extend the reach of their measurement capabilities.

The Purpose of Scientific Investigation   The main objective of science is to explain things. A scientific explanation is one based on strict procedures, and it is called a theory. A **scientific theory** is *a set of interrelated, logically organized statements that* *explain a phenomenon of special interest and that have been corroborated through obser-vation and analysis.* Theories describe situations and how they work or proceed. The collection of ideas that constitute a theory is tested against observed facts. A theory is "corroborated" when its ideas successfully predict these observable facts. A theory is not a fact in and of itself; rather, it is a well-organized explanation of facts. As a phenomenon is better understood, a theory is modified and refined to improve its predictive ability. Thus, theory development is a cumulative process that occurs over a long period.

An adequate scientific theory accomplishes two things. First, it provides a sense of understanding about a phenomenon: how, when, why, and under what conditions it occurs. Simply put, it makes sense of things. Second, a theory allows us to make empirical predictions, to answer the question of under what conditions and to what degree a phenomenon will occur. Such predictions are possible because changes in one phenomenon are related to changes in other phenomena. For instance, we predict a greater chance of rain when atmospheric moisture (humidity) increases and predict an increase in the crime rate of a community when economic times are tough.

Scientific Skepticism and the Statistical Imagination

Science *requires* that its ideas withstand the test of being able to predict observations. Well-trained scientists are skeptics; they have a critical and doubting attitude. They are willing to tolerate uncertainty and are not too quick to draw conclusions. A skeptic is hesitant to believe something simply because it is reported to be true by trusted friends, the mass media, or people in positions of authority, such as government leaders and even parents. A look at popular culture, especially the ideas thrown about in the mass media, suggests that most people are highly credulous—inclined to believe things—even in the absence of evidence and even in the presence of contradictory evidence. The late renowned scientist Carl Sagan, a spokesperson for the value of science, observed that many people are very quick to "suspend *dis*belief." He noted, for example, how gullible people were in falling for the "crop circles" hoax, believing for 15 years that huge elegant pictograms discovered in English grainfields were left there by space aliens. (A couple of rogues named Bower and Chorley eventually confessed to the hoax.) Sagan argued that we are not skeptical enough of much that is only alleged to be fact. He beckoned us to take science more seriously because the scientific process is especially designed to separate fact from fiction (Sagan 1995a, 1995b). He made a good case that a society that encourages the learning of science will produce better-informed citizens. He noted:

> In College . . . I began to learn a little about how science works . . . how rigorous the standards of evidence must be . . . how our biases can color our interpretation of the evidence, how belief systems widely . . . supported by the political, religious and academic hierarchies often turn out to be not just slightly in error but grotesquely wrong . . .
>
> The tenets of skepticism do not require an advanced degree to master . . . All science asks is to employ the same levels of skepticism we use in buying a used car . . .
>
> (Sagan 1995b:10–13)[*]

---

[*]From Carl Sagan, *The Demon-Haunted World.* Copyright © 1995 by Random House. Reprinted by permission of the publisher.

Scientific explanations based on observation, strict procedures, and the collective scrutiny of the scientific community often contradict common sense as well as the ideas put forth by political leaders. This does not mean that science forgoes common sense. Instead, science uses **informed common sense**, *that which is weighed and double-checked against carefully gathered data.* Uninformed common sense is all too common! Scientific skepticism requires learning procedural skills and developing a questioning attitude. Similarly, having the statistical imagination involves learning skills (e.g., how to compute probabilities and think proportionally) and being ready to ask whether an observed phenomenon is reasonable.

At the same time, science has limitations. First, it is restricted to examining empirical—observable and measurable—phenomena. Faith, not science, must resolve, for example, the question of whether God and heaven exist. Second, many sound, factually based scientific arguments lack political or taxpayer support. For example, research reveals that poverty in the United States could be reduced by expanding government family assistance programs such as employment training and child care services. These "workfare" measures, however, are costly and typically lack taxpayer support, and so recent legislation simply gives public assistance recipients a limited time to solve these issues for themselves. A third limitation of science is that it creates ethical dilemmas and resistance to its application. For instance, an economist could make a convincing argument that euthanasia, or "mercy killings," would save billions of dollars in medical expenses incurred by the terminally ill. Obviously, many would question this argument not on a factual but on a moral basis. There is more to human existence than cost accounting.

Science does not have all the answers, and scientists must be skeptical of the answers they have. When it comes to explaining empirical reality, however, the scientific method is the best approach. A key feature of the scientific method is statistical analysis.

Conceiving of Data

Variables and Constants   *Measurable phenomena that vary (change) over time or that differ from place to place or from individual to individual* are called **variables**. Variables are features of the subjects (students, the homeless, the people of St. Louis, lab rats) or objects (buildings, trees, floods, bacteria, crimes) under study. (From here on, we will use the term *subject* to mean people *or* objects.) For instance, in studying individuals, we might note differences in the variables of age, weight, height, personality traits, race, and socioeconomic status.

---

a variable   A measurable phenomenon that varies (changes) over time or that differs from place to place or from individual to individual.

We use the term **variation** to refer to *how much the measurements of a variable differ among study subjects,* and we compare differences in variation between groups. For example, there is much variation in ages among students on commuter college campuses in large cities, ranging perhaps from 17 to 70 years. In contrast, the variation in ages in traditional, day-class colleges in small "campus towns" is typically much smaller, say, 17 to 25 years.

Some variables exhibit little variation or do not vary at all within a group, such as the ages of first-grade pupils. *Characteristics of study subjects that do not vary* are called **constants**. Sometimes we intentionally "hold variables constant." For instance, in an experiment on the effects of alcoholic beverages on driving behavior, we would use subjects of about the same weight because lighter people are known to get drunk more quickly than heavier people. This way, reduced reaction time in driving can be attributed to the amount of alcohol consumed rather than to differences in weight. By "holding weight constant," we eliminate its effects on driving behavior; since weight did not vary, a variation in weight cannot possibly explain the results of the experiment. By holding weight constant and holding constant any other variables that affect drunkenness, we are able to isolate the effects of alcohol consumption on driving behavior.

The Dependent Variable and Independent Variables That Explain It   Typically, in gathering data, our purpose is to research a single variable that is of special interest to us. We want to know what causes an increase or decrease in the amount of this variable. What causes "variation" in it? What are its scores dependent on? This variable of main interest is called the **dependent variable**, *the variable whose variation we want to explain.* For example, the 1960s were characterized by urban strife, with rioting in over 40 cities in a three-year period. In an effort to understand and prevent riots, a National Advisory Commission on Civil Disorders (1968) was formed to conduct a scientific study. The incidence of riot behavior was the dependent variable. The commission wished to explain why riots occurred in some cities but not in others.

Variables suspected of being related to an increase or decrease in riot behavior also were measured. These variables included the rate of poverty in communities, the number of complaints of police brutality, racial disturbances in the weeks before a riot, and the number of known "Communist sympathizers" in a city. These *predictor variables that are related to or predict variation in the dependent variable* are called **independent variables**.[3] Table 1–2 distinguishes the characteristics of independent and dependent variables.

A predictive statement about the relationship between variables is called a hypothesis. Specifically, a **hypothesis** is *a prediction about the relationship of two variables, asserting that differences among the measurements of an independent variable will correspond to differences among the measurements of a dependent variable.*

---

a hypothesis A prediction about the relationship between two variables, asserting that differences among the measurements of an independent variable will correspond to differences among the measurements of a dependent variable.

The Commission on Civil Disorders examined cities as its subject of investigation. The commission's research team hypothesized that the incidence of riots (the dependent variable) was related to independent variables such as the percentage of households living in poverty, the adequacy of family assistance programs, the degree of governmental participation by minorities, the occurrence of "tension heightening incidents," and, especially, persistent reports of police brutality. To say that a relationship exists between the incidence of police brutality and the incidence of riots is to say that cities with lots of police brutality tended also to have lots of riots. This hypothesis and similar ones involving the other independent variables constituted a *protest theory of riot behavior.* This theory advanced the argument that people riot in response to oppressive police actions and because of frustration with poor government services. The ideas and data stimulated by this theory ultimately led to changes in local government policies and a reduction in civil disorders (Johnson 1973: 376).

The findings of the Commission on Civil Disorders disproved some common **myths**, *widely held beliefs that are false.* Specifically, it discredited the *Communist conspiracy theory,* a political argument that the riots were part of an organized revolution aimed at overthrowing the U.S. government (Johnson 1973: 376). Why were people so quick to believe that the riots were Communist-inspired? Myths often arise from commonsense explanations reinforced by isolated or sporadic events and by political rhetoric aimed at stoking the fears of the electorate. The urban strife of the 1960s occurred during a period of rapid social change and uncertainty. On the domestic front there was a civil rights movement with racial minorities, especially African-Americans, demanding the elimination of discrimination in hiring, schooling, and the use of public facilities. At the same time, on the world scene there was a "Cold War" between the capitalist countries of the West and Communist countries, especially the former Soviet Union and the People's Republic of China. These Communist governments made open calls to arms and vowed to infiltrate the United States with spies who would encourage the poor and "repressed minorities" to revolt. In this atmosphere, the occurrence of riots in poor minority neighborhoods throughout the United States seemed to many people a plausible result of a Communist conspiracy.

As it turned out, the facts showed that Communists among the riot participants were extremely hard to come by. Furthermore, there was no difference in the number of Communist sympathizers in cities where riots occurred and cities where they did not.

TABLE 1–2 | Possible relationships between independent and dependent variables

Independent Variable		Dependent Variable
Cause	$\rightarrow$	Effect
Predictor	$\rightarrow$	Outcome
Stimulus	$\rightarrow$	Response
Intervention (action taken)	$\rightarrow$	Result
Correlation: change in one variable	$\rightarrow$	Associated change in another variable

The Communist conspiracy argument was disproved; it was not supported by data and did not withstand the scrutiny of statistical analysis.

A scientific theory is an organized argument that must be corroborated by empirical evidence. A theory is "corroborated" when its ideas successfully predict observable measurements.[4] As more data are acquired, theories are modified and refined to improve their predictability and sense of understanding.

The Research Process

The research process involves organizing ideas into a theory, making empirical predictions that support that theory, and then gathering data to test the predictions. The research process is a cumulative one, a continual process of accumulating knowledge. The research process for scientific investigation involves seven steps. Steps 1 through 3 are the major themes of social science theory courses, steps 4 and 5 are covered in methodology courses, and steps 6 and 7 are covered in statistics courses. The seven steps are as follows:

1. *Specify the research question.*   We raise a question and identify the dependent variable. For example, we may ask: Why are riots occurring in some cities?

2. *Review the scientific literature.*   We do this to make sure that time and money are not wasted collecting data that already exist. We seek to extend the "frontier of knowledge," the outer limits of what has already been learned.

3. *Propose a theory and state hypotheses.*   Theory involves organizing ideas into a logical form that can explain variation in the dependent variable. In developing a theory, we identify independent variables and state hypotheses about how we think they affect the dependent variable, assuming the theory is meaningful.

Hypotheses are generated or "motivated" by theory—established ideas found in the scientific literature, with innovative modifications of the researcher. The theory directs us to expect certain observed outcomes from data. If these outcomes are then found to occur, the theory is corroborated. For example, the protest theory of riot behavior motivates the following hypothesis:

H_1: Cities with a high incidence of police brutality (independent variable) are likely to have a high incidence of civil disorders (dependent variable).

In contrast, the Communist conspiracy theory of riot behavior motivates the following hypothesis:

H_2: Cities with a large number of Communists (independent variable) are likely to have a high incidence of civil disorders (dependent variable).

The theory, based on the literature review, also guides us in selecting "control" variables. For example, in measuring civil disorders, we must control for the crime rate. This assures us that cities with a large incidence of riots are not simply high-crime cities, in which case crime rate, not simply police brutality, would explain part of the incidence of civil disorders.

We should also note that not all scientific studies employ theory. Much *research is done simply to solve immediate practical problems or explore new phenomena about which so little is known that formulating a theory is impossible.* Such studies are called **exploratory studies**. For example, someone exploring privacy issues about cell phone transmissions may begin with loosely organized ideas and questions.

4. *Select a research design.*   The research design details how data are to be measured, sampled, and gathered. Common social science methods include direct observation of behavior, laboratory experiment, survey, content analysis of media, and analysis of existing or "secondary" data (such as police reports and the census of the population).

5. *Collect the data.*   This is usually the most expensive part of research. It involves "going into the field" to inform people about the study and gathering data by using the plan developed in step 4. This is also one of the most enjoyable parts of research. Data collection allows the researcher to get out of the office and meet new and often interesting people.

6. *Analyze the data and draw conclusions.*   This involves statistical analysis, the main topic of this text. Hypotheses are tested by comparing observations to theoretical predictions. In the riot example, the data collected by the Commission on Civil Disorders supported hypothesis 1 and disproved hypothesis 2, giving greater credibility to the protest theory.

7. *Disseminate the results.*   To disseminate means to scatter widely and thus share. Scientific findings are shared with two "audiences": the public and the scientific community.

Public audiences include not only citizens but also politicians and business, church, charity, and educational groups. Researchers may speak at public forums such as press conferences, talk shows, city council meetings, community organization meetings, and high school classes. Such talks must be kept conceptually and statistically simple.

For the scientific audience, dissemination of research findings involves presenting findings at scientific conferences and publishing books or, more commonly, short articles in professional journals. Research publication is a strenuous process of peer review—a system of checks and balances—that ideally maximizes the chance that a published work will be accurate and unbiased. A scientific manuscript follows a strict form. When completed, it is submitted to the editor of a journal in the field. The editor sends copies without author identification to similarly trained scientists. This "blind" review minimizes personal bias. Reviewers, however, are obliged to be highly skeptical of the manuscript. They scrutinize every detail, searching for faulty logic, biased interpretations, unsound sampling, poor measurement or analysis, and misguided conclusions. If several reviewers agree that the research is sound and would advance knowledge, the editor may accept it for publication if print space is available. Leading journals in most fields are extremely selective, publishing as few as 1 of every 10 submissions. This screening process ensures that the research selected for publication meets professional standards. Researchers who publish on a regular basis are highly skilled practitioners of science.

Proportional Thinking: Calculating Proportions, Percentages, and Rates

The term *proportion* is a mathematical concept related to fractions and percentages. A good sense of proportion about a phenomenon requires more than having a good feel for what that phenomenon is about. Understanding proportions requires **proportional thinking**: *weighing the part against the whole and calculating the likelihood of the phenomenon occurring over the long run.* Having a sense of proportion and calculating mathematical proportions are essentially the same thing. Mathematical proportions are simply precise expressions of our intuitions about the significance of certain facts. Computing a proportion is a way to measure and evaluate a sense of likelihood and significance about the observations we make.

To get started properly, we will briefly review basic calculations of fractions, proportions, and percentages. (Additional review is provided in Appendix A.) Every aspect of statistical work—from measurement and graphical presentation to the computation of statistical probabilities—involves working with mathematical proportions; therefore, this review provides a good orientation to statistical calculations.

Mathematical proportions are simply *division problems that weigh a part (the numerator) against a whole (the denominator).* To compute a proportion, we start with a **fraction**, *a way of expressing what part of the whole (or total number) a category of observations constitutes.*

$$\text{Fraction} = \frac{\text{numerator}}{\text{denominator}} = \frac{\text{part}}{\text{whole}}$$

Calculating a Fraction

$$\text{Fraction} = \frac{\text{\# in a category}}{\text{\# in total group}}$$

where # is read "number" or "number of."

For example, in a study of the inmates occupying the Washington County jail, we determine that among the total jail population of 149 inmates, 112 have been charged with drug-related offenses (DROs) such as the possession or sale of an illegal substance. Is this a large part of the jail population? If so, what does this say about the nature of crime and law enforcement in Washington County? To have a good sense of proportion, the two figures, 112 and 149, should be constructed into a fraction:

$$\text{Fraction of Washington County jail inmates charged with DROs} = \frac{\text{\# charged with DROs}}{\text{total inmate population}} = \frac{112}{149}$$

An easier interpretation of this fraction can be found by transforming it into a proportion. **Proportion** means *part of a whole, or part of the total amount or number of observations, expressed in decimal form.* Fractions are reduced to proportions (or "decimalized") by dividing a fraction's numerator by its denominator to obtain a quotient. (A quotient is *the answer to a division problem.*) Thus,

$$p \text{ [of Washington County jail inmates charged with DROs]} = \frac{\text{\# charged with DROs}}{\text{total inmate population}} = \frac{112}{149} = .7517$$

where *p* stands for proportion, the bracketed information describes the targeted population total (the denominator) followed by the targeted characteristic (the numerator), and the pound symbol (#) is read as "number."

> **proportion**   Part of the total amount or number of observations, expressed in decimal form.

Calculating a Proportion

$$p \text{ [of total group in a category]} = \frac{\text{\# in a category}}{\text{\# in total group}} = \text{quotient}$$

where p = proportion of and the quotient is rounded to four decimal places (i.e., the nearest ten-thousandth). The quotient will always have a value between 0 and 1.

This proportion for Washington County is correctly—but awkwardly—stated as "point seven-five-one-seven" or "seven thousand five hundred and seventeen ten-thousandths." For a general audience, then, we go a step further and transform this proportion into the more recognizable expression *percentage.* Percent means "per hundred," and a **percentage** is equal to *a proportion multiplied by 100.* The percentage tells us how many out of every 100 inmates are charged with DROs. Thus,

$$\% \text{ [of Washington County jail inmates charged with DROs]} = p(100) = (.7517)(100) = 75.17\%$$

Calculating a Percentage

$$\% \text{ [of total group in a category]} = p(100)$$

where p = proportion of total group in a category. The quotient will always have a value between 0 percent and 100 percent.

At this point we should have a sense that substance abuse is a serious problem for law enforcement in Washington County. Indeed, more than 75 of every 100 inmates are jailed on DRO charges. Clearly, *it is very likely and usual* for an incarcerated person to have gotten into trouble with drugs. The justice system in this county is heavily burdened by these cases.

Proportions and percentages are preferred ways of expressing "the part to the whole." Proportions will always have answers between 0 (none) and 1 (all). Similarly, percentages always range between 0 percent and 100 percent. Aside from their simplicity compared to the fractional form, proportions and percentages are useful for quickly producing common denominators for two or more fractions. Proportions provide the common denominator 1.00, and percentages provide the common denominator 100. For instance, suppose we compare the DRO cases of Jefferson County's and Washington County's jails. Jefferson County has only 42 DRO cases in a total jail population of 45 inmates. Which fraction is larger, then, 112 out of 149 or 42 out of 45? We obtain a common denominator by computing proportions and percentages. For Jefferson County, then,

$$p \text{ [of Jefferson County jail inmates charged with DROs]} = \frac{\text{\# charged with DROs}}{\text{total inmate population}} = \frac{42}{45} = .9333$$

$$\% \text{ [of Jefferson County jail inmates charged with DROs]} = p(100) = (.9333)(100) = 93.33\%$$

The percentages allow us to see that, in fact, Jefferson County's jail population is more heavily populated by drug-related offenders than is Washington County's (93.33 percent versus 75.17 percent, respectively), even though there are more DRO cases in Washington County.

We can observe from these calculations that to change a fraction into a proportion, we divide the numerator by the denominator to obtain the "decimalized" quotient. To change a proportion into a percentage, we multiply the proportion by 100 by moving the decimal point two places to the right. To transform a percentage into a proportion, we move the decimal point two places to the left, which is simply a matter of dividing by 100. To express a proportion as a fraction, we must have good mastery over decimal places. If necessary, review decimal place locations in Appendix A. Finally, as a general rule (with only a few exceptions) we round proportions to four decimal places to the right of the decimal point and round percentages to two decimal places to the right.

A percentage is a very common way to standardize statistics from different groups. Sometimes, however, percentages do not convey a meaningful sense of proportion. For example, what is the likelihood of being killed by lightning? From data for 2000, we find the U.S. population to be 281,421,906 (U.S. Bureau of the Census 2000). We determine that 51 people were killed by lightning during that year (National Oceanic and Atmosphereic Administration 2003). The proportion and percentage of the population killed by lightning would compute as:

$$p \text{ [of 2000 U.S. population killed by lightning]} = \frac{\text{\# killed by lightning}}{\text{total population size}} = \frac{51}{281,421,906} = .00000018$$

$$\% \text{ [of 2000 U.S. population killed by lightning]} = (p)(100) = .000018\%$$

Thus, assuming that 2000 is a typical year, the likelihood of being killed by lightning is 18 hundred-thousandths of a percent. This is difficult to conceive of even for the mathematically astute. A denominator of 100 is confusing when fewer than one in a hundred are at risk. The statistical imagination beckons us to find another way to convey this risk.

Another way to standardize is to compute a **rate**, *the frequency of occurrence of a phenomenon in relation to some specified, useful "base" number of subjects in a population.* The base number is placed in the denominator so that the rate may be stated as cases per thousand, per ten thousand, per hundred thousand, per million, and so forth. A useful base number is one that clearly specifies the "population at risk" for a phenomenon. With a large group such as the population of the United States, a larger base number is needed in place of the "per 100" used with percentages. Recall that when we transform a proportion into a percentage, we multiply by 100. Similarly, we can multiply a proportion by other multiples of 10 to get rates with larger denominators.

Calculating a Rate

Rate of occurrence $= (p)$ (a useful base number)

where $p =$ proportion of total group in a category and the useful base number is a multiple of 10.

A useful base number for a rate is one that conveys the counting of a phenomenon. In this example, we count persons killed. Our rate, then, should be presented in whole persons with numbers to the left of the decimal point. Observing our proportion of .00000018, to get to a count of persons, we must move the decimal point seven places to the right. A review of decimal place locations in Appendix A shows that this is equivalent to multiplying by 10,000,000. Thus,

$$\text{Rate of lightning deaths per ten million population} = (p)\ (10,000,000)$$

$$= (.00000018)(10,000,000) = 1.8 \text{ lightning deaths per } 10,000,000 \text{ people}$$

This calculation is explicit and useful. It states that only about two out of 10 million people are killed by lightning each year. We can conceive of 10 million as the population of a large city (such as New York City). Imagining a city and thinking proportionately, we get a sense that the risk of a lightning death is very tiny. Only about two persons in an entire large city are likely to be killed each year. (In fact, if we were in a desert city where it seldom rains, we could adjust this figure downward.)

Another quick calculation allows us to set the numerator of this rate to 1 person rather than 1.8. This gives us the number of persons in the population per each lightning death. A ratio of 1.8 to 10,000,000 is equal to a ratio of 1 to 5,555,556. This is obtained by dividing 10,000,000 by 1.8:

$$\frac{1.8 \text{ lightning deaths}}{10,000,000 \text{ people}} = \frac{1 \text{ lightning death}}{X \text{ people}}$$

$$X = \frac{10,000,000}{1.8} = 5,555,556 \text{ people}$$

where X is the number of people in the population for each person killed by lightning. Thus, our chance of being killed by lightning in a year is about 1 in $5\frac{1}{2}$ million, the population of, say, the Boston, Massachusetts, metropolitan area. Hence, our chances of dying by a lightning strike are quite small.

To Compare Two or More Groups of Different Size

Standardize the fraction by using a common denominator:

Proportions have a common denominator of 1.

Percentages have a common denominator of 100.

Rates have a selected useful common denominator in multiples of 10.

We have not gotten very far in our introductory discussion of statistics, and we already have encountered the importance of accurate communication. Mathematical formulas are rather strict in form. All of our formulas will have the following elements:

Presenting Answers in a Way That Encourages Proportional Thinking

Symbol = formula = contents of formula = answer

Observe these elements in our calculations of inmates with DROs.

These basic calculations are introduced early in this book because having a sense of understanding about reality and understanding the mathematics of proportions go hand in hand. Measures of "part of the whole" are typically the first calculations made in any statistical analysis. Proportional thinking is a basic feature of the statistical imagination.

How to Succeed in This Course and Enjoy It

Through years of teaching statistics I have learned that students must be willing to work and keep up with this course. Attention to and success with early assignments make later, more abstract assignments much easier to grasp. Succeeding in a statistics course is much like an airliner taking off. A great deal of energy is used reaching altitude (Chapters 1 through 9), but then the plane can cruise the rest of the way (Chapters 10 through 15). This text is designed for early success to allay your fears and reveal how enjoyable and interesting the subject is. Even an average student who is willing to put in the time and effort can earn an A in this course and have fun doing it. But this course does require hands-on assignments. Learning statistics is like learning to play a musical instrument. You can study music theory all day long, but until you practice your instrument, you will not learn how to play it. The key to success for playing an instrument or learning statistics is well-organized "practice."

If you fear that this course will doom you because of your perceived weaknesses in math, put those fears aside. The course starts with simple calculations and builds on them. If you work hard and keep up, the math will not be an issue. Start by reviewing the basic mathematical procedures in Appendix A. Here are some study guides:

- Organize your study notes, assignments, returned papers, and the like in a three-ring binder. This allows you to insert corrected materials and returned papers in their proper place and makes exam preparation highly efficient.

- Use proper reading technique. That is, look over a chapter for 20 to 30 minutes before reading it in detail. Read chapters before they are presented in class.

- Never miss a class or lab session. The material in this course is cumulative. Everything learned early on is applied in later chapters. Each chapter is a link in a chain, and a chain is only as strong as its weakest link. Keep up and this course is fun. Get behind and it becomes unnecessarily troublesome.

- In this course, do not be afraid to give back what is in the book. Complete sample exercises are provided for all procedures, and there is a summary of formulas at the end of each chapter. Exercises and tables distinguish between "givens" (information provided by a research problem) and "calculations" (what must be done to complete the problem). Follow the form of these exercises and "show the work" as well as the answer. In fact, answers to some of the problems are provided in Appendix C so that you may check your progress at home. A lifeless computer also can generate numbers. Proper interpretation of the answer is what is important, and detailed work is necessary for learning the logic behind a procedure.

- Turn in work on time. Go over returned assignments and correct them immediately.

- Ask for assistance when needed. There is no such thing as a stupid question in this course, but failing to ask *is* stupid.

- Accept the fact that this course is fun. Concentrated effort will be rewarded not only in terms of earning a grade but also in terms of learning valuable job skills.

TABLE 1–3 | Percentage change in the number of deaths from AIDS reported in Alabama Public Health Area 11 by gender

Gender	Number of AIDS Deaths in 1995	Number of AIDS Deaths in 1996	Percent (%) Change from 1995 to 1996
Men	43	44	2
Women	6	10	67
Total	49	54	10

Source: Data from Alabama Center for Health Statistics.

Statistical Follies and Fallacies: The Problem of Small Denominators

Care must be taken in interpreting proportions and percentages based on extremely small groups. Small baseline numbers in reports of percentage change are a particular source of confusion. Table 1–3 presents an example from the AIDS epidemic (Alabama Center for Health Statistics 2004).

Percentage change is calculated as follows:

$$\text{Percentage change} = \frac{\text{\# at time 2} - \text{\# at time 1}}{\text{\# at time 1}}(100)$$

The table shows that the *percentage increase* in the incidence of AIDS deaths was much higher for women than men between the two years. Such statistics were often reported as evidence that the epidemic was spreading much more rapidly among women than men, suggesting that AIDS had suddenly become a "female" disease. In fact, in 1996 only 10 deaths occurred among women compared with 44 among men. The apparent "female" phenomenon was due to the problem of a small denominator. In such a situation, a good statistician would simply report that there were too few female cases to make meaningful comparisons of percentage change.

SUMMARY

1. Statistics is a fun, imaginative, and informative way of looking at the empirical world. It is not simply a mathematical exercise. It involves careful observation, measurement, and analysis, and creatively putting the results to practical and scientific use.

2. The statistical imagination involves a balanced way of observing the world, the ability to think through a problem and maintain a sense of proportion when weighing evidence against preconceived notions. It looks at the larger picture and takes a critical view.

3. Consumer statistics designed for public audiences are called descriptive statistic Statistical analysis that involves testing scientific theory (hypothesis testing) called inferential statistics.

4. The purpose of scientific investigation is to explain the empirical world. These explanations take the form of theory—organized ideas that provide a sense of understanding and the ability to make predictions. Scientists are trained to be skeptical; that is, they accept the results of statistical analysis only after careful scrutiny and criticism.

5. Science has limitations. It involves the investigation of empirical phenomena only. Many sound, factually based scientific arguments lack political or taxpayer support. Ethical dilemmas often arise from scientific research and create resistance to its application.

6. For scientific research, statistical analysis involves collecting data and testing hypotheses about relationships between independent and dependent variables.

7. An important part of statistical analysis is controlling statistical error.

8. The seven steps of the research process are: specify the research question, review the scientific literature, propose a theory and state hypotheses, select a research design, collect the data, analyze the data and draw conclusions (the stage covered by this course), and disseminate the results.

9. Fractions, proportions, percentages, and rates are simply ways to measure a sense of proportion, gaining a sense of balance by weighing a part against the whole.

10. By providing a common denominator, proportions, percentages, and rates provide a way to standardize an assortment of observations of several groups of varying size.

CHAPTER EXTENSIONS ON *THE STATISTICAL IMAGINATION* WEB SITE

Chapter 1 Extensions of text material available on *The Statistical Imagination* Web Site at www.mhhe.com/ritchey2 has additional material for each chapter that expounds on a chapter's topics or provides advanced techniques. These materials are upgraded periodically.

FORMULAS FOR CHAPTER 1

Showing the work when making calculations:

Symbol = formula = contents of formula = answer

Calculating a fraction:

$$\text{Fraction} = \frac{\text{numerator}}{\text{denominator}} = \frac{\text{part}}{\text{whole}}$$

Calculating a proportion:

$$\text{Proportion} = p\,[\text{of total group in a category}] = \frac{\text{\# in a category}}{\text{\# in total group}} = \text{quotient}$$

Calculating a percentage:

$$\text{Percentage} = \% \,[\text{of total group in a category}] = p(100)$$

Calculating a rate:

$$\text{Rate of occurrence} = (p)\,(\text{a useful base number})$$

Calculating percentage change:

$$\text{Percentage change} = \left(\frac{\#\text{ at time 2} - \#\text{ at time}}{\#\text{ at time 1}} \right)(100)$$

QUESTIONS FOR CHAPTER 1

1. An interviewer in a survey misunderstood a respondent and incorrectly recorded that respondent's age. Was this a mistake or a statistical error? Explain.

2. Mary Jones is upset about natural disasters, noting that in a single year there were floods in the Midwest, drought in the South, and major earthquakes in the West. She believes that these events are proof that the end of the world is near. While Mary has a vivid imagination, explain why she lacks the statistical imagination.

3. In a study of college *seniors* at a major university, you measure major curriculum (psychology, sociology, chemistry, English, art, and so on) and year of schooling (first year, sophomore, junior, senior). In your study, which of these measurements is a variable, and which is a constant?

4. In a study of college seniors, you measure grade point average (GPA) and alcohol consumption in the previous month. State a hypothesis for these two variables and indicate which is the independent variable and which is the dependent variable. Could the results of your study of college *seniors* be "generalized" to *the entire student body* of the college? Why or why not?

5. For a sample of homeless persons, you are interested in the relationship between gender and types of sleeping places (where the subject spent the previous night). Which variable is the independent variable and which is the dependent variable?

6. Bob owns a book and computer store named InfoManiacs. He calculated the proportion of his profits that result from selling computer software and got an answer of 2.49. Could this be correct? Explain.

7. What is the essential feature of science that separates it from other forms of inquiry into nature?

8. Identify a commonly held belief that you suspect is a myth. Suggest what types of data might be collected to expose the myth. How might proportional thinking be applied to challenge this widely believed falsehood?

9. To get an idea of how organized scientific procedures are, go to the library or the Web and page through several scientific journals, such as the *American Sociological Review,* the *American Journal of Sociology,* the *Journal of the American Psychological Association,* the *Journal of Health and Social P*

Administrative Science Quarterly, Criminology, Social Services Review, American Journal of Psychology, American Political Science Review, Review of Public Administration, and *Political Science Quarterly.* Note the abundance of statistical tables and graphs in these articles. Note also that all articles in the various volumes have similar section headings.

a. List the headings of at least five articles from at least three different journals.

b. Compare these lists to the seven stages of the research process and comment.

10. Suppose one state in the United States had an infant mortality rate of 8.6 deaths per 1,000 live births in 1998. In the year 2000, the state public health department holds a conference called Goals 2010, in which policy makers and government officials vow to improve public health in the new millennium. They set a target rate of 6.0 infant deaths per 1,000 live births to be reached by the year 2010. This target rate is a _____.

11. In most states the interstate speed limit is 70 miles per hour. Random samples of vehicle speed are made with a speed detector radar gun. The average speed is found to be 74 miles per hour. The set speed limit is a statistical _____, and 74 miles per hour is a statistical _____.

12. Solve this ancient riddle.
As I was going to St. Ives, I met a man with seven wives.
Every wife had seven sacks, every sack had seven cats,
Every cat had seven kits.
Kits, cats, sacks, and wives; how many were going to St. Ives?

EXERCISES FOR CHAPTER 1

Problem Set 1A

1A-1.   Fill the blanks in the following table (see Appendix A for review).

	Fraction	Proportion	Percentage (%)
a.	$\dfrac{27}{198}$	.1364	_____
b.	$\dfrac{1}{598}$	_____	_____
c.	$\dfrac{36}{12,000}$	_____	_____
d.	_____	.2321	_____
e.	_____	_____	44.63
f.	_____	_____	91.35

1A-2. As an introductory statistics student, your professor asked that you calculate the accuracy of field goals kicked during the past season's games played at University Stadium. The kickers for the home team kicked 16 field goals in 21 attempts, and the kickers for the visiting teams kicked 17 field goals in 24 attempts. Which team had the better field goal kickers, home or visiting? Why?

1A-3. According to the U.S. Federal Bureau of Prisons (2003), 19.7 percent of federal prison inmates are in minimum-security facilities, 38.7 percent are in low security facilities, 24.7 percent are in medium-security facilities, and 10.8 percent are in high-security facilities. The total 2003 federal prison inmate population is 145,290. How many inmates are in each of these security categories?

1A-4. You are interested in conducting a research project involving levels of educational attainment in Alaska. The U.S. Bureau of the Census (2000) indicates that the Alaskan population aged 25 years and older is 379,556. Complete the table below by inserting the proportion (p) of this population that has completed various educational levels. Show the general formula and calculations for persons with less than a ninth-grade education.

Educational Level	n	p
Less than ninth grade	15,663	
Ninth to twelfth grade, no diploma	28,619	
High school graduate (or equivalency)	105,812	
Some college, no degree	108,442	
Associate degree	27,213	
Bachelor's degree	61,196	
Graduate or professional degree	32,611	
Totals		

1A-5. The North Atlantic Treaty Organization (NATO) consists of 19 member countries. Of these nations, only 2, the United States and Canada, are located in North America. What proportion of NATO member nations are *not* in North America? What percentage?

1A-6. Five academic departments have been selected to send 50 graduate and 150 undergraduate students to represent the university at a national leadership conference. However, department affiliation and degree level must be represented proportionally. For example, a proportion of .1945 of undergraduates come from the Department of Sociology, so .1945 of the representatives will come from that department. The following table shows numbers of students by department and degree level. Complete the proportion (p) and number (#) of students to attend in each empty cell. Show the general formula and calculations for at least one computation.

Department	Graduate	p	# to Attend	Undergraduate	p	# to Attend
Sociology	58			135		
Psychology	69			189		
History	50			122		
Anthropology	44			118		
Political Science	48			130		
Totals			50			150

1A-7. You are interested in examining marital status in the state of California. The population aged 15 years or older in California is 26,076,163 (U.S. Bureau of the Census 2000). Using the following figures, fill in the rates per 100,000 population for each of the categories shown in the table. Show the general formula and an example of calculations for the never married category.

Marital Status	n	Rate per 100,000 population (>15 yrs)
Never married	7,843,907	
Now married, except separated	13,657,201	
Separated	642,670	
Widowed	1,457,818	
Divorced	2,474,567	
Totals	26,076,163	

1A-8. Cockerham, Snead, and DeWaal (2002) examined the impact of socialist ideology on negative health behaviors in Russia. Among a sample of 8,701 Russian residents, 4,437 reported regular alcohol use and 3,704 reported smoking cigarettes. In addition, 3,292 of the sample reported that they assumed a prosocialist orientation, and 4,868 were married.
  a.   What proportion of the sample reported regular alcohol use?
  b.   What percentage of the sample did *not* report smoking?
  c.   What percentage of respondents did not report having a prosocialist orientation?
  d.   What proportion of respondents was married?

Problem Set 1B

1B-1. Fill in the blanks for the following table (see Appendix A for review).

	Fraction	Proportion	Percentage (%)
a.	$\dfrac{51}{207}$	.2464	_____
b.	$\dfrac{24}{503}$	_____	_____
c.	$\dfrac{663}{13,200}$	_____	_____
d.	_____	.0784	_____
e.	_____	_____	38.35

1B-2. During the 2003 regular season, the university baseball team played two catchers, David "Plate Guarder" Feinberg and Byron "Face Mask" Taylor. Coach Smith must decide which of them will start in the upcoming conference tournament against a team that is noted for stealing bases. His choice will rest on regular season success in throwing out opponents who attempted stolen bases. David threw out 17 base-stealers in 48 attempts and Byron threw out 14 of 32. Which catcher will start? Why?

1B-3. The U.S. Federal Bureau of Investigation (FBI) (2002a; 2002b) periodically compiles Uniform Crime Report statistics for all types of criminal activity. For 2002, the FBI's statistics revealed 9,721 single-bias instances of hate crimes. Of these, 44.9 percent were motivated by racial bias, 21.6 percent by ethnic bias, 18.8 percent by religious bias, and 14.3 percent by bias against sexual orientation. How many hate crimes occurred for each category?

1B-4. As part of an investigation of housing unit composition in the state of Louisiana, you are to examine the ages of householders across the state. There are 1,656,053 occupied housing units in the state (U.S. Bureau of the Census 2000). Complete the following table for the proportion (p) of householders in each age category. Show the general formula and calculations for householders aged 15 to 24 years.

Ages of Householders	n	p
15 to 24 years	102,760	
25 to 34 years	282,345	
35 to 44 years	367,556	
45 to 54 years	335,157	
55 to 64 years	228,754	
65 years and over	339,481	
Totals	1,656,053	

1B-5. An international car and heavy equipment manufacturer runs 112 plants worldwide. Only 42 of these plants are located in the eastern hemisphere. What proportion of these manufacturing plants are located in the western hemisphere? What percentage?

1B-6. Better Bodies Health Spa is to select 100 members to attend the Winter Olympics, half male and half female. Age groups are to be represented according to their proportional membership. For example, the proportion of males in the age group 21–30 is .0992, so that proportion of the males making the trip will fall in that age category. The following chart gives the membership breakdown by age and gender. Fill in the proportion (p) and number (# to attend) for each age group for each gender. Show the general formula and the computation for the males in the 21–30-year-old-group.

Age Group	Males	p	# to Attend	Females	p	# to Attend
21–30	49			80		
31–40	170			217		
41–50	169			176		
51–60	84			91		
61+	22			48		
Totals			50			50

1B-7. Roughly 20 percent of the U.S. population is affected by mental disorder every year (U.S. Dept. of Health and Human Services 1999). The total population, according to the 2000 decennial census, is 281,421,906 (U.S. Bureau of the Census 2000). The following table lists several mental disorders and their estimated prevalence in the general population. Calculate the numbers (n) and rates of these disorders per 100,000 population in the United States, and fill in the appropriate cells in the table. Show the general formulas and calculations for simple phobia.

Disorder	Estimated % Prevalence	n	Rate per 100,000 Population
Simple phobia	8.3		
Schizophrenia	1.3		
Mood disorder	7.1		
Post-traumatic stress disorder	3.6		
Anorexia nervosa	0.1		

1B-8. In their analysis of Russian health lifestyles, Cockerham, Snead, and DeWaal (2002) reported the following distribution of educational attainment among a sample of 8,657 respondents. Complete the proportion and percent columns in the following table. Show the general formula and calculations for those with no professional courses.

Education	n	p	(%)
No professional courses	2,113		
Professional courses	1,037		
Professional training without secondary education	713		
Professional training with secondary education	1,154		
Technical school	1,854		
University	1,700		
Graduate school	86		
Totals	8,657		

Problem Set 1C

1C-1.   Fill in the blanks for the following table (see Appendix A for review).

	Fraction	Proportion	Percentage (%)
a.	_____	_____	60.46
b.	_____	.2736	_____
c.	_____	_____	94.32
d.	$\dfrac{1,922}{8,998}$	_____	_____
e.	$\dfrac{163}{7,231}$	_____	_____

1C-2.   The Graduate Student Association (GSA) sponsored a new-release movie night and bowling night. Both events were advertised, the movie in print media and bowling night on campus radio. The GSA projected a turnout of 200 students for movie night and 150 for bowling night. However, 92 students showed up for movie night and only 84 showed up for bowling night. Based on the proportion of projected turnout, which advertising medium appeared to be a more effective way to advertise GSA events?

1C-3.   According to the Federal Bureau of Investigation (FBI) (2002b), there were a total of 11,451 hate-crime offenses reported in 2001. Of these, 67.8 percent were crimes against persons and 31.5 percent were crimes against property. Of crimes reported against persons, 55.9 percent were acts of intimidation. Of crimes against property, 83.7 percent were classified as destruction, damage, or vandalism.

     a.   How many hate crimes were committed against persons?

     b.   How many hate crimes were committed against property?

     c.   How many hate crimes against persons were deemed acts of intimidation?

     d.   How many hate crimes against property were deemed acts of destruction/damage/vandalism?

1C-4. Scott, Sam, and Sid, three friends who sack groceries at the local market, decided to pool their tips one afternoon to buy a gift for their friend Cindy, who was in the hospital. Scott put in $15, Sam $12, and Sid $10. What proportion of the gift money was contributed by each one?

1C-5. You are interested in the phenomenon of personalized license plates, plates on which the owner has his or her name or a saying. In a random sample of 341 plates, you find that 73 are personalized. What proportion is *not* personalized? What percentage?

1C-6. Representatives to the Graduate Student Association (GSA) and the Undergraduate Student Association (USA) at a large university are elected by the student body. Available seats are allotted in proportion to student enrollment for each department. For example, if 10 percent of the undergraduates are enrolled in the biology department, then 10 percent of the USA representatives will come from biology students. The following table shows student enrollment for selected academic departments, which together will fill 22 GSA and 62 USA representative seats. Complete the table to show the proportion (p) and number (#) of representatives to each student organization from each department. Show the general formula and calculations for the proportion and number of representatives to the GSA for biology.

Department	Graduate	p	# to GSA	Undergraduate	p	# to USA
Biology	43			119		
Chemistry	33			98		
Computer Science	45			122		
Mathematics	29			88		
Physics	28			76		
Totals			22			62

1C-7. Complete the following table by calculating the rate of institutionalization (in prisons and mental hospitals) per 100,000 population. Show the general formula and the computation for Anderson, Indiana.

City	Population	Number of Persons Institutionalized	Rate per 100,000 Population
Anderson, Indiana	130,669	3,981	
Bellingham, Washington	127,780	1,602	
Duluth, Minnesota	239,971	4,610	
Modesto, California	370,522	4,456	

1C-8. Turner (1995) investigated the effects of unemployment. He contacted 5,612 persons whom he deemed eligible for study because they had been unemployed at least once since joining the labor force. Of these eligible persons, 3,617 were actually interviewed, among whom 1,252 were tagged for long-term study. In the long-term study group, 154 were "recently unemployed," having lost their jobs in the past three years. Of the recently unemployed, 45 remained unemployed.

   a. What proportion of eligible subjects was interviewed?
   b. What percentage of those interviewed was not accepted for long-term study?
   c. What percentage of the long-term study group became unemployed in the past three years?
   d. What percentage of the recently unemployed had returned to work?

Problem Set 1D

1D-1. Fill in the blanks for the following table (see Appendix A for review).

	Fraction	Proportion	Percentage (%)
a.	_____	_____	29.67
b.	_____	.7243	_____
c.	_____	_____	87.63
d.	$\frac{2,485}{6,773}$	_____	_____
e.	$\frac{9,228}{11,621}$	_____	_____
f.	_____	.6827	_____

1D-2. According to the U.S. Bureau of the Census (2000), the population of Alabama is 4,447,100, the population of Oregon is 3,421,399, and the population of Texas is 20,851,820. The state with the highest proportion of persons 65 years of age and older will receive federal funding to support senior citizen programs. The number of citizens over 65 years of age is

579,798 in Alabama, 438,177 in Oregon, and 2,072,532 in Texas. Which state will receive the federal funds?

1D-3. According to the U.S. Federal Bureau of Prisons (2003), in the first half of 2003, a total of 153,205 inmates were sentenced to prisons. Of these, 55.6 percent were sentenced for drug offenses; 11.3 percent for weapons, explosives, or arson; 10.7 percent for immigration violations; 6.7 percent for robbery; and 15.7 percent for other offenses. How many inmates were sentenced for each of these crimes?

1D-4. In a casual conversation after class, Jane and Anne discover that they have a common habit. To relieve stress, they keep tabs on how frequently they can ring the recycle bin when throwing away a ball of paper. Jane brags that of 250 tosses, she rang the bin 128 times. In 265 tosses, Anne made 157 "baskets." Who is the better tosser? Why?

1D-5. In order to meet Environmental Protection Agency (EPA) guidelines, the quantity of particulate matter in the city's air can exceed 69 parts per million only 15 percent of the days in the year without incurring cautions. How many days is this?

1D-6. A corporation with offices in Los Angeles and New York will train its administrative assistants in a new software program. Each training session accommodates 40 persons from each city. So that some employees in every department will receive training right away, participants are chosen by using quotas based on the number of employees in a department. For instance, if 10 percent of the administrative assistants are in a particular department in Los Angeles, then 10 percent of the 40 trainees will come from that department. The following chart gives the membership breakdown by department and city. Fill in the proportion (p) and number (# to attend) for each department and city. Show the formula and computation for the personnel department in Los Angeles.

Department	Los Angeles	p	# to Attend	New York	p	# to Attend
Personnel	36			43		
Marketing	81			93		
Shipping	65			78		
Management	24			31		
Accounting	25			38		
Totals			40			40

1D-7. Complete the following table by calculating the rate of institutionalization (in prisons and mental hospitals) per 100,000 population. Show the general formula and the computation for Bakersfield, California.

City	Population	Number of Persons Institutionalized	Rate per 100,000 Population
Bakersfield, California	543,477	10,808	
Burlington, North Carolina	108,213	1,158	
Great Falls, Montana	77,691	787	
Poughkeepsie, New York	259,462	11,082	

1D-8. Turner (1995) investigated the effects of unemployment. He contacted 5,612 persons whom he deemed eligible for study because they had been unemployed at least once since joining the labor force. Of these eligible persons, 3,617 were actually interviewed, among whom 1,252 were tagged for long-term study. Imagine that of the 1,252 persons in the long-term study group, 732 were males and 520 were females. Of the 154 recently unemployed, 80 were males and 74 were females. Among the 45 still unemployed, 25 were males and 20 were females.

    a. In this long-term study group, which gender had the higher proportion of recent unemployment?

    b. Among the recently unemployed, were men or women more successful in returning to the workforce?

OPTIONAL COMPUTER APPLICATIONS FOR CHAPTER 1

If your instructor assigns exercises on the computer, the text comes with a compact disk that contains the *Statistical Package for the Social Sciences (SPSS)* software, *SPSS for Windows, Student Version*. The software is time restricted. It will work for 13 months from the date on which you load it onto your computer. This software includes a tutorial and good help menus that facilitate its operation.

Appendix D of this text, "Guide to *SPSS for Windows*," provides a concise overview of the basic operations of the software package and chapter-by-chapter instructions. In addition, *The Statistical Imagination* Web site at www.mhhe.com/ritchey2 provides specific chapter exercises and more instructions on running procedures and interpreting output. Use Appendix D to get started.

The *SPSS for Windows, Student Version* is more than adequate for learning basic statistics. If you desire to conduct your own research, however, you may wish to gain access to the full base system of the regular (nonstudent) version of *SPSS for Windows*, or the *SPSS for Windows Graduate Pack,* which is available on campuses with full version site licenses. These versions of *SPSS* have several advantages, including a "Syntax Editor" window that pastes and saves mouse commands for later use. Moreover, in the regular version of *SPSS* there are no limitations on the number of variables or sample sizes of data sets.

All computer application exercises are on *The Statistical Imagination* Web site. The site provides easily downloadable computer exercises for each chapter, detailed instructions on the statistical procedures used in a chapter, data sets around which chapter exercises are built, and codebooks that describe the variables in each data set.

The data sets on *The Statistical Imagination* Web site have been modified in minor ways to facilitate instruction and, therefore, do not suffice for true research purposes. You may request unmodified original data sets from the sources listed in the codebooks on the Web site. Other data sets are available with Internet access from government agencies, and research foundations, such as the Inter University Consortium for Political and Social Research (ICPSR) and the National Opinion Research Center (NORC). The Web site provides links to these sources and others. The Web site also provides links to statistical-related sites that reveal the many applications of statistical work. These sites include population reports of the U.S. Bureau of the Census, U.S. Department of Justice crime data, statistical abstracts, sports statistics sites, interesting marketing surveys, and quizzical games.

Getting Started with SPSS

Start by looking over Appendix D and reading the Chapter 1 instructions. To download *SPSS for Windows, Student Version* onto your computer, insert the *SPSS* compact disk into your CD drive. Click "Install *SPSS for Windows Student Version*" and follow instructions. Appendix D provides additional information on saving an *SPSS for Windows* icon on your computer desktop and opening the program for use. Once you open *SPSS,* you may wish to follow the tutorial to become familiar with basic windows, icons, and menus.

Chapter 1 Exercises

Go to *The Statistical Imagination* Web site www.mhhe.com/ritchey2 to access Chapter 1 computer applications exercises. This first exercise involves an orientation to *SPSS for Windows* statistical software with directions on how to download and retrieve data files.

NOTES

1. When someone makes an objective statement about an object (or person or situation), the statement describes a characteristic that is truly part of the object, for example, the statement "The stop sign is red." When someone makes a subjective statement, the statement actually describes a characteristic of the "subject" observer rather than the object. Subjective statements therefore are personal views or opinions that reflect the biases, distortions, personal opinions, or prejudices of the person making the statement. For example, someone who is color-blind might say, "The stop sign is gray." The "grayness" is not part of the sign but instead is only the perception of the subject observer.

2. The Latin abbreviation *i.e.* means "that is" (*id est*); *e.g.* means "for example" (*exempli gratia*).

3. The term *independent* comes from laboratory science, where predictor variables are manipulated independently of outcomes. For example, in a study of the effects of a drug

on rats, the drug is given to some rats (the experimental group), while a placebo (or fake drug) is given to a matched group of rats (the control group). The choice of which rats are assigned to each group is done independently of measuring which rats get well.

4. The term *theory* is often used to mean an uncorroborated idea, as in "That is just a theory." This is a nonscientific use of the term. Scientific theories are based *not* on conjecture or opinion but on objective analysis of carefully gathered data.

2

Organizing Data to Minimize Statistical Error

CHAPTER OUTLINE

Introduction

Whether done for scientific investigation, product marketing, weather forecasting, or placing a bet, attempting to predict the future is a common pastime. Scientists make empirical predictions to test the accuracy of their ideas. For example, what are your chances of being a victim of a crime at your workplace? Madriz (1996) found three predictive factors based on the idea that the risk of victimization can be reduced by means of the careful study of routine activities. One risk factor is exposure—situational vulnerability—such as working alone in a convenience store late at night. A second is proximity to potential offenders, such as working at a store in a high-crime area. A third is target attractiveness, the desirability of a victim's property, such as having large amounts of cash on hand.

If a store owner put his or her employees at unnecessary risk, a robbery or murder would not be a random occurrence or mistake; it would be an error. In Chapter 1 we noted that **errors** are *known degrees of imprecision.* Knowing the relationship between circumstances and the likelihood of robbery allows one to institute preventive measures that reduce the calculated chances that "errors" will occur. Risk reduction measures might include having at least two employees present, closing at 11:00 P.M., locating in a high-traffic area, keeping only small amounts of cash on hand, and installing surveillance systems. Error reduction hinges on understanding the predictive relationships among variables.

As we briefly noted in Chapter 1, statistics is about the precise understanding and control of **statistical error**, *known degrees of imprecision in the procedures used to gather and process information.* Errors are not mistakes. Errors are known amounts of imprecision that can be calculated and reduced by careful, informed selection of sampling designs, measurement instruments, and statistical formulas.

---

statistical error   Known degrees of imprecision in the procedures used to gather and process information.

Statistical analysis typically involves sampling: observing only a small part of the group or population under study. For example, to learn about all convenience stores, we might study a sample of 20 stores. Can the data from a sample of 20 stores accurately reveal how all convenience stores operate? Research also involves observation and measurement. Can we assume that our measurements are completely accurate? Sampling and measurement are two potential sources of error in drawing conclusions in research. **Sampling error** is *inaccuracy in predictions about a population that results from the fact that we do not observe every subject in the population.* **Measurement error** is *inaccuracy in research which derives from imprecise measurement instruments, difficulties in the classification of observations, and the need to round numbers.* After discussing each of these types of error, we will show how they are related.

Controlling Sampling Error

To analyze means to pick something apart and examine it in fine detail in an organized way. In doing statistical work, we analyze groups of persons, objects, or events and measure variables to get averages, tendencies, or percentages. *Measurement of a single person,* say, recording Mary Smith's age as 19 years, does not provide a statistic; this is simply an **observation**. However, determining that the average age of a class of 30 students is 19.5 years is computing a statistic based on a set of observations. The field of statistics involves **summary calculations** of many observations, *the summing up of a group of measurements.* Our interests are in observing many cases, gathering precise information about them, and making summary statements about the group, not about individuals.

The group of subjects we observe is usually quite small. Our purpose is to study the small number of subjects to draw conclusions about the larger population from which those subjects came. Studying every instance of a phenomenon is impractical, costly, and unnecessary. For example, we do not have to poll every likely voter to determine candidate A's support. Instead, we can poll a cross section of likely voters, perhaps 500. This smaller group is called a sample, while the larger, complete group from which it came is called a population or universe.

Figure 2–1 depicts the notion of sampling. The **population** (or universe) is *a large group of people of particular interest that we desire to study and understand.* Commonly studied populations include the people of a country, state, or community; the inmates at a state correctional facility; currently enrolled students at a college; families with school-age children; hospital patients; head chefs in New York City restaurants; and corporation executives. A **sample** is *a small subgroup of the population; the sample is observed and measured and then used to draw conclusions about the population.*

---

a population (or universe)   A large group of people (or objects) of particular interest that we desire to study and understand.

a sample   A small group of the population; the sample is observed and measured and then used to draw conclusions about the population.

Sampling is something we do all the time. We taste a spoonful (a sample) to decide whether to add more chili powder to the pot (the population). To explore an academic major, say, sociology, we may take one or two courses (a sample) to determine whether the universe of ideas and activities of sociology appeals to us. A first date with someone is a sampling of that individual's personality, a first exposure to the universe of his or her behavioral and attitudinal tendencies. Sampling is a common and efficient human behavior.

FIGURE 2–1

The relationship of a population (universe) of measurements to a sample of measurements

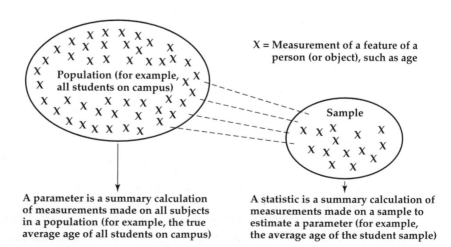

X = Measurement of a feature of a person (or object), such as age

Population (for example, all students on campus)

Sample

A parameter is a summary calculation of measurements made on all subjects in a population (for example, the true average age of all students on campus)

A statistic is a summary calculation of measurements made on a sample to estimate a parameter (for example, the average age of the student sample)

Our interest, however, is not in the sample per se. Instead, we want to learn about the entire population. To acquire absolutely correct information about an entire population, we would ideally measure *all* of its members and summarize the results in mathematical terms, reporting percentages, rates, and averages. *A summary calculation of measurements made on all subjects in a population* is called a **parameter**. For example, the average age of inmates at Sharpwire Prison is a parameter. The percentage of executives who are female at the Menrule Plastics Corporation is a parameter. Unfortunately, most populations are so large that we cannot afford the time and expense of measuring all members. For example, it would be absurd to measure the heights of all American adults. Because of the high costs of measuring every subject in a population, the true values of parameters are typically unknown.

Fortunately, sampling allows us to accurately *estimate* parameters. With samples we compute statistics rather than parameters. A **statistic** is *a summary calculation of measurements made on a sample to estimate a parameter of the population*. For instance, in a sample of 800 registered Republicans in New Jersey we might find that 74 percent support the governor. This percentage constitutes a statistic, only an estimate of the governor's true support. A sample and the statistics computed on it are simply tools for drawing *conclusions about a population in general*—the population as a whole. Such conclusions, if made by following proper statistical procedures, are called statistical generalizations.

---

a parameter   A summary calculation of measurements made on all subjects in a population.

a statistic   A summary calculation of measurements made on a sample to estimate a parameter of the population.

We must never lose sight of the fact that it is the population that is of concern to us. For example, an "exit poll" sample of voters (taken as people leave a voting place) may suggest that candidate A is the winner. This, however, is an estimate, an approximation of the true level of support. The true winner will be known only after all the votes are counted, that is, when the entire population of voters has been measured.

One way to remember that a single sample only provides estimates is to compare the results of several samples from the same population. If a statistics professor sent each of 30 class members out to gather a sample of 10 fellow students and estimate average student age, each class member would get a slightly different result. (If you are not convinced, draw two samples yourself.) This variability in sampling outcomes simply reflects the fact that a statistic from a single sample is only an estimate of the true population parameter.

How, then, are we to trust the results of a single sample? The answer to this question presents good news and bad news. The bad news is that statisticians must acknowledge that conclusions from a sample are not absolutely correct, that statistics are only estimates of parameters. The good news is that statistical procedures and the logic of probability theory allow statisticians to specify a known degree of error in predictions and therefore stipulate the degree of confidence we may place in a conclusion based on statistics. Put simply, although statistical estimates are not perfect, we know how close to perfect they are.

Careful Statistical Estimation versus Hasty Guesstimation

The statistical imagination emphasizes understanding a point of detail in its proper context, taking care not to draw simplistic or fantastic conclusions. Statistical estimation is different from commonsense "guesstimation," which is often biased. A **statistical estimate** is *the report of a summary measurement based on systematic sampling and precise measurements and reported with known degrees of error and confidence.* A **guesstimate** is *a report of a summary measurement based on limited and usually subjective personal experiences, anecdotal evidence, or hasty casual observations.*

Guesstimation might occur when a news reporter picks candidate A as the sure winner because an exit poll reports support by 52 percent of likely voters. In contrast, taking note of the sample size, a statistician would be more cautious and emphasize that 52 percent means 52 plus or minus 5 percentage points; therefore, support lies somewhere between 47 percent and 57 percent. Candidate A's victory is not assured because support could be *as low as* 47 percent. Moreover, the statistician provides a degree of confidence for the estimate, such as 95 percent. (We cannot claim 100 percent confidence until all the votes are in.) Careful statistical estimation is different from even a good guess. Statisticians differ from other prognosticators in two important ways: Statisticians (1) control and manage the degree of error in reported statistics and (2) precisely state confidence in their conclusions.

A particularly insidious type of guesstimation is a prejudicial **stereotype**, *a false generalization that implies that all individuals in a category share certain, usually undesirable, traits.* For example, there is the racist stereotype that African-Americans are too ignorant, lazy, or immoral to support their families and that this is the cause of poverty in America. In fact, nearly 7 of every 10 poor Americans are white and most poor people are employed. Guesstimates are often guided by feelings that reinforce stereotypes, feelings such as hate, fear, and superiority. In contrast, statistical generalizations are interpreted with caution and within the larger context of scientific testing with its safeguards against subjectivity. Table 2–1 compares guesstimates to statistical estimates.

TABLE 2–1 | Commonsense "guesstimates" versus statistical estimates

Commonsense Guesstimates	Statistical Estimates
The idea is based on limited and usually subjective personal experiences, anecdotal evidence, or hasty observations.	The idea is based on systematic sampling and measurement.
Produces conjectures and mistaken conclusions.	Produces reliable estimates with known degrees of error and confidence.
Produces and reinforces stereotypes.	Produces statistical generalizations.
Usually a matter of opinion.	Usually a matter of fact.

Sampling Error and Its Management with Probability Theory

Because the only way to know a true parameter is to survey the entire population, each statistic computed from a sample is an estimate. Just by chance, the statistics of some samples are closer to the true parameter value than are those of others. **Probability theory** (Chapter 6) is *the analysis and understanding of chance occurrences.* It provides a set of rules for determining the accuracy of sample statistics and computing the degrees of confidence we have in conclusions about a population.

To successfully manage sampling error we must focus on its specific sources: sample size and sample representativeness. **Sample size** refers to *the number of cases or observations in a sample: the number of persons or objects observed.* Generally speaking, the larger the sample, the smaller the range of error. Suppose a researcher sent two assistants out to determine the average age of the student body. One asked 3 students for their ages, while the second asked 1,000. Intuition leads us to place greater trust in the results from the larger sample because the smaller sample could more easily bunch up with all young or all old students. In a later chapter we will learn to compute and report statistics with a "confidence interval" of plus or minus an exact amount of error for any given sample size. With a sample of 1,000 we may find that the average age on campus is 22.4 years plus or minus 0.3 year, which asserts that the average age lies between 22.7 years (i.e., 22.4 + 0.3) and 22.1 years (i.e., 22.4 − 0.3). The computation of "plus or minus some sampling error" is based on mathematical probabilities or probability theory.

Probability theory also allows us to say exactly how often a statistic will incorrectly predict the parameter, that is, how often errors may cause a wrong answer. For example, we may note that 5 percent of the time our procedures produce a false conclusion. By noting this level of error, however, we are also noting our level of confidence. If our estimate is wrong only 5 percent of the time, then it is correct 95 percent of the time; thus, we are 95 percent confident in it.

A second factor affecting sampling accuracy is the extent to which all segments of a population actually land in the sample—sample representativeness. A **representative sample** is one in which *all segments of the population are included in the sample in their correct proportions in the population.* For example, if a campus population is actually 54 percent male and 46 percent female, a representative sample will have close to these percentages of men and women.

---

representative sample   A sample in which all segments of the population are included in the sample in their correct proportions in the population.

A **nonrepresentative sample** is *one in which some segments of the population are overrepresented or underrepresented in the sample.* This is a dangerous type of sampling error because it can lead to totally bogus results. Suppose, for instance, the campus administration wishes to poll students on their support for expanding the football stadium. Nursing Student Association volunteers do the polling and are told to poll every 10th student, but instead they poll every 10th student coming out of the nursing building. Unsurprisingly, the results show that only 23 percent of students favor the expansion. Why? Because the association members actually surveyed the population of nursing students, which is disproportionately female and not representative of the campus as a whole. We would say that this sample is *biased* by a disproportionately high share of females. This nonrepresentative sample allowed one segment of the population to have more than its fair share of "votes" on an issue.

There are a variety of sampling designs, but one of the most commonly used is a simple random sample. A **simple random sample** is *one in which every person (or object) in the population has the same chance of being selected for the sample.* (In technical terms, we say that everyone in the population has *an equal probability of inclusion* in the sample.) This design is like a raffle or lottery in which every person in the population may enter only once. A simple random sample of sufficient size usually will produce a representative sample.

> **simple random sample**   A sample in which every person (or object) in the population has the same chance of being selected for the sample.

Controlling Measurement Error

In addition to avoiding sampling errors, we must precisely define how measurements are to be made and carefully code the responses once the data are acquired. *The set of procedures or operations for measuring a variable* is called its **operational definition**. For example, suppose we use U.S. Census data to conduct a study of urban poverty with a sample of 300 cities. There are various ways to *operationalize* a measure of poverty. The challenge is to select the way that most accurately depicts how many of a city's households are occupied by poor families. One measure is the percentage of households receiving food stamps. A second is the city's unemployment rate. A third is the percentage of households living below the federally defined poverty level (a specific income adjusted for household size). In fact, the third option generally is recognized as the best approximation of poverty for a community, and so we would choose this as our operational definition. The choice of an operational definition is guided by identifying common types of measurement error and doing everything possible to minimize them.

Levels of Measurement: Careful Selection of Statistical Procedures

Measurement

Measurement is *the assignment of symbols, either names or numbers, to the differences we observe in a variable's qualities or amounts. The measurement of a particular sample subject on a single variable* is that subject's **score** for that variable or, to use computer terminology, a code. Suppose for a moment that your statistics class is a sample. We could score the variables age, class level, gender, grade point average (GPA), and race. For one student, Joanie, these scores are 20 on age, junior on class level, female on gender, 3.25 on GPA, and white on race; for another, Ron, the respective codes are 19, sophomore, male, 3.48, and African-American. We will use the terms *score* and *code* interchangeably. The *value* of a score is its amount.

As this simple illustration reveals, not all variables are measured in the same way. Some are scored with names or categories that identify differences in kind or quality, such as African-American and white for the variable race. Other variables allow for distinctions of degree or distance between quantities, such as the variables age and GPA. These variables have a **unit of measure**, a *set interval or distance between quantities of the variables*. We score them numerically, like the numbered marks on a ruler or meter stick. The unit of measure for a temperature scale is a degree; for weight, a pound; for height, an inch; and so on.

To capture the fine distinctions among the measurement properties of variables, we use a scheme called levels of measurement. The **level of measurement of a variable** *identifies its measurement properties, which determine the kind of mathematical operations (addition, multiplication, etc.) that can be appropriately used with it and the statistical formulas that can be used with it in testing theoretical hypotheses*. These levels are called nominal, ordinal, interval, and ratio. The level of measurement of a variable is an important guide for selecting statistical formulas and procedures.

---

level of measurement of a variable   Identifies the variable's measurement properties, which determine the kind of mathematical operations (addition, multiplication, etc.) that can be appropriately used with it and the statistical formulas that can be used with it in testing theoretical hypotheses.

Nominal Variables

Nominal variables are those for which *codes merely indicate a difference in category, class, quality, or kind*. The word *nominal* comes from the Latin word for *name,* and these variables have named categories. Examples include place of birth (Chicago, Atlanta, Portland, etc.), favorite flavor of ice cream (vanilla, chocolate, cookies and cream, etc.), make of automobile (Ford, Lexus, Pontiac, etc.), and academic major (psychology, chemistry, electrical engineering, etc.).

Nominal variables do not allow for meaningfully ordered numerical scores. Nonetheless, because computers more efficiently process numbers, we sometimes number the categories of these variables in computer codes. For instance, with the variable *gender* we may set the codes as $0 =$ male and $1 =$ female. The choice of numbers for such codes is arbitrary; we could just as well have coded $0 =$ female and $1 =$ male. Additionally, the categories of a nominal variable cannot be meaningfully ranked in magnitude (from high to low) even if ordered numbers are assigned as codes. For example, to code female as 1 and male as 0 does not imply that females are a score of 1 higher than males. There is no sense of degree with nominal variables. A person is either male or female, not one or the other to some degree. Even some apparently numerical scores are actually nominal variables. For example, a Social Security number is actually a category, and there is no point in computing its average.

Since many nominal variables have only two categories, there is a special name for them. A **dichotomous variable** is *one with only two categories*. A common dichotomous survey variable is any with the answers "yes" and "no" and, in laboratory research designs, one that distinguishes "presence" (the experimental group) or "absence" (the control group). For example, in testing the effectiveness of a new hay fever medication, the experimental group is administered the new drug and scored 1. The control group is given an imitation drug (or placebo) and scored 0. In the computer we name this variable LABGROUP. When we desire to isolate the experimental group for analysis, we instruct the computer to search the codes of LABGROUP and pull out those cases with a code of 1.

Ordinal Variables

Like nominal variables, **ordinal variables** *name categories, but they have the additional property of allowing categories to be ranked* from highest to lowest, best to worst, or first to last. Typical ordinal variables include social class ranking (upper, middle, working, poverty), educational class level (senior, junior, etc.), and quality of housing (standard, substandard, dilapidated). Survey questions that measure attitudes and opinions often employ ranked scores. For example, the variable "attitude toward legal abortion" might rank the extent of agreement using the response categories: *strongly agree, agree, don't know, disagree, strongly disagree*. This widely used set of codes is called Likert scoring after its originator, Rensis Likert (1932).

Interval Variables

Interval variables have the characteristics of nominal and ordinal variables, plus *a defined numerical unit of measure*. Interval variables identify differences in amount, quantity, degree, or distance and are assigned highly useful numerical scores. Examples include temperature (scored to the nearest thermal degree) and intelligence quotient (IQ) score, ranging from 0 to 200 points. With interval variables, the intervals or distances between scores are the same between any two points on the measurement scale. For example, with the variable temperature, the difference between 10 degrees and 11 degrees Fahrenheit is the same as that between 40 degrees and 41 degrees. A set, ordered unit of measure provides the ability to add, subtract, multiply, and divide scores and compute averages.

Interval variables give a sense of "how much" or "what size," such as how hot, how opinionated, how conservative, how depressed, how long, and how heavy. With interval variables we think in terms of distances between scores on a straight line. For example, if the average test grade in a class is 80 and Carl got an 85 and Brett got a 90, then Brett's score was twice as far above average as Carl's. Furthermore, the ranges of error with interval variables are more definite and easier to manage because, for instance, numerical scores can be rounded.

Comparing the properties of interval and ordinal variables is informative. Unlike interval variables, ordinal variables lack the property of a set unit of measure even if the ordered categories are numbered. For instance, position of finish in a horse race (1, 2, 3, etc.) is merely ordinal; it simply says which horses crossed the finish line first, second, third, and so on, but not how far apart they finished. For this ordinal variable to be treated as an interval variable, the horses would have to finish in single-file order and equal distances apart. Furthermore, subtraction of the ranked numbers of an ordinal variable provides only differences in rank, not distance between scores. For example, if One Leg Up and Trouble at the Gate finished third and sixth, respectively, then One Leg Up came in three positions ahead. These horses could have been separated by a few inches or hundreds of yards. Although ordinal variables do allow some calculations, such as differences in rank and average rank, they have limited mathematical usefulness. Interval variables have much greater mathematical usefulness than do ordinal variables.

Ratio Variables

Ratio variables have the characteristics of interval variables plus *a true zero point, where a score of zero means none*. Weight, height, age, distance, population size, duration of time, and GPA are examples of ratio variables.

Comparing ratio variables to interval variables is informative because both have set intervals in their unit of measure, but only ratio variables have a meaningful zero point. Some *interval* variables may have a score of zero, but the zero point is arbitrary; that is, it could be set at any point in a variable's possible score range because the zero does not mean none. For instance, zero temperature does not mean no temperature. Thus, on the Fahrenheit scale it is set at 32 degrees below the freezing point, while on the Celsius scale it is set at the freezing point itself.

The true zero points of ratio variables allow even greater flexibility in computations and statistical analysis. Like interval variables, ratio variables can be multiplied and divided, but we can also compute ratios, hence the name. A **ratio** is *the amount of one observation in relation to another*. For example, if John eats three slices of pizza and Jessica eats one, the ratio is three to one, written as 3:1. With a ratio level variable the answer for a computed ratio makes sense, but with an interval-level variable it does not. For example, an 80-pound boy is twice as heavy as a 40-pound boy, a ratio of 2:1. But it makes no sense to say of the interval-level variable *temperature* that it is four times warmer in Miami, where it is 80 degrees, than in New York, where it is 20 degrees. In New York it is not warm at all! One way, then, to determine whether a variable has a true zero is to attempt to interpret a ratio. If the ratio is meaningless, the variable is at best interval level and its zero point is arbitrary.

Because of the similarities of statistical procedures applied to interval and ratio variables, we often lump these distinctions together by referring to interval/ratio variables. Similarly, we often refer to nominal/ordinal variables. Table 2–2 summarizes the properties of the four conventional levels of measurement.

In summary, to determine the level of measurement of a variable, ask these questions and follow the tree diagram below:

1. Is the variable scored using category names, such as "male" or "female"? If so, then the level of measurement is nominal. Can these category names be ranked from low to high, such as lower class, working class, middle class, and upper class? If so, then the level of measurement is ordinal.
2. Is the variable scored using numerical values, such as 1, 2, 3, and so on, but the scores simply designate ranks, such as 1st, 2nd, and 3rd? If so, then the level of measurement is ordinal.

TABLE 2–2 | Characteristics of the four levels of measurement

Level of Measurement	Examples	Qualities	Mathematical Operations Permitted
Nominal	Gender, race, religious preference, marital status	Classification into categories; naming of categories	Counting of the number of cases (i.e., the frequency) of each category of the variable; comparing the sizes of categories
Ordinal	Social class rank, attitude and opinion questions	Classification of categories; rank ordering of categories from low to high	All the above plus judgments of greater than and less than and computations of differences and averages of ranks
Interval	Temperature, summary indexes, attitude and opinion scales	All the above plus distances between scores have a fixed unit of measure	All the above plus mathematical operations such as addition, subtraction, multiplication, division, square roots
Ratio	Weight, income, age, years of education, size of population	All the above plus a true zero point	All the above plus the computation of meaningful ratios

3. Is the variable scored using numerical values that have a set interval or unit of measure, such as inches, miles, or degrees? If so, then the level of measurement is interval. Does this variable also have a true zero point? If so, then the level of measurement is ratio.

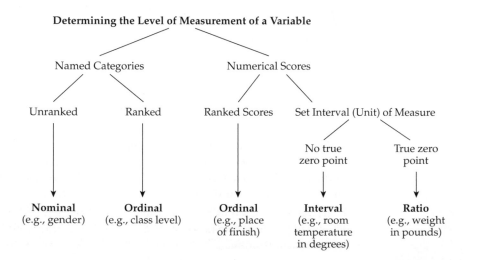

Determining the Level of Measurement of a Variable

TABLE 2–3 I Creating an index to transform several nominal variables into a ratio variable

Variable Number and Name	Operational Definition (how the variable is measured)	Level of Measurement	Codes (how scored)
1. SMOKES	Current smoker?	Nominal	0 = no 1 = yes
2. BINGE	Has consumed five or more alcoholic beverages on a single occasion in the past month.	Nominal	0 = no 1 = yes
3. EXERCISE	Does not exercise regularly.	Nominal	0 = no 1 = yes
4. DRUGS	Has used an illicit drug in the past month.	Nominal	0 = no 1 = yes
5. DROVEDR	Has driven while intoxicated.	Nominal	0 = no 1 = yes
6. RISKIND	Number of risk behaviors reported.	Ratio	Sum of yes answers for variables 1 through 5

Improving the Level of Measurement

To take advantage of set units of measure, scientists often devise ways to change nominal/ordinal variables into interval/ratio forms. Table 2–3 lists several nominal variables that have been transformed into a ratio-level variable called the Index of Health Risk Behavior. The nominal variables are scored 0 for no and 1 for yes. This is called dummy coding because the numerical scores are artificial; 0 and 1 do not distinguish amounts or quantities. Instead, 0 means the risk factor is not present, and 1 means that it is. The ratio variable RISKIND is an individual's total number of risk factors, and this variable has a true zero point. If Jeremy smokes, drinks, drives drunk, and takes drugs and Adam only smokes, then Jeremy experiences four times as many risky behaviors as Adam, a ratio of 4:1. We hope your own RISKIND score computes low.

Distinguishing Level of Measurement and Unit of Measure

Take care to distinguish the terms *level of measurement* from *unit of measure*. The level of measurement applies to the entire variable and provides information on the strengths and weaknesses of a variable's measurement. For example, can we calculate averages for a variable? If the level of measurement of the variable is interval or ratio, such as the variable *age,* then yes. On the other hand, if the level of measurement is nominal (e.g., gender), then the answer is no. The unit of measure, however, is a term *used only* with interval/ratio variables. It fixes the set interval for the numerical values used as scores for an interval/ratio variable. For example, we may choose to measure the width of a desk with an inch as a unit of measure. If we chose instead to measure the desk with a centimeter ruler, then a centimeter is our unit of measure. Careless attention to units of measure can result in costly mistakes. For example, in 1999, the guidance system of the National Aeronautics and Space Administration's (NASA) Mars Climate Orbiter inadvertently sent the spacecraft into the Martian atmosphere, causing the destruction of the orbiter. One engineering project team used metric units of measure (i.e., parts of meters) in communicating with another team that assumed the numbers were in English units (parts of inches). This confusion about the units of measure cost NASA $125 million (http://www.cnn.com/TECH/space/9909/30/mars.metric/).

Coding and Counting Observations

Once data collection is complete, the next step in managing data is to code and record all measurements on a spreadsheet or in a computer data file. Table 2–4 is an example of a simple **codebook**, *a concise description of the symbols that signify each score of each variable.* These data come from a survey of students at the fictional college Apple Pond Institute. In this codebook we substitute number symbols for the categories male and female and for class levels. This is done because computers have an easier time counting and sorting numbers (in computer lingo, *numeric* symbols) than they do sorting words (*character* or *string* symbols).

In a codebook, care is taken to be very precise because response coding may introduce measurement error. Every variable is coded by following two basic principles: inclusiveness and exclusiveness. The **principle of inclusiveness** states that for a given variable *there must be a score or code for every observation made.* Simply put, did we include a response category or score for every possible answer? For example, with the nominal variable *race,* we might list the categories white, African-American, Native American, Asian-American, Hispanic, and Other. The response category Other avoids the need to waste questionnaire space for categories expected to get few responses in a given study locale (such as Eskimo in Kansas). Other is a *residual category* that picks up the leftovers (think of the word *residue*).

Even if we ignore the issue of how to code persons of mixed heritage, if we merely use white and African-American, the tabulation of race will not be inclusive of, say, Asian-Americans. Without their own or an Other category, we cannot assume that all Asian-Americans will score themselves the same way. Some may check white, but others may leave the question blank. After computing totals, we would not be able to say exactly how

TABLE 2–4 | Codebook for questionnaire responses of criminal justice majors at Apple Pond Institute

Variable Name	Description of Variable Codes
STUDENT NAME	Record first name, middle initial without period, and last name; blank = missing.
AGE	Record self-reported age up to 97 years; 98 = 98 years or more; 99 = missing.
GENDER	0 = male, 1 = female, 9 = missing.
GPA	Grade point average on a four-point scale = number of quality points earned per credit hour earned (rounded to two decimal places); 9.99 = missing.
CLASS LEVEL	1 = first year, 2 = sophomore, 3 = junior, 4 = senior, 8 = other, 9 = missing.

many we have of *any* race. We missed Asian-Americans who left the question blank, and some of our "whites" are Asian-Americans, but we have no idea how many. Such a careless loss of control over measurement error can make the data on race useless.

The **principle of exclusiveness** states that for a given variable *every observation can be assigned one and only one score*. Simply put, each category must exclude scores that do not belong there, and any two categories must not share a response. For example, with the variable *religious affiliation in childhood,* the response categories Protestant, Baptist, Catholic, Jewish, and Other would not be mutually exclusive because one Baptist may check Baptist, while another may check Protestant. When the totals for each category were summed, we could not say how many Baptists were in the sample. Some might have checked "Protestant," but we have no way of telling who did and how many. Table 2–5 presents the results of the 1994 General Social Survey for this variable. Exclusiveness is assured by asking Protestants a "probe" or follow-up question to determine their specific denominations. (To aid your understanding of table information in this text, we modified tables to stipulate "Givens" [i.e., the data available] and "Calculations." In published reports of these tables these terms would not appear.)

TABLE 2–5 I Distribution of religious affiliation in childhood, response to questions: in what religion were you raised? if Protestant: what specific denomination is that, if any?

	Givens	Calculations
Response Category	**(a)** **Number**	**(b)** **Percent (%) of Total Sample**
Protestant		
Baptist	706	23.73
Methodist	319	10.72
Lutheran	220	7.39
Presbyterian	139	4.67
Episcopalian	68	2.29
Other	309	10.39
No denomination or		
nondenominational church	69	2.32
Total Protestant	1,830	61.51
Catholic	882	29.65
Jewish	55	1.85
None	127	4.27
Other	74	2.49
No answer	7	0.23
Total	2,975	100.00

Source: National Opinion Research Center, General Social Survey 1994.
www.icpsr.umich.edu/gss/codebook/relig16.htm
www.icpsr.umich.edu/gss/codebook/denom16.htm

TABLE 2–6 I Computational spreadsheet of questionnaire responses of 10 criminal justice majors at Apple Pond Institute (fictional data)

Student Name	Age	Gender	Grade Point Average	Class Level
		Givens		
Jessica A Cortland	19	1	3.21	2
Mark E Pippin	22	0	2.75	4
Stayman V Winesap	19	0	2.43	1
Barry D McIntosh	21	0	3.39	3
Harriet G Smith	20	1	3.87	3
Antonio B Rome	22	0	2.32	3
Robert J Cox	18	0	3.25	1
Rodney I Greening	20	0	9.99	2
Thomas R York	22	0	2.47	4
Goldie D Licious	19	1	3.68	2

Return to the codebook of Table 2–4 and note that the principle of inclusiveness is met by supplying *codes for missing data,* called **missing values**. We say, for example, that gender and class level have a missing value of 9. In surveys, missing values occur when an interviewer accidentally skips a question or a respondent does not answer. When we compute statistics for a variable, we disregard cases that score a missing value.

Table 2–6 is a simple spreadsheet of the results of a questionnaire survey administered to 10 criminal justice majors at Apple Pond Institute. A spreadsheet is a matrix listing the scores of all variables, organized in columns, and all cases, organized in rows.

A spreadsheet is useful for summarizing data in an efficient way. For example, we can quickly count the number of females in the sample by summing the ones listed under "Gender." From this simple spreadsheet we can quickly see that the sample is composed of seven males and three females; there are two first-year students, three sophomores, three juniors, and two seniors; ages range from 18 to 22 years; and GPAs range from 2.43 to 3.87 with one unreported case. Of course, for a large sample, an efficient procedure involves entering these spreadsheet codes into a computer data file and allowing computer software to handle the computations. Computer data files are organized like spreadsheets.

Frequency Distributions

Once all the data are organized onto a spreadsheet or computer file, the next step in the analysis is to focus separately on each variable and answer the question: How many subjects fall into each category or score? We organize the data of each variable into a **frequency distribution**, *a listing of all observed scores of a variable and the frequency (f) of each score (or category)*. We use capital English letters to represent a variable. If X is defined as the variable *gender,* the frequency distribution of X simply shows how many men and women are in the sample. Table 2–5 above provides the frequency distribution for religious affiliation in childhood.

---

frequency distribution A listing of all observed scores of a variable and the frequency (f) of each score (or category).

Standardizing Score Distributions

Knowing the frequency of a category is not very informative by itself. For example, someone may note that there are five millionaires living in a city. Five is not many for New York City, but is a lot for a town of 800 people. Thus, it is more informative to report a category frequency as a proportion or percentage of the total number of subjects in the sample. The statistical imagination beckons us to express a category frequency in a larger context, as a part in relation to a whole. We address the question: Five millionaires out of how many people? As we noted in Chapter 1, fractions, proportions, and percentages provide common denominators or "standard measures" for easy comparison of categories and samples. For a sample as a whole, the **proportional frequency distribution** *is a listing of the proportion of responses for each category or score of a variable.* The **percentage frequency distribution** is *a listing of the percent of responses for each category or score of a variable.*

---

proportional frequency distribution A listing of the proportion of responses for each category or score of a variable.

percentage frequency distribution A listing of the percent of responses for each category or score of a variable.

To obtain these distributions for each response category or score of a variable, we write a fraction and then divide it to obtain the proportion and percentage. For ease of interpretation, the percentage frequency distribution is the one usually reported. For example, with data from the spreadsheet in Table 2–6, the percentage of the Apple Pond Institute sample that are males is

$$p\,[\text{of student sample that are males}] = \frac{\#\,\text{males}}{n} = \frac{7}{10} = .7000$$

$$\%\,[\text{of student sample that are males}] = (p)(100) = (.7000)(100) = 70.00\%$$

where p stands for proportion and n is the sample size. After doing the same for females, we have the percentage frequency distribution of the variable *gender,* as in the rightmost column of Table 2–7. This table also provides the frequency and proportional frequency distributions. The total of all proportions and percentages for a distribution will equal 1.0000 and 100.00 percent, respectively, within rounding error.

TABLE 2–7 | Frequency, proportional frequency, and percentage frequency distributions of the variable gender for a sample of 10 Apple Pond Institute students

Givens		Calculations	
Gender (X)	Frequency (f)	Proportional Frequency	Percentage Frequency (%)
Male	7	.7000	70.00
Female	3	.3000	30.00
Total	10	1.0000	100.00

Calculating the Proportional and Percentage Frequencies of a Category

$$p \text{ [of total sample } (n) \text{ in a category]} = \frac{f \text{ of category}}{n} = \frac{\# \text{ in category}}{n}$$

$\%$ [of total sample (n) in a category]

$$= (p \text{ [of total sample } (n) \text{ in a category]})(100)$$

where

p [of total sample (n) in a category] = proportion of all cases that fall in the category,

f = frequency of cases (or number of cases) in the category,

n = sample size

Table 2–5 (on page 49) provides both the frequency and percentage frequency distributions for the variable religious affiliation in childhood.

Coding and Counting Interval/Ratio Data

Variables with interval/ratio levels of measurement are distinguished from nominal/ordinal variables by their numerical qualities, especially their set units of measure, such as miles, kilometers, inches, seconds, and pounds. Such "quantitative" variables allow us to picture a ruler and think linearly, in terms of distance between points on a straight line. Moreover, we can make very precise measurements.

A **precise measurement** is *one in which the degree of measurement error is sufficiently small for the task at hand*. Precision depends on practical circumstances and is controlled by specifying rounding error. For instance, in cutting two-foot-long fireplace logs, a small degree of precision will suffice because we can afford a large degree of error, say, "give or take a half foot." By contrast, for a quality test of microcomputer circuit boards, a precision of one-thousandth of an inch may be required. The degree of precision is a question of tolerance. We ask: How much measurement error can we tolerate (or put up with) without encountering practical problems or drawing faulty scientific conclusions?

Rounding Interval/Ratio Observations

An observation of an interval/ratio variable may not give us the true score because its measurement often can be made endlessly more precise. For example, we can measure distances to the nearest kilometer, meter, centimeter, and so on. Therefore, we round interval/ratio scores to some specified, chosen degree of precision. In doing so, we acknowledge that the recorded code for the score has some measurement error in it. **Rounding error** is *the difference between the true or perfect score (which we may never know) and our rounded, observed score*. Rounding error depends on what *decimal place we choose as our level of precision*—our rounding unit. (If necessary, review decimal place locations in Appendix A.) If we decide to measure time to the nearest hundredth of a second, such as in Olympic track events, then our rounding unit is the hundredths place.

The procedure for rounding a score of an interval/ratio variable is as follows:

1. Specify the rounding unit according to its decimal place.
2. Observe the number *to the right* of the rounding unit and follow these rules.
   A. If it is 0, 1, 2, 3 or 4, round down.
   B. If it is 6, 7, 8, or 9, round up.
   C. If it is 5, look at the next decimal place to the right, and, if the number in it is 5 or greater, round up. If there is no number in this next decimal place, round to an even number.

Think of rounding as moving to the nearest point on a line. For instance, if we are rounding to *the nearest integer* (the ones place), we are simply moving to the nearest integer.

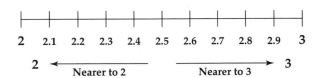

Here, for example, 2.1, 2.2, 2.3, and 2.4 are rounded down to 2 simply because they are closer to 2 than to 3. Additional examples are provided in Appendix A.

The Real Limits of Rounded Scores

Once we are presented with rounded scores, the numbers *in the rounding unit's decimal place* must be recognized as estimates. A score's true value could be any of the scores that are rounded to get the recorded score. Suppose, for example, we measure Jonathan's height to the nearest inch and record 69 inches. Several hours later, with Jonathan absent, Alan asks us how tall Jonathan is. We look at our data spreadsheet and see a code of 69 inches. At this instant, all we can say is that Jonathan's true height is somewhere between $68^1/_2$ and $69^1/_2$ inches, or 69 plus or minus one-half inch. This *range of possible true values of an (already) rounded score* is called the **true limits** or **real limits** of the score.

The real limits of a rounded score specify the range of numbers that could have been rounded to get the recorded score. In this sense, computing the real limits is the reverse of rounding. For example, suppose we score how long it takes each of 150 students to complete a chemistry lab project and round to the nearest hour. Suppose also that 56 of these students receive a score of two hours. Some of them took a little less than two hours, and some took a little more. Precisely, a student scoring two hours could have taken as little as 90 minutes ($1^1/_2$ hours), the *lower real limit,* or as much as 150 minutes ($2^1/_2$ hours), the *upper real limit*. A score of two hours *really* means between $1^1/_2$ and $2^1/_2$ hours, and so we call this range of times the real limits.

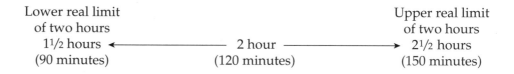

Lower real limit of two hours		Upper real limit of two hours
$1^1/_2$ hours ←—————	2 hour —————→	$2^1/_2$ hours
(90 minutes)	(120 minutes)	(150 minutes)

We calculate real limits by moving a half rounding unit in each direction, using the following procedure:

Calculating Real Limits of an Interval/Ratio Score

1. Observe the score and identify the "rounding unit," the decimal place to which the score was rounded (as in column B below). (For decimal place locations, review Figure A–1 in Appendix A.)

2. Divide this rounding unit by 2 (as in column C below). *Caution:* Do not divide the number in the rounding unit's decimal place by 2.

3. Subtract the result of (2) from the observed rounded score to get the lower real limit (LRL, as in column D below).

4. Add the result of (2) to the observed rounded score to get the upper real limit (URL, as in column E below).

	(A) Calculate Real Limits of:	(B) Identify Rounding Unit	(C) Divide Rounding Unit by 2	(D) LRL Subtract (C) from (A)	(E) URL Add (C) to (A)
(a)	.48	.01	$\dfrac{.01}{2} = .005$	.475	.485
(b)	17	1	$\dfrac{1}{2} = .5$	16.5	17.5
(c)	4,000	1,000	$\dfrac{1,000}{2} = 500$	3,500	4,500
(d)	0.7	.1	$\dfrac{.1}{2} = .05$	.65	.75

Examples:

For example, for the 56 students who scored 2 hours on the chemistry lab project, we rounded to the nearest hour (the ones place). We divide *this rounding unit of 1 hour* by 2 to get one-half hour. Then we subtract this result from the observed rounded score of 2 hours to get the lower real limit (1½ hours) and add it to the observed score of 2 hours to get the upper real limit (2½ hours). It is unlikely that even one of these 56 students took exactly 2 hours to complete the project; two hours is a rounded estimate. We can rest assured, however, that each of the 56 finished somewhere between 1½ and 2½ hours. Our degree of precision is the rounding unit of 1 hour.

The principles of inclusiveness and exclusiveness also apply to interval/ratio variables. For a variable such as age, sticking to the principle of inclusiveness would appear straightforward; we simply record "age at last birthday." To ensure inclusiveness, however, a survey question should include the responses "refused" and "don't know." Exclusiveness is straightforward as long as all measurements are made the same way, in this case, age to the last birthday. If a respondent says she or he is 26 years old, then record 26, not 27 or 25.

Proportional and Percentage Frequency Distributions
for Interval/Ratio Variables

Proportional and percentage frequency distributions for interval/ratio variables are calculated the same way as they are for nominal/ordinal variables except that in place of categories we have scores. For instance, if Smithville University has 10,000 students and 3,000 are 19 years old, the proportional and percentage frequencies for the score of 19 years is

$$p\,[\text{of 19 year olds at Smithville University}] = \frac{f \text{ of 19 year olds}}{n} = \frac{3,000}{10,000} = .3000$$

$$\% \,[\text{of 19 year olds at Smithville University}] = (p)(100) = 30.00\%$$

TABLE 2–8 | Illustration of a cumulative percentage frequency distribution: years of formal education among elderly caregivers of Alzheimer patients

	Givens		Calculations	
Years of Formal Education (X)	Frequency (f)		Percentage Frequency	Cumulative Percentage (%) (f)
5	1		5%	5
6	1		5	10
7	1		5	15
9	2		10	25
10	1		5	30
11	1		5	35
12	10		50	85
14	2		10	95
16	1		5	100
Total	20		100%	100

If these calculations are made for all ages, the results are presented as the percentage frequency distribution of the variable *age* for the population of Smithville University students.

Cumulative Percentage Frequency Distributions

Table 2–8 presents the frequency, percentage frequency, and cumulative percentage frequency distributions of the education levels of 20 caregivers—relatives who accompany Alzheimer patients to a clinic (Clair, Ritchey, and Allman 1993). These three pieces of information are standard parts of computer output because together they generate quick answers to a series of questions. Obviously, the raw score frequency (f) provides an answer for how many subjects received a specific score and the percentage frequency standardizes the frequency for sample size. The additional piece of information in Table 2–8, the cumulative percentage frequency, is a valuable way to view the frequency of scores in a distribution up to and including a score of interest. This is the **cumulative percentage frequency**, *the percentage frequency of a score plus that of all the scores preceding it in the distribution*. For example, for the caregivers in Table 2–8, what percentage has an education up to and including the high school level? To obtain the cumulative percentage frequencies, we list scores from lowest to highest and calculate the percentage frequency of each score. Then we add the percentage frequencies of a target score and all lesser scores. In Table 2–8, 85 percent had 12 years of schooling or less. By subtracting this cumulative percentage frequency from 100 percent, we can promptly see that only 15 percent of the sample went beyond high school.

The following box provides a guide on how to set up frequency distributions.

How to Set Up Frequency Distributions

Let us suppose that we wish to produce a frequency distribution table for the variable age in Table 2–6 for a sample from fictional Apple Pond Institute. Table 2–6 presents the data in a spreadsheet format. We are to complete the following Table A to present the frequency distribution, percentage frequency distribution, and cumulative percentage frequency distribution for the variable *age*. Follow these steps:

1. Construct a template with the proper title and headings (the information above the columns of numbers in Table A).

2. Observe the scores for age among the 10 students in Table 2–6 and list, only once, each value of *X* from the lowest to the highest. This goes under "Age (*X*)" in Table A.

3. Count the number of students for each age in Table 2–6 and insert this count under "Frequency (*f*)" in Table A. Check to see that the total frequency is the sample size, *n* = 10, and record this total.

4. Calculate the proportional frequency for each value of *X* by dividing each frequency by the total *n* of 10. These results go under "Proportional Frequency" in Table A. Check to see that the total proportional frequency sums to 1.0000. If the calculations are correct and the total does not sum to 1.0000, then insert a footnote indicating "Total did not add to 1.0000 because of rounding error."

5. Calculate the percentage frequency of each value of *X* by multiplying the proportional frequency by 100 (i.e., by moving the decimal point two places to the right). These results go under "Percentage Frequency" in Table A. If the calculations are correct and the total does not sum to 100.00%, then insert a footnote indicating "Total did not add to 100 percent because of rounding error."

6. For Table A, calculate the cumulative percentage frequency, the percentage frequency of a score plus that of all the scores preceding it. Start by recording 10.00 percent for *X* = 18. Now add this cumulative percentage frequency of *X* = 18 to the *percentage* frequency of *X* = 19 to get the cumulative percentage frequency of *X* = 19, which is 10.00 percent + 30.00 percent = 40.00 percent. Now add this cumulative percentage frequency of *X* = 19 to the *percentage* frequency of *X* = 20 to get the cumulative percentage frequency of *X* = 20, which is 40.00 percent + 20.00 percent = 60.00 percent, and so on. Make sure that the cumulative percentage frequency of the highest value of *X* sums to 100.00 percent.

TABLE A. | Frequency, proportional frequency, and percentage frequency distributions of the variable *age* for a sample of 10 Apple Pond Institute students

Age (*X*)	Frequency (*f*)	Proportional Frequency	Percentage Frequency (%)	Cumulative Percentage Frequency (%)
18	1	.1000	10.00	10.00
19	3	.3000	30.00	40.00
20	2	.2000	20.00	60.00
21	1	.1000	10.00	70.00
22	3	.3000	30.00	100.00
Totals	10	1.0000	100.00	

Percentiles and Quartiles

We often visualize a distribution of scores as being broken or "fractured" into groups above and below a score or into groups with equal percentages of cases. Cumulative frequency distributions provide the tool for identifying **fractiles**, *scores that separate a fraction of a distribution's cases.* Percentile ranks (or, simply, percentiles) are one common fractile. *Among the cases in a score distribution,* a **percentile rank** is *the percentage of cases that fall at or below a specified value of X.* For example, from the cumulative percentage frequencies in Table 2–8, we see that a caregiver with 14 years of education has a level of education equal to or exceeding 95 percent of the sample, a percentile rank of 95. Percentiles often are used in education circles as a way to rank grades or test scores. For instance, on a college admissions test a student who scores at the 90th percentile or better may qualify for admission to an exclusive college. The following box shows how to calculate a percentile without a cumulative percentage frequency distribution.

Steps for Calculating Percentiles

The calculation of a percentile addresses the following question: A particular score is equal to or higher than what percentage of scores? Following are fictional data for a course exam. Notice that the scores are ranked in ascending order (i.e, from lowest to highest). *Before calculating a percentile, the scores must be ranked from lowest to highest or highest to lowest.*

Let us calculate Taylor's percentile rank on this exam. Her score of 78 is equal to or higher than 14 of the 27 students. First, calculate the proportion of cases equal to or less than 78, and then the percentage.

$$p\,[\text{of scores} \le 78] = \frac{14}{27} = .5185 \qquad \%\,[\text{of scores} \le 78] = (p)(100) = 51.85 = 52\%$$

Thus, Taylor's percentile rank is 52. She scored equal to or higher than 52 percent of the students. Notice that we rounded the percentage to two places because percentile ranks are reported to whole percentages (i.e., without decimal places).

Now let us calculate John's percentile rank:

$$p\,[\text{of scores} \le 91] = \frac{23}{27} = .8518 \qquad \%\,[\text{of scores} \le 91] = (p)(100) = 85.18 = 85\%$$

Thus, John's percentile rank is 85. Notice that Barry's score was included in the calculation because it is equal to John's.

Student Rank	Student Name	Exam Grade (Ranked)	Student Rank	Student Name	Exam Grade (Ranked)
1	Kevin	54	15	Shannel	79
2	Carl	58	16	William	80
3	Robert	61	17	Angie	82
4	Brian	61	18	Akilah	83
5	Maria	65	19	Daniel	85
6	Sean	69	20	Kaitlin	88
7	Jim	70	21	Marcy	90
8	Jessica	72	22	John	91
9	Carol	73	23	Barry	91
10	Brooke	75	24	Wanda	93
11	Kia	75	25	Sarah	95
12	Terry	77	26	Charles	96
13	Jackie	77	27	Elisa	97
14	Taylor	78			

SUMMARY OF STEPS FOR CALCULATING PERCENTILES:

Step 1. Rank the scores

Step 2. Calculate the proportion and percentage of cases with scores equal to or less than the case of interest.

Step 3. Report the percentile in whole percentages.

Note: Keep in mind that percentiles are easily obtained from a cumulative percentage distribution.

Quartiles are *fractiles that identify the score values that break a distribution into four equally sized groups (i.e., 25 percent of the cases in each group).* When a distribution has a large range of scores, quartiles are easily obtainable from cumulative percentage frequency distributions. The first quartile, Q_1, is the 25th percentile; the second, Q_2, is the 50th percentile; and the third, Q_3, is the 75th percentile. Computer statistical software typically is programmed to identify quartiles and other fractiles, such as deciles, which break a distribution into 10 equally sized groups.

Table 2–9 presents the distribution of grades on a midterm exam (X) and illustrates the utility of quartiles. In this class of 20 students, the lowest 25 percent (or the five lowest grades) are from $X = 69$ and below, the next quarter of students are from $X = 72$ to 84, the third quarter are from $X = 85$ to 91, and the highest quarter are from $X = 93$ and above. We can also see that one-fourth of the students scored 69 or below, failing to make a C; one-half scored above 84, three-fourths scored 91 or below, half scored between 72 and 91, and so on.

TABLE 2-9 | Quartiles of a distribution of midterm exam grades

			Givens		Calculations		
		Exam Grade (X)	f	Percentage f	Cumulative Percentage (%) f	Location of Quartiles (Q)	
		31	1	5.0%	5.0		
		58	1	5.0	10.0		
		63	1	5.0	15.0		
		68	1	5.0	20.0		
Q_1	→	69	1	5.0	25.0	←	Q_1 = 25th percentile
		72	1	5.0	30.0		
		76	1	5.0	35.0		
		77	1	5.0	40.0		
		82	1	5.0	45.0		
Q_2	→	84	1	5.0	50.0	←	Q_2 = 50th percentile
		85	1	5.0	55.0		
		86	2	10.0	65.0		
		88	1	5.0	70.0		
Q_3	→	91	1	5.0	75.0	←	Q_3 = 75th percentile
		93	2	10.0	85.0		
		94	1	5.0	90.0		
		95	1	5.0	95.0		
		97	1	5.0	100.0		
		Total	20	100.0%			

Finally, it is important to remember to rank the scores of a distribution before calculating fractiles.

> **fractiles**   Scores that separate a fraction of a distribution's cases.
>
> **percentile rank**   Among the cases in a score distribution, the percentage of cases that fall at or below a specified value of X.
>
> **quartiles**   Fractiles that identify the score values that break a distribution into four equally sized groups.

Grouping Interval/Ratio Data

Sometimes, for clarity of presentation in a table or graph, interval/ratio distributions are grouped or "collapsed" into a smaller number of ordinal categories. For example, in a study of adults in the United States, the variable age will vary from 20 to about 100, providing 80 scores. It is confusing to present a table listing the frequency and percentage frequency of all 80 ages. For clarity, we combine ages into 10-year categories, as in Table 2–10.

TABLE 2–10 | The ratio variable age grouped into 10-year ordinal categories

	Givens		Calculations
Ordinal Code	Age Group	f	Percent (%)
1	20–29	47	10.49
2	30–39	68	15.18
3	40–49	106	23.66
4	50–59	96	21.43
5	60–69	53	11.83
6	70–79	45	10.04
7	80–89	24	5.36
8	90 and over	9	2.01
	Total	448	100.00

There is an important thing to note about grouping interval/ratio data. When we group data, we throw away detail, which results in *grouping error*. For instance, Table 2–10 shows that there were 106 respondents between 40 and 49 years of age. But were most of them closer to 40 or to 49? We have no way of knowing by observing the grouped scores. If the ungrouped data are available, we can use them to obtain more precise computations of averages. In general, any time we move from a "higher" level of measurement to a "lower" level (i.e., from ratio to interval, from interval to ordinal, or from ordinal to nominal), we lose information and this limits what can be done mathematically.

Nonetheless, in reading the work of others, we may be presented grouped data without the accompanying statistics. In these situations, attempt to contact the author for descriptive statistics. If this is not possible, then averages and other statistics can be computed from the grouped data, but these statistics will include grouping error. See Freund and Simon (1991: 70) for a discussion of computing statistics with grouped data.

Statistical Follies and Fallacies: The Importance of Having a Representative Sample

Sample size and sample representativeness are separate concerns. A large sample does not guarantee a representative sample. A systematic, repetitious mistake in sampling can produce a large but biased sample. A classic case of systematic sampling error occurred in the 1936 presidential campaign, in which *Literary Digest* magazine selected a large sample from telephone directories and automobile owners. The results showed overwhelming support for the Republican candidate, Alf Landon, over Franklin D. Roosevelt, the Democratic candidate. When election day rolled around, it was not Landon but Roosevelt who won the election—and by a landslide no less! The *Literary Digest* poll systematically ignored voters without telephones or automobiles and thus failed to adequately poll the poor, who constituted the bulk of Roosevelt's support (Babbie 1992: 192–93). There are methods to verify the representativeness of a sample, and we will cover them in Chapter 10. Suffice it to say here that a small representative sample is better than a large nonrepresentative one. A teaspoonful of chili with all the ingredients constitutes a better taste test than does a cupful drawn from only the top of the pot.

SUMMARY

1. Statistical error is known degrees of imprecision in the procedures used to gather and process information. Statistical analysis involves controlling error and, thus, knowing whether a conclusion is sound.

2. The two main sources of error are sampling error and measurement error.

3. A population is a large group of people of particular interest that we desire to study and understand. We sample the population, gather data from it, and calculate statistics on these data to obtain estimates of population parameters and draw conclusions about the population.

4. Statistical estimates are based on sound scientific methods wherein sampling and measurement error are taken into account when results are reported. Guesstimates are poorly derived conclusions about a population.

5. To manage sampling error, we must focus on its two specific sources. The first is sample size. The larger the sample, the smaller the range of error. Given a sample size, probability theory allows us to say exactly how often a sample statistic will correctly predict a parameter. The second source of sampling error is sample representativeness. A nonrepresentative sample can lead to faulty conclusions.

6. To control measurement error, we must first specify an operational definition and determine the level of measurement of a variable.

7. Nominal level is the simplest level of measurement. *Nominal* comes from the Latin word for *name*. A nominal variable is one that is measured simply by naming categories.

8. An ordinal variable is one with named categories and the additional property of allowing categories to be ranked from highest to lowest, best to worst, or first to last. Variables with numerical ranks, such as 1st, 2nd, or 3rd, are also ordinal variables.

9. Interval variables have the characteristics of nominal and ordinal variables plus a defined numerical unit or "interval" of measure. With its established unit of measure, such as inches, pounds, or miles, an interval variable is scored numerically and subject to many informative mathematical calculations.

10. Ratio variables have the characteristics of interval variables, plus a true zero point, where a score of zero means *none*. The true zero point allows for even greater flexibility in computations than is found with interval variables. With a ratio variable, we can compute ratios—the amount of one observation in relation to another.

11. Whereas the codes of nominal and ordinal variables merely indicate a difference in category, class, quality, or kind, the codes of interval and ratio variables identify differences in amount, quantity, degree, or distance.

12. It is important to distinguish level of measurement (nominal, ordinal, interval or ratio) from unit of measure (inches, pounds, etc.).

13. A codebook is a concise description of the symbols that signify each score of each variable in a data set. Every variable is coded following the principles of inclusiveness and exclusiveness.

14. Efficient ways to grasp the character of the data for a variable—how the scores differ among subjects of a population—is to organize the data into a frequency distribution, a proportion frequency distribution, and a percentage frequency distribution. Percentages are easier to interpret than are proportions. To get the percentage frequency distribution, multiply each proportional frequency by 100.

15. A cumulative percentage frequency is used to identify fractiles—scores that separate a fraction of a distribution's cases. Percentile ranks and quartiles are commonly reported fractiles. It is important to rank order a variable's scores before calculating fractiles.

CHAPTER EXTENSIONS ON *THE STATISTICAL IMAGINATION* WEB SITE

Chapter 2 Extensions of text material available on *The Statistical Imagination* Web site at www.mhhe.com/ritchey2 include: (a) A discussion of when an ordinal variable may be treated as though it were of interval level of measurement. Such "interval-like" ordinal variables may be used with more advanced statistical procedures for interval/ratio variables. (b) A discussion of how establishing the validity and reliability of a measurement are important considerations for minimizing measurement error. (c) An illustration of why it is mandatory that both measurement and sampling error be minimized. Perfect measures are useless with poor sampling and vice versa.

FORMULAS FOR CHAPTER 2

Calculating the proportional frequency of a category or score:

$$p \text{ [of total sample } (n) \text{ in a category]} = \frac{f \text{ of category}}{n} = \frac{\# \text{ in category}}{n}$$

Calculating the percentage frequency of a category or score:

$$\% \text{ [of total sample } (n) \text{ in a category]}$$
$$= (p \text{ [of total sample } (n) \text{ in a category]})(100)$$

Calculations for percentiles and quartiles:
Set up a spreadsheet with the following headings:

Score (X)	f	Percentage f	Cumulative Percentage f

The percentile of a score is its cumulative percentage frequency. Quartiles are located at the 25th, 50th, and 75th percentiles.

QUESTIONS FOR CHAPTER 2

1. Discuss the difference between an observation and a statistic.

2. Discuss the difference between a statistic and a parameter.

3. What is a good way to prove that the statistics from a single sample are only estimates of a population's parameters?

4. Although brought up far removed from any minority neighborhood, Karen fancied herself an open-minded individual without prejudices. She became a social worker and got a job at the human resources department tracking minority children who were abused by substance-addicted parents. Karen developed overwhelming feelings of racism and is now convinced that minorities are morally inferior. In terms of sampling bias, what has happened to Karen?

5. A self-proclaimed expert on female sexuality reports that three-fourths of women state that they hate men. Talk show hosts challenge this statistic. The expert responds by noting that her sample of over 6,000 is the largest sample ever collected on the subject and that her results have a range of error of less than one-tenth of 1 percent. Her sampling method was a mail-in questionnaire inserted in a popular women's magazine. Name the ways in which her sample might be biased.

6. By way of a telephone survey, you want to assess the public's opinion on the mayor's proposal for raising taxes to build a new zoo. If you randomly selected every 100th number from the area telephone directory, would you obtain a representative sample? Explain in terms of sample bias.

7. Dr. Burnett tests a new antidepressant drug at a mental hospital. The drug is found to be quite effective. Will the drug necessarily have the same effectiveness for all persons suffering from depression? Explain in terms of sample bias.

8. Suppose we are measuring weight among a sample of body builders and record Sam the Ham's weight as 246 pounds. He actually weighs between 245½ and 246½ pounds, this range of weights being the _____ and _____ limits of a score of 246 pounds.

9. Holly and Cheryl both conducted studies of social science majors at their colleges, asking them how many expected to be employed in industry after graduation. Holly, with a sample of 650, got an estimate of 31 percent. Cheryl, with a sample of 45, got an estimate of 23 percent. Which estimate can we place more "faith" in, and why? In terms of controlling sampling error, what else do we need to know about Holly's and Cheryl's samples? Why?

10. Bob bought firewood for his 36-inch-wide fireplace. To make sure the pieces would fit, he took a two-foot-long stick with him and made sure each piece of

wood was roughly within 6 inches of the length of the stick. Shara designs microcomputer circuits. Her measurement instrument measures to the nearest tenth of an inch, but this instrument is less precise than Bob's stick. Explain.

11. Distinguish among the concepts level of measurement, unit of measure, and rounding unit. Illustrate with examples.

EXERCISES FOR CHAPTER 2

Problem Set 2A

2A–1. Indicate the level of measurement of the following variables.

Variable Name	Operational Definition and Coding (how the variable is measured and scored)	Level of Measurement
a. GPA	Grade point average: the number of academic quality points earned divided by the number of earned credit hours	
b. HEIGHT	Physical height in inches	
c. CPUNISH	10-item attitude scale on support for the death penalty with summary scores ranging from 0 to 40	
d. AUTOTAG	Automobile license plate number: seven-digit number with county identifiers	
e. LABORSTA	Labor status: 1 = unskilled; 2 = semiskilled; 3 =skilled	
f. CITYPOP	Population within the city limits	
g. CARMAKE	Make of automobile: Ford, Buick, Toyota, etc.	

2A–2. In a study of abused women in South Africa (Jewkes et al. 2002), 1,279 women are surveyed in a cross-sectional sample. Identify the levels of measurement of the following sociodemographic variables from the study.

Variable Name	Operational Definition and Coding (how the variable is measured and scored)	Level of Measurement
a. PROVENCE	Provence of residence: 1 = Eastern Cape; 2 = Mpumalanga; 3 = Northern Province	
b. EDUCATION	Education: 1 = None; 2 = Primary; 3 = Lower Secondary; 4 = Higher Secondary; 5 = Any postschool	
c. AGE	Age in years: self-reported.	
d. OCCUPATION	Ocupational status: 1 = unemployed; 2 = trader; 3 = domestic worker; 4 = professional; 5 = etc.	
e. MARRIED	Marital status: 1 = marrried in church ceremony; 2 = married in traditional ceremony; 3 = widow/divorce/separated; 4 = single.	
f. CROWDED	Household crowding index: number of people per room	

2A–3. Imagine that a sample of physicians is asked the following items on a questionnaire. With the provided response categories, does each variable follow the principles of both inclusiveness and exclusiveness? If not, how can they be improved to be in accordance with these principles?

a. What is your medical specialty? (Please check one.)
___ Primary Care   ___ Endocrinology   ___ Oncology
___ Rheumatology   ___ Otolaryngology   ___ Psychiatry

b. How many patients do you see in the average workweek?
___ less than 10   ___ 10–20   ___ 20–30   ___ 30–40
___ 40–50

c. Please check the category that most closely fits your total annual income from medical practice.
___ $0–$25,000   ___ $26,000–$40,000   ___ $51,000–$75,000
___ $76,000–$100,000   ___ $100,000–$150,000
___ $151,000 and above

d. In what region did you complete your medical education? (Please select one.)
___ South   ___ Northeast   ___ West
___ Southwest   ___ Midwest

2A–4. Round the following numbers to the stipulated rounding unit.
a. 39.7246 to nearest ten
b. 26.3194 to nearest tenth
c. 29.1352 to nearest hundredth
d. 29.1352 to nearest thousandth
e. 692 to nearest hundred
f. 41.755 to nearest hundredth
g. 24.721 to nearest tenth

2A–5. Specify the real limits of the following rounded numbers.
a. .059
b. .0060
c. 2,890 rounded to nearest ten
d. 5,400 rounded to nearest hundred
e. Age 3 rounded to nearest birthday
f. Age 3 rounded to last birthday
g. 12 inches
h. 12.0 inches

2A–6. The following is the distribution of family caregivers' relationships to Alzheimer patients. Calculate the ratio of the number of female to male caregivers.

Family Caregiver's Relationship to Patient	f
Wife	114
Husband	17
Daughter	37
Son	4
Sister	8
Brother	1
Mother	2
Daughter-in-law	13
Other female relative	24
Other male relative	2

2A–7. The following are data on the number of vehicles registered for a random sample of 20 households in Madison County: 2, 1, 2, 4, 2, 3, 4, 2, 1, 4, 2, 1, 0, 3, 2, 4, 3, 4, 2, 2.

    a. Compile the data into a frequency distribution table with columns for the frequency, the proportional frequency, the percentage frequency, and the cumulative percentage frequency. (No need to show formulas.)

    b. If a household has three registered vehicles, what is that household's percentile rank? Interpret your answer.

2A–8. Below is a list of midterm exam scores for a group of 14 graduate students.

Student Name	Midterm Exam Score
Jonathan	76
Susan	82
Jason	95
Andrea	52
Kelli	64
Jennifer	94
James	79
Brian	88
William	69
Caroline	95
Patricia	90
Kevin	98
Mark	88
Jeffrey	92

    a. Calculate Jeffrey's percentile rank based on the set of exam scores listed.

    b. Calculate Brian's percentile rank.

Problem Set 2B

2B–1. Indicate the level of measurement of the following variables.

Variable Name	Operational Definition and Coding (how the variable is measured and scored)	Level of Measurement
a. WEIGHT	Physical weight in pounds	
b. DENSITY	Population (number of people residing in a defined area) per square mile of area	
c. IMRATE	Infant mortality rate: number of deaths in the first year of life per 1,000 births	
d. STUDENT	Student status: 1 = undergraduate; 2 = graduate; 3 = special	
e. ESTEEM	Self-assessment of self-esteem: 15-item summary scale with scores ranging from 0 to 60	
f. JOBSAT	Satisfaction with job: 0 = very dissatisfied; 1 = dissatisfied; 2 = satisfied; 3 = very satisfied	
g. LIFEEXP	Life expectancy: average number of years newborns may expect to live (usually sex- and age-adjusted)	

2B–2. In a study of caregivers of elderly family members, 293 women are interviewed concerning the stresses of caregiving and maintaining employment at the same time. Identify the levels of measurement of each of the following variables from the study.

Variable Name	Operational Definition and Coding (how the variable is measured and scored)	Level of Measurement
Caregiver Variables		
a. WORKMILE	Distance from home to workplace in miles	
b. CGAGE	Caregiver's age in years	
c. CGHEALTH	Self-reported health rating: 1 = poor; 2 = fair; 3 = good; 4 = excellent	
Care Recipient Variables		
d. PGENDER	Gender: 0 = male; 1 = female.	
e. ADL	Activities of daily living: Number of activities able to do without help, such as bathe and dress	
f. LIFESAT	Satisfaction with life: 12-item summary scale with scores ranging from 0 to 36	

2B–3. Imagine that caregivers are asked the following items on a questionnaire. With the provided response categories, does each variable follow the principles of both inclusiveness and exclusiveness? If not, how can they be improved to be in accordance with these principles?

    a. Do you have a religious preference? If so, what is it? (Please check one.)
       ___ Protestant ___ Catholic ___ Jewish
       ___ Baptist   ___ None

    b. What is your marital status? (Please check one.)
       ___ Single ___ Married

    c. Please check the category that most closely fits your total annual family income from all sources.
       ___ $0–$10,000 ___ $11,000–$20,000 ___ $21,000–$30,000
       ___ $31,000–$40,000 ___ $41,000–$50,000 ___ $50,000 and above

    d. Are you currently employed outside of the home? (Please check one.)
       ___ Full-time ___ Part-time ___ Unemployed
       ___ Employed

2B-4. Round the following numbers to the stipulated rounding unit.
    a. 28.349 to nearest tenth
    b. 31.666 to nearest hundredth
    c. 587 to nearest hundred
    d. 25.6385 to nearest thousandth
    e. 25.6558 to nearest hundredth
    f. 25.6388 to nearest tenth
    g. 25.6388 to nearest ten

2B-5. Specify the real limits of the following rounded numbers.
    a. 4.0 inches
    b. 4 inches
    c. Age 5 rounded to last birthday
    d. Age 5 rounded to nearest birthday
    e. 3,300 rounded to nearest hundred
    f. 3,360 rounded to nearest ten
    g. .0030
    h. .068

2B–6. The following is the distribution of the number of times each course is scheduled during the year at a major university by academic discipline. Calculate the ratio of the number of psychology to sociology course offerings.

Courses	f
Psychology	
PY 101	5
PY 109	5
PY 212	2
PY 214	3
PY 217	4
Sociology	
SOC 100	7
SOC 120	2
SOC 220	2
SOC 235	1
SOC 240	1

2B-7. Funk et al. (2003) examined the relationship between playing violent video games and feelings of empathy in a sample of children. Suppose the following data represent empathy scale scores for a sample of 20 children after playing a violent video game: 4, 1, 3, 1, 2, 5, 3, 1, 2, 4, 2, 3, 5, 0, 2, 3, 4, 2, 1, 2.

a.   Compile the data into a frequency distribution table with columns for the frequency, the proportional frequency, the percentage frequency, and the cumulative percentage frequency. (No need to show formulas.)

b.   If a child scores a 2 on the experimental empathy scale, what is that child's percentile rank? Interpret your answer.

2B-8. Below is a list of midterm exam scores for a group of 14 graduate students.

Student Name	Midterm Exam Score
Jeremy	76
Susanna	82
Jack	95
Andrew	52
Anika	64
Jennifer	94
James	79
Brad	88
William	69
Carol	95
Patricia	90
Kevin	98
Mark	88
Jeffrey	92

a.   Calculate Jennifer's percentile rank based on the set of exam scores listed.

b.   Calculate Carol's percentile rank.

Problem Set 2C

2C-1.   Indicate the level of measurement of the following variables.

Variable Name	Operational Definition and Coding (how the variable is measured and scored)	Level of Measurement
a AGE	Numeric age in years	
b. EDUCATION	Educational status: 0 = no high school diploma; 1 = high school; 2 = some college; 3 = college degree	
c. REGBIRTH	Region of birth: 1 = South; 2 = Northeast; 3 = West; 4 = Southwest; 5 = Midwest; 6 = Outside U.S.	
d. FINREF	Attitudes toward campaign finance reform: 15-item summary scale with scores ranging from 0 to 65	
e. VOTSTAT	Voter Status: 1 = Noncitizen; 2 = Citizen, unregistered; 3 = Citizen, registered voter; 4 = Citizen, disenfranchised (i.e., convicted felon)	
f. POPCON	Voting population within political constituency	
g. AVGINC	Average income (of registered voters residing within a defined geographic area)	

2C-2.   In a study conducted by Macassa et al. (2003), survey data are used to examine inequalities in child mortality in Mozambique, based on parental socioeconomic position. Identify the levels of measurement of each of the following variables from the study.

Variable Name	Operational Definition and Coding (how the variable is measured and scored)	Level of Measurement
a. MOMOCCUP	Mother's occupation: 1 = not working; 2 = unskilled manual; 3 = skilled manual; 4 = professional; 5 = etc.	
b. CHILDSEX	Gender of child: 0 = male; 1 = female	
c. MOMAGE	Age of mother in years	
d. MAGEBORN	Age group of mother at birth: 1 = 15–18; 2 = 19–23; 3 = 24–28; 4 = 29–33; 5 = 34 and above	
e. BIRTHORD	Birth order: 1 = first birth; 2 = second birth; 3 = third birth; 4 = fourth birth or higher	
f. RESIDE	Place of residence: 1 = urban; 2 = rural	

2C-3.   Franks et al. (2003) studied the relationship between sociodemographic characteristics, self-rated health, and mortality in the United States, using the following variables. With the hypothetical response categories given here, does

each variable follow the principles of both inclusiveness and exclusiveness? If
not, how can they be improved to be in accordance with these principles?

a. To what age group do you belong?

___ 25–34   ___ 35– 44   ___ 45–54   ___ 55–64
___ 65–74   ___ 74 or above

b. What is your race/ethnicity?

___ white   ___ black   ___ Latino   ___ Asian

c. What is your educational attainment (in years of schooling)?

___ 9 or less   ___ 9–11   ___ 12   ___ 13–15
___ 15 or more

d. What is your current level of income?

___ $0–$10,000   ___ $11,000–$15,000   ___ $21,000–$30,000
___ $31,000–$40,000   ___ $41,000–$50,000
___ $50,000 and above

2C-4. Round the following numbers to the stipulated rounding unit.

a. 62.5982 to nearest ten
b. 62.5982 to nearest tenth
c. 62.5982 to nearest hundredth
d. 62.5985 to nearest thousandth
e. 723 to nearest hundred
f. 54.7652 to nearest hundredth
g. 17.823 to nearest tenth

2C-5. Specify the real limits of the following rounded numbers.

a. .327
b. .02381
c. 6,720 rounded to nearest ten
d. 63,000 rounded to nearest hundred
e. Age 7 rounded to nearest birthday
f. Age 7 rounded to last birthday
g. 8 kilograms
h. 8.00 kilograms

2C-6. The following is the distribution of students by class level at a major urban
university. Calculate the ratio of the number of undergraduate students to the
number of graduate students.

Class Level	f
Undergraduate	
Freshman	65
Sophomore	73
Junior	61
Senior	48
Graduate	
Master's Degree (M.A.)	18
Doctoral Degree (Ph.D.)	22

2C-7.   Reynolds (1997) examined the effects of industrial employment and job conditions on workers' levels of psychological distress using a modified version of the Center for Epidemiological Studies' Scale of depression (CES-D). Suppose the following data represent CES-D scores for a sample of 20 respondents: 3, 2, 2, 5, 4, 6, 4, 3, 7, 6, 5, 2, 4, 3, 4, 5, 7, 6, 4, 5.

    a.   Compile the data into a frequency distribution table with columns for the frequency, the proportional frequency, the percentage frequency, and the cumulative percentage frequency. (No need to show formulas.)

    b.   If a worker scores a 6 on the CES-D scale, what is that worker's percentile rank? Interpret your answer.

2C-8.   Following is a list of Graduate Record Examination (GRE) scores for a group of 20 potential graduate students applying at a major university.

Student Name	GRE Scores
Jack Jones	1,380
Valerie Jackson	1,400
Robin Schmidt	1,220
Jerome Gonzalez	1,410
Richard Roper	1,100
James Filer	1,190
Rashan Miller	1,200
Jeff Wong	1,470
Kevin McMillan	1,420
Joseph Polanski	1,510
Stephanie Nicholson	1,450
Alexandra Zimmerman	1,520
Jennifer Fitzsimmons	1,210
William van der Bergh	1,180
Nicholas Andropov	1,550
Jacqueline Sheets	1,110
Chris Chang	1,400
Michael McKee	1,450
Sharon Johnson	1,380
Ronald Lucie	1,220

    a.   Calculate Kevin McMillan's percentile rank based on the set of GRE scores listed.

    b.   Calculate Michael McKee's percentile rank.

Problem Set 2D

2D-1.   Indicate the level of measurement of the following variables.

Variable Name	Operational Definition and Coding (how the variable is measured and scored)	Level of Measurement
a. PARTYAFF	Political party affiliation: 1 = Republican; 2 = Democrat; 3 = Independent; 4 = Other; 5 = None	
b. EDCOMP	Years of formal education completed	
c. RELATT	Attitudes toward the display of religious icons in federal and state legislative/judicial buildings: 12-item summary scale with scores ranging from 0 to 48	
d. RELDOM	Religious denomination you most identify with: 1 = Baptist; 2 = Lutheranism; 3 = Catholicism; 4 = Judaism; 5 = Islam; 6 = Episcopalian; 7 = Other	
e. POLSAT	Satisfaction with current political system: 1 = very dissatisfied; 2 = dissatisfied; 3 = satisfied; 4 = very satisfied	
f. CESD	Center for Epidemiological Studies Depression Scale: 20-item instrument that detects possible clinical depression in adolescents and adults with scores ranging from 0 to 60	

2D-2.   In a study of caregivers of disabled children, 141 women are interviewed concerning the stresses of caregiving (fictional data). Identify the levels of measurement of each of the following variables from the study.

Variable Name	Operational Definition and Coding (how the variable is measured and scored)	Level of Measurement
a. QUALITY	Perceived quality of care provided to patient: 1 = excellent; 2 = good; 3 = fair; 4 = poor	
b. INCOME	Annual income of household from all sources in U.S. dollars	
c. DIAGNO	Medical diagnosis of patient: standard medical insurance industry numerical codes	
d. BATHSELF	Can person being cared for bathe him/herself?	
e. TEMP	Body temperature of patient in Fahrenheit degrees	

2D-3.   Sibicky et al. (1995) studied empathetic concern as a motivation for helping behaviors. With the response categories provided, does each variable follow the principles of both inclusiveness and exclusiveness? If not, how can they be improved to be in accordance with these principles?

  a. Were you motivated to help by (check one):

  _____ Warmth _____ Compassion _____ Sympathy

  b. Are you:

  _____ Over 25 years of age _____ Under 25 years of age

  c. How many times would you be willing to help the same person?

  _____ 0–4 _____ 6–10 _____ 11–15 _____ None

2D-4. Round the following numbers to the stipulated rounding unit:

  a. 5.455 to nearest tenth
  b. 5.455 to nearest hundredth
  c. 20.821 to nearest hundredth
  d. 381 to nearest hundred
  e. 467,988 to nearest thousand
  f. 467,988 to nearest hundred thousand
  g. .00051 to nearest thousandth

2D-5. Specify the real limits of the following rounded numbers.

  a. 5.00 kilograms
  b. 5 kilograms
  c. Age 9 rounded to last birthday
  d. Age 9 rounded to nearest birthday
  e. 71,000 rounded to nearest hundred
  f. 9,680 rounded to nearest ten
  g. .01605
  h. .248

2D-6. The following is the distribution of workers by title of position in a communications firm. Calculate the ratio of the number of other employees to the number of managers.

Title	Number of Workers
Management Positions	
President	1
Chief executive officer	1
Vice president	3
Assistant vice president	8
Administrative assistant	8
Chief of floor staff	12
Other Positions	
Secretary	16
Sales associate	42
Office clerk	18
Technical/professional	14
Housekeeping	3

2D-7.   Pearson et al. (1990) showed that when a grandmother lives with a family, she is likely to become involved in parenting activities. Suppose the following data represent the number of parenting commands given to 25 children by their grandmothers: 5, 4, 3, 3, 6, 5, 3, 2, 4, 7, 5, 6, 2, 3, 4, 8, 7, 5, 6, 4, 2, 1, 5, 7, 3.

a.   Compile the data into a frequency distribution table with columns for the frequency, the proportional frequency, the percentage frequency, and the cumulative percentage frequency. (No need to show formulas.)

b.   If a grandmother gave two commands, what is her percentile rank? Interpret your answer.

2D-8.   Below is a list of Graduate Record Examination (GRE) scores for a group of 20 potential graduate students applying at a major university.

Student Name	GRE Scores
Jack Jones	1,380
Valerie Jackson	1,400
Robin Schmidt	1,220
Jerome Gonzalez	1,410
Richard Roper	1,100
James Filer	1,190
Rashan Miller	1,200
Jeff Wong	1,470
Kevin McMillan	1,420
Joseph Polanski	1,510
Stephanie Nicholson	1,450
Alexandra Zimmerman	1,520
Jennifer Fitzsimmons	1,210
William van der Bergh	1,180
Nicholas Andropov	1,550
Jacqueline Sheets	1,110
Chris Chang	1,400
Michael McKee	1,450
Sharon Johnson	1,380
Ronald Lucie	1,220

a.   Calculate Jeff Wong's percentile rank based on the set of GRE scores listed.

b.   Calculate Chris Chang's percentile rank.

OPTIONAL COMPUTER APPLICATIONS FOR CHAPTER 2

If your class uses the optional computer applications that accompany this text, download the Chapter 2 exercises on *The Statistical Imagination* Web site at www.mhhe.com/ritchey2. The exercises involve (1) creating and saving data (*.SAV) files using *SPSS for Windows;* (2) producing frequency distributions, quartiles, and percentiles; and (3) managing and saving output files. Additional instructions appear in Appendix D of this text.

Quality control of data coding and entry is very important for minimizing mistakes. To meet scientific and ethical standards, a researcher must be able to look colleagues in the eye and honestly assure them that the data set has no random mistakes in it. Aside from ethics, poor data entry wastes time and energy in the later stages of analysis. An ethical but careless researcher may spend months analyzing a data set and then find incorrect data entries. The discovery of a single incorrect entry requires a complete reanalysis of data. Thus, we must diligently check the accuracy of a data set before analysis begins.

Here are some guidelines for the detection of coding and entry mistakes for self-coded data or existing data files.

Quality Control Guidelines for Data Entry

1. Make sure entered code values are consistent with the codebook and measurement instruments (such as questionnaires).

2. If your typing skills or eyesight is poor, have an assistant read and double-check data entries.

3. Double-check codes on a printout that lists all variables and their codes.

4. Use frequency distribution printouts to check for stray codes (i.e., codes that should not be present in the data).

Charts and Graphs: A Picture Says a Thousand Words

Introduction: Pictorial Presentation of Data

Ultimately, statistical analysis is about simplifying and summarizing large amounts of information. Whether you are a scientist or just a casual observer of what goes on around you, your interests are likely to lie with understanding the behavior of a large population of subjects or objects. For example, recall your first day on campus. Many questions probably popped into your mind as you attempted to adjust to all of the new activities tied to this interesting environment. You may have inquired: How large is the campus? How many students are enrolled here? Are there many from my hometown or majoring in my subject? When it comes to my ability to succeed, am I at least average? Is this a place where I will fit comfortably?

It is only natural for human beings to wish to simplify and organize their percep- tions of the world around them by summing things up. In order to orient ourselves to a new situation, we quickly search for a few broad generalizations that describe the big picture. We wish to simplify the complexities that assault us so that we behave appro- priately and efficiently and not be fooled. As we noted in Chapters 1 and 2, there is so much information out there that we must take care to maintain a sense of proportion and balance in how we interpret and react to it. A sense of proportion about reality can be gauged with numbers or with pictures.

To convey a sense of proportion, we can describe the score distribution of a variable numerically with percentage frequencies as we did in Chapter 2. Numerical distributions, however, make sense only if a person tends to think proportionately. Therefore, we often substitute graphs and "pictorial" drawings such as pie charts to encourage proportional thinking directly. Graphs provide strong support for the maxim

"A picture says a thousand words." When some of those words are numerical, a picture clarifies a thousand words and calculations.

With today's user-friendly software, the mass media bombard us with graphs, pie charts, and pictographs (pictures of objects, stick figures, or shaded maps). Sometimes the software takes on a life of its own and draws a graph incorrectly. To avoid such mishaps, it is important to know the mathematical computations behind graph construction and not rely solely on software programmers.

Graphical and pictorial designs are chosen on the basis of (1) the level of measurement of a variable, (2) the study objectives and points to be made, and (3) the targeted audience. For public audiences, colorful, uncluttered graphs work best, providing an overview of descriptive statistics such as percentages and averages. In contrast, professional audiences are accustomed to inferential statistics—those designed to explain and test hypotheses. Along with statistical tables, graphs may assist us in discerning the shapes of frequency distributions. Even descriptive graphs can alert an analyst to potential sources of error that may influence additional analysis.

Graphing and Table Construction Guidelines
Graphical presentations must follow some simple rules and guidelines which also apply to tables and report construction.

Graphing and Table Construction Guidelines

1. Choose the design on the basis of (*a*) the level of measurement of a variable, (*b*) the study objectives, and (*c*) the targeted audience.

2. Above all, a good graphical presentation should be clear and understandable. It should simplify, not complicate.

3. A graph, table, or chart should be self-explanatory and convey information without reference to a text or speaker. Careful selection of titles, scale designations, captions, and other legend material accomplishes this objective. Submit each graph or table to the "lost in the parking lot" test. Ask: If this graph were dropped in the parking lot, could a complete stranger pick it up and interpret it?

4. Before deciding on the type of pictorial presentation (e.g., pie chart versus bar chart), produce rough drafts of several options. Computer software makes this relatively easy. To broaden the choices, seek advice and peruse other materials, such as organizational reports.

5. Adhere to the principles of inclusiveness and exclusiveness (Chapter 2). Footnote any exceptions.

6. If the data are not your own, indicate the source at the bottom of the graph or table.

Graphing Nominal/Ordinal Data

Pie Charts

A simple style of presentation for nominal/ordinal data is the pie chart. A **pie chart** is *a circle that is dissected (or sliced) from its center point with each slice representing the proportional frequency of a category.* All of us have sliced pies, and sometimes we fail to get a fair share. When a researcher wants to provide a sense of proportion in regard to a nominal/ordinal variable, pie charts are especially useful. They convey fairness, relative size, or inequality among the categories. The relative size of a pie slice is a form of proportional thinking with which everyone is familiar.

---

pie chart   A circle that is dissected (or sliced) from its center point with each slice representing the proportional frequency of a category of a nominal/ordinal variable. It is especially useful for conveying a sense of fairness, relative size, or inequality among categories.

Figure 3–1 portrays the distribution of marital status in a sample of 161 homeless persons. The area within the entire circle represents 100 percent of the subjects in the sample. The area of a slice represents the percentage in a specific category. It is easy to see that over half the homeless respondents had never been married.

A computer program readily produced the pie chart in Figure 3–1. To relate the pie to the frequency distribution of marital status, let us construct the chart by hand. It is important to understand how charts are constructed because a computer program may produce a design other than the one intended. The first step in drawing any graph is to produce the variable's frequency distribution. In addition, for pie charts we compute the proportional frequency and percentage frequency of each category. The proportional frequencies, together with knowledge about the dimensions of a circle, are used to compute the sizes of the slices.

Correct slicing of the pie depends on knowing that the angles that dissect a circle from its center are measured in degrees with a protractor (a half-moon-shaped circular

FIGURE 3–1

Pie chart of marital status of homeless adults, *n* = 161

ruler). Regardless of the size of a circle, its circumference is defined as having a total distance around of 360 degrees (°). A half circle is 180° around, or a proportion of .5 times 360 degrees. A quarter circle is 90° around, or one-fourth of 360 degrees. These benchmarks of a circle are illustrated in Figure 3–2. Any part of the pie can be sliced by multiplying the proportion in a category by 360 degrees.

Table 3–1 provides calculations for the pie chart shown in Figure 3–1. How is each category awarded its portion of the pie? A category's portion is the proportional frequency p times 360°, the total circumference of the pie. If .51 (51 percent) of the respondents had never married, they should "get" 51 percent of the pie—185° worth—or just over one-half. Once the 360 degrees are awarded for all categories, a protractor is used to cut the pie into correctly proportioned pieces. Percentages are placed on the pie chart for the sake of clarity. If the chart is presented to a public audience, we round to a whole percentage (i.e., the ones place).

Interpreting Pie Charts   Let us return to Figure 3–1, which portrays the distribution of marital statuses for a sample of 161 homeless persons, and systematically interpret its meaning. First, focus on the largest pie slices, which represent categories with the greatest frequencies of occurrence. In Figure 3–1 it is easy to see that over half of homeless respondents had never been married and substantial portions had divorced or separated. Second, compare slice sizes to one another. A higher percentage of homeless persons had never married than all other categories combined. Unattached persons—those who have never married, divorced, or separated—constitute a large segment of homeless persons. Third, compare the results to other populations. Look for unexpectedly small or large slices in this population compared to others. The most striking revelation in Figure 3–1 is the small piece dedicated to "married." For example, in the general adult population, 56.7 percent of adults over age 18 are married compared to only 4 percent in this sample of homeless persons (U.S. Bureau of the Census 2003). In summary, homelessness is not beneficial to marital stability.

Note in Table 3–1 that the percentage in the "Never married" category is rounded down to 51 percent instead of up to 52 percent. Moreover, we award this category 185° instead of 186°. These adjustments for rounding error are necessary to keep the total degrees of the circle from exceeding 360, since a circle has a defined space of that amount. Adjusting the "Never married" category has the smallest effect on error compared with adjusting other categories.

FIGURE 3–2

Degrees of a circle for one-quarter circle, one-half circle, and full circle

Benchmarks

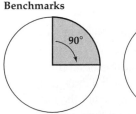
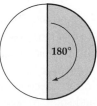
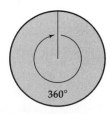

TABLE 3–1 | Computational spreadsheet for constructing a pie chart: The distribution of marital status for a sample of 161 homeless persons

Givens			Calculations		
Marital Status	f		p	(p)(360°)	Percent (%)
Never married	83		.5155	185°	51
Divorced	43		.2671	96	27
Separated	22		.1366	49	14
Married	7		.0435	16	4
Widowed	3		.0186	7	2
No answer	3		.0186	7	2
Totals	161		.9999*	360°	100

*Total did not add to 1.0000 because of rounding error.

Computer software packages (such as the *SPSS for Windows,* which is an option with this text) provide a wide range of pie chart styles. One or more slices can be brought out in relief or "exploded," and pairs of pie charts can be presented for comparison of groups or time periods.

How to Construct and Interpret a Pie Chart

To construct a pie chart:

1. Set up a frequency distribution table with the following headings:

Category	f	p	(p)(360°)	%

where

"Category" = the category name of a nominal/ordinal variable,

f = the frequency of cases (or number of cases) in a category,

$p = p$ [of the total n in a category] = (f of category)/n, with n = sample size,

$(p)(360°)$ = degrees for each slice,

% = percent [of the total n in a category] = $(p)(100)$.

2. Draw a circle and place a dot in its center. Draw a straight line from the dot to the circle. Place a protractor on this line, mark the number of degrees for the first category, and draw a line to create the pie slice. Place a protractor on this second line, mark the number of degrees for the second category, and soon. Make sure that exactly 360° are accounted for.

3. Clearly label each slice and indicate the percent of cases it represents. Make sure the labels are horizontal (i.e., do not wind them to the shape of the slice). Use artistic judgment to place the labels inside or outside the slices.

4. Properly title the pie chart. Identify the source of data at the bottom of the graph.

To interpret a pie chart:

1. Focus on the largest pie slices. Stipulate which categories had the greatest frequencies of occurrence.

2. Compare slice sizes to one another.

3. If appropriate, compare the results to other populations. Look for unexpectedly small or large slices (such as the small percentage of married persons among homeless adults in Figure 3–1).

Bar Charts

Another way to graph nominal/ordinal data is to use a bar chart. A **bar chart** is *a series of vertical or horizontal bars with the length of a bar representing the percentage frequency of a category of a nominal/ordinal variable.* Like a slice of a pie chart, the area of a bar—which is determined by its length—conveys a sense of the proportional frequency of a category. Bar charts are especially good at conveying competition among categories ([i.e., which category finishes with the greatest frequency (longest bar)]. Bar charts are constructed on two axes: one lying flat, or horizontal (the *abscissa*), and the other standing straight up, or vertical (the *ordinate*). In other words, the two lines are joined at a 90°, or "square," angle. The categories of a variable are situated on one axis, and markings for percentages are made on the other axis. We need only compute the percentage frequency of each category to construct a bar chart.

> **bar chart**   A series of vertical or horizontal bars with the length of a bar representing the percentage frequency of a category of a nominal/ordinal variable. Bar charts are especially useful for conveying a sense of competition among categories.

Interpreting Bar Charts   Figure 3–3 provides a bar chart of the percentage frequency distribution of employment of homeless adults in the week prior to an interview. First, observe the heights of the bars. The tallest bar is the category with the highest frequency. Comment on the rank order of categories. In Figure 3–3, we see that more homeless persons did not work in the previous week than did work. Second, compare the bars and comment on any that are especially tall or short. In Figure 3–3, we note that the bars are about the same height. Third, if appropriate, compare the results to other populations. Look for unexpectedly tall or short bars. A knowledgeable researcher

FIGURE 3–3

Bar chart of employment in the previous week among homeless adults, $n = 161$

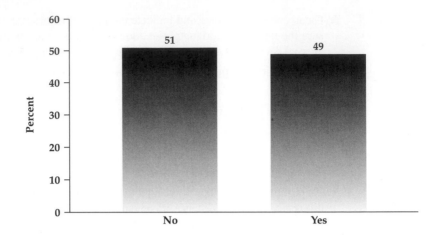

would point out that the results contradict a common stereotype that homeless persons are shiftless. Considering the circumstances of homelessness, one would expect a much lower rate of recent work than revealed in this sample. In this regard, then, the percentage of those working is higher than expected. In summary, the similarity of bar heights quickly conveys that almost as many homeless adults work as not.

How to Construct and Interpret a Bar Chart

To construct a bar chart:

1. Set up a frequency distribution table with the following headings:

Category	f	p	%

where

"Category" = category name of a nominal/ordinal variable,

f = frequency of cases (or number of cases) in a category,

$p = p$ [of the total n in a category] = (f of category)/n, with n = sample size

% = percent [of the total n in a category] = $(p)(100)$.

2. Draw the horizontal axis of the bar chart, its width appropriate to the number of bars.

3. Draw the vertical axis. Observe the highest frequency (f) or percentage frequency in the frequency distribution table and label the axis from zero to just beyond this highest frequency.

4. Draw the bars using a width that is visually appealing. You may choose to rank order the bars from highest to lowest. Space apart the bars of each category. Use frequencies (f) or percentage frequencies on the vertical axis as markers for bar heights. Clearly label the category names under the bars.

5. Properly title the bar chart. Make sure that axis labels are correct and clear. Identify the source of data at the bottom of the graph.

To interpret a bar chart:

1. Observe the heights of bars. The tallest bar indicates the category with the highest frequency. Comment on the rank order of categories.

2. Compare the bars, commenting on any that are especially tall or short.

3. If appropriate, compare the results to other populations. Look for unexpectedly tall or short bars.

Figure 3–4 shows a "clustered" bar chart, which is good for comparing two or more groups for a nominal/ordinal variable. This figure compares the functional ability of 104 clinic patients at a veterans hospital and reveals how low functional ability is very characteristic of ill veterans over age 70.

Finally, the vertical axis of a bar chart does not always simply measure number or percentage. Among the categories of a nominal/ordinal variable, bar charts may be used to convey relative amounts of any variable. For example, exercise 3B–2 in the end-of-chapter exercises involves a bar chart for alcohol consumption for five European countries. The nominal variable is country, and the countries' names will be labeled across the horizontal axis of the bar chart. On the vertical axis, instead of indicating number or percentage, the scale will be "liters of alcohol consumed." The values to be plotted are directly available in the table provided with the exercise. Similarly, we could construct a bar chart comparing the median incomes of these five countries with dollar amounts indicated on the vertical axis.

FIGURE 3–4

Clustered bar chart of the functional ability of clinic patients served at a veterans hospital by age, $n = 104$

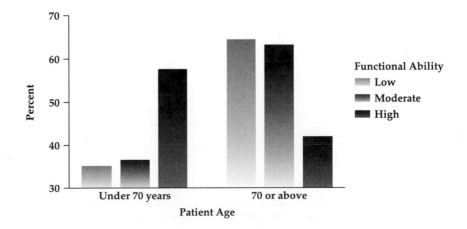

Graphing Interval/Ratio Variables

Histograms

A histogram is a type of graph used with interval/ratio variables. One such ratio variable, which we will define as X, is the fuel economy ratings provided by the Environmental Protection Agency (U.S. Department of Energy 2004). These ratings are the estimated miles per gallon (MPG) posted on new vehicle models. Again, the first step for any graph is to produce a frequency distribution. The calculation spreadsheet in Table 3–2 presents the frequency distribution of fuel economy ratings for in-city driving for 4-cylinder compact car models for model year 2004 (excluding electric/gasoline hybrid models). Our interest is in how the scores are clustered and how they are spread out. We can readily see, for example, that the minimum rating was 18 MPG and the maximum, 38 MPG. Observing the fuel economy ratings with high frequencies of occurrence (i.e., those for which f is large), we can see that many

TABLE 3–2 I Computational spreadsheet for constructing histograms and polygons: Frequency distribution of fuel economy ratings for city driving in miles per gallon (MPG); 106 Compact car models; Model year 2004

Givens		Calculations
X Fuel Economy Rating (MPG)	f	Real Limits
18	1	17.5–18.5
20	4	19.5–20.5
21	6	20.5–21.5
22	19	21.5–22.5
23	10	22.5–23.5
24	17	23.5–24.5
25	9	24.5–25.5
26	13	25.5–26.5
27	5	26.5–27.5
28	5	27.5–28.5
29	4	28.5–29.5
30	1	29.5–30.5
31	1	30.5–31.5
32	3	31.5–32.5
33	3	32.5–33.5
35	2	34.5–35.5
36	1	35.5–36.5
38	2	37.5–38.5
Total	106	

Source: U.S. Department of Energy, 2004.

compact car models are projected to get between 22 and 26 MPG in city driving conditions. (For persons accustomed to gauging fuel economy in metric units, multiply MPG by .42 to obtain the equivalent kilometers per liter of gasoline.)

By graphing the data we get an even better sense of proportion about how fuel economy ratings are distributed for compact cars. Figure 3–5 presents the fuel economy ratings in Table 3–2 in the form of a frequency histogram. A **frequency histogram** is *a 90-degree plot presenting the scores of a variable along the horizontal axis and the frequency of each score in a column parallel to the vertical axis.* In other words, *X* is plotted on the horizontal axis and *f* on the vertical axis. A histogram is similar to a bar chart except the columns of a histogram touch one another (unless a score has a frequency of zero cases, in which case there will be a column missing). The markings on the horizontal axis are called tick marks and they represent the *X*-scores (in this instance, ratings in MPG). Notice that the lowest and highest labeled tick marks, 17 MPG and 39 MPG, respectively, extend just below the minimum and maximum observed scores of 18 and 38 MPG. To draw and label the vertical axis, in the frequency distribution table identify the highest frequency (*f*) recorded. In Table 3–2, this is a frequency of 19 for a score of 22 MPG. Label the vertical axis from 0 to just beyond 19. The width of each column of the histogram is the same. The columns touching one another accounts for the real limits of each score. For example, the scores in Table 3–2 are rounded to the nearest integer; in other words, every model rated at 22 MPG did not get exactly 22 MPG in the Environmental Protection Agency's calculations. Accounting for real limits of the scores widens the columns such that adjacent columns will touch one another and meet the principle of inclusiveness.

---

frequency histogram   A 90-degree plot presenting the scores of an interval/ratio variable along the horizontal axis and the frequency of each score in a column parallel to the vertical axis.

Interpretation of Histograms   What message does the histogram in Figure 3–5 convey? There are several characteristics of histograms that convey information. First, observe the heights of columns. We can see that the most frequently occurring fuel economy rating is 22 MPG and ratings of 24 and 26 MPG are also quite common. Second, look for clusters of scores and see if there is a "central tendency," a score value around which the distribution centers. We can see that the bulk of the models get between 20 and 29 MPG. Moreover, with the exception of a few especially high scores, the ratings tend to center around 24 MPG. Third, let us look for symmetry or balance in the distribution of scores. We can see that this histogram is not symmetrical. The bulk of *X*-scores rests on the lower end of the distribution and a few models, those above about 30 MPG, have especially high fuel economy ratings. (In Chapter 4, we will define the shape of this score distribution as a right skew.)

FIGURE 3–5

Frequency
histogram of
fuel economy
ratings of 106
compact car
models; model
year 2004

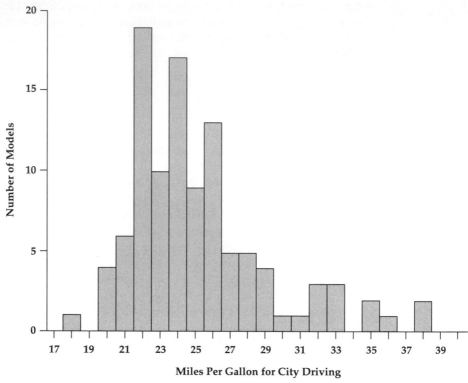

Source: U.S. Department of Energy, 2004.

How to Construct and Interpret Histograms

To construct a histogram:

1. Set up a frequency distribution table with the following headings:

Score (*X*)	*f*	Real Limits of Score

where

Score = a score of an interval/ratio variable

f = the frequency of cases (or number of cases) for a score

2. Calculate the real limits of each score. (See Chapter 2 for real limits.)

3. Draw the horizontal axis of the histogram. Observe the lowest and highest scores in the frequency distribution table. Put tick marks on the axis and label the values of *X* accordingly; allow extra space at each end of the axis beyond the values of the lowest and highest scores.

4. Draw the vertical axis. Observe the highest frequency (f) in the frequency distribution table and label the axis from zero to just beyond this highest frequency.

5. Draw the columns using real limits as markers for column widths and frequencies (f) as markers for column heights.

6. Properly title the histogram. Make sure that axis labels are correct and clear. Identify the source of data at the bottom of the graph.

To interpret a histogram:

1. Observe the heights of columns. The tallest column indicates the value of the X-score with the highest frequency (f).

2. Look for clusters of scores and see if there is a "central tendency," an X-score value around which the distribution centers.

3. Look for symmetry or balance in the distribution of scores. Do the scores tend to fall evenly around a central score, or are there especially low or high scores (as in Figure 3–5)?

Polygons and Line Graphs

Another graphing technique for interval/ratio variables is the frequency polygon or *line graph*. A **frequency polygon** is *a 90-degree plot with the interval/ratio score plotted on the horizontal axis and score frequencies depicted by the heights of dots located above scores and connected by straight lines.* The axes of a polygon are designed like those of a histogram. The values of a variable (X) are marked on the horizontal axis, or baseline. Frequencies (f) are plotted up the vertical axis. But to indicate the frequency of the variable at a particular score, we use dots in place of columns and connect the dots to obtain a graph line. Figure 3–6 is the polygon for the fuel economy ratings in Table 3–2, which we used for the histogram in Figure 3–5. Whereas histograms draw attention to the tallest columns where the bulk of scores lie, polygons communicate a sense of trend or movement. That is, we observe the flow of peaks and valleys in the graph line as we compare the fuel economy ratings from lowest to highest across the baseline.

frequency polygon (line graph)   A 90-degree plot with the interval/ratio score plotted on the horizontal axis and score frequencies depicted by the heights of dots located above scores and connected by straight lines.

Interpretation of Polygons (Line Graphs)   What message does the polygon in Figure 3–6 convey? The notable characteristics of polygons are similar to those of histograms. First, identify the highest peak of the polygon. This peak occurs for a fuel economy rating of 22 MPG and this is the most frequently occurring score. Slightly lower peaks occur for fuel economy ratings of 24 and 26 MPG, revealing these values

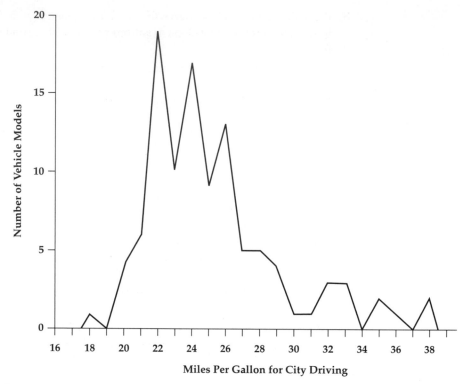

FIGURE 3–6

Frequency polygon of the distribution of fuel economy ratings for city driving in miles per gallon (MPG) for 106 compact car models; model year 2004

Source: U.S. Department of Energy, 2004.

to also occur quite frequently. Second, look for an expanse of space under the graph line and see if there is a central tendency. We can see that most of the area under the graph line rests between scores of 20 and 29 MPG, and the ratings tend to center around 24 MPG. There are a few especially high scores, beyond a score of 30 MPG. Third, look for symmetry or balance in the distribution of scores and look for a trend in the shape of the graph line. See if the tails of the graph line are evenly situated. In Figure 3–6, the "dragon's tail" extending to the right highlights the imbalance in the distribution. While most compact car models have MPG ratings below 30, a few models are especially fuel efficient. Overall, the polygon conveys the message that as one moves up the scale of fuel economy ratings toward the higher MPG range, there are fewer models available.

Frequency polygons are especially useful for comparing two or more samples. For example, let us compare the distributions of fuel economy ratings for compact cars with those of 4-wheel-drive sports utility vehicles (SUVs). Table 3–3 provides the frequency and percentage frequency distributions for both types of vehicles. Notice that the sample sizes of vehicle types differ. There are 106 compact car models but only 68 SUV models. If we use raw frequencies to construct the polygons, the polygon for the more numerous compact cars will dwarf the polygon for the SUVs. Thus, we use a common

How to Construct and Interpret Polygons (Line Graphs)

To construct a polygon:

1. Set up a frequency distribution table with the following headings (exactly like the table used in constructing histograms):

Score (*X*)	*f*	*Real Limits* of Score

where

Score = a score of an interval/ratio variable

f = the frequency of cases (or number of cases) for a score

2. Calculate the real limits of each *X*-score. (See Chapter 2 for real limits.)

3. Draw the horizontal axis or "baseline" of the polygon. Observe the lowest and highest scores in the frequency distribution table. Put tick marks on the axis and label the values of *X* accordingly; allow extra space at each end of the axis beyond the lowest and highest scores.

4. Draw the vertical axis. Observe the highest frequency (f) in the frequency distribution table and label the axis from zero to just beyond this highest frequency.

5. Progressing from the lowest to the highest values of *X*, draw dots above each value of *X* to the height of its frequency (f).

6. Connect the dots with lines. *Caution:* If a value of *X* has a frequency of zero (e.g., the score of 34 MPG in Table 3–2), the graph line extends down to the baseline.

7. Close off the ends of the graph line. Tie the lowest value of *X* to the baseline by drawing a line between its dot and its lower real limit. Tie the highest value of *X* to the baseline by drawing a line between its dot and its upper real limit.

8. Properly title the polygon. Make sure that axis labels are correct and clear. Identify the source of data at the bottom of the graph.

To interpret a polygon:

1. Look for peaks. The tallest peak indicates the value of *X* with the highest frequency.

2. Look for an expanse of space under the graph line to see if there are clusters of scores and to see if there is a central tendency.

3. Look for symmetry or balance in the distribution of scores. Look for a trend in the shape of the graph line. See if the tails of the graph are evenly situated around a central score. If not, note especially low or high scores by identifying which tail extends out.

denominator of 100 by calculating the percentage frequencies. Figure 3–7 presents the two polygons with "Percent of Vehicle Models" stipulated in the vertical axis. Once these two distributions are graphically depicted together, their differences become quite clear. The peaks of the two lines convey a difference in central tendency or average, the topic of the next chapter. SUVs tend to have relatively low fuel ratings ranging in a rather narrow span from about 15 to 20 MPG. In contrast, compact cars have higher ratings and a broader range from about 20 to 29 MPG. One of the most striking features of this graph is the small overlap between the two lines. The *most*-fuel-efficient SUVs have fuel economy ratings equal to the *least*-efficient compact cars.

TABLE 3–3 | A comparison of fuel economy ratings for city driving in miles per gallon (MPG) for compact car and 4-wheel drive sports utility vehicle (SUV) models; model year 2004

Fuel Economy Rating (MPG)	Compact Car Models		SUV Models	
	f	Percent (%)	f	Percent (%)
11	0	.0	1	1.5
12	0	.0	1	1.5
15	0	.0	21	30.9
16	0	.0	12	17.6
17	0	.0	15	22.1
18	1	.9	9	13.2
19	0	.0	8	11.8
20	4	3.8	1	1.5
21	6	5.7	0	.0
22	19	17.9	0	.0
23	10	9.4	0	.0
24	17	16.0	0	.0
25	9	8.5	0	.0
26	13	12.3	0	.0
27	5	4.7	0	.0
28	5	4.7	0	.0
29	4	3.8	0	.0
30	1	.9	0	.0
31	1	.9	0	.0
32	3	2.8	0	.0
33	3	2.8	0	.0
35	2	1.9	0	.0
36	1	.9	0	.0
38	2	1.9	0	.0
Totals	106	99.8	68	100.1*

*Total percentages do not sum to 100 because of rounding error.
Source: U.S. Department of Energy, 2004.

FIGURE 3–7

A comparison of fuel economy ratings for city driving in miles per gallon for 106 compact car models and 68 sports utility models; model year 2004

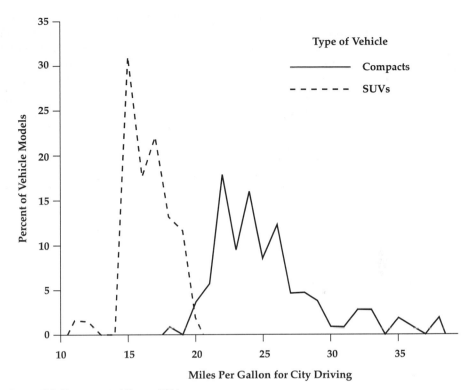

Source: U.S. Department of Energy, 2004.

Finally, both histograms and polygons are useful devices for identifying unusually high or low scores in a distribution. For example, in Figure 3–7 notice that there are a couple of SUV models with especially low fuel economy ratings (11 and 12 MPG). Similarly, there are a few compact car models with especially high ratings, above 34 MPG. We call these unusual scores *outliers*. Aside from drawing our attention to "outstanding" scores, it is important to identify outliers and consider their effects on inferential statistical analysis.

Using Graphs with Inferential Statistics and Research Applications

Graphs are used primarily for descriptive purposes with public audiences. In scientific research and inferential statistics, however, we sometimes graph a variable to become familiar with its distribution and to prepare it for later analysis. To expedite this preparation phase, we computer-generate histograms and polygons (line graphs). In inferential statistics, these graphics are especially useful for detecting atypical scores in a distribution. For example, a graph depicting divorce rates in the 50 states reveals that Nevada, with its liberal divorce laws, *is* markedly different. Such an atypical case is called a **deviant score or outlier**, *a score that is markedly different from the others in the score distribution.* As we will learn later, outliers distort statistical calculations such as averages. If the distortions are great, it is necessary to discard or adjust these deviant scores. For example, in the case of divorce rates the appropriate procedure might be to discard the Nevada data. We inform the reader that it is an exceptional state that is worthy of a case study (individualized analysis) and stipulate that our conclusions apply only to the other 49 states. Another way to modify the distorting effects of outliers is to mathematically adjust extreme scores. One method involves taking the logarithm of the scores, a mathematical transformation that compresses scores into a smaller range. A second method is simply to reduce the value of the outlier to the next lowest or highest score, a procedure called truncating. A final caution: It is inappropriate to omit or adjust outliers simply because they do not fit the expected pattern. The researcher must clearly explain the theoretical and practical reasons for such adjustments. More will be said about outliers in later chapters.

---

deviant score or outlier   A score that is markedly different from the others in the score distribution.

Statistical Follies and Fallacies: Graphical Distortion

Graphs and charts provide mental maps of large sets of data. The procedures for designing graphs are normative; that is, different people have different ideas about what is pleasing to the eye. In other words, pictorial presentation is part art.

Since the norms of the presentation of data are aesthetic as well as technical, often they are unclear. For example, how wide should the bars in a bar chart be? Should we paint the bars a variety of colors? The conventions that apply to these and similar questions are flexible and often follow fashion. Art inspires creativity and individuality.

When the rules are unclear, however, they are easy to break, intentionally or unintentionally. For example, with the assortment of computer graphics programs available today, users are often willing to leave the details of graphing to the unknown

FIGURE 3–8

Poster presented to Mortimer Mainstreet by his campaign staff to report the results of the most recent gubernatorial campaign poll

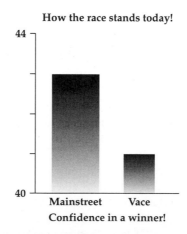

How the race stands today!

Confidence in a winner!

individual who designed the software. As a result, popular (as opposed to scientific) media assault us with rapidly conceived computer-generated graphs and charts. As you become astute in statistical thinking, you will begin to see that many if not most of these "quickies" are at best unreliable (i.e., open to multiple interpretations) and at worst misleading.

The following parable depicts a common graphical distortion. Fictional gubernatorial candidate Mortimer Mainstreet had a comfortable two-to-one margin in early electoral polls over the only serious contender, Harry Vace. For Mortimer, however, it has been downhill ever since. Rumor has it that he is about to scrap his campaign staff, whose members are beginning to fear that their dreams of ruling the state and their jobs are in peril.

The latest poll has come out, and it shows that Mortimer's lead has dwindled to 2 percentage points, 43 to 41 percent, with 16 percent undecided and a margin of error of plus or minus 3 percent. The race has become too close to call. In an attempt to avoid losing their jobs, the staff members inform Mortimer of the poll results on page 94 (Figure 3–8). (If Mortimer Mainstreet lets this get by, he does not deserve to be governor!) Can you identify all the things wrong with this chart?

SUMMARY

1. Charts and graphs provide a sense of proportion about a distribution of scores without requiring a reader to have extensive mathematical knowledge.

2. Choose a graphic design on the basis of (*a*) the level of measurement of the variable, (*b*) the study objectives, and (*c*) the targeted audience.

3. There are sound guidelines for constructing graphs and tables. A graph should simplify, not complicate. A chart or table should stand on its own and make sense without reference to text.

4. Pie charts and bar graphs are commonly used to illustrate the distribution of categories of a nominal/ordinal variable.

5. Pie charts are especially useful for conveying a sense of fairness, relative size, or inequality among categories.

6. Bar charts are especially useful for conveying a sense of competition among categories.

7. Clustered bar charts are good for comparing two or more groups for a nominal/ordinal variable.

8. For interval/ratio variables, use a frequency histogram or frequency polygon (line graph).

9. Frequency histograms draw attention to where the bulk of scores in a distribution falls.

10. Frequency polygons (or line graphs) portray a sense of trend or movement in a distribution of scores.

CHAPTER EXTENSIONS ON *THE STATISTICAL IMAGINATION* WEB SITE

Chapter 3 Extensions of text material available on *The Statistical Imagination* Web site at www.mhhe.com/ritchey2 include (*a*) graphing of histograms and polygons with grouped data, (*b*) graphing of *ogives*—cumulative frequency distributions, and (*c*) graphing of box-and-whisker plots, which are useful for identifying outliers.

FORMULAS FOR CHAPTER 3

Calculations for pie charts:
    Set up a spreadsheet with the following headings:

Category	f	p	(p)(360)°	%

Calculations for bar charts:
    Set up a spreadsheet with the following headings:

Category	f	p	%

Calculations for histograms and polygons:
    Set up a spreadsheet with the following headings:

Score	f	Real Limits of Score

QUESTIONS FOR CHAPTER 3

1. What are three things to consider in choosing a graphical style or design?
2. What is the foremost objective of graphing data?
3. What is the "parking lot" test?
4. Pie charts and bar charts are used with variables of what levels of measurement?
5. Histograms and polygons (line graphs) are used with variables of what levels of measurement?
6. Under what circumstances is a pie chart especially useful?
7. Under what circumstances is a bar chart especially useful?
8. Explain the relationship between rounded scores and the real limits of scores.
9. Mrs. Barker is on a bus with the 24 pupils in her fifth-grade class. She is chatting with the bus driver, Kevin Braughn. If you were to construct a frequency

histogram of ages of the bus's occupants, how would it appear? What would be peculiar about Mrs. Barker's and Kevin's ages? What statistical term is used to describe these two scores?

EXERCISES FOR CHAPTER 3

Problem Set 3A

3A-1.   According to the U.S. Federal Bureau of Prisons (2003), the percentage distribution of inmates by security level of prison is as follows. Construct a pie chart.

Security Level	Percent (%)
Minimum	19.4
Low	38.9
Medium	24.8
High	10.7
No security level	6.1

3A-2.   For European countries, Lueschen et al. (1995) examined 1990 health care expenditures as a percentage of gross domestic product (GDP). Construct a bar chart and comment on their findings.

Country	Percentage of GDP Spent on Health Care in 1990 (%)
Belgium	7.6
France	8.8
Germany	8.3
Netherlands	8.2
Spain	6.6

3A-3.   Following are U.S. Bureau of the Census (2000) data on gender and educational attainment for individuals 25 years of age and older.
  a.   Construct a clustered bar chart of gender and educational attainment.
  b.   Comment on the nature of gender and educational attainment in the United States.

	Gender	
Educational Attainment	Male (%)	Female (%)
Less than high school diploma	19.9	19.3
High school diploma	27.6	29.6
Some college	20.6	21.5
Associate/Bachelor's degree	21.9	21.8
Master's degree	6.0	5.8
Professional degree	2.6	1.4
Doctoral degree	1.4	0.6
Totals	100.0	100.0

3A-4.   Alba, Logan, and Crowder (1997) examined the makeup of white ethnic neighborhoods in New York City. One area of interest is migration from the central city between 1980 and 1990. The following table presents ethnic group populations for a neighborhood for those two years.

	1980			1990		
	Germans	Irish	Italians	Germans	Irish	Italians
Population	46,920	9,570	50,773	18,300	9,436	41,429

a.   Construct separate pie charts for each of these two years to depict the populations of each ethnic group.
b.   Construct a clustered bar chart for these two years to depict the population of each ethnic group.
c.   Compare the two types of charts. In general, what do the charts convey? Which graphical style is better at depicting the phenomenon? Explain your choice.

3A-5.   Assume that the following are the ages of students on a college debate team: 20, 19, 20, 21, 20, 21, 22, 24, 23, 22, 19, 20, 21, 21, 22, 23, 22, 20, 21, 21, 23, 29.
a.   Prepare a frequency distribution and construct a frequency histogram of these data.
b.   Construct a frequency polygon of these data.
c.   Which of the two graphs would you choose to present to a public audience? Why?
d.   One of the scores is peculiar. What is this peculiarity called?

3A-6. The following are frequency distributions of distances (in kilometers) traveled daily by high school students in suburban and rural school districts (fictional data).

    a. Construct frequency polygons for the two distributions on the same graph. (Caution: The sample sizes differ.)

    b. What is the obvious conclusion drawn in comparing distance traveled for the two school districts?

Kilometers	Suburban *f*	Rural *f*
1	2	0
2	4	1
3	9	0
4	13	3
5	14	5
6	8	6
7	6	9
8	5	13
9	4	17
10	2	24
11	0	15
12	0	8
13	0	7
14	0	2
15	0	1

Problem Set 3B

3B-1. The following table presents the percentage distribution of murders in the United States for 2002 by the relationship of the victim to the offender (Federal Bureau of Investigation 2002a). Construct a pie chart.

Relationship of Victim to Offender	Percent (%)
Family	12.7
Stranger	14.0
Other known	30.5
Unknown	42.8
Total	100.0

3B-2. Lueschen et al. (1995) analyzed alcohol consumption for five European countries. Construct a bar chart of their data and comment on their findings.

Country	Liters Consumed per Person over 24 Years of Age in 1990
Belgium	12.4
France	16.7
Germany	12.3
Netherlands	9.9
Spain	15.5

3B-3. The Federal Bureau of Investigation (2002a) provides data on arrest percentages for drug sale/manufacturing and simple drug possession by region, shown next.
- *a.* Create a clustered bar chart of drug arrests by type and region.
- *b.* Comment on the percentages of drug arrests by type and region.

Drug Abuse Violation	Northeast (%)	Midwest (%)	South (%)	West (%)
Sale/Manufacturing	27.9	23.1	17.2	16.4
Possession	72.1	76.9	82.8	83.6
Totals	100.0	100.0	100.0	100.0

3B-4. Data regarding the principal activities and accomplishments of the Immigration and Naturalization Service Investigations Program are compiled by the Office of Immigration Statistics of the U.S. Department of Homeland Security (2003). Data for selected years are presented.
- *a.* Construct pie charts for these two years (on the same page) to depict the activities and accomplishments of the INS Investigations Program.
- *b.* Construct a clustered bar chart for these two years to depict the activities and accomplishments of the INS Investigations Program.
- *c.* Compare the two types of charts. In general, what do the charts convey? Which graphical style is better at depicting the phenomenon? Explain your choice.

Cases	1992 Investigations			2002 Investigations		
	Criminal	Employer	Smuggling	Criminal	Employer	Smuggling
Completed	38,716	7,053	7,073	78,841	2,061	2,395

3B-5.   Suppose a small college is interested in increasing participation in campus activities. A random sample of students was asked to check events that they attended on a checklist for the previous term. The results for the number of events attended were as follows: 2, 2, 4, 8, 5, 2, 3, 1, 6, 5, 4, 12, 1, 4, 2, 7, 6, 3, 2, 4, 7, 4, 2, 3.

    a.   Construct a frequency histogram of these data.

    b.   Construct a frequency polygon of these data.

    c.   Which of the two graphs would you choose to present to a public audience? Why?

    d.   One of the scores is peculiar. What is this peculiarity called?

3B-6.   Suppose that the following are frequency distributions of the ages of inpatients at a substance abuse treatment hospital by the major diagnoses of cocaine and alcohol addiction.

    a.   Construct overlying frequency polygons of these data. (*Caution:* The sample sizes differ.)

    b.   What does the graph reveal?

Age	Cocaine Addicts f	Alcohol Addicts f
26	2	1
27	5	2
28	6	2
29	11	3
30	13	5
31	8	6
32	4	9
33	4	15
34	0	17
35	1	15
36	0	7
37	0	5
38	0	2

Problem Set 3C

3C-1.   The United States Bureau of the Census (2000) provides data on educational attainment (among persons aged 25 years and over) in the United States. Use the following percentage distribution to construct a pie chart.

Educational Attainment	Percent (%)
12th grade or less, no diploma	19.6
High school graduate	28.5
Some college, no degree	21.1
Associate/Bachelor's degree	21.8
Master's degree	5.9
Professional degree	2.0
Doctorate degree	1.0

3C-2.   The Central Bank of the Russian Federation (2000, 2002, 2003) reports several macroeconomic indicators on the state of the Russian economy. Shown is a summary of selected years with regard to gross domestic product (GDP) in billions of rubles. Construct a bar chart and comment on the findings.

Year	GDP (in billions of rubles)
1998	2,696
1999	4,545
2000	7,302
2001	9,039
2002	10,863

3C-3.   The following table provides the percentage distribution of the United States population by gender and age for the year 2000 (U.S. Bureau of the Census 2000).

  a.   Construct a clustered bar chart to compare the age distributions of males and females.

  b.   Comment on the nature of gender and age in the United States.

Age Group	Gender	
	Male (%)	Female (%)
Under 18	26.8	24.6
18–24	10.0	9.3
25–44	30.8	29.6
45–64	21.8	22.2
65 and over	10.4	14.4

3C-4.   Nishi et al. (2004) examined the effects of socioeconomic indicators on several health indicators among Japanese civil servants. Some selected characteristics of their study population are shown here, specifically pertaining to employment grade and gender.

    a.   Construct pie charts for these two years (on the same page) to depict the distribution of study subjects by employment grade and gender.

    b.   Construct a clustered bar chart for males and females to depict the distribution of employment grades by gender. (Use numbers of cases rather than percentages.)

    c.   Compare the two types of charts. In general, what do the charts convey? Which graphical style is better at depicting the nature of gender and employment grade among selected Japanese civil servants? Explain your answer.

Employment Grades	Males *n*	Females *n*
Higher-level nonmanual	239	95
Lower-level nonmanual	585	174
Manual	135	118

3C-5.   Assume that the following are the ages of students in a pool of intramural football team players: 18, 19, 22, 20, 22, 21, 19, 24, 28, 23, 22, 19, 18, 19, 22, 21, 20, 24, 23, 18, 19, 21.

    a.   Construct a frequency histogram of these data.

    b.   Construct a frequency polygon of these data.

    c.   Which of the two graphs would you choose to present to a public audience? Why?

    d.   One of the scores is peculiar. What is this peculiarity called?

3C-6.   Assume that the following are frequency distributions of the ages of males and females in a large introductory sociology class.

    a.   Construct overlying frequency polygons of these data. (*Caution:* The sample sizes differ.)

    b.   What does the graph reveal?

Age	Males f	Females f
18	4	3
19	5	5
20	4	4
21	3	6
22	2	7
23	5	4
24	4	3
25	1	5
26	2	2
27	3	1
28	4	3
29	3	1
30	1	2

Problem Set 3D

3D-1. Cockerham, Snead, and DeWaal (2002) examined health lifestyles in the former Soviet Union. The educational distribution of their sample is shown. Construct a pie chart for these data. This chart is to be presented to a professional audience, so there is no need to round the percentages.

Level of Education	Percent (%)
No professional courses	24.4
Professional courses	12.0
Professional training without secondary education	8.2
Professional training with secondary education	13.3
Technical school	21.4
University/graduate school	20.6

3D-2. Pikhart et al. (2004) examined psychosocial factors at work and their role in mental health outcomes. Three countries were examined and marital status data from the Czech Republic sample are shown. Construct a bar chart and comment on the nature of this distribution.

Marital Status	n
Married	255
Single	11
Divorced	37
Widowed	3

3D-3.   Abbotts et al. (2004) examined the relationship between religiosity and mental health among children in two main Christian denominations in west Scotland. The frequency distribution of religious attendance for selected religious groups is shown.

Attendance	Church of Scotland	Catholic	Other	None
Every day	7	17	0	0
Most days	27	63	9	3
Weekly	202	450	50	20
Less often	229	143	13	64
Never	481	71	20	249

   a.   Construct a clustered bar chart comparing frequency of religious attendance among religious denominations, or lack of specified denominations.
   b.   Comment on the distribution of religious attendance for the selected groups.

3D-4.   Cardano, Costa, and Demaria (2004) examined social mobility and health in a longitudinal study of men in Turin, Italy. The social class percentage distribution of male Turin residents aged 25 to 49 in 1981 and 1991 is shown in the table (in modified form).

Social Class	1981 (%)	1991 (%)
Upper middle	8.8	16.6
White collar	25.3	25.5
Self-employed	15.3	16.2
Working class	50.6	41.7

   a.   Construct pie charts for social class for each of these two years.
   b.   Construct a clustered bar chart for these two years to depict the social class distribution shown.
   c.   Compare the two types of charts. In general, what do the charts convey? Which graphical style is better at depicting the phenomenon? Explain your choice.

3D-5.   Suppose that the following are the ages of students in a local sociology graduate program: 24, 25, 26, 25, 24, 22, 27, 33, 25, 22, 24, 25, 26, 23, 27, 25, 26, 25, 24, 22.
   a.   Construct a frequency histogram of these data.
   b.   Construct a frequency polygon of these data.
   c.   Which of the two graphs would you choose to present to a public audience?
   d.   One of the scores is peculiar. What is this peculiarity called?

3D-6. Assume that the following are frequency distributions of the ages of senior citizens in two different retirement centers.
  a. Construct overlying frequency polygons of these data. (*Caution:* The sample sizes differ.)
  b. What does the graph reveal?

Age	Center I f	Center II f
67	6	2
68	5	1
69	5	0
70	3	1
71	4	2
72	4	3
73	3	2
74	2	2
75	1	4
76	1	3
77	2	5
78	1	3
79	0	4
80	2	3

OPTIONAL COMPUTER APPLICATIONS FOR CHAPTER 3

Chapter computer exercises are available on *The Statistical Imagination* Web site at www.mhhe.com/ritchey2. These exercises involve how to produce graphs and charts using *SPSS for Windows* and how to choose appropriate graphical styles. In addition, Appendix D of this text, *An Introduction to SPSS,* provides basic instructions for producing graphs and charts.

As is the case for all graphic software, the graphics in *SPSS* have preset features (default settings) that may produce a graph different from that intended. Thus, graphics output usually requires editing. A cautionary note is in order: Treat a computerized graphics program as a mere drawing tool. Always carefully examine a graph to make sure that it is accurate. Follow the Graphing and Table Construction Guidelines at the front of this chapter. You, not the software package, are ultimately responsible for the final product.

Measuring Averages

CHAPTER OUTLINE

Introduction

Everyone is familiar with the general concept of an average in situations such as an average grade, an average income, a bowling average, and a batting average. If someone is "average" in some way—average height, weight, intelligence, and so forth—this person is not unusual. To be average is to be like most other people.

In a distribution of scores, an average will fall between the extreme scores—somewhere in the middle area of the score distribution. For instance, most men are not too tall or too short; they are "about average." We call this typical, average score the central tendency of the variable. A **central tendency statistic** *provides an estimate of the typical, usual, or normal score found in a distribution of raw scores*. For example, the heights of American males tend to cluster around five feet, eight inches, and healthy infants weigh around seven pounds at birth. If Bob has a bowling average of 165, we do not expect him to bowl that exact score every game, but to bowl around that score most of the time.

---

central tendency statistic   A statistic that provides an estimate of the typical, usual, or normal score found in a distribution of raw scores.

There are three common central tendency statistics: the mean, the median, and the mode. Why three? Because each has strengths but also potential weaknesses, depending on the particular shape of a variable's score distribution. Depending on a distribution's shape, one measure of average may be more accurate than another, and sometimes reporting any central tendency statistic alone may mislead or fail to provide enough information.

The Mean

The arithmetic mean of a distribution of scores (or, simply, the mean) is a central tendency statistic that is familiar to any student who has calculated the average of examination grades for a course. The **mean** is *the sum of all scores divided by the number of scores observed (i.e., the sample size).* To compute the mean of a variable, we simply add all scores and divide by the sample size.

---

the mean   The sum of all scores in a distribution divided by the number of scores observed (i.e., the sample size).

The mean is the most useful central tendency statistic. With a quick mathematical calculation, it furnishes a summary of the typical or average scores in a distribution. Because it uses the mathematical operation of division, the mean applies only to interval/ratio variables.

In mathematical formulas, the conventional symbol used to represent a variable name is a capital English letter. The letters X and Y are fashionable here. For example, we might set X to stand for age and set Y to stand for height. Often, Y is used for a dependent variable and subscripted X's are used for a set of independent variables. For example, we might set Y = college grade point average (GPA), with the following set of predictor variables: X_1 = high school GPA, X_2 = college admissions test score, X_3 = reading comprehension ability, and X_4 = year of schooling.

For a variable X, whatever we define it to be, the symbol for the mean *computed on sample data is $\overline{X}$,* which is stated "X-bar." For example, if X = age and the mean age of a statistics class is 20.5 years, we say, "X-bar equals 20.5 years." Remember to state the units of measure of the variable, in this case, years. The mean is calculated as follows (Σ is read as "the sum of").

Calculating the Mean

$$\overline{X} = \frac{\Sigma X}{n}$$

where

$\overline{X}$ = the mean of the interval/ratio variable X computed on sample data

ΣX = the sum of all the individual scores for the variable X

n = the number of observations (i.e., the sample size)

If there are 12 children in a sample, ages 6, 12, 5, 10, 9, 10, 8, 7, 9, 11, 8, and 10 years, their mean age is

$$\overline{X} = \frac{\Sigma X}{n} = \frac{6 + 12 + 5 + 10 + 9 + 10 + 8 + 7 + 9 + 11 + 8 + 10}{12}$$

$$= \frac{105 \text{ years}}{12} = 8.75 \text{ years}$$

Technically, the mean is 8.75 years *per child,* but we leave off the unit of the denominator. Conceptually, the value of the mean tells us what the X-scores in a sample would be *if* every sample subject had the same score. In the preceding example, 8.75 years (i.e., eight years, nine months) would be the age of every child if all the children had the very same age. It is useful, mathematically speaking, to think of the mean as a measure of "equal share." For example, if we wanted to know the mean amount of pocket cash among students in a classroom, we would put all the cash in a pot and divide it equally. (Any volunteers?) The amount each person received would be the mean value of pocket cash. The mean also can be viewed as a balance point, the point at which *differences between* the mean of X and the individual X-scores in the distribution balance out. In Chapter 5 we will pursue this notion further.

Finally, in calculating central tendency statistics, particularly the mean, care must be taken not to include the scores coded as missing cases. Only "valid" cases are included in the calculation of the mean. For example, if in a sample of 49 persons, 2 failed to report their ages, the sum of ages would be divided by 47—the number of valid scores—instead of the sample size of 49. Moreover, with computer files, care must be taken not to add the "missing value" codes (such as 999) to the sum of scores.

Proportional Thinking About the Mean

Combining the Means of Two Different-Size Samples   The mean is the most widely used central tendency statistic for interval/ratio variables. Thus, it is important that we have a good sense of proportion about its calculation. First, let us examine a situation where a common mistake is made: combining the means of two groups by adding the two means and dividing by 2. [The only time this is not a mistake is when the two groups have the same sample sizes (i.e., when the n's are equal).] For example, observe the mean number of vacation days per year (X) for group 1, the eight secretaries of a local bank, and group 2, the three vice presidents. For the eight secretaries:

$$\overline{X}_{(group1)} = \frac{\Sigma X_{(group1)}}{n_{(group1)}} = \frac{7 + 10 + 7 + 12 + 16 + 7 + 14 + 10}{8}$$

$$= \frac{83 \text{ days}}{8} = 10.38 \text{ vacation days}$$

For the three vice presidents:

$$\overline{X}_{(group2)} = \frac{\Sigma X_{(group2)}}{n_{(group2)}} = \frac{60 + 30 + 30}{3}$$

$$= \frac{120 \text{ days}}{3} = 40.00 \text{ vacation days}$$

If we *incorrectly* calculated the mean of the entire office by summing these two means and dividing by 2, we would obtain the erroneous answer of 25.19 vacation days. The correct calculation for the combined mean is

$$\overline{X}_{(groups\ 1\ plus\ 2\ combined)} = \frac{\Sigma X_{(group1)} + \Sigma X_{(group2)}}{n_{(group1)} + n_{(group2)}}$$

$$= \frac{83 + 120}{8 + 3} = \frac{203}{11} = 18.45 \text{ vacation days}$$

With a moment's thought we can see that this formulation is equivalent to treating all 11 employees as one sample. Additional illustrations of mistakenly "averaging" group means are provided in "Statistical Follies and Fallacies" at the end of this chapter.

Calculating the Combined Mean of Two Different Size Samples

Given the means and sample sizes of two groups:

$$\overline{X}_{(groups\ 1\ plus\ 2\ combined)} = \frac{\Sigma X_{(group1)} + \Sigma X_{(group2)}}{n_{(group1)} + n_{(group2)}}$$

where

$\overline{X}$ = the mean of the interval/ratio variable, X, computed on sample data

$$\Sigma X_{(group)} = (n)_{(group)}(\overline{X})_{(group)}$$

and

n = the number of observations (i.e., the sample size)

Example: Suppose X = grade on the final exam; the mean grade for the 13 seniors in the class is 87 and the mean grade for the 16 juniors is 79. What is the mean grade for the two groups combined?

1. Calculate the ΣX for each group:

$$\Sigma X_{(seniors)} = (13)(87) = 1{,}131 \text{ exam points}$$

$$\Sigma X_{(juniors)} = (16)(79) = 1{,}264 \text{ exam points}$$

2. Substitute the sums into the preceding equation:

$$\overline{X}_{(seniors\ and\ juniors)} = \frac{\Sigma X_{(seniors)} + \Sigma X_{(juniors)}}{n_{(seniors)} + n_{(juniors)}}$$

$$= \frac{1{,}131 + 1{,}264}{13 + 16} = \frac{2{,}395}{29} = 82.59 \text{ exam points}$$

Potential Weaknesses of the Mean: Situations Where Reporting It Alone May Mislead

When a central tendency statistic is reported, we tend to presume that its value is representative of typical scores in the middle of a distribution. There are times, however, when reporting the mean can mislead in this regard. This is the case because the calculation of the mean can be inflated (pulled up) or deflated (pulled down) by extreme scores, or outliers. Extremely high scores, or positive outliers, inflate the value of the mean by "boosting up" the sum of X (i.e., ΣX) in the numerator of the formula. Extremely low scores in a distribution, or negative outliers, deflate the value of the mean by "shrinking" ΣX. For an example with high-value outliers, suppose we compute the mean amount of pocket cash for 10 students. Ideally, this mean should tell us what the typical amount is. But suppose one student cashed a $400 paycheck and our calculation comes out as follows, where X = amount of cash on each student (for simplicity, rounded to the nearest dollar):

$$\overline{X} = \frac{\Sigma X}{n} = \frac{5 + 2 + 6 + 10 + 8 + 3 + 9 + 11 + 5 + 400}{10}$$

$$= \frac{\$459}{10} = \$45.90 \approx \$46$$

Obviously, this computed mean of $46 does not represent the typical, average, or central tendency amount of pocket cash. Most students have less than $10, and to report a mean of $46 is misleading. The calculation of the mean is distorted by the presence of an outlier. To obtain a sense of proportion about how the formula for the mean is calculated, examine the relationship between the numerator (ΣX) and the denominator (n). When ΣX is large and n is small, the mean will be large. If ΣX is large because of the presence of one or two high-value outliers, the mean will "inflate" to a large value.

Keep in mind that our objective is to use sample statistics to estimate the parameters of a population. If an inflated or deflated *sample* mean is reported, this will present a distorted summary of how subjects *in a population* score. This limitation of the mean is a special problem with small samples; the smaller the sample, the greater the distortion resulting from an outlier. For example, compute the mean age of the following sample of five college students at Crosstown University, where one student in the sample has an extremely high age: 19, 19, 20, 21, and 54 years. The answer will leave the impression that this sample is quite above the typical college age when in fact four of the five students *are* of the typical age. See also what happens when there is an extremely low score as with this sample of ages: 8, 19, 19, 20, and 21 years. In such cases, the outlier should be removed and the mean should be recalculated without it. In reporting this "adjusted mean," we note why the adjustment was made.

Any time we compute a mean, especially with a small sample, we first examine the raw score frequency distribution for outliers. One handy device for this is a histogram (Chapter 3). Because the mean is more useful than the median and the mode are, we often adjust the scores in a distribution to reduce the effects of outliers on the computation of the mean. The distorting effects of outliers are noted throughout the text.

The Median

The **median** (Mdn) is *the middle score in a ranked distribution*—that value of a variable which divides the distribution of scores in half, *the score for which half of the cases fall above and half fall below*. For example, if the median income of households in Cornbelt City is $26,000, half the households in that city have incomes higher than $26,000 and half have incomes lower than $26,000. Conceptually, the median is a location point—the middle position score. The median brings to mind a geographic location between equal areas, such as the median of a highway. The median score is also equal to the 50th percentile, the point at which 50 percent of the observations fall below it. Among the three central tendency statistics, the median is most useful when a distribution is skewed (i.e., has a few scores to one side). For example, the median price of recent housing sales is preferable to the mean price because a few high-price sales inflate the value of the mean.

the median   For an ordinal or interval/ratio variable, the middle score in a ranked distribution, the score for which half of the cases fall above and half fall below.

To compute the median of a distribution, the scores for a variable X must first be ranked; that is, the scores must be arranged in order of size from the smallest to the largest or from the largest to the smallest. Divide the sample size n by 2 to get near the middle score in the distribution. If n is an odd number, the median will be an actual case in the sample. Suppose, for instance, we have a sample of five families with the following monthly household incomes (X):

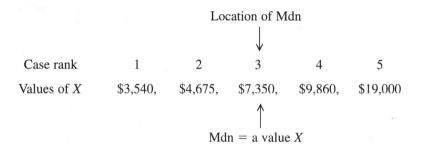

The median income is $7,350, the value of X for the third-ranked score.

If n is an even number, the median is located between two middle scores and is calculated by taking the mean of those two scores. For example, if a sixth family with an income of $20,000 is inserted into the sample,

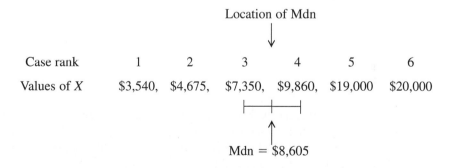

The median is situated between the third and fourth cases. It is calculated by summing the scores of $7,350 and $9,860 and dividing by 2.

With a small sample, locating the median is a straightforward task. With a large sample (and in computer software), the median is mathematically located by dividing the sample size by 2 and adding .5. Note that this result gives *the ranked location* of the median, not the median itself. Rank the scores, then count to this position. The X-score in this position is the median. After finding the median, double-check by seeing whether your answer indeed splits the cases in half. The median can be used with interval/ratio variables. Finally, do not confuse the median with another statistic called the *midrange,* the halfway point between the minimum and maximum values of X.

Calculating the Median (Mdn)

1. Rank the distribution of scores from lowest to highest.
2. Locate the position of the median. Divide the sample size, *n*, by 2 to get near the middle score in the distribution. If *n* is an odd number, the median will be an actual case in the sample. If *n* is an even number, the median will be located between two middle scores and is calculated by taking the mean of those two scores. (Mathematically, the rank position of the median is found by dividing the sample size by 2 and adding .5.)

Potential Weaknesses of the Median: Situations Where Reporting It Alone May Mislead

The median is based on the ranked location of scores in a distribution. It is *insensitive to the values of the scores* in a distribution; that is, regardless of the values of the *X*'s around it, the median is the middle score determined by the number of scores (*n*) in the sample. For example, the following two distributions of exam scores have the same median even though they are composed of markedly different scores.

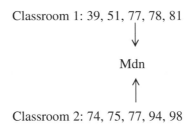

Classroom 1: 39, 51, 77, 78, 81

Mdn

Classroom 2: 74, 75, 77, 94, 98

To say that the average examination grade in both classes is 77 is misleading because it suggests that the two classes performed equally. (In fact, classroom 2 did much better with a *mean* of 83.6 compared with a *mean* of 65.2 for classroom 1.) The median is not affected by the values of *X*.

While insensitive to score values, the median is sensitive to (or affected by) a change in sample size. For example, suppose that in classroom 1 two students take the examination late; they do poorly, which is typical of students who take a test late. When their scores are included in the distribution, the median shifts drastically from 77 to 51:

Classroom 1 (including late scores): 34, 36, 39, 51, 77, 78, 81

Mdn

The median, then, has two potential weaknesses: (1) It is *in*sensitive to the values of the scores in a distribution, and (2) it is sensitive to (or affected by) a change in sample size.

Before reporting the median make sure that neither of these potential weaknesses will lead to faulty conclusions. Finally before locating the median be sure to rank the scores.

The Mode

The **mode** (Mo) is *the most frequently occurring score in a distribution.* Conceptually, the mode is the "most popular" score. Table 4–1 presents the distribution of ages for a sample of college students. The mode is 19 years because more people (49 of them) scored this age than any other. Note that the mode is an X-score (19 years), *not* a frequency, f (49 cases).

TABLE 4–1 | The distribution of ages for a sample of 125 college students

		Givens		Calculations
		Age	*f*	*Percent (%)*
		18	31	24.8
Mo	$\longrightarrow$	19	49	39.2
		20	20	16.0
		21	18	14.4
		22	7	5.6
		Total	125	100.0

---

the mode   The most frequently occurring score in a distribution.

Calculating the Mode (Mo)

1. Compile the scores into a frequency distribution.
2. Identify Mo = value of X with the most cases (i.e., the greatest frequency, f).

A cautionary note is in order. Do not confuse the mode (the "most frequently occurring score") with the "majority of scores." A simple majority would be "more than half," or 50 percent of the cases in a sample plus at least one. Note that in this distribution, although the most frequently occurring score is 19 years, the majority of the sample is not 19 years old; only 39.2 percent of the sample is that age. No age in this distribution has a majority.

The mode is useful with variables of all levels of measurement. The mode is easy to spot in charts. In a pie chart, it is the category with the largest slice; in a bar chart, the tallest bar; on a histogram, the tallest column; and on a polygon, the score for the highest point, or peak.

Potential Weaknesses of the Mode: Situations Where Reporting It Alone May Mislead

Generally speaking, *by itself* the mode is the least useful central tendency statistic because it has a narrow informational scope. While it identifies the most frequently occurring score, it suggests nothing about scores that occur around this score value. Thus, the mode is most useful when it is reported in conjunction with the median

FIGURE 4–1

Variously shaped score distributions with the same mode

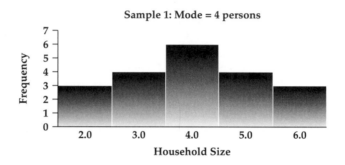

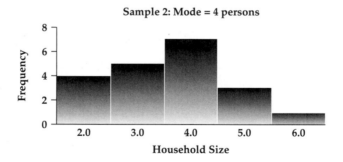

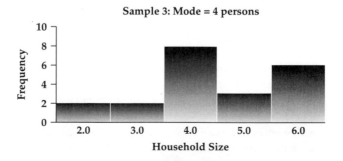

TABLE 4–2 | Distribution of wages in a fast-food restaurant

Wage $	f	Employee Classification
5.75	13	Regular employees
10.50	2	Night managers
18.90	1	Head manager
Total	16	

and the mean. As we will see, reporting all three central tendency statistics is quite informative.

The mode can be misleading when it is used alone because it is insensitive to both the values of scores in a distribution and the sample size. This means that you may have any number of totally different-shaped distributions, yet all could have the same mode, as is depicted in Figure 4–1. Moreover, a variable may have more than one mode or no meaningful mode at all.

There is at least one situation in which the mode is an appropriate central tendency statistic by itself and reporting the mean and the median is misleading. This occurs when the scores of X are essentially of the same value for all cases except a few. An example is the wage structure of a fast-food restaurant where everyone (except the manager) is paid the same low wage. This distribution is shown in Table 4–2, where X is the hourly wage and f is the frequency of scores. The mean here is $7.17, and it is "pulled up" by the extreme scores of the managers' wages. To a job seeker, this mean leaves the false impression that the restaurant on average provides quite a bit more than the minimum wage. The median is $5.75, the same as the mode, but reporting this median leads to the incorrect interpretation that half the employees make above that amount, which is not the case. To report the mode, $5.75, is to say that lots of the employees are paid this low salary. This is the most accurate depiction of this distribution of wages.

Central Tendency Statistics and the Appropriate Level of Measurement

Recall from Chapter 2 that the level of measurement of a variable tells us what mathematical formulas and statistics are appropriate for that variable. The mean and the median are clearly appropriate with interval/ratio variables. It makes sense to talk about mean weight, height, or income. Novice statisticians, however, should avoid using the mean and the median with ordinal variables. With nominal variables, means and medians are meaningless. The nominal variable *gender* is a case in point. A person cannot be an average of so much male and so much female; he or she is one or the other. Recall Table 2–5, which gives the distribution of religious affiliations in childhood for a sample of U.S. adults. It makes no sense to ask what the mean religion is.

Whereas the mean and the median apply best to interval/ratio variables, the mode can be used with variables of all levels of measurement. From Table 2–5 we could report that the modal religion is "Total Protestant" for major religions, "Catholic" for any single denomination, or "Baptist" for any single Protestant denomination.

Frequency Distribution Curves: Relationships Among the Mean, Median, and Mode

Given that each of the three central tendency statistics has potential weaknesses, it is worthwhile to view them as a set of statistics to be interpreted together. These three statistics are especially useful when they are examined graphically. An imaginative way to understand the relationship among these three statistics is to locate the values of each one on a frequency distribution curve.

A **frequency distribution curve** is *a substitute for a frequency histogram or polygon in which we replace these graphs with a smooth curve.* This substitution is appropriate because the smooth curve is viewed not so much as a depiction of the sample distribution, but more as an estimate of the way scores are distributed *in the population.* As with a histogram, the scores of a variable are depicted from left (lowest) to right (highest); that is, the scores are ranked on the horizontal axis. The area under a frequency distribution curve represents *the total number of subjects in the population and is equal to a proportion of 1.00 or a percentage of 100 percent.* Our concern is with assessing the shape of a distribution, *examining the relative locations of the mean, median, and mode to estimate the shape of a frequency distribution.* Frequency distribution curves apply only to variables of interval/ratio levels of measurement.

---

frequency distribution curve   A substitute for a frequency histogram or polygon in which we replace these graphs with a smooth curve. The area under the curve represents the total number of subjects in the population and is equal to a proportion of 1.00 or a percentage of 100 percent.

Figure 4–2 shows three very common shapes of score frequency distribution curves. As with our histograms, the horizontal axis of the curves represents the scores of a variable X. The vertical axis (which we often do not bother to draw) represents the proportional frequency or percentage frequency; thus, the height of the curve at any value of X represents the proportion of a sample or population with that score.

The Normal Distribution

A **normal distribution** is one in which *the mean, median, and mode of a variable are equal to one another and the distribution of scores is bell-shaped.* We also refer to this as "a normal curve." Figure 4–2A depicts IQ scores, which are normally distributed with a mean of 100. A normal distribution is symmetrical (i.e., balanced on each side). Its mean, median, and mode are located in the center of the distribution. The presence of the median there assures symmetry because, by definition, the median splits a ranked distribution of scores in half. Since the mode is at the center point of a normal distribution, the peak of the curve is located there.

FIGURE 4–2

Common frequency distribution curves and the relative locations of the mean, median, and mode, where *X* is an interval/ratio variable (fictional data)

A. The Normal Distribution or Normal Curve

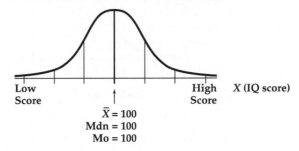

Low Score   High Score   *X* (IQ score)

$\bar{X} = 100$
Mdn = 100
Mo = 100

B. Positively Skewed Distribution or Right Skew

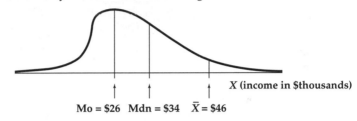

X (income in $thousands)

Mo = $26   Mdn = $34 $\bar{X}$ = $46

C. Negatively Skewed Distribution or Left Skew

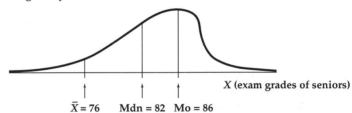

X (exam grades of seniors)

$\bar{X}$ = 76   Mdn = 82   Mo = 86

> **a normal distribution**   A frequency distribution curve in which the mean, median, and mode of a variable are equal to one another and the distribution of scores is bell-shaped.

Skewed Distributions

A **skewed distribution** is *one in which the mean, median, and mode of the variable are unequal and many of the subjects have extremely high or low scores*. When this is the case, the distribution stretches out in one direction like the blade of a sword or barbecue skewer; hence, the name *skewed* (Figure 4–2B and C).

> **skewed distribution**   A frequency distribution curve in which the mean, median, and mode of the variable are unequal and many of the subjects have extremely high or low scores.

FIGURE 4–3

Bimodal
distribution of
the weights
of men and
women

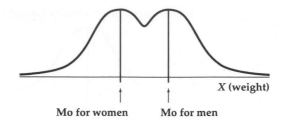

The positions of the mean, median, and mode are predictable for skewed distribution curves. A **right (or positive) skew** is *one with extreme scores in the high or positive end of the score distribution* (Figure 4–2B). For example, household income in the United States is positively skewed; most households make only so much money, but a few are extremely wealthy. The high extreme scores inflate the mean, "pulling" it in the positive direction. The mode is the central tendency measure with the lowest computed score. The median will equal either the mean or the mode or, most likely, will fall between them.

A **left (or negative) skew** is *one with extreme scores in the low or negative end of the score distribution* (Figure 4–2C). For example, test scores in a senior-level college course tend to be left-skewed. Most seniors get high scores, but a few tail off in the negative direction. These few extreme low scores deflate the mean, pulling it in the negative direction. The mode is the highest computed score, and the median falls between the mean and the mode.

With either a left or a right skew, if the median does not fall between the mean and the mode, this suggests that the distribution is oddly shaped. One such oddly shaped distribution is a bimodal distribution, one with two modes or peaks. For example, the variable weight for a sample that includes both men and women may produce a bimodal distribution, with the higher mode resulting from the fact that men are heavier on average (Figure 4–3).

Using Sample Data to Estimate the Shape of a Score Distribution in a Population

With interval/ratio variables when computing central tendency statistics and histograms for *sample* data, the data for a variable often appear slightly skewed. This does not guarantee, however, that the variable's scores are skewed in *the population* from which the sample was drawn. The skew in the sample data may be due to sampling error. In other words, a second sample from the population may appear normal or skew slightly in the other direction.

Skewness statistics are used to determine whether sample data are so skewed that they suggest that the population scores are skewed. We will not compute a skewness statistic by hand. Computer programs, however, provide skewness statistics, and a common one is available with the optional computer applications that accompany this text. When this skewness statistic's absolute value (its value ignoring the plus or minus sign) is greater than 1.2, the distribution may be significantly skewed, depending on the shape of the distribution as well as the sample size. A few outliers in a large sample will have little effect on statistics. If this skewness statistic's absolute value is greater than 1.6, however, regardless of sample size, the distribution probably is skewed; then reporting the sample mean of X as an estimate of the population central tendency can be misleading because of the mean's potential distortion by extreme scores. Aside from the issue of accurately describing the shape of a distribution, skewness is a concern with inferential statistics. As we shall see in later chapters, in testing a hypothesis about the relationship between two variables, a skewed variable requires extra work to avoid incorrect conclusions. Such instances will be identified as they are encountered.

As we will see in Chapter 5, when a distribution is not skewed or otherwise oddly shaped, the mean is the central tendency statistic of choice. This is especially true for reports to public audiences whose members may be overloaded by more than one statistic. However, if a distribution is skewed, the median is the statistic to report. The median minimizes error in describing a skewed distribution because it falls between the mean and the mode, as is depicted in Figure 4–2B and C. As the most central of the three statistics, the median is the best of three poor choices for a skewed distribution when only one statistic is to be reported.

For scientific audiences, skewed distributions are noted by reporting all three central tendency statistics and perhaps including a graph to convey the distribution's shape accurately. Sometimes a skewed distribution is very informative. For example, *hospital stays* is positively skewed. In a given year, most people stay no days or very few days in the hospital. But a substantial percentage stays longer, and a few

TABLE 4–3 I Characteristics, strengths, and potential weaknesses of the mean, median, and mode

| Central Tendency Statistic | Definition | Strengths and Applications | | Potential Weaknesses |
		Appropriate Levels of Measurement	Application to Shapes of Score Distribution	
Mean	Value of X if all scores were conceivably the same	Interval Ratio	Open to many mathematical operations when a distribution is normally shaped	Its calculation is distorted by outliers or a skew in the distribution curve
Median	Middle score in a ranked distribution; score for which half the scores fall above and half fall below; the 50th percentile	Interval Ratio	Preferred when the distribution is skewed	Insensitive to the values of X in the distribution but sensitive to changes in sample size
Mode	Most frequently occurring score in a distribution; the "most popular" score	Nominal Ordinal Interval Ratio	Preferred when virtually all scores (or categories) in the distribution are the same	Insensitive to the values of X and insensitive to how scores are distributed around it

"skew out," spending weeks or months in the hospital. Such a skew stimulates thinking about predictors of long stays. Can you think of hypotheses that explain the skew of hospital stays?

As we shall see in Chapter 5, overall the mean is the most valuable central tendency statistic. It allows much greater flexibility in mathematical calculations. For the most part, the median and the mode are dead-end streets because they offer no additional worthwhile mathematical operations. Little is gained beyond reporting them. Whenever possible, the mean is the summary measurement to use, especially with inferential statistics. Because of this, we often adjust skewed distributions to "bring them down to normal" so that we can use the mean. The specifics of this type of error control are discussed later in this text. Table 4–3 summarizes the properties of the three central tendency statistics.

Organizing Data for Calculating Central Tendency Statistics

There are two common formats for organizing data and computing central tendency statistics on those data. One format is a spreadsheet of the raw score distribution. As was indicated in Chapter 2, a spreadsheet format typically is used for computer data entry or input, but spreadsheets also are commonly used by business, government, and community groups to maintain organization records. Spreadsheet computer software programs, such as *Lotus 1-2-3, Excel,* and *Corel Quattro Pro,* are especially designed for this purpose. Spreadsheet formats evolved from the logical way to do problems by hand—simply listing the scores of a variable in a vertical column.

The second common format for calculations is a frequency distribution format. In this format, the scores of a variable are listed in one column and the frequency of each score is listed in another (like the frequency distributions in Chapter 2). This format is typical of computer *output*. The frequency distribution format is especially useful for identifying the mode. Now let us do a simple problem to illustrate both formats.

Spreadsheet Format for Calculating Central Tendency Statistics

Suppose we are interested in how often film students in a college communications department study their art by going to new-release movies. We collect a random sample of 19 students. We ask each one to name the new movies he or she saw in the past month at theaters and record the following results: 2, 6, 4, 5, 2, 3, 4, 3, 6, 4, 3, 3, 5, 4, 5, 2, 3, 4, 3. Table 4–4 presents these data in a spreadsheet format with the calculations necessary for computing the mean. The scores are ranked to facilitate calculation of the median and the mode.

First, let us calculate the mean:

$$\overline{X} = \frac{\Sigma X}{n} = \frac{72}{19} = 3.79 \text{ movies}$$

Second, let us calculate the median. We have already ranked the scores, something necessary for computing the median. The sample size ($n = 19$) divided in half is about

TABLE 4–4 I Data organized in a spreadsheet format: Number of new-release movies seen in past month (X)

Subject's Number	Subject's Initials	X
	Givens	
1	BH	2
2	KP	2
3	JN	2
4	TW	3
5	JD	3
6	WA	3
7	KM	3
8	BC	3
9	CR	4
10	ML	4
11	MW	4
12	MF	4
13	JS	4
14	BY	4
15	LL	5
16	WF	5
17	CM	5
18	BL	6
19	SH	6
$n = 19$		$\Sigma X = 72$ movies

nine cases, and since n is odd, we determine that the tenth case is the median. On the spreadsheet, we count down to the tenth case and find that the median is four movies:

$$Mdn = 4 \text{ movies}$$

Finally, we calculate the mode. Observation of the ranked data in Table 4–4 reveals that the most frequently occurring score is 4:

$$Mo = 4 \text{ movies}$$

Obviously, using a spreadsheet for doing calculations by hand would be cumbersome with a large number of cases. The purpose of a pencil-and-paper exercise is to grasp the underlying features of a statistic. In real-world research work, computer spreadsheets or statistical software packages are utilized to save time and reduce calculation errors.

Frequency Distribution Format for Calculating the Mode

Table 4–5 presents the same data on the 19 film students, but it uses a frequency distribution format. Working off of the spreadsheet of Table 4–4 (as a computer would), in

TABLE 4–5 | Data organized in a frequency distribution format: Number of new-release movies seen in past month (X)

Givens	
X	f
2	3
3	5
4	6
5	3
6	2
$n = 19$	

Table 4–5 we see that there is a frequency of three students who score two movies, five who score three movies, and so on.

Calculation of the mode is quite easy with the frequency distribution format. In Table 4–5 we simply observe the column listing frequencies (i.e., the f column) and see which score occurred with the highest frequency. More students (six of them) saw four movies than any other number of movies for the month:

$$Mo = 4 \text{ movies}$$

Frequency distribution output and basic descriptive statistics are standard features of statistical computer software packages.

Statistical Follies and Fallacies: Mixing Subgroups in the Calculation of the Mean

Because the mean is susceptible to distortion by outliers and extreme scores, we must clearly describe which cases or subjects are included in its calculation. Organizations such as businesses and school systems, intentionally or not, commonly report means that are unrealistic. For example, a public school district may report that the mean salary of its teachers is $45,000. When this occurs, teachers are likely to congregate in the faculty lounge and ask one another: Who around here makes that much money? Of course, teachers are not stupid. They know right away that whoever did the calculations "mixed the status ranks" by including higher-paid personnel—such as student counselors, assistant principals, and principals—all of whom are certified to teach but seldom do. These administrators might have been included because the "statistician" simply asked the computer to calculate the mean salary for all certified teachers without regard to rank. When these higher-paid personnel are included, their high salaries skew the mean. To avoid such statistical follies, means should be reported separately for distinct subgroups.

Mixing status ranks sometimes results in a mean that fits no group at all. For example, a company may have only two ranks of employees: blue-collar workers averaging about $30,000 per year, and managers averaging about $70,000. If these two groups are about the same size, the mean salary for the entire company will come out to about $50,000. Interestingly, not a single employee in the company earns a salary near that amount.

Another example is the mean age of attendees of parents' night at a third-grade class at an elementary school. The mean age will calculate to about 20 years, yet everyone there will be either eight or nine years old (the kids) or in his or her thirties (the parents). The mean is certainly inappropriate for summarizing this distribution of ages.

SUMMARY

1. A central tendency statistic is one that provides an estimate of the typical, usual, normal, or average score found in a distribution of raw scores.

2. There are three measures of central tendency—the mean, the median, and the mode. Each has strengths and weaknesses.

3. The relative values of the three central tendency statistics inform us as to the shape of a score distribution.

4. The mean and median are appropriate with interval/ratio variables. With nominal variables, means and medians are meaningless. The mode can be used with variables of all levels of measurement.

5. The mean is the most useful central tendency statistic.

6. Calculation of the mean is affected by outliers and by a skew in the distribution of scores.

7. The median is a positional score, the middle score in a ranked distribution. It is equal to the 50th percentile.

8. When a distribution is skewed, the median is the statistic of choice because its value will fall between the mean and the mode and, thus, minimize error.

9. Remember to rank the scores from smallest to largest before calculating the median.

10. The median is insensitive to the values of the scores in a distribution. The median is sensitive to a change in sample size.

11. The mode is the most frequently occurring score or category in a distribution. The mode may be envisioned as the most popular score or category. However, do not confuse the mode with "the majority of scores."

12. The mode is easy to spot on charts and graphs. In identifying the mode, take care to remember that it is a score (X), not a frequency (f).

13. The mode is the least useful measure of central tendency by itself because it has a narrow informational scope; that is, it tells us little. The mode is insensitive to the values of scores in a distribution and insensitive to the sample size. Two distributions of scores can have radically different shapes yet have the same mode.

14. A frequency distribution curve is a substitute for a frequency histogram or polygon in which we replace these graphs with a smooth curve.

15. The relative locations of the mean, median, and mode on the X-axis are predictable for certain shapes of distribution curves. In a normal distribution or "normal curve," the mean, median, and mode of the variable are equal. In a negatively skewed distribution, the mean will have the lowest value of X, the mode the highest, and the median will fall between. In a positively skewed distribution, the mean will have the highest value of X, the mode the lowest, and the median will fall between.

16. Typically, the mean of two groups combined is *not* simply the sum of the means divided by 2. This only works when the two groups are of the same sample size.

CHAPTER EXTENSIONS ON *THE STATISTICAL IMAGINATION* WEB SITE

Chapter 4 Extensions of text material available on *The Statistical Imagination* Web site at www.mhhe.com/ritchey2 include illustrations where the mean and median may be used with rank-ordered ordinal variables with certain characteristics.

FORMULAS FOR CHAPTER 4

Calculating the mean:
Working from a spreadsheet:

$$\overline{X} = \frac{\Sigma X}{n}$$

Calculating the combined mean of two groups (given individual scores):

$$\overline{X}_{(groups\ 1\ plus\ 2\ combined)} = \frac{\Sigma X_{(group1)} + \Sigma X_{(group2)}}{n_{(group1)} + n_{(group2)}}$$

Calculating the combined mean of two groups (given group means):

$$\text{Since } \overline{X} = \frac{\Sigma X}{n}, \Sigma X = (n)(\overline{X})$$

Substitute to obtain:

$$\overline{X}_{(groups\ 1\ plus\ 2\ combined)} = \frac{n_{(group1)}\overline{X}_{(group1)} + n_{(group2)}\overline{X}_{(group2)}}{n_{(group1)} + n_{(group2)}}$$

Calculating the median:

1. Rank the distribution of scores from lowest to highest.

2. Locate the position of the median. Divide the sample size, n, by 2 to get near the middle score in the distribution. If n is an odd number, the median will be an actual case in the sample. If n is an even number, the median will be located

between two middle scores and is calculated by taking the mean of these two scores. (Mathematically, the rank position of the median is found by dividing the sample size by 2 and adding .5.)

Calculating the mode:

1. Compile scores into a ranked raw score spreadsheet or frequency distribution format.
2. Identify Mo = value of X with the greatest frequency.

QUESTIONS FOR CHAPTER 4

1. For each central tendency statistic, variables of what levels of measurement are appropriate?
2. Define the mean, the median, and the mode. Specify the potential limitations of each one.
3. Why is it better to compute all three measures—the mean, median, and mode—than to rely on one?
4. As a general rule, it is incorrect to calculate the mean for two groups combined by simply dividing the sum of their separate means by 2. What is the exception to this rule?
5. If a score distribution is skewed, what single central tendency statistic is most appropriate for a public audience? Why?
6. In general, the mode of a distribution is the least useful central tendency statistic. Under what circumstances, however, is it the most appropriate central tendency statistic to report?
7. If the modal age of a distribution is 22 years, does this mean that a majority of the persons in this population is 22 years old? Explain.
8. How is the mode located on a histogram, a polygon, and a frequency distribution curve?
9. On a frequency distribution curve, what do the horizontal and vertical axes represent?
10. Describe the characteristics of a normal frequency distribution curve.
11. State in general terms how a left skew in a frequency distribution affects the three common averages: mean, median, and mode.
12. State in general terms how a right skew in a frequency distribution affects the three common averages: mean, median, and mode.
13. Suppose a distribution of ages has a mean of 55 years, a mode of 28 years, and a median of 34 years. What is the likely shape of the frequency distribution curve of this variable?
14. As illustrated in "Statistical Follies and Fallacies" in this chapter, a variable's mean can be a poor measure of central tendency when there is a mixture of status ranks within a population. Provide an example of how mixing status ranks can result in a mean that fits no rank at all.

EXERCISES FOR CHAPTER 4

Problem Set 4A

Remember to include formulas, stipulate units of measure, and answer the question.

4A-1. Given the following data with X = age, calculate the modal age, median age, and mean age. Start by organizing the data into a spreadsheet table with the scores ranked under a column labeled "X (ranked)."

X	X (cont.)
14	14
15	17
19	19
19	22
22	28

4A-2. Seven office workers entered a weight-loss competition. After a few weeks of dieting, their weight losses (in pounds) were as follows: 5, 7, 3, 0, 2, 4, and 3. Calculate the median and mean weight loss. Set X = pounds lost.

4A-3. Demographers study the populations of various states, communities, and countries. One subject of interest is the growth or decline in a population's size, which is affected by birth rates, longevity (how long people live based on ages at which they typically die), and how many are moving into and out of an area (migration). One variable is age of mortality (i.e., age of death). Suppose in nation A, the modal age of mortality is 55, the median is 60, and the mean is 65. In nation B, the mean is also 65, but the mode is 75 and the median is 70.

  a. From this information, construct the frequency curves of age of mortality for each nation.

  b. Which nation appears better off in terms of longevity?

4A-4. All five members of a family work. Their hourly wages are: $30, $10.50, $5.15, $12, and $6. Set X = hourly wage.

  a. Compute the mean and median.

  b. Compared to the other scores, what would we call the $30 hourly wage?

  c. What is its effect on the calculation of the mean?

  d. Adjust for this peculiarity by recalculating the mean without it.

4A-5. The following are annual tuition prices for five major American universities: $10,000, $29,000, $8,000, $12,500, $11,300. Set Y = price of tuition.

  a. Compute the mean and median.

  b. Compared to the other scores, what would we call the tuition price of $29,000?

  c. What is its effect on the calculation of the mean?

  d. Adjust for this peculiarity by recalculating the mean without it.

4A-6. The mean age of the 47 men in the Sparkesville Bridge Club is 54.8 years. The mean age of the 62 women in the club is 56.4 years. What is the mean age of all 109 members? Set X = age.

4A-7. In an experiment to see whether chickens can distinguish colors, rewards of corn kernels are supplied when a chicken correctly pecks a pad matching colors. Reaction times are measured to the nearest one-hundredth of a second. Flossy's reaction times are as follows: 1.32, 1.45, 1.21, 1.05, .97, .91, .93, .93, .96, .93, .88, .94, .98.

Set X = reaction time (in seconds).
a. Organize the data into a spreadsheet table with the scores ranked under a column labeled "X (ranked)."
b. Calculate Flossy's mean, median, and modal reaction times.
c. Describe the shape of the distribution of Flossy's reaction times.

4A-8. Given the following statistics and what we know about how they are related within a distribution of scores, describe the likely shape of the distribution for each variable listed. Sketch the curve indicating the relative locations of the mean, median, and mode.

Variable	$\bar{X}$	Mdn	Mo	Shape of Curve	Sketch of Curve
Age (years)	30	35	39		
Household size	4.1	3.0	2.0		
Years employed	11	8	7		
Weight (pounds)	160	132	134		

Problem Set 4B

Remember to include formulas, stipulate units of measure, and answer the question.

4B-1. The following data are for the variable Y = distance from workplace (in miles) for the employees of a copy machine retailer. Compute the mean and median scores. Start by organizing the data into a spreadsheet table with the scores ranked under a column labeled "Y (ranked)."

Y	Y (cont.)
13	10
9	11
6	14
3	5
12	7

4B-2. Scores on the analytical portion of the Graduate Records Examination (GRE) of five candidates to a graduate program were as follows: 700, 625, 640, 590, and 600. Compute the mean and median scores. Set X = GRE score.

4B-3.   In evaluating crime rates between two cities, a criminologist calculates $X =$ the average number of vehicles stolen per day (over a six-month period). For city A, the mode of X is 15 vehicles, the median is 20, and the mean is 25. For city B, the mean is also 25, but the mode is 35 and the median is 30.

    a.   From this information, construct the frequency curves for each city.

    b.   In which city would you feel safer parking your car on the street? Why?

4B-4.   The following are grade point averages (GPAs on a 4-point scale) of students in a tutorial program: 1.7, 2.6, 2.3, 3.9, 2.2, 1.9, 2.1. Set $Y =$ GPA.

    a.   Organize the data into a spreadsheet table with the scores ranked under a column labeled "Y (ranked)."

    b.   Compute the mean and median of Y.

    c.   Compared to the other scores, what would we call the GPA of 3.9?

    d.   What is its effect on the calculation of the mean?

    e.   Adjust for this peculiarity by recalculating the mean without it.

4B-5.   The following are final exam grades for five undergraduate social science students at a large urban university: 90, 88, 64, 92, 87. Set $X =$ exam grade.

    a.   Compute the mean and median exam grade.

    b.   Compared to the other scores, what would we call the score of 64?

    c.   What is its effect on the calculation of the mean?

    d.   Adjust for this peculiarity by recalculating the mean without it.

4B-6.   Suppose that the following are the mean ages of substance-addicted patients at a local treatment facility separated out by type of primary addiction. Calculate the mean age of all substance-addicted patients at the facility. Set $X =$ age.

	Primary Addiction			
	Cocaine ($n = 44$)	Crack Cocaine ($n = 29$)	Heroin ($n = 24$)	Alcohol ($n = 69$)
Mean age (years)	29.8	23.4	34.6	42.9

4B-7.   The batting averages of the starting lineup of the little league team, the Fastball Dodgers, are as follows: .360, .200, .350, .355, .230, .345, .360, .380, and .400. Set $X =$ individual batting average.

    a.   Organize the data into a spreadsheet table with the scores ranked.

    b.   Calculate the team's mean, median, and modal batting averages.

    c.   Describe the shape of the distribution.

4B-8.   Given the following statistics and what we know about how they are related within a distribution of scores, describe the likely shape of the distribution for each variable listed. Sketch the curve, indicating the relative locations of the mean, median, and mode.

Variable	$\bar{X}$	Mdn	Mo	Shape of Curve	Sketch of Curve
Height (inches)	70	68	66		
Exams this semester	10	13	15		
Spirituality score	30	30	30		
Grocery budget	$130	$109	$104		

Problem Set 4C

Remember to include formulas, stipulate units of measure, and answer the question.

4C-1.   Given the following series of height measurements (in inches), calculate the modal, median, and mean heights. Set X = height (in inches). Start by organizing the data into a spreadsheet table with the scores ranked under a column labeled "X (ranked)."

X	X (cont.)
60	78
70	59
68	67
72	74
69	70

4C-2.   Assume that the following are the number of interconference victories among seven college basketball teams: 12, 8, 7, 9, 11, 5, and 4. Organize the data into a spreadsheet table with the scores ranked. Calculate the median and mean number of wins among these teams. Set X = number of victories or "wins."

4C-3.   In comparing test scores among undergraduate psychology students, a department chair calculates the exam grades for two classes. For class A, the mode is 75 test points, the median is 80, and the mean is 85. For class B, the mean is also 85, but the mode is 95 and the median is 90. Set X = exam grade.
   a.   From this information, construct the frequency curves of exam grades for each class.
   b.   Which class appears to have fared better on this particular exam?

4C-4.   The following are annual salaries (Y) among seven physicians employed in a large urban area: $88,000, $94,000, $86,000, $110,000, $212,000, $115,000, and $97,000.
   a.   Organize the data into a spreadsheet table with the scores ranked under a column labeled "Y (ranked)."
   b.   Compute the mean and median salary.
   c.   Compared to the other scores, what would we call the salary of $212,000?
   d.   What is its effect on the calculation of the mean?
   e.   Adjust for this peculiarity by recalculating the mean without it.

4C-5. The following are employee performance evaluations (completed by supervisors) of a major computer software company. Each employee is rated on a scale from 0 to 10, based upon her or his performance on a number of established indicators. Set Y = employee rating.
  a. Organize the data into a spreadsheet table with the scores ranked under a column labeled "Y (ranked)."
  b. Compute the mean and the median.
  c. Compared to the other scores, what would we call the rating of 3?
  d. What is its effect on the calculation of the mean?
  e. Adjust for this peculiarity by recalculating the mean without it.

Y
8
3
9
7
8
6
9
8
7

4C-6. Assume that the mean weight of 34 men involved in a local weight-loss program is 228 pounds, while the mean weight of the 46 women involved in the same program is 194 pounds. What is the mean weight of all 80 participants? Set X = weight (in pounds).

4C-7. Assume that nine friends are competing against one another in a timed, 40-yard footrace. Each participant's time (in seconds) is as follows: 4.8, 5.2, 4.7, 4.9, 5.4, 4.8, 4.9, 4.8, and 5.3. Set X = time (in seconds).
  a. Organize the data into a spreadsheet table with the scores ranked.
  b. Calculate the group's mean, median, and modal 40-yard sprint times.
  c. Describe the shape of the distribution.

4C-8. Given the following statistics and what we know about how they are related within a distribution of scores, describe the likely shape of the distribution for each variable listed. Sketch the curve indicating the relative locations of the mean, median, and mode.

Variable	$\bar{X}$	Mdn	Mo	Shape of Curve	Sketch of Curve
Weight (pounds)	195	205	215		
Spending money	$150	$140	$125		
Depression scale score	25	25	25		
Age (years)	30	40	50		

Problem Set 4D

Remember to include formulas, stipulate units of measure, and answer the question.

4D-1. Given the following weight measurements for a number of friends, calculate the modal, median, and mean weights. Set X = weight (in pounds). Start by organizing the data into a spreadsheet table with the scores ranked under a column labeled "X (ranked)."

X	X (cont.)
158	180
180	195
169	200
190	195
180	160

4D-2. Under the supervision of their teachers, a small group of adolescent students decided to assess their overall growth in height (in inches) over an 18-month period. The differences in their heights between start (time 1) and finish (time 2) are as follows: 4.4, 6.0, 3.6, 2.9, 4.3, 3.6, 2.9, 4.2, and 2.8. Calculate the median and mean growth. Set X = growth in 18 months (in inches).

4D-3. A researcher is interested in comparing patterns of family income in U.S. dollars (X) between two upper-middle-class communities. For Community 1, the modal family income is $80,000, the median is $90,000, and the mean is $100,000. For Community 2, the mean is also $100,000, but the mode is $120,000 and the median family income is $110,000.
  a. From this information, construct the frequency curves of family income for each community.
  b. Which community appears to be more affluent with regard to family income?

4D-4. The following are class sizes for seven introductory sociology classes at a major urban university: 65, 79, 72, 115, 84, 87, and 78. Set Y = number of students.
  a. Organize the data into a spreadsheet table with the scores ranked under a column labeled "Y (ranked)."
  b. Compute the mean and the median.
  c. Compared to the other scores, what would we call the class size of 115?
  d. What is its effect on the calculation of the mean?
  e. Adjust for this peculiarity by recalculating the mean without it.

4D-5. The following are the number of paid employees among nine subsidiaries of a large international finance firm. Set X = number of employees.

    a. Organize the data into a spreadsheet table with the scores ranked under a column labeled "X (ranked)."

    b. Compute the mean and the median.

    c. Compared to the other scores, what would we call the subsidiary with only 67 employees?

    d. What is its effect on the calculation of the mean?

    e. Adjust for this peculiarity by recalculating the mean without it.

X
212
198
283
176
191
254
67
187
193

4D-6. The mean Graduate Record Examination (GRE) score of the 39 male applicants to the department of sociology at Central University is 1,140 GRE points. The mean score for the 54 female applicants is 1,210. What is the mean GRE score for all 93 applicants? Set X = GRE score.

4D-7. Nine friends are competing against one another in a fantasy American football league. The passing yards for each competitor's star quarterback for the previous week are as follows: 283, 205, 183, 197, 296, 315, 304, 227, and 296. Set X = passing yards.

    a. Organize the data into a spreadsheet table with the scores ranked under a column labeled "X (ranked)."

    b. Calculate the mean, median, and modal passing yards.

    c. Describe the shape of the distribution.

4D-8. Given the following statistics and what we know about how they are related within a distribution of scores, describe the likely shape of the distribution for each variable listed. Sketch the curve indicating the relative locations of the mean, median, and mode.

Variable	$\bar{X}$	Mdn	Mo	Shape of Curve	Sketch of Curve
Entertainment expenses	$163	$154	$139		
Religiosity scale score	30	30	30		
Cholesterol levels	182	207	219		
Body mass index	25	30	33		

OPTIONAL COMPUTER APPLICATIONS
FOR CHAPTER 4

The optional computer exercises for Chapter 4 are found on *The Statistical Imagination* Web site at www.mhhe.com/ritchey2. These exercises include generating central tendency statistics with *SPSS Windows* and using the output to gain a sense of proportion about the shapes of score distributions for interval/ratio variables. Central tendency statistics may be calculated using the Descriptives command or the Frequencies command, which are described in Appendix D.

)

CHAPTER

5

Measuring Dispersion or Spread in a Distribution of Scores

Introduction

For an interval/ratio variable, reporting a central tendency statistic by itself is not enough to convey the shape of a distribution of scores. Two samples with the same means can have radically different shapes. Figure 5–1 shows two distributions of ages: for a sample of elementary school pupils (grades kindergarten through six, or K–6) and for a third-grade class from a second school. The mean age of the pupils in both schools is 8.5 years. In the K–6 school, however, children are as young as 5 and as old as 12. In the third-grade class of the other school, none of the pupils is under 7 or over 10 years of age. Although these two distributions of ages have the same central tendency, their scores are dispersed very differently, with a greater spread of ages at the K–6 school.

    The topic of this chapter is **dispersion**, *how the scores of an interval/ratio variable are spread out from lowest to highest and the shape of the distribution in between.* There are an infinite number of possible distribution shapes for a variable with a given mean. All scores could be lumped around the mean with the distinct shape of a bell curve, but the curve could be of different sizes, depending on the sample size. Or scores could be slightly or greatly skewed to one side. Furthermore, a single variable may have very different spreads from one population to another. For example, yearly household income for residents of the United States ranges from zero to tens of millions of dollars

FIGURE 5-1

Comparison of
the spreads of
ages of pupils
in two samples
with the same
means

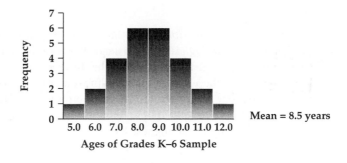

Mean = 8.5 years

Ages of Grades K–6 Sample

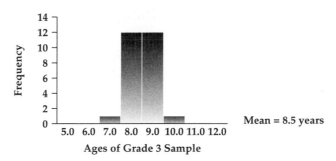

Mean = 8.5 years

Ages of Grade 3 Sample

while the household income of the poor living in housing projects ranges from zero to a few thousand dollars.

> **dispersion**   How the scores of an interval/ratio variable are spread out from lowest to highest and the shape of the distribution in between.

Dispersion statistics *describe how the scores of an interval/ratio variable are spread across its distribution.* Dispersion statistics allow precise descriptions of the frequency of cases at any point in a distribution. For instance, if the federal government decides to increase taxes for "the rich," by using dispersion statistics, we can identify the income level of the wealthiest 5 percent of all households. Similarly, if a public welfare program is budgeted to cover only 10,000 city households, we can establish what household income level qualifies for assistance. Studying dispersion is like taking a walk back and forth across the X-axis of a histogram and observing where cases are concentrated. Do most cases fall around the mean, or are they off to one side? How many cases fall between any two points? What value of the variable lops off the top 10 percent of cases? The two most used dispersion statistics are the range and the standard deviation.

> **dispersion statistics**   Statistics that describe how the scores of an interval/ratio variable are spread across its distribution.

The Range

The **range** is *an expression of how the scores of an interval/ratio variable are distributed from lowest to highest*—the distance between the minimum and maximum scores found in a sample. It is computed as the difference between the maximum and minimum scores plus the value of the rounding unit. The value of the rounding unit (e.g., 1 if scores are rounded to the nearest whole number, 0.1 if scores are rounded to the nearest tenth, and so on) is added to account for the lower real limit of the lowest score and the upper real limit of the highest score.

Computing the Range of an Interval/Ratio Variable X

1. Rank the scores in the distribution from lowest to highest.
2. Identify the minimum and maximum scores.
3. Identify the value of the rounding unit (see Appendix A for a review).
4. Calculate the range:

Range = (maximum score − minimum score) + value of rounding unit

---

the range   An expression of how the scores of an interval/ratio variable are distributed from lowest to highest.

Let us compute the range for a sample problem. Suppose X = age (calculated from date of birth and rounded to the nearest year) and we have the following distribution of scores:

$$21, 23, 43, 26, 20, 21, 25$$

Start by ranking the scores:

$$20, 21, 21, 23, 25, 26, 43$$

Identify the minimum and maximum scores of 20 and 43, respectively, and identify that the rounding unit is 1.

Compute the range:

Range = (maximum score − minimum score) + value of rounding unit
= (43 − 20) + 1 = 24 years

As a result of rounding, the individual who scored 20 could be as young as 19.5 years and the 43-year-old could be as old as 43.5 years. The range of 24 years is the distance between these lower and upper real limits of the scores; that is, 43.5 years − 19.5 years = 24 years.

FIGURE 5–2

Comparison of two differently shaped distributions that have the same range

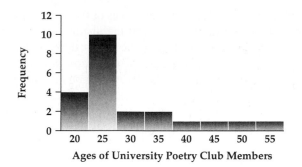

Ages of University Poetry Club Members

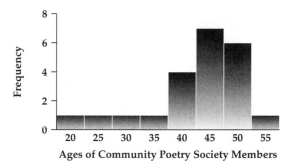

Ages of Community Poetry Society Members

Often it is more informative to report the minimum and maximum scores themselves by saying that these ages range from 20 to 43. This way we indirectly show that there is no one in the sample under about 20 years of age or over about 43 years of age.

Limitations of the Range: Situations Where Reporting It Alone May Mislead

Since the range uses the most extreme scores of the distribution, an outlier will greatly inflate its calculation. This happened for the seven ages shown above. The 43-year-old made the range appear to be spread out over 24 years. Reporting this would give the impression that the sample has a considerable number of 30- and 40-year-olds. A more accurate report would stipulate that with the exception of the 43-year-old student, the ages had a range of 7 years ($26 - 20 + 1 = 7$). Removing the outlier and noting it as an exception is a reasonable way of adjusting for this limitation of the range.

The range also is limited by its narrow informational scope. It tells us nothing about the shape of the distribution between the extreme scores. For example, the two distributions depicted in Figure 5–2 have the same range of ages, suggesting similar shapes, but in fact their shapes are radically different. Finally, there is little one can do mathematically with the range. In sum, the range has limited usefulness, especially when reported alone.

The Standard Deviation

The standard deviation is another summary measurement of the dispersion or spread of scores in a distribution. This dispersion statistic is fundamentally different from the range. By focusing on the extremes of the distribution, the range approaches dispersion from the "outsides" or ends of the distribution. Viewing the range is like watching a basketball game from high in the stands; the court appears boxed in by the goals at each end. In contrast, the **standard deviation** *describes how scores of an interval/ratio variable are spread across the distribution in relation to the mean score.* The mean is a central tendency statistic and as such provides a point of focus that is centered "inside" the distribution. Viewing spread from the mean with its standard deviation is like watching from center court; the focus is on distance from center court to other points in either direction. Like the mean, the standard deviation is most appropriate with interval/ratio variables.

> **the standard deviation**   Describes how scores of an interval/ratio variable are spread across the distribution in relation to the mean score.

Proportional and Linear Thinking about the Standard Deviation

For an interval/ratio variable, the standard deviation is computed by determining how far each score is from the mean—how far it *deviates* from the mean. In this sense, the standard deviation is a derivative (or offspring) of the mean, and the two measures are always reported together. In fact, the phrase "the mean and standard deviation" is the one most often used by statisticians. The standard deviation—as a summary measurement of all the scores in a distribution—tells how widely scores cluster around the mean. As we shall see shortly, the standard deviation also is useful in conjunction with the normal curve.

The following is the formula for computing the standard deviation:

Computing the Standard Deviation

$$s_X = \sqrt{\frac{\Sigma (X - \overline{X})^2}{n - 1}}$$

where

s_X = standard deviation for the interval/ratio variable X
$\overline{X}$ = mean of X
n = sample size

It is worthwhile to take a step-by-step approach to the computation of the standard deviation. This removes the mystery from the formula (with its Σ, square, and square root symbols) and helps us appreciate that the standard deviation is an essential part of the normal curve.

Identify Givens   We start by identifying the information given.

Given: X = an interval/ratio variable, n = sample size, and a distribution of raw scores for X.

Compute the Mean   We compute the mean because the standard deviation is designed to measure spread around the mean.

$$\overline{X} = \frac{\Sigma X}{n}$$

Compute Deviation Scores: Linear Thinking   Next we determine how far each subject's score falls from the mean. The difference between a score and its mean is called a **deviation score**, *how much an individual score differs or "deviates" from the mean:*

$$X - \overline{X} = \text{deviation score for a value of } X$$

Think of a deviation score as a measure of distance on the X-axis. What does the deviation score tell us? Suppose X is the variable weight and the mean weight for a sample of women volleyball players from Elmstown University is 138 pounds. The star player, Sandra "Soul Spiker" Carson, weighs 173 pounds; this is her raw score or "X-score." Her deviation score is plus 35 pounds:

$$\text{Deviation score} = X - \overline{X} = 173 - 138 = 35 \text{ pounds}$$

The deviation score tells us two things about a score in the distribution: (1) the amount or distance the X-score falls from the mean and (2) the direction of the X-score: whether it is below or above the mean. When an X-score is greater than the mean, the deviation score will compute to a positive value, like Sandra's, meaning that the X-score lies to the right on a distribution curve. When an X-score is less than the mean, the deviation score will compute to a negative, meaning that the X-score lies to the left of the mean. Sandra's deviation score of $+35$ pounds tells us that she is 35 pounds *above* the mean weight of the team.

---

deviation score   How much an individual score differs or "deviates" from the mean.

The deviation score is the central mathematical computation in computing the standard deviation. As a summary measurement for the whole sample, the standard deviation is a summation and average of these deviation scores squared, as in the steps below.

Sum the Deviation Scores   The next step in computing the standard deviation is to sum the deviation scores. This sum will always equal zero (within rounding error):

$$\Sigma (X - \overline{X}) = 0 = \text{sum of the deviation scores}$$

The summation of deviation scores is a check on the accuracy of computations because the sum of deviation scores will *always* equal zero (within rounding error). We spoke in Chapter 4 of how the mean is a balance point in the distribution. What the mean does is balance the deviations so that they cancel one another out and result in a sum of deviation scores of zero. In fact, another mathematical definition of the **mean** is *that point in a distribution where the deviation scores sum to zero.*

Square the Deviation Scores and Sum the Squares   The dispersion of a variable is often compared for two or more samples. Summing the deviation scores will not detect a difference in spread between two samples because the sum for both will be zero. This potentially leaves us on a dead-end street. If one sample's scores are widely spread out and the other's are only narrowly spread out, what good is it to report that both have a sum of deviation scores of zero? None! Therefore, in comparing two samples, we must find a way to sum the deviation scores so that the sum is larger for a sample with a greater spread. The most useful solution is to square each deviation score and then sum the squares. Squaring eliminates negative signs in deviation scores. *The sum of squared deviation scores* is the **variation** (often referred to as the **sum of squares**), *a statistic that summarizes deviations for the entire sample:*

$$\Sigma (X - \overline{X})^2 = \text{the variation (or "sum of squares")}$$

> **the variation or the sum of squares**   The sum of squared deviation scores; a statistic that summarizes deviations for the entire sample.

Divide the Sum of Squares by $n - 1$ to Adjust for Sample Size and Error: Proportional Thinking   The sum of squares, or variation, is a good measure of the spread of a distribution, but this statistic presents two problems. First, suppose we wish to compare distributions from two samples of different sizes. For instance, we may compare the distributions of grade point averages (GPAs) for student samples from Crosstown University ($n = 88$) and State University ($n = 104$). When we sum the squares for each sample, we may find a higher sum for State University simply because we summed more numbers—104 cases rather than a mere 88. Each X-score adds some amount to the computation. In other words, everything else being equal, the more observations, the larger the sum of squares. To make a balanced comparison of two different-size samples, then, we need to adjust for the number of observations in each sample by dividing each by its sample size (n). This gives us the average variation (the mean of the sum of squares) in each sample. In this manner we adjust the sum of squares in proportion to the number of cases in the sample.

A second consideration regarding sample size is that it will encompass sampling error; the larger the sample, the less the sampling error. Statisticians have determined that if we subtract 1 from n, this slight adjustment results in a sample statistic that more accurately estimates the parameter of the population. Put simply, by subtracting 1 from the sample size, we make an adjustment for sampling error. (Note that with large samples, this adjustment would have very little effect on the calculation, whereas with small samples, it would have a great effect.)

In summary, we divide the variation (sum of squares) by $n - 1$ to account for the effects of sample size on the sum and to account for sampling error. The result is called the variance, and its symbol is $s_X{}^2$:

$$s_X{}^2 = \frac{\Sigma (X - \overline{X})^2}{n - 1} = \text{ variance of a sample}$$

The **variance** is *the average variation of scores in a distribution.* To avoid confusing variance and variation, note the accented *n* sound in "variance" and note that *n* is in its denominator. (Finally, we should note that if the standard deviation is computed for the scores of an entire population, sampling error is not an issue. Therefore, we do not need to subtract 1 from *n* to obtain the variance of a population, which would be symbolized as $\sigma_X{}^2$.)

---

the variance   The average variation of scores in a distribution (i.e., the mean of the sum of squares).

Take the Square Root of the Variance to Obtain the Standard Deviation   A final step is required to produce a good measure of spread. The variance is perfectly acceptable for calculations, but it is not directly interpretable because the units of measure are squared. Thus, we might compute the variance of weight for Crosstown University's football team and find it to be 1,391.45 squared pounds. Well, what is a "squared pound"? It is a pound times a pound, but who knows what that really means except perhaps a mathematician? We need a directly interpretable unit of measure—pounds instead of squared pounds. To "get back to" pounds, we take the square root of the variance. (The square root of a squared unit of measure is the unit of measure itself.) The result is the standard deviation:

$$s_X = \sqrt{\frac{\Sigma (X - \overline{X})^2}{n - 1}} = \sqrt{s_X{}^2}$$

In the case of the Crosstown team's weight, the standard deviation would be 37.30 pounds:

$$s_X = \sqrt{\frac{\Sigma (X - \overline{X})^2}{n - 1}} = \sqrt{s_X{}^2}$$

$$= \sqrt{1{,}391.45} = 37.30 \text{ pounds}$$

The elements of the standard deviation equation—deviation scores, the sum of squares or variation, and the variance—are important in and of themselves. These elements appear by themselves in many statistical formulas (see, for example, Chapter 12). The steps for calculating the standard deviation are summarized in Table 5–1, which you will find useful in later chapters.

It is a good practice to set up a spreadsheet for these computations. Table 5–2 presents a spreadsheet for computing the standard deviation of the weights of 12 of the 98 players on Crosstown's football team.

To compute the deviation scores, $X - \overline{X}$, we calculate the mean and subtract each score from it to produce the third column of the spreadsheet:

$$\overline{X} = \frac{\Sigma X}{n} = \frac{2{,}856}{12} = 238 \text{ pounds}$$

TABLE 5–1 | Understanding the standard deviation through its computation

Step in Computing the Standard Deviation	What the Step Accomplishes
1. Identify the givens.	**1.** X must be an interval/ratio variable.
2. Compute the mean: $$\overline{X} = \frac{\Sigma X}{n}$$	**2.** Because the standard deviation is based on deviations from the mean.
3. Compute deviation scores: $$X - \overline{X}$$	**3.** To determine each score's distance from the mean.
4. Sum the deviation scores: $$\Sigma(X - \overline{X})$$	**4.** Make sure that $$\Sigma(X - \overline{X}) = 0$$
5. Square the deviation scores and sum them to obtain the variation or sum of squares: $$\text{Variation} = \Sigma(X - \overline{X})^2$$	**5.** The deviation scores are squared to remove negative signs and obtain a sum other than zero.
6. Compute the variance: $$s_X^2 = \frac{\Sigma(X - \overline{X})^2}{n - 1}$$	**6.** Divide the sum of squares by $n - 1$ to adjust for sample size and sampling error.
7. Compute the standard deviation, s_X: $$s_X = \sqrt{\frac{\Sigma(X - \overline{X})^2}{n - 1}} = \sqrt{s_X^2}$$	**7.** Take the square root of the variance to obtain directly interpretable units of measure (units instead of squared units).

TABLE 5–2 | Spreadsheet for computing the standard deviation: Weight of crosstown football players ($n = 12$)

	Givens		Calculations	
(1) Player	(2) X	(3) $X - \overline{X}$	(4) $(X - \overline{X})^2$	
1	165	−73	5,329	
2	200	−38	1,444	
3	216	−22	484	
4	217	−21	441	
5	226	−12	144	
6	236	−2	4	
7	239	1	1	
8	244	6	36	
9	261	23	529	
10	268	30	900	
11	283	45	2,025	
12	301	63	3,969	
$n = 12$	$\Sigma X = 2{,}856$ pounds	$\Sigma(X - \overline{X}) = 0$	$\Sigma(X - \overline{X})^2 = 15{,}306$ squared pounds	

Finally, we square the deviation scores in column 3 to obtain column 4. The sum in column 4 of Table 5–2 and the sample size n are all we need to compute the standard deviation:

$$s_X = \sqrt{\frac{\Sigma(X - \overline{X})^2}{n - 1}} = \sqrt{\frac{15{,}306}{11}} = \sqrt{1{,}391.45} = 37.30 \text{ pounds}$$

Limitations of the Standard Deviation

Since the standard deviation is computed from the mean, like the mean it is inflated by outliers. Outliers produce large deviation scores. When squared, these large deviations, whether positive or negative, produce a large positive, inflated result. Thus, the standard deviation can be very misleading when reported for a skewed distribution in which a few scores are strung out in one direction. To convince yourself of the effect of extreme scores on both the mean and the standard deviation, complete the spreadsheet in Table 5–2 but add the following two cases to obtain a new sample with $n = 14$: player 13 who weighs 115 pounds and player 14 who weighs 125 pounds. Then compare the answers from the original and new samples.

How to Calculate the Range and Standard Deviation

Problem: Calculate the range, mean, and standard deviation of the gasoline excise taxes charged by 10 selected states in the western United States. These states and their taxes are presented in Table 5–3, where X = gasoline excise tax per gallon.

TABLE 5–3 | State excise taxes on gasoline in selected western states in May 1996

Givens		Calculations	
State	Tax (¢) per Gallon X	$X - \bar{X}$	$(X - \bar{X})^2$
New Mexico	17	−4.7	22.09
California	18	−3.7	13.69
Arizona	18	−3.7	13.69
Utah	19	−2.7	7.29
Colorado	22	.3	.09
Washington	23	1.3	1.69
Nevada	23	1.3	1.69
Oregon	24	2.3	5.29
Idaho	25	3.3	10.89
Montana	28	6.3	39.69

$\Sigma X = 217¢$ $\Sigma(X - \bar{X})^2 = 116.10$ squared ¢

$n = 10$ $\Sigma(X - \bar{X}) = 0$

Source: Tax rates from http://www.api.org/news/596sttax.htm. Copyright © 1996 by American Petroleum Institute. Reprinted by permission of the Institute.

1. Make sure that the variable is of interval/ratio level of measurement (as is the case of gasoline excise taxes).

2. Organize the data into a spreadsheet with scores ranked from lowest to highest, and with the following column headings:

Case	X	$X - \bar{X}$	$(X - \bar{X})^2$

where "Case" = the case number or name,

X = the raw, observed score of the interval/ratio variable,

$X - \bar{X}$ = the deviation score,

$(X - \bar{X})^2$ = the squared deviation score.

3. Calculate the range. With these ranked scores, we see that the minimum score is 17 cents and the maximum is 28 cents. Our rounding unit is a whole number.

Range = (maximum score − minimum score) + value of rounding unit

$$= (28 - 17) + 1 = 12¢$$

4. Compute the mean.

$$\overline{X} = \frac{\Sigma X}{n} = \frac{217}{10} = 21.7¢$$

5. Subtract each raw score (*X*) from the mean to obtain its deviation score. Sum the deviation scores to make sure that they sum to zero (within rounding error).

6. Square each deviation score and sum the squares.

7. Calculate the standard deviation:

$$s_X = \sqrt{\frac{\Sigma (X - \overline{X})^2}{n - 1}} = \sqrt{\frac{116.10}{9}} = 3.59¢$$

The Standard Deviation as an Integral Part of Inferential Statistics

The features of the mean and the standard deviation make them highly useful for getting a sense of proportion about individual variables under study. The standard deviation and the deviation scores from which it is computed are also essential for examining the relationships between two variables. The focus of inferential statistics is to gain an understanding of why the individual scores of a dependent variable deviate from its mean.

Suppose, for instance, we are studying alcohol abuse. For a sample of adult drinkers, we find that the mean consumption of alcoholic beverages is 4.3 gallons per year. Gary consumed 7.3 gallons last year, 3 gallons over the mean. Sam consumed only 1 gallon, 3.3 gallons less than the mean. What accounts for these high and low deviations? Perhaps we could hypothesize some predictor (independent) variables we believe are related to this dependent variable. For example, the mealtime consumption hypothesis might explain part of Gary's positive deviation score: Drinkers from families that consume wine with meals have a higher mean alcohol consumption. There is also the social drinker hypothesis, which might explain part of Sam's negative deviation score: Drinkers who consume alcohol only when it is served at social functions have a lower mean alcohol consumption.

For an entire sample, our interest is in explaining the variation—the sum of squared deviation scores. Deviation scores, the variation, and the standard deviation are simply measures of differences in scores for a variable among the subjects of a population. Is the mean amount of yearly alcohol consumption higher for persons in some regions, among different age or religious groups, or between the sexes? The answers to such questions hinge on the mathematical properties of the mean, the standard deviation, and the normal curve.

Why Is It Called the "Standard" Deviation?

The standard deviation gets its name from the fact that it provides a *common unit of measure* (a standard) for comparing variables with very different *observed units of measure*. For example, imagine that Mary Smith and Jason Jones are both applying for a scholarship based on college admissions test performance. Mary took the Academic College Testing Service (ACT) test and scored 26 ACT points. Jason took the Stanford Admissions Test (SAT) and scored 900 SAT points. These two test scores have very different observed units of measure: ACT test points range from 0 to 36, and SAT test points range from 200 to 1,600. Raw scores for the two tests cannot be compared directly. By using the means and standard deviations for both tests, however, we can devise a way of comparing them. With the following statistics, we find that in comparison to others taking these tests, Mary had the higher score:

X = ACT test score $\overline{X}$ = 22 ACT points s_X = 2 ACT points

Y = SCT test score $\overline{Y}$ = 1000 SAT points s_Y = 100 SAT points

Mary's ACT score of 26 is 2 standard deviations above the mean for those taking the ACT test; that is, her score is 4 ACT points—2 times 2 standard deviations—above the average of 22. Jason scores *1 standard deviation below* the mean for those taking the SAT test; that is, his score is 100 SAT points—1 standard deviation—below the average of 1,000. Without hesitation we can award the scholarship to Mary. By using standard deviations as units of measure in place of "ACT test points" and "SAT test points," we have a common yardstick or standard of measure for these two variables— hence the name *standard* deviation. Who said you cannot compare apples to oranges?

Standardized Scores (Z-Scores)

The preceding example illustrates the fact that a research subject's score on any interval/ratio variable may be expressed in several ways. First, we can *express it in its original, observed units of measure* as a **raw score**. For example, Mary's raw score of X is 26 ACT points. Second, we can *express it as a deviation from the mean,* i.e., the deviation score $(X - \overline{X})$; Mary's deviation score is +4, meaning that she scored 4 ACT points above the mean for those who took the ACT. Third, we can express her score as *a number of standard deviations from the mean* ACT score. We call this her **standardized score** (or **Z-score**), which is computed as follows for the variable X:

Computing Standardized Scores (Z-Scores)

$$Z_X = \frac{X - \overline{X}}{s_X}$$

where

Z_X = standardized score for a value of X

    = number of standard deviations a raw score

      (X-score) deviates from the mean

X = an interval/ratio variable

$\overline{X}$ = the mean of X

s_X = the standard deviation of X

If we set X = ACT score with $\overline{X}$ = 22 ACT points and s_X = 2 ACT points, Mary's Z-score is

$$Z_X = \frac{X - \overline{X}}{s_X} = \frac{26 - 22}{2} = \frac{4}{2} = 2.00 \text{ SD}$$

where SD means "standard deviations." A Z-score is an X-score's distance from the mean (i.e., its deviation score) divided into standard deviation unit distances.

A key to keeping track of these three ways of expressing score is to focus on the units of measure. Raw scores *and* deviation scores for a variable are presented in the original observed unit of measure, which of course is defined by a variable. For example, the observed unit of measure for age is years; for weight, pounds; for height, inches; and so on. But no matter what the unit of measure of a variable is, its Z-scores are measured in SD. Table 5–4 summarizes these distinctions.

Here are some examples from a random sample of women students at Crosstown University:

1. Where X = weight, $\overline{X}$ = 120 pounds, s_X = 10 pounds:

Case	X (weight)	X − X̄ (deviation score)	Z_X (standardized score)
Cheryl Jones	110 pounds	−10 pounds	−1 SD
Jennifer Smith	125 pounds	5 pounds	.5 SD
Terri Barnett	107 pounds	−13 pounds	−1.3 SD

2. Where Y = height, $\overline{Y}$ = 65 inches, s_Y = 3 inches:

Case	Y (height)	Y − Ȳ (deviation score)	Z_Y (standardized score)
Cheryl Jones	64 inches	−1 inch	−.33 SD
Jennifer Smith	65 inches	0 inch	0 SD
Terri Barnett	68 inches	3 inches	1 SD

TABLE 5–4 | The different ways in which a variable's scores can be presented

Form of Score for a Variable and Its Symbol	Units of Measure of the Variable	Example: X = Height
Raw score (X-score): X	The variable's unit of measure	Inches
Deviation score = $X - \overline{X}$	The variable's unit of measure	Inches
Standardized score (Z_X) or "Z-score": $$Z_X = \frac{X - \overline{X}}{s_X}$$	Standard deviations of the variable (SD)	SD

Keep in mind that both deviation scores *and* Z-scores are measures of the distance from a variable's raw score to its mean. The deviation score is obtained by subtracting the mean from the raw score (i.e., $X - \overline{X}$). In dividing this deviation score by the standard deviation, we cut this deviation score into parts and multiples of standard deviations from the mean. Recall that after computing the mean, computing the deviation scores is the next thing we do when we calculate the standard deviation. The essence of the standard deviation is viewing an individual's raw score as a deviation from the mean.

To gain a good sense of proportion about the formulas for deviation scores and Z-scores, let us examine the relationships among the sizes of raw scores, deviation scores, and Z-scores. First, the farther from the mean an X-score is, the larger are its deviation score and Z-score. Moreover, the sign of any deviation score and Z-score indicates the **direction of a score**: *whether that observation fell above the mean (the positive direction) or below the mean (the negative direction)*. The sign "−" (minus sign) indicates that a raw score is below the mean; the sign "+" (plus sign) which is implied, not written, indicates that it is above the mean. In the preceding examples Cheryl and Terri are below average on weight and Terri is above average on height. In fact, we can tell from these Z-scores that Terri is a tall, thin person—more than 1 SD below on weight but 1 SD above on height. Jennifer is the mean height; thus, her deviation score and Z-score for Y are zero: she deviates none from the mean height.

Since we will be using Z-scores or similar measures of deviation in every chapter in the remainder of this text, it is wise to practice computing deviation scores and Z-scores and to study the directions (signs) of those scores. A simple double check is in order. If a raw score is below the mean, its deviation and Z-scores are negative. Also keep in mind that Z-scores are just another way to express raw scores. Every raw score has a corresponding Z-score, and vice versa.

The Standard Deviation and the Normal Distribution

In addition to providing a standard of comparison between different variables and samples, under the appropriate conditions the mean and the standard deviation provide a wealth of information. This is the case when a variable has a distribution of scores that is normal—shaped like the normal distribution curve. As we defined it in Chapter 4, a normal distribution is symmetrical, with its mean, median, and mode equal to one another and located in the center of the curve. Symmetry or balance in the curve is not

FIGURE 5–3

The relationship
of the standard
deviation to the
normal curve

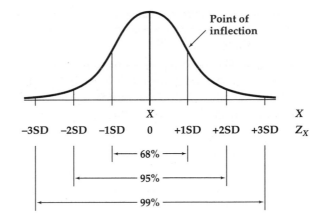

the whole picture, however. The normal curve also has a distinct bell shape that is not too flat or too peaked. Many variables are normally distributed (such as height, weight, and intelligence). Regardless of which variable is examined, if it is normally distributed, it carries the properties of a normal curve.

What makes the standard deviation such a valuable statistical tool is that it is a mathematical part of the normal curve. As you follow the curve from its center (i.e., its peak) out in either direction, the curve changes shape to approach the X-axis. From the peak, the point at which the curve begins to shift outward is 1 standard deviation from the mean. This point is called the point of inflection, and it is highlighted in Figure 5–3. This indicates that the mean and the standard deviation are mathematical aspects of a natural phenomenon: the tendency for a bell-shaped, normal distribution to occur for many natural events.

Understanding the phenomenon of normality is an important aspect of the statistical imagination. Many naturally occurring phenomena have frequency distributions that take the bell shape of the normal curve. The normal curve depicts the fact that as we deviate farther from the mean, we can expect fewer and fewer cases. For many variables, there is an average around which most scores fall, and as we move away from this average, case frequencies diminish. For example, physical height is normally distributed; most people are about average, with just a few really tall people and really short people.

One of the best features of the naturally occurring phenomenon of normality is that it allows precise predictions of how many of a population's scores fall within any score range. As illustrated in Figure 5–3, *for any normally distributed variable:*

1. Fifty percent of the scores fall above the mean, and 50 percent fall below. This is due to the fact that the median is equal to the mean.

2. Virtually all scores fall within 3 standard deviations of the mean in both directions. This is a distance of 3 Z-scores below to 3 Z-scores above the mean, a width of 6 standard deviations across. The precise amount is 99.7 percent. The remaining .3 percent of cases (that is, 3 cases out of 1,000) fall outside 3 standard

deviations, and theoretically the curve extends into infinity in both directions. (Practically speaking, the scores for some variables, such as personal weight, have finite limits.)

3. Approximately 95 percent of the scores of a normally distributed variable fall within 2 standard deviations distance in both directions from the mean. This is plus and minus 2 Z-scores from the mean.

4. Approximately 68 percent of the scores of a normally distributed variable fall within 1 standard deviation (plus or minus 1 Z-score) distance in both directions from the mean.

Keep in mind that the normal distribution has very predictable features. *If a variable is distributed in this peculiar bell shape,* we can use sample statistics and what we know about the normal curve to estimate how many scores *in a population* fall within a certain range.

To illustrate the utility of the normal curve, let us follow through on our example, a sample of women students from Crosstown University, where X = weight, the mean weight is 120 pounds, and s_X = 10 pounds. First, we need to make sure that the distribution of scores is indeed normal, that is, that it is bell-shaped. This could be done by producing a histogram of the scores from a sample (not shown). If this graph appears roughly bell-shaped, we can assume that this variable is normally distributed not only in the sample but also in the population. We refer to this as "assuming normality." (The shape of a sample histogram can be slightly off from normal as a result of sampling error.) As is graphed in Figure 5–4, assuming normality, we can make the following estimates of the weights of the population of female students at Crosstown University:

1. Half these female students weigh over 120 pounds.

2. Approximately 68 percent of Crosstown University's female students weigh between 110 and 130 pounds.

FIGURE 5–4

Using the normal curve to estimate the weight (*X*) distribution of female students at Crosstown University

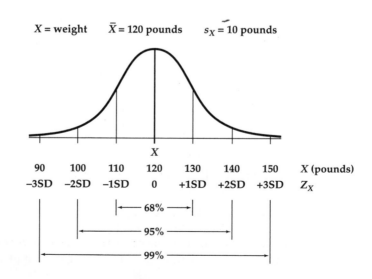

3. Approximately 95 percent of Crosstown University's female students weigh between 100 and 140 pounds.

4. Very few weigh under 90 pounds or over 150 pounds.

Remember, a Z-score is just another way to express a raw score (i.e., the X-score for an individual observation). If Susannah weighs 110 pounds, she is 1 SD below the mean weight and has a Z-score of –1.00 SD.

Tabular Presentation of Results

In research articles, a basic descriptive statistics table is one that lists all variables and their means and standard deviations. Table 5–5 presents a descriptive statistics table from a study of the psychological well-being of homeless persons at two points in time.

TABLE 5–5 | Descriptive statistics for psychological symptoms, life satisfaction, and self-mastery

Subscales	Follow-Up 1		Follow-Up 2	
	M	SD	M	SD
Psychological symptoms				
Anger	4.17	.80	4.14	.85
Anxiety	3.97	.79	3.97	.80
Depression	3.60	.76	3.68	.77
Mania	3.59	.87	3.68	.90
Psychoticism	4.51	.72	4.52	.72
Life satisfaction				
Clothing	4.33	1.59	4.49	1.60
Food	4.79	1.53	4.98	1.42
Health	4.81	1.38	4.77	1.41
Housing	4.37	1.49	4.51	1.54
Leisure	3.74	1.53	3.84	1.56
Money	2.98	1.57	3.19	1.67
Social	4.42	1.44	4.51	1.79
Self-mastery				
Mastery-1	3.21	.85	3.24	.84
Mastery-2	3.36	.87	3.28	.85

Note: $n = 298$. Higher scores reflect greater subjective well-being.
Source: Modified from Marshall et al., 1996: 49. Reprinted with permission of the American Sociological Association.

Statistical Follies and Fallacies: What Does It Indicate When the Standard Deviation Is Larger than the Mean?

As we noted in Chapter 4, the mean is susceptible to distortion by the presence of extreme scores, outliers, and skewed distributions. Because it is based on deviations from the mean, the standard deviation is susceptible to the same problem. The distortion is compounded by the fact that the deviation scores are squared.

A common type of skewed distribution is a positive (or right) skew in which most people score low but a few score high. For example, "hospital stays," or the number of times a random sample of persons over age 65 have stayed in a hospital in the past year, is right skewed. Most persons will score zero stays, a few will score one stay, slightly fewer will score two stays, and a few severely ill persons will score frequent stays. This type of distribution is presented in Table 5–6.

TABLE 5–6 I The skewed distribution of hospital stays in the past year among people over 65 years of age (fictional data)

Givens		Calculations	
(1) Case	(2) X	(3) $X - \bar{X}$	(4) $(X - \bar{X})^2$
1	0	−2.41	5.81
2	0	−2.41	5.81
3	0	−2.41	5.81
4	0	−2.41	5.81
5	0	−2.41	5.81
6	0	−2.41	5.81
7	0	−2.41	5.81
8	0	−2.41	5.81
9	1	−1.41	1.99
10	1	−1.41	1.99
11	1	−1.41	1.99
12	2	−.41	.17
13	2	−.41	.17
14	5	2.59	6.71
15	9	6.59	43.43
16	10	7.59	57.61
17	10	7.59	57.61

$\Sigma X = 41$ times $\Sigma(X - \bar{X})^2 = 218.15$ times

$n = 17$ $\Sigma(X - \bar{X}) = .03^*$

*Did not sum to zero because of rounding error.

Even without a histogram, the relative values of the mean and standard deviation for this distribution provide a signal that the distribution is skewed. These statistics compute as follows:

X = hospital stays = for the past year, the number of times a person is admitted to a hospital and stays at least one night

$$\overline{X} = 2.41 \text{ times} \qquad s_X = 3.69 \text{ times} \qquad n = 17 \text{ cases}$$

Note that the standard deviation is larger than the mean. This suggests that one or more extreme scores inflated the mean and the standard deviation. Moreover, since numbers are squared in the standard deviation, a few extreme scores can quickly "explode" its value. Note, for instance, the large contribution to the sum of squares the three largest cases made with their stays of 9, 10, and 10 times.

Why should a standard deviation larger than the mean indicate a skew? Recall that if a distribution is not skewed (i.e., it has a normal bell shape), its range will be about 4 to 6 standard deviations wide. When the curve is drawn, 2 or 3 standard deviations' width will fit on each side of the mean. If the lower limit of a variable's X-scores is zero, at least 2 standard deviations distance should fit between an X-score of zero and the mean. When the standard deviation is larger than the mean, as in the case of hospital stays, not even a single width of the standard deviation can make this fit. Another way to put it is that the standard deviation should be about half the size of the mean or less.

Two general rules apply to the relative sizes of the mean and the standard deviation:

1. If the standard deviation is larger than the mean, this probably indicates a skew, the presence of outliers, or another peculiarity in the shape of the distribution, such as a bimodal distribution.

2. If the standard deviation is not half the size of the mean or less, care should be taken to examine the distribution for skewness or outliers.

As we will discuss in later chapters, when a skewed variable is correlated with other variables, the results may be misleading (Chapter 14). In such cases, adjustments must be made to statistics to avoid such mistakes.

SUMMARY

1. Dispersion refers to how the scores of an interval/ratio variable are spread out from lowest to highest and the shape of the distribution in between. Dispersion statistics measure this spread.

2. The most commonly used dispersion statistics are the *range* and the *standard deviation*.

3. The range is an expression of how the scores of an interval/ratio variable are distributed from lowest to highest. It is the distance between the minimum and maximum scores in a sample.

4. The range has limitations. It is greatly affected by outliers. In addition, it has narrow informational scope. It provides the width of a distribution of scores but tells us nothing about how scores are spread between the maximum and minimum scores.

5. The standard deviation describes how scores of an interval/ratio variable are spread across the distribution in relation to the mean score. The standard deviation is computed by determining how far each score is from the mean—how far it "deviates" from the mean. Thus, the standard deviation is based on deviation scores.

6. The standard deviation has limitations. It is greatly inflated by outliers. It can be misleading if the distribution of scores is skewed.

7. The standard deviation provides a standard unit of comparison—a common unit of measure for comparing variables with very different observed units of measure. Standardized scores (Z-scores) express a raw score as a number of standard deviations (SD) from the mean score. Two variables with different units of measure may be compared if both variables are standardized by calculating Z-scores.

8. The direction of a Z-score is determined by its sign. A positive Z-score occurs when a raw score is higher than the mean. A negative Z-score occurs when a raw score is less than the mean.

9. There are three ways to express the value of any score of an interval/ratio variable:

   a. As a *raw score,* the observed value of *X* in its original unit of measure (such as inches, or pounds).

   b. As a *deviation score,* the difference between the mean and a raw score. Deviation scores are also expressed in the variable's original unit of measure.

   c. As a *Z-score* (i.e., the *standardized score*), the difference between the mean and a raw score, but expressed as a number of standard deviations (SD).

10. The standard deviation is a mathematical part of the normal curve. It is the distance on the *X*-axis from the mean to the score directly under the point of inflection of the curve.

11. If a variable is normally distributed, we can use sample statistics and what we know about the normal curve to estimate how many scores in a population fall within a certain range. (*a*) 50% of the scores fall above the mean and 50% fall below. (*b*) Virtually all scores (99.7%) fall within 3 standard deviations of the mean in both directions. (*c*) Approximately 95% of the scores fall within 2 standard deviations of the mean in both directions. (*d*) Approximately 68% of the scores of a normally distributed variable fall within 1 standard deviation of the mean in both directions.

12. If the standard deviation is larger than the mean, the distribution of scores *cannot* be normally shaped. A histogram of the variable is likely to reveal a skew or oddly shaped score distribution.

CHAPTER EXTENSIONS ON *THE STATISTICAL IMAGINATION* WEB SITE

Chapter 5 extensions of text material available on *The Statistical Imagination* Web site at www.mhhe.com/ritchey2 include how an estimate of the standard deviation based on the range may be used to detect whether a score distribution is skewed.

FORMULAS FOR CHAPTER 5

Organize a spreadsheet with cases in rank order:

Givens		Calculations	
(1) Case	(2) X	(3) $X - \overline{X}$	(4) $(X - \overline{X})^2$
•	•	. . .	. . .
•	•	. . .	. . .
•	•	. . .	. . .
$\Sigma X = \ldots$		$\Sigma(X - \overline{X})^2 = \ldots$	
$n = \ldots$	$\Sigma(X - \overline{X}) = 0$		

Calculating the range:

1. Rank the scores in the distribution from lowest to highest.
2. Identify the minimum and maximum scores.
3. Identify the value of the rounding unit (see Appendix A).
4. Calculate the range:

    Range = (maximum score − minimum score) + value of rounding unit

Calculating the standard deviation:

1. Start by computing the mean of X and completing a spreadsheet similar to the one in Table 5–2.
2. Calculate the standard deviation:
   Working with a spreadsheet

$$s_X = \sqrt{\frac{\Sigma (X - \overline{X})^2}{n - 1}}$$

Calculating standardized scores (Z-scores):

$$Z_X = \frac{X - \overline{X}}{s_X}$$

QUESTIONS FOR CHAPTER 5

1. Dispersion statistics are computed only on variables of what levels of measurement?

2. Both the range and the standard deviation are measures of the dispersion of scores within a distribution. Explain the differences in perspective between these two statistics.

3. What effect does an extreme score or outlier have on the computation of the range?

4. The standard deviation is "derived from" the mean. What does this mean?

5. In computing the range, the value of the rounding unit of the variable is added to the difference between the maximum and minimum scores. Why is the value of the rounding unit added?

6. In computing the standard deviation, why is it necessary to square the deviation scores?

7. In computing the standard deviation for sample data, why must we divide by $n - 1$?

8. In computing the standard deviation, why must we take the square root?

9. What is the mathematical relationship between the variance and the standard deviation?

10. What is another name for the variation?

11. What is the significance of the word *standard* in the term *standard deviation?*

12. An expression of how far a raw score is from the mean of a distribution in the original units of measure of the variable X is called a _____ score.

13. An expression of how far a raw score is from the mean of a distribution in units of measure of standard deviations (SD) is called a _____ score.

14. What are the properties of a normal distribution?

15. In a normal distribution, approximately what percentage of scores fall within 1 standard deviation of the mean in both directions? Within 2 standard deviations of the mean in both directions? Within 3 standard deviations of the mean in both directions?

16. In a normal distribution, exactly what percentage of scores falls above the mean? What central tendency statistic besides the mean accounts for this phenomenon?

17. In a normal distribution, the curve peaks at the value of the mean. What central tendency statistic besides the mean accounts for this phenomenon?

18. If a raw score falls below the mean in a distribution, will the sign of its Z-score be positive or negative? Illustrate your answer by using the formula for calculating a Z-score.

19. In any interval/ratio score distribution, there is a score for which the deviations from it sum to zero. What central tendency statistic is located at this point?

20. For his age group, Charles is 1 standard deviation below the mean height but 1.5 standard deviations above the mean weight. Describe his general body build.

21. Daniel is 3 standard deviations above the mean in terms of his intelligence quotient (IQ). Describe his general intellect.

22. Explain why a distribution probably is not normal when the standard deviation is larger than the mean.

EXERCISES FOR CHAPTER 5

Problem Set 5A

5A-1. Use the formula for the standard deviation to complete the blanks in the following table. The table presents calculations on interval/ratio variables from different samples of size n.

Sum of Squares	n	Variance	Standard Deviation
11,828.52	88	135.96	_____
3,120.00	21	_____	_____
893.49		30.81	_____
_____	347	124.65	11.16

5A-2. Hughes and Waite (2002) examined living arrangements and health in the late middle-age years of the life course. Suppose that the following are a series of ages from their study: 74, 81, 83, 77, 76, 79, 79.
  a. Organize a spreadsheet with cases in rank order with X = age.
  b. Compute the mean, median, and modal age.
  c. Compute the range of ages.
  d. Compute the standard deviation of ages.

5A-3. Hoff (2003) examined the work lives of physicians employed by health maintenance organizations (HMOs). Suppose that the following data depict the daily patient load (i.e., the number of patients seen per day) of seven HMO physicians: 8, 7, 11, 4, 5, 13, 7.
  a. Organize a spreadsheet with cases in rank order with Y = number of patients seen per day.
  b. Compute the mean, median, and modal patient loads for the seven physicians.
  c. Compute the range of patients seen per day.
  d. Compute the standard deviation.

5A-4. Takao et al. (2003) examined the relationship between occupational class and physical activity among Japanese employees. Suppose that the following data represent a sample of scores on a scale measuring individuals' positions

within the Japanese occupational hierarchy: 27, 26, 28, 30, 31, 29, 27, 31, 29. Set X = occupational class scale score.
a. Organize the data using a spreadsheet format with the scores of X ranked.
b. Calculate the mean and standard deviation.

5A-5. It's homecoming week and crazy things are happening around campus. One of those crazy things is a footrace among sororities. A random sample of racing sisters, pledges, and alumnae produces the following ages: 19, 18, 20, 19, 29, 18, 20, 18, 22, 21. Set X = age.
a. Organize the data using a spreadsheet format with the scores of X ranked.
b. Calculate the mean and standard deviation.
c. Is there something peculiar in this distribution? Adjust for it by recalculating the statistics.
d. Comment on the differences between the original and adjusted statistics.

5A-6. Ellickson and colleagues (2003) examined adolescent smoking behavior and subsequent smoking behavior. Suppose that the following data are from a sample of 16- to 20-year-old smokers.

Y = the number of cigarettes smoked per day.

$$\bar{Y} = 15 \text{ cigarettes} \qquad s_Y = 5 \text{ cigarettes}$$

a. Complete the columns in the following table for a few selected cases from the data. Be sure to specify the units of measure.
b. Who stands out as a heavy smoker?

Case	Y (cigarettes per day)	Y − Ȳ (deviation score)	Z_Y (standardized score)
Bob Smith	17		
Spencer Byrd	30		
Sonya Turnham	4		
Chuck Martin	20		

5A-7. Ferraro and Yu (1995) studied the relationship between body weight and self-ratings of health. Suppose you were given the following summary statistics on weight from this study.

$$X = \text{weight} \qquad \bar{X} = 169 \text{ pounds} \qquad s_X = 18 \text{ pounds}$$

a. Draw and label the normal curve for these weights.
b. The following table includes data for just a few of the observations. Complete the middle column by estimating each Z_X by sight (i.e., by simply observing X on the curve).
c. For each X-score, compute the exact Z-score and insert it in the right column. (Show the formula and computation for X = 128 pounds.)

X (pounds)	Sight Estimate of Z-score (SD)	Computed Z-score (SD)
169		
128		
192		
177		
151		
109		

Problem Set 5B

5B-1. Use the formula for the standard deviation to complete the blanks in the following table. The table presents calculations on interval/ratio variables from different samples of size n.

Sum of Squares	n	Variance	Standard Deviation
38.76	7	_____	_____
347,295.92	1,041	_____	18.27
_____	91	40.89	_____
5,865.04	_____	17.56	_____

5B-2. Goesling (2001) examined the phenomenon of world income inequality, both within and between nations around the world. Suppose the following are a sample of monthly incomes for residents of the United States: $2,347; $2,434; $1,636; $1,963; $2,358; $1,968; $2,683.
a. Organize a spreadsheet with cases in rank order with X = monthly income.
b. Compute the mean, median, and modal monthly income.
c. Compute the range.
d. Compute the standard deviation.

5B-3. Wiesner (2003) examined reciprocal relations between depressive symptoms and delinquent behavior among male and female adolescents. Suppose that the following are ages of adolescents involved in this study: 10, 8, 9, 11, 12, 9, 13.
a. Organize a spreadsheet with cases in rank order with Y = age.
b. Compute the mean, median, and modal ages for the selected adolescents.
c. Compute the range of ages.
d. Compute the standard deviation.

5B-4. Groome and Soureti (2004) studied the relationship between post-traumatic stress disorder and anxiety symptoms in children following a 1999 earthquake near Athens, Greece. Suppose that the following set of data represents Richter scale magnitude measurements for several earthquakes

around the Mediterranean Sea during the late twentieth century: 5.8, 2.4, 2.2, 6.0, 3.1, 2.4, 2.2, 5.8, 2.4. Set X = Richter scale magnitude points.
a. Organize the data using a spreadsheet format with X-scores ranked.
b. Calculate the mean and standard deviation.

5B-5. Betts and Morell (1999) analyzed the effects of personal background (i.e., family background, high school, resources, peer group, etc.) on undergraduate grade point average (GPA). Suppose that the following were GPAs for a sample of undergraduate university students: 3.6, 3.8, 3.6, 3.9, 2.6, 3.8, 3.8, 3.9. Set X = GPA.
a. Organize the data using a spreadsheet format with the scores ranked.
b. Calculate the mean and standard deviation.
c. Is there something peculiar in this distribution? Adjust for it by recalculating the statistics.
d. Comment on the differences between the original and adjusted statistics.

5B-6. Green et al. (2001) studied the phenomenon of hate crime and discussed the practical difficulties associated with collecting data on this phenomenon. However, assume that you have been able to secure reliable data on hate crime in the United States. Set Y = hate crime rate = number of hate crimes reported per 100,000 population covered by reporting agencies. The following are rates for a selected sample of states:

$$\bar{Y} = 1.19 \text{ hate crimes per 100,000 population}$$

$$s_Y = .32 \text{ hate crimes per 100,000 population}$$

a. Complete the columns in the following table. Be sure to specify the units of measure.
b. What state stands out as having a relatively high rate of hate crimes?

State	Y (hate crimes rate)	$Y - \bar{Y}$ (deviation score)	Z_Y (standardized score)
Florida	1.15		
Indiana	1.08		
Iowa	1.02		
Mississippi	.97		
Texas	1.75		

5B-7. Slater et al. (2003) examined the relationship between violent media content and aggressive behavior among adolescents. In order to replicate their results, suppose we conduct a similar analysis of aggressive behavior among 13- to 16-year-old boys in a youth detention facility. The variable is operationalized as the number of aggressive acts—verbal insults and threats, acts of physical violence, and destruction of property—committed over the past week. The acts are tabulated by observing videotapes of the facility's recreation rooms and grounds, library, rest rooms, and cafeteria. We compute descriptive statistics on this variable and obtain the following results with X = number of aggressive acts:

$$\overline{X} = 16.8 \text{ acts} \qquad s_X = 4.4 \text{ acts}$$

a. Draw and label the normal curve for these aggressive acts.
b. The following table includes data for just a few of the observations. Complete the middle column by estimating each Z_X by sight (i.e., by simply observing X on the curve).
c. For each X-score, compute the exact Z-score and insert it in the right column. (Show the formula and computation for X = 9 acts.)

X (aggressive acts)	Sight Estimate of *Z*-score (SD)	Computed *Z*-score (SD)
9		
12		
19		
26		
3		
14		

Problem Set 5C

5C-1. Use the formula for the standard deviation to complete the blanks in the following table. The table presents calculations on interval/ratio variables from different samples of size n.

Sum of Squares	*n*	Variance	Standard Deviation
12,654.27	97	131.82	_____
2,876.54	18	_____	_____
975.46	_____	34.82	_____
_____	526	142.53	_____

5C-2. For research subjects in low-income communities in Kenya, Molyneux et al. (2004) examined parental comprehension of informed consent documents. As part of the study's quantitative component, suppose the following are incomes for residents within the authors' research area: $627, $435, $569, $615, $796, $715, $615.
a. Organize a spreadsheet with cases in rank order with X = income.
b. Compute the mean, median, and modal income.
c. Compute the range of incomes.
d. Compute the standard deviation of incomes.

5C-3. Siebert (2004) studied the determinants of depression among social workers in North Carolina. Assume that the following data represent the number of case contacts in the past week for a sample of social workers: 10, 8, 13, 7, 6, 15, 6.

   a. Organize a spreadsheet with cases in rank order with Y = case contacts in past week.

   b. Compute the mean, median, and modal number of case contacts.

   c. Compute the range.

   d. Compute the standard deviation.

5C-4. Roose et al. (2004) attempted to determine the efficacy of antidepressant medication for the treatment of depressive symptoms in patients 75 years of age and older. Assume that the following data are Center for Epidemiologic Studies Depression Scale (CESD) scores for a small number of study participants: 38, 31, 42, 27, 19, 49, 31, 19, 38. Set X = CESD scale points.

   a. Organize the data using a spreadsheet format with the scores ranked.

   b. Calculate the mean and standard deviation.

5C-5. Ebrahim et al. (2004) assessed the association between socioeconomic position and self-reported disability among older males. Suppose that the following are ages of a number of men in this study: 74, 69, 76, 72, 72, 78, 87, 74, 69, 74. Set X = age.

   a. Organize the data using a spreadsheet format with the scores ranked.

   b. Calculate the mean and standard deviation.

   c. Is there something peculiar in this distribution? Adjust for it by recalculating the statistics.

   d. Comment on the differences between the original and adjusted statistics.

5C-6. Ramstedt (2004) examined alcohol consumption and alcohol-related mortality in Canada. The following statistics are from a subsample of alcohol-addicted subjects from the author's investigation. Set Y = the number of alcoholic drinks consumed per day.

$$\bar{Y} = 6 \text{ drinks}$$

$$s_Y = 2 \text{ drinks}$$

   a. Complete the columns in the following table for a few selected cases from the sample. Be sure to specify the units of measure.

   b. Who stands out as the heaviest drinker?

Subject	Y (drinks per day)	$Y - \bar{Y}$ (deviation score)	Z_Y (standardized score)
Jill Williams	4		
Thomas Wilke	8		
Jason Schmidt	12		
Jenny Pence	7		

5C-7. Body mass index (BMI) is a measure of healthy weight level taking into account one's height. It is calculated in kilograms of weight per squared meters of height. Xiaoxing and Baker (2004) investigated the relationship between BMI, physical activity, and the risk of decline in both overall health and physical functioning. Suppose you were given the following summary statistics on BMI from this study. Set X = BMI score.

$$\bar{X} = 31 \text{ kg/m}^2$$
$$s_X = 9 \text{ kg/m}^2$$

a. Draw and label the normal curve for these body mass indices.
b. The following table includes data for just a few of the observations. Complete the middle column by estimating each Z_X by sight (i.e., by simply observing X on the curve).
c. For each X-score, compute the exact Z-score and insert it in the right column. (Show the formula and computation for $X = 11$.)

X (pounds)	Sight Estimate of Z-score (SD)	Computed Z-score (SD)
31		
11		
42		
38		
22		
2		

Problem Set 5D

5D-1. Use the formula for the standard deviation to complete the blanks in the following table. The table presents calculations on interval/ratio variables from different samples of size n.

Sum of Squares	n	Variance	Standard Deviation
29.57	5	_____	_____
426,113.21	1,986		14.65
	82	35.43	_____
8,450.35	_____	22.12	_____

5D-2. Garroutte et al. (2004) examined the relationship between ethnic identity and satisfaction among chronically ill American Indian patients at a Cherokee

Nation clinic. Suppose that the following are a series of ages from their study: 56, 64, 62, 57, 64, 59, 58.

a. Organize a spreadsheet with cases in rank order with X = age.
b. Compute the mean, median, and modal age.
c. Compute the range of ages.
d. Compute the standard deviation of ages.

5D-3. Henning and Feder (2004) compared the various characteristics of men and women incarcerated for domestic violence. Suppose that the following sample represents the number of reported incidents of domestic violence among the men and women included in this study: 5, 2, 3, 4, 3, 6, 1.

a. Organize a spreadsheet with cases in rank order with Y = incidents of domestic violence.
b. Compute the mean, median, and modal number of incidents.
c. Compute the range.
d. Compute the standard deviation.

5D-4. Tohill et al. (2004) reviewed the epidemiologic evidence assessing the relationship between fruit and vegetable consumption and body weight. Assume that the following are the average body weights of a small number of study participants: 168, 181, 144, 159, 181, 204, 168, 144, 181. Set X = body weight (pounds).

a. Organize the data using a spreadsheet format with the scores ranked.
b. Calculate the mean and standard deviation.

5D-5. Grove and Wasserman (2004) examined life-cycle patterns of grade point average (GPA) among five collegiate cohorts at a large private university. Suppose that the following are a sample of collegiate GPAs from a number of study subjects in this investigation: 3.8, 3.4, 2.4, 3.8, 3.7, 3.4, 3.4, 3.8. Set X = GPA.

a. Organize the data using a spreadsheet format with the scores ranked.
b. Calculate the mean and standard deviation.
c. Is there something peculiar in this distribution? Adjust for it by recalculating the statistics.
d. Comment on the differences between the original and adjusted statistics.

5D-6. Varano et al. (2004) explored the correlation between drug use and homicide. Suppose that the following statistics represent the homicide rates of the research areas included in this analysis. Set Y = homicide rate = number of homicides reported per 100,000 population.

$$\overline{Y} = 6.59 \text{ homicides per } 100,000 \text{ population}$$

$$s_Y = 1.74 \text{ homicides per } 100,000 \text{ population}$$

a. Complete the columns in the following table for a few selected areas. Be sure to specify the units of measure.
b. Which area stands out as having a relatively high rate of homicides?

State	Y (homicide rate)	Y − Ȳ (deviation score)	Z_Y (standardized score)
Area 1	4.97		
Area 2	8.99		
Area 3	5.99		
Area 4	6.95		
Area 5	6.29		

5D-7.   Boardman (2004) evaluated the relationship between residential stability and physical health among black and white adults. Part of the variation in health levels was due to differences in levels of stress among neighborhoods. Suppose you were given the following summary statistics from a scale used to analyze neighborhood stress levels. Set X = stress scale score.

$$\bar{X} = 11.3 \text{ stress scale points}$$

$$s_X = 3.2 \text{ stress scale points}$$

a.   Draw and label the normal curve for these stress scale scores.

b.   The following table includes data for just a few of the observations. Complete the middle column by estimating each Z_X by sight (i.e., by simply observing X on the curve).

c.   For each X-score, compute the exact Z-score and insert it in the right column. (Show the formula and computation for $X = 7$ stress scale points.)

X (stress scale points)	Sight Estimate of Z-score (SD)	Computed Z-score (SD)
7		
10		
14		
19		
1		
16		

OPTIONAL COMPUTER APPLICATIONS FOR CHAPTER 5

Chapter computer exercises are available on *The Statistical Imagination* Web site at www.mhhe.com/ritchey2. In addition, Appendix D of this text, *Guide to SPSS for Windows,* provides basic instructions for calculating dispersion statistics and standardized scores. As is emphasized in this chapter, the standard deviation is typically reported with the mean. Thus, these "descriptive statistics" are found together in computational software. The mean, range, and standard deviation may be calculated from several places in *SPSS* and are part of optional statistics for many statistical test procedures, such as those in Chapters 9–12.

6

Probability Theory and the Normal Probability Distribution

Introduction: The Human Urge to Predict the Future

Human mental capacity is distinguished from that of other animals by an ability to forecast the future—to conceive of what happens "in the long run." To predict future events is to understand them, and the development of human culture depends on prediction. The field of statistics is about making predictions with highly precise measurements. Statisticians gain status and authority from successful prediction and understanding. With its applications in the sciences, business, industry, weather forecasting, medicine, public health, public services, government, the gambling industry, entertainment, and sports, statistical work is an example of forecasting the future.

Human desires to forecast events are not new. From the earliest times of human social organization, "seers" (such as priest-doctor shamans) acquired great authority by predicting climactic cycles and important events such as rain. Applying mathematics to practical problem solving also has a long history. Measurement and computing techniques are as old as human culture and were very well established 4,000 years ago. The pyramids of ancient Egypt exemplify a precise mathematical organization of the physical world. In fact, many scholars argue that the extent of Egyptian knowledge is greatly underrated (Gillings 1972, Neugebauer 1962, Struik 1948). As Tompkins (1971: xiv–xv) notes:

> Whoever built the Great Pyramid . . . knew the precise circumference of the planet, and the length of the year to several decimals—data which were not rediscovered till the seventeenth century.

Modern mathematics, trigonometry, and "exact sciences" such as physics have their origins in ancient Mediterranean cultures in which the systematic study of nature was revered. Underlying the development of science is the recognition that physical nature is highly cyclical and thus predictable to the extent that it follows strict scientific laws. For example, a physicist standing on the ground can rest assured that any object heavier than air will drop to the earth. Human behavior, however, is not quite as predictable. Therefore, social and behavioral scientists often must qualify their conclusions by noting that their predictions are based on limited *but calculable* degrees of accuracy. For instance, a social scientist studying the relationship of, say, high school grades to college grades may only be able to assert a correlation between them, stating that there is a calculable *chance* that an A student in high school will get A's in college. The laws of chance are tools for determining the degree of accuracy in social science predictions. We refer to *the analysis and understanding of chance occurrences* as **probability theory**.

---

probability theory   The analysis and understanding of chance occurrences.

Discovery of the laws of chance began in ancient times and perhaps was stimulated as much by leisure activities such as gaming as by work activities (David 1962: 4–10). Among the artifacts of Egypt's first dynasty (3500 B.C.E.) are board games, playing pieces, and animal *astralagi* (joint bones), the precursors of dice. In Egypt, cubical dice were in common use by 3000 B.C.E. Gaming was so common in Roman times that it was prohibited on certain days. In Roman literature there are references to a book by Claudius (10 B.C.E.–C.E. 54) titled *How to Win at Dice*. Astute gamblers had the statistical imagination. They could think proportionately, recognizing that some "tosses of the bones" occurred a greater proportion of the time than did others. By successfully advising members of the ruling classes on how to increase their gambling winnings, these early statisticians gained high status. Successful stock market analysts and survey researchers as well as horse race handicappers are the modern equivalent of these highly respected statistical advisers.

We may surmise that human interest in predicting the outcomes of future events was not limited to games of chance. As far as humans are concerned, the forces of nature (especially climate) involve chance, and environmental adaptation is wrought with fate and good or bad luck. Cultural evolution is stimulated by a society's need to anticipate what will happen next. For example, by the middle dynastic period (circa 2000 B.C.E.) the ancient Egyptians had developed complex irrigation and canal systems to regulate the annual flooding of the Nile River. With data managed by a highly efficient bureaucracy, they monitored the river's depth with "nilometers" placed at strategic points along the Nile's vast 4,145-mile length. By studying and anticipating flows, they used floodwater advantageously for crop irrigation (David 1962). The accuracy of their predictions produced a stable economy that enhanced the political power of the ruling dynasties. Many ancient cultures had their share of empiricists: individuals who believed in the merits of observation and measurement. Empiricism and the popularity of gambling, religion, and fortune-telling attest to an innate human interest in betting on what will happen next and preparing for it. Everything from predicting enemy troop strength to deciding whether to carry an umbrella, invest in stocks, or propose marriage requires measurements and estimations of the likelihood of success or failure. Statistical analysis using probability theory is the tool by which predictions are made with a maximum degree of accuracy. For statisticians, many of these predictions are based on the normal curve. The normal curve and similar curves are used to calculate probabilities. The ideas behind modern probability theory were well established by 1800 [Laplace 1951 (1820)].

What Is a Probability?

A **probability** (*p*) is *a specification of how frequently a particular event of interest is likely to occur over a large number of trials (situations in which the event can occur).* We call the probability of this interesting event occurring the probability of success. Similarly, the probability of the event *not* occurring is called the probability of failure.

By observing the results or "outcomes" of a large number of trials, we are able to identify all possible outcomes. To take a very simple example, suppose we wish to determine the probability of tossing a coin and getting "heads." To determine the possible outcomes of a coin flip, we could flip one repeatedly, say 10,000 times or trials. We would quickly see that the only possible outcomes are "heads" (success) and "tails" (failure). To calculate the probability of getting heads (success), we divide the number of times heads occurs by 10,000. We would find that heads occurs very close to half the time. This example illustrates, however, that to calculate a probability, often we can simply "do the math." Obviously, a coin has two possible outcomes. These outcomes have an equal chance of occurring, so the probability of tossing heads is one-half or .5000. Thus, another way to conceive of a probability is the number of possible successful events over the number of possible outcomes. When it is possible to readily identify all possible outcomes, such as for tossing coins or rolling dice, repeated trials are unnecessary.

To symbolize a probability, brackets are used to distinguish the targeted event of interest, and a lowercase *p* is used to indicate "the probability" of a specific calculation. Note that this symbol is the same one used in previous chapters for *proportion*. This is done because probabilities *are* proportions, *as* we will discuss shortly.

---

a probability (*p*)   A specification of how frequently a particular event of interest is likely to occur over a large number of trials.

The general formula for presenting a probability is as follows:

Computing a Probability

$$p \, [\text{of success}] = \frac{\# \text{ successes}}{\# \text{ trials}} = \frac{\# \text{ possible successful outcomes}}{\text{total } \# \text{ possible outcomes}}$$

where p [of success] = probability of "the event of interest."

For consistency in instruction, in this text answers to computations of probabilities will be rounded and presented to four decimal places. Of course, probabilities also may be presented as percentages by multiplying p by 100. Here are some examples that reveal how simple the notion of probability is:

Example A: When flipping a single coin, what is the probability of getting heads?

For a coin there are two possible outcomes, and heads is one of them. Thus,

$$p \, [\text{heads}] = \frac{\# \text{ heads}}{\# \text{ of possible outcomes}} = \frac{1}{2} = .5000$$

Example B: When randomly drawing a single card from a well-shuffled standard deck of 52 playing cards:

$$a. \quad p \, [\text{king}] = \frac{\# \text{ kings in deck}}{\text{total } \# \text{ cards in deck}} = \frac{4}{52} = .0769$$

$$b. \quad p \, [7] = \frac{\# \text{ 7s in deck}}{\text{total } \# \text{ cards in deck}} = \frac{4}{52} = .0769$$

$$c. \quad p \, [\text{heart}] = \frac{\# \text{ of hearts in deck}}{\text{total } \# \text{ cards in deck}} = \frac{13}{52} = .2500$$

Example C: When randomly drawing a single marble from a well-mixed box of 300 marbles in which 100 are red and 200 are green:

$$a. \quad p \, [\text{red}] = \frac{\# \text{ of reds in box}}{\text{total } \# \text{ marbles in box}} = \frac{100}{300} = .3333$$

$$b. \quad p \, [\text{green}] = \frac{\# \text{ of greens in box}}{\text{total } \# \text{ marbles in box}} = \frac{200}{300} = .6667$$

As these illustrations reveal, computing a probability is simply a matter of proportional thinking in regard to the long-term occurrence of an event of interest. To ask, What is the probability? is to wonder, out of all the times a category of events occurs, how many of those times we can expect a certain outcome. This expectation is then expressed as a proportion or percentage.

Basic Rules of Probability Theory

There are just a few basic rules to follow in computing any probability. All calculations of probabilities employ these essential rules.

Probability Rule 1: Probabilities Always Range Between 0 and 1

Because probabilities are proportions, their lower numerical limit is zero (the event cannot happen) and their upper numerical limit is 1.00 (the event must happen). In other words, probabilities always calculate between 0.00 and 1.00 (or 0 percent and 100 percent). If this is not the case, a mathematical mistake has occurred.

Some events do have a zero probability of occurring—they never occur (e.g., remaining alive underwater for 24 hours without life-support devices). Some events occur with a 100 percent probability—they always happen (e.g., the sun will rise tomorrow). Many events, however, are not so definite; their probabilities of occurrence are somewhere between never and always.

Probability Rule 2: The Addition Rule for Alternative Events

Sometimes we may desire to define *success* as more than a single characteristic event. For example, what is the probability of drawing a king *or* an ace from a deck of cards? Here we have two alternatives for success: a king or an ace. The **addition rule for alternative events** states that *the probability of alternative events is equal to the sum of the probabilities of the individual events.* Therefore,

$$p \text{ [king or ace]} = p \text{ [king]} + p \text{ [ace]}$$

$$= \frac{\text{\# kings in deck}}{\text{total \# cards in deck}} + \frac{\text{\# aces in deck}}{\text{total \# cards in deck}}$$

$$= \frac{4}{52} + \frac{4}{52} = \frac{8}{52} = .1538 \text{ (about 15\%)}$$

A simple trick to follow with the addition rule is to replace the word *or* with an addition sign, +.

Do not make this complicated. The addition rule is just a guide to help us calculate a probability when there are several ways to gain success. In the case of drawing an ace or a king, there are eight ways. (If you are not convinced, count the aces and kings in a deck of cards.)

In later chapters we will use the symbol P (capitalized) to represent the probability of success and Q to represent the probability of failure. (These symbols probably evoked the old adage "Mind your p's and q's.") The addition rule leads to an important point: The probability of success *or* failure must be 1.00; that is, $P + Q = 1$. It follows from this that if we know P, then Q can be computed quickly. That is,

$$Q = 1 - P$$

Similarly,

$$P = 1 - Q$$

For example, if $P = p$ [king or ace], then

$$Q = p \text{ [any card other than a king or ace]} = 1 - p = 1 - .1538 = .8462 \text{ (about 85\%)}$$

In other words, if we have about a 15 percent chance of drawing a king or ace, then we have about an 85 percent chance of not doing so.

Probability Rule 3: Adjust for Joint Occurrences

Sometimes success for an event is not straightforward because a single outcome is successful in more than one way. For example, in drawing a single card from a standard deck of 52, there is a problem in the following computation, which uses the addition rule:

$$p \text{ [king or queen or heart]} = p \text{ [king]} + p \text{ [queen]} + p \text{ [heart]}$$

Incorrect

$$= \frac{\# \text{ kings} + \# \text{ queens} + \# \text{ hearts in deck}}{\text{total \# cards in deck}} = \frac{21}{52} = .4038$$

This answer is incorrect. If we take a deck of cards and count the "success cards" (kings, queens, and hearts), we will find 19, not 21. This is the case because when adding the separate probabilities, we counted both the king of hearts and the queen of hearts twice. By being a king *and* a heart, the king of hearts is successful in two ways (put another way, the characteristics are not mutually exclusive). Similarly, double success occurs for the queen of hearts.

When we have *an event that double-counts success or joins two aspects of success,* we call this a **joint occurrence**. To compute the correct probability, we must subtract every joint occurrence to eliminate these double counts. In this case, the queen of hearts and the king of hearts each is a joint occurrence. Thus,

$$p \text{ [king or queen or heart]}$$

$$= \{p \text{ [king]} + p \text{ [queen]} + p \text{ [heart]}\} - \{p \text{ [joint occurrences]}\}$$

$$= \frac{\# \text{ kings} + \# \text{ queens} + \# \text{ hearts in deck}}{\text{total \# cards in deck}} - \frac{2 \text{ joint occurrences}}{\text{total \# cards in deck}}$$

$$= \frac{21}{52} - \frac{2}{52} = \frac{19}{52} = .3654$$

Probability Rule 4: The Multiplication Rule for Compound Events

Some events have two or more parts to them. We call these *multiple-part events* **compound events** (from chemistry, where a *compound* such as water is defined as a substance composed of two or more elements, in this case hydrogen and oxygen). For example, we may define success as drawing a pair of aces from the deck, that is, drawing an ace, putting it back in, reshuffling (i.e., randomizing), and then drawing an ace again. The **multiplication rule for compound events** states that *the probability of a compound event is equal to the multiple of the probabilities of the separate parts of the event.* Thus,

$$p \text{ [ace then ace]} = p \text{ [ace]} \cdot p \text{ [ace]}$$

$$= \frac{4}{52} \cdot \frac{4}{52} = \frac{16}{2{,}704} = .0059$$

A simple trick to follow is to replace the word *then* (or *and*) with the multiplication sign, •.

Do not make this complicated. Mathematically, the multiplication rule simply extracts the number of successes in the numerator of the fraction and the total number of possible events in the denominator. Accordingly, it turns out that if we spent months drawing a card, replacing it, reshuffling, drawing a second card, and recording the outcomes, we would discover that there are 2,704 possible combinations of two cards. And we would discover that there are 16 possible combinations of ace pairs, as is shown in Figure 6–1. Thank goodness for mathematicians! They astutely noticed that instead of having to sort these combinations out piecemeal, we need only multiply the separate probabilities.

A simple coin-flipping exercise will further reinforce the simplicity of the multiplication rule. Let us compute the probability of flipping a coin twice and getting heads both times:

$$p \text{ [heads then heads]} = p \text{ [heads]} \cdot p \text{ [heads]}$$

$$= .5 \cdot .5 = .2500 \text{ (or 1 out of 4)}$$

As is shown in Figure 6–2, flipping two coins (or flipping a single coin twice) results in four possible outcomes, and only one of those outcomes is heads then heads.

To really grasp this, make your own similar chart for the probability of getting all heads when tossing three coins. (Mathematically, the probabilities of dichotomous events are calculated by expanding the binomial distribution formula; see Chapter 13.)

Probability Rule 5: Account for Replacement with Compound Events

When we illustrated rule 4, the multiplication rule for compound events, we computed the probability of drawing a pair of aces and found that $p = .0059$. We stipulated that the first card drawn was to be returned to the deck before the second card was drawn. This stipulation for calculating the probability of a compound event is called "with

FIGURE 6–1

Possible pairings of aces when randomly drawing a card, replacing it, and randomly drawing a second card

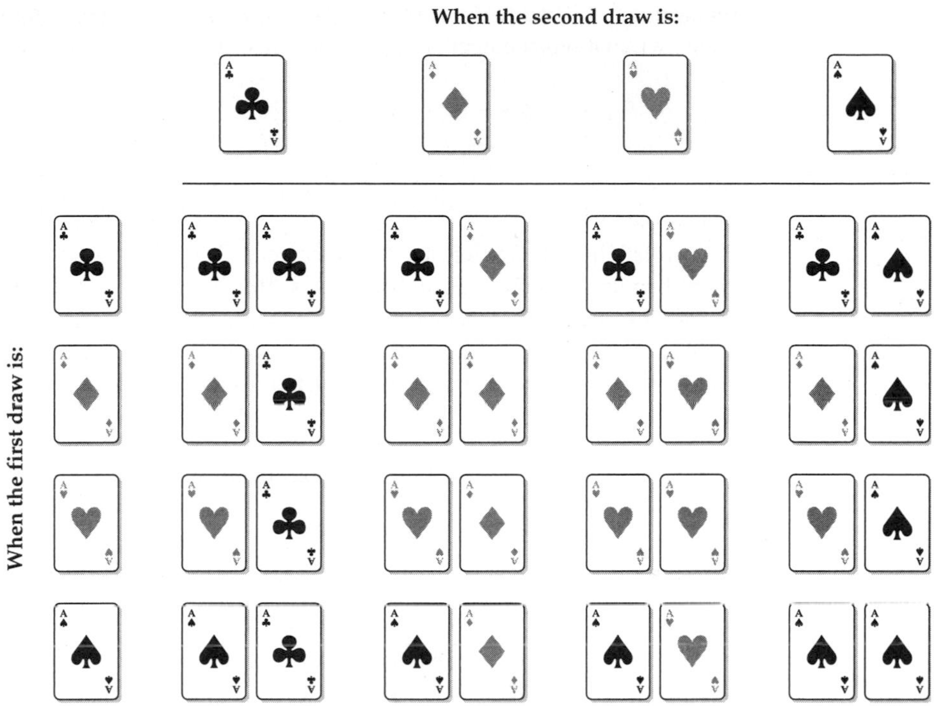

When the second draw is:

When the first draw is:

FIGURE 6–2

Possible outcomes of two flipped coins

First Coin   Second Coin

replacement." If we had not returned the first card, the calculation would have been done "without replacement" and the computed probability would have been different:

$$p \text{ [ace then ace] without replacement} = p \text{ [ace]} \cdot p \text{ [ace]}$$

$$= \frac{4}{52} \cdot \frac{3}{51} = \frac{12}{2,652} = .0045$$

The probability of the first ace is the same with or without replacement because the event begins with 52 cards and four aces. But if the first card drawn is an ace *and it is not replaced,* then for the second draw there are only 51 cards in the deck and only 3 are aces. Close attention must be paid to issues of replacement in compound events. Numerators and denominators are adjusted accordingly. For instance, let us compute the following:

$$p \text{ [ace then king then ace] without replacement} = p \text{ [ace]} \cdot p \text{ [king]} \cdot p \text{ [ace]}$$

$$= \frac{4}{52} \cdot \frac{4}{51} \cdot \frac{3}{50} = \frac{48}{132,600} = .0004$$

Finally, not all compound events involve issues of replacement. For example, replacement is not an issue with coin tossing. The calculated probabilities are the same for "heads then heads" in tossing two coins at once or tossing one coin twice.

The five rules of probability are fundamental; that is, they must be considered in computing the probability of any event, no matter how simple or complicated that event is. The simple examples presented in this chapter illustrate these basic principles. Much more complex formulations of probabilities are presented in advanced texts such as that of Lee and Maykovich (1995). Fortunately for students and scholars today, it is not necessary to have extensive mathematical skills to compute probabilities. Computer software writers require us to learn only which buttons to push or what table to read to obtain the answers to probability questions. A thorough understanding of basic probability theory, however, is necessary to avoid misinterpreting such computer output. Moreover, an understanding of probability theory is essential for acquiring the statistical imagination.

Using the Normal Curve as a Probability Distribution

Proportional Thinking About a Group of Cases and Single Cases
As we noted in Chapter 5, the standard deviation is used to examine the way scores in a distribution are spread out and to compare the spread of two or more samples. We can, however, do much more with the standard deviation. With a single interval/ratio variable *that we have reason to believe is normally distributed in its population,* we can compute standardized scores (Z-scores) and use them to determine the proportion (p) of a population's scores falling between any two scores in the distribution. Since the normal curve has a distinct shape, we can identify and measure areas because the areas represent a proportion of cases.

Recall from Chapter 5 that a Z-score tells us how many standard deviations away from the mean a raw (or X-score) lies:

$$Z_X = \frac{X - \overline{X}}{s_X} = \text{number of standard deviations (SD) from the mean}$$

We noted that roughly 68 percent of the cases in a normally distributed population have X-scores within 1 standard deviation distance to both sides of the mean (i.e., between a Z-score of plus and minus 1). For example, suppose we have the following information where X = height for a sample of men at a health and fitness club:

$$\overline{X} = 69 \text{ inches} \qquad s_X = 3 \text{ inches} \qquad \text{Distribution is normal}$$

Since this distribution is normal, let us draw the normal curve to get a sense of proportion about how many of the men are how tall. Our basic knowledge of the normal curve tells us that roughly 68 percent are between 66 inches and 72 inches, as noted on the curve shown next. Moreover, since the median is located at the mean, we know that half the men are below 69 inches (5 feet, 9 inches) and half are above. And since over 99 percent of a normally distributed population falls within three Z-scores to both sides of the mean, very few are shorter than 60 inches or taller than 78 inches.

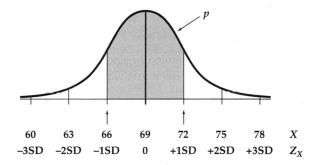

60	63	66	69	72	75	78	X
–3SD	–2SD	–1SD	0	+1SD	+2SD	+3SD	Z_X

Thus,

$$p \text{ [of } X = 66 \text{ to } X = 72] = \text{approximately } 68\%$$

In fact, with the help of a statistical table, we can compute Z-scores and use them to determine any area under the curve. This procedure is called partitioning areas under the normal curve, and we will do some partitioning shortly.

As it turns out, areas under the normal curve represent probabilities of occurrence. Notice that we use the symbol *p* to represent proportions *and* probabilities. Probabilities are proportions of time for which success occurs out of all possible occurrences. Knowing the proportion of success for the population as a whole gives us the probability of success for a single subject. In other words, a specified area under the normal curve provides the probability of occurrence of any single score falling between any two score values.

To illustrate this connection, suppose we are hanging out at the health and fitness club, killing time. To entertain ourselves, we play a whimsical game called "guess the height." The rules of the game are such that when we hear someone approaching from around the corner, we guess his height and then ask him when he appears. If we are within 3 inches of the correct height, we win.

How can we improve our chances of winning? We know that the fitness club members' heights are normally distributed around a mean of 69 inches with a standard deviation of 3 inches. This tells us that about 68 percent of the men are between 66 and 72 inches tall. Let us think probabilistically; that is, let us look at the long run. For every 100 men that approach, 68 will fall in the "success" range:

$$p \text{ [of next man being 66 to 72 inches tall]} = \frac{\text{\# that tall}}{100 \text{ who approach}} = \frac{68}{100} = .6800$$

If we guess 69 inches, our chance of winning, then, is about 68 percent—not bad odds. To get a sense of proportion on this, imagine that the club members are 100 marbles in a box, with green marbles representing those with heights of 66 to 72 inches. There are 68 green marbles, and the probability of randomly drawing one is .6800, or 68 percent.

In a normal distribution of scores, (1) the proportion of cases between two scores, (2) the area under the curve between these two scores, and (3) the probability of randomly selecting a case between these scores *are all the same.* This is why we use p to represent all these ideas. For instance, the symbol p [of $X = 66$ to $X = 72$] can be stated and interpreted in three ways:

1. *A distributional interpretation that describes the result in relation to the distribution of scores in a population or sample.* Thus, roughly .6800 (or 68 percent) of the men in the club are between 66 and 72 inches tall.

2. *A graphical interpretation that describes the proportion of the area under a normal curve* (assuming the distribution is normal in shape). Thus, roughly 68 percent of the area under the normal curve falls between the X-scores of 66 and 72 inches.

3. *A probabilistic interpretation that describes the probability of a single random drawing of a subject from this population.* Thus, if a random member of the club approaches, there is about a .6800 chance that he is between 66 and 72 inches tall.

Three Ways to Interpret the Symbol p

1. A distributional interpretation that describes the result in relation to the distribution of scores in a population or sample.

2. A graphical interpretation that describes the proportion of the area under a normal curve (assuming the distribution is normal in shape).

3. A probabilistic interpretation that describes the probability of a single random drawing of a subject from this population.

These three interpretations are saying the same thing: About 68 percent of the men are between 66 and 72 inches in height. Because of its probabilistic interpretation, the normal curve often is referred to as a probability curve.

These distinctions also highlight an important point about the probabilities of events. Although stated for a single type of "success," any probability is based on the entire distribution of all possible events. A singular event is assessed relative to a larger set of occurrences. This type of proportional thinking is central to grasping the statistical imagination.

Partitioning Areas Under the Normal Curve

To **partition an area under the normal curve** is *to identify part of the curve and compute the proportion (p) of the total curve this part represents*. We use the normal distribution table (Statistical Table B in Appendix B) when we do partitioning. Where do the numbers in this table come from? Statisticians long ago discovered how the occurrences of many natural phenomena fit the bell shape of the normal curve. They worked out the mathematics of this phenomenon and came up with the mean, the standard deviation, and Z-scores. Then they formulated areas or proportions (*p*) under the curve. These areas are fixed and apply to any normally distributed variable because normality is a natural occurrence—just like gravity. The normal curve table provides precisely calculated areas under the curve. One thing must be emphasized here: Such partitioning of areas using the mean, the standard deviation, Z-scores, and the normal distribution curve *works only if we have reason to believe that the scores in a population are normally distributed*. If the distribution of scores is skewed or otherwise oddly shaped, the normal curve table cannot be used in calculations.

---

to partition an area under the normal curve To identify part of the curve and compute the proportion (*p*) of the total curve this part represents.

The normal curve table provides what is needed to calculate exactly how much area is under the curve between any two scores or to the sides of any individual score. Remember that an area under the curve represents a proportion (*p*) of the population between the raw scores corresponding to that section of the curve. These *p*'s are computed to four decimal places. The information in the normal curve table is depicted in Figure 6–3. As is noted in Figure 6–3A, column A of the normal curve table lists Z-scores, where Z_X is the number *of standard deviations* an X-score deviates from the mean. Column A provides only *positive* Z-scores, or those that apply to the right side of the normal curve. But the curve is symmetrical (i.e., the left side is a mirror image of the right side). Therefore, column A can be used with negative Z-scores by simply imagining a negative sign in front of the entries.

Column B of the normal curve table gives the area from the mean out to a Z-score, as depicted in Figure 6–3B. For example, observe in the normal curve table a Z-score of 1.00 in column A. The column B entry is .3413 (about 34 percent). For the fitness club we can state that 34 percent of members are between the heights of 69 and 72 inches.

FIGURE 6–3

Information
provided in the
columns of
the normal
distribution
table (Statistical
Table B in
Appendix B)

A. In column A: Computed Z-scores for one side of the curve or the other

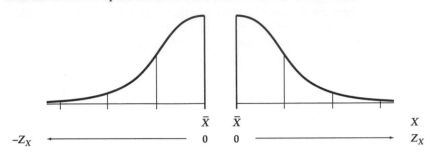

B. In column B: Area under the curve from the mean of X to the Z-score for a value of X

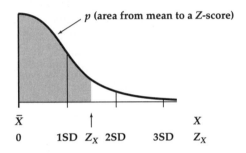

C. In column C: Area under the curve from the Z-score for a value of X and beyond

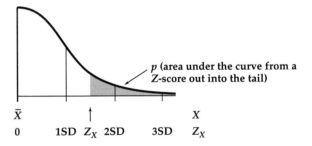

Similarly, we can view this Z-score as -1.00, and again, column B reads .3413, the proportion of members between the heights of 66 and 69 inches. Two times .3413 is .6826,
or about 68 percent—the proportion between 66 and 72 inches—that we noted falls
within 1 standard deviation to both sides of the mean. Similarly, we said that approximately 95 percent of the scores in any normal distribution fall within about 2 standard
deviations of the mean. Actually, 95 percent fall within 1.96 SD (a Z-score) to both sides
of the mean. Start learning how to use the table by finding these Z-scores in column A
and comparing the areas in column B.

Column C of the normal curve table gives the area under the curve from a Z-score and beyond in the "tail" of the curve, as in Figure 6–3C. For example, .1587 (or 15.87 percent) of scores in a normal distribution fall to the right of a Z-score of 1.00 or to the left of a Z-score of -1.00. This is found by looking at a Z-score of 1.00 in column A and then observing the entry .1587 in column C.

We noted earlier that any normally distributed variable has a median equal to the mean. Thus, 50 percent of the scores in any normal distribution fall in either direction from the mean. Since the table provides half the curve, note that for any Z-score, columns B and C sum to .5000, or 50 percent. Finally, keep in mind that Z-scores may be positive or negative, depending on whether a raw score is above or below the mean, respectively. Z-scores can be infinitely large, although in practice they typically fall between about -3.00 and 3.00 because in a normal distribution nearly 100 percent of cases fall within 3 standard deviations to both sides of the mean. The *areas* in columns B and C of the normal curve table, however, are always positive; these areas depict space. Zero space is the smallest amount we can have, and 100 percent space is the largest.

Sample Problems Using the Normal Curve

To show the usefulness of the normal curve table, let us work some sample problems. Keep in mind that partitioning is based on the mean and the standard deviation; therefore, the variable must be interval/ratio. In addition, to use the normal curve table we must be assured that the variable is normally distributed in the population. The distribution cannot be skewed, peaked, flat, bimodal, or otherwise shaped. Normality is best determined by observing the histogram of the variable to identify the distinctive bell shape. However, if the histogram of a variable is made *for a sample* and the score distribution is not perfectly bell-shaped, the variable still could be normally distributed *in the population*. The difference in shape could be due to sampling error. In this text we will not deal with this fine point. We will simply state that we assume that the variable is normally distributed in the population; in shorthand, we "assume normality."

How to Partition Areas Under the Normal Curve

OVERVIEW:

When working with the normal curve there are three essential elements: (*a*) X-scores (raw scores), (*b*) Z-scores (standardized scores), and (*c*) p's (proportions of area taken from the normal curve table, Appendix B, Statistical Table B). If you are given any one of these three elements, you can determine the other two:

If given X, calculate Z and get p from the normal curve table.

If given Z, get p from the normal curve table and calculate X.

If given p, get Z from column A of the normal curve table and calculate X.

1. Make sure your variable is of the interval/ratio level of measurement and that the distribution of scores is assumed to be normal.

2. Calculate the mean and standard deviation of X (if these statistics are not provided in the exercise).

3. Draw the normal curve and mark the location of the mean and 3 standard deviations to either side of it. Label the curve for Z-scores (i.e., -3 SD to $+3$ SD).

4. Label the curve for X-scores. Start by adding the standard deviation to the mean to obtain the X-score that falls 1 standard deviation above the mean.

5. Identify and shade the target area, p, as determined by the exercise. With reference to the normal curve table, determine whether the target area is a column B-type area or column C-type area. The answer sometimes lies in making additional calculations using the figures from column B or C. (See, for example, Problem Types 3, 4, and 6 that follow.)

6. Calculate Z-scores for the X-scores stipulated in the exercise.

7. Refer to the normal curve table for proportions (p) under the curve.

Let us suppose that we have conducted interviews of 500 women who are receiving family assistance support payments. We will refer to these women as assistance recipients. (In common parlance, such women are called welfare mothers, a somewhat politically biased term.) One interest we have in these women is how poverty affects self-esteem, an individual's feeling of "worthiness, adequacy, competence, and likeability" (Ensminger 1995: 351). Suppose we measure self-esteem with a 20-point attitude scale that has an interval level of measurement. The mean self-esteem score is found to be 8 with a standard deviation of 2. A histogram assures us that the distribution is normally shaped. We begin these exercises by taking an inventory of known information, that which is "given" in the problem.

Givens: An interval variable X = self-esteem and its raw scores (not shown).

From these scores we obtain the following statistics:

$$\overline{X} = 8 \text{ self-esteem points} \qquad s_X = 2 \text{ self-esteem points}$$

$$n = 500 \qquad \text{Assume a normal distribution}$$

[*Study Hint: Draw the bell-shaped curve on all problems.* It is a good practice always to draw the normal curve. Mark the mean and 3 standard deviations from it in both directions. Label the curve for X (in this case, self-esteem scores) and for Z-scores. *Remember:* X is a raw score with a unit of measure of self-esteem points, Z_X is a standardized or Z-score with units of measure of standard deviations (SD), and p is a proportion of the area under the curve.]

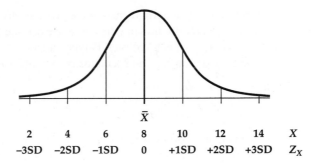

Our basic knowledge of the normal distribution readily tells us the following: (1) 50 percent of the assistance recipients score above 8, and 50 percent score below 8, (2) approximately 68 percent score between 6 and 10 on the self-esteem measure, (3) approximately 95 percent score between 4 and 12, and (4) nearly all—over 99 percent—score between 2 and 14.

We can use the normal curve table to answer several types of questions about the distribution of self-esteem among recipients of family assistance. [*Important Study Hint:* The normal curve table requires Z-scores. When in doubt about how to start a problem, compute Z-scores.]

Problem Type 1: *p* [of Cases from the Mean to an *X*-Score].   Find the proportion (*p*) of cases between the mean and some *X*-score.

Solution Plan: Draw and label the normal curve for the variable *X;* shade the target area (*p*) from the mean out to the specified *X*-score; compute the Z-score for that *X*-score; locate the Z-score in column A of the normal curve table; get *p* from column B; report the answer in everyday terms.

Illustration: Where *X* = self-esteem score, what percentage of assistance recipients have self-esteem scores between 5 and 8?

Identify this target area, *p*.

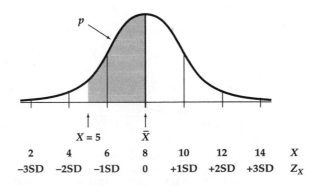

Column B in the normal curve table provides areas under the curve from the mean out to any Z-score. By drawing the curve, we can see that the target area (p) is bordered by the mean; thus, p is a "column B-type" area.

The next step in solving problems is to transform a raw score into a Z-score:

$$Z_X = \frac{X - \bar{X}}{s_X} = \frac{5 - 8}{2} = \frac{-3}{2} = -1.50 \text{ SD}$$

Remember that a Z-score is just another way to express a raw score. An assistance recipient scoring 5 on self-esteem falls 1.50 SD *below* the mean, the *negative* Z-score of −1.50; she is among those with rather low self-esteem. In column A of the normal curve table, find 1.5 and treat it as −1.5. Look in column B and report the answer as follows:

$$p \ [\text{of } X = 5 \text{ to } X = 8] = .4332 \qquad \% = p \ (100) = 43.32\%$$

Finally, answer the question in everyday terms: A little over 43 percent of assistance recipients scored between 5 and 8 on the self-esteem measure. (This is a distributional interpretation describing the result in relation to the distribution of scores of the population of recipients of family assistance.) If a randomly selected name is chosen from the case files, there is about a 43 percent chance that this person will score between 5 and 8 on the self-esteem measure. (This is a probabilistic interpretation, the probability of a single randomly drawn assistance recipient falling in the targeted area.) We compute percentages and substitute the term *chance* for *probability* for clarity of expression to a public audience.

Problem Type 2: *p* [of Cases Greater Than an *X*-Score].   Find the proportion (p) of cases greater than a specified X-score.

Solution Plan: Draw and label the normal curve for the variable X; shade the target area (p) from the X-score out into the tail in *the positive or "greater than" direction;* compute the Z-score and locate it in column A; get p from column C.

Illustration: Where X = self-esteem score, what proportion of the assistance recipients score at or above 13 on the self-esteem scale?

Shade the target area, p:

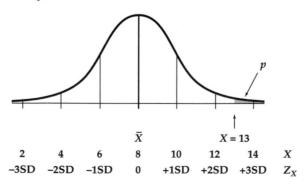

			$\bar{X}$		X = 13		
2	4	6	8	10	12	14	X
−3SD	−2SD	−1SD	0	+1SD	+2SD	+3SD	Z_X

Compute the Z-score for $X = 13$:

$$Z_X = \frac{X - \overline{X}}{s_X} = \frac{13 - 8}{2} = \frac{5}{2} = 2.50 \text{ SD}$$

Find 2.50 in column A of the normal curve table. Look in column C and report the proportion of area greater than or equal to 13 as follows:

$$p \ [\text{of } X \geq 13] = .0062$$

Answer the question in everyday terms: Only 62 of every 10,000 assistance recipients score 13 or above on the self-esteem scale. (In a sample of 500 this would be about 3 persons.) Very few assistance recipients have extremely high self-esteem. If a randomly selected name were chosen from case files, there would be less than a 1 percent chance that this person scored above 13.

Problem Type 3: p [of Cases Between Two X-Scores on Different Sides of the Mean]. Find the proportion of cases between two X-scores, one below the mean and one above the mean.

Solution Plan: Draw and label the normal curve; shade the target area (p) from one X-score to the other; compute the Z-scores for the two X-scores; locate them in column A of the normal curve table; get areas PA and PB (drawn below) from column B; compute the area (p), which will be the sum of PA and PB.

Illustration: Where $X = $ self-esteem score, what proportion of the assistance recipients score between 4 and 10 on the self-esteem scale? (*Study Hint:* Only by drawing the curve can we readily see that this problem involves two areas that adjoin the mean: two column B-type areas.)

Shade the target area, p:

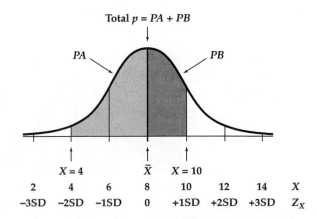

Compute the Z-scores for $X = 4$ and $X = 10$:

$$Z_X = \frac{X - \bar{X}}{s_X} = \frac{4 - 8}{2} = \frac{-4}{2} = -2.00 \text{ SD}$$

$$Z_X = \frac{X - \bar{X}}{s_X} = \frac{10 - 8}{2} = \frac{2}{2} = 1.00 \text{ SD}$$

Now use the normal curve table. In column A find each of the two Z-scores. Look in column B to get areas PA and PB and report the answer as follows:

$$PA = p \ [\text{of } X = 4 \text{ to } X = 8] = .4772$$
$$PB = p \ [\text{of } X = 8 \text{ to } X = 10] = .3413$$
$$p \ [\text{of } X = 4 \text{ to } X = 10] = PA + PB = .4772 + .3413 = .8185$$
$$\% = p(100) = 81.85\%$$

Answer the question in everyday terms: About 82 percent of assistance recipients have self-esteem scores between 4 and 10. If a randomly selected name is chosen from the case files, there is an 82 percent chance that this person will have a self-esteem score between 4 and 10.

Problem Type 4: p[of Cases Between Two X-Scores on One Side of the Mean]. Find the proportion (p) of cases between two X-scores *on one side* of the mean.

Solution Plan: Draw and label the curve; shade the target area (p) from one X-score to the other; compute the Z-scores and locate them in column A of the normal curve table; get areas PA and PB from column B; compute the area p, which is PA minus PB.

Illustration: What proportion of the assistance recipients scored between 11 and 13 on the self-esteem scale? In the sample of 500, *how many* assistance recipients is this? (*Study Hint:* By drawing the curve, we see that the target area p does not touch the mean. Therefore, it is *not* a column B-type area in the normal curve table; neither is it a tail-shaped, column C-type area. Thus, to solve this illustration, we must compute p indirectly.)

Shade the target area p:

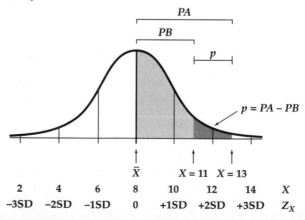

Compute the Z-scores for $X = 13$ and $X = 11$:

$$Z_X = \frac{X - \overline{X}}{s_X} = \frac{13 - 8}{2} = \frac{5}{2} = 2.50 \text{ SD}$$

$$Z_X = \frac{X - \overline{X}}{s_X} = \frac{11 - 8}{2} = \frac{3}{2} = 1.50 \text{ SD}$$

In column A find each of the two Z-scores. Look in column B to get areas *PA* and *PB* and report the answer as follows:

$$PA = p \text{ [of } X = 8 \text{ to } X = 13] = .4938$$
$$PB = p \text{ [of } X = 8 \text{ to } X = 11] = .4332$$
$$p \text{ [of } X = 11 \text{ to } X = 13] = PA - PB = .4938 - .4332 = .0606$$
$$\% = p(100) = 6.06\%$$

[*Study Hint:* Subtract *p*'s (i.e., areas under the curve), not Z-scores.]
To determine how many of the 500 assistance recipients score in this range, take the proportion of the sample size *n* as follows:

Computing the Number of Sample Cases Corresponding to an Area

$$\# = p\ (n)$$

where

   $\#$ = number of cases in the sample for the designated area, p

   p = proportion of area under the curve

   n = sample size

The number of assistance recipients scoring between 11 and 13 on the self-esteem scale is

$$\# = p\ (n) = .0606\ (500) = 30.3 = 30 \text{ recipients}$$

Finally, answer these questions in everyday terms: Only 6 percent of assistance recipients have self-esteem scores between 11 and 13. This is only 30 of the 500 assistance recipients. If a randomly selected name were chosen from the case files, there would be only a 6 percent chance that this person would score between 11 and 13.

Problem Type 5: *p* [of Cases Less Than an *X*-Score That Is Less Than the Mean].
Find the proportion (*p*) of cases less than or equal to a specified *X*-score that is less than the mean.

Solution Plan: Draw and label the normal curve; shade the target area (*p*) from the X-score out into the tail *in the negative direction;* compute the Z-score and locate it in column A of the normal curve table; get *p* from column C.

Illustration: If a randomly selected name were chosen from the case files, what is the probability that this assistance recipient would score at or below 6.5 on the self-esteem scale?

Shade the target area *p*:

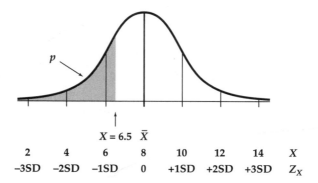

X = 6.5 $\overline{X}$

2	4	6	8	10	12	14	X
–3SD	–2SD	–1SD	0	+1SD	+2SD	+3SD	Z_X

Compute the Z-score for X = 6.5:

$$Z_X = \frac{X - \overline{X}}{s_X} = \frac{6.5 - 8}{2} = \frac{-1.5}{2} = -.75 \text{ SD}$$

In column A of the normal curve table, find .75 and treat it as though it were −.75. Look in column C and report the answer as follows:

$$p \,[\text{of } X \leq 6.5] = .2266$$
$$\% = p(100) = 22.66\%$$

Answer the question in everyday terms: The probability that a randomly selected assistance recipient scored at or below 6.5 on the self-esteem scale is about 23 percent.

Problem Type 6: *p* [of Cases Less Than an *X*-Score That Is Greater Than the Mean].
Find the proportion (*p*) of cases *less than* a specified X-score that is *greater than* the mean.

Solution Plan: Draw the curve; shade the target area (*p*); compute the Z-score and locate it in column A; get *p* from column B and add .5000.

Illustration: Where X = self-esteem score, what is the probability (*p*) that a randomly selected assistance recipient scores at or below 10.5 on the self-esteem scale?

[*Study Hint:* Remember that the normal curve table gives areas only for one side of the curve. Remember also that a normal curve has a median equal to the mean; therefore, half (or a proportion of .5000) of the scores fall below the mean. This illustration is solved by working with the area above the mean and then adding the area below the mean. (Incidentally, to find the proportion, *p*, of cases *more than* a specified *X*-score which is *less than* the mean, work from the left side over. Calculate the area below the mean and then add it to .5000, which is the area above the mean.)]

Shade the target area *p:*

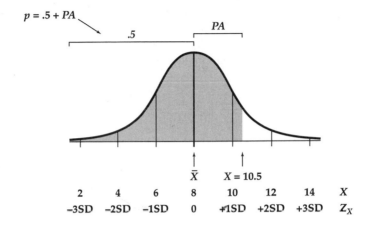

Compute the *Z*-score for $X = 10.5$

$$Z_X = \frac{X - \overline{X}}{s_X} = \frac{10.5 - 8}{2} = \frac{2.5}{2} = 1.25 \text{ SD}$$

In column A of the normal curve table, find 1.25. Look in column B and report the answer as follows:

$$PA = p \text{ [of } X = 8 \text{ to } X = 10.5] = .3944$$
$$p \text{ [of } X \le 10.5] = PA + .5000 = .3944 + .5000 = .8944$$

Answer the question in everyday terms: The probability that a randomly selected assistance recipient scored at or below 10.5 on the self-esteem scale is over 89 percent.

Problem Type 7: Find the X-Score That Has a Specified *p* [of Cases] Above or Below It.
Find the value of a raw score *X* for which a specified percentage of the sample or population falls above or below that value.

Solution Plan: Whereas the previous problem types provided an *X*-score and asked for an area (*p*), this problem provides information on *p* and asks for an *X*-score. Draw and label the normal curve; *roughly* identify and shade the target area *p;* find this area in column B or column C of the normal curve table, whichever column is apparently appropriate from the drawing; read column A to get the *Z*-score; solve for *X* as follows:

$$Z_X = \frac{X - \overline{X}}{s_X}, \qquad \text{thus, } X = \overline{X} + (s_X)(Z_X)$$

Illustration: The Department of Mental Health has a program designed to ward off episodes of acute psychological depression by building the self-esteem (X) of assistance recipients. The program has funding for only 50 people among the 500 who were measured for self-esteem. Let us choose the 50 with the lowest self-esteem because they are presumably at the greatest risk of depression. What is the highest self-esteem score a recipient can have to qualify for the program?

To identify the target area, p, we compute the proportion of assistance recipients who are to qualify:

$$p \, [\text{qualifying for program}] = \frac{\# \, \text{qualifying}}{n} = \frac{50}{500} = .1000$$

In drawing the target area, keep in mind that it will be a tail in the *negative* direction of scores because we are looking for the *lowest* 50 assistance recipients. Note that the target area is a column C-type area.

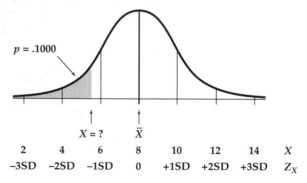

[*Study Hint:* At this point, estimate the answer from the graph. Our marking of the position of X should be close. We know by now that only 15.87 percent of cases fall below -1 SD, and so the 10 percent mark must be just below that. Thus, our X-score should be slightly below 6. Estimating the answer in this fashion not only encourages proportional thinking but also provides a warning if our calculated answer is incorrect.]

Now use the normal curve table. In column C find .1000 or the nearest amount to it, in this case, .1003. Look in column A to find the corresponding Z-score of -1.28 and solve for X:

$$X = \overline{X} + (s_X)(Z_X) = 8 + (2)(-1.28) = 8 - 2.56 = 5.44 \text{ self-esteem points}$$

Answer the question in everyday terms: Those assistance recipients who score less than or equal to 5.44 on the self-esteem scale fall in the lowest 10 percent and therefore qualify for the depression-avoidance program.

Study Hint: Problem Type 7 shows that as long as we know the mean and the standard deviation of a distribution and can assume that the distribution of scores in the population is normally shaped, only one additional piece of information is needed to solve any problem. This piece of information can be a raw X-score, a standardized Z-score, or an area under the normal curve (p).

Thus:

* If given an X-score, compute Z_X and use the normal curve table to get p.
* If given a Z-score, use the normal curve table to get p or solve for X, where $X = \overline{X} + (s_X)(Z_X)$.
* If given a percentage or area, p, use the normal curve table to get the corresponding Z-score and solve for X, where $X = \overline{X} + (s_X)(Z_X)$.

Computing Percentiles for Normally Distributed Populations

Normal curve Problem Types 5, 6, and 7 deal with areas under the curve that are below a particular raw score X. These areas define **percentile ranks**, *the percentage of a sample or population that falls at or below a specified value of a variable* (see Chapter 2). For example, with regard to Problem Type 6, someone who scored 10.5 on the self-esteem scale scored higher than did 89 percent of the assistance recipients in the sample—a percentile rank of 89. When a variable is normally distributed, we can use the normal curve table to quickly compute percentile ranks.

Many distributions, especially achievement, intelligence, and school admissions tests, are especially designed to produce a score distribution that is normally distributed. We all remember receiving percentile ranks in addition to the raw scores for such tests. The companies that distribute the tests intentionally "normalized" them so that score distributions fit the normal curve. Once this normalization is accomplished, the normal curve table is used to generate percentile ranks.

One commonly used standardized test is the Stanford-Binet Intelligence Scale. (For an overview, see http://www.chclibrary.org/micromed/00066170.html). This test is designed to assess cognitive development in children. Normal level of development is the mean test score of 100 scale points. Let us assume that the distribution of scores is normal and that the standard deviation is 16 scale points.

Illustration: Stanley Jones scored 120 on the Stanford-Binet Intelligence Scale. What is his percentile rank on the scale? That is, what percentage of test takers did he score equal to or better than?

Shade the target area p:

$p = .5 + PA = .8944$, the 89th percentile

			$\overline{X}$	$X = 120$			
52	68	84	100	116	132	148	X
–3SD	–2SD	–1SD	0	+1SD	+2SD	+3SD	Z_X

Compute the Z-score for $X = 120$:

$$Z_X = \frac{X - \bar{X}}{s_X} = \frac{120 - 100}{16} = \frac{20}{16} = 1.25 \text{ SD}$$

In column A of the normal curve table, find 1.25. Look in column B and report the answer as follows:

$$PA = p \text{ [of } X = 100 \text{ to } X = 120] = .3944$$
$$p \text{ [of } X \leq 120] = PA + .5000 = .3944 + .5000 = .8944$$

Answer the question in everyday terms: Stanley Jones's percentile rank on the Stanford-Binet Scale is 89.

In using the normal curve to calculate percentile ranks, when an X-score is greater than the mean, we will find a column B-type area like PA above and add it to .5000. This is a Problem Type 6 calculation. However, if an X-score is less than the mean, we will calculate the negative Z-score and look in column C of the normal curve table. This is a Problem Type 5 calculation. Using these two problem types, we can readily make the calculations for a series of Stanford-Binet scores. This is illustrated in Table 6–1. For practice, calculate these percentile ranks. Notice that the reported percentile ranks are rounded for simplicity, but they are rounded down in every case. A percentile rank states the percentage of a sample or population that falls "at or below a specified value." A score rounded up would not be correct. For example, the person in Table 6–2 who scored 126 on the Stanford-Binet could *not* say that he or she scored equal to 95% of those who took the test. Thus, a Stanford-Binet score of 126 is at the 94th percentile.

Finally, we should mention that percentile ranks can be determined for distributions that are not normally distributed. All that is necessary to compute any percentile is to determine what percentage of a distribution falls below a specified X-score. Most

TABLE 6–1 I Using the normal curve to obtain percentile ranks

Givens		Calculations		
Stanford-Binet Score	Z-score	From Column C Problem Type 5	.5000 + Column B Problem Type 6	Percentile Rank
68	−2.00	.0228	—	2nd
80	−1.25	.1056	—	10th
90	−.62	.2672	—	26th
100	0.00	.5000	—	50th
108	.50	—	.6915	69th
126	1.62	—	.9474	94th
133	2.06	—	.9803	98th

TABLE 6–2 | Comparing raw scores (X), Z-scores, and percentile ranks to gain a sense of proportion about normally distributed variables

Givens		Calculations	
Student	**X**	**Z_X**	**Percentile Rank**
Ronald	24	0	50
Barry	28	1	84
Sophia	32	2	98

computer programs provide this information as the "cumulative percentage" of a distribution (see Chapter 2).

The Normal Curve as a Tool for Proportional Thinking

Once we have gotten over learning the details of chopping the normal curve into areas, we should begin to truly appreciate its usefulness. As a descriptive tool, normalizing score distributions on tests is done because experience has shown that intelligence, learning, and achievement are normally distributed; that is, most people are about average in intelligence and achievement, and this is why the normal curve "bells up" in the middle. Very few people are geniuses and very few are extremely below normal, and this is why the curve begins to hug the horizontal axis as we observe scores more than 1 standard deviation from the mean in either direction.

Working with the normal curve also makes us more cautious in the interpretation of data. We are now aware, for example, that scores from different tests (such as the ACT and SAT) can be compared by looking at the relative positions of scores within their own distributions; a simple way to do this is to compare percentile ranks.

After working with the normal distribution, we become aware that equal differences between scores do not always indicate that one score is just as far away from another in terms of how unusual it is. For example, suppose the 2,000 entering first-year students at State University had a mean ACT score (X) of 24 with a standard deviation of 4 and the distribution was normally shaped. Ronald made a 24, Barry made a 28, and Sophia made a 32. Observation of the raw scores suggest that Barry falls precisely between Ronald and Sophia in their ranks on these scores. Our sense of a normal distribution should convince us, however, that Barry is considerably above average although his score of 28 is only 4 points better than a 24. This is apparent when the raw scores (X), standardized scores (Z_X), and percentile ranks are compared, as they are in Table 6–2.

This illustrates the importance of knowing how a distribution of scores is spread. Barry is only 4 points better than Ronald on the raw score, but he is 34 percentage points better in terms of percentile rank. Barry, like Sophia, scored better than the great majority of entering students. Raw scores by themselves suggest otherwise and can be very misleading. The standard deviation as a unit of measure with normal distributions is a powerful tool for gaining accurate insight into the significance of a raw score.

The phenomenon of normality is the essence of statistical analysis. It is very important that we learn how to roam about the normal curve and develop the skills to partition areas under it. A quick look through the remainder of this text should convince you of the importance of mastering the problems in this chapter. Nearly every chapter after this one has depictions of the normal curve or similar curves. Because it so handily provides probabilities, the normal curve distribution and predictable curves similar to it are called probability distributions. As we shall see in Chapter 7, sampling events have predictable patterns of occurrence, and their probability curves are used to determine how usual or unusual a sampling event is. Probabilities in general and the normal probability distribution in particular are key elements in statistical analysis.

Finally, an interesting thought quiz about probabilities involves the matter of low-occurrence events. Any natural or human event has *some* probability of occurring. Occasionally, for instance, someone is struck by a meteorite. Most of us, however, do not check the sky constantly for these objects. We understand probabilities and know that "you just have to be really unlucky" for this to happen to you. Similarly, 40 million people enter a lottery. One person wins. He or she is very lucky! It snows in Florida once every five years, but it happens to snow on your wedding day. You are very unlucky! In terms of the ideas of probability theory, what does it mean to say someone is very lucky or unlucky? What is luck?

Statistical Follies and Fallacies: The Gambler's Fallacy: Independence of Probability Events

Imagine that Bob and Terri are gambling by playing a coin-tossing game. Bob wins with heads, and Terri wins with tails. They take turns deciding how much the next flip will be worth, choosing an amount from 5 cents to 25 cents. Bob just won three flips in a row at 10 cents a flip. Should Terri increase the bet to 25 cents for the next toss? Does the fact that heads fell three times in a row increase the chances that tails will come up next?

The answer is no. A common statistical mistake in computing probabilities involves the independence of the parts of compound events. Each coin is flipped independently of what happened to it in previous flips. If we flip a coin twice and get heads both times, this does not increase the probability of a third flip coming up tails. That probability remains .5000.

This tendency to imagine that independent events are tied together is one type of gambler's fallacy. When a gambler hits a streak of bad luck, he or she may start to believe that a streak of good luck must follow. In the long run, indeed, good and bad luck balance out. But what is the long run? Is it 3 tosses, 10 tosses, 1 million tosses? For a given gambler, is the long run longer than his or her money will hold out? Moreover, the balance between good and bad luck occurs among all gamblers, not within a single gambler. Thus, if 100 couples were playing this coin-tossing game, over the course of an evening, chances are great that about as many heads will be tossed as tails. But Bob and Terri may end up tossing more heads, while Joe and Maggie may toss more tails.

To assume that coin tosses are linked is to think mistakenly that we know the length of a "series," a sequence of tosses over the long run. Unfortunately, there are an infinite number of possible sequences, because each toss is independent of the next. For example, Bob's three heads in a row could be part of any of the following series in which heads and tails fall an equal number of times:

*T, T, **H, H, H**, T, H, H, T, T*

*T, T, T, T, H, T, **H, H, H**, H, H, T*

*H, T, H, T, T, H, T, T, T, H, H, T, **H, H, H**, T*

***H, H, H**, H, T, T, H, H, T, T, T, H, T, T, H, T, H, T, T, H*

For a gambler to assume that he or she somehow knows the future sequence of outcomes is to assume that the future can be seen to a greater extent than what the basic probabilities of occurrence tell us. This obviously is not a sensible way to gamble.

SUMMARY

1. Probability theory is the analysis and understanding of chance occurrences. In the field of statistics, probability theory is used to calculate statistical error.

2. A probability is a specification of how frequently a particular event of interest is likely to occur over a large number of trials (i.e., situations in which the event can occur).

3. The probability of success (P) is the probability of an event of interest occurring. The probability of failure (Q) is the probability of an event of interest *not* occurring. $P + Q = 1$.

4. There are five basic rules of probability.

5. The normal curve is a probability distribution for an interval/ratio variable that is normally distributed. Areas under the normal curve can be partitioned, where Z-scores and the normal curve table are used to compute proportions of a population's scores falling between any two scores in the distribution or beyond any score in its tails. The area under the curve is symbolized as p, because it may be interpreted as a probability.

6. For a normal distribution, there are three ways to interpret p: (1) a distributional interpretation that describes the result in relation to the distribution of scores in a population or sample; (2) a graphical interpretation that describes the proportion of the area under a normal curve; and (3) a probabilistic interpretation that describes the probability of a single random drawing of a subject from this population.

7. If a distribution of interval/ratio scores is normal in shape, then the normal curve and Z-scores can be used to quickly calculate percentile ranks.

CHAPTER EXTENSIONS ON *THE STATISTICAL IMAGINATION* WEB SITE

Chapter 6 Extensions of text material available on *The Statistical Imagination* Web site at www.mhhe.com/ritchey2 include how to calculate probabilities for common games of chance and skill, such as Texas Hold 'Em poker.

FORMULAS AND RULES OF PROBABILITY IN CHAPTER 6

Calculating a probability:

$$p \text{ [of success]} = \frac{\text{\# successes}}{\text{\# trials}} = \frac{\text{\# possible successful outcomes}}{\text{total \# possible outcomes}}$$

Calculating a *Z*-score:

$$Z_X = \frac{X - \overline{X}}{s_X}$$

Calculating a raw score (X) when Z_X is known:

$$X = \overline{X} + (s_X)(Z_X)$$

Computing the number of cases that correspond to an area under the normal curve:

$$\# = p(n)$$

Basic Rules of Probability Theory

1. Probability rule 1: Probabilities always range between 0 and 1.
2. Probability rule 2: The addition rule for alternative events: The probability of alternative events is equal to the sum of the probabilities of the individual events.
3. Probability rule 3: Adjust for joint occurrences, events that double-count success or join two aspects of success.
4. Probability rule 4: The multiplication rule for compound events: The probability of a compound event is equal to the multiple of the probabilities of the separate parts of the event.
5. Probability rule 5: Account for replacement with compound events.

QUESTIONS FOR CHAPTER 6

1. What is probability theory?

2. Name three recent actions in your everyday life where you used probability theory (even though you did not calculate actual probabilities).

3. What does the denominator of a probability formula typically denote?

4. What does the numerator of a probability formula typically denote?

5. If someone reports a probability of 150 percent, what rule of probability has been broken?

6. Name two events that have a 100 percent probability of occurrence.

7. Name two events that have a 0 percent probability of occurrence.

8. State the addition rule of probability and specify when it is used. Give an example.

9. State the multiplication rule of probability and specify when it is used. Give an example.

10. When calculating a probability, an event that double-counts success or joins two aspects of success is called a _____.

11. For a proportion of cases fitting success, what distinguishes a distributional interpretation from a probabilistic interpretation? Illustrate with an example.

12. The mean, standard deviation, and normal curve are used most appropriately with variables of what levels of measurement?

13. Why is it appropriate to use the same symbol, p, for proportion, probability, and area under a normal curve?

14. When a score of a normally distributed variable is to the right of the mean, it is in the _____ direction.

15. Explain why it is inappropriate to use Z-scores and the normal curve table for any distribution of scores that is not normally shaped.

16. What information does a percentile rank provide?

17. Explain what it means to be very lucky or very unlucky.

EXERCISES FOR CHAPTER 6

Problem Set 6A

6A-1. Compute the following probabilities for the roll of one gaming die:
   - *a.* p [6]
   - *b.* p [2 or 4]
   - *c.* p [2 then 3 then 4]

6A-2. Suppose you have a box of well-stirred dry beans: 150 red, 70 white, and 80 black. Compute the probabilities of randomly drawing the following from this box.
  a.   *p* [white then red then black] without replacement
  b.   *p* [red then red then black] with replacement
  c.   *p* [white then black then white] with replacement of blacks only

6A-3. For the toss of one coin (*H* = heads, *T* = tails), compute the following.
  a.   *p* [*H*]
  b.   *p* [*T* then *T*]
  c.   *p* [*T* then *H* then *H*]

6A-4. Compute the following probabilities for drawing cards from a standard deck of 52 playing cards.
  a.   *p* [10]
  b.   *p* [7 or king]
  c.   *p* [jack or diamond]
  d.   *p* [king then king, or ace then ace] without replacement

6A-5. Steelman, Powell, and Carini (2000) explored the relationship between teacher unions and student educational performance as measured by standardized tests, such as the American College Testing exam (ACT). Use the ACT statistics shown here to answer the following questions. The distribution is normally shaped. Draw the normal curve and label all target areas. Set *X* = ACT score.

$$\overline{X} = 22 \text{ ACT points}$$
$$s_X = 2 \text{ ACT points}$$
$$n = 441,574 \text{ students}$$

  a.   What proportion of students scored *above* 26?
  b.   What number of students who took the ACT scored *between* 17 and 19?
  c.   What proportion of the scores fell *between* 18 and 23?
  d.   Determine the score below which 90 percent of the scores fell.
  e.   If an applicant had to make at least the 90th percentile rank to get into a college program, what score would he or she need to achieve (short answer)?

6A-6. Lynch, Maciejewski, and Potenza (2004) examined the relationship between various psychiatric conditions and gambling behavior in adolescents and young adults. To replicate their results, you obtain data from a sample of young adults with a mean age of 22 years and a standard deviation of 2 years. Ages in this population are normally distributed. You are to randomly select an individual from this population. Compute the following probabilities. Draw the normal curve for each problem. Set *X* = age.
  a.   *p* [of randomly drawing someone between the ages of 20 and 24]
  b.   *p* [of randomly drawing someone "19 years old or younger" or "25 years old or older"]

      c.   If the youngest 10 percent of the population of young adults are to be mailed a letter, to what ages will the letters be targeted?

6A-7.   Bastiaens (2004) examined patient responses to antidepressant treatment in a community mental health clinic. The Center for Epidemiologic Studies Depression Scale (CESD) is used to assess the severity of depressive symptoms. Assume that you have normally distributed CESD scores for some mental health patients. The mean CESD score is 27.2 scale points and the standard deviation is 3.2. You are interested in isolating extremely low and high CESD scores for these patients, those that fall outside the middle 95 percent (or .95) of scores. These areas will fall in the tails of the normal curve with 2.5 percent (or .025) in each tail. Set X = CESD score.

      a.   Draw and label the normal curve. Use the normal curve table to identify the Z-score that isolates a proportion of .025 of the area in each tail.

      b.   Determine the CESD scores (i.e., X-scores) that define the extremes outside the middle 95 percent area. Interpret your answer in everyday language.

6A-8.   One commonly used standardized test is the Stanford-Binet Intelligence Scale (Hollinger and Baldwin 1990). This test is designed to assess cognitive development in children. The test is "normalized," designed so that scores fall in a normal distribution around a mean of 100 scale points with a standard deviation of 13 scale points. Set X = Stanford-Binet Intelligence score.

      a.   Suppose that one test taker, Jack McGinley, scored a 130 on the Stanford-Binet Intelligence Scale. What is Jack's percentile rank on the scale? That is, Jack's score was equal to or higher than what percentage of test takers?

      b.   Bob Harris scored 89 on the Stanford-Binet Intelligence Scale. What is his percentile rank?

Problem Set 6B

6B-1.   Compute the following probabilities for the roll of one gaming die:

      a. p [5]

      b. p [5 then 6]

      c. p [1 or 3 or 6]

6B-2.   Suppose you have a box of 100 red marbles, 50 blue marbles, and 50 green marbles. Compute the probabilities of randomly drawing the following from the box:

      a. p [red then red then green] without replacement

      b. p [red then red then green] with replacement

      c. p [blue then red then green] with replacement of reds only

6B-3.   For the toss of one coin (H = heads, T = tails), compute the following:

      a. p [T]

      b. p [H then T]

      c. p [T then T then T]

6B-4. Compute the following probabilities for drawing cards from a standard deck of 52 playing cards.

    a. p [ace]

    b. p [king or jack]

    c. p [queen or spade]

    d. p [ace then ace, or king then king] without replacement

6B-5. Gardner, Van Dyne, and Pierce (2004) examined the motivational effects of pay level on employee performance. Suppose that we have the following descriptive statistics for job performance scores, where a high score indicates good work. Use these data to answer the following questions. The distribution is normal. Draw the normal curve and label all target areas. Set Y = job performance score.

$$\bar{Y} = 78 \text{ points}$$

$$s_Y = 8 \text{ points}$$

$$n = 473 \text{ employees}$$

    a. What proportion of employees scored *above* 90 on job performance?

    b. How many of the employees scored *between* 88 and 98?

    c. What proportion of the scores fell *between* 70 and 90?

    d. Determine the score below which 95 percent of the scores fell.

    e. If an applicant had to make at least the 95th percentile rank to obtain bonus pay, what score would he or she need to make (short answer)?

6B-6. For a large homeless population, Wong and Piliavin (2001) examined stressors, resources, and psychological distress using the Center for Epidemiological Studies Depression Scale (CESD), a community screening questionnaire. Among homeless persons, the mean CESD score is 23.5 with a standard deviation of 7.5 and the distribution is normal. As an intake worker at a homeless shelter, you wish to apply their research. When new clients arrive, you administer the CESD. Answer the following questions. Draw a normal curve with each solution. Set X = CESD score.

    a. Any client scoring 16 or higher is to be sent to a doctor. What is the probability that your next client will be sent to a doctor?

    b. What is the probability that your next client will score 10 or below?

    c. If those homeless scoring in the highest 15 percent on the CESD are to be targeted for suicide prevention services, what score qualifies a client for these services?

6B-7. He and Sutton (2004) evaluated a proposed method for tracking the prevalence of childhood obesity in Canada. Suppose you have a sample of children that you wish to track on the basis of body mass index (BMI), which measures weight relative to height. The mean BMI of your sample is 26.8 kilograms (kg) per meters squared and the standard deviation is 1.9 kg per meters squared. Those children who are in the top 5 percent for BMI are to be sent to a special program. Set X = BMI score.

a.   Draw and label the normal curve. Use the normal curve table to identify the Z-score that isolates .05 of the area in the positive end of the curve.

b.   Determine what BMI score (i.e., X-score) isolates the top 5 percent of the children. Interpret your answer in everyday language.

6B-8.   The American College Testing (ACT) examination is the most widely accepted college entrance exam. This test assesses students' abilities over four distinct skill areas. For this exercise, assume that this distribution of ACT scores is normal with a mean of 22 points and a standard deviation of 4 points. Draw the normal curve. Set X = ACT score.

a.   Jennifer O'Neal scored 31 on the test. What is her percentile rank? That is, Jennifer's score is equal to or higher than what percentage of test takers?

b.   Carl Lane scored 19 on the ACT test. What is his percentile rank?

Problem Set 6C

6C-1.   Compute the following probabilities for the roll of one gaming die.

a. p [2]

b. p [1 or 5]

c. p [2 then 5 then 6]

6C-2.   Suppose you have a large, well-mixed barrel of 70 black balls, 200 blue balls, and 120 red balls. Compute the probabilities of randomly drawing the following from the barrel:

a. p [black then black then red] without replacement

b. p [blue then red then black] with replacement

c. p [blue then red then blue] with replacement of reds only

6C-3.   For the toss of one coin (H = heads, T = tails), compute the following.

a. p [H]

b. p [H then H]

c. p [H then T then T]

6C-4.   Compute the following probabilities for drawing cards from a standard deck of 52 playing cards.

a. p [4]

b. p [9 or jack]

c. p [queen or club]

d. p [jack then jack, or 8 then 8] without replacement

6C-5.   The Scholastic Aptitude Test (SAT) is a college entrance exam. Although Freedle (2003) argues that the test is culturally and statistically biased against some minority groups, it is still widely used. Suppose that the following descriptive statistics correspond to a sample of students who took the SAT. The distribution is normally shaped. Draw the normal curve and label all target areas. Set Y = SAT score.

$$\bar{Y} = 1{,}100 \text{ SAT points}$$
$$s_Y = 100 \text{ SAT points}$$
$$n = 322{,}763 \text{ students}$$

a.   What proportion of students scored *above* 1,300?
b.   How many students scored *below* 1,080?
c.   What proportion of the scores fell *between* 900 and 1,150?
d.   Determine the score below which 85 percent of the scores fell.
e.   If an applicant had to make at least the 85th percentile rank to get into a college program, what score would he or she need to achieve (short answer)?

6C-6.   Browning, Leventhal, and Brooks-Gunn (2004) examined the impact of neighborhood context and race on initiation of sexual activity among young adolescents. Assume that you have a population of young adolescents with a mean age of 13 years and a standard deviation of 1 year. Ages in this population are normally distributed. You are to randomly select individuals from this population. Compute the following probabilities and draw the normal curve for each problem. Set X = age.
a. p [of randomly drawing someone between the ages of 12 and 14]
b. p [of randomly drawing someone "11.5 years or younger" or "14.5 years or older"]
c.   The youngest 10 percent of the adolescents are to be selected for follow-up interviews. What age and below will qualify a subject for this interview?

6C-7.   Egan and Kadushin (2004) examined job satisfaction among home health social workers within the environment of the Medicare interim payment system. You use a similar job satisfaction scale (ranging from 0 to 36) for another sample of home health workers. Your sample mean is 23.6 job satisfaction scale points and the standard deviation is 2.3. The distribution is normal. You are to isolate a total of 5 percent of scores, the 2.5 percent that are extremely low and the 2.5 percent that are extremely high. Set X = job satisfaction scale.
a.   Draw and label the normal curve. Use the normal curve table to identify the Z-scores that isolate the proportion of respondents scoring in the top and bottom 2.5 percent.
b.   Determine the two satisfaction scale scores (i.e., X-scores) for the top 2.5 percent and bottom 2.5 percent of workers. Interpret your answer in everyday language.

6C-8.   The Scholastic Assessment Test (SAT) is a college admissions exam that assesses verbal and quantitative abilities. Ram (2004) used the SAT to study

the effects of school expenditures on student achievement in the
United States. SAT scores are normally distributed with a mean of
1,100 points and a standard deviation of 150. Set X = SAT score.

a. Brian Fitzsimmons scored 1,420 on the test. What is his percentile rank?
   That is, Brian's score is equal to or higher than what percentage of test
   takers?

b. Marie Larelle scored 974 on the ACT test. What is her percentile rank?

Problem Set 6D

6D-1. Compute the following probabilities for the roll of one gaming die.
   a. p [4]
   b. p [2 then 4]
   c. p [1 or 4 or 5]

6D-2. Suppose you have a large, well-mixed container of soft drinks: 100 regular,
   50 caffeine-free, and 70 diet drinks. Compute the probabilities of randomly
   drawing the following from the container. You are not to open them. You are
   simply trying to impress your friends.
   a. p [regular then diet then caffeine-free] without replacement
   b. p [diet then diet then regular] with replacement
   c. p [regular then diet then regular] with replacement of diet drinks only

6D-3. For the toss of one coin (H = heads, T = tails), compute the following.
   a. p [H]
   b. p [T then H]
   c. p [H then H then H]

6D-4. Compute the following probabilities for drawing cards from a standard deck
   of 52 playing cards.
   a. p [king]
   b. p [queen or ace]
   c. p [queen or spade]
   d. p [five then five, or queen then queen] without replacement

6D-5. Klem and Connell (2004) examined dimensions of teacher support and its
   relationship to student achievement as measured by midterm exam score.
   Use these statistics to answer the following questions. The distribution is
   normal. Draw the normal curve and label all target areas. Set X = midterm
   exam score.

$$\overline{X} = 81 \text{ points}$$
$$s_X = 4 \text{ points}$$
$$n = 212 \text{ students}$$

a. What proportion of students scored *above* 90?
b. What number of students scored *between* 86 and 91?
c. What proportion of the scores fell *between* 77 and 87?

     d. Determine the exam score below which 95 percent of the scores fell.

     e. If a student had to make at least the 95th percentile rank in this group of students, what score would he or she need to make (short answer)?

6D-6. Greiner et al. (2004) examined the impact of occupational stressors on hypertension among urban transit operators. You wish to validate this study using a sample of 200 transit workers in another city. You administer a stress scale and find a mean score of 18.5 stress scale points with a standard deviation of 4.5. The distribution is normal. Draw normal curves to answer the following questions. Set X = stress scale score.

     a. Any worker who scores 14 or higher on the stress scale is eligible to participate in an intensive interview portion of your study. Given your statistics, how many of the 200 workers in your sample will be given an intensive interview?

     b. What is the probability that the next worker tested will score 10 or below?

     c. Those workers scoring in the highest 15 percent on the stress scale are to be given extensive cardiac testing. What stress score qualifies a participant for these services?

6D-7. Riebschleger (2004) studied the experiences of children living with a family member who had been diagnosed with a psychiatric disability. Suppose you are conducting a similar study. The mean age of your sample of children is 11.7 years and the standard deviation is 1.4 years. The distribution is normal. You are to isolate the oldest 5 percent of children and conduct a follow-up interview of them. Identify this age range. Set X = age.

     a. Draw and label the normal curve. Use the normal curve table to identify the Z-score that isolates the top .05 of the area under the curve.

     b. Determine the age (i.e., X-score) that cuts off the top 5 percent of children. In other words, above what age do 5 percent of children in this sample fall? Interpret your answer in everyday language.

6D-8. The Graduate Record Exam (GRE) is an admissions test for postgraduate study in the United States. Goldberg and Pedulla (2002) assessed performance differences for various methods of taking the examination. The test is "normalized" (i.e., designed to fit the normal curve). You have a sample of 897 students who took the exam electronically. The mean of the sample is 1,000 points and the standard deviation is 140 points. Use the normal curve to answer the following questions. Set X = GRE score.

     a. One student, Caroline van Nostren, scored a 1,340 on the test. What is her percentile rank? That is, Caroline's score is equal to or higher than what percentage of test takers?

     b. John Riley scored 843. What is his percentile rank?

OPTIONAL COMPUTER APPLICATIONS
FOR CHAPTER 6

For classes using computers, go to *The Statistical Imagination* Web site at www. mhhe.com/ritchey2 and open the Computer Application Exercises for Chapter 6. These exercises focus on using score frequency distributions as probability distributions and using *Z*-scores to compute probabilities with normally distributed interval/ratio variables. In addition, Appendix D of this text provides a brief overview of the *SPSS* command sequences for procedures covered in this chapter.

7

Using Probability Theory to Produce Sampling Distributions

Introduction: Estimating Parameters

To review briefly, a population is a large set of persons about whom we desire information. Typically, to save time and money, we sample rather than observe such a large group. Sample statistics provide estimates of the parameters of the total population. Suppose our population of interest is the 16,000 students in a four-year college. From this campus we select a random sample of 200 students. We are interested in parameters such as the following: What is the mean grade point average (GPA)? What percentage of students supports opening the campus library 24 hours a day? What is the mean age? Our interest, however, is not in the means or proportions of the 200 students in the sample. It is the entire student body of 16,000 for which we seek answers. The sample is merely a tool to obtain information about the parameters of this total campus population.

    The statistics calculated on a sample, however, provide only estimates. How can we acknowledge and deal with this fact? Are there statistical tools that allow us to refine these estimates by stating them with a degree of confidence and known levels of sampling error? The answers to these questions lie in a good understanding of what are called sampling distributions.

Point Estimates

Suppose we set X as GPA and for a sample of 200 students we find a mean of 2.46 "GPA points" (i.e., credits earned per credit hour taken). Does this assure us that the population mean is also 2.46? Of course not. There is sampling error to consider. **Sampling error** is *the difference between the calculated value of a sample statistic and the true value of a population parameter,* which is usually unknown. By definition, sample statistics are merely estimates of parameters. If we report this single figure of 2.46 GPA points, we are providing what is called a **point estimate**, *a statistic provided without indicating a range of error.* This is not much better than a best guess. Why? Because if we draw a second, a third, and a fourth sample, we are likely to get slightly different computed means from each one. In other words, there is variability in statistical outcomes from sample to sample.

---

sampling error   The difference between the calculated value of a sample statistic and the true value of a population parameter.

point estimate   A statistic provided without indicating a range of error.

Predicting Sampling Error

It was the discovery of sample variability—the recognition that each sample's statistics differ slightly from those of the next—that underlies a basic understanding of sampling error. Like the ancient statisticians who repeatedly rolled dice, later statisticians learned about sampling error through **repeated sampling**—*drawing a sample and computing its statistics and then drawing a second sample, a third, a fourth, and so on.* These "bean-counting" statisticians learned two important natural facts about repeated sampling from a population. First, calculated results will differ from one sample to the next. Second, the calculations made on a sample—a group that is smaller than the entire population—are only estimates. That is, a sample's statistics will be slightly off from the true values of its population's parameters.

---

repeated sampling   Drawing a sample and computing its statistics and then drawing a second sample, a third, a fourth, and so on. Repeated sampling reveals the nature of sampling error.

Repeated random sampling and the resulting variability in statistical outcomes are illustrated in Figure 7–1, which presents a population of children whose ages range from zero (infant under one year) to nine years. For sample statistics—calculations made on sample data—we typically use English letter symbols such as $\overline{X}$ and s_X (with which we are already familiar). When feasible, we use Greek letters for population parameters. Specifically, we use the following symbols to represent population parameters for interval/ratio variables:

For the interval/ratio variable X,

μ_X = the mean of a population (pronounced *mu*-sub-X)
σ_X = the standard deviation of a population (pronounced *sigma*-sub-X)

FIGURE 7–1

Sampling
variability with
repeated
sampling:
X = ages of
children, zero to
nine years

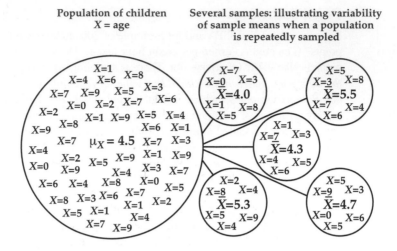

Population of children
X = age

Several samples: illustrating variability
of sample means when a population
is repeatedly sampled

Mathematical Symbols Typically Used to Distinguish Populations and Samples

For sample statistics: English letters
For population parameters: Greek letters

In Figure 7–1, X = age and the mean age *in the population* of children is μ_X = 4.5 years. Note that the depicted sample means $\overline{X}$'s in the smaller balloons vary around this population mean of 4.5 years. Each sample mean is slightly higher or lower than 4.5, reflecting sample variability caused by the natural occurrence of random sampling error. For example, the sample on the upper right where $\overline{X}$ = 5.5 years misses the true parameter of 4.5 by 1.0; that is, the sampling error calculates as follows:

$$\overline{X} - \mu_X = 5.5 - 4.5 = 1.0 \text{ year}$$

A good way, then, to show that the sample statistics are not exact values of population parameters is to sample repeatedly. If you are unconvinced of this, draw a couple of random samples from the population (i.e., the large circle) of children's ages in Figure 7–1. Chances are great that you will come up with slightly different sample means. Each sample is a very small part of the larger population, and each is composed of a different set of six children. In one sample—just by chance—more older than younger children may appear, resulting in a sample mean slightly higher than 4.5 years. In a second sample—just by chance—more younger than older children may appear, resulting in a lower sample mean. Repeated sampling results in varied statistical outcomes.

Over 200 years ago probability theorists recognized some "bad news": A statistic from a single sample is only an estimate of a population parameter. But through repeated sampling—many hours spent drawing one sample after another—these theorists discovered some good news: Sampling error is patterned and systematic and therefore is predictable.

The first predictable thing found from repeated sampling was that the resulting sample means were similar in value and tended to cluster around a particular value. Probability theorists suspected that this central value was the true value of the population parameter—the population mean itself (μ_X). Using models similar to Figure 7–1, they compared sample outcomes to known parameters and found that a distribution of sample statistics indeed centers on the actual population parameter. This makes sense. If the average age of a population of children is 4.5 years, the mean calculated on a truly random sample should be close to this value. Second, probability theorists discovered that sampling variability was mathematically predictable from probability curves. They took the results from repeated samples and plotted histograms. Most of their computed sample means fell very close in value to the population parameter, and as one moved away from this parameter in either direction, there were fewer and fewer outcomes. In other words, they discovered that statistical outcomes occur according to probability curves such as the normal curve. Finally, when comparing samples of different sizes, these theorists determined that the larger the sample size, the smaller the range of errors in repeated samples.

Sampling Distributions

When the distributions of statistics from repeatedly drawn samples are plotted on histograms, we get an informative picture of the predictability of sampling error. We call such a distribution a sampling distribution. *From repeated sampling,* a **sampling distribution** is *a mathematical description of all possible sampling outcomes and the probability of each one.*

---

sampling distribution   From repeated sampling, a mathematical description of all possible sampling outcomes and the probability of each one.

Sampling Distributions for Interval/Ratio Variables

To illustrate the particulars of a sampling distribution of means, let us see what happens if we sample repeatedly from a population *with a known mean.* Suppose we determine from licensing records that the mean age *of the population* of all licensed practicing physicians in the United States is 48 years. Since these data are for the entire population, this mean is a known parameter, symbolized as μ_X, where X = physician age. Suppose also that the standard deviation of this population is six years, symbolized as σ_X. The *raw score* frequency distribution of this *population* of ages is presented in Figure 7–2. Note that this distribution is not a bell-shaped normal curve. It is important to keep in mind that on the horizontal axis of Figure 7–2 we plot raw scores (X-scores)—the actual ages of physicians.

FIGURE 7–2

Raw score
frequency
distribution of
ages for the
entire popula-
tion of actively
practicing
physicians in
the United
States (fictional
data)

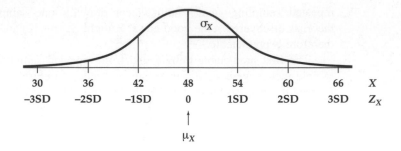

30	36	42	48	54	60	66	X
−3SD	−2SD	−1SD	0	1SD	2SD	3SD	Z_X

$$\mu_X$$

FIGURE 7–3

The sampling
distribution of
the mean age of
physicians in
the United
States

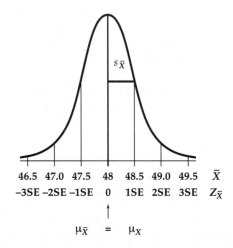

46.5	47.0	47.5	48	48.5	49.0	49.5	$\bar{X}$
−3SE	−2SE	−1SE	0	1SE	2SE	3SE	$Z_{\bar{X}}$

$$\mu_{\bar{X}} = \mu_X$$

   Now let us move our focus away from the raw score distribution in Figure 7–2 and think about a sampling distribution of means. To determine all possible sampling outcomes, we must imagine repeatedly drawing samples from this population. Say we draw 10,000 samples of 144 physicians. For each sample, we compute the sample mean age, $\bar{X}$. A moment's thought should convince us that most sample means will calculate to around 48 years. But because of sampling error, we would *not* be surprised if each sample mean were slightly off, say 47.9 years or 48.2 years.

   Now let us imagine that we plot the values of these 10,000 sample means on a histogram. That is, for each sample we treat the calculated mean age as a single observation. Thus, we plot $\bar{X}$'s in place of X's on the horizontal axis. Guess what shape this histogram will take? Yes, a normal distribution. As it turns out, when the sample size, n, is greater than 121 cases, *a sampling distribution of means is normal in shape*. This normality is illustrated in the bell-shaped curve in Figure 7–3. Most of the 10,000 sample means fall on or right around 48 years. As we move away from 48 years in either direction, the curve slopes downward, indicating fewer and fewer outcomes. Moreover, if we sum the values of all 10,000 sample means and divide by 10,000, this *mean of sample means* is 48 years—the mean age of physicians in the population. *The mean of a sampling distribution of means* is symbolized as $\mu_{\bar{X}}$ and will always equal the population mean (μ_X). Furthermore, as with any normal curve, the standard deviation is the distance to the point of inflection of the curve. In summary, the curve in Figure 7–3 is a sampling distribution of means (X-bars, not X's). It mathematically describes *all possible sampling outcomes and the probability of each outcome.* (Why the standardized scores appear in units of "SE" instead of "SD" will be explained shortly.)

What does this sampling distribution tell us? First, any sampling distribution (by definition) depicts all possible sampling outcomes. Figure 7–3 reveals all statistical outcomes that occur if we repeatedly draw samples of size 144 from the physician population and compute the mean of each sample. Second, since a sampling distribution of means takes a normal shape when $n > 121$ cases, the normal curve table is used to compute the probability of occurrence of any sample outcome. Thus, with this normal distribution, about 68 percent of the observations fall within 1 standard deviation on both sides of the mean. Specifically, about 68 percent of the time our sample means ($\bar{X}$'s) will compute to between 47.5 and 48.5 years; approximately 95 percent of the time, between 47.0 and 49.0 years; and almost 100 percent of the time, between 46.5 and 49.5 years. In summary, this distribution provides a description of all possible sampling outcomes when $n = 144$ and the population mean is 48 years. A sampling distribution tells us how often a sample statistic is likely to miss the true population parameter value and by how much.

The Standard Error

The standard deviation of a sampling distribution has a special name—the standard error—because it is a measure of predictable sampling errors. The **standard error** is *the standard deviation of a sampling distribution.* Note that for the sampling distribution in Figure 7–3, the units of measure are labeled SE (standard errors) rather than SD (standard deviations). The standard error measures the spread of sampling error that occurs when a population is sampled repeatedly.

---

standard error   The standard deviation of a sampling distribution. The standard error measures the spread of sampling error that occurs when a population is sampled repeatedly.

Mathematicians have determined that a good estimate of *the standard error of a sampling distribution of means* is the sample's standard deviation divided by the square root of the sample size (*n*). Note the English symbol that indicates this estimated standard error is based on sample data.

Computing the Standard Error of a Sampling Distribution of Means when σ_X Is Unknown (for an interval/ratio variable)

$$s_{\overline{X}} = \frac{s_X}{\sqrt{n}}$$

where

$s_{\overline{X}}$ = estimated standard error of means for the variable X
s_X = the standard deviation of a sample
n = sample size

For the sampling distribution of the mean ages of physicians depicted in Figure 7–3, the standard error is one-half year:

$$s_{\overline{X}} = \frac{s_X}{\sqrt{n}} = \frac{6}{\sqrt{144}} = \frac{6}{12} = .5 \text{ year}$$

Let us return to Figure 7–3 and observe the horizontal axis. We may view this axis as a measuring stick for sampling error. The standard error tells us where to make the markings on the stick.

The Law of Large Numbers

A close look at the formula for the standard error of a sampling distribution of means reveals an important point about the spread of sampling error. *The larger the sample size, the smaller the standard error.* This principle, called the **law of large numbers**, makes sense (Sheynin 1970). A big sample works better than a small one. This is apparent in the makeup of the formula for the standard error. When n is replaced with increasingly larger values, this increases the size of the denominator and reduces the size of the quotient. For samples of physicians, replace n with increasingly larger values and note how the calculated standard error decreases.

the law of large numbers   The larger the sample size, the smaller the standard error (i.e., the smaller the range of error in the sampling distribution).

The Central Limit Theorem

To help us distinguish raw score and sampling distributions, note the similarities and differences between the curves in Figures 7–2 and 7–3. In both distributions the means are equal to the population mean, μ_X. In the sampling distribution of Figure 7–3, however, on the horizontal axis we plot *sample means* (X-bars, not raw X-scores), and the standard deviation is the standard error. Furthermore, the standard error in Figure 7–3 has a different formula and symbol than does the standard deviation in Figure 7–2. (Review Chapter 5.)

Note also the differences in the size of the spread of these distributions. In the raw score distribution of Figure 7–2, the actual ages of the physicians range from about 30 to 66 years. In the sampling distribution of Figure 7–3, *the computed sample means have a much narrower range, from a sample mean of about 46 years to one of about 50 years.* This is highlighted in Figure 7–4, which superimposes the distributions. It makes intuitive sense that the sampling distribution has a smaller range. As a central tendency statistic, the mean for any sample is likely to compute within a central area of a raw score distribution. An average is likely to be average. Thus, when we plot a large number of means, they cluster *narrowly* around a center value that happens to be the mean of the population, μ_X. Mathematically, the narrower spread of a sampling distribution is apparent in the formula for the standard error. The standard deviation is in the numerator and thus is divided into smaller pieces. The standard error will always calculate to a smaller value than will the standard deviation.

The tendency is strong for a sampling distribution to have a small range of values within the center of the raw score distribution. In fact, this tendency is so strong that it occurs even when the raw score distribution itself is not normally shaped. *Regardless*

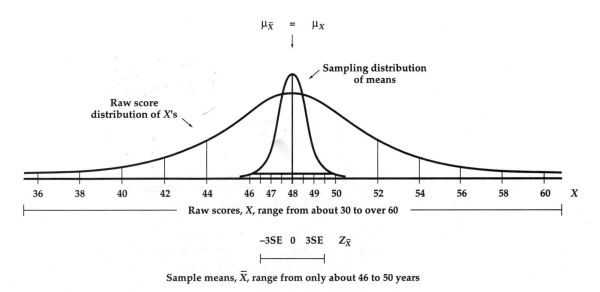

FIGURE 7–4

Comparison of the spreads of a distribution of raw scores to its sampling distribution: ages of physicians in the United States

of the shape of a raw score distribution, its sampling distribution will be normal when the sample size, n, is greater than 121 cases and will center on the true population mean. Among mathematicians this discovery is referred to as the **central limit theorem**, which was first conceived by Pierre Laplace (Fischer 2000). (As we will explain in Chapter 10, even when the sample size is less than 121, the shape of the distribution will approximate a normal curve.)

---

the central limit theorem   Regardless of the shape of a raw score distribution of an interval/ratio variable, its sampling distribution will be normal when the sample size, *n,* is greater than 121 cases and will center on the true population mean.

To illustrate the central limit theorem, let us look at the random number table (Statistical Table A in Appendix B). Each single number in the table is called a digit. These "single random digits" range from 0 to 9. Each digit can be viewed as a score of the variable *X,* such as the ages of children nine and under in Figure 7–1. How was this random number table generated? Let us imagine producing it by hand. We start by writing each of the digits (0 through 9) on separate slips of paper. We place these 10 slips into a hat and stir them up—randomize them—so that each has an equal chance of being selected. We draw a slip, record the result, replace it in the hat, and repeat the process an infinite number of times. Since every digit has an equal chance of selection on each draw, over the long run we will record just as many 0s as 1s, 2s, and so on, through 9. The frequency distribution of these raw scores (i.e., *X*-scores) would appear as it does in Figure 7–5. This distribution is "rectangular" in shape; each column of the histogram is equal in height to all the others. This is the case because all digits have an equal chance of selection and therefore each will occur with the same frequency. Thus, this distribution is not even remotely normal—it lacks "tails."

FIGURE 7–5

Raw score frequency distribution of an infinite set of single random digits

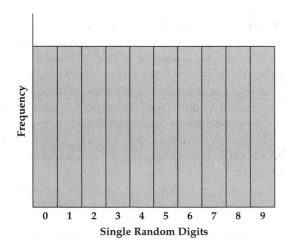

FIGURE 7–6

Sampling
distribution
of means of
samples of
single random
digits

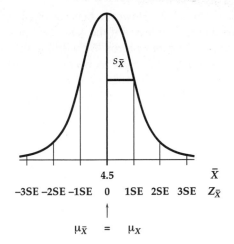

Now let us imagine that we are taking *samples* from this random number table with $n > 121$. We select a sample, compute the sample mean $(\overline{X})$, and repeat this process many times. Demonstrating the central limit theorem, the shape of a histogram of the resulting sampling distribution is normal even though the raw score distribution is not remotely normal in shape. This is illustrated in Figure 7–6.

It is a good idea to gain a sense of this phenomenon by treating the random number table (Statistical Table A in Appendix B) as though it were a population of random digits and drawing repeated samples from it. (See the exercises at the end of the chapter.)

Fortunately, to determine the shape of a sampling distribution, we do not have to sample repeatedly. Probability theorists, the bean counters of the past, spent their time doing this and provided standard error formulas. We need only draw one sample and use its standard deviation to estimate the standard error of a sampling distribution.

Sampling Distributions for Nominal Variables

With nominal variables we count the frequency of categories and calculate proportions. We often target a particular "success" category and wish to determine its parameter in the population. To obtain a sampling distribution of the proportion of success, we ask the question: What happens if we draw a sample, calculate the proportion for this category, and then repeat these procedures over and over? What shape will the distribution of sample outcomes take? As it turns out, a sampling distribution of proportions takes the shape of a normal distribution when n is sufficiently large as discussed below.

To illustrate a sampling distribution of proportions, let us examine the proportion of female physicians among all physicians in active practice in the United States. Specifically, data from the American Medical Association's (1997) *Physician Characteristics and Distribution in the U.S., 1996–1997* reveal that in 1995 there were 720,325 physicians in active practice, of whom 149,404 were female. That is, the known population parameter of the proportion female was .2074 (approximately 21 percent). A moment's thought should convince us that if we draw, say, 10,000 random samples of, say, 300 physicians, the proportion female in each sample should come out to around .21. However, because of expected sampling error, for a given sample we would not be surprised if the calculated proportion was slightly off—say, .20 or .22—because of sampling error. We will find that the bulk of the 10,000 sample proportions fall right around .21, and as we move out in either direction, we will obtain fewer and fewer outcomes. A histogram of these outcomes is normal in shape. Moreover, the mean of *these 10,000 sample proportions* is .21; that is, if we add all 10,000 proportions together and divide by 10,000, the result will be .21—the proportion of female physicians in the population. The standard deviation of this sampling distribution of proportions is called the standard error of proportions.

As with the sampling distribution of means, the sampling distribution of proportions has its own symbols. Since our interest is in the proportion of female physicians (a nominal variable), we will denote *the proportion of females among U.S. physicians* as P (i.e., success) and *the proportion of males among U.S. physicians* as Q (i.e., failure). Thus,

$$P = p\,[\text{of U.S. physicians who are female}]$$
$$Q = p\,[\text{of U.S. physicians who are male}]$$

We will use the following subscripted symbols to represent population parameters. To avoid nesting the letter p in the symbols, we use the subscript u for *universe*, another term for population. Thus,

$$P_u = p\,[\text{of the population of U.S. physicians who are female}] = .21$$
$$Q_u = p\,[\text{of the population of U.S. physicians who are male}] = 1 - P_u$$
$$= 1 - .21 = .79$$

We will use a subscripted s to represent sample statistics. Thus,

$$P_s = p\,[\text{of the sampled U.S. physicians who are female}]$$
$$Q_s = p\,[\text{of the sampled U.S. physicians who are male}]$$

We want to know, based on the relative proportions of male and female physicians in the population, how much error is expected in repeated sampling. As with means, the size of the error is related to sample size: the larger the sample, the smaller the range of error. To determine sampling error, we compute the standard deviation of this sampling distribution—its standard error—for a sample size of 300 physicians. If the values of P and Q are known, as is the case with physicians, the standard error of proportions is symbolized by sigma-sub-P-sub-s (σ_{P_s}) with the following formula:

Computing the Standard Error of a Sampling Distribution of Proportions When P_u and Q_u are known (for a nominal variable)

$$\sigma_{P_s} = \sqrt{\frac{P_u Q_u}{n}}$$

where

σ_{P_s} = standard error of proportions for a nominal variable, with
$P = p$ [of the success category]
$P_u = p$ [of the success category in the population]
$Q_u = p$ [of the failure category in the population]
n = sample size

For the standard error of the proportion of female physicians with samples of size 300,

$$\sigma_{P_S} = \sqrt{\frac{P_u Q_u}{n}} = \sqrt{\frac{(.21)(.79)}{300}} = .02$$

Figure 7–7 shows the distribution of these samples, with P_s, the proportion female in a sample, plotted along the horizontal axis. As with any normal curve, this one tells us what to expect if we repeatedly draw samples from the physician population: About 68 percent of the time our sample outcomes, P_s, will compute between .19 and .23 (i.e., $.21 \pm \sigma_{P_s}$; about 95 percent of the time, P_s will compute between .17 and .25 (i.e., $.21 \pm 2\sigma_{P_s}$; and only a very small percentage of the time will any P_s be less than .15 or greater than .27 (i.e., $.21 \pm 3\sigma_{P_s}$). This sampling distribution, then, tells us how often to expect a sample outcome to miss the true parameter (P_u) and by how much. Moreover, since this distribution of sampling outcomes is normal, we can mathematically describe its mean and a standard error (as in Figure 7–7). Finally, by calculating Z-scores, we can partition the curve and compute the probability of the occurrence of any single sampling outcome or any range of sampling outcomes. Thus, this mathematically derived normal distribution is a sampling distribution—a description of all possible sample outcomes and the probability of each one.

This illustration is unusual in that the true population parameters of the proportions of female and male physicians are known. In much research the sample is the only source of data available and sample statistics are used to estimate the standard error of

FIGURE 7–7

The sampling distribution of the proportion of female physicians in the United States in 1995

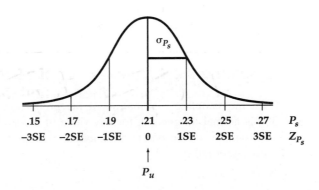

proportions. Thus, if P_u and Q_u are not known, σ_{P_s} is estimated as follows, using sample proportions P_s and Q_s.

Computing the Standard Error of a Sampling Distribution of Proportions When P_u and Q_u are Unknown (for categories of a nominal variable)

$$s_{P_S} = \sqrt{\frac{P_s Q_s}{n}}$$

where

s_{P_S} = estimated standard error of proportions for a nominal variable, with
　　　$P = p$[of the success category]
P_s = p[of the success category in the sample]
Q_s = p[of the failure category in the sample]
n = sample size

Rules Concerning a Sampling Distribution of Proportions

Repeated sampling and calculation of sample proportions (P_s) reveal the following qualities about a sampling distribution of proportions:

1. The mean of a sampling distribution of proportions is equal to the population parameter, P_u.

2. A sampling distribution of proportions will be normal in shape when the smaller parameter (P_u or Q_u) times $n \geq 5$. (If the parameter is unknown, the sample estimates—P_s and Q_s—apply in making this judgment.) In the preceding example P_u (the proportion of female physicians = .21) is smaller than Q_u (the proportion of males = .79). Thus, we set $p_{smaller}$ at .21. To see if a normal distribution is appropriate, we must determine that $p_{smaller}$ times n is greater than or equal to 5:

$$(p_{smaller})(n) = (.21)(300) = 63 \qquad 63 \geq 5$$

Thus, the sampling distribution of the proportion of female physicians where $n = 300$ is normal. In general, for any value of P_u or Q_u (whichever is smaller), the minimum sample size needed to assume a normal distribution is determined by using the following formula:

> ## Computing the Minimum Sample Size Needed to Assume That a Sampling Distribution of Proportions Is Normally Shaped
>
> $$\text{Minimum } n = \frac{5}{p_{smaller}}$$
>
> where
>
> $\qquad$ Minimum n = minimum sample size needed to assume normality
>
> $\qquad p_{smaller}$ = the smaller of P_u or Q_u (if these parameters are known)
>
> $\qquad\qquad\quad$ or the smaller of P_s or Q_s (if P_u and Q_u are unknown)

For example, when $P_s = .1$, the minimum $n = 50$; when $P_s = .3$, the minimum $n = 17$; and when $P_s = .5$, the minimum $n = 10$. These examples illustrate that when P_s is moderate (i.e., around .5) rather than extreme, a smaller sample will suffice to assure that the sampling distribution is normal. Finally, when the minimum n is less than 5, the appropriate sampling distribution is called the binomial distribution, which is described in Chapter 13.

Finally, note that for our illustration of the sampling distribution of female physicians we use the dichotomous variable *gender of physician*. Recall that a dichotomous variable is one with only two categories, such as male and female. If you have a nominal variable with more than two categories, as always the success category is defined as P. The failure category Q, however, is the proportion of all other categories combined and this proportion equals $1 - P$. For example, if $P = p$ [of students at State University who are seniors], then $Q = 1 - P = p$ [of students at State University who are juniors, sophomores, first-year students, and other classifications]. In summary, the sampling distribution for a nominal variable focuses on the proportion of success. The remaining "failure" categories are viewed as "not P"; therefore, $Q = 1 - P$.

Bean Counting as a Way of Grasping the Statistical Imagination

Sampling distributions are depictions of what happens if we repeatedly draw samples from a population and compute statistics on a variable. Through this repeated sampling we discover all possible statistical outcomes and the probability of each one. The standard error, the size of which depends on sample size, gives us a ruler to compute these probabilities.

Sampling distributions are an essential feature of statistical analysis because they are useful as probability curves. Having discovered these predictable tendencies in sampling outcomes, probability theorists began to ask questions: Can we use knowledge about the predictability of sampling outcomes in a way that allows us to avoid having to "sample" the entire population to determine a variable's true mean? Can we, for instance, forgo the expense of interviewing all 16,000 students on a campus? Can we examine a single sample and simply estimate errors? For instance, if a single student sample has a mean GPA of 2.44, can we use our knowledge about the predictability of repeated samples to infer a range of error, say, plus or minus .1? Is there a way to compute the degree of confidence we have in the accuracy of a statistic from a single sample? We know that a sample statistic is an estimate—not 100 percent correct. But can we say that we are 90 percent, 95 percent, or 99 percent sure of our results?

You may realize by now that a sampling distribution is a probability distribution. For a given sample size, a sampling distribution tells us how frequently to expect any and all sampling outcomes when we draw random samples. This is no different from calculating, say, the probability of tossing heads and then heads with two coins, as we did in the previous chapter (Figure 6–2). In fact, some of the simple illustrations of probability distributions in that chapter are useful as sampling distributions. And our hard work in Chapter 6, partitioning areas of the normal curve, was done to prepare us for treating the sampling distribution as a normal curve.

Producing sampling distributions by hand—through repeated sampling—is important for truly understanding the concept. This is what early statisticians probably did. First, they set out to determine what happens when a nominal variable is sampled repeatedly. To represent a category of a variable such as gender, they could have substituted a box of beans for the population, letting white beans represent men and red beans represent women. They repeatedly scooped samples from the box with a sample size of, say, 100 beans. For each sample they computed the proportion female (i.e., P_s, where $P = p$) [of beans that are red]). They plotted these sample proportions on a histogram and discovered the normal curve and the formula for the standard error. They tried various sample sizes ($n = 90, 80, 70$, etc.) and found that as long as the sample size is sufficiently large, a sampling distribution of proportions takes the bell shape of a normal curve.

For interval/ratio variables the early statisticians used random number tables such as Statistical Table A in Appendix B, treating the digits as though each represented a case for a variable such as age. After repeatedly drawing samples, computing the means, and plotting them on histograms, they discovered yet again the natural phenomenon of normality. Ultimately, these "bean-counting" mathematicians worked out standard error formulas and discovered the law of large numbers and the central limit theorem. Modern statisticians are thankful for the tireless efforts of these early mathematicians and statisticians. Today we need draw only one random sample and use formulas to estimate the shape of a sampling distribution.

The central limit theorem essentially states that random sampling results in normal curves: symmetrical distributions that bunch in the middle and tail out to the sides. Normality in random sampling is a natural phenomenon that existed long before statisticians measured and formulated it, just as gravity existed long before Isaac Newton measured and explained it.

It is one thing for us to talk about how early statisticians learned about sampling distributions and another thing for us to experience the process of generating them for ourselves. The exercises and computer applications for this chapter provide simple ways to produce sampling distributions the old-fashioned way—by actually counting beans. *Bean counter* is a negative term that often is thrown at stingy bureaucrats who pinch pennies, but being a literal bean counter is not such a bad thing for gaining insight into the natural processes behind random sampling error. If you want the remainder of the course to go smoothly, generate enough sampling distributions to gain a sense of mastery over the idea. Become a bean counter.

Distinguishing Among Populations, Samples, and Sampling Distributions

It is helpful at this point to review some of the symbols and formulas we have used thus far. We have to use our imagination a lot in dealing with statistics because the only thing we touch is the sample. Meanwhile, we have to imagine what the larger population is like. Furthermore, we must imagine a sampling distribution and describe its shape mathematically and graphically.

FIGURE 7–8

Distinguishing among measurements made on samples, populations, and sampling distributions (for the interval/ratio variable *X*)

	Sample	Population	Sampling Distribution
Symbols			
Mean	$\bar{X}$	μ_X	$\mu_{\bar{X}} = \mu_X$
Standard deviation	s_X	σ_X	$s_{\bar{X}}$ = (standard error estimated by s_X)
Description	Statistic = summary measurement of *X* computed on a sample of *n* (actual observation).	Parameter = summary measurement of *X* if every subject in the population is observed (usually unknown).	*Hypothetical* distribution of an infinite number of samples of size *n*. (Hypothetical implies that not even a large number of samples is usually drawn. This distribution is mathematically produced.)
	Actual sample of size *n*	Population of *X*'s	Hypothetical infinite set of samples of size *n*

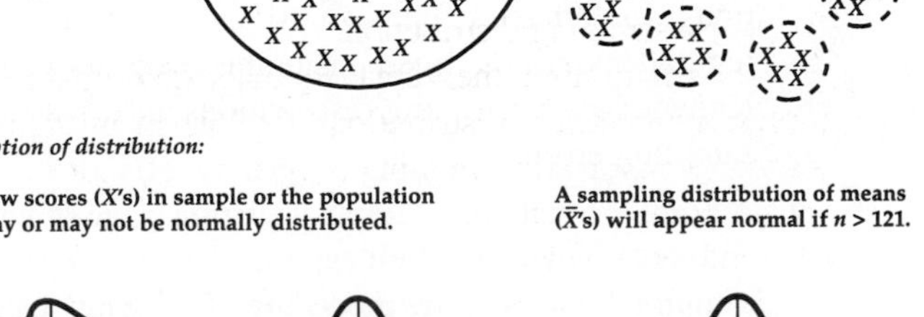

Description of distribution:

Raw scores (*X*'s) in sample or the population may or may not be normally distributed.

A sampling distribution of means ($\bar{X}$'s) will appear normal if $n > 121$.

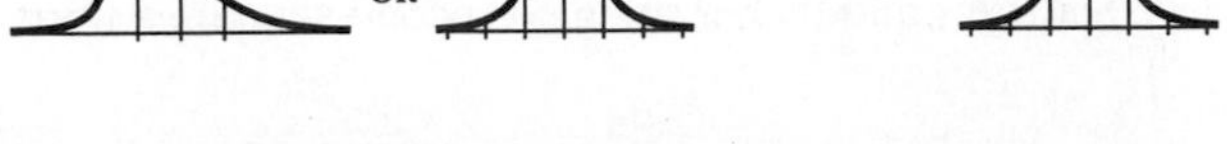

Figure 7–8 provides a summary of the symbols used for sample statistics, population parameters, and sampling distribution statistics for means. From here on it will be very important to keep these ideas and symbols straight.

Statistical Follies and Fallacies: Treating a Point Estimate as Though It Were Absolutely True

As we have learned in this chapter, no single statistic—a summary measure based on sample data—is the last word on estimating a parameter of the population. Repeated sampling shows that the next sample from the same population is likely to result in a slightly different statistical outcome. Yet it is not uncommon, especially in the mass media, for point estimates to be accepted quickly and then treated as though they were absolutely true.

Among political pollsters there may be advantages to having a less than perfect estimate. For instance, a single poll may show that just over 50 percent of the respondents—a simple majority—support a legislative bill. The pollster and the supporters of the legislation are likely to broadcast this result and then speak of it as though it were absolute fact. A second poll may show that considerably less than 50 percent support the bill. If the politicians are not interested in the absolute truth but simply want to support their positions, they are not likely to make an issue of the indefinite conclusions made with point estimates. A trained statistician or a skeptical citizen may not fall for this ruse, but many citizens may. Not only do such pollsters deceive us, they insult the intelligence of the populace. In Chapter 8 we will see that there is a way to specify the error in a point estimate and express the degree of confidence we have that it is an accurate estimate of a population parameter.

SUMMARY

1. Understanding sampling distributions is a key element in conducting statistical analysis. Sampling distributions are probability curves that allow us to calculate the range of error and level of confidence we can assert when using sample statistics to draw conclusions about population parameters.

2. Sample statistics are usually noted with English letters. When feasible, population parameters are noted with Greek letters.

3. To determine the value of a population parameter with absolute certainty, calculations would have to be made for every subject in a population. Typically, this is too expensive and time-consuming to do, so we rely on random sampling. Knowledge of sampling distributions allows us to calculate the probability of sampling error.

4. A point estimate is a sample statistic provided without indicating a range of error and must be viewed with caution. This becomes apparent through repeated sampling, which is the procedure of drawing a sample and computing its statistics and then drawing a second sample, a third, a fourth, and so on.

5. Repeated sampling reveals several things about the nature of sampling error: (*a*) Calculated statistics will differ from one sample to the next; (*b*) a given sample's statistic will be slightly off from the true value of its population's parameter; (*c*) sampling error is patterned and systematic and therefore mathematically predictable from probability curves called sampling distributions.

6. The central limit theorem states that regardless of the shape of the raw score distribution of an interval/ratio variable, the sampling distribution of means will be normal in shape when the sample size, *n,* is greater than 121. This normal distribution will center on the true population mean. Even if a raw score distribution in a population is skewed, a sampling distribution of means from this population will nonetheless take the shape of a normal curve.

7. The standard error is the standard deviation of a sampling distribution. Formulas allow us to quickly estimate a standard error using statistics from a single sample.

8. The law of large numbers states that the larger the sample size, the smaller the standard error of a sampling distribution. Large samples with their small standard errors provide more accurate estimates of population parameters than do small samples.

9. A sense of proportion about the relationship between sample size and sampling error is apparent in the formula for the standard error of the mean, where the standard deviation of a sample is divided by the square root of *n*. A large *n* in the denominator of the equation produces a small quotient, indicating that the larger the sample, the smaller the range of error in sampling.

10. For a nominal/ordinal variable, proportions calculated for a repeatedly sampled population will calculate to similar values that cluster around the value of the population parameter—the population proportion. A sampling distribution of proportions will be normal when the smaller parameter (the probability of success or failure in the population) multiplied by the sample size is greater than or equal to 5 (i.e., when $p_{smaller} \geq 5$).

CHAPTER EXTENSIONS ON *THE STATISTICAL IMAGINATION* WEB SITE

Chapter 7 Extensions of text material available on *The Statistical Imagination* Web site at www.mhhe.com/ritchey2 include additional pointers on understanding sampling distributions.

FORMULAS FOR CHAPTER 7

Computing the standard error of a sampling distribution of means:

$$s_{\overline{X}} = \frac{s_X}{\sqrt{n}}$$

Computing the standard error of a sampling distribution of proportions (for a nominal variable):

When P_u and Q_u are known   When P_u and Q_u are unknown

$$\sigma_{P_s} = \sqrt{\frac{P_u Q_u}{n}} \qquad\qquad s_{P_s} = \sqrt{\frac{P_s Q_s}{n}}$$

Computing the minimum sample size needed to assume that a sampling distribution of proportions is normally shaped:

$$\text{Minimum } n = \frac{5}{p_{smaller}}$$

Thus, assume a normal distribution when $(p_{smaller})(n) > 5$.

QUESTIONS FOR CHAPTER 7

1. What is the difference between a statistic and a parameter? Which one is usually unknown for the variable? Illustrate the symbols we use for the statistics and parameters of interval/ratio variables and nominal variables.

2. Define a sampling distribution. Distinguish it from a distribution of raw scores from a population.

3. How can we demonstrate that a statistic computed on a single sample only provides *an estimate* of a parameter?

4. If we draw a histogram to portray a *raw score* distribution—say, the distribution of ages for a sample of 200 students—what points are plotted along the horizontal axis of the histogram?

5. If we draw a histogram to portray the distribution of *mean ages* for 1,000 *samples* of 200 students, what points are plotted along the horizontal axis? What is this distribution called?

6. For an interval/ratio variable, provide the symbols for the standard deviation and the standard error. What does each dispersion statistic measure? How are the two related mathematically?

7. State and explain the law of large numbers.

8. Under what circumstances will a sampling distribution of proportions fit the normal distribution?

9. Match the symbols on the left with their definitions on the right.
   a. X _____ The standard deviation for a *sample* of raw scores X
   b. μ_X _____ The standard deviation for a *population* of raw scores X
   c. $\bar{X}$ _____ The symbol for an interval/ratio variable and its raw scores
   d. s_X _____ The standard error of a *sampling distribution* of means for the variable X, estimated from the sample standard deviation

e. σ_X _____ The mean of a *sample* of raw scores of the variable X

f. $s_{\overline{X}}$ _____ The mean of a *population* of raw scores of the variable X

10. The symbols in question 9 apply to variables of what levels of measurement?

11. Match the symbols on the left with their definitions on the right.

a. P _____ The proportion in the "success" category in a *population* of subjects

b. Q _____ p [of the success category]

c. P_u _____ The proportion in the "success" category in a *sample* of subjects

d. Q_u _____ The standard error of a distribution of sample proportions computed with known values of P_u and Q_u

e. P_s _____ The standard error of a distribution of sample proportions estimated from the sample statistics P_s and Q_s

f. σ_{P_s} _____ The proportion of the "failure" category in a *population* of subjects

g. s_{P_s} _____ p [of failure], where "failure" is the absence of a defined category or characteristic of a variable

12. The symbols in question 11 apply to variables of what levels of measurement?

13. Explain and illustrate with formulas why a standard error of means will always be smaller than the standard deviation of that variable.

EXERCISES FOR CHAPTER 7

Problem Set 7A

7A-1.   Elder et al. (2004) analyzed the prevalence and characteristics of alcohol-related hospital visits among a sample of emergency departments and found frequent visits related to assault. Suppose that you gather a random sample of 190 records from the files of young adults charged with assault over the past six months. You find that the mean age of those charged is 20.8 years with a standard deviation of 3.1 years. Use these statistics to calculate the standard error of a sampling distribution of ages.

7A-2.   The following (fictional) data are from a random sample of 437 employees of a multinational corporation. Complete the following table by calculating standard errors.

Variable	Standard Deviation or *P*	Standard Error
a. Monthly salary	$1,200	
b. Age	4 years	
c. Proportion female	.39	
d. Years of service	2.7 years	
e. Proportion of workers in manufacturing divisions	.57	

7A-3. Produce a sampling distribution of the proportion of heads in the repeated tossing of 10 coins. Take 10 dimes. Toss them at once. Do this 100 times. (Works best when tossed on a bed.)

    a. With each toss, count the number of "heads" and record the result in the following table under column A with a slash or stem (i.e., /). This is called a stem plot.

    b. After the 100 tosses, count the stems and record the frequency of each combination of heads in column B (e.g., ### // = seven times).

    c. Plot the resulting distribution of sample tosses on graph paper as a frequency histogram.

    d. Compute the probability of each sample outcome and record it under column C as "p of outcome."

    e. Exhibit your statistical imagination by describing in everyday terms why the sampling distribution took the shape it did.

No. Heads	(A) Stem Plot of Frequency	(B) Recorded Frequency of Occurrence	(C) *p* of Outcome
0			
1			
2			
3			
4			
5			
6			
7			
8			
9			
10			

7A-4. Produce a sampling distribution of means for a sample size of 60. (*Note:* This problem is less cumbersome if done as a group project in the classroom or laboratory.)

    a. Using the random number table (Statistical Table A in Appendix B), randomly select 60 *single* random digits; that is, X = a single random digit. Compute the mean of this sample and record it to one decimal place. Do this 100 times to obtain 100 sample means ($\overline{X}$) of $n = 60$.

    b. On graph paper, draw a histogram of this sampling distribution.

    c. From observation (without computing) provide an estimate of the mean of the population of random digits (μ_X) of a random number table.

    d. From observation (without computing) give an estimate of the standard error ($s_{\overline{X}}$) of this sampling distribution.

    e.   Use your basic knowledge of the normal curve to approximate how often sample outcomes occur within 1, 2, and 3 standard errors to both sides.

    f.   From this repeated-sampling experience, what did you learn about the dynamics of sampling interval/ratio variables?

7A-5.   The objective of this exercise is to produce a sampling distribution of means for a sample size of 7.

    a.   Using the random number table (Statistical Table A in Appendix B), randomly select seven *single* random digits; that is, X = a single random digit. Compute the mean of this sample and record it to one decimal place. Do this 120 times to obtain 120 sample means $(\overline{X})$ of $n = 7$.

    b.   On graph paper, draw a histogram of this sampling distribution.

    c.   From observation (without computing) provide an estimate of the mean of the population of random digits (μ_X) of a random number table.

    d.   From observation (without computing) give an estimate of the standard error $(s_{\overline{X}})$ of this sampling distribution.

    e.   From this repeated-sampling experience, what did you learn about the dynamics of sampling interval/ratio variables?

    f.   If you were assigned exercise 7A-4, compare the results of exercises 7A-4 and 7A-5 and comment with reference to the law of large numbers.

7A-6.   Produce a sampling distribution of proportions. In a box (or large bowl), dump one pound of (dry, uncooked) red beans and one pound of northern white beans; mix thoroughly (i.e., randomize). This is a population of beans. Take a tablespoon and draw *two* scoops to obtain a sample of beans from this population. To two decimal places, compute P_s, the proportion of red beans in the sample, where $P = p$ [of the beans that are red]. Replace the beans and mix thoroughly. Do this 100 times and plot the resulting sampling distribution of P_s's as a histogram. Observe the sampling distribution and answer the following questions *without making calculations.*

    a.   Give an estimate of the proportion of red beans in the population (i.e., the parameter for the entire box, P_u).

    b.   Give an estimate of the standard error of this sampling distribution (i.e., s_{P_s})

    c.   Use your basic knowledge of the normal curve to describe how often sample outcomes occur within 1, 2, and 3 standard errors to both sides.

    d.   From this bean-counting experience, what did you learn about the dynamics of sampling nominal variables?

7A-7.   Harmelink and VanDenburgh (2003) discuss the role of certified public accountants (CPAs) in guarding clients' investments. Suppose that you want to describe the sampling distribution of the proportion of persons satisfied with services received from a CPA. You survey a random sample of clients of 40 CPAs and find that 36 of the clients are satisfied.

    a.   Would it be appropriate to use a normal distribution to describe the sampling distribution? Why or why not?

b. Assuming that this sample proportion of those who are satisfied is a
    good estimate for the population of CPA clients, how large a sample is
    needed to use a normal curve as a description of this sampling
    distribution?

Problem Set 7B

7B-1. Guo (2004) discusses the relationship between marketing research and
marketing practices. As a marketing researcher at the Yeasty Feasty Bakery,
you conduct product purchase surveys, implementing a number of Guo's
suggestions. In your marketing area you find that the mean number of loaves
of bread consumed per month per household is 5.3 loaves with a standard
deviation of 1.5 loaves. These data are based on a sample of 200 households.
Use these statistics to calculate the standard error of a sampling distribution
of the mean loaves consumed per month.

7B-2. A marketing firm has surveyed 395 households to assess television-watching
habits. Complete the following table by calculating standard errors.

Variable	Standard Deviation or P	Standard Error
a. Age of household head	5 years	
b. Hours TV is on after 5:00 P.M.	1.5 hours	
c. Proportion of households owning their homes	.59	
d. Years of schooling	1.9 years	
e. Proportion of households with more than two TVs	.32	

7B-3. Produce a sampling distribution of the proportion of heads in the repeated
tossing of eight coins. Take eight dimes. Toss them at once. Do this 100
times. (Works best when tossed on a bed.)

a. With each toss, count the number of "heads" and record the result in the
    table on page 229 under column A with a slash or stem (i.e., /). This is
    called a stem plot.

b. After the 100 tosses, count the stems and record the frequency of each
    combination of heads in column B (e.g., ### // = seven times).

c. Plot the resulting distribution of sample tosses on graph paper as a
    frequency histogram.

d. Compute the probability of each sample outcome and record it under
    column C as "p of outcome."

e. Exhibit your statistical imagination by describing in everyday terms why
    the sampling distribution took the shape it did.

No. Heads	(A) Stem Plot of Frequency	(B) Recorded Frequency of Occurrence	(C) p of Outcome
0			
1			
2			
3			
4			
5			
6			
7			
8			

7B-4. Produce a sampling distribution of means for a sample size of 50. (*Note:* This problem is less cumbersome if done as a group project in the classroom or laboratory.)

    a. Using the random number table (Statistical Table A in Appendix B), randomly select 50 *single* random digits; that is, $X =$ a single random digit. Compute the mean of this sample and record it to one decimal place. Do this 100 times to obtain 100 sample means $(\overline{X})$ of $n = 50$.

    b. On graph paper, draw a histogram of this sampling distribution.

    c. From observation (without computing) provide an estimate of the mean of the population of random digits (μ_X) of a random number table.

    d. From observation (without computing) give an estimate of the standard error $(s_{\overline{X}})$ of this sampling distribution.

    e. Use your basic knowledge of the normal curve to describe how often sample outcomes occur within 1, 2, and 3 standard errors to both sides.

    f. From this repeated-sampling experience, what did you learn about the dynamics of sampling interval/ratio variables?

7B-5. Produce a sampling distribution of means for a sample size of 6. (*Note:* This problem is less cumbersome if done as a group project in the classroom or laboratory.)

    a. Using the random number table (Statistical Table A in Appendix B), randomly select six *single* random digits; that is, $X =$ a single random digit. Compute the mean of this sample and record it to one decimal place. Do this 120 times to obtain 120 sample means $(\overline{X})$ of $n = 6$.

    b. On graph paper, draw a histogram of this sampling distribution.

    c. From observation (without computing) provide an estimate of the mean of the population of random digits (μ_X) of a random number table.

    d. From observation (without computing) give an estimate of the standard error $(s_{\overline{X}})$ of this sampling distribution.

    e.   From this repeated-sampling experience, what did you learn about the dynamics of sampling interval/ratio variables?

    f.   If you were assigned exercise 7B-4, compare the results of exercises 7B-4 and 7B-5 and comment with reference to the law of large numbers.

7B-6.   Produce a sampling distribution of proportions. In a box (or large bowl), dump one pound of (dry, uncooked) red beans and one pound of northern white beans; mix thoroughly (i.e., randomize). This is a population of beans. Take a tablespoon and draw *two* scoops to obtain a sample of beans from this population. To two decimal places, compute P_s, the proportion of white beans in the sample, where $P = p$ [of the beans that are white]. Replace the beans and mix thoroughly. Do this 100 times and plot the resulting sampling distribution of P_s's as a histogram. Observe the sampling distribution and answer the following questions *without making calculations*.

    a.   Give an estimate of the proportion of white beans in the population (i.e., the parameter for the entire box, P_u).

    b.   Give an estimate of the standard error of this sampling distribution (i.e., s_{P_s}).

    c.   Use your basic knowledge of the normal curve to describe how often sample outcomes occur within 1, 2, and 3 standard errors to both sides.

    d.   From this bean-counting experience, what did you learn about the dynamics of sampling nominal variables?

7B-7.   Spoge and Trewin (2003) discuss the rising popularity of paperless electronic income tax filing, which gives individuals a faster turnaround time on their tax refunds. You are to describe the sampling distribution of the proportion of persons satisfied with how quickly the Internal Revenue Service returned their tax refunds. You obtain a random sample of 20 persons who received refunds and find that 16 are satisfied.

    a.   Would it be appropriate to use a normal distribution to describe the sampling distribution? Why or why not?

    b.   Assuming that this sample proportion of those satisfied is a good estimate for the population of those receiving refunds, how large a sample is needed to use a normal curve as a description of this sampling distribution?

Problem Set 7C

7C-1.   Wee et al. (2005) estimated health care expenditures associated with obesity in the United States, examining the influence of age, race, and gender. Suppose that you gather a random sample of 275 medical records from a small community health center in the Southeast, calculating each patient's most recent body mass index (BMI) in kg/m^2. You discover that the mean BMI for this sample is 30.4 kg/m^2, with a standard deviation of 3.2 kg/m^2. Use these statistics to calculate the standard error of a sampling distribution of body mass indexes.

7C-2.   Assume that the following data are from a random sample of 511 full- and part-time students at a major urban university. Complete the following table by calculating standard errors.

Variable	Standard Deviation or *P*	Standard Error
a. Monthly financial aid	$300	
b. Age	5 years	
c. Proportion male	.41	
d. Weekly work hours	3.7 hours	
e. Proportion of students currently employed	.71	

7C-3.   Produce a sampling distribution of the proportion of tails in the repeated tossing of 10 coins. Take 10 dimes. Toss them at once. Do this 100 times. (Works best when tossed on a bed.)

   a.   With each toss, count the number of "tails" and record the result in the following table under column A with a slash or stem (i.e., /). This is called a stem plot.

   b.   After the 100 tosses, count the stems and record the frequency of each combination of tails in column B (e.g., *HH* // = seven times).

   c.   Plot the resulting distribution of sample tosses on graph paper as a frequency histogram.

   d.   Compute the probability of each sample outcome and record it under column C as "*p* of outcome."

   e.   Exhibit your statistical imagination by describing in everyday terms why the sampling distribution took the shape it did.

No Tails	(A) Stem Plot of Frequency	(B) Recorded Frequency of Occurrence	(C) *p* of Outcome
0			
1			
2			
3			
4			
5			
6			
7			
8			
9			
10			

7C-4. Produce a sampling distribution of means for a sample size of 60. (*Note:* This problem is less cumbersome if done as a group project in the classroom or laboratory.)

    a. Using the random number table (Statistical Table A in Appendix B), randomly select 60 *single* random digits; that is, X = a single random digit. Compute the mean of this sample and record it to one decimal place. Do this 100 times to obtain 100 sample means ($\overline{X}$) of $n = 60$.

    b. On graph paper, draw a histogram of this sampling distribution.

    c. From observation (without computing) provide an estimate of the mean of the population of random digits (μ_X) of a random number table.

    d. From observation (without computing) give an estimate of the standard error ($s_{\overline{X}}$) of this sampling distribution.

    e. Use your basic knowledge of the normal curve to approximate how often sample outcomes occur within 1, 2, and 3 standard errors to both sides.

    f. From this repeated-sampling experience, what did you learn about the dynamics of sampling interval/ratio variables?

7C-5. Produce a sampling distribution of means for a sample size of 5. (*Note:* This problem is less cumbersome if done as a group project in the classroom or laboratory.)

    a. Using the random number table (Statistical Table A in Appendix B), randomly select five *single* random digits; that is, X = a single random digit. Compute the mean of this sample and record it to one decimal place. Do this 120 times to obtain 120 sample means ($\overline{X}$) of $n = 5$.

    b. On graph paper, draw a histogram of this sampling distribution.

    c. From observation (without computing) provide an estimate of the mean of the population of random digits (μ_X) of a random number table.

    d. From observation (without computing) give an estimate of the standard error ($s_{\overline{X}}$) of this sampling distribution.

    e. From this repeated-sampling experience, what did you learn about the dynamics of sampling interval/ratio variables?

    f. If you were assigned exercise 7C-4, compare the results of exercises 7C-4 and 7C-5 and comment with reference to the law of large numbers.

7C-6. Produce a sampling distribution of proportions. In a box (or large bowl), dump one pound of (dry, uncooked) red beans and one pound of northern white beans; mix thoroughly (i.e., randomize). This is a population of beans. Take a tablespoon and draw *two* scoops to obtain a sample of beans from this population. To two decimal places, compute P_s, the proportion of red beans in the sample, where $P = p$ [of the beans that are red]. Replace the beans and mix thoroughly. Do this 100 times and plot the resulting sampling distribution of P_s's as a histogram. Observe the sampling distribution and answer the following questions *without making calculations*.

    a. Give an estimate of the proportion of red beans in the population (i.e., the parameter for the entire box, P_u).

      b.   Give an estimate of the standard error of this sampling distribution (i.e., s_{P_s}).

      c.   Use your basic knowledge of the normal curve to describe how often sample outcomes occur within 1, 2, and 3 standard errors to both sides.

      d.   From this bean-counting experience, what did you learn about the dynamics of sampling nominal variables?

7C-7.   Martin (2003) discusses the impact of voting rewards (e.g., fund allocation, budget benefits, etc.) on political participation and voter turnout. Suppose that you are interested in describing the sampling distribution of the proportion of students that voted in the 2004 presidential election. You obtain a random sample of 30 students on campus, survey them, and discover that 18 of them voted.

      a.   Would it be appropriate to use a normal distribution to describe the sampling distribution? Why or why not?

      b.   Assuming that this sample proportion of student voters is a good estimate for the population of students who turned out to vote, what is the smallest sample needed to use a normal curve as a description of this sampling distribution?

Problem Set 7D

7D-1.   In the United Kingdom, Prosser and Walley (2005) explored the extent to which general practitioners consider financial costs when prescribing drugs. Suppose you are interested in the same phenomenon. You discover that the mean cost of 650 British patients' prescriptions is 32 pounds sterling (£) with a standard deviation of 9 pounds sterling (£). Use these statistics to calculate the standard error of a sampling distribution of prescription costs.

7D-2.   Assume that the following data are from a random sample of 298 mothers of children enrolled in an educational day camp program. Complete the following table by calculating standard errors.

Variable	Standard Deviation or *P*	Standard Error
a. Age of oldest child	1.9 years	
b. Hours worked per week	1.5 hours	
c. Proportion renting their homes	.36	
d. Years of education	2.8 years	
e. Proportion of mothers with more than one child	.44	

7D-3.   Produce a sampling distribution of the proportion of tails in the repeated tossing of 10 coins. Take 10 dimes. Toss them at once. Do this 100 times. (Works best when tossed on a bed.)

      a.   With each toss, count the number of "tails" and record the result in the following table under column A with a slash or stem (i.e., /). This is called a stem plot.

b. After the 100 tosses, count the stems and record the frequency of each combination of tails in column B (e.g., ⧾⧾ // = seven times).

c. Plot the resulting distribution of sample tosses on graph paper as a frequency histogram.

d. Compute the probability of each sample outcome and record it under column C as "p of outcome."

e. Exhibit your statistical imagination by describing in everyday terms why the sampling distribution took the shape it did.

No Tails	(A) Stem Plot of Frequency	(B) Recorded Frequency of Occurrence	(C) p of Outcome
0			
1			
2			
3			
4			
5			
6			
7			
8			
9			
10			

7D-4. Produce a sampling distribution of means for a sample size of 60. (*Note:* This problem is less cumbersome if done as a group project in the classroom or laboratory.)

a. Using the random number table (Statistical Table A in Appendix B), randomly select 60 *single* random digits; that is, X = a single random digit. Compute the mean of this sample and record it to one decimal place. Do this 100 times to obtain 100 sample means $(\bar{X})$ of $n = 60$.

b. On graph paper, draw a histogram of this sampling distribution.

c. From observation (without computing) provide an estimate of the mean of the population of random digits (μ_X) of a random number table.

d. From observation (without computing) give an estimate of the standard error ($s_{\bar{X}}$) of this sampling distribution.

e. Use your basic knowledge of the normal curve to describe how often sample outcomes occur within 1, 2, and 3 standard errors to both sides.

f. From this repeated-sampling experience, what did you learn about the dynamics of sampling interval/ratio variables?

7D-5. Produce a sampling distribution of means for a sample size of 8. (*Note:* This problem is less cumbersome if done as a group project in the classroom or laboratory.)

a. Using the random number table (Statistical Table A in Appendix B), randomly select eight *single* random digits; that is, X = a single random digit. Compute the mean of this sample and record it to one decimal place. Do this 120 times to obtain 120 sample means $(\overline{X})$ of $n = 8$.
b. On graph paper, draw a histogram of this sampling distribution.
c. From observation (without computing) provide an estimate of the mean of the population of random digits (μ_X) of a random number table.
d. From observation (without computing) give an estimate of the standard error $(s_{\overline{X}})$ of this sampling distribution.
e. From this repeated-sampling experience, what did you learn about the dynamics of sampling interval/ratio variables?
f. If you were assigned exercise 7D-4, compare the results of exercises 7D-4 and 7D-5 and comment with reference to the law of large numbers.

7D-6. Produce a sampling distribution of proportions. In a box (or large bowl), dump one pound of (dry, uncooked) red beans and one pound of northern white beans; mix thoroughly (i.e., randomize). This is a population of beans. Take a tablespoon and draw *two* scoops to obtain a sample of beans from this population. To two decimal places, compute P_s, the proportion of white beans in the sample, where $P = p$ [of the beans that are white]. Replace the beans and mix thoroughly. Do this 100 times and plot the resulting sampling distribution of P_s's as a histogram. Observe the sampling distribution and answer the following questions *without making calculations*.
a. Give an estimate of the proportion of white beans in the population (i.e., the parameter for the entire box, P_u).
b. Give an estimate of the standard error of this sampling distribution (i.e., s_{P_s}).
c. Use your basic knowledge of the normal curve to describe how often sample outcomes occur within 1, 2, and 3 standard errors to both sides.
d. From this bean-counting experience, what did you learn about the dynamics of sampling nominal variables?

7D-7. *Medical adherence* is a term used to refer to when a patient follows a doctor's orders. Kim, Kaplowitz, and Johnston (2004) examined the effects of physician empathy on adherence. Along similar lines, you are to describe the sampling distribution of the proportion of patients who adhere to their doctors' recommendations. You obtain a random sample of 57 patients from a physician's office and find that 33 of them adhered.
a. Would it be appropriate to use a normal distribution to describe the sampling distribution? Why or why not?
b. Assuming that this sample proportion of patients who adhered is a good estimate for the population of patients, what is the smallest sample needed to use a normal curve as a description of this sampling distribution?

OPTIONAL COMPUTER APPLICATIONS
FOR CHAPTER 7

If your class uses the optional computer applications that accompany this text, open the Chapter 7 exercises on *The Statistical Imagination* Web site at www.mhhe.com/ritchey2. These exercises involve producing sampling distributions by using the computer's random number generator. These exercises reinforce your understanding of sampling distributions and will help you achieve a sense of proportion on the relationship between sample size and sampling error. In addition, Appendix D of this text provides a brief overview of the *SPSS* command sequences for procedures covered in this chapter.

CHAPTER

8

Parameter Estimation Using Confidence Intervals

Introduction

Last night Kristi attended a rock concert at the campus stadium. Upon returning to her residence hall, she discovered that in the revelry of the event she had lost an inexpensive but sentimentally valuable ring, one passed down from her grandmother. She has spent most of today searching the stadium's ball field and is beginning to lose hope. Finally, Kristi remembers that her friend Sarah has a metal detector and gives her a call. As it turns out, Sarah's metal detector is not very astute at pinpointing objects, but it is quite reliable within a span of error. Specifically, the detector beeps when it is within 2 yards of a metal object. Sarah arrives and walks the field with her metal detector, and it beeps. But then she says that she must scoot to meet another friend for dinner. Kristi asks, "Where is my ring?" Sarah tells her to look a couple of yards to either side of the 50-yard line, near the far hash mark. Kristi asks: "Are you sure I will find it?" Sarah responds that her detector is precise to within 4 yards 95 percent of the time. Sarah is quite confident—95 percent—so she bets Kristi a dinner that she will find the ring. Sarah could not point to the ring's exact location, but she has a high degree of confidence that it is within the 4-yard area she described. (Kristi, incidentally, found her ring within a few minutes and treated Sarah to a meal the next evening.)

Searching for the location of an object is similar to estimating the value of a population parameter by using the statistics from a sample. As we learned in Chapter 7, the statistics of a sample are estimates—calculations that only fall near the value of the true population parameter—just as Sarah's metal detector only got Kristi close to the location of her ring. Can we do as Sarah did and not only point to a spot but also give a reliable span of area within which to look for a parameter? For example, can we take one sample of 10th-graders and estimate the mean height of all 10th-graders to within one inch—a point estimate give or take a half inch (say, 67.5 inches $\pm$ .5 inch)? Our conclusion would be that the mean height is between 67 and 68 inches—not exact but close. And can we, like Sarah, declare that we are 95 percent confident of this interval estimate? As we noted in Chapter 7, repeated sampling reveals that any single point estimate only gets us close when estimating a population parameter, just as Sarah pinpointed a spot on the field. In this chapter we learn to say confidently just how close this single point estimate is to the true parameter *within a range of error,* just as Sarah sent Kristi to search within two yards to either side of the detector's beeping point. Such an estimation is called a confidence interval.

A **confidence interval** is *a range of possible values of a* **parameter** *expressed with a specific degree of confidence*. With confidence intervals we take a point estimate and couple it with knowledge about sampling distributions. We project a known, calculable span—or "interval"—of error around the point estimate. For example, where X = grade point average (GPA), suppose we take a sample of 300 Crosstown University students and compute a sample mean GPA ($\overline{X}$) of 2.46. Our knowledge of repeated sampling and sampling distributions tells us that this sample statistic should be close to the true population parameter. How close? In Chapter 7 we saw that a sampling distribution of means, produced by repeatedly sampling a population, takes the shape of a normal curve when $n > 121$. With a sample of 300 Crosstown students, we can report the results of repeated sampling in a distributional way and say, for example, that 95 percent of the samples fall within about 2 standard errors of the true parameter. We may interpret this percentage in a probabilistic way and say that *if we draw only one sample,* there is a 95 percent probability that this single sample's mean falls within about 2 standard errors of the parameter, whatever that parameter may be. This predictable error, the product of about 2 times the standard error, is called the error term of a 95 percent confidence interval for this situation when n is greater than 121. This error term allows us to provide a probabilistic interpretation of a single-sample calculation.

In calculating confidence intervals, we do *not* repeatedly sample, plot, and compute areas under a sampling distribution curve. Instead, we draw only one sample and

---

confidence interval A range of possible values of a parameter expressed with a specific degree of confidence.

compute a point estimate such as the mean. We then compute a standard error and multiply it by a Z-score that is chosen for a desired level of confidence. The result is a range of error based on knowing about the predictability of error from repeated sampling. Then we add and subtract this amount from the point estimate to obtain an interval within which the parameter is likely to fall. This error term is a "give or take some error" amount (just as Sarah said to look a couple yards to either side of the 50-yard line). For instance, if we calculate the 95 percent confidence interval of the mean GPA of Crosstown University students, our answer may take the form of an interval of values, say, 2.16 to 2.76 GPA points—the sample mean of 2.46 (a point estimate) plus or minus .30 (an error term). The result is an interval estimate of the true mean GPA (μ_X), a range of GPA values in which the true campus mean is likely to fall. While we do not say that we know the exact value of the mean GPA of the entire student body, we are 95 percent sure that this parameter is between 2.16 and 2.76. The calculated value of 2.16 sets the lower confidence limit (LCL), the smallest value we think μ_X could have. Similarly, 2.76 sets the upper confidence limit (UCL), the highest value we think μ_X could have. We acknowledge that the population mean GPA could be as low as 2.16 or as high as 2.76 or anywhere in between. That is, μ_X could be 2.16, 2.17, 2.18, 2.28, 2.34, or any value up to 2.76. We do not insist that we have found the exact value any more than Sarah insisted that she found the exact spot where Kristi's ring lay. But just like Sarah, we can bet with 95 percent confidence that the computed interval has the true population value within it. The objective of computing a confidence interval, then, is to estimate a population parameter within a specific span or "interval" of values.

Confidence intervals are used frequently in exploratory studies. Recall from Chapter 1 that exploratory studies seek information about new phenomena for which so little is known that formulating a theory is impossible. Confidence intervals ask the first, basic question: What is the value of an unknown parameter? If your course uses *SPSS* statistical software, you will note that confidence intervals are computed under the menu item "Explore."

Computing a confidence interval is like casting a fishing net into a pond in which there is only one fish. The location of the fish at a given moment represents the unknown parameter. Is it 10 feet upshore, 20 feet, or 30 feet, and so on? We have one opportunity to cast the net and wish to feel 95 percent confident of catching the fish. A point estimate of the location provides some rough information, telling us in which part of the pond to cast the net, say, by a stump that is down the shore a ways. Computing the confidence interval tells us how wide to cast the net. Our stipulated level of confidence tells us our success rate—how often we will catch the fish if we use a net of a certain width: the width of the computed confidence interval. The **level of confidence** is *a calculated degree of confidence that a statistical procedure conducted with sample data will produce a correct result for the sampled population.*

---

level of confidence   A calculated degree of confidence that a statistical procedure conducted with sample data will produce a correct result for the sampled population.

Confidence Interval of a Population Mean

For any interval/ratio variable X, such as GPA, we set out to estimate the mean of a population. The question we want to answer is: What is the value of μ_X? Sample statistics are the tools we use to obtain this estimate. This is depicted in Figure 8–1.

Suppose, for example, we are studying the wage structure of an industrial plant that employs several thousand computer assemblers but do not have access to all company files. We obtain a random sample of 129 personnel files with data on hourly wages, a ratio variable X. Our purpose is to use these sample data to make statements about the entire population of computer assemblers. Thus, we compute a confidence interval for the mean wage, μ_X, of all assemblers. Our research question is: Within a specified span of dollar amounts, what is the parameter μ_X, the mean hourly wage of *the population* of computer assemblers? Is it between, say, $9 and $10, or between $14 and $15, or what? With a 95 percent confidence interval, we will be 95 percent confident that the mean wage is within the span of dollar amounts we compute.

By relying on a sample, we know that there is error in our conclusion because we know about sampling error. In fact, the only way to be perfectly confident, or 100 percent confident, is to eliminate any sampling error by gathering data on the entire population and computing the correct parameter μ_X. This is too costly and time-consuming. Thus, we settle on using a sample, knowing that we will have some degree of error in our conclusion. Fortunately, the amount of this expected error is known. The **level of expected error** is *the difference between the stated level of confidence and "perfect confidence" of 100 percent.* In other words, if we are 95 percent confident about our stated conclusion, we are 5 percent unsure about it. Thus, we have a 5 percent level of expected error.

FIGURE 8–1

Using sample statistics to obtain an interval estimate of a population parameter for an interval/ratio variable X = GPA

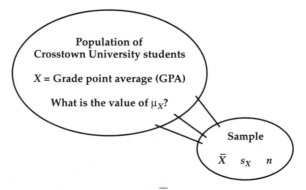

Conclusion about μ_X based on observing $\overline{X}$: We are 95 percent confident that the mean GPA of Crosstown University students is between 2.16 and 2.76.

In computing a confidence interval, we use the Greek letter *alpha* (α) to symbol-ize the level of expected error. This level of expected error also is called the *level of significance,* a term thoroughly covered in Chapter 9. In computing the 95 percent con-fidence interval, our level of significance or expected error is 5 percent:

$$\text{Level of confidence} = 95\%$$
$$\text{Level of significance (expected error)} = \alpha = 100\% - \text{level of confidence}$$
$$= 100\% - 95\% = 5\%$$

In general, then, the level of confidence and the level of significance are inversely related; as one increases, the other decreases. Together, the level of confidence and the level of significance sum to 100 percent. Thus:

Calculating the Level of Confidence and the Level of Significance

$$\text{Level of confidence} = 100\% - \alpha$$

Therefore,

$$\alpha = 100\% - \text{level of confidence}$$

where

$$\alpha = \text{level of significance (or expected error)}$$

To calculate a confidence interval, we calculate a standard error. Then, from the normal curve table (Statistical Table B in Appendix B), we obtain a Z-score that corre-sponds to chosen levels of confidence and significance (α). We call this a *critical* Z-score, symbolized by Z_α. We multiply Z_α by the standard error to obtain an "error term." The error term is the amount of plus and minus error, such as ± 3 percent that we report with our interval estimate. To calculate the confidence interval, we add and subtract this error term from the sample mean. The resulting spread of values is a con-fidence interval estimate of the population mean:

$$\text{Confidence interval} = \text{a point estimate} \pm \text{an error term}$$

Calculating the Standard Error for a Confidence Interval of a Population Mean

The purpose of a confidence interval is to determine an approximation of the popula-tion parameter. The parameter, then, is unknown. For an interval/ratio variable, both the mean and the standard deviation of the population are unknown. Therefore, we must use the sample standard deviation to estimate the standard error of the mean. Recall from Chapter 7 that this estimated standard error is as follows:

Computing the (Estimated) Standard Error of a Confidence Interval of a Population Mean

$$s_{\overline{X}} = \frac{s_X}{\sqrt{n}}$$

where

$s_{\overline{X}}$ = estimated standard error of means for an interval/ratio variable X
s_X = standard deviation of a sample
n = sample size

Choosing the Critical Z-Score, Z_α

With confidence intervals we use our knowledge of sampling distributions to determine the levels of significance and confidence. Confidence intervals traditionally are stated for 95 percent and 99 percent confidence. Recall from Chapter 7 that a sampling distribution of means takes the shape of a normal curve when $n > 121$. Moreover, the standard deviation of a sampling distribution is called the standard error. As we noted earlier, in repeated sampling approximately 95 percent of sample means will fall within 2 standard errors of the population mean. To be more exact, 95 percent of sample means fall precisely within 1.96 standard errors and 5 percent fall in the two tails. In the normal curve table, observe a Z-score of 1.96 in column A. In column C we find that .0250 (or 2.5 percent) of cases fall outside this score on each side of the distribution.

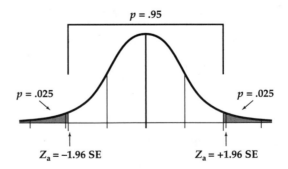

This Z-score of ± 1.96 is referred to as a *critical* Z-score for the 95 percent level of confidence. We use Z_α to symbolize it, where α is the level of significance, which, again, is 1 − the level of confidence. In repeated sampling we are confident that 95 percent of sample outcomes will fall within this range and 5 percent outside of it in the two tails of the curve.

For the 99 percent level of confidence, the level of significance is 1 percent or .01. Split into two tails, we have .005 (one-half of 1 percent) of the area of the curve in each tail. The critical Z-score (Z_α) that isolates these areas of the curve is ± 2.58.

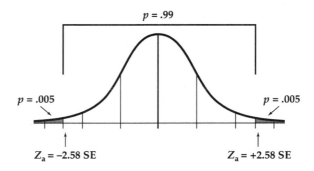

Calculating the Error Term

Once the standard error is computed, it is multiplied by Z_α to obtain the error term.

Calculating the Error Term of a Confidence Interval of a Population Mean (when $n \geq 121$)

$$\text{Error term} = (Z_\alpha)(s_{\bar{X}})$$

where

α = level of significance (or expected error)

Z_α = critical Z-score that corresponds to the stated levels of significance and confidence

$s_{\bar{X}}$ = estimated standard error of a confidence interval of the mean

Calculating the Confidence Interval

Keeping in mind that a confidence interval of a population mean is a sample mean plus and minus an error term, the general formula for computing the confidence interval of a population mean is as follows:

Calculating a Confidence Interval (CI) of a Population Mean (when $n > 121$)

$$(100\% - \alpha)\ CI \text{ of } \mu_X = \overline{X} \pm (Z_\alpha)\,(s_{\overline{X}})$$

where

α = level of significance (or expected error, expressed as a percentage)

$(100\% - \alpha)$ = level of confidence

CI of μ_X = "confidence interval of a population mean"

$\overline{X}$ = sample mean

Z_α = critical Z-score that corresponds to the stated level of significance and confidence

$s_{\overline{X}}$ = (estimated) standard error of a confidence interval of the mean

---

Again, two very commonly reported confidence intervals are the 95 percent and 99 percent CIs. In the common situation of a sample size of n greater than 121, the following formulas are used:

Calculating 95 Percent and 99 Percent Confidence Intervals of a Population Mean for the Common Situation of $n > 121$

$$95\%\ CI \text{ of } \mu_X = \overline{X} \pm (1.96)\,(s_{\overline{X}})$$

and

$$99\%\ CI \text{ of } \mu_X = \overline{X} \pm (2.58)\,(s_{\overline{X}})$$

where

X = an interval/ratio variable

$95\%\ CI$ of μ_X = "95% confidence interval of the population mean of X"

$99\%\ CI$ of μ_X = "99% confidence interval of the population mean of X"

$\overline{X}$ = sample mean

$s_{\overline{X}}$ = estimated standard error of the mean

When to Calculate a Confidence Interval of a Population Mean (when $n > 121$)

1. The research question calls for estimating a population parameter.
2. The variable of interest (X) is of interval/ratio level of measurement. Thus, we are to provide an interval estimate of the value of a population parameter μ_X.
3. We are working with a single representative sample from one population.
4. The sample size is greater than 121.

The Five Steps for Computing a Confidence Interval of a Population Mean, μ_X

We will compute confidence intervals by following these five steps: (1) State the research question, identify the level of measurement of the variable, list "givens," and draw a diagram (like Figure 8–1) representing the target population, its parameter to be estimated, the sample, and its statistics; (2) compute the standard error and the error term; (3) using the general formula for confidence intervals, compute the LCL and UCL; (4) provide an interpretation of findings in everyday language directed to individuals and groups that know little about statistics (e.g., college or company administrators, city officials, news reporters, and the public); and (5) provide a statistical interpretation illustrating the notion of "confidence in the procedure." The following checklist is handy for remembering these steps. A complete sample problem follows.

Brief Checklist of Five Steps for Computing Confidence Intervals

Step 1. State the research question. Draw conceptual diagrams depicting givens, including the population and sample under study, the variable (e.g., $X = \ldots$) and its level of measurement, and given or calculated statistics.

Step 2. Compute the standard error and error term.

Step 3. Compute the LCL and UCL of the confidence interval.

Step 4. Provide an interpretation in everyday language.

Step 5. Provide a statistical interpretation illustrating the notion of "confidence in the procedure."

How to Calculate a Confidence Interval of a Population Mean

Problem: We are conducting a study of the wage structure of an industrial plant that employs several thousand computer assemblers. We need to get a rough idea of the mean hourly wage of this population of assemblers. We randomly select 129 personnel files and record the hourly wages. In this sample we find a mean of $8.00 and a standard deviation of $1.70. Compute the 95 percent confidence interval for the mean hourly wage of the plant's assemblers. (In doing a problem, it is not necessary to state the instructions provided in parentheses.)

Step 1. Research question: Within a specified span of dollar amounts, what is the parameter μ_X, the mean hourly wage of the population of computer assemblers? *Givens:*

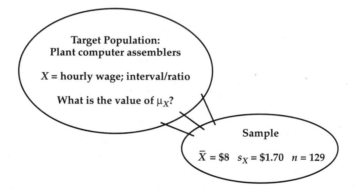

Step 2. (standard error, critical Z-score, and error term)

$$s_{\bar{X}} = \frac{s_X}{\sqrt{n}} = \frac{1.70}{\sqrt{129}} = \$.15$$

For 95 percent confidence, $Z_\alpha = 1.96$.

$$\text{Error term} = (Z_\alpha)(s_{\bar{X}}) = (1.96)(\$.15) = \$.29$$

Step 3. (LCL and UCL)

$$95\% \ CI \text{ of } \mu_X = \bar{X} \pm (1.96)(s_{\bar{X}})$$
$$= \text{sample mean} \pm \text{error term}$$
$$= \$8.00 \pm (1.96)(\$.15) = \$8.00 \pm \$.29$$
$$LCL = \$8.00 - \$.29 = \$7.71$$
$$UCL = \$8.00 + \$.29 = \$8.29$$

> **Step 4.**   (interpretation in everyday language): "I am 95 percent sure that the mean hourly wage of the plant's computer assemblers is between $7.71 and $8.29."
>
> **Step 5.**   (statistical interpretation illustrating the notion of "confidence in the procedure"): "If the same sampling and statistical procedures are conducted 100 times, 95 times the true population parameter μ_X will be encompassed in the computed intervals and 5 times it will not. Thus, I have 95 percent confidence that this single confidence interval I computed includes the true parameter."

Proper Interpretation of Confidence Intervals

When we use the statement "I am 95 percent confident," we are *actually expressing confidence in our method.* For the sample problem above, this is stated as the **statistical interpretation** of our results. For a 95 percent confidence interval of the mean, our statistical interpretation begins: If the same sampling and statistical procedures are conducted 100 times, 95 times the true population mean μ_X will be encompassed in the computed intervals. Remember, since we did not gather data for every member of the population, we cannot declare an exact, true value of the population mean (the parameter). Therefore, there is a chance that the computed confidence interval does not include the true parameter. To return to our fishing analogy, we do not know exactly where the fish is located. We may cast the net and not catch the fish. With a 95 percent confidence interval, this chance of failure is 5 percent (100 percent − 95 percent = 5 percent), the level of significance (or expected error). While we are going to cast the net only once, our knowledge of sampling error and its predictability with a normal curve assures us that if we cast it 100 times, we will net the fish 95 times. In the long run, a 95 percent confidence interval based on a single sample is correct 95 percent of the time.

To properly understand confidence intervals we must use the statistical imagination and employ what we know about repeated sampling, sampling distributions, and probability theory. Figure 8–2 portrays the notion of repeatedly sampling *and* computing confidence intervals for a sample size greater than 121. Ninety-five of every 100 sample means will compute to within 1.96 standard errors of the true population mean. This is because in repeated sampling 95 out of 100 samples fall that close. Figure 8–2 conveys that the statistical procedure of repeatedly calculating confidence intervals results in the true population mean falling within the interval a predictable 95 percent of the time (19 times out of 20). This means, of course, that the computed confidence interval will miss the correct parameter a predictable 5 percent of the time (as is the case for sample number 7). Which samples hit and miss? *For the 95 means within 1.96 standard errors,* the computed confidence intervals will include the population's true parameter—its true mean. These sample means are close enough for their confidence intervals to stretch over to μ_X. For the five means that calculate outside 1.96 standard errors, the computed confidence intervals will miss the true parameter. In real life, we only take one sample and compute its confidence interval. We are banking on the probability that this single

FIGURE 8-2

The success rate of a 95 percent confidence interval in providing an interval estimate that encompasses the true population parameter value

μ_X = **unknown** mean of X in the population (i.e., the parameter)

LCL = lower confidence limit
UCL = upper confidence limit

Let us imagine drawing 100 samples with a sample size of, say, 122. We compute the $\bar{X}$ for each sample and plot the outcomes as a sampling distribution. This distribution will be normal in shape, with sample means centering on the true population parameter value, μ_X (whatever its value may be.) Since $n > 121$, a critical Z-score of ± 1.96 leaves 5 percent of the area in the tails of the curve and 95 percent in between. Thus, 95 percent of these means fall within 1.96 standard errors of the true parameter as it is depicted in the normal curve below. Let us imagine also that we compute 95 percent confidence intervals for each of these 100 sample means. For the 95 means that calculate to within 1.96 standard errors, their confidence intervals will be spread widely enough to encompass (or "catch") the true parameter, μ_X. For the five sample means outside of 1.96 standard errors, their computed confidence intervals will *not* be spread widely enough to catch the true parameter. In other words, the procedure of calculating a 95 percent confidence interval works 95 percent of the time. The following diagram presents 20 of 100 samples with calculated confidence intervals. Ninety-five percent (19 of 20) encompass the population parameter (μ_X). Sample number 7 depicts the one of 20 (i.e., 5 percent) that fails to encompass the population mean.

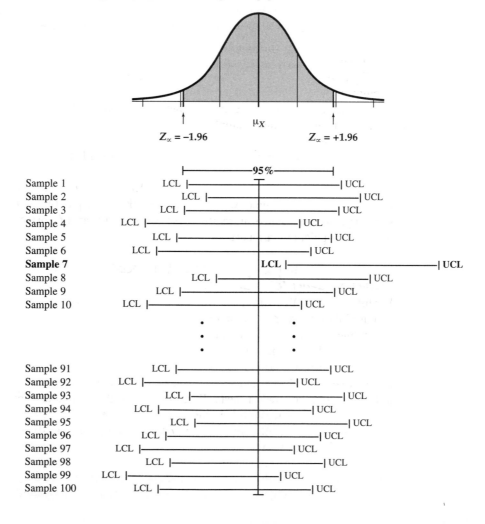

sample is one of the 95 that fall within 1.96 standard errors of the true parameter. If it is one of those 95, when we cast out 1.96 standard errors we will catch the true μ_X whatever its value is. Of course, we still do not know the true parameter and our confidence interval is only an interval estimate; sometimes this estimate is quite broad. We will never know the true parameter, μ_X, unless we have the time and money to obtain data from every member of the population, but odds of 95 out of 100 are pretty good.

Common Misinterpretations of Confidence Intervals

A confidence interval addresses the size of parameters, not individual scores. Thinking in terms of individual scores is a common misinterpretation of a confidence interval. In the example of a confidence interval of the mean wage of a plant's computer assemblers, we stated: "I am 95 percent sure that *the mean hourly wage* of the plant's computer assemblers is between \$7.71 and \$8.29." We are *not saying* that 95 percent of the computer assemblers earn hourly wages between those two figures! If our purpose had been to describe a score span in which 95 percent of the assemblers fall, we would have used the standard deviation of the sample—not the standard error—to make such a projection (as in Chapter 6). The confidence interval addresses issues of summary statistics, not individual scores.

We also must take care not to begin treating our sample mean as though it were the population mean itself. We learned in Chapter 7 that repeated sampling produces a sampling distribution with sample means centered on the population mean, μ_X. But it would be wrong to take the single sample mean, $\overline{X}$, of our study and treat it as though all other sample means centered on it. In other words, with a confidence interval, we are *not* saying that 95 percent of repeated samples will have means between the upper and lower confidence limits computed *from this single sample mean*. It is the unknown population mean around which these other samples fall. The confidence interval interpretation is based on our single sample, whose mean is unlikely to equal the population mean. In summary, the confidence interval simply gives us a span of possible values for the unknown population parameter.

The Chosen Level of Confidence and the Precision of the Confidence Interval

For the sample of 129 computer assemblers, we chose the 95 percent level of confidence and used the critical Z-score of 1.96 to compute the error term. The use of Z-scores in computing confidence intervals is related to our knowledge of sampling distributions from repeated sampling. In Chapter 7 we learned that if we draw many samples and compute their means (as did our ancestral bean counters), the sampling distribution will be a normal distribution when $n > 121$. The Z-scores measure how far off a sample mean is from the true population mean. With the help of the normal distribution probability table, these scores determine the probability of occurrence of sampling outcomes.

In calculating a confidence interval, *once a sample has been drawn,* its mean, standard deviation, and sample size are "givens." That is, we are stuck with them. These givens determine the standard error of the confidence interval and therefore greatly influence the width of the calculated confidence interval. If the standard deviation is large or the sample size is small, the confidence interval is going to calculate widely; it will not be very precise. After the sample is "given," however, we may still influence the precision of a confidence interval through our choice of the level of confidence. The chosen level of confidence determines the size of the critical Z-score (Z_α). The greater the chosen level of confidence, the larger the Z_α. Therefore, in the calculation of the confidence limits, a large Z_α produces a large error term and a less precise (or broader) confidence interval.

For example, let us substitute a Z_α of 2.58 in place of 1.96 in the example problem of the confidence interval of the mean wage of computer assemblers. In the normal distribution table, this is the Z_α that corresponds to a 99 percent confidence interval:

$$99\% \ CI \ of \ \mu_X = \overline{X} \pm (2.58)(s_{\overline{X}}) = \$8.00 \pm (2.58)(\$0.15)$$

$$= \$8.00 \pm \$.39 = \$7.61 \text{ to } \$8.39$$

Comparing the two confidence intervals, we can see that we have greater confidence at the 99 percent level but that our estimate is less precise:

$$95\% \ CI \ of \ \mu_X = \$7.71 \text{ to } \$8.29; \text{ this interval is } \$0.58 \text{ wide}$$
$$99\% \ CI \ of \ \mu_X = \$7.61 \text{ to } \$8.39; \text{ this interval is } \$0.78 \text{ wide}$$

---

the relationship between the level of confidence and the degree of precision   The greater the stated level of confidence, the greater the error term and therefore the less precise the confidence interval.

This makes sense. If we are going to place a lot of faith (or confidence) in an answer, we must play it safe by allowing for a lot of error. For example, we might say we are 99.9999 percent confident (and be willing to bet $100 on our answer) that the mean wage of computer assemblers is between $3 and $100 per hour. In this absurd situation we are confident, but the degree of precision is so low that it is meaningless. On the other hand, if we provide an estimate with a high degree of precision of, say, 10 cents—$7.95 to $8.05—we will not bet too much on it. To return once again to the fishing analogy, someone might say that he or she is 100 percent confident that the fish is between one shore and the other, but this "help" is so imprecise that it is useless. On the other hand, if we asked whether the fish was between us and a dock 20 steps away, he or she might respond, "I'm not so sure."

Sample Size and the Precision of the Confidence Interval
There is a way to obtain a high degree of precision *and* maintain a high level of confidence: *Make sure before collecting data* that the sample size is sufficiently large to produce small standard errors and precise confidence intervals. Let us see how sample size affects the width of a confidence interval. Let us recompute the 95 percent confidence interval for the population of computer assemblers but use a sample size of 1,000

instead of 129. Let us assume that the sample mean and standard deviation remain the same, and recalculate the standard error, error term, and confidence interval:

$$s_{\bar{X}} = \frac{s_X}{\sqrt{n}} = \frac{1.70}{\sqrt{1000}} = \$.05$$

$$\text{Error term} = (Z_\alpha)(s_{\bar{X}}) = (1.96)(\$0.05) = \$0.10$$

$$95\% \; CI \text{ of } \mu_X = \bar{X} \pm (Z_\alpha)(s_{\bar{X}})$$
$$= \$8.00 \pm (1.96)(\$0.05)$$
$$= \$8.00 \pm \$0.10 = \$7.90 \text{ to } \$8.10$$

Comparing this sample of 1,000 to the sample of 129, we can see that the larger sample estimate is more precise:

With $n = 129$: 95% CI of $\mu_X = \$7.71$ to $\$8.29$; this interval is $\$0.58$ wide.

With $n = 1,000$: 95% CI of $\mu_X = \$7.90$ to $\$8.10$; this interval is only $\$0.20$ wide.

The more precise confidence interval for the sample of $n = 1,000$ makes intuitive sense and follows from the law of large numbers (Chapter 7). The larger the sample size, the smaller the sampling error and therefore the greater the precision of the confidence interval.

---

the relationship between sample size and degree of precision
The larger the sample size, the more precise the confidence interval.

Confidence Intervals of the Mean for Small Samples   For a confidence interval of the mean when the sample size (n) is less than or equal to 121, the critical scores of ± 1.96 and ± 2.58 are not appropriate. These scores are based on knowledge that samples of over 121 cases produce sampling distributions that fit the normal curve. Because the mean is susceptible to distortion by extreme scores, "small" samples of $n \le 121$ produce sampling distributions that are flatter than the bell shape of a normal curve. These distributions are called approximately normal distributions and their critical scores are called t-scores instead of Z-scores. In the formula for the confidence interval for small samples, t-scores are substituted for Z-scores. We will discuss this modification for small samples in Chapter 10.

Large-Sample Confidence Interval of a Population Proportion

With nominal/ordinal variables, confidence intervals provide an estimate of the proportion of a population that falls in the "success" category of the variable. Let us suppose that we are conducting election polling for a political candidate, Chantrise Jones. We wish to obtain an interval estimate of her support by conducting a telephone poll of likely voters two days before the election. We define $P = p$ [of likely voters supporting Chantrise]. Of course, we cannot afford to poll all likely voters; thus, we sample them. The sample proportion, P_s, is used to estimate the population parameter, P_u, within an interval with a calculated sampling error. Just as in the case of confidence intervals of the mean, we use a sample statistic, P_s, as a point estimate of P_u, and add and subtract an error term. The complete formula for computing the confidence interval of population proportion is

$$(100\% - \alpha) \; CI \; of \; P_u = P_s \pm (Z_\alpha)(s_{P_s})$$

$$= \text{sample proportion} \pm \text{error term}$$

Here $P = p$ [of the success category] of a nominal/ordinal variable, $\alpha = $ the level of significance (or expected error), $(100\% - \alpha) = $ the level of confidence, CI of P_u is read as "the confidence interval of a population proportion," $P_s = $ the sample proportion, $Z_\alpha = $ the critical Z-score (from the normal distribution table) that corresponds to the stated level of confidence and significance, and $s_{P_s} = $ the estimated standard error of a confidence interval of a proportion.

Here are the circumstances in which calculating a confidence interval of a population proportion is appropriate:

When to Calculate a Confidence Interval of a Population Proportion (for a nominal/ordinal variable)

1. We are to provide an interval estimate of the value of a population parameter, P_u, where $P = p$ [of the success category] of a nominal/ordinal variable.
2. We have a single representative sample from one population.
3. The sample size (n) is sufficiently large that $(p_{smaller})(n) \geq 5$, resulting in a sampling distribution that is normal.

The requirement that the sample size (n) be sufficiently large that $(p_{smaller})(n) \geq 5$ is the only restriction on sample size. The critical Z_α for a 95 percent confidence interval will always be ± 1.96, and for the 99 percent confidence interval it will be ± 2.58.

We compute an estimated standard error based on sample data (as in Chapter 7) and calculate the error term as follows:

Computing the Standard Error of a Confidence Interval of a Population Proportion (for a nominal/ordinal variable)

$$sp_S = \sqrt{\frac{P_s Q_s}{n}}$$

where

sp_S = estimated standard error of proportions for a nominal variable with
$\quad\quad P = p$ [of the success category]
$P_s = p$ [of the success category in the sample]
$Q_s = p$ [of the failure category in the sample] $= 1 - P_s$
$\quad n$ = sample size

Calculating the Error Term of a Confidence Interval of a Population Proportion

$$\text{Error term} = (Z_\alpha)(sp_S)$$

where

α = level of significance (or expected error)
Z_α = critical Z-score that corresponds to the stated level of confidence
$\quad\quad$ and significance
sp_S = estimated standard error of proportions for a nominal/ordinal variable
$\quad\quad$ where $P = p$ [of the success category]

For the traditional 95 percent and 99 percent levels of confidence we use the following two equations:

Calculating 95 Percent and 99 Percent Confidence Intervals of a Population Proportion when ($p_{smaller}$) (n) $\geq$ 5 (for a nominal/ordinal variable)

$$95\% \; CI \text{ of } P_u = P_s \pm (1.96)\,(s_{p_s})$$

and

$$99\% \; CI \text{ of } P_u = P_s \pm (2.58)\,(s_{p_s})$$

where

$$P = p \; [\text{of the success category}] \text{ of a nominal/ordinal variable}$$
$$95\% \; CI \text{ of } P_u = 95 \text{ percent confidence interval of a population proportion}$$
$$99\% \; CI \text{ of } P_u = 99 \text{ percent confidence interval of a population proportion}$$
$$P_s = \text{sample proportion}$$
$$s_{p_s} = \text{estimated standard error of a confidence interval}$$
$$\text{of a proportion}$$

As we noted in Chapter 7, a sampling distribution of proportions is normally distributed only when the smaller of P_s and Q_s times n is greater than or equal to 5. If ($p_{smaller}$) (n) $<$ 5, the best solution is to increase the sample size.

Let us now calculate 95 percent confidence interval of the proportion of support for Chantrise Jones's U.S. Senate run. We follow the Checklist of Five Steps for Computing Confidence Intervals.

How to Calculate a Confidence Interval of a Population Proportion

Problem: We work for Chantrise Jones, who is running for the U.S. Senate. It is two days before the election. With 95 percent confidence, she wants to know if she is likely to win. What is her level of support among likely voters? In a telephone poll of 1,393 likely voters, 752 indicate that they intend to vote for her.

Step 1. Research question: With 95 percent confidence, can we conclude that Chantrise Jones is likely to win the election? That is, does she appear likely to get more than .50 (50 percent) of the vote? Within a specified range of percentage of support, what is the parameter P_u, the proportion of the population of likely voters intending to vote for Chantrise Jones? *Givens:*

$P = p$ [of likely voters supporting Chantrise]

$Q = p$ [of likely voters supporting someone else]

Sample: $n = 1{,}393$ likely voters   # supporting Chantrise $= 752$

$$P_s = \frac{\text{\# supporting Chantrise}}{\text{total number polled}} = \frac{752}{1{,}393} = .54$$

$$Q_s = 1 - P_s = 1 - .54 = .46$$

[Check to see if n is large enough. See if $(p_{smaller})(n) > 5$.]

$$(p_{smaller})(n) = (.46)(1{,}393) = 640.78, \qquad 640.78 > 5$$

(Thus, we can proceed with calculations)

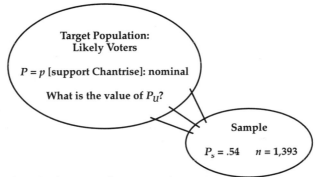

Step 2.   (standard error and error term)

$$s_{P_s} = \sqrt{\frac{P_s Q_s}{n}} = \sqrt{\frac{(.54)(.46)}{1{,}393}} = .0134$$

(For 95 percent confidence, $Z_\alpha = 1.96$.)

$$\text{Error term} = (Z_\alpha)(s_{p_s}) = (1.96)(.0134) = .0263$$

Step 3.   (the LCL and UCL of the confidence interval)

$$95\% \text{ CI of } P_u = P_s \pm (1.96)(s_{p_s})$$

$$= .54 \pm (1.96)(.0134)$$

$$= .54 \pm .0263$$

$$= \text{sample proportion} \pm \text{error term}$$

$$LCL = .54 - .0263 = .5137 = 51.37\%$$

$$UCL = .54 + .0263 = .5663 = 56.63\%$$

Step 4.   (interpretation in everyday language): "I am 95 percent sure that the percentage of likely voters supporting Chantrise Jones is between 51 percent and 57 percent." Chantrise's chances of winning are good. If the election were held today, she would get at least 51 percent of the vote. (*Note:* We rounded to a whole percentage for the benefit of a public audience.)

Step 5.   (statistical interpretation illustrating the notion of "confidence in the procedure"): "If the same sampling and statistical procedures are conducted 100 times, 95 times the true population parameter, P_u, will be encompassed in the computed intervals and 5 times it will not. Thus, I am 95 percent confident that the single confidence interval I computed includes the true parameter."

Choosing a Sample Size for Polls, Surveys, and Research Studies

Sample Size for a Confidence Interval of a Population Proportion

A question that every researcher encounters is: How large a sample do I need? As we just learned, sample size is an important component in the size of a standard error. In the standard error equations for both means and proportions, the sample size (*n*) is in the denominator of the equations. Thus, a large sample size is better because it will produce a small standard error. Because of cost factors, however, we cannot simply choose an enormous sample size. Nevertheless, we can choose an *appropriate* sample size for the degree of precision we desire for the reported results. The degree of precision depends on the research objectives, the amount of time and money available for the research, and other considerations. For example, a political polling firm may use small samples early but increase the sample size to improve precision as the election approaches. Depending on these issues, we may choose to report results with plus or minus 1 percent error, 3 percent error, 5 percent error, and so on. The chosen precision hinges on the size of the error term of the confidence interval equation.

Let us demonstrate the choice of sample size for a confidence interval of proportions. Nominal/ordinal level variables, such as the proportion of likely voters favoring a candidate or supporting an issue, are used very commonly in political polling. A traditional standard in political polls as well as marketing surveys is to report results with 95 percent confidence and a ± 3 percent range of error. Once the size of the error term is chosen, the sample size required to reach that level of error is determined by solving for *n* in the error term equation. The error term for a confidence interval of proportions can be expanded as follows:

$$\text{Error term} = (Z_\alpha)(s_{P_s}) = (Z_\alpha))\sqrt{\frac{P_s Q_s}{n}}$$

Solving for *n* results in the following equation for calculating the needed sample size:

Calculating Sample Size for the Confidence Interval of a Population Proportion (for a nominal/ordinal variable)

$$n = \frac{(P_s Q_s)(Z_\alpha)^2}{\text{error term}^2}$$

where

　　n = sample size needed

　　Z_α = Z-score that corresponds to the stated level of confidence and
　　　　significance (for example, Z_α = 1.96 for a 95% level of confidence)

　　P_s = *p* [of the success category in the sample]

　　Q_s = *p* [of the failure category in the sample]

　　Error term = desired precision in the results to be reported

---

To solve for *n*, all the other terms in the equation must be known or otherwise estimated. We *choose* the level of confidence, which determines Z_α. If we choose the 95 percent level, Z_α = 1.96. We also choose the degree of precision—how large we want the error term to be. For example, we might choose the traditional ±3 percent (i.e., ±.03). Since we have not gathered data yet, we must estimate P_s and Q_s for the important variables in the study, such as the percentage supporting a candidate. These figures may be estimated on the basis of previous research. If such research is unavailable, a conservative estimate is to set P_s at .5. Since $Q_s = 1 - P_s$, then Q_s also will be estimated at .5. (These estimates are conservative in the sense that they will err on the large size; that is, the 3 percent error reported will be a worst-case scenario where error is overreported rather than underreported.) With all the previously unknown terms now specified, let us solve for the needed sample size when we desire ±3 percent error at the 95 percent level of confidence:

$$n = \frac{(P_s Q_s)(Z_\alpha)^2}{\text{error term}^2} = \frac{(.5)(.5)(1.96)^2}{.03^2} = 1,067 \text{ survey respondents}$$

We can see that a considerable sample size is needed for a ±3 percent reporting error at the 95 percent level of confidence. Because of the high cost of sampling, many polling firms have begun to settle for smaller samples and a larger error (such as ±5 percent). This is especially true of overnight telephone pollsters, whose costs have increased as a result of time delays caused by encountering answering machines and cellular phones. For the procedure of calculating needed sample size for a confidence interval of a population mean, see the Chapter 8 Extensions of text material available on *The Statistical Imagination* Web site at www.mhhe.com/ritchey2.

Statistical Follies and Fallacies: It Is Plus *and* Minus the Error Term

In popular media reports of survey polls, a common mistake is to treat the error term as equal to the width of the confidence interval itself. For example, in a recent presidential contest, a major network reported results of a poll of likely voters a week before the election. The Republican candidate was reported to have 42 percent of the vote to 36 percent for the Democratic candidate with the remainder undecided. The range of error was reported as plus-or-minus 3.5 percent. Because the difference in candidate support was 6 percent and this is greater than 3.5 percent, the nightly news led off with the story that the Republican candidate had "a substantial lead." This statement was incorrect. The lower confidence limit for the Republican candidate was $42 - 3.5 = 38.5$ percent; in the population of likely voters his support could have been that low. The upper confidence limit for the Democratic candidate was $36 + 3.5 = 39.5$ percent; his support could have been that high. In other words, the two confidence intervals overlapped and it was possible that the Democratic candidate held the lead. A correct interpretation of the poll would have been that the election was a dead heat. There was insufficient data to conclude that either candidate had the lead.

The person who scripted the news story probably made the common mistake of simply noting that the two point estimates of 42 and 36 percent were six percentage points apart and that this was more than 3.5 percent. To show separation between the candidates' levels of support, however, the two point estimates must be more than 7.0 percent apart, 2 times the error term of 3.5 percent. Recall that sample statistics are only tools to draw conclusions about population parameters. It is essential that sampling error be properly evaluated. A *sample* difference of 6 percent may have looked impressive, but for that sample it was not enough to establish a difference in the *population* of likely voters.

A major news network's misreporting of error terms and confidence intervals is not unusual. In fact, many times popular media reporters simply ignore the error term and treat a point estimate as though it were true. As we have learned, no single statistic—a summary measure based on sample data—is the last word on estimating a parameter of the population. Repeated sampling shows that the next sample from the same population is likely to result in a slightly different statistical outcome. Yet, it is not uncommon for point estimates to be quickly accepted and thereafter treated as though they were absolutely true. Proper attention to an error term, the width of a confidence interval, and the level of confidence is essential to complete understanding and proper interpretation of statistical findings.

SUMMARY

1. Based on the analysis of the statistics in a sample, a confidence interval is a range of possible values of a population parameter expressed with a specific

degree of confidence. The purpose of a confidence interval is to provide an interval estimate of the value of an unknown population parameter and precisely express the confidence we have that the parameter falls within that interval. With a confidence interval we answer the question: What is the value of a population parameter, give or take a little known sampling error?

2. To construct a confidence interval, we take a point estimate and use knowledge about sampling distributions to project an interval of error around it. The formula is set up as follows: Confidence interval = point estimate ± error term.

3. A confidence interval is calculated using a sample mean or proportion, a standard error, and a critical Z-score from the normal curve table. This critical score corresponds to a level of significance (i.e., expected error) and its level of confidence. For large samples, critical scores of 1.96 and 2.58 are used for the 95 percent and 99 percent levels of confidence, respectively. The error term is calculated by multiplying a standard error by the critical score.

4. The level of confidence and the level of significance, alpha (α), are inversely related—as one increases, the other decreases. The level of confidence plus the level of significance sum to a proportion of 1.00 or a percentage of 100 percent. Thus, for example, a level of confidence of 95 percent has a level of significance of 5 percent (i.e., $\alpha = .05$).

5. A large standard error occurs when either n is small or the sample standard deviation is large.

6. A large error term results when either the standard error or the critical Z-score is large.

7. A confidence interval of a population mean is calculated when the variable of interest (X) is of interval/ratio level of measurement.

8. The "everyday language" interpretation of the confidence interval of a population mean addresses the question: What is the estimate of the parameter, μ_X (mu-sub-X)? The interval reported is an estimate of *the population mean,* not an estimate of the range of X-scores.

9. The statistical interpretation of the confidence interval describes the logical process by which we may stipulate a level of confidence. With a 95 percent confidence level, we are asserting that the calculated interval is a good estimate 95 percent of the time. (Review Figure 8–2.)

10. With nominal/ordinal variables, confidence intervals provide an estimate within a range of error of the proportion of a population that falls in the "success" category of the variable. For a confidence interval of a population proportion, the sample size must be sufficiently large that $(p_{smaller})(n) \geq 5$, resulting in a sampling distribution that is normal in shape.

11. The precision of a confidence interval (i.e., its width) is the difference between the UCL and LCL. The greater the stated level of confidence, the less precise the confidence interval. The larger the sample size, the more precise the confidence interval.

12. To obtain a high degree of precision *and* maintain a high level of confidence, a researcher must use a sufficiently large sample, one that will produce a small standard error and, therefore, a more precise confidence interval. Sample size can be chosen to fit a desired level of confidence and range of error.

CHAPTER EXTENSIONS ON *THE STATISTICAL IMAGINATION* WEB SITE

Chapter 8 Extensions of text material available on *The Statistical Imagination* Web site at www.mhhe.com/ritchey2 include calculation of minimum sample size for a confidence interval of the mean.

FORMULAS FOR CHAPTER 8

Calculating a confidence interval of a population mean when $n > 121$

Given: An interval/ratio variable X

Research question: What is the value of the population mean, μ_X

$$95\% \ CI \text{ of } \mu_X = \bar{X} \pm (1.96) \, (s_{\bar{X}})$$

$$99\% \ CI \text{ of } \mu_X = \bar{X} \pm (2.58) \, (s_{\bar{X}})$$

$$s_{\bar{X}} = \frac{s_X}{\sqrt{n}}$$

Calculating confidence interval of a population proportion (when $[(p_{smaller}) \, (n)] \geq 5$)

Given: A nominal/ordinal variable with $P = p$ [of the success category]

Research question: What is the value of the population proportion, P_u?

$$95\% \ CI \text{ of } P_u = P_s \pm (1.96) \, (s_{p_s})$$

$$99\% \ CI \text{ of } P_u = P_s \pm (2.58) \, (s_{p_s})$$

$$s_{P_s} = \sqrt{\frac{P_s Q_s}{n}}$$

The precision or width of a confidence interval $= \text{UCL} - \text{LCL}$

Sample size for the confidence interval of a population proportion (for a nominal/ordinal variable):

$$n = \frac{(P_s Q_s) \, (Z_\alpha)^2}{\text{error term}^2}$$

QUESTIONS FOR CHAPTER 8

1. In plain language, what is a confidence interval?

2. What is the purpose of computing a confidence interval?

3. In computing a confidence interval, what two factors go into the size of the interval?

4. In computing confidence intervals, what is the relationship between sample size and the size of the standard error?

5. In computing confidence intervals, what is the relationship between the size of the confidence interval and the critical Z-score used to compute it?

6. State the statistical interpretation of any confidence interval for which you have 99 percent confidence.

7. List the five steps in computing a confidence interval.

8. The level of significance (or expected error) in the computation of a confidence interval is symbolized by the Greek letter α. Mathematically, what is the relationship between α and the level of confidence?

EXERCISES FOR CHAPTER 8

Problem Set 8A

8A-1. Following the five steps for computing a confidence interval, compute and interpret the 95 percent confidence interval for the following data:

$$X = \text{age} \qquad n = 189 \text{ corporate executives}$$
$$\text{Mean} = 57 \text{ years} \qquad \text{Standard deviation} = 9 \text{ years}$$

8A-2. Redo the last three steps for computing a confidence interval to compute the 99 percent confidence interval for the data in exercise 8A-1. Compare the results to the answer in exercise 8A-1 and discuss.

8A-3. You wish to compute an interval estimate of the mean incomes of city planners in 150 Metropolitan Statistical Areas (MSAs) in the Sun Belt. You obtain a random sample of 214 city planners and find a mean income of $43,571 with a standard deviation of $4,792. Following the five steps, construct the 99 percent confidence interval. As part of step 4, explain your results to the head of the Urban Studies Department at the local university.

8A-4. It is the year 2010. You work for President Shirley D. Fendus as a pollster. She desires to know what proportion of her 8,469 party officials supports her legislative bill to increase defense spending. You poll 306 randomly selected party officials and find that 108 support her bill. To inform her, compute and interpret the 95 percent confidence interval. Follow the five steps.

8A-5. You have secured an appointment as an assistant to a representative in the United States House of Representatives. Your candidate, and her party, are seeking to get an important security bill through Congress. Accordingly, you wish to know how many of the 434 other representatives intend to cast a supporting vote for the bill. You randomly select 137 members of the house and discover that 76 support the proposed legislation. Compute and interpret the 95 percent confidence interval. Follow the five steps.

8A-6. You are to conduct a survey to determine the percentage of registered voters currently supporting candidate A. The results are to be reported with 95 percent confidence and a 2 percentage point error term. What size sample should you obtain? (*Hint:* P_s is unknown at this time, but assume it will be .5.)

8A-7. Complete the following table, where $n = 1,000$ and $P_s = .5$. Answer the questions that follow.

Level of Confidence	Z_α	SP_s	Error Term	LCL	UCL	Width of Confidence Interval
95%	1.96	.0158	.0310	.4690	.5310	.0620
99%	___	___	___	___	___	___
99.9%	___	___	.0520	___	___	___

a. What is the relationship between the size of the level of confidence and the width of the confidence interval? Explain.

b. How is the width of the confidence interval computed?

c. What is the relationship between the size of the level of confidence and the size of the error term? Explain.

Problem Set 8B

8B-1. Following the five steps for computing a confidence interval, compute and interpret the 95 percent confidence interval for the following (fictional) data from a random sample of men in a national nutrition study:

X = weight $n = 147$ men

Mean = 174 pounds   Standard deviation = 6 pounds

8B-2. Redo the last three steps for computing a confidence interval to compute the 99 percent confidence interval for the data in exercise 8B-1. Compare the results to the answer in exercise 8B-1 and discuss.

8B-3. Dr. Latisia Latham, a marriage counselor, administers the Global Distress Scale (GDS), which measures overall marital discord. It consists of 43 true/false questions with a total score combined for the two partners (Snyder, Willis, and Grady-Fletcher 1991). She asks you to provide a rough estimate of the average score of her clientele. You obtain a random sample of 125 couples and find a mean GDS score of 59 GDS scale points with a standard deviation of 5.2. Following the five steps, provide a 95 percent confidence interval of the mean GDS score of Dr. Latham's clients.

8B-4. Senator Daniel "Dandy" Barker is contemplating a run for the presidency. He has someone poll 90 randomly selected registered voters and finds that 51 percent support him against the incumbent. If the election were held today, could Senator Barker be assured of victory? Explain using a 95 percent confidence interval. Follow the five steps.

8B-5. The elected president of the Student Association of the School of Social and Behavioral Sciences (SBS) has decided to seek another term. Random polling among 219 undergraduate and graduate students indicate that about 63 percent support her next term as president. If the election were conducted today, could the candidate be assured of victory? Explain using a 95 percent confidence interval.

8B-6. You are to conduct a survey to determine the percentage of a health maintenance organization's patients who are satisfied with their primary physicians. You wish to report the results with 99 percent confidence and a 3 percentage point error term. What size sample will you need to draw? (*Hint:* P_s is unknown at this time, but assume it will be .5.)

8B-7. Complete the following table, where $n = 225$ and $P_s = .6$. Answer the questions that follow.

Level of Confidence	Z_α	SP_s	Error Term	LCL	UCL	Width of Confidence Interval
95%	1.96	.0327	.0641	.5359	.6641	.1282
99%	___	___	___	___	___	___
99.9%	___	___	.1076	___	___	___

    a. What is the relationship between the size of the level of confidence and the width of the confidence interval? Explain.

    b. How is the width of the confidence interval computed?

    c. What is the relationship between the size of the level of confidence and the size of the error term? Explain.

Problem Set 8C

8C-1. Following the five steps for computing a confidence interval, compute and interpret the 95 percent confidence interval for the following data:

        X = years of education n = 226 job applicants

        Mean = 15 years   Standard deviation = 1.5 years

8C-2. Redo the last three steps for computing a confidence interval to compute the 99 percent confidence interval for the data in exercise 8C-1. Compare the results to the answer in exercise 8C-1 and discuss.

8C-3. You need to compute an interval estimate of the mean ages of voting-age adults in a congressional district. You obtain a random sample of

274 voting-age adults and find a mean age of 36.3 years with a standard deviation of 9.7 years. Following the five steps, construct the 99 percent confidence interval.

8C-4. You have been elected by a majority of your classmates as a representative to the University Congress. While attempting to get a reform-oriented bill on the congressional ballot, you wish to know how many of your 516 fellow representatives intend to support your bill. You randomly select 112 representatives, discovering that 68 support your reforms. Compute and interpret the 95 percent confidence interval. Follow the five steps. Based on your results, can you be 95 percent confident that your bill will win a majority vote in the congress?

8C-5. You have been hired by Chairman William Burns of the Senate Appropriations Committee. He wants to know what proportion of his 6,421 party officials intend to support his new budget spending resolution. You randomly poll 279 party officials and discover that 101 support the resolution. In order to keep Senator Burns informed of the latest polling numbers, compute and interpret the 95 percent confidence interval. Follow the five steps.

8C-6. You are to conduct a survey to determine the percentage of a business's employees that support extending store hours during the coming holiday season. The results are to be reported with 95 percent confidence and a 3 percentage point error term. What size sample of employees should be obtained? (*Hint: P_s is unknown at this time, but assume it will be .5.*)

8C-7. Complete the following table, where $n = 550$ and $P_s = .4$. Answer the questions that follow.

Level of Confidence	Z_α	sP_s	Error Term	LCL	UCL	Width of Confidence Interval
95%	1.96	.0209	.0410	.3590	.4410	.0820
99%	____	____	____	____	____	____
99.9%	____	____	.0690	____	____	____

a. What is the relationship between the size of the level of confidence and the width of the confidence interval? Explain.
b. How is the width of the confidence interval computed?
c. What is the relationship between the size of the level of confidence and the size of the error term? Explain.

Problem Set 8D

8D-1. Following the five steps for computing a confidence interval, compute and interpret the 95 percent confidence interval for the following data from a random sample of students in a university-wide study.

X = grade point average (GPA) n = 314 students

Mean = 2.9 points   Standard deviation = .3 points

8D-2.   Redo the last three steps for computing a confidence interval to compute the 99 percent confidence interval for the data in exercise 8D-1. Compare the results to the answer in exercise 8D-1 and discuss.

8D-3.   You wish to calculate an interval estimate of the mean Graduate Record Examination (GRE) scores among incoming graduate students at a large urban university. You have collected a random sample of 129 students and find a mean GRE score of 1,200 points with a standard deviation of 60 points. Following the five steps, construct the 99 percent confidence interval.

8D-4.   Governor Jackson Fitzpatrick is seeking a second gubernatorial term. Polling among 324 registered voters indicates that about 61 percent support his reelection. If the election were conducted today, could Governor Fitzpatrick be assured of victory? Explain using a 95 percent confidence interval. Follow the five steps.

8D-5.   Professor William Carr is thinking about a run for United States Senate. He has commissioned you to randomly poll 126 registered voters, and you discover that 54 percent support him at this time. If the election were conducted today, could Professor Carr be assured of victory? Explain using a 95 percent confidence interval. Follow the five steps.

8D-6.   As a statistician in a brokerage firm, you are to conduct a survey to determine the percentage of investors satisfied with their financial advisors. You wish to report the results with 99 percent confidence and a 2 percentage point error term. What size sample would you need to select. (*Hint: P_s* is unknown at this time, but assume it will be .5.)

8D-7.   Complete the following table, where n = 185 and P_s = .7. Answer the questions that follow.

Level of Confidence	Z_α	sp_s	Error Term	LCL	UCL	Width of Confidence Interval
95%	1.96	.0337	.0661	.6339	.7661	.1322
99%	___	___	___	___	___	___
99.9%	___	___	.1112	___	___	___

a.   What is the relationship between the size of the level of confidence and the width of the confidence interval? Explain.

b.   How is the width of the confidence interval computed?

c.   What is the relationship between the size of the level of confidence and the size of the error term? Explain.

OPTIONAL COMPUTER APPLICATIONS
FOR CHAPTER 8

If your class uses the optional computer applications that accompany this text, open the Chapter 8 exercises on *The Statistical Imagination* Web site at www.mhhe.com/ritchey2. The exercises are on computing confidence intervals in *SPSS for Windows* with an emphasis on the importance of examining the effects of skewness on the computations. In addition, Appendix D of this text provides a brief overview of the *SPSS* command sequences for procedures covered in the chapter.

C H A P T E R

9

Hypothesis Testing I: The Six Steps of Statistical Inference

Introduction: Scientific Theory and the Development of Testable Hypotheses

As was noted in Chapter 1, inferential statistics are computed to show cause-and-effect relationships and to test hypotheses and scientific theories. A theory is tested by making specific predictions about data. For example, in studying civil disorders such as riots, we might posit a "protest theory" which says that riot behavior is stimulated by the practice of suppressive authority, such as incidents of police brutality. This theory provides concepts (such as civil disorder, riots, suppression, and protest) as well as ideas about how the social world works (such as the idea that abusive state authority leads to protest). Most important, a theory steers our thoughts so that we are able to conceive of a set of propositions about relationships among measured variables. For instance, if suppressive authority leads to protest, measures of protest should be high (such as a high incidence of civil disorders and riots) in situations where state suppression is also high (such as lots of police brutality). In summary, a theory is a set of logically organized, interrelated ideas that explains a phenomenon of interest *and* allows testing of the soundness of those ideas against observable facts. The process of determining which facts are valid and which are not is called hypothesis testing, the topic of this chapter.

Relating the well-organized ideas of a theory to real events is the creative side of the statistical imagination. It requires "seeing the future," at least with regard to how a phenomenon of interest will behave. A theory "motivates" hypotheses by moving us to think in terms of proving our points. A **hypothesis** is *a prediction about the relationship between two variables, asserting that differences among the measurements of an independent variable will correspond to differences among the measurements of a dependent variable*. A hypothesis is a prediction in need of corroboration by observation and analysis of data. (The word *hypothesis* shares its root with the word *hypothetical*, meaning "Let's imagine for the moment.") Hypotheses put theoretical ideas into practice by stipulating that given the logic of the theory, observable facts should appear in a certain way. If data turn out as a theory suggests, that theory may be a worthwhile explanation of the phenomenon of interest. By contrast, if predictions are not supported by fact, that theory is not sound and must be rejected or greatly modified. In a broad sense, hypothesis testing serves the purpose of corroborating theory.

---

a hypothesis A prediction about the relationship between two variables, asserting that differences among the measurements of an independent variable will correspond to differences among the measurements of a dependent variable.

The theoretical purpose of a hypothesis test is to corroborate theory by testing ideas against facts.

Making Empirical Predictions

One challenge of scientific hypothesis testing is figuring out how to make empirical predictions. Actually, making such predictions is not difficult. We do so frequently in our everyday lives. Here are some questions you may raise and some hypotheses you may test today, along with the empirical observations you could make to test them.

Question 1. Should I carry an umbrella today?

Hypothesis: An increase in cloudiness (independent variable) is associated with an increase in rain (dependent variable).

Observation: Look out the window.

Question 2. Will I get better grades on my statistics quizzes if I study more for each one?

Hypothesis: The longer the study time (independent variable), the better the quiz grade (dependent variable).

Observation: Study more and see what happens.

Question 3.   Will I suffer injury if I step in front of a moving bus?

1. *A physical science hypothesis:* Given the known physical laws that two objects cannot occupy the same space at the same time and that objects of greater mass moving at higher speeds will displace objects of lesser mass and speed, the massive bus should crush the less massive person.

Observation: Step in front of the bus.

2. *A behavioral science hypothesis:* There will be a greater incidence of head and body injuries (dependent variable) to victims of pedestrian bus crashes than to persons who have not experienced such crashes (independent variable).

Observation: Analyze hospital records. (This would be called a retrospective study, because we would be looking back at past experiences.)

Suggestion: Test this one with the retrospective data or crash dummies.

The last question illustrates the fact that we actually use tremendous amounts of empirically corroborated information as we go about our daily lives. We do not have to step in front of a bus to know that injuries will occur.

Statistical Inference

To infer is to draw a conclusion about something. **Statistical inference** entails *drawing conclusions about a population on the basis of sample statistics*. As was discussed in Chapter 2, statistical inferences must take into account sampling error. And as we learned in Chapter 7, a measurement made on a sample can be expected to be slightly off from the true population parameter.

---

statistical inference   Drawing conclusions about a population on the basis of sample statistics.

An awareness of how sampling error varies and how it may be predicted with sampling distributions is the key to understanding statistical inference. Let us illustrate with a simple example. Let us suppose that we are sitting in class one day when a handsome stranger walks into the room dressed like a rodeo cowboy or country-and-western musician. He is wearing a feathered 10-gallon hat, a sequined western shirt, a turquoise-bejeweled string tie, a large belt buckle shaped like the state of Texas, and the shiniest pointy-toed boots we have ever seen. He introduces himself as Billy "Tex" Cooper from Dallas, Texas.

Tex says that he heard that statistics courses deal with predicting the future and that he would like to learn more about this because he wants to become a professional gambler. He pulls a pair of dice from his pocket and proposes a game. He says, "I'll tell you what. I will roll these dice. If they come up 2, 'snake eyes,' then all of you will pay me a dollar. If they come up any other combination—3, 4, 5, and so on—then I will pay each of you one dollar." We ask to see his dice, and they appear legitimate.

Sounds like a very good deal. Why? Because our knowledge of probability tells us that we should have an advantage here. Probability theory allows us to figure out *what happens in the long run*, that is, when dice are rolled over and over again. If we can mathematically project how often each side of a die will come up, we can determine whether some combinations of two dice will come up more frequently than others. In other words, we can produce the sampling distribution for the event of rolling two dice.

As we learned in Chapter 7, a sampling distribution is a mathematical description of all possible sampling outcomes and the probability (p) of each. Figure 9–1 is a matrix illustrating the sampling distribution for the roll of two dice, that is, all possible combinations and the probability of each combination. The matrix reveals that there are 36 possible outcomes. When the first die comes up 1, the second die can come up 1 or 2 or 3 or 4 or 5 or 6. When the first die comes up 2, the second die can, again, come up 1 or 2 or 3 or 4 or 5 or 6, and so on. Looking, then, at the upper left-hand corner of the matrix, we see that when both dice roll up as 1, the combination is 2, or snake eyes, the lowest possible outcome. This is the only way to obtain an outcome of 2, and there are 36 total possible outcomes; thus, the probability of rolling a 2 with two dice is 1 out of 36. The combination of 3 can occur two ways: first die 1 and second die 2 and first die 2 and second die 1; thus, the probability of rolling a 3 is 2 out of 36. The rest of the matrix gives the combinations for all other possible rolls, with each possible outcome (from 2 to 12) situated crosswise on the diagonals.

The matrix of Figure 9–1 is summarized in Table 9–1, which provides a clear description of the sampling distribution for a single roll of two dice. It is a list of all possible outcomes and the probability (p) of each one. Note the familiar, close-to-normal shape of the stargraph or "curve" of these outcomes. Like the means and proportions we produced with repeated sampling in Chapter 7, this distribution peaks (in this case at a score of 7) with gradually lower frequencies as we move into the "tails" of the curve. Taking note that 7 occurs 6/36 of the time, we can quickly calculate the probabilities of other outcomes by moving away from 7 and subtracting 1. Thus, the probability of rolling 6 is 5/36, that of rolling 8 is 5/36, that of rolling 5 is 4/36, and so forth. (Figure 9–1 and Table 9–1 are worth the cost of tuition for this course! They should be invaluable if you shoot craps or play Monopoly, backgammon, or any other game of chance that uses dice.)

FIGURE 9–1

Matrix of all possible combinations of side pairings for the roll of two dice

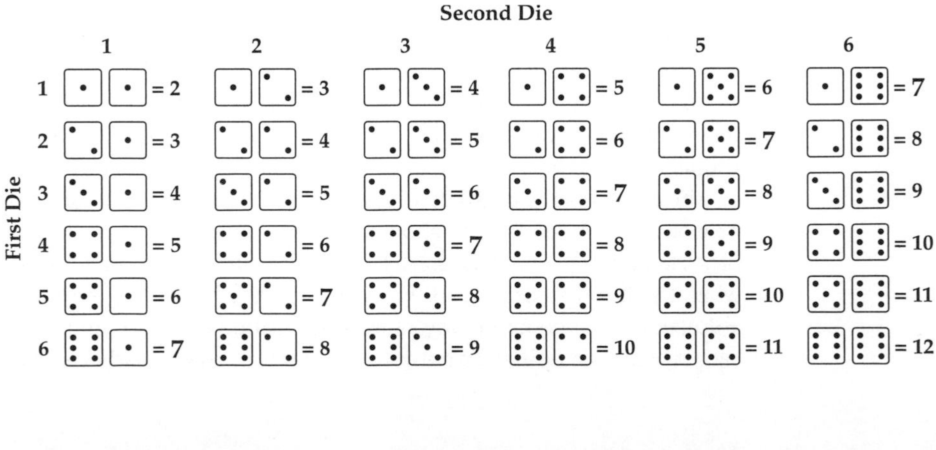

TABLE 9–1 | The sampling distribution of the roll of two dice

Possible Outcome	Fraction *p*	Stargraph
2	1/36 = .0278	*
3	2/36 = .0556	**
4	3/36 = .0833	***
5	4/36 = .1111	****
6	5/36 = .1389	*****
7	**6/36 = .1667**	******
8	5/36 = .1389	*****
9	4/36 = .1111	****
10	3/36 = .0833	***
11	2/36 = .0556	**
12	1/36 = .0278	*
Totals	36/36 = 1.0001*	

*Total does not sum to 1 because of rounding error.

Getting back to Tex, we should have an advantage. The probability of his winning with a single roll with snake eyes is 1/36, or .0278. Using the addition rule for alternative events, the probability of us winning a single roll is 35/36, or .9722—the probabilities of all other possible outcomes combined, or simply, $1 - .0278$. We should be feeling pretty good right now. Here's this charming guy, dressed elaborately, who says that he is rather ignorant about probability, which is the essence of gaming and gambling. (And we're thinking we are pretty smart right now because we have survived a statistics course to this point!)

But let's suppose he rolls the dice and 2 rolls up. Wait a minute! Something's not right here. At this point we may suspect that Tex is a con artist and that the dice are loaded (weighted in such a way that only 2 will come up) or that he is using sleight of hand to switch to a loaded pair before he rolls. Why are our suspicions raised? Partly because his appearance at class is unexpected and we are prejudiced against people who dress differently and talk us out of our money. But we are also suspicious because probability theory tells us what to expect from the rolls of two dice even before they are rolled. We have determined that *an honest pair of dice* would come up 2 only .0278 of the time. This is less than 3/100. In other words, if 100 gamblers had dropped by and rolled their dice *and all the dice were honestly marked and weighted,* fewer than three would have rolled snake eyes. Tex just arrives out of nowhere and does it? Kind of hard to believe. We cannot be absolutely sure (Tex may just be really lucky), but we suspect that we "got taken" and that Tex is a crook. We probably will conclude that the outcome was *the effect* of loaded dice, not the effect of very good luck in the random fall of honest dice.

Although we did not follow strict procedures, we tested the hypothesis that Tex is a crook. All hypothesis tests have the elements of this event. First, a question is raised: Is Tex honest or is he a crook? Second, predictions of normal sampling outcomes are made with a sampling distribution: Honest dice predictably fall as in Table 9–1. Third, we observe the statistics of a single sample and calculate the probability of occurrence up against the sampling distribution: Tex rolls snake eyes. With honest dice the probability of this outcome is unusually small, only .0278. Fourth, we decide whether this outcome is the effect of normal sampling error or the effect of loaded dice. Tex's rolls appear highly unusual for honest dice. Therefore, we reject the assumption that the dice are honest and conclude that his rolls are the effect of loaded dice. Finally, we state a conclusion: Tex is a crook! In simple terms, the dice did not behave like honest dice so they must not be honest.

In addition to the purpose of corroborating a theory, all hypothesis tests have a statistical purpose. They answer the general questions: Does an observed sampling outcome appear normal, the effect of sampling error? Or is the outcome highly unusual and therefore the effect of something else? The sampling distribution provides a measuring stick against which to compare a single observed sample's statistic to determine if it is unusual. When the probability of a sampling outcome is low, such as .0278, we reject the notion that this outcome is simply due to sampling error. The only reason we are able to call Tex a crook is that we know how *honest* dice fall. This knowledge is described with mathematical certainty in the sampling distribution of Table 9–1.

---

statistical purpose of a hypothesis test   To determine whether sampling outcomes indicate (1) real effects in the population or (2) sampling error.

When you decided whether to carry an umbrella today, you followed the same logical procedure:

Research Question: Is it going to rain?

Hypothesis: If there is a dark, cloudy sky, there is a good likelihood of rain.

Observation: The sky is a clear blue. This does not fit the empirical predictions of the hypothesis. The probability of rain with no clouds is extremely low.

Conclusion: Reject the notion that it is going to rain. Leave the umbrella home.

Essentially, the logic of hypothesis testing involves deciding whether to accept or reject a statement based on observations of data. We compare predictions to empirical evidence.

The Importance of Sampling Distributions for Hypothesis Testing

We now have a general idea behind the logic of hypothesis testing. Let us take an example that uses the statistics we learned in earlier chapters and begin to assemble the details of hypothesis testing. Suppose we are conducting a study of high school athletes. We wish to examine whether the common stereotype that athletes are "dumb jocks"— all brawn and no brains—has any merit. More specifically: On average, are athletes less intelligent than other high school students? Using our statistical imaginations, we search for a way to compare athletes to students in general. We obtain an intelligence quotient (IQ) test that has a national average of 100 for all high school students. This is a target value to which high school athletes may be compared. Our research question is: Is the mean IQ of high school athletes less than the mean IQ of all high school students?

Having this specific numerical value of 100 IQ points allows us to test a hypothesis. To do so, we draw a single sample of 144 high school athletes and find a sample mean of 99 IQ points with a standard deviation of 12 IQ points. Our sample mean is 1 point below the average IQ. If we did not know better, we would immediately conclude that, indeed, athletes have lower IQs and this supports the dumb-jocks stereotype. We are hesitant to draw this conclusion, however, because we did not calculate the mean IQ *of the population* of all high school athletes. We simply used a sample of 144 of them. We know from our experience of having repeatedly sampled a population and calculated means from it (Chapter 7) that a second sample from a population would likely provide a slightly different result. For example, it would be just as likely to obtain a sample mean of 101, which is 1 point above average. And a third sample would provide yet another result. In other words, even if the mean score of the *population* of athletes is 100 IQ points and no different from that of all high school students, *a sample* can calculate slightly off from 100 due to expected sampling error. So does this −1-point difference between the empirical observation and the predicted value indicate something meaningful or is it simply sampling error?

Fortunately, we have a way to calculate how far off sample means can be. We learned in Chapter 7 that if a population has a known mean, μ_X, when samples are drawn repeatedly from the population, the sample means, $\bar{X}$'s, will center on the value of μ_X. For the case in point, if the mean IQ of athletes is no different from that of all students, sample means will center around 100. Moreover, sampling error is predictable. When the sample size is greater than 121, a graph of means from repeated sampling will take the shape of a normal curve. To precisely describe the sampling distribution, we calculate the standard error of means using the sample size and standard deviation of our sample:

$$s_{\bar{X}} = \frac{s_X}{\sqrt{n}} = \frac{12}{\sqrt{144}} = 1.00 \text{ IQ point}$$

Now we draw the normal curve for this sampling distribution (Figure 9–2).

What does the curve in Figure 9–2 tell us? We can see that *if the mean IQ of the population of student athletes is indeed 100,* in repeated sampling about 68 percent of the time we can expect to obtain a sample mean, $\bar{X}$, between 99 and 101 IQ points. About 95 percent of the time we can expect to obtain a sample mean between 98 and 102 IQ points.

Now we know what sampling outcomes occur under the assumption that there is *no difference* between the mean IQs of athletes and all students. The sampling distribution provides a measuring stick against which we can compare our actual sample outcome of $\bar{X} = 99$ IQ points. We ask the questions: Is a sample mean of 99 IQ points a usual result—simply sampling error—when the population mean, $\mu_X = 100$ IQ points?

FIGURE 9–2

Sampling
distribution of
the mean IQ of
high school
athletes
assuming the
normal mean of
100 IQ points

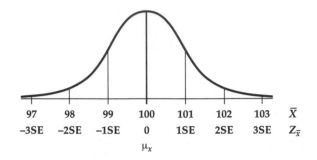

Or, as an alternative explanation, is a sample mean of 99 highly unusual when repeatedly sampling from a population with a mean of 100? Just as we did with Tex, we can calculate the probability of the "unusualness" of a sampling outcome. We will make the precise calculation of the probability of this sampling outcome in a moment. In Figure 9–2 we can see already, however, that a sample mean of 99 is not unusual coming from a population whose mean IQ is 100. A difference of -1 IQ point is within 1 standard error of the predicted value of 100 IQ points. About 68 percent of means calculate in this range. Thus, we conclude: The average IQ of athletes appears no different from that of all students; therefore, the dumb-jocks notion is a false stereotype. We draw this conclusion because the observed sample mean of 99 could easily have resulted from sampling error.

With the Tex-the-gambler question we got an unusual, low probability sampling outcome, so we rejected "honest dice." With our dumb-jocks question we got a high probability outcome leading us not to reject normal intelligence. The general idea behind hypothesis testing is the same for all scientific disciplines and all statistical applications. Identify a hypothesis statement that allows predictions of all possible sampling outcomes in the form of a sampling distribution. Make an empirical observation of a single sample's statistic and see how it measures up against predictions. The ability to conceive of sampling distributions is the central feature of hypothesis testing.

There are many types of hypothesis tests. A particular test is shaped around the sampling distribution that is appropriate to it. The particulars of a sampling distribution depend on how many variables are involved, their levels of measurement, sample size, and other features.

The Six Steps of Statistical Inference for a Large Single-Sample Means Test

Let us proceed to define the specifics of hypothesis testing using our "dumb-jocks" stereotype example. For this situation, we employ what is called a large single-sample means test. In this instance, *large* is defined as a sample with more than 121 cases, which allows us to use the normal curve as our sampling distribution. Specifically, we use a large single-sample means test when the following criteria are met:

When to Use a Large Single-Sample Means Test (Z-distribution, $n > 121$ cases)

In general: Useful for testing a hypothesis that the mean of a population is equal to a target value.

1. There is only one variable.
2. The level of measurement is interval/ratio.
3. There is a single sample and population.
4. The sample size is greater than 121 cases.
5. There is a target value of the variable to which we may compare the mean of the sample.

For the "dumb-jocks" example, we have a single variable: IQ score. It is of interval/ratio level of measurement. We have a single population of interest: high school athletes. Our sample size of 144 athletes is greater than 121. We have a target value that provides a prediction of how sampling outcomes fall: normal IQ is a score of 100. Thus, we may use a large single-sample means test.

Every hypothesis test follows the same logical process comprised of six parts. We refer to this process as "the six steps of statistical inference" or "the six steps of hypothesis testing." Prior to the test itself, we must prepare for it. Here is a brief outline of the logical process.

Brief Checklist for the Six Steps of Statistical Inference

TEST PREPARATION
State the research question. Draw conceptual diagrams depicting givens, including the population(s) and sample(s) under study, variables (e.g., $X = \ldots$, $Y = \ldots$,) and their levels of measurement, and given or calculated statistics and parameters. State the proper statistical test procedure.

SIX STEPS
Using the symbol H for *hypothesis:*

1. State the H_0 and the H_A and stipulate test direction.
2. Describe the sampling distribution.
3. State the level of significance (α) and test direction and specify the critical test score.

4. Observe the actual sample outcomes and compute the test effects, the test statistic, and *p*-value.

5. Make the rejection decision.

6. Interpret and apply the results and provide best estimates in everyday terms.

Test Preparation

We begin a hypothesis test with test preparation. This is similar to gathering the ingredients of a recipe prior to mixing them. First, we identify and state a research question, "a goal that can be stated in terms of a hypothesis" (Bailey 1978:10). As we noted, research questions are asked to resolve practical matters or answer theoretically motivated questions. For the dumb-jocks example, our research question is: Is the mean IQ of high school athletes less than the mean IQ of all high school students, which is 100 IQ points? Then we identify the "givens," including the variables involved, the population, the sample size, parameters provided, and statistics provided or computed. To help distinguish these elements, we organize them in a diagram that distinguishes the population from the sample. This is presented in Figure 9–3. Notice that the symbols in the population oval pertain to parameters and those in the sample oval pertain to statistics.

Our hypothesis test is about the population and its parameters. A sample's statistics are only estimates of population parameters and the sample is merely a tool to make statistical inferences about the population. The final step in test preparation is to state what statistical test is to be used. In this case we are using the large single-sample means test.

The Six Steps

Step 1: The Null Hypothesis   In a test of the dumb-jocks hypothesis, just as we did with the Tex-the-gambler case, we must place our statistical observations in a larger context that takes into account sampling error. We must find a "statistical hypothesis," a statement that provides a numerical value and projects a sampling distribution around it. Such a hypothesis is called the **null hypothesis**, *a hypothesis stated in such a way that we will know what statistical outcomes will occur in repeated sampling if this hypothesis is true.*

FIGURE 9–3

Depiction of "givens" for a hypothesis test

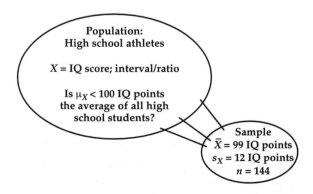

Population:
High school athletes

X = IQ score; interval/ratio

Is $\mu_X < 100$ IQ points the average of all high school students?

Sample
$\bar{X}$ = 99 IQ points
s_X = 12 IQ points
n = 144

We symbolize the null hypothesis as H_0. For our dumb-jocks hypothesis, the null hypothesis is stated as:

$$H_0: \mu_{X\,(high\ school\ athletes)} = 100 \text{ IQ points} \text{ (the known mean, } \mu_X,$$
$$\text{of all high school students)}$$

That is, the mean IQ of high school athletes is no different from that of all high school students.

Notice the form of presentation, which is consistent for all hypothesis tests. The null hypotheses always pertain to parameters of the population, not statistics from a sample. The population to which the parameter applies, in this case high school athletes, is subscripted under the parameter's symbol.

We cannot conduct a hypothesis test unless we can identify a null hypothesis related to the research question. To do so we ask: Is there a way to predict sampling outcomes assuming no effect, zero effect, or no difference? The dictionary definition of the word *null* is "*none.*" In fact, that is why we use the symbol H_0 (*H*-sub-zero). Although our research question asks whether athletes have a lower mean IQ, our null hypothesis posits an equal mean IQ (i.e., no difference). We have to state it this way in order to construct a sampling distribution, which we describe in step 2.

Another way to make sense of the word *null* is to notice that often we test a hypothesis by examining a statement that "nullifies" the research question by reversing or negating its wording. We want to know if the mean IQ of high school athletes is different, so we test the null hypothesis that it is no different. In this sense, we are making an indirect evaluation of the research question. We try to prove something by rejecting something else, just as we sought to prove that Tex is a crook by disproving that he is honest. It is easier to disprove something than to prove it. If we wish to prove that all birds are white, the simple approach is to disprove it by pointing at colorful birds. Oftentimes, the null hypothesis is found by reversing the wording of the research question.

---

null hypothesis (or statistical hypothesis): *H*₀   A hypothesis stated in such a way that we will know what statistical outcomes will occur in repeated sampling if this hypothesis is true.

A null hypothesis is a statement of "no effect" or "no difference." It guides us in selecting a sampling distribution for a hypothesis test. Oftentimes, the null hypothesis is the negation or reversal of the research question, which is proven by rejecting the null hypothesis.

In laboratory research, a "no effect" baseline is established with a control group. For example, suppose we wish to test the effectiveness of an allergy medication. We give an experimental group of subjects the actual medication, while a control group receives a *placebo* or fake, look-alike pill. Subjects in both groups are exposed to pollen and we calculate the mean numbers of allergy symptoms for both groups. The mean number of symptoms among subjects in the control group provides a baseline measure of "no effect," because the placebo pill has no medication. We would test the null hypothesis that the medication has "no effect," which is to say that there is no difference in the mean number of symptoms with or without the medication. If the mean number of symptoms of the experimental group is significantly lower, however, we would reject "no effect" and conclude that the drug *is* effective. To prove a research question, we reject the null hypothesis.

The important thing about a null hypothesis, however, is that it must be a *statistical hypothesis*. It is a statement that provides a sampling distribution, predictions of statistical outcomes as though we draw an infinite number of samples to determine the nature of sampling error. The sampling distribution provides a measuring stick to calculate the probability of statistics calculated for the one sample we actually draw.

Returning to the dumb-jocks example, why not build the sampling distribution around the research question itself? Because the assertion that the mean IQ *of the population* of student athletes is less than 100 does not provide a target value for the sampling distribution. If the population mean is less than 100, what is it? This has yet to be determined. Moreover, it would be a terrible mistake to use our observed sample mean of 99 IQ points to construct the sampling distribution. If several researchers each draw samples of 144 athletes, each researcher will obtain a different sample mean—due to sampling error—and each would therefore have a misguided sampling distribution centering on a different, random value. On the other hand, centering our sampling distribution on 100 IQ points provides a firm prediction. In the end, we may or may not stick with this prediction. We will either reject the null hypothesis or fail to reject it.

The Alternative Hypothesis, H_A In every hypothesis test the null or "no effect" hypothesis is required in order to project sampling outcomes. We must also decide ahead of time what we will conclude if we reject the null hypothesis. This statement is called the **alternative hypothesis (H_A)**, *the hypothesis we will accept if the null hypothesis is rejected.* Typically, the alternative hypothesis is the one that directly addresses the research question, and this is the case for our dumb-jocks research question:

$$H_A: \mu_{X \text{ (high school athletes)}} < 100 \text{ IQ points}$$

That is, the mean IQ of high school athletes is less than that of all high school students, one-tailed.

---

alternative hypothesis: H_A The hypothesis we will accept if the null hypothesis is rejected. Oftentimes, the alternative hypothesis is a direct statement of the research question.

Possible Alternative Hypotheses For any hypothesis test, there is a single null hypothesis and a single alternative hypothesis. However, there are three *possible* alternative hypotheses and we use the term *direction* to distinguish them. When we predict a direction, we are asserting that we have reason to believe that the sample mean will fall above or below the hypothesized mean of 100. For reasons that we will discuss momentarily, we also use the terms *one-tailed* and *two-tailed* to refer to tails in the sampling distribution curve. Here are three possible alternative hypotheses for our dumb-jocks hypothesis.

Option 1: A positive direction, one-tailed alternative hypothesis:

$$H_A: \mu_{X \text{ (high school athletes)}} > 100 \text{ IQ points}$$

That is, the mean IQ of high school athletes is *greater than* that of all high school students, one-tailed.

Here, *positive* means on the high side of the mean IQ. We will use a sampling distribution curve to calculate the probability of our sample outcome. When we predict the positive direction, we will calculate positive Z-scores in the tail of the curve to the right above the mean.

Option 2: A negative direction, one-tailed alternative hypothesis:

$$H_A: \mu_{X \text{ (high school athletes)}} < 100 \text{ IQ points}$$

That is, the mean IQ of high school athletes is *less than* that of all high school students, one-tailed.

Here, *negative* means on the low side of the mean IQ. When using a sampling distribution curve to calculate the probability of our sample outcome, we will calculate negative Z-scores to the left side or left tail of the curve.

Option 3: A nondirectional, two-tailed alternative hypothesis:

$$H_A: \mu_{X \text{ (high school athletes)}} \neq 100 \text{ IQ points}$$

That is, the mean IQ of high school athletes is *not equal to* that of all high school students. Two-tailed.

The third option is nondirectional. It does not propose that the mean IQ of athletes is higher or lower, just different. Calculation of the probability of outcomes will use both sides or tails of the sampling distribution curve.

When we test a hypothesis, we must decide which of these three alternative hypotheses applies. We test only one of them. That determination is made on the basis of theory or practical considerations. The common stereotype about "dumb jocks" proposes that they are less intelligent, so we choose option 2. But another researcher may propose that high school athletes have a higher mean IQ, because it takes smarts to keep up with studies and play a sport. This researcher states the H_A in the positive direction as in option 1. A third researcher may be aware of both theories and wish to resolve the debate by proposing a nondirectional H_A. This researcher states the H_A as option 3. While there are three optional alternative hypotheses for any hypothesis test, we must choose only one option. Moreover, for reasons that will become clear later, this option is chosen before observing sample data in step 4. Finally, by not claiming to predict a direction ahead of time, a two-tailed test is more conservative than a one-tailed test. It is more difficult to reject the H_0 and accept the H_A when conducting a two-tailed test. The reasons for this are presented in Chapter 10.

To establish the direction of a statistical test, examine the research question closely. If there are positive directional words (*greater than, more than, increase, heavier than, larger than, faster, gain*), a positive one-tailed test is in order. If there are negative directional words (*less than, decrease, lost, shorter than, slower than*), a negative one-tailed test is in order. Of course, when there is no stipulation of direction, we use a two-tailed test.

Deciding on the Direction of a Hypothesis Test: State the Alternative Hypothesis in One of Three Ways

1. One-tailed in the positive direction
    Content of research question includes terms such as *greater than, more, increase, faster, heavier*, and *gain*.   →   Use a positive one-tailed test in the alternative hypothesis and a $>$ sign.

2. One-tailed in the negative direction
    Content of research question includes terms such as *less than, fewer, decrease, slower, lighter*, and *loss*.   →   Use a negative one-tailed test in the alternative hypothesis and a $<$ sign.

3. Two-tailed, nondirectional;
    Content of research question includes no statements about direction or simply asserts inequality.   →   Use a neutral two-tailed test in the alternative hypothesis and a $\neq$ sign.

Step 2: Describe the Sampling Distribution   The second step in a hypothesis test is to describe the sampling distribution. For a hypothesis test, the sampling distribution is a description of all possible sampling outcomes and the probability of each outcome *when the H_0 is true*. The sampling distribution is constructed around the hypothesized parameter of the null hypothesis. If it is true that the mean IQ of the population of athletes is equal to 100, then repeated sampling from this population and a plot of the resulting $\bar{X}$'s produces a normal distribution curve when $n > 121$. The complete description of the sampling distribution for the dumb-jocks hypothesis is stated as: If H_0 is true and samples of size 144 are repeatedly drawn from the population of high school athletes, sample means ($\bar{X}$'s) will center on 100 as a normal distribution with a standard error:

$$s_{\bar{X}} = \frac{s_X}{\sqrt{n}} = \frac{12}{\sqrt{144}} = 1.00 \text{ IQ point}$$

When completing an exercise, we draw the sampling distribution curve as in Figure 9–2 above. The logical transition between steps 1 and 2 is as follows: Step 1 provides a statement, the H_0, that allows precise predictions of sampling outcomes. Step 2 imagines (i.e., hypothesizes) that this statement is true and describes these sampling predictions. Moreover, this description of sampling outcomes is exhaustive. Every possible sampling outcome is presented. And using the partitioning skills we learned in Chapter 6, we can calculate the probability of any combination of outcomes. Again, the sampling distribution is the essence of hypothesis testing and we do not even have to count beans to get it. Mathematicians provide us with knowledge of the shapes of sampling distribution curves and the standard error formulas required to accurately draw them. The standard error formula takes into account sample size, which is an important factor in the size of sampling errors.

Step 3: The Level of Significance   In step 3, we state a level of significance (symbolized by the Greek letter alpha, α). Recall from Chapter 8 that we referred to the level of significance as the level of expected error. We will return to the notion of error later in this chapter. For the time being, let us focus on an important function of the level of significance in the six steps: It helps determine whether to reject the null hypothesis (H_0) or fail to reject it. For hypothesis testing, the level of significance is the critical probability amount that defines just how unusual a sampling outcome must be to reject the parameter value predicted by H_0. For our example, how far from the normal IQ of 100 must the sample mean IQ of athletes fall before we conclude that their mean IQ is significantly lower? Will a difference of 1 point below 100 be enough, or 2 points, or 3 points, etc.? The level of significance, however, is presented as a probability on a sampling distribution curve. This allows us to use standard tables, such as the normal curve table, to calculate probabilities. We do not have a table for IQ point differences.

It is very common in social science survey research to set $\alpha = .05$. We do this in step 3. In step 4 we will calculate the probability of obtaining a sample mean of 99 IQ points. If this probability is low, less than our α of .05, we will reject the H_0 that the mean is 100 and accept the alternative hypothesis (H_A) that it is less. If the probability of obtaining a mean of 99 IQ points turns out to be high (i.e., greater than .05), we will conclude that it is not unusual coming from a population with a mean of 100. We will "fail to reject" the H_0. Since we do not have a table for IQ points, we must calculate a Z-score in order to use the normal curve table to obtain a probability of occurrence.

Step 4: Observe the Actual Sample: Compute the Test Effects, the Test Statistic, and the *p*-Value   In step 4 we finally look at our sample data. We observe the sample mean and compare it to the hypothesized value of 100. To determine the probability of occurrence, we calculate a Z-score to transform IQ points into standard errors. Then we take the Z-score to the normal curve table to obtain the probability of occurrence of the sampling outcome.

To calculate the Z-score, we take the difference between the value of the sample statistic and the parameter value predicted by the H_0. This difference is called the "**test effect**." With our dumb-jocks hypothesis, the test effect is -1 IQ point:

$$\bar{X} - \mu_X = 99 - 100 = -1 \text{ IQ point}$$

> **the test effect of a hypothesis test**   The difference between the value of the sample statistic and the parameter value predicted by the null hypothesis.
>   The test effect is a deviation score. It addresses the question: How much does the value of the sample statistic deviate from the value of the population parameter predicted by the null hypothesis?

A test effect is a deviation score. Recall from Chapter 5 that a deviation score is the difference (or distance) between the mean in the center of a normal curve and some point (i.e., score) on the horizontal or *X*-axis. Recall also that deviation scores are expressed in the original unit of measure of the raw score. With the example above, this would be IQ points. To calculate the probability of a test effect, we must standardize the score—transform it into standard deviation units—so that we can use probability tables such as the normal distribution table. (We do not have a table with IQ points in it!) For hypothesis tests, these standardized scores are expressed in standard error units. A **test statistic** to be used in conjunction with probability curves and statistical probability tables *is a formula for measuring statistical test effects in standard error units*.

> **a test statistic**   A formula for measuring statistical test effects in standard error units. These formulas are used in conjunction with probability curves and the statistical tables in Appendix B.

The sampling distribution for our dumb-jocks hypothesis is the normal curve and our test statistic is a *Z*-score. Statistical test effects usually are measured in the numerator of the test statistic and then standardized by dividing them by the standard error. This is the case for a large single-sample means test.

Calculating the Test Statistic for a Single-Sample Means Test

$$Z_{\bar{X}} = \frac{\bar{X} - \mu_X}{s_{\bar{X}}}$$

$$= \frac{\text{the test effect}}{\text{standard error}} = \begin{array}{l} \text{number of standard errors (SE)} \\ \text{difference between what was} \\ \text{observed and what was hypothesized} \end{array}$$

where

$Z_{\bar{X}}$ = number of standard errors a sample mean ($\bar{X}$) deviates from the hypothesized population mean (μ_X)

$s_{\bar{X}}$ = estimated standard error of the sampling distribution of means

A look at the terms of this formula in relation to the distribution curve is informative. Any Z-score (review Chapter 6) is a measure of the deviation ("how far off" the observed sample statistic falls) from an expected value. Any Z-distribution curve has a mean and a standard deviation (SD) and an interval/ratio score measured across its horizontal axis.

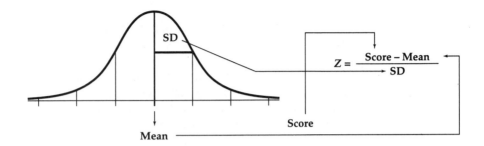

For instance, as we saw in Chapter 6, when the interval/ratio measurement is a raw score X, then Z_X is computed as follows:

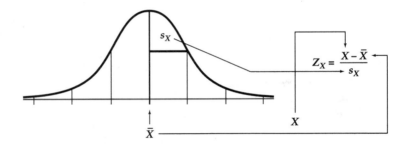

The parallel elements of a normal distribution of sample means are as follows:

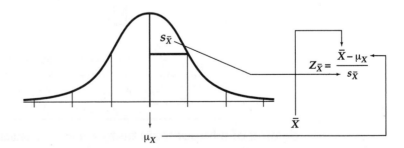

Take care to distinguish the standard error of this distribution of means, $s_{\bar{X}}$, from the standard deviation of the raw score distribution, s_X.

Before calculating the test statistic, let us estimate its value by sight. Observe Figure 9–2 on page 274. We can see that a sample outcome of 99 IQ points is 1 standard error below the hypothesized mean of 100; therefore,

$$\text{Test statistic} = Z_{\bar{X}} = \frac{\bar{X} - \mu_X}{s_{\bar{X}}} = \frac{99 - 100}{1.00} = -1.00 \text{ SE}$$

The p-value   To determine if a test effect is significantly large enough to lead us to reject a null hypothesis, we must compute the probability of its occurrence. We did this with the Tex-the-gambler hypothesis. We found that the probability of rolling snake eyes is .0278. This *unusually low* probability of occurrence for honest dice led us to reject his honesty. Similarly, for our dumb-jocks stereotype hypothesis, we can precisely determine the probability of the observed effect. This probability is called the *p*-value. The **p-value of the hypothesis test** is *a measurement of the unusualness of a sample outcome when the null hypothesis is true*. In general, the *p*-value is the following calculation:

> *p* [a sampling outcome as unusual as or more unusual than the one observed when the null hypothesis is true]

For sampling distributions that fit probability curves, such as the normal curve, the *p*-value is calculated as an area in one or both tails of the curve. If the alternative hypothesis (H_A) is a one-tailed test in the negative "less than" direction, such as our dumb-jocks hypothesis, the *p*-value is calculated as the area in the curve from the observed sample mean value of 99 IQ points and beyond to the left. To avoid confusion, let us shade the target area of the *p*-value:

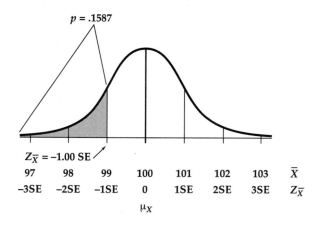

$$p = .1587$$

$$Z_{\bar{X}} = -1.00 \text{ SE}$$

97	98	99	100	101	102	103	$\bar{X}$
–3SE	–2SE	–1SE	0	1SE	2SE	3SE	$Z_{\bar{X}}$

$$\mu_X$$

---

the *p*-value of a hypothesis test   A measurement of the unusualness of a sample outcome when the null hypothesis is true.
   On probability curves such as the normal curve, the *p*-value will be an area in the tail of the curve.

We use the normal curve table (Statistical Table B in Appendix B) to obtain its numerical value. The shaded area is a column C-type area. In column A of the table we locate a Z-score of 1.00 and imagine a negative sign since our test statistic value is -1 SE. In column C we find the proportion of area in the tail is .1587. Thus, we state our p-value as follows:

> p-value: p [drawing a sample with a mean ($\bar{X}$) as unusual as or more unusual than 99 when the true population mean (μ_X) is 100] = .1587.

What does the phrase "as unusual as or more unusual than" convey? In calculating the p-value in the tail of the curve, the word *or* is a cue for using the addition rule of probability, and what we do is add the probabilities. Our p-value is the probability of obtaining a sample with a mean as unusual as 99 plus the probability of any outcome more unusual, such as a mean IQ of 98 or 97 or 96 or 95, etc. The null hypothesis (H_0) is rejected when the p-value is small. If we had taken only the probability of a sampling outcome of 99, it would be a tiny area in the curve above that single score. We would have rejected the H_0 very quickly, even though 99 is not an unusual outcome. So one reason for taking the area beyond the observed outcome is to avoid this miscalculation. The real reason for including "or more unusual than" is this: If we were to consider a sample mean of 99 IQ points unusual enough to reject H_0, we would surely reject the H_0 for sample outcomes more extreme, such as 98, 97, or 96. The curve is swooping down in the tail. Outcomes beyond 99 IQ points have even lower probabilities.

What if we use a different alternative hypothesis (H_A)? If the H_A is a one-tailed test in the positive "greater than" direction, the p-value is calculated as the area in the curve from the observed sample mean and beyond to the right. If the H_A is a two-tailed, nondirectional test, the p-value is calculated to include the areas of both tails of the curve. Remember, the calculation of the p-value assumes that H_0 is true. If no direction is stipulated ahead of time in the H_A, in repeated sampling it would be just as unusual to miss the hypothesized parameter of 100 IQ points on the high side as on the low side. Since the normal curve is symmetrical (i.e., a mirror reflection on each side), for a two-tailed test we simply multiply the column C area by 2. For example, if the H_A for the dumb-jocks hypothesis had been simply "not equal to 100," our p-value would have been (.1587) (2) = .3174, the area beyond 1 SE on both sides of the curve.

Step 5: The Rejection Decision   Once we determine the p-value in step 4, we compare it to the level of significance (α) from step 3, which is .05. If the p-value is less than or equal to α, then we reject the H_0 and accept the H_A. On the other hand, if the p-value is greater than α, we "fail to reject" the H_0. This step of the hypothesis test is called the rejection decision. For our dumb-jocks question, our p-value of .1587 is greater than .05, so we fail to reject the H_0.

Step 6: Interpret and Apply the Results and Provide Best Estimates in Everyday Terms   The final step in hypothesis testing is to provide an interpretation of results. We take into account the audience to which the results are to be reported. For a public audience, one that is not well versed in statistical terms, the interpretation is restricted to everyday language. For a professional presentation or submission to a scientific journal, additional statistical information is provided.

For our dumb-jocks stereotype hypothesis, let us imagine that we are presenting to a public audience. Essentially, we address three things in the interpretation:

1. Restate the H_0 or H_A, whichever we decided on in step 5.

2. Provide best estimates based on the sample data. Observe the sample statistic. When H_0 is rejected and H_A is accepted, present the sampling outcome as a best estimate of the parameter. When H_0 is not rejected, present the sampling outcome and the test effect as simply due to sampling error.

3. Provide a straightforward answer to draw the hypothesis test procedure to a close.

With our dumb-jocks hypothesis we failed to reject the H_0. Thus, we rule out the H_A and, instead, restate and interpret the H_0 in straightforward language: The mean IQ score of high school athletes appears no different than the mean IQ of 100. *Best estimate:* We estimate that the mean IQ of athletes is 100—the same as that of other students. The -1-point difference between the mean IQ score of the sample of high school athletes and the normal mean IQ of 100 is due to expected sampling error. *Answer:* The "dumb-jocks" stereotype is wrong. High school athletes are, on average, just as intelligent as other students.

Notice the elements of step 6. First, we revert back to step 1 and restate the H_0. Therefore, in step 1, the H_0 and H_A must be stated properly and clearly to avoid confusion. Second, in the restatement of the H_0, we use the conservative language "*appears no different*" rather than "*is no different*" or "*is the same.*" Since we are relying on sample data, we cannot state a conclusion about the population with 100 percent confidence. Third, in providing best estimates, since we failed to reject the H_0, we should at least mention that the test effect is due to sampling error. A public audience may desire to know why we stuck with a mean IQ of 100 when sample data seem to show that athletes average 1 IQ point lower. A public audience may ask why we chose to ignore the effect and may even accuse us of bias or "political correctness." To answer, we must clearly explain the notion of random sampling error. For example, we mention that a second sample could have had a mean of 101—1 point higher than the general mean— and we would have drawn the same conclusion. In providing best estimates, there is also the option of calculating a confidence interval (Chapter 8). For example, for our dumb-jocks sample, the 95 percent confidence interval would read: We are 95 percent confident that the mean IQ (μ_X) of the population of high school athletes is between 97 and 101 points (calculations not shown). Notice that a μ_X of 100 IQ points falls within this confidence interval. That is why we conclude that the mean IQ of athletes appears no different than that of all students.

Finally, remember to answer the question, even if this is a restatement of other parts of the interpretation. The null and alternative hypotheses are stated in mathematical and statistical language. The answer to the research question may address broader conceptual questions. In this case we tested mean IQ, while our broader question was whether the dumb-jocks stereotype is true.

Special Note on Symbols

For reasons explained in Chapter 10, computer software programs such as *SPSS* refer to any single sample means test, regardless of sample size, as a *t*-test. This applies to the Z-test presented in this chapter. In your computer software, look for a *t*-test of means to run the Z-test procedure.

Understanding the Place of Probability Theory in Hypothesis Testing

Computing probabilities is the essential mathematical operation in hypothesis testing. Note that in the six steps of statistical inference we discussed "probability" many times. First, in step 2, the sampling distribution is a prediction of all possible sampling outcomes and the probability of each outcome when the null hypothesis (from step 1) is imagined to be true. Second, in step 3, we set the level of significance (α), the probability level that may lead us to reject the null hypothesis. Third, in step 4, we compute the probability of our actual sampling outcome, still imagining that the null hypothesis is true. In step 5, we compare two probabilities: the one computed in step 4 and the one stated in step 3. This comparison leads us to a conclusion: We either reject the null hypothesis and accept the alternative hypothesis, or we "fail to reject" the null hypothesis and let it stand. *If you begin to lose sight of what hypothesis testing is about, remember that it is based on comparing two probabilities: that of what actually occurs in our single observed sample and that of what we expect to occur in repeated sampling.*

A Focus on p-Values

Understanding *p*-values is essential for grasping the logic of hypothesis testing. Let us apply some proportional thinking by asking these questions: What happens as the magnitude of a *p*-value increases? What does it mean when the *p*-value calculates small or large?

When the *p*-Value Is Large Relative to Alpha, That Is, when $p > \alpha$, We Fail to Reject the Null Hypothesis   A large *p*-value tells us that our observed sample outcome is not much different or "far off" from the outcome predicted by the null hypothesis; in other words, the test effect is small. For example, suppose we had obtained a mean of 99.9 IQ points for our sample of jocks. Our test effect would have been $-.10$ IQ points. The sampling distribution in Figure 9–2 suggests that this small test effect could very well have resulted from normal sampling error. It has a high probability of occurrence and that is what the *p*-value measures. When we obtain a small test effect and its large *p*-value, in scientific lingo we say: There is not "a statistically significant difference" between what is observed and what is hypothesized. The difference could easily have resulted from normal sampling error.

When the p-*Value is Small Relative to Alpha, That is, when* p ≤ α, *We Reject the Null Hypothesis A small *p*-value tells us that *assuming* the null hypothesis is true, our sample outcome is unusual. Suppose, for example, that our sample mean IQ had calculated to 97 IQ points. The test effect would have been −3 IQ points. Looking at Figure 9–2, we can see that this large effect is 3 standard errors below the hypothesized mean of 100 and there is not much area beyond that point in the tail of the curve. In fact, our *p*-value would have been .0013 (from column C of the normal curve table). This is so unusual that perhaps the population mean is not 100. Small *p*-values occur when the sample outcome does not reasonably fit the hypothesized parameter. Recall the simple illustration: When no clouds are observed, reject the hypothesis that it is to rain soon. The probability (or *p*-value) of getting rain from a cloudless sky is surely small, so the hypothesis of rain is rejected. When we obtain a large test effect and small *p*-value, in scientific lingo we say: There is "a statistically significant difference" between what is observed and what is hypothesized. In summary, there is an inverse relationship between the size of the test effect and its computed *p*-value, as summarized in the following box.

---

the relationships among effect size, *p*-values, and rejection decisions

A small test effect → a large *p*-value → "fail to reject" the H_0

A large test effect → a small *p*-value → "reject" the H_0

The Level of Significance and Critical Regions of the Sampling Distribution Curve

As we have demonstrated, the *p*-value is the probability of an outcome as unusual as or more unusual than the one observed. As we noted in Chapter 6 when partitioning the normal curve, a probability can be represented graphically. We did so in our sample problem by shading the sampling distribution curve to indicate that the *p*-value area is equal to .1587. We also can shade the area that represents the level of significance, α = .05. To do so we partition .05 of the area in the negative/left tail of the curve, because in the alternative hypothesis (H_A) we predicted one-tail in that direction. This task is a Problem Type 5 from Chapter 6. We look in column C of the normal curve table (Statistical Table B in Appendix B) for the value of .0500 or that closest to it. In column A we find 1.64 and add a negative sign to indicate that we are working with the lower half of the curve. This indicates that a Z-score of −1.64 cuts off the lower .05 of the curve. This Z-score is referred to as the **critical test score**, *the one that is large enough to indicate a significant difference between the observed sample statistic and the hypothesized parameter.* It is symbolized as Z_α. *The area in the tail of the curve that is beyond Z_α* is called **the critical region** of the curve. Let us superimpose this α = .05 area on the curve along with the *p*-value area.

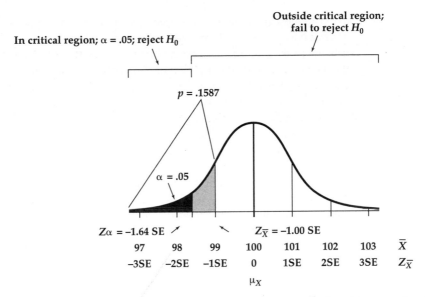

The word *critical* is used because the critical region comprises Z-scores that lead us to criticize the validity of the null hypothesis. On a sampling distribution curve the relative locations of the critical test score, Z_α, and the calculated value of the test statistic, $Z_{\bar{X}}$, provide a quick way to evaluate the rejection decision in step 5 of the six steps. Observe the curve and compare the *absolute values* (the scores ignoring the signs) of $Z_{\bar{X}}$ from step 4 to the critical test score (Z_α) from step 3. For the jocks stereotype problem, $Z_\alpha = -1.64$. If the test statistic $(Z_{\bar{X}}$ from step 4) falls in the critical region of the curve, we reject the H_0, because this means that $p \leq \alpha$. In our dumb-jocks stereotype problem we did not fall in that critical region and, therefore, we failed to reject the H_0.

---

the critical test score (Z_α)   The test statistic score that is large enough to indicate a significant difference between the observed sample statistic and the hypothesized parameter.

the critical region of the sampling distribution curve   The area in the tail of the curve that is beyond the critical test score (Z_α) of the stated level of significance (α).

In general, there is an inverse relationship between these two scores, as indicated in the box that follows.

---

the relationships among the test statistic, the critical test score, and the *p*-value

If $Z_{\bar{X}} \geq Z_\alpha$, then $p \leq \alpha$; that is, the *p*-value area is smaller than the critical region area. Reject H_0 and accept the H_A.

If $Z_{\bar{X}} < Z_\alpha$, then $p > \alpha$; that is, the *p*-value area is larger than the critical region area. Fail to reject H_0.

The most frequently used critical Z-score is ± 1.96. Ninety-five percent of the area under a normal curve falls between $+1.96$ and -1.96, leaving 5 percent of the area distributed in the two tails (2.5 percent in each tail). It is the area in the tails of the curve that constitutes the critical region or α-probability. Since the focus is on two tails, this is called a two-tailed critical region. A critical Z-score of ± 1.96, then, corresponds to the critical region "$\alpha = .05$, two tails."

We can also have a critical region concentrated on one side of the curve—a one-tailed critical region. As shown above, the critical Z-score of 1.64 is a one-tailed critical region; 5 percent of the curve is beyond 1.64 on one side. A critical Z-score of 1.64, then, corresponds to the critical region "$\alpha = .05$, one tail." These two critical scores and their critical regions are illustrated in Figure 9–4. Table 9–2 lists several commonly used Z-scores and the sizes of their critical regions (i.e., α-probabilities). Note that these critical regions are "comfortable" sizes (i.e., 5 percent, 1 percent, and 0.1 percent). For instance, if asked to rate the performance of the members of a rock-and-roll group, you might respond that the group rates in the top 5 percent or 1 percent. You are not likely to use an awkward percentage such as 4 percent.

FIGURE 9–4

Critical Z-scores for $\alpha = .05$

Illustration A: Critical two-tailed Z-score of ± 1.96; critical region area totals .05 (5%) distributed in the two tails.

Designated: Critical region for $\alpha = .05$, two tails.

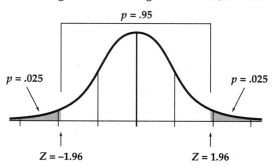

$p = .95$

$p = .025$ $p = .025$

Z = –1.96   Z = 1.96 $\alpha = (.025) + (.025) = .05$

Illustration B: Critical one-tailed Z-score of 1.64; critical region area totals .05 (5%) in one tail.

Designated: Critical region for a = .05, one tail.

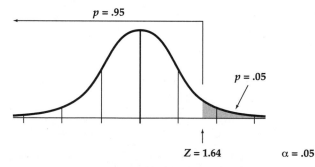

$p = .95$

$p = .05$

Z = 1.64 $\alpha = .05$

TABLE 9–2 | Commonly used critical *Z*-scores and α-probabilities
(*p* in the critical region)

Critical Region (α)	Critical Z-score (Z_α)	In One Tail		In Two Tails		
		p	%	*p*	Σ% from Both Sides	(% on one side)
α = .05, 1 tail	1.64	.05	5%			
α = .01, 1 tail	2.33	.01	1%			
α = .001, 1 tail	3.08	.001	0.1%			
α = .05, 2 tails	1.96			.05	5%	(2.5%)
α = .01, 2 tails	2.58			.01	1%	(0.5%)
α = .001, 2 tails	3.30			.001	0.1%	(.05%)

The Raw-Score Unit of Measure for a Critical Region   The notion of critical region allows us to look at the rejection decision in yet another way. Both the test statistic, $Z_{\bar{X}}$, and critical test score, Z_α, are in standard error (SE) units. The test statistic, $Z_{\bar{X}} = -1.00$ SE is simply a standardized version of the observed $X = 99$ IQ points. We can also calculate the critical test score in the raw-score units of IQ points. A critical test score of -1.64 standard errors corresponds to a $\bar{X}$ of 98.3 IQ points. This calculation is a Problem Type 7 in Chapter 6. We solve for $\bar{X}$ and substitute the critical test score of $Z_\alpha = -1.64$ for $Z_{\bar{X}}$:

$$Z_{\bar{X}} = \frac{\bar{X} - \mu_X}{s_{\bar{X}}}$$

thus:

$$\bar{X} = \mu_X + (Z_{\bar{X}})(s_{\bar{X}})$$
$$= 100 + (-1.64)(1.00) = 98.36 \text{ IQ points}$$

This result tells us that a sample mean lower than *98.36 IQ points* has less than a .05 probability of occurrence from a population with a mean of 100. Since our observed mean of 99 IQ points is greater than 98.36, we fail to reject the H_0.

Obtaining a good sense of the relationships among observed sample outcomes, their representation as test scores, their *p*-values, the chosen level of significance, critical test scores, and critical regions is best acquired by observing the sampling distribution curve. Drawing this curve is an important learning tool for hypothesis testing.

Choosing the Level of Significance   It is in step 3 of the six steps of statistical inference that we set the level of significance, α. We come back to α in step 5, where we make the "rejection decision" by comparing the *p*-value to α. When $p \leq \alpha$, we reject the null hypothesis; when $p > \alpha$, we fail to reject the null hypothesis. As we noted

TABLE 9–3 | Possible results of rejection decisions

Our Rejection Decision	The Unknown Truth about Parameters	
	When the H_0 Is Actually True	When the H_0 Is Actually False
We reject the H_0	Type I error	Correct decision
We fail to reject the H_0	Correct decision	Type II error

above, unless we observe the entire population, our results are only estimates and the rejection decision and the conclusions made from it may be wrong. Any sampling-based conclusions have expected error, as we saw in Chapter 8, where we referred to α as expected error. We call this an error rather than a mistake because we are able to stipulate its chances of occurrence precisely. Setting the level of significance allows us to control the chances of making a wrong decision or "error."

Table 9–3 depicts the relationship between true outcomes and the rejection decision and reveals four possible occurrences. Keep in mind that we will never know whether the null hypothesis is true or false *unless we "sample" the entire population and get the true parameter.* We conduct a statistical test with the knowledge that we may draw a wrong conclusion.

Although we will never know for sure when we do it, when we reject the null hypothesis when it is false, we have made the correct decision. Similarly, when we fail to reject the null hypothesis when it is true, we have made the correct decision. However, when we *reject a true null hypothesis,* we make a **type I error**. In any test where we reject the null hypothesis, there is a chance that we should not have rejected it. For example, could it be that Tex the gambler was simply lucky? Similarly, in any hypothesis test where we fail to reject the null hypothesis, there is a chance that we should have rejected it. This is a matter of *failing to reject a false null hypothesis,* and we call this error a **type II error**. This would have been the case of concluding that Tex was honest when in fact he was not.

We will never know for sure whether we made the correct decision or made an error. We can, however, manage and control the magnitude of such errors in a number of ways. First, if we reject the null hypothesis, we could not have made a type II error because a type II error involves *not* rejecting a hypothesis. Similarly, when we fail to reject the null hypothesis, we know we could not have made a type I error because this error involves *rejecting* a hypothesis. Second, we can easily control the amount of type I error we are willing to chance. This is the case because the level of significance, α, which we set at our own discretion, is the probability of making a type I error. Thus,

$$\alpha = p \text{ [of making a type I error]}$$

Again, the null hypothesis is rejected when the *p*-value from step 4 is small. If we had chosen to set α low (say, .001), we would have made it difficult to reject the null hypothesis because the *p*-value would have had to be very small to "get under" .001. By making the null hypothesis difficult to reject at all, we make it difficult to reject in error. Thus, when we set α low, we reduce the chance of a type I error—of rejecting the null hypothesis when in fact it is true.

By contrast, if we choose to set α high (say, .10), we make it easier to reject the null hypothesis because the *p*-value from step 4 would not have had to compute very small to be less than an α of .10. By making it easy to reject the null hypothesis, we reduce the chance of making the mistake of not rejecting it when it is false (i.e., we reduce the chance of making a type II error).

We use the Greek symbol *beta* (β) to signify the probability of a type II error. Thus,

$$\beta = p \ [\text{of making a type II error}]$$

Unfortunately, controlling β is very difficult. Setting α is possible because it is based on the expected distribution of outcomes described by the sampling distribution—when the null hypothesis is true. Beta, however, depends on the null hypothesis being false. Since a hypothesis can be false in any number of ways, we have no easy mathematical basis for calculating the probabilities of these false outcomes. We can, however, indirectly control β when we set our alpha level. This is because α and β are inversely related; that is, as α increases, β must necessarily decrease, and vice versa. Although we typically do not calculate β, we know that when α is set high, this makes it easier to reject the null hypothesis. This lessens the chance of failing to reject it at all and therefore lessens the chance of failing to reject it *when it is false*.

---

type I error   Unknowingly making the incorrect decision of rejecting a true null hypothesis.

$$\alpha = p \ [\text{of making a type I error}]$$

type II error   Unknowingly making the incorrect decision of failing to reject a false null hypothesis.

$$\beta = p \ [\text{of making a type II error}]$$

Again, it is α, the level of significance, that we set. Deciding on its value is not troublesome, however, because scientists in a particular field follow conventions (traditions) that are based on the types of questions being studied and on what other scientists will accept. The four conventional α levels are presented in Table 9–4, which shows the relationship between these levels and the likelihood of rejecting a null hypothesis. The level of significance (α) should be set low when the consequences of a type I error are serious. For instance, if our null hypothesis is that a new prescription drug is toxic (i.e., poisonous), we do not want to reject this hypothesis prematurely and make a type I error. Thus, we would set α low (say, .001). This would require strong evidence that the drug was safe before we would reject its toxicity. In social survey research the conventional α-level is .05, a moderate level. Unless you have a good reason to do otherwise, follow this convention. If you do encounter a situation with ethical implications, see the Chapter 9 Extensions on *The Statistical*

TABLE 9–4 | Conventional levels of significance and the likelihood of rejecting a null hypothesis (H_0)

Likelihood of Rejecting the H_0	Level of Significance* (α)	Typical Uses
High	.10	Exploratory research, where little is known about a topic
Moderate	.05 and .01	Conventional levels in survey research and psychometric and educational assessment instruments
Low	.01 and .001	Conventional levels in biological, laboratory, and medical research, especially when a type I error is life-threatening (such as testing the toxicity of drugs)

*These conventional levels apply to bivariate statistical analysis. In multivariate statistical modeling such as LISREL, model fit may be tested with an α set as high as .5. Such analysis is beyond the scope of this text.

Imagination Web site at www.mhhe.com/ritchey2 for a systematic procedure for setting the level of significance.

Choose the Level of Significance Before Observing Data It is essential that we decide how critical we are going to be of the null hypothesis (H_0) *before* making our sample observation. That is, we must set α in step 3 of the six steps, before looking at the sample data in step 4. Why? If we waited until after observing the sample outcome in step 4, we could set α to a level slightly larger than the computed p-value and this would assure us of rejecting the H_0. That is, we could rig the hypothesis test to obtain the result we desire. For instance, suppose we are dead set on proving that athletes are dumb jocks. We could observe our p-value of .1587 and then set $\alpha = .20$. Upon "finding" $p < \alpha$, we would reject the H_0. From the standpoint of scientific integrity, however, this would be cheating. It would allow personal bias to enter into the scientific process. Aside from scientific integrity, this would be dishonest. If done unintentionally, it would reveal ignorance about the logic of hypothesis testing. We would become the "dumb statisticians."

In analyzing data, it is tempting to peek at the results before setting the level of significance. In the world of scientific research, getting the results we desire may support the arguments of our theory, lead to publications in reputable journals, and make us famous. In the business world, getting the results we desire may enhance our status with the boss (by showing, for example, that there was a statistically significant increase in company profits). In political polling, getting the results we desire may sway undecided voters. Indeed, statistical analysis can be manipulated by setting an advantageous α-level. But do not be tempted! Properly trained professional scientists view data tampering as unethical. Furthermore, as we discussed in Chapter 1, the scientific research process has checks and balances (such as blind reviews of journal article submissions) to catch unethical or careless behavior. These checks and balances minimize not only human error but also human vanity.

The Level of Confidence

When we reject the null hypothesis (H_0) at, say, the .05 level of significance, we are taking a 5 percent chance of rejecting the H_0 when it is in fact true. For example, suppose we examine the research question that Tex the gambler is a crook. Our H_0 is that he is honest. We set α at .05, a conventional level of significance. We calculated the p-value of rolling snake eyes and it is .0278; therefore, $p < \alpha$ and we reject H_0 and call Tex a crook. We will never know for sure, however, if he really is. (He took his dice with him and got away!) There was a 5 percent chance that he was simply very lucky and that we falsely accused him. But by the same token, there was a 95 percent probability that we made the correct decision and did not falsely reject his honesty. We call this the **level of confidence**, *the confidence we have that we did not make a type I error,* and it is equal to $1 - \alpha$.

---

the level of confidence

Level of confidence = 1 – level of significance = $1 - \alpha$

A .05 level of significance corresponds to a 95 percent level of confidence. Similarly, a .01 level of significance corresponds to a 99 percent level of confidence, and so on.

We defined these terms in Chapter 8 with regard to confidence intervals. The mathematical properties are the same here. The level of confidence and the level of significance (or expected sampling error) are statements about the confidence we have in our sampling and statistical procedures. At the .05 level of *significance* we are asserting that *if the null hypothesis is actually true* and we conduct our procedures 100 times, we will *incorrectly* reject this true null hypothesis only 5 times. Therefore, we will make the correct decision 95 times. Thus, we are 95 percent confident in the conclusion we draw from this single hypothesis-testing procedure. Our level of confidence is inversely related to the chance we take of making a type I error. The less chance we take of rejecting the null hypothesis (i.e., the lower we set α), the more confident we are in our conclusion *when we do happen to reject it.*

The only time we have 100 percent confidence in a conclusion is when every subject in a population is observed. In this uncommon situation, the resulting computations are not estimates (i.e., statistics) but actual parameters. Also, sampling error is not an issue; that is, we have a zero probability of sampling error. For example, the records office of Crosstown University may use computerized records to provide an exact mean grade point average of its current student body, the actual population parameter. In most research, such as a telephone survey of households in the United States, we do not have access to every observation for a population. Fortunately, our ability to manage and control sampling error makes it unnecessary to spend large sums of money surveying entire populations.

Study Hints: Organizing Problem Solutions

The ins and outs of hypothesis testing are best learned through doing. The task is much like learning to read music. It takes practice and is best approached systematically.

All hypothesis tests follow the logic of the six steps of statistical inference. The general statement of these steps is presented in Table 9–5. It is wise to go ahead and learn the wording of the six steps even if you are not completely comfortable with the meaning of them all. This way, you will not be lost when your instructor refers to a particular step in class.

TABLE 9–5 | The six steps of statistical inference or hypothesis testing

Test Preparation

State the research question. Draw conceptual diagrams depicting the givens, including the population(s) and sample(s) under study, variables (e.g., $X = \ldots, Y = \ldots$) and their levels of measurement, and given or calculated statistics and parameters. Using the criteria for selecting a statistical test, choose and state the proper statistical test procedure.

Six Steps

Using the symbol *H* for *hypothesis:*

1. State the null hypothesis (H_0). State the alternative hypothesis (H_A) and stipulate the direction of the test (whether it is one-tailed or two-tailed).

   The H_0 is a statistical hypothesis, one stated in such a way that you will know what statistical outcomes will occur in repeated random sampling *if this hypothesis is true.* The H_A is accepted if the H_0 is rejected.

2. Describe the sampling distribution and draw the sampling distribution curve.

   The sampling distribution is a projection of sampling outcomes likely to occur in repeated sampling *when the H_0 is true.* A sampling distribution consists of a listing of all possible sampling outcomes and a stipulation of the probability of each one.

3. State the chosen level of significance (α). Indicate again whether the test is one-tailed or two-tailed. Specify the critical test score and mark the critical region on the curve in step 2.

   Alpha is the amount of sampling error we are willing to tolerate in coming to a conclusion. The critical test score is obtained from statistical tables in Appendix B.

4. Observe the actual sample outcomes. Compute the test effects, the test statistic, and *p*-value, and mark the *p*-value on the curve in step 2.

   The *test effect* is the difference between what was observed in the sample and what was hypothesized for the H_0 (in step 1). The *test statistic* is a formula for measuring the likelihood of the observed effect. The *p-value* is the probability (p) of sampling outcomes as unusual as or more unusual than the outcome observed under the assumption that the H_0 is true.

5. Make the rejection decision.

   Compare the *p*-value to α.

   > If $p \leq \alpha$, reject the H_0 and accept the H_A at the $1 - \alpha$ level of confidence.
   > If $p > \alpha$, fail to reject the H_0.

   To determine if $p \leq \alpha$, compare the absolute value of the test statistic to the absolute value of the critical test score. Observe the *p*-value relative to the critical region on the curve in step 2.

6. Interpret and apply the results, and provide best estimates in everyday terms.

Solution Boxes Using the Six Steps

Each statistical procedure in the remaining chapters includes solution boxes to facilitate completion of chapter exercises. The following two boxes present concise presentations of large single-sample means test solutions. The first box pertains to our dumb-jocks stereotype problem where we failed to reject the null hypothesis, H_0. The second box presents a solution where the H_0 is rejected. In all hypotheses tests, the first four steps assume that the H_0 is true; therefore, these steps are quite consistent from test to test. The main distinctions between solutions with different rejection decisions occur in steps 5 and 6. Compare these two solutions and pay close attention to these two final steps.

Solution for a Large Single-Sample Means Test (When $n > 121$): Where the Null Hypothesis Is Not Rejected

TEST PREPARATION

Research question: Is the mean IQ of high school athletes less than the mean IQ of all high school students, which is 100 IQ points? *Statistical procedure:* Large single-sample means test. *Givens:*

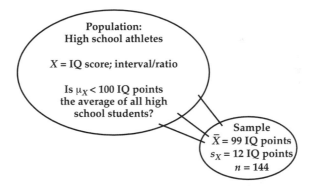

SIX STEPS

1. H_0: $\mu_{X(high\ school\ athletes)} = 100$ IQ points (the known mean (μ_X) of all high school students)

    That is, the mean IQ of high school athletes is no different from that of all high school students.

    H_A: $\mu_{X(high\ school\ athletes)} < 100$ IQ points

    That is, the mean IQ of high school athletes is *less than* that of all high school students. One-tailed.

2. *Sampling distribution:* If H_0 is true and samples of size 144 are repeatedly drawn from the population of high school athletes, sample means ($\overline{X}$'s) will center on 100 as a normal distribution with a standard error:

$$s_{\overline{X}} = \frac{s_X}{\sqrt{n}} = \frac{12}{\sqrt{144}} = 1.00 \text{ IQ point}$$

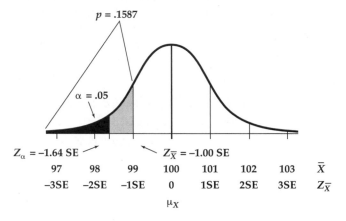

(Shading of the curve is done with steps 3 and 4.)

3. *Level of significance:* $\alpha = .05$. One-tailed. Critical test score $Z_\alpha = -1.64$ SE.

(Shade and mark the critical region as "$\alpha = .05$" on the curve in step 2.)

4. *Observation:*

$$\text{Test effect: } \overline{X} - \mu_X = 99 - 100 = -1 \text{ IQ point}$$

$$\text{Test statistic: } Z_{\overline{X}} = \frac{\overline{X} - \mu_X}{s_{\overline{X}}} = \frac{99 - 100}{1.00} = -1.00 \text{ SE}$$

p-value: *p* [drawing a sample with a mean ($\overline{X}$) as unusual as or more unusual than 99 when the true population mean (μ_X) is 100] = .1587 (In the normal curve table, .1587 is found in column C for $Z = -1.00$. Shade and mark the area of the *p*-value on the curve in step 2.)

5. *Rejection decision:* $|Z_{\overline{X}}| < |Z_\alpha|$ (i.e., 1.00 < 1.64); thus, $p > \alpha$ (i.e., .1587 > .05); fail to reject H_0.

6. *Interpretation:* The mean IQ score of high school athletes appears no different than the mean IQ of 100. *Best estimate:* We estimate that the mean IQ of athletes is 100, the same as that of other students. The -1-point difference between the mean IQ score of the sample of high school athletes and the normal mean IQ of 100 is due to expected sampling error.

Answer: The "dumb-jocks" stereotype is wrong. High school athletes are, on average, just as intelligent as other students.

Solution for a Large Single-Sample Means Test (When $n > 121$): Where the Null Hypothesis Is Rejected

Problem.   You are a quality management consultant for a large national Health Maintenance Organization (HMO). You conduct a study of neurosurgeons' requests for an expensive diagnostic procedure. It is measured as the "Request Rate" of the procedure, the number of requests per hundred patients examined. Five years ago, the mean request rate for all 1,567 neurosurgeons in the HMO was 19.7 requests. You obtain current records on a sample of 130 neurosurgeons in the HMO. You find the mean request rate to be 20.9 requests with a standard deviation of 5.7 requests. Has the mean request rate of HMO neurosurgeons for an expensive diagnostic procedure increased since five years ago? Use the six steps of statistical inference and round the standard error to two decimal places.

TEST PREPARATION

Research question: Has the mean request rate of HMO neurosurgeons for an expensive diagnostic procedure increased since five years ago? *Statistical procedure:* Large single-sample means test. *Givens:*

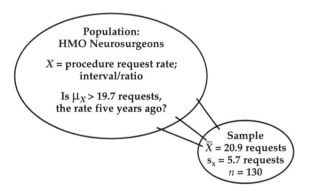

SIX STEPS

1. H_0: $\mu_{X \,(HMO \; neurosurgeons \; today)}$ = 19.7 requests (the known mean (μ_X) of HMO neurosurgeons five years ago)

   That is, the mean request rate of HMO neurosurgeons for the procedure is no different from five years ago.

   H_A: $\mu_{X \,(HMO \; neurosurgeons \; today)}$ > 19.7 requests

   That is, the mean request rate is greater than it was five years ago. One-tailed.

2. *Sampling distribution:* If H_0 is true and samples of size 130 are repeatedly drawn from the population of HMO neurosurgeons, sample means ($\bar{X}$'s) will center on 19.7 as a normal distribution with a standard error:

$$s_{\bar{X}} = \frac{s_X}{\sqrt{n}} = \frac{5.7}{\sqrt{130}} = .50 \text{ requests}$$

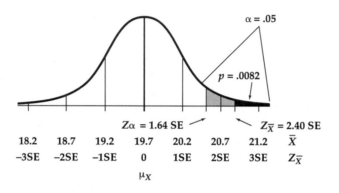

(Shading of the curve is done with steps 3 and 4.)

3. *Level of significance:* $\alpha = .05$. One-tailed. Critical test score $Z_\alpha = -1.64$ SE. (Shade and mark the critical region as "$\alpha = .05$" on the curve in step 2.)

4. *Observation:*

Test effect: $\bar{X} - \mu_X = 20.9 - 19.7 = 1.20$ requests

Test statistic: $Z_{\bar{X}} = \dfrac{\bar{X} - \mu_X}{s_{\bar{X}}} = \dfrac{20.9 - 19.7}{.50} = 2.40$ SE

p-value: p [drawing a sample with a mean ($\bar{X}$) as unusual as or more unusual than 20.9 when the true population mean (μ_X) is 19.7] = .0082 (In the normal curve table, .0082 is found in column C for $Z = 2.40$. Shade and mark the area of the *p*-value on the curve in step 2.)

5. *Rejection decision:* $|Z_{\bar{X}}| > |Z_\alpha|$ (i.e., 2.40 > 1.64); thus, $p < \alpha$ (i.e., .0082 < .05); reject H_0 and accept H_A at the 95% level of confidence.

6. *Interpretation:* The mean request rate for the procedure appears to be greater than 19.7 now. *Best estimate:* We estimate that the mean request rate of HMO neurosurgeons is now 20.9 procedures per hundred patients examined. *Answer:* The mean request rate of HMO neurosurgeons for an expensive diagnostic procedure has increased since five years ago.

Interpreting Results When the Null Hypothesis Is Rejected: The Hypothetical Framework of Hypothesis Testing

Again, the word *hypothetical* means "Let us imagine for the moment." For both of the preceding solution boxes, in steps 1 through 4 of the six steps of statistical inference, we make hypothetical or "if this is true" statements. Observe the second solution box. In step 1, although we suspect that the mean request rate for an expensive procedure has increased, we state the null hypothesis (H_0) to "imagine for the moment that it has not," and we proceed to step 2 as though this is the case. In step 2, we continue to imagine by predicting sampling outcomes for "when the H_0 is true;" that is, we assume the request rate has not changed. The request rate may or may not have changed, but we describe what happens in repeated sampling *if it has not,* because this is a way for us to make firm mathematical predictions about sampling outcomes. In step 3, by setting the level of significance and stipulating the critical score, we state how unusual a sampling outcome must be for us to reject the H_0 which we are *assuming to be true*. In step 4, when we compute the *p*-value, this probability of our sampling outcome is calculated *as though the H_0 is true*. Steps 1 through 4 are imaginary in the sense that we use our statistical knowledge and imaginations to foresee what to expect when we observe data if the null hypothesis is true. Only in step 5 do we firm up a decision and decide what we really believe is true—the null hypothesis or the alternative. In testing a hypothesis, we say in each of steps 1 through 4: "Hold this thought. If the H_0 is true, then here is what happens in repeated sampling." In step 5, we decide if our sample data fit the predictions.

It is in steps 5 and 6, then, that distinct differences appear between hypotheses tests where the H_0 is and is not rejected. In step 5, if the H_0 is rejected, we accept the alternative hypothesis (H_A). In doing so, we are taking an α chance of making a type I error, so we have $1 - \alpha$ confidence in our conclusion. Thus, notice in step 5 in the procedure request rate solution box that, since $\alpha = .05 = 5\%$, we accept the H_A at the 95% level of confidence. We now proceed in step 6 to interpret the alternative hypothesis. The observed sample mean value of 20.9 requests for the expensive procedure is now accepted as a worthy estimate of the population parameter.

If the H_0 is not rejected in step 5, as was the case with the jocks stereotype solution, we do *not* accept the H_0 as true—we simply fail to reject it. We are conservative in stating the rejection decision here because there is the possibility of a type II error. That is, the conclusion that athletes have the same IQ as other students may be false. Unless we go to the considerable trouble of calculating *beta*, the probability of a type II error, we have no way of knowing how much confidence to place in our conclusion. Subsequently, in step 6 we use conservative language such as "appears no different" or "we did not find a significant difference." A valuable learning tool is to continually compare the six-step solutions for each new hypothesis test in the remaining chapters.

Selecting Which Statistical Test to Use

How do we know the correct statistical formulas for a particular problem? The most difficult part of hypothesis testing is choosing the proper sampling distributions and

TABLE 9–6 | Criteria for the selection of a statistical test

1. ASK:	How many variables are we observing for this test?
2. ASK:	What are the levels of measurement of the variables? That is, are the variables nominal/ordinal (for calculating counts and proportions) or interval/ratio (for calculating means)?
3. ASK:	Are we dealing with one representative sample from a single population or more?
4. ASK:	What is the sample size?
5. ASK:	Are there peculiar circumstances to consider?

statistical formulas. These tasks are made easier if systematic criteria are followed in making the choices. These criteria are presented in Table 9–6.

Although each one of these criteria is important in determining the type of test to use, criterion 2 is especially useful. You may want to review the four levels of measurement (Chapter 2). One helpful point to remember is that the mean, deviation scores, variance, and standard deviation are computed only for interval/ratio variables. Thus, statistical tests for these variables often carry the name *means test, differences of means,* or *analysis of variance.* In contrast, nominal/ordinal level variables typically involve counting frequencies, percentages, or proportions of cases in categories and often carry the name *proportions test.* To assist you in selecting the proper procedure, decision trees are provided on the inside front cover of the text and at the ends of chapters.

Statistical Follies and Fallacies: Informed Common Sense: Going Beyond Common Sense by Observing Data

In both the social and the physical world much can be learned through common sense—applying a clear reasoning process to a situation. But scientists stay in business because many of the processes of nature are not so obvious. In fact, social scientists have long established that as humans, we are prone to prejudices and simplistic falsehoods that we come to believe because common sense tells us they are true. There are many myths and superstitions about reality, especially social reality. Science and the statistical imagination with its hypothesis-testing procedure encourage us to question observations more closely, weigh them against predictable outcomes, and challenge myths and prejudices.

Common sense, for instance, leads many people to conclude that women are "obviously" physically and emotionally weaker than men. Clearly, on average, men have greater upper-body strength. But physical strength has many dimensions that challenge the male dominance claim. For instance, fewer females are stillborn, and girls have a lower infant death rate and greater life expectancy. Emotional strength is also hard to pin down. Many people assume that men are emotionally stronger than women because women are quicker to cry. But then, why do men commit over 90 percent of all emotionally charged violent crimes such as assaults and murders? Does the confusion lie with cultural restraints on how men and women express emotions? How can emotional strength be measured reliably and fairly? To fully understand physical and emotional strength, we must start with a clear definition of what strength truly is. Although common sense explains much of reality, a greater understanding requires astute reasoning, meaningful prediction, and accurate observation and measurement. Methodical observation extends and *informs* common sense.

This is not to say that a given scientific report is the last word on an issue. Any scientific theory is always open to further modification. Nor is it to say that scientists are above creating and adhering to their own myths. For example, much scientific research in the late 1800s supported the notion that women were innately less intelligent than men. But in science such myths tend not to stand the test of time. The scientific research process has built-in systems of checks and balances that increase the opportunities for exposing myths. Hypothesis testing is a key process in separating essential facts from apparent but prejudicial facts.

⬥ SUMMARY

1. A hypothesis is a prediction about the relationship between two variables that asserts differences among the measurements of an independent variable will correspond to differences among the measurements of a dependent variable.

2. The theoretical purpose of a hypothesis test is to corroborate theory by testing ideas against facts.

3. The statistical purpose of a hypothesis test is to determine whether statistical effects computed from a sample indicate (1) real effects in the population or (2) sampling error.

4. Statistics from a sample are merely tools for drawing conclusions about a population. It is the population about which we will ultimately make statements.

5. A hypothesis test is based on predicting sampling outcomes for a null hypothesis (H_0). Assuming the H_0 is true, we predict all possible sampling outcomes factoring in sampling error. The resulting sampling distribution is a measuring stick to which our actual, single sampling outcome is compared to see if it is "significantly different" from the outcome predicted by the H_0.

6. The chosen level of significance (α), the direction of the test, and the critical score from a statistical table such as the normal curve table establish the point at which we reject H_0 and the amount of sampling error we will tolerate in coming to a conclusion. This is depicted graphically as the critical region under the sampling distribution curve.

7. The test effect is the difference between what was observed in the sample and what was hypothesized in step 1.

8. The test statistic transforms the test effect into standard errors so that a statistical table may be used to calculate the p-value.

9. The rejection decision compares the p-value to α. A small p-value, one less than α, tells us that our sample outcome is unusual when H_0 is true and justifies rejecting the truth of the H_0.

10. The criteria listed in Table 9–6 assist us in selecting the proper statistical test procedure. The level of measurement of variables and sample size are important criteria.

11. A type I error is rejecting a true H_0. The level of significance, α, is equal to the probability of making a type I error. Type I error is easily controlled by choosing the size of α. A type II error is failing to reject a false H_0. *Beta* is the probability of making a type II error and it is more difficult to control.

12. A large single-sample means test is used with a single interval/ratio variable from one population with a sample size greater than 121 cases. In addition, there must be a target value around which to frame sampling predictions for the test. The normal Z-distribution curve is the sampling distribution.

CHAPTER EXTENSIONS ON *THE STATISTICAL IMAGINATION* WEB SITE

Chapter 9 Extensions of text material available on *The Statistical Imagination* Web site at www.mhhe.com/ritchey2 include a systematic way of choosing the level of significance for hypothesis tests involving ethical situations or situations where the consequences of the test are controversial.

STATISTICAL PROCEDURES COVERED TO THIS POINT

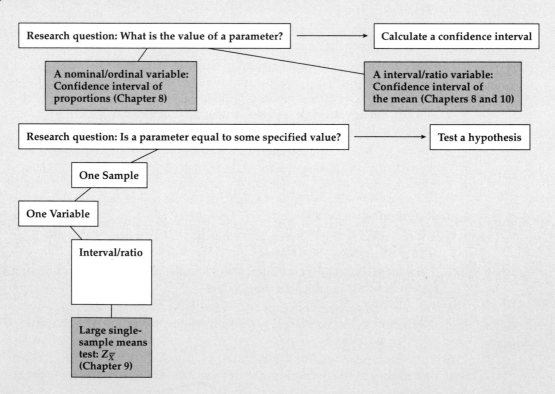

FORMULAS FOR CHAPTER 9

Large single-sample means test (Z-test)

> *Given:* An interval/ratio variable X, a single sample and population, and $n > 121$ cases
>
> *Research question:* Is μ_X (i.e., the mean of X in the population) equal to a target value?

H_0: $\mu_X =$ a target value

Sampling distribution: Normal Z-distribution; standard error estimated using the sample standard deviation.

Standard error:

$$s_{\overline{X}} = \frac{s_X}{\sqrt{n}}$$

Test effect $= \overline{X} - \mu_X$

Test statistic (for use with the normal curve, Z-distribution Table, Statistical Table B, Appendix B):

$$Z_{\overline{X}} = \frac{\overline{X} - \mu_X}{s_{\overline{X}}}$$

QUESTIONS FOR CHAPTER 9

1. A theory (a set of ideas about how the empirical world works) motivates hypotheses (specific predictions of which observations can be expected when a theory is true). Suppose we are testing a racial discrimination theory to account for residential segregation (i.e., the tendency for a neighborhood to be occupied by a single race). In regard to the behavior of real estate agents, what hypothesis is motivated by this theory?

2. Define and distinguish theoretical and statistical purposes for testing a hypothesis. Illustrate with an example.

3. In testing a hypothesis, we determine whether observed sample effects are due to real differences in population parameters or simply are due to sampling error. Mathematically, what two things must we predict in order to begin such a test?

4. Do we reject a null hypothesis when the *p*-value is large or small? Explain.

5. What is the relationship between the size of the effect of a statistical test and the *p*-value calculated for that test? Illustrate with an example.

6. In plain language, what is the level of significance of a hypothesis test and what is its function in the test?

7. Match the following:
   a. Type I error   _____ p [type I error]
   b. Type II error   _____ Rejecting the H_0 when in fact it is true
   c. Alpha (α)   _____ p [type II error]
   d. Beta (β)   _____ Failing to reject the H_0 when in fact it is false

8. A sampling distribution is hypothetical. What does this mean?

9. We use means tests for variables with what levels of measurement?

10. Why must we choose the level of significance before observing the statistical outcomes from our sample?

11. List the six steps of statistical inference.

12. List the criteria for the selection of a statistical test.

13. Now that you know the sampling distribution for the roll of a pair of dice (Table 9–1), use your statistical imagination to improve your strategy for the board game Monopoly. (You may wish to inspect the actual game to answer these questions.)
   a. Winning the game hinges on owning the more valuable properties and frequently collecting rent on them. Given this, if you could choose to own one color of properties (or streets) to start the game, what color would you choose? Why?
   b. What is the most foolish thing a player just sent to jail can do on the next turn if he or she does not own the purple or orange properties?
   c. The four railroads do not pay very much rent and thus often are not worth purchasing and holding. However, there are circumstances when it is advantageous to own them. When would these be? (*Hint:* The addition rule of probability is helpful here.)

EXERCISES FOR CHAPTER 9

Problem Set 9A

On all hypothesis tests, follow the six steps of statistical inference, including test preparation, a conceptual diagram, and probability curves. For consistency, round standard errors to two decimal places. Use $\alpha = .05$ unless otherwise stipulated.

9A-1.   Practice the art of identifying null hypotheses and conceiving of sampling distributions. In general terms, predict what sampling outcomes may be expected to occur with repeated sampling when the following null hypotheses (H_0) are true. (A review of Chapter 7 may be helpful.)
   a. H_0: The mean age of students on campus is 21 years.
   b. H_0: Among the Fortune 500 corporations, the percentage of corporate board members that is female is 20 percent.
   c. H_0: The mean weight of Lot-O-Chocolate candy bars is .75 ounces.
   d. H_0: The instructor is not biased toward men or women in awarding A's.

9A-2. A research question is a project goal that can be stated in terms of a hypothesis. Practice the art of determining whether each of the following research questions constitutes the null hypothesis (H_0) or the alternative hypothesis (H_A). Explain your answer.

    a. On average, there are over six acts of violence per week in every prime-time television drama series.

    b. On a bet, Elbert just flipped 10 coins and got all heads. Are his coins double-headed?

    c. Is the stereotype true that over 90 percent of homeless persons are addicted to alcohol or drugs?

9A-3. The direction and sign of a hypothesis test are specified in the alternative hypothesis. Decide whether the following alternative hypotheses (H_A) are one-tailed in the positive direction, one-tailed in the negative direction, or two-tailed nondirectional. Also, indicate the mathematical sign and explain your choice.

    a. H_A: Over 50 percent of lung cancer victims are or have been smokers.

    b. H_A: The mean grade point average of male and female students is not the same.

    c. H_A: In the central city school district less than 60 percent of high school graduates go on to college.

9A-4. In a study of work patterns among attorneys, a researcher hypothesizes that those specializing in corporate law work more hours per week than do those specializing in estate law. In the H_0, the researcher hypothesizes that the mean number of hours worked per week for the two groups is equal.

    a. Why does she state the H_0 that way instead of saying that the mean for corporate lawyers is higher?

    b. In the H_A, should she use a one-tailed or a two-tailed test? Why?

    c. In step 3 of the test, she states a level of significance (α) of .05. In step 4 of the test, she computes a *p*-value of .23. In step 5, will she reject the H_0 or fail to reject it?

9A-5. This exercise will familiarize you with the relationships among levels of significance, *p*-values, and rejection decisions. For the following levels of significance and *p*-values, indicate whether you would reject or fail to reject the null hypothesis, H_0.

	Level of Significance (α from step 3 of the six steps)	*p*-value (from step 4 of the six steps)	Rejection Decision: Reject H_0 or Fail to Reject H_0
a.	.001	.0007	
b.	.05	.0650	
c.	.01	.0099	
d.	.05	.0399	
e.	.001	.0110	
f.	.01	.0101	

9A-6. Someone asks you if the average grade point average (GPA) of Greene County High School students is equal to a B (i.e., a GPA of 3.0). You do not think so and have reason to believe that it is less than 3.0. Test the hypothesis with the following sample data:

$$n = 155 \qquad \overline{X} = 2.91 \text{ GPA points} \qquad s_X = .9 \text{ GPA points}$$

9A-7. A large regional bank seeks to locate branch offices in residential communities. The objective is to focus on home improvement loans, so a community's homes must have an average age over 15 years. You randomly select 130 city property records for Clarksdale and find the mean age of homes to be 15.78 years with a standard deviation of 3.1 years. Is Clarksdale a good candidate for a branch office?

9A-8. In step 3 of the six steps of a hypothesis test we decide on a level of significance (α), the amount of p-value below which we will define the sampling outcome as unusual and reject the H_0. On the sampling distribution curve, this is the critical region with a critical score expressed as a number of standard errors.

  a. For exercise 9A-6, what is its critical score expressed in the raw score units of GPA points?

  b. For exercise 9A-7, what is its critical score expressed in the raw score units of years?

Problem Set 9B

On all hypothesis tests, follow the six steps of statistical inference, including test preparation, a conceptual diagram, and probability curves. For consistency, round standard errors to two decimal places. Use $\alpha = .05$ unless otherwise stipulated.

9B-1. Practice the art of identifying null hypotheses and conceiving of sampling distributions. In general terms, predict what sampling outcomes may be expected to occur with repeated sampling when the following null hypotheses (H_0) are true. (A review of Chapter 7 may be helpful.)

  a. H_0: Half the television-viewing public watches a network nightly news program.

  b. H_0: The mean speed of automobiles on the death alley stretch of the interstate is 80 miles per hour.

  c. H_0: Forty percent of high school seniors have illegally consumed alcohol.

  d. H_0: The mean age of corporate vice presidents is 49 years.

9B-2. A research question is a project goal that can be stated in terms of a hypothesis. Practice the art of determining whether each of the following research questions constitutes the null hypothesis (H_0) or the alternative hypothesis (H_A). Explain your answer.

  a. On average, do the drivers on the death alley stretch of the interstate exceed the speed limit of 70 miles per hour?

    b.   Using a sample of 30 of the 125 players, is the average weight of this year's football team the same as last year's, which was 224 pounds?

    c.   Does this casino use loaded dice?

9B-3.   The direction and sign of a hypothesis test are specified in the alternative hypothesis. Decide whether the following alternative hypotheses (H_A) are one-tailed in the positive direction, one-tailed in the negative direction, or two-tailed nondirectional. Also, indicate the mathematical sign and explain your choice.

    a. H_A: Over 80 percent of county jail inmates are imprisoned on drug-related charges.

    b. H_A: For the new drug Fixitall, the cure rate of the experimental group that received the drug is higher than that of the control group that received a placebo (i.e., a sugar pill).

    c. H_A: The percentages of Baptists and Methodists who believe that the Bible is free of errors is not the same.

9B-4.   Professor Smith is studying gender inequality in a large communications firm. On the basis of past experience and theories from the literature, she has reason to believe that the firm's women have a mean income below that of men. In the H_0, she hypothesizes that the mean incomes of men and women are equal.

    a.   Why does she state the H_0 that way instead of saying that the mean for men is higher?

    b.   In the H_A, should she use a one-tailed or a two-tailed test? Why?

    c.   In step 3 of the test, she states a level of significance (α) of .05. In step 4 of the test, she computes a *p*-value of .03. In step 5, will she reject the H_0 or fail to reject it?

9B-5.   This exercise will familiarize you with the relationships among levels of significance, *p*-values, and rejection decisions. For the following levels of significance and *p*-values, indicate whether you would reject or fail to reject the null hypothesis, H_0.

	Level of Significance (α from step 3 of the six steps)	*p*-value (from step 4 of the six steps)	Rejection Decision: Reject H_0 or Fail to Reject H_0
a.	.05	.0476	
b.	.05	.3297	
c.	.01	.0476	
d.	.001	.0028	
e.	.01	.0006	
f.	.05	.4996	

9B-6.   Someone asks you if the average body mass index (BMI) of Jackson Middle School students is equal to the ideal BMI suggested by the Centers for Disease Control (i.e., a BMI of 25). You do not think so and have reason to believe that it is higher than 25. Test the hypothesis with the following sample data:

$$n = 170 \qquad \overline{X} = 27.6 \text{ kg per meters squared} \qquad s_X = .9 \text{ kg per meters squared}$$

9B-7.   Someone asks you if the average grade point average (GPA) of Highlands University students is equal to a B (i.e., a GPA of 3.0). You do not think so and have reason to believe that it is less than 3.0. Test the hypothesis with the following sample data:

$$n = 210 \qquad \overline{X} = 2.92 \text{ GPA points} \qquad s_X = .9 \text{ GPA points}$$

9B-8.   In step 3 of the six steps of a hypothesis test, we decide on a level of significance (α), the amount of p-value below which we will define the sampling outcome as unusual and reject the H_0. On the sampling distribution curve, this is the critical region with a critical score expressed as a number of standard errors.

a.   For exercise 9B-6, what is its critical score expressed in the raw score units of kilograms per meters squared?

b.   For exercise 9B-7, what is its critical score expressed in the raw score units of GPA points?

Problem Set 9C

On all hypothesis tests, follow the six steps of statistical inference, including test preparation, a conceptual diagram, and probability curves. For consistency, round standard errors to two decimal places. Use $\alpha = .05$ unless otherwise stipulated.

9C-1.   Practice the art of identifying null hypotheses and conceiving of sampling distributions. In general terms, predict what sampling outcomes may be expected to occur with repeated sampling when the following null hypotheses (H_0) are true. (A review of Chapter 7 may be helpful.)

a. H_0: The mean age of a large company's employees is 32 years.

b. H_0: The mean weight for a Division 1-A football team's players is 207 pounds.

c. H_0: The mean number of students enrolled in introductory sociology courses at a large, urban university is 82.

d. H_0: Women constitute 65 percent of licensed physicians among pediatric specialties.

9C-2.   A research question is a project goal that can be stated in terms of a hypothesis. Practice the art of determining whether each of the following research questions will constitute the null hypothesis (H_0) or the alternative hypothesis (H_A). Explain your answer.

       a.   Using a sample of 120 undergraduates, is the average age of this year's incoming class of first-year students the same as past years, which was 18.4 years?

       b.   Does the poker player mark cards in order to increase his advantage over his fellow players?

       c.   Is it true that over 60 percent of new Ph.D.'s in sociology are female?

9C-3.   The direction and sign of a hypothesis test are specified in the alternative hypothesis. Decide whether the following alternative hypotheses (H_A) are one-tailed in the positive direction, one-tailed in the negative direction, or two-tailed nondirectional. Also, indicate the mathematical sign and explain your choice.

       a. H_A: Greater than 60 percent of college seniors have engaged in binge-drinking behavior in the past six months.

       b. H_A: Less than 6 percent of the U.S. population have a doctoral graduate degree.

       c. H_A: The percentages of sociologists and psychologists that attribute mental illness to structural attributes within society is not the same.

9C-4.   In a study of academic achievement patterns among high school students, a researcher hypothesizes that, in grades 10–12, females make better grades in core curriculum classes. In the H_0, the researcher hypothesizes that the mean grades assigned to both gender groups are equal.

       a.   Why does the researcher state the H_0 that way instead of saying that the mean for females is higher?

       b.   In the H_A, should the researcher use a one-tailed or a two-tailed test? Why?

       c.   In step 3 of the test, the researcher states a level of significance (α) of .05. In step 4 of the test, he computes a *p*-value of .41. In step 5, will he reject the H_0 or fail to reject it?

9C-5.   This exercise will familiarize you with the relationships among levels of significance, *p*-values, and rejection decisions. For the following levels of significance and *p*-values, indicate whether you would reject or fail to reject the null hypothesis, H_0.

	Level of Significance (α from step 3 of the six steps)	*p*-value (from step 4 of the six steps)	Rejection Decision: Reject H_0 or Fail to Reject H_0
a.	.05	.3610	
b.	.01	.0031	
c.	.001	.0149	
d.	.01	.0067	
e.	.05	.0549	
f.	.05	.0476	

9C-6. Suppose that someone asks you if the average number of children among families in a large Midwestern city is 4. You disagree and believe that this average is less than 4. Test the hypothesis with the following sample data:

$$n = 195 \qquad \bar{X} = 3.68 \text{ children} \qquad s_X = 1.1 \text{ children}$$

9C-7. Someone asks you if the average grade point average (GPA) of State University students is equal to a B (i.e., a GPA of 3.0). You do not think so and have reason to believe that it is less than 3.0. Test the hypothesis with the following sample data:

$$n = 140 \qquad \bar{X} = 2.87 \text{ GPA points} \qquad s_X = .8 \text{ GPA points}$$

9C-8. In step 3 of the six steps of a hypothesis test, we decide on a level of significance (α), the amount of p-value below which we will define the sampling outcome as unusual and reject the H_0. On the sampling distribution curve, this is the critical region with a critical score expressed as a number of standard errors.

    a. For exercise 9C-6, what is its critical score expressed in the raw-score units of number of children?

    b. For exercise 9C-7, what is its critical score expressed in the raw-score units of GPA points?

Problem Set 9D

On all hypothesis tests, follow the six steps of statistical inference, including test preparation, a conceptual diagram, and probability curves. For consistency, round standard errors to two decimal places. Use $\alpha = .05$ unless otherwise stipulated.

9D-1. Practice the art of identifying null hypotheses and conceiving of sampling distributions. In general terms, predict what sampling outcomes may be expected to occur with repeated sampling when the following null hypotheses (H_0) are true. (A review of Chapter 7 may be helpful.)

    a. H_0: The mean speed of drivers at a local police speed trap is 78 miles per hour.

    b. H_0: The mean age of tenured faculty at a small, liberal arts university is 42 years.

    c. H_0: 70 percent of college students report engaging in binge drinking over the past six months.

    d. H_0: The mean starting income among business school graduates is $47,000 per year.

9D-2. A research question is a project goal that can be stated in terms of a hypothesis. Practice the art of determining whether each of the following research questions constitutes the null hypothesis (H_0) or the alternative hypothesis (H_A). Explain your answer.

    a. Jane just rolled five boxcars (two 6s) in a row with a pair of dice. Is she playing with dice that have been tampered with (e.g., loaded)?

  b. On average, do first-year chemistry majors drop out of their intended major more than first-year students in other academic disciplines?

  c. In one large metropolitan area, police officers average more than six arrests per week involving driving under the influence (DUI).

9D-3. The direction and sign of a hypothesis test are specified in the alternative hypothesis. Decide whether the following alternative hypotheses (H_A) are one-tailed in the positive direction, one-tailed in the negative direction, or two-tailed nondirectional. Also, indicate the mathematical sign and explain your choice.

  a. H_A: Study trials indicate that the rates of absorption and rehydration attributed to consumption of a newly developed sports drink are higher than the corresponding rates among already existing formulas.

  b. H_A: More than 10 percent of instructors at a local community college report having experience with academic misconduct in their classes within the past year.

  c. H_A: The mean ages among males and females in a county-wide study sample are not the same.

9D-4. In a study of professions in the United States, a researcher postulates that females average lower levels of occupational esteem than males in identical professional and managerial positions. In the H_0, the researcher hypothesizes that the mean levels of professional esteem among men and women are equal.

  a. Why does the researcher state the H_0 that way instead of saying that the mean for women is lower?

  b. In the H_A, should the researcher use a one-tailed or a two-tailed test? Why?

  c. In step 3 of the test, the researcher states a level of significance (α) of .05. In step 4 of the test, she computes a p-value of .024. In step 5, will she reject the H_0 or fail to reject it?

9D-5. This exercise will familiarize you with the relationships among levels of significance, p-values, and rejection decisions. For the following levels of significance and p-values, indicate whether you would reject or fail to reject the null hypothesis, H_0.

	Level of Significance (α from step 3 of the six steps)	p-value (from step 4 of the six steps)	Rejection Decision: Reject H_0 or Fail to Reject H_0
a.	.01	.0124	
b.	.001	.0025	
c.	.05	.0059	
d.	.01	.0027	
e.	.05	.3110	
f.	.001	.0009	

9D-6. Studies of homeless persons in the mid-twentieth century consistently found the average age of this population to be over 40 years. A recent study of 150 homeless persons in a southern city found a mean age of 37.7 years with a standard deviation of 9.6 years. Is the average age of homeless persons there *less than* 40?

9D-7. You are to determine whether or not students who apply to graduate school have a higher mean IQ score than other students. To do so, you administer an IQ test to a random sample of 125 students who are applying to graduate school. It is known that the national average IQ score of students is 100. Your sample produces an average IQ score of 105 with a standard deviation of 10 points. What do you conclude?

9D-8. In step 3 of the six steps of a hypothesis test, we decide on a level of significance (α), the amount of *p*-value below which we will define the sampling outcome as unusual and reject the H_0. On the sampling distribution curve, this is the critical region with a critical score expressed as a number of standard errors.

    a.   For exercise 9D-6, what is its critical score expressed in the raw-score units of years?

    b.   For exercise 9A-7, what is its critical score expressed in the raw-score units of IQ points?

OPTIONAL COMPUTER APPLICATIONS FOR CHAPTER 9

If your class uses the optional computer applications that accompany this text, open the Chapter 9 computer exercises on *The Statistical Imagination* Web site at www.mhhe.com/ritchey2. The exercises involve the large single-sample means test and an orientation to bivariate statistical procedures for *SPSS for Windows*. In addition, Appendix D of this text provides a brief overview of the *SPSS* command sequences for procedures covered in this chapter.

Hypothesis Testing II: Single-Sample Hypothesis Tests: Establishing the Representativeness of Samples

CHAPTER OUTLINE

Introduction

In many respects Chapter 10 is an extension of Chapter 9, where the large single-sample means test is used to introduce the logic of hypothesis testing. In Chapter 10, we continue with single-sample hypotheses tests and start with a discussion of their common applications. Two hypotheses tests are presented, the small single-sample means test (when $n \leq 121$ cases) and the large single-sample proportions test. For the latter hypothesis test, we show an important application: testing for sample representativeness. Finally, you will recall that the calculation of a confidence interval of a population mean (Chapter 8) carried the restriction that the sample size be greater than 121 cases. In Chapter 10, we show the minor adjustments needed to calculate a confidence interval of a population mean for samples with fewer cases.

As we learned in Chapter 8, when we want to estimate an unknown parameter of a population, say, the mean age of managers of fast-food restaurants, we compute a confidence interval. With confidence intervals we address the question: *What is* the score value of the parameter? The confidence interval provides an interval or span estimate. In this chapter we address a different type of question. Rather than ask, *What is* the value of the parameter? we ask, *Is the parameter equal to some chosen target value?*

Where do these target values come from? There are several sources:

1. *A known population parameter from a comparison group.* For example, it is known that the mean intelligence quotient (IQ) score for all persons is 100. Where H_0 is the null hypothesis and H_A is the alternative hypothesis, we can test the hypothesis that the mean IQ of a specific group, say, inventors, is higher:

   H_0: $\mu_{X(inventors)} = 100$ IQ points (the known mean, μ_X, of all adults)

   H_A: $\mu_{X(inventors)} > 100$ IQ points (the known mean, μ_X, of all adults). One-tailed.

   Note that on the left sides of these equations we subscript the name of the population under study and on the right we indicate the source of the target value.

2. *Known parameters from a past time period.* For example, 2000 U.S. Census data provide actual parameters, such as the proportion of U.S. households headed by women. Using a current national sample of 1,500 households, we can test the hypothesis that the proportion has changed since then:

   H_0: $P_{u(female\text{-}headed\ households\ today)} = .19$ (the known proportion, P_u, of female-headed households in 2000)

   H_A: $P_{u(female\text{-}headed\ households\ today)} \neq .19$ (the known proportion, P_u, of female-headed households in 2000). Two-tailed.

3. *A statistical ideal.* For example, as the quality control manager of the Smellishou Perfume Company, you select a random sample of half-ounce bottles from store shelves and determine whether this desired volume was maintained throughout the production and delivery process.

   H_0: $\mu_{X(bottles\ of\ Smellishou\ on\ store\ shelves)} = .5$ ounce (the desired target value)

   H_A: $\mu_{X(bottles\ of\ Smellishou\ on\ store\ shelves)} < .5$ ounce (the desired target value). One-tailed.

4. A *population is sampled, and the sample statistics are compared to some known population parameters to determine whether the sample is representative of the population.* For example, suppose we have sampled 250 nurses in the state. Complete state licensing records show that 64 percent of all state nurses are registered nurses (RNs). This is a known parameter for our sampled population.

If our sample is representative, about 64 percent of the nurses in the sample will be RNs.

H_0: $P_{u(sampled\ population)}$ = .64 (the known parameter (P_u) of the

targeted state nursing population)

That is, the sample *is* representative of state nurses with regard to the proportion of nurses holding RN licenses.

H_A: $P_{u(sampled\ population)}$ ≠ .64 (the known parameter (P_u) of the targeted

state nursing population)

That is, the sample *is not* representative of state nurses with regard to the proportion of nurses holding RN certificates.

Later in this chapter we will illustrate complete hypothesis tests for some of these source target values.

---

purpose of a single-sample hypothesis test   To determine whether a parameter of a population is equal to a specified "target" value. Sources of target values: (1) comparison groups, (2) known parameters from a past time period, (3) statistical ideals, and (4) known parameters of a sampled population (for establishing sample representativeness).

The Small Single-Sample Means Test

In Chapter 9, to illustrate the logic of hypothesis testing we learned how to do a *large* single-sample means test. In doing so, we were careful to say many times that this test, which used the normal curve as a sampling distribution, required a minimum sample size of more than 121 cases. Why does this matter? Recall from Chapter 4 that the mean has a limitation: The calculation of a mean can be distorted by outliers or by a skewed distribution.

A sampling distribution of means describes what sample outcomes would occur if we repeatedly sample and calculate means. The sampling distribution reveals how each sample mean will differ slightly and how often to expect a sample mean to miss the true parameter. We used the normal curve table and Z-scores to calculate the probability of sampling outcomes. As it turns out, when the sample size, n, is 121 cases or fewer, the chances are great that extreme scores will distort the calculation of sample means. If a high extreme score is included, the mean will be inflated in value. If a low extreme score is included, the mean will be deflated. When n is 121 or fewer cases, the effects of extreme scores are so great in repeated sampling that the sampling distribution curve has a large spread in sampling error and this flattens the curve. We call this flattened curve a t-distribution.

The "Student's t" Sampling Distribution

As the law of large numbers asserts, for a sampling distribution of means, the larger the sample size n, the smaller the standard error. Conversely, especially small samples have standard errors so large that the probability curve is stretched and flattened. This flattening begins to appear with sample sizes less than 122 and is especially apparent when n is less than 30.

The sampling distribution curve we use with especially small samples is called Student's t, or simply a t-distribution. This distribution curve is approximately normal. Like the normal curve, the t-distribution curve is symmetrical; that is, the mean, median, and mode are equal and one side of the curve is a mirror image of the other. But a t-distribution curve is flatter than the normal curve (i.e., a t-distribution is *platykurtic,* or flattened out like a plate).

When testing a hypothesis, the test statistic—a measure of distance on the horizontal axis of this sampling distribution curve—is symbolized by t instead of Z to indicate that the curve is only approximately normal. To identify critical scores and evaluate p-values, we use the t-distribution table (Statistical Table C in Appendix B).

---

approximately normal *t*-distribution   A sampling distribution that is like the normal curve in that it is symmetrical, but the curve is flattened rather than bell-shaped. For test statistics, use the symbol t instead of Z. Use the t-distribution table rather than the normal curve table to identify critical scores and evaluate p-values.

To illustrate the flattening of a sampling distribution, let us focus on sample size. Figure 10–1 compares the sampling distributions for three sample sizes of 10, 20, and more than 121 cases. With a sample size above 121, the curve will be normal with its distinctive bell shape. A sample size of 121 or fewer cases produces a t-distribution curve that is only approximately normal. The smaller the sample size, the flatter the t-distribution.

The shape of a particular t-distribution curve depends on an adjustment called degrees of freedom (df), which are defined and explained later in this chapter. For a sampling distribution of means, degrees of freedom are computed as the sample size minus 1.

FIGURE 10–1

Flattening of
sampling
distributions of
means when
n is less
than 121

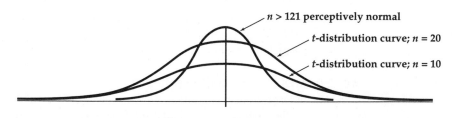

$n > 121$ perceptively normal

t-distribution curve; $n = 20$

t-distribution curve; $n = 10$

Calculating Degrees of Freedom for a Sampling Distribution of Means

$$df = n - 1$$

where

$$df = \text{degrees of freedom}$$
$$n = \text{sample size}$$

As Figure 10–1 indicates, the smaller the sample, the flatter the curve. To calculate probabilities from a t-distribution curve, we need 120 t-distribution tables just like the normal curve table—one for each sample size from 121 down to 2. To save space, a single t-distribution table (Statistical Table C in Appendix B) consolidates information from all 120 curves. This table, however, is designed differently from the normal curve table; these differences are illustrated in Table 10–1.

The key difference is that the t-distribution table provides information only for the traditional *critical regions* of $\alpha = .05$, $\alpha = .01$, and $\alpha = .001$ (chapter 9). In the t-distribution table, the left column provides degrees of freedom (df) and the top row provides areas under the curve—but only for these critical regions. The body of the table contains critical t-scores (t_α's). In a t-distribution curve, these t-scores are used the same way as critical Z-scores (Z_α).

Observe the two-tailed and one-tailed t-distributions on the right side of Table 10–1. For any number of degrees of freedom (df), as you move to the right across the table, the t-scores increase while the levels of α decrease from .05 to .001. This simply reflects the fact that the larger the value of the critical score, the smaller the area in the tail of the curve.

Notice that the t_α-scores in the bottom row of Table 10–1 are essentially equivalent to Z_α-scores. The differences are so small that they do not appear when the t-scores are rounded. That is, Z-scores and t-scores are the same when the sample size (n) is 122 or more and, therefore, degrees of freedom compute to 121 or more. But going up any α-column of the t-distribution table, the t-score will always be larger than the Z-score that appears at the bottom of the table. This makes intuitive sense because both Z-scores and t-scores measure variability in sampling error—distance from the mean of the curve. When the sample size is small, calculated means have greater error because of the sensitivity of the mean to extreme scores of X. It is not unusual with a small sample to get sampling outcomes ($\overline{X}$'s) farther out in the tail of the curve—quite far removed from the parameter (μ_X). This "pushing" of a critical region farther from the mean (μ_X) of the sampling distribution for a small sample is illustrated in Figure 10–2, which shows the critical Z- and t-values at the .05 level, one-tailed when $n > 121$ and $n = 20$, respectively. With an n of 20, it would be just as unusual to draw a sample whose mean is 1.725 standard errors from μ_X as it would to draw a mean only 1.64 standard errors from μ_X when n is greater than 121.

TABLE 10–1 | Locations of information in the normal distribution and *t*-distribution tables

Statistical Table B in Appendix B The Normal Distribution Table		Statistical Table C in Appendix B The *t*-Distribution Table							
			Two-Tailed				One-Tailed		
Column A Z-scores	Column C Area beyond Z	df	.05	.01	.001	df	.05	.01	.001

α-probabilities for critical regions are located here

Column A Z-scores	Column C Area beyond Z	df	.05	.01	.001	df	.05	.01	.001
1.64	.0505 (≈ .05) one-tailed	•	•	•	•	•	•	•	•
•	•	5	2.571	4.032	6.869	5	2.015	3.365	5.893
2.33	.0099 (≈ .01) one-tailed	•	•	•	•	•	•	•	•
•	•	10	2.228	3.169	4.587	10	1.812	2.764	4.144
3.08	.0010 one-tailed	•	•	•	•	•	•	•	•
•	•	•	•	•	•	•	•	•	•
1.96	.0250 (× 2 = .05) two-tailed	•	•	•	•	•	•	•	•
•	•	20	2.086	2.845	3.850	20	1.725	2.528	3.552
2.58	.0049 (≈ .005 × 2 = .01) two-tailed	•	•	•	•	•	•	•	•
•	•	•	•	•	•	•	•	•	•
3.30	.0005 (× 2 = .001) two-tailed	•	•	•	•	•	•	•	•
•	•	30	2.042	2.750	3.646	30	1.697	2.457	3.385
•	•	120	1.980	2.617	3.373	120	1.658	2.358	3.160
•	•	∞	1.96	2.58	3.30	∞	1.64	2.33	3.08
↑			↑	↑	↑		↑	↑	↑

Critical Z's (Z_α's) are in column A
of the normal distribution table

Critical *t*'s (t_α) are in these columns
of the *t*-distribution table

FIGURE 10–2

Comparison of one-tailed critical regions and critical scores for sample sizes of 121 or more (a normal distribution) and 20 (a *t*-distribution)

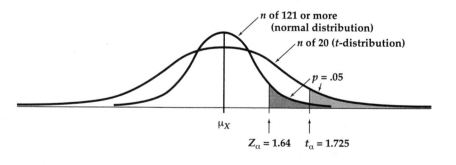

n of 121 or more
(normal distribution)

n of 20 (*t*-distribution)

$p = .05$

μ_X

$Z_\alpha = 1.64$ $t_\alpha = 1.725$

Do not be thrown off by this. A t-distribution is simply an approximately normal curve—a normal curve that is flattened out by a greater spread of sampling error. The t-scores in the t-distribution table are like Z-scores except that they are for critical regions only. Calculated t-scores and Z-scores measure the same thing on these curves.

Selecting the Critical Probability Score, t_α, from the t-distribution Table

In step 3 of the six steps of statistical inference we must identify the proper critical score, t_α, from the t-distribution table (Statistical Table C in Appendix B). The particular t_α score depends on the chosen level of significance (α), the direction of the test (two-tailed/nondirectional or one-tailed/directional), and the number of degrees of freedom implied by the sample size, with $df = n - 1$. Here are some example t_α values taken from the t-distribution table:

Example 1: We desire the .05 level of significance, the test is two-tailed/ nondirectional, and $n = 15$. Calculate $df = n - 1 = 14$. In Statistical Table C, observe the left four columns under "Two-tailed or nondirectional test." Find 14 under the "df" column. Move over to the critical score listed under $\alpha = .05$. The critical score, $t_\alpha = 2.145$.

Example 2: We desire the .01 level of significance, the test is one-tailed/directional, and $n = 27$. Calculate $df = n - 1 = 26$. In Statistical Table C, observe the right four columns under "One-tailed or directional test. " Find 26 under the "df" column. Move over to the critical score listed under $\alpha = .01$. The critical score, $t_\alpha = 2.479$.

Example 3: We desire the .05 level of significance, the test is two-tailed/ nondirectional, and $n = 339$. Calculate $df = n - 1 = 338$. In Statistical Table C, observe the left four columns under "Two-tailed or nondirectional test." Find "∞" under the "df" column, meaning $n > 121$ and, therefore, $df > 120$. Move over to the critical score listed under $\alpha = .05$. The critical score, $t_\alpha = 1.96$. This critical score is the same as one taken from the normal curve table (Statistical Table B in Appendix B). It applies to the large sample test we learned in Chapter 9 and to large-sample confidence intervals in Chapter 8. Since it is not unusual to have samples larger than 121 and to conduct two-tailed tests at the .05 level of significance, the t_α of 1.96 is used frequently.

Finally, the name *Student's t* has an interesting story behind it. The discovery and mathematical derivation of the t-distribution were made early in the twentieth century by a mathematician named W. S. Gossett, who worked for the Guinness Brewing Company in Dublin, Ireland. To protect its competitive advantage in the ale business, the company did not allow its employees to publish their work. His findings on dealing with small samples were so important for statisticians, however, that the company made an exception and allowed Gossett to publish under the pseudonym Student. Hence, he signed his work that way, and to this day statisticians refer to this sampling distribution as Student's t.

Special Note on Symbols

As we mentioned in Chapter 9, computer software programs such as *SPSS* refer to any single-sample means test, regardless of sample size, as a t-test. Now you should understand why. When $df > 120$, a sampling distribution of means will fit the normal curve and Z is certainly an appropriate symbol to indicate that the distribution is normal. But to avoid complicating computer programs, regardless of sample size, we use the symbol t and refer to all single-sample means tests as t-tests. This is okay. In a sense, the normal Z-curve may be viewed as a special case of a t-curve, the case where $n > 121$, providing 121 or more degrees of freedom. Again, in your computer software, look for a t-test of means to run any single-sample means test for any size sample. In addition, in the remainder of this text we will refer to the t-test even when $n > 121$.

What Are Degrees of Freedom?

In doing a statistical analysis on a sample, care must be taken to prevent research procedures from leading to inaccurate conclusions about the population. Every measurement instrument and statistical technique has limitations that potentially distort the interpretation of data. For example, the famous Hubble telescope (which rides on a satellite outside the atmosphere) provides distorted images because of a microscopic misalignment in the curvature of its lens. As a result, the photographic images appear blurred. The stars themselves are not blurred; the blurring is a function of the measurement instrument's limitations. The faulty telescope gets in the way of an accurate assessment of the true shapes of distant galaxies. On-site adjustments (via the space shuttle) compensate for the bent lens up to a point, but the Hubble's images are still not pure. The telescope has a peak degree of accuracy, and this level is fixed. The conclusions drawn about the nature of its photographic subjects (stars, galaxies, quasars, etc.) are restricted by the tools and methods used to gather data. Even with computer enhancements, Hubble scientists inevitably confront a lack of flexibility in correcting the distortions of their measurement instrument. The picture they see is only a close approximation of what truly appears there.

Similarly, statistical procedures have limitations that potentially get in the way of an accurate assessment of population parameters. To estimate the spread of a sampling distribution of means, we must consider the effects of the major limitation of the mean (Chapter 4): The calculation of the mean is affected by extreme scores or outliers. This distorting effect is especially troublesome with small samples. Being aware of this limitation, we adjust calculations to account for the sensitivity of the mean to outliers, just as Hubble scientists computer-enhance their photographic images. Any statistical procedure has limits: a lack of total freedom in how it is used. We use the term *degrees of freedom* to refer to how flexible a statistical procedure is. The more degrees of freedom we have, the better, because **degrees of freedom** are *the number of opportunities in sampling to compensate for limitations, distortions, and potential weaknesses in statistical procedures.*

Why are the degrees of freedom for the approximately normal t-distribution calculated as $n - 1$? For a variable, an extreme score in the sample can produce an inflated or deflated mean, one that does not reflect the true population parameter value of that variable. When the sample size is small, this distortion can be rather large. Once a high-value extreme score is randomly drawn into a small sample, there are not many opportunities left for a low-value case to be selected to pull the computed mean closer to the true population parameter. An extremely high score fixes the calculation of the mean into the high-value end of the score range of the variable. The small sample is inflexible, not free of the mean's limitation of sensitivity to extreme scores. It has few degrees of freedom.

To illustrate these principles, we noted in chapter 7 (Figures 7–5 and 7–6) that an infinite set of single random digits ranges from 0 to 9 with a mean of 4.5 (as in Statistical Table A in Appendix B). That is, the true population parameter, μ_X, is 4.5. Suppose, however, we did not know this, and to get an estimate of this population parameter, we sampled these digits and computed the sample mean, $\overline{X}$. Ideally, this estimate would be close to the true parameter of 4.5. This is accomplished when in the random draw process each chosen score on the high side (e.g., 9, 8, 7, or 6) is balanced out by a score on the low side (e.g., 0, 1, 2, or 3). With a true parameter average of 4.5, a perfectly accurate random sample would include as many 0's as 9's because the mean of these two scores is 4.5. Similarly, this perfect sample would include as many 1's as 8's, 2's as 7's, 3's as 6's, and 4's as 5's. But suppose our sample size is small, say, $n = 5$. Imagine further that the first random digit drawn for the sample is a 9, an extreme score. When 9 is added to ΣX in computing the sample mean, it is likely to cause our estimate of the parameter to be on the high side. For example, the following sequence of sample draws could occur and result in a "high-side" sample mean of 6.2:

Sampling sequence: 9, 5, 3, 8, 6

$$\overline{X} = \frac{\Sigma X}{n} = \frac{31}{5} = 6.2$$

With this small sample, after we draw the 9, it is very likely that our estimate will be high because we have only four sampling opportunities left ($n - 1$) to pick up a 0 to balance out the calculation of the mean. We would say that we have only 4 degrees of freedom. Drawing a 9 locks us into a high-side estimate. A sample of five is not very flexible once an extreme score enters the sample.

With a large sample, say, size 130, the drawing of a 9 early on is not as large a problem. We have 129 more chances to draw a 0 to bring the sample calculation of the mean back into the 4.5 range. With a large sample there is greater freedom of adjustment in the sampling procedure.

Another way to look at the concept of degrees of freedom is to consider "independence of sampling events. "For instance, suppose someone said he or she collected five random digits and computed a mean of 6.2, as in the preceding illustration. If this researcher told us the values of four of the digits, we could mathematically determine the fifth. That is, if the first four digits are 9, 5, 3, and 8, for the ΣX to add to 31 to produce a mean of 6.2, the last digit has to be 6. In other words, the last digit is not free to vary; its value is dependent on how the mean is calculated. Thus, in calculating the degrees of freedom for a mean, we subtract 1 from the sample size. In this example that leaves us 4 degrees of freedom. Four of the digits are "free to vary." Degrees of freedom, then, can be viewed as the number of independent sampling events—events that are independent of the limitations of the statistical formula used.

It is only with a sampling distribution of means that degrees of freedom are calculated as $n - 1$. With other statistical procedures, adjustments for degrees of freedom depend on the particular limitations of a procedure. In the remaining chapters, the limitations of various statistical procedures are discussed and degrees of freedom adjustments are made. It may be worthwhile to look through the remaining chapters for the symbol df to become familiar with the notion that sample statistics include this adjustment.

---

degrees of freedom (df)   The number of opportunities in sampling to compensate for limitations, distortions, and potential weaknesses in statistical procedures or the number of independent sampling events. Degrees of freedom are calculated in different ways for various statistical procedures.

Degrees of freedom calculations represent a recognition of the limitations of a procedure. We will use wording such as "*adjust* for degrees of freedom" and "*correct* for degrees of freedom." We often say that a particular limitation causes us to "*lose* degrees of freedom." For instance, the sensitivity of the mean to outliers causes us to lose 1 degree of freedom. Adjusting for the degrees of freedom of a procedure is an essential part of assessing sampling error. We must constantly be aware that to sample is to look through a narrow lens. We must ask: Are what we see and what is truly there one and the same? If we know our lens is blurred, we must take this into account, just as the Hubble scientists "correct" their digital photographic images with computer enhancements. The calculation of degrees of freedom is our mode of correction.

The Six Steps of Statistical Inference for a Small Single-Sample Means Test

In Chapter 9, we learned the six steps of statistical inference for a large single-sample means test. Now that we have determined that special considerations are in order for a means test when n is small (121 or fewer cases), let us apply the six steps of statistical inference to this circumstance.

In 2005, the United States experienced a historical natural disaster when Hurricane Katrina devastated the Gulf of Mexico Coast from east Texas to Alabama. Over one-quarter of a million people were displaced and many lost their property and belongings. The social sciences have a long tradition in disaster research, including the study of how such events affect mental and physical health. Let us suppose that in the weeks following the hurricane, we survey persons displaced from the Gulf Coast who are now living in public emergency shelters in a city a few hundred miles north. The study involves an array of variables related to emergency services, social and capital resources, future prospects, and health effects of the disaster. Suppose that among our measures of health is a series of questionnaire items called the Acute Stress Disorder Scale (ASDS; Bryant, Moulds, and Guthrie, 2000). The scale measures *acute* distress: the *immediate reactions* to a traumatic event. Its 19 survey items require respondents to indicate how often they have experienced symptoms since the event. The list includes dissociative symptoms, such as numbness, a sense of unreality, and the feeling of being outside oneself watching events unfold. In addition, the scale measures fears of reexperiencing trauma, avoidance of thinking about and discussing it, and psychological arousal, such as irritability, jumpiness, overreaction to stimuli, and feelings of distress. The scale is especially useful at predicting which populations of stressed persons are likely to experience the *chronic,* long-term stress disorder Post-Traumatic Stress Syndrome (PTSS).

The ASDS is of interval level of measurement, with scores ranging from 19 to 95, where a high score indicates greater stress. Previous studies using the ASDS reveal that individuals with a score greater than 56 have a good likelihood of developing PTSS (Bryant, Moulds, and Guthrie 2000:64–65). We can use this cutoff score as an indicator of whether our *population* of disaster victims is at risk of long-term PTSS. If so, public health interventions are in order, such as screening of individuals in shelters. Mental health services may then be provided to individuals with high ASDS scores to lessen the risk of PTSS.

Our interest, then, is in the mean ASDS of this population of publicly sheltered Hurricane Katrina victims. If the mean ASDS score is above 56, then this group is at risk of PTSS. We interview 24 randomly selected sheltered adults. We find a mean of 64.54 ASDS scale points with a standard deviation of 19.27 scale points.

Let us think a moment about our research question and how we might test it. Our research question is: On average, do Hurricane Katrina victims experience mean ASDS scores above the cutoff score of 56, putting them at risk of PTSS? For any single-sample hypothesis test, we must have a target value to state the null hypothesis (H_0) and this is provided by the cutoff score of 56 ASDS scale points. We will assume that this value is true and then make sampling predictions as though it were. In other words, the target value for the H_0 allows us to describe the sampling distribution, assuming that this H_0 is true. Our alternative hypothesis (H_A) will be that the mean ASDS for this population is greater than 56. We can compare our sample mean of 64.54 to our cutoff score of 56. The difference is the test effect:

$$\overline{X} - \mu_X = 64.54 - 56 = 8.54 \text{ ASDS scale points}$$

We see that on average our sample subjects score 8.54 points above the cutoff mark. We cannot, however, quickly conclude that this *population* of sheltered victims has a high mean ASDS. Why? Because the test effect could be the result of sampling error, especially since we have a small sample. In other words, we might take a second sample and find its mean to be 8.54 points *below* 56. Recall that the statistical purpose of any hypothesis test is to determine whether a statistical effect computed from a sample indicates a real effect in the population or simply sampling error. Our hypothesis test will determine whether the mean of 64.54 ASDS for the sample is so far above 56 ASDS points as to be statistically significant from 56.

Now we will examine the criteria for the selection of the *t*-test and present the six steps of statistical inference.

When to Use a Small Single-Sample Means Test ($n \leq 121$; t-distribution, $df = n - 1$)

In general: Useful for testing a hypothesis that the mean of a population, μ_X, is equal to a target value.

1. Only one variable.
2. The level of measurement is interval/ratio.
3. A single sample and population.
4. The sample size, n, is 121 or fewer cases (although this test may be used for larger samples, it is required when n is small).
5. There is a target value of the variable to which we may compare the mean of the sample.

Let us examine our research question and determine if this hypothesis test is in order. First, we have the single variable, ASDS. Second, it is of interval level of measurement. Third, we have one sample from the population of sheltered Hurricane Katrina victims. Fourth, our sample size of 24 is "small" (i.e., 121 or fewer). Finally, we have a target value around which to project a sampling distribution.

Now let us apply the six steps of statistical inference to our question of whether publicly sheltered victims of Hurricane Katrina experience high levels of ASDS. The following box presents the solution. Notice that it parallels the steps in Table 9–5 on page 296. As with all of hypothesis tests, study the solution and compare it to Table 9–5 as well as to the hypothesis tests you have learned.

Brief Checklist for the Six Steps of Statistical Inference

TEST PREPARATION
State the research question. Draw conceptual diagrams depicting givens, including the population(s) and sample(s) under study, variables (e.g., $X = \ldots$, $Y = \ldots$,) and their levels of measurement, and given or calculated statistics and parameters. State the proper statistical test procedure.

SIX STEPS
Using the symbol H for *hypothesis:*

1. State the H_0 and the H_A and stipulate test direction.
2. Describe the sampling distribution.

3. State the level of significance (α) and test direction and specify the critical test score.

4. Observe the actual sample outcomes and compute the test effects, the test statistic, and *p*-value.

5. Make the rejection decision.

6. Interpret and apply the results and provide best estimates in everyday terms.

Solution for a Small Single-Sample Means Test (when $n \leq 121$)

TEST PREPARATION

Research question: On average, do Hurricane Katrina victims experience mean ASDS scores above the cutoff score of 56, putting them at risk of PTSS? *Statistical procedure:* Small single-sample means test. *Givens:*

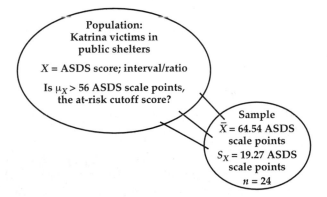

SIX STEPS

1. H_0: $\mu_{X(sheltered\ Katrina\ victims)} = 56$ ASDS points (the mean cutoff score, μ_X, above which a population is at risk of PTSS)

   That is, the mean ASDS of sheltered Katrina victims is no different from the cutoff score.

   H_A: $\mu_{X(sheltered\ Katrina\ victims)} > 56$ ASDS points,

   That is, the mean ASDS of sheltered Katrina victims is above the cutoff score, indicating that this population is at risk of PTSS. One-tailed.

2. *Sampling distribution:* If H_0 is true and samples of size 24 are repeatedly drawn from the population of sheltered Katrina victims, sample means

($\bar{X}$'s) will center on 56 as an approximately normal *t*-distribution, $df = n - 1 = 23$, with a standard error:

$$s_{\bar{X}} = \frac{s_X}{\sqrt{n}} = \frac{19.27}{\sqrt{24}} = \frac{19.27}{4.90} = 3.93 \text{ ASDS scale points}$$

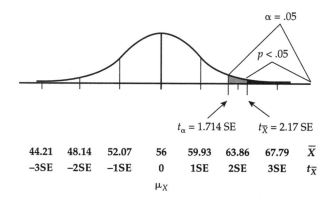

44.21	48.14	52.07	56	59.93	63.86	67.79	$\bar{X}$
-3SE	-2SE	-1SE	0	1SE	2SE	3SE	$t_{\bar{X}}$
			μ_X				

(Shading of the curve is done with steps 3 and 4.)

3. *Level of significance:* $\alpha = .05$. One-tailed. Critical test score $t_\alpha = 1.714$ SE. (Shade and mark the critical region on the curve in step 2.)

4. *Observation:*

   Test effect: $\bar{X} - \mu_X = 64.54 - 56 = 8.54$ ASDS scale points

   Test statistic: $t_{\bar{X}} = \dfrac{\bar{X} - \mu_X}{s_{\bar{X}}} = \dfrac{64.54 - 56}{3.93} = 2.17$ SE

   p-value: *p* [drawing a sample with a mean ($\bar{X}$) as unusual as or more unusual than 64.54 when the true population mean (μ_X) is 56] $< .05$.

   (Shade and mark the area of the *p*-value on the curve in step 2.)

5. *Rejection decision:* $|t_{\bar{X}}| > |t_\alpha|$ (i.e., $2.17 > 1.714$); thus, $p < \alpha$ (i.e., $p < .05$); reject H_0 and accept H_A at the 95 percent level of confidence.

6. *Interpretation:* The mean ASDS scale score of sheltered Katrina victims appears significantly greater than the cutoff score of 56. *Best estimate:* We estimate that the mean ASDS scale score of sheltered Katrina victims is 64.54. *Answer:* Publically sheltered Hurricane Katrina victims appear at great risk of acute stress disorder. They should be targeted for mental health services geared toward detecting and preventing the effects of this disorder as well as Post Traumatic Stress Disorder.

Some things to note about this hypothesis test:

- In step 1, note that the hypothesis is about parameters (μ_X), not statistics $(\overline{X})$. Every hypothesis test is about the population and its parameters. Sample statistics are only estimates of population parameters and the sample is merely a tool to make statistical inferences about the population.

- In step 1, we state the alternative hypothesis, H_A, as a positive, one-tailed test and focus on the right side of the curve. This decision was *not* made by examining the sample mean to see if it was higher than 56. Instead, the positive direction was chosen on the basis of practicality. Scores *higher than* 56 ASDS scale points are of interest for predicting PTSS.

- In step 2, we describe the sampling distribution for the parameter hypothesized in step 1. The sampling distribution tells us that if this population has a mean ASDS of 56, not higher or lower, and if we repeatedly sample with $n = 24$, about 68 percent of the time the sample mean ASDS scores, $\overline{X}$, will fall between 52.07 and 59.93; about 95 percent of the time between 48.14 and 63.86; and so on.

- In step 3, we observe the t-distribution table for the critical t_α-score for a one-tailed test at the .05 level of significance with $df = 23$ and find it to be 1.714 standard errors (SE). This critical score defines the critical region, the area shaded and marked on the curve in step 2 as $\alpha = .05$. If, indeed, the mean ASDS score of our Katrina victim population is 56, only 5 percent of the time in repeated sampling do sample means fall more than 1.714 SE above 56. Our sample mean of 64.54 ASDS points falls in the critical region, so we consider it significantly different from 56 points and reject the H_0 in step 5.

- In step 4, rather than focus on the critical region we focus on the p-value. The computation of the p-value tells us how unusual the observed sample outcome is *when the H_0 is true*. It answers the question: With repeated sampling, how often does a mean of 64.54 ASDS points or more occur when the population mean is 56? Since $p < .05$, we consider the sample mean as so unusual as to reject 56 as the true population mean.

- In step 4, we return to step 2 and draw the p-value area on the sampling distribution curve. Regardless of whether the H_0 is true or not, in step 2 we predict what occurs in sampling "if the H_0 is true" and in step 4 the calculation of the p-value assumes this for the moment. Remember that steps 1 through 4 are predicated on the assumption that the H_0 is true.

- In step 5, take note of the careful wording of the rejection decision. When we reject the H_0, we accept that H_A, but not without caution. An outcome of 64.54 ASDS points does occur in repeated sampling when H_0 is 56, albeit less than 5 percent of the time. Because we did not sample the entire population, we cannot be 100 percent sure of our result. But by setting α at .05, we are taking only a 5 percent chance of rejecting the H_0 when in fact it is true. That is, we are taking a 5 percent chance of making a type I error and drawing the wrong conclusion. On the other hand, we have a 95 percent chance of not making that error. Thus, we are 95 percent confident in our result.

- In step 6, because we rejected the null hypothesis, H_0, the interpretation focuses on the accepted H_A. At this point, we can disregard the H_0. Notice also that the tone of step 6 is substantive. It is a discussion of the research question and addresses concepts and variables. The earlier steps address technical aspects of the statistical procedure and focus on probability theory.

- In step 5, we rejected the H_0 that $\mu_X = 56$ ASDS points. In step 6, a public or professional audience will desire to know what we accepted in place of 56. Thus, we provide a *best estimate*. Since we are the only researchers around with a statistical estimate of ASDS for this population, we provide our sample result of 64.54 ASDS points. This is a point estimate. For a professional audience, a calculation of the confidence interval (Chapter 8) might be called for.

Gaining a Sense of Proportion About the Dynamics of a Means Test

Thus far, we have learned two hypotheses tests, the large and small single-sample means tests. Essentially, we could call both of them t-tests and use the t-distribution with the knowledge that when $n > 121$, the sampling distribution is normal rather than merely approximately normal. This is apparent in Table 10–1 where, when $n > 121$, the critical t-scores of the t-distribution table equal the critical Z-scores of the normal curve table. As noted, computer programs refer to all single-sample means tests as t-tests.

Single-sample means tests are good for learning the basic idea behind hypothesis testing. The target value of the null hypothesis of a means test is easy to conceive. The logic of the hypothesis test is simple. We hypothesize a mean score of an interval/ratio variable X in the H_0, say, for example, the hypothesis that the mean grade point average on campus, μ_X, is 3.0 (a B). We observe a sample mean, $\overline{X}$. If the sample mean is close to the hypothesized parameter value, say, 2.9 GPA points, we stick with the value of X in the H_0 and treat the difference (i.e., the effect) as due to sampling error. If the sample mean is not in the vicinity of the hypothesized value of X in the H_0, say, 2.4 GPA points, then we reject H_0. We conclude that the effect is so large that it likely did not occur due to sampling error. Although this concept is simple enough, we must determine exactly what "close" is. The six steps of statistical inference define "close" relative to sample error. Now let us further examine the elements of the hypothesis test to gain a better sense of how the parts connect.

Relationships among Hypothesized Parameters, Observed Sample Statistics, Computed Test Statistics, p-Values, and Alpha Levels

It is important to have a sense of proportion about the relationships among the hypothesized parameter (μ_X), the observed sample statistic ($\overline{X}$), the computed test statistic ($t_{\overline{X}}$), the level of significance and its critical score (α and t_α), and the p-value. This list of concepts may appear overwhelming, but once their interrelationships are grasped, things fall into place and hypothesis testing appears quite simple. Let us think in terms of the likelihood of the null hypothesis (H_0) being rejected, after which the alternative hypothesis (H_A) is accepted. In other words, under what conditions are we no longer willing to accept that the null hypothesis is true? What sample observations lead to a rejection of the null hypothesis?

Rule 1: The Null Hypothesis Is Rejected when the Effect of the Test Is Large—Large Enough That the Test Statistic Value Is Greater Than the Critical Test Score

Again, the effect of the test is the difference between the observed sample statistic and the hypothesized parameter. It is a deviation score on the curve. The null hypothesis will be rejected when the test effect is large. Recall the simple example of hypothesizing that it is going to rain soon. We expect to see dense dark clouds in the sky. If we observe a clear blue sky, this test effect is so different from what we expect that we reject the hypothesis of rain.

When the test effect is large, the test statistic value will also be large. For the single-sample means test, the test statistic is $t_{\bar{x}}$, which is calculated in step 4 of the six steps. It measures the test effect *as a number of standard errors (SE)*. When $|t_{\bar{x}}| > |t_\alpha|$, $p < \alpha$; we reject the null hypothesis. When $|t_{\bar{x}}| < |t_\alpha|$, $p > \alpha$; we fail to reject the null hypothesis. With a means test, for example, the test effect is calculated as $\bar{X} - \mu_X$, and this term appears in the numerator of the test statistic. In any division problem, when the numerator is large, the quotient will be large. Suppose we hypothesize that the mean grade point average (GPA) of students is greater than 2.6. This will be the alternative hypothesis, because we must state the null hypothesis as equal to 2.6 to produce a sampling distribution (i.e., H_0: $\mu_X = 2.6$ GPA points). Let us compare samples of students with large and small test effects, one sample from State University and another from Crosstown University. For simplicity's sake, let us imagine that the standard errors are the same and are equal to .2 GPA point and that the sample sizes are 500. The sample means from the two campuses differ as follows:

From State University (a large test effect and test statistic):

Step 1. H_0: $\mu_X = 2.6$ GPA points.

H_A: $\mu_X > 2.6$ GPA points   One-tailed

Step 4. Observed sample mean:

$$\bar{X} = 3.0 \text{ GPA points}$$

$$\text{Test effect} = \bar{X} - \mu_X = 3.0 - 2.6 = .4 \text{ GPA point}$$

$$\text{Test statistic} = t_{\bar{x}} = \frac{\bar{X} - \mu_X}{s_{\bar{X}}} = \frac{3.0 - 2.6}{.2} = \frac{.4}{.2} = 2.00 \text{ SE}$$

From Crosstown University (a small test effect and test statistic):

Step 1. H_0: $\mu_X = 2.6$ GPA points.

H_A: $\mu_X > 2.6$ GPA points   One-tailed

Step 4. Observed sample mean:

$$\overline{X} = 2.7 \text{ GPA points}$$

$$\text{Test effect} = \overline{X} - \mu_X = 2.7 - 2.6 = .1 \text{ GPA point}$$

$$\text{Test statistic} = t_{\overline{X}} = \frac{\overline{X} - \mu_X}{s_{\overline{X}}} = \frac{2.7 - 2.6}{.2} = \frac{.1}{.2} = .50 \text{ SE}$$

The sample mean of State University misses by .4 GPA point—almost one-half of a letter grade. This is 2.00 standard errors away from the 2.6 GPA that we expect. This is a large difference between the observed sample GPA of 3.0 and the hypothesized parameter of 2.6. It is so large that we can confidently say that it is *not* due to random sampling error. We reject the null hypothesis that the GPA at State University is 2.6 and conclude that it is higher. On the other hand, for the Crosstown University sample, the effect of the test was small—only .1 GPA point—and therefore $t_{\overline{X}}$ is small. The sample mean is only one-half a standard error from the expected mean. Our experience with sampling distributions suggests that this small difference could easily result from sampling error. To summarize rule 1, when the test effect and therefore the absolute value of the test statistic $t_{\overline{X}}$ are large, the likelihood of rejecting the null hypothesis goes up.

Rule 2: The Larger the Test Effect and the Test Statistic, the Smaller the *p*-Value
Large test effects and test statistic values are unusual when the null hypothesis is true. The observed sample outcome is quite unusual (i.e., has a low probability of occurrence) when the test effect is large. In the *t*-distribution curve, the low probability of a large test effect is apparent in the small area in the tail of the curve beyond a large $t_{\overline{X}}$.

The approximately normal *t*-distribution curve is useful for gaining a sense of proportion about the relationship between the value of the test statistic and the *p*-value. Since the *t*-distribution table provides areas in the curve only for critical regions, we can only estimate the *p*-value of a particular test statistic value $t_{\overline{X}}$. Let us illustrate by examining the Crosstown and State University samples using a one-tailed test. In both samples, $df = n - 1 = 499$. The critical t_α values are found in the "∞" row of the *t*-distribution table.

For State University:

$$H_0: \mu_X = 2.6 \text{ GPA points}$$

$$\overline{X} = 3.0 \text{ GPA points}$$

$$\overline{X} - \mu_X = 0.4 \text{ GPA points}$$

$$t_{\overline{X}} = 2 \text{ SE}$$

This is a relatively large test effect and test statistic value. The *p*-value is relatively small. To see this, observe the *t*-distribution table to get the *p*-value. The calculated *t*-value, $t_{\overline{X}} = 2$ SE, falls between the critical t_α-values of 1.64 and 2.33; thus, $p\ [t_{\overline{X}} = 2 \text{ SE}]$ is less than .05 but greater than .01.

The *p*-value is stated: p [drawing a sample with a mean ($\overline{X}$) as unusual as or more unusual than 3.0 GPA points when the true population mean (μ_X) is 2.6 GPA points] $< .05$.

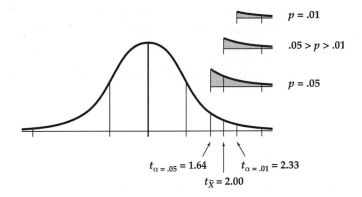

For Crosstown University:

$$H_0: \mu_X = 2.6 \text{ GPA points}$$
$$\overline{X} = 2.7 \text{ GPA points}$$
$$\overline{X} - \mu_X = 0.1 \text{ GPA points}$$
$$t_{\overline{X}} = .5 \text{ SE}$$

This is a relatively small test effect and test statistic value. The *p*-value is relatively large. Observing the *t*-distribution table, the calculated *t*-value, $t_{\overline{X}} = .5$ SE, falls to the left of the critical t_α-score of 1.64; thus, $p \, [t_{\overline{X}} = .5]$ is greater than .05.

The *p*-value is stated as *p* [drawing a sample with a mean ($\overline{X}$) as unusual as or more unusual than 2.7 GPA points when the true population mean (μ_X) is 2.6 GPA points] > .05.

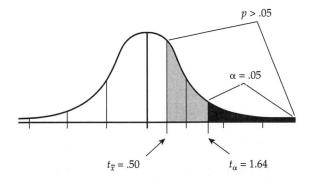

In this comparison, we can see for the Crosstown University sample that it would *not* be unusual to draw a sample mean of 2.7 GPA points from this population if its mean is 2.6 GPA points. In fact, if the population parameter is indeed 2.6 GPA points, in repeated sampling, a large proportion of the time, we would draw sample means that are close to the hypothesized mean. The high probability of this outcome is apparent in the large shaded area of the Crosstown University curve. In testing at the .05 level of significance, we would fail to reject the null hypothesis for Crosstown University. In contrast, with the State University sample, we would conclude that it *is* unusual to draw a sample mean of 3.0 GPA points from a population with a mean equal to 2.6 GPA points. In fact, this effect of .4 GPA point seldom occurs as a result of chance sampling error—fewer than 5 times out of 100 samples. On the State University curve, this is apparent in the comparably small area beyond $t_{\bar{X}} = 2.00$ SE. In testing at the .05 level of significance, we would reject the null hypothesis for the State University case.

To summarize this second rule about the relationship of statistics and *p*-values, the larger the test effect and thus the larger the test statistic, the smaller the probability that the sample outcome occurred as a result of random sampling error. Now let us discuss levels of significance (alpha levels) in relation to test direction.

Rule 3: It Is Easier to Reject with a One-Tailed Test Than with a Two-Tailed Test
Another exercise that will help you gain a sense of proportion about hypothesis testing involves examining whether it is easier to reject the null hypothesis with a one-tailed test or a two-tailed test. As we mentioned in Chapter 9, the answer is a one-tailed test because with a one-tailed test the test effect—the difference between the observed sample outcome and the hypothesized parameter—does not have to be as great for the test statistic $t_{\bar{X}}$ to fall beyond the critical test statistic score, t_α. When $t_{\bar{X}}$ falls beyond t_α into the critical region, the *p*-value will fall below α, and the null hypothesis will be rejected. With a one-tailed test, the critical region is clustered to one side and the t_α is smaller (1.64 compared to 1.96 for the two-tailed test), placing the critical region closer to the hypothesized mean. Therefore, the test effect can be smaller to reach the area of the critical region for a one-tailed test.

To illustrate this, let us suppose that two researchers, Jerome and Charlotte, unbeknown to each other, are testing the hypothesis that State University's mean GPA is 2.6. Jerome has no reason to state a direction in his alternative hypothesis, and so he does a two-tailed test. Charlotte, however, is aware that State University, compared to other colleges in the area, has more scholarships to offer its students and thus attracts better students. Therefore, her alternative hypothesis states that State University's mean GPA is higher than 2.6, and she uses a positive one-tailed test. In step 1 of the statistics test, both Jerome and Charlotte state their null hypotheses as follows:

Step 1. H_0: $\mu_{X(State\ University)} = 2.6$ GPA points

Their alternative hypotheses, however, will be stated differently:

Jerome: H_A: $\mu_{X(State\ University)} \neq 2.6$ GPA points. Two-tailed.

Charlotte: H_A: $\mu_{X(State\ University)} > 2.6$ GPA points. One-tailed.

Suppose that both of them collect samples of 122 and find sample means of 2.95 (i.e., $\bar{X} = 2.95$ GPA points). Their sample standard deviations (s_X) are both 2.2 GPA points, and therefore their computed standard errors are .20 GPA point. Both of their sampling distributions would look like this:

$$s_{\bar{X}} = \frac{s_X}{\sqrt{n}} = \frac{2.2}{\sqrt{122}} = .20 \text{ GPA point}$$

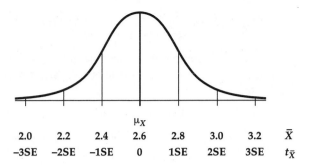

μ_X

2.0	2.2	2.4	2.6	2.8	3.0	3.2	$\overline{X}$
−3SE	−2SE	−1SE	0	1SE	2SE	3SE	$t_{\overline{X}}$

In step 3, although they both stipulate a level of significance (α) of .05, their critical (t_α) scores will differ. Jerome will find his t_α to be 1.96 under the "two-tailed or nondirectional test" columns on the left side of the t-distribution table. Charlotte will find her t_α to be 1.64 under the "one-tailed or directional test" columns on the right side of the t-distribution table. In step 4 of their statistical tests, their calculated test effects and test statistics will be identical.

Step 4. *Observation:*

$$\overline{X} = 2.95 \text{ GPA points} \qquad s_X = 2.2 \text{ GPA points} \qquad n = 122$$
$$\text{Test effect} = \overline{X} - \mu_X = 2.95 - 2.6 = .35 \text{ GPA point}$$

$$\text{Test statistic} = t_{\overline{X}} = \frac{\overline{X} - \mu_X}{s_{\overline{X}}} = \frac{2.95 - 2.6}{.2} = \frac{.35}{2} = 1.75 \text{ SE}$$

Their p-values (step 4) will differ, however, because they will be estimated from different columns of the t-distribution table. And in step 5 their rejection decisions will differ.

Jerome's p-value and rejection decision:

p [drawing a sample with a mean ($\overline{X}$) as unusual as or more unusual than 2.95 GPA points when the true population mean (μ_X) is 2.6 GPA points] > .05

Jerome's sample mean must be 1.96 SE from the hypothesized parameter to reject it, but the test statistic is only 1.75 SE, and so it falls short of the critical region.

$t_{\alpha = .05, \text{ two-tailed}} = 1.96 = \text{deviation (in SE)}$ ⟶ ☐ = a distance of 1.96 SE
needed for rejection for two-tailed test

$t_{\overline{X}} = \text{deviation of observed sample mean}$ ⟶ ☐ = a distance of only 1.75 SE

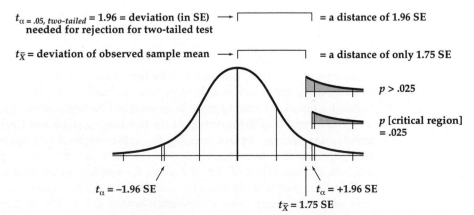

$p > .025$

p [critical region] = .025

$t_\alpha = -1.96 \text{ SE}$ $t_\alpha = +1.96 \text{ SE}$

$t_{\overline{X}} = 1.75 \text{ SE}$

Step 5. *Rejection decision:* $|t_{\bar{x}}| < |t_{\alpha}|$ (i.e., 1.75 < 1.96); thus, $p > \alpha$ (i.e., $p > .05$). Fail to reject H_0.

Charlotte's sample mean need be only 1.64 SE from the hypothesized parameter to reject it. Since the test statistic is 1.75 SE, it reaches her critical region for a one-tailed test.

Charlotte's *p*-value and rejection decision:

p [drawing a sample with a mean ($\bar{X}$) as unusual as or more unusual than 2.95 GPA points when the true population mean (μ_X) is 2.6 GPA points] < .05.

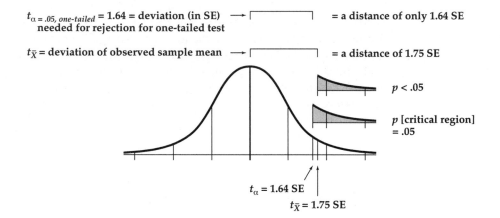

$t_{\alpha = .05,\ one\text{-}tailed} = 1.64$ = deviation (in SE) → ▢ = a distance of only 1.64 SE
needed for rejection for one-tailed test

$t_{\bar{X}}$ = deviation of observed sample mean → ▢ = a distance of 1.75 SE

$p < .05$

p [critical region] = .05

$t_{\alpha} = 1.64$ SE

$t_{\bar{X}} = 1.75$ SE

Step 5. *Rejection decision:* $|t_{\bar{x}}| > |t_{\alpha}|$ (i.e., 1.75 > 1.64); thus, $p < \alpha$ (i.e., $p < .05$). Reject the H_0 and accept the H_A at the 95 percent level of confidence.

For both Jerome and Charlotte, the *test effect*—the difference between what is observed in the samples and what is expected when the null hypothesis is true—is .35 GPA point. In step 5 of the six steps of the test, however, Jerome will not reject the null hypothesis while Charlotte will reject it. Charlotte's critical region is larger with its 5 percent area lumped to one side. This pushes her critical score ($t_{\alpha} = 1.64$) back toward the hypothesized mean, reducing the size of the test effect needed for rejection. Jerome's 5 percent critical region is split to both sides for his two-tailed test, leaving his critical score ($t_{\alpha} = \pm 1.96$) way out in the tail, and this requires a larger test effect to reach the critical region. What this amounts to is that by splitting the 5 percent area in two, Jerome's *p*-value must actually be less than .025 for him to reject the null hypothesis. The *p*-value of a two-tailed test is split to both sides, just like the area of the critical region. In other words, his test effect must be twice as unusual as Charlotte's before he can reject.

The selection of the direction of the test leads Jerome and Charlotte to different conclusions. Jerome, by not rejecting the null hypothesis that the mean GPA is 2.6, will conclude that State University's mean GPA could be that value, and he will attribute the test effect of .35 GPA point to sampling error. Charlotte, however, by rejecting the null hypothesis, will conclude that the test effect of .35 GPA point is very unusual coming from a population with a mean GPA of 2.6; therefore, State

University's mean GPA must not be 2.6. She will state that it is significantly higher than 2.6 GPA points. Charlotte increased her chances of rejecting the null hypothesis by selecting a one-tailed test.

By selecting a one-tailed test we load the dice in favor of rejecting the null hypothesis and accepting the alternative hypothesis. If this is the result we desire to prove a theory or impress a boss, we must have good reasons for using a one-tailed test. Moreover, the choice of direction is not made by observing sample statistics. The direction of the test is determined by the research *question,* which pertains to parameters of the population. The direction of the test is *not* determined by the research answers that are found in sample statistics.

Rule 4: The Lower the Level of Significance, the Harder It Is to Reject the Null Hypothesis   When the level of significance, α, is small, the critical region of the test will be smaller and its boundary on the probability curve will lie farther from the hypothesized parameter. This means that a test effect must be very large for the absolute value of the test statistic to reach the value of the critical t-score (t_α). For example, suppose a third researcher, Roger, is testing the hypothesis that State University's mean GPA is 2.6. His data are just like those of Charlotte and Jerome—a sample mean of 2.95 GPA points and so on—and the test statistic $t_{\bar{X}}$ computes to 1.75 standard errors. Moreover, like Charlotte, Roger conducts a one-tailed test, *but he states his level of significance as .01.* His critical score from the t-distribution table is quite large: $t_\alpha = 2.33$. Thus, to reject the null hypothesis, his test effect must be large enough that his test statistic will equal at least 2.33 standard errors (SE). Let us look at Roger's p-value and rejection decision and compare it to Charlotte's above.

Roger's p-value and rejection decision:

Step 4. p [drawing a sample with a mean ($\bar{X}$) as unusual as or more unusual than 2.95 GPA points when the true population mean (μ_X) is 2.6 GPA points] $< .05$ but $> .01$.

Step 5. *Rejection decision:* $|t_{\bar{X}}| < |t_\alpha|$ (i.e., $1.75 < 2.33$); thus, $p > \alpha$ (i.e., $p > .01$). Fail to reject H_0.

Both Roger and Charlotte have the same *test effect,* .35 GPA point, which is 1.75 standard errors distance from the hypothesized mean of 2.6. In step 5 of the hypothesis test, however, Roger *will fail to* reject the null hypothesis with $\alpha = .01$, while Charlotte *will* reject it with $\alpha = .05$. Roger will conclude that State University's mean GPA could be 2.6, but Charlotte will conclude that State University's mean GPA is significantly higher than 2.6 GPA points. While the test statistic value of 1.75 SE reached Charlotte's critical region of .05, it fell short of Roger's critical region of .01. It is harder to reject when the level of significance is low (say, $\alpha = .01$ or .001). Conversely, it is easier to reject when it is moderate to high (say, $\alpha = .05$ or .10).

Rule 5. When the Observed Sample Outcome Is in the Opposite Direction of That Predicted by the Alternative Hypothesis, Immediately Fail to Reject the Null Hypothesis   One must take care in calculating the p-value when conducting a one-tailed test where the observed sample outcome falls in the opposite direction than that predicted by the alternative hypothesis (H_A). For example, suppose Shelia, another researcher at State University, examines the research question that the mean GPA is *less than* 2.6, a prediction in the negative direction. With $n = 500$ her sample mean calculates to 3.0, which is in the *positive* direction. Selected steps in the test are as follows:

Step 1. H_0: $\mu_X = 2.6$ GPA points

H_A: $\mu_X < 2.6$ GPA points. One tailed.

Step 3. *Level of significance:* $\alpha = .05$. One-tailed.

Critical test score $t_\alpha = -1.64$ SE

Step 4. *Observed sample mean:* $\overline{X} = 3.0$ GPA points

Test effect: $= \overline{X} - \mu_X = 3.0 - 2.6 = .4$ GPA point

Test statistic: $t_{\overline{X}} = \dfrac{\overline{X} - \mu_X}{s_{\overline{X}}} = \dfrac{3.0 - 2.6}{.2} = \dfrac{.4}{.2} = 2.00$ SE

If we blindly proceed with this test by observing the absolute values of the critical test score and test statistic, we would conclude that the observed sample mean of 3.0 GPA points is significantly different from 2.6 GPA points and reject the H_0. Indeed, the absolute value of the test statistic, $t_{\overline{X}}$, is greater than the absolute value of the critical score t_α; that is, $|2.00| > |-1.64|$. The outcome, however, is not in the direction predicted by the H_A and it does not fall in the critical region. How can we justify accepting the H_A that the mean GPA is *less than* 2.6 when the observed sample mean of 3.0 is *greater than* 2.6? The proper computation of the *p*-value is as follows:

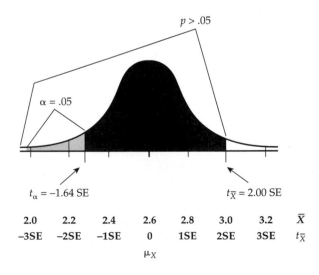

$p > .05$

$\alpha = .05$

$t_\alpha = -1.64$ SE $t_{\overline{X}} = 2.00$ SE

2.0	2.2	2.4	2.6	2.8	3.0	3.2	$\overline{X}$
-3SE	-2SE	-1SE	0	1SE	2SE	3SE	$t_{\overline{X}}$

μ_X

In the H_A Shelia predicted the negative direction. Therefore, the area of the p-value is calculated in that direction, from the observed test statistic value of 2.00 SE *to the left* in the negative direction. When the outcome is in the wrong direction, obviously the p-value must be greater than .50, and therefore greater than .05, because at least half the curve is encompassed by the p-value's area. This illustrates the importance of drawing the sampling distribution curve.

This circumstance also reveals the importance of clearly justifying choice of test direction with a practical or theoretical reason. If you predict a direction, you are giving yourself the advantage of making it easier to reject the H_0. If the sample outcome falls in the opposite direction, you cannot abandon the original prediction. Instead, you must do some fast explaining. Incidentally, if Shelia had not predicted a direction and had used a two-tailed test, she could have legitimately rejected the H_0. She cannot, however, run a double-barreled, one-tailed test using one-tailed critical values but waiting to see the direction in which an outcome occurs.

When using a computer to test hypotheses, pay close attention to whether the sampling outcome of your test falls in the predicted direction. The computer is programmed to do either a one- or two-tailed test, but it assumes you predicted the correct direction. If Shelia had done this problem on the computer and simply observed the p-value provided on output, she would have seen that $p < .05$ on the output and jumped to the wrong conclusion. These kinds of tricky situations reveal the value of learning statistics by completing pencil-and-paper exercises and not relying solely on the whims of computer programming.

Although an easy way to make the rejection decision is to observe the value of the test statistic, $t_{\bar{X}}$, and compare it to the critical score, t_α, understanding the calculation and meaning of the p-value is important. This is the case especially if you are using computers. Computer output typically reports the value of the test statistic and the p-value, but not the critical score. Poor understanding of any of these elements of a hypothesis test can lead to faulty conclusions.

Relationships Among Hypothesized Parameters, Observed Sample Statistics, Computed Test Statistics, *p*-Values, and Alpha Levels

Rule 1:   The statistical hypothesis (H_0) is rejected when the test effect is large enough that the test statistic value is greater than the critical test score value, for example, with a single-sample means test when

$$|t_{\bar{X}}| > |t_\alpha|$$

Rule 2:   The larger the test effect and the test statistic, the smaller the p-value.

Rule 3:   It is easier to reject the H_0 with a one-tailed test than a two-tailed test.

Rule 4:   The lower the level of significance, the harder it is to reject the H_0.

Rule 5:   When the observed sample outcome is in the opposite direction of that predicted, immediately fail to reject the H_0.

Using Single-Sample Hypothesis Tests to Establish Sample Representativeness

Single-sample hypothesis tests are especially useful in determining whether a sample is representative of the population from which it was drawn. In Chapter 2 we discussed the importance of a representative sample, one in which all segments of the population (such as males, females, whites, blacks, the young, the old, the wealthy, and the poor) are included in correct proportion to their representation in the population. For example, suppose a researcher in the fictional Delaney County conducts a telephone survey to see whether the citizens support a property tax increase. Her population of interest is all heads of households in the county. To obtain a sample of 387 household heads, the researcher uses a random dialing system that assures the inclusion of unlisted telephone numbers. Obviously, however, her poll excludes households without phones. Since most households without phones are occupied by poor people, she must determine whether using a phone survey unfairly excludes the poor. She therefore wishes to determine whether her sample is representative of the county's households with respect to poverty rate. The poverty rate of a county is the percentage or proportion of households that are below the government's defined minimum income to survive, a point called the *poverty threshold.*

How can a nonrepresentative sample lead to an incorrect conclusion about support for the property tax increase? Suppose adults from wealthy households are more likely to own their homes. Homeowners directly see the amounts charged to their tax bills and are less inclined to support an increase. If homeowners are overrepresented in the sample, their responses will count more than will those of the members of poorer households. The results may indicate that the majority of county residents oppose a tax increase when in fact the poorer residents who are more in favor of it are not given a fair opportunity to voice their opinions.

Let us examine a small population to illustrate the consequences of under- and overrepresentation. Suppose a county has 10 households: 7 with phones and 3 without. Of the 7 with phones, 3 support the tax increase and 4 oppose it. All 3 households without phones support it. Thus, the true support of the entire county is 6 *for* and 4 *against.* A correctly done poll, then, should show support for the tax increase. But what if those without phones were not polled? The poll results would make it appear incorrectly that county residents were against the increase 4 to 3. Sample representativeness is an essential requirement for making statistical generalizations: statements about an entire population made on the basis of a sample.

Target Values for Hypothesis Tests of Sample Representativeness

To establish the representativeness of a sample, data must be acquired on some *known parameters* of the population. If we have a few known parameters, we can use them as hypothesized target values in a series of single-sample hypotheses tests. Demographic variables such as age, gender, marital status, income, poverty rate, and race typically are used as known parameters to evaluate the representativeness of a sample. This is the case because the U.S. Bureau of the Census provides these parameters by ZIP code area, census enumeration district, neighborhood, metropolitan area, county, or state. For groups and organizations such as companies, schools, clubs, and voluntary groups, organization records are a good source of such parameter data.

Much of the data from a country's census bureau is of nominal/ordinal level of measurement. The reliability of data for nominal variables such as gender, race, and poverty rate is typically better than that for interval/ratio variables, such as household income, which is highly skewed. A large single-sample means test can be used to establish sample representativeness with respect to an interval/ratio variable, but these tests must be done carefully. Therefore, common nominal variables are typically chosen for establishing sample representativeness. The known parameters for these nominal/ordinal variables provide the proportions of the population fitting a category, such as the proportion female and the proportion nonwhite. These proportions provide target values for what is called a large single-sample proportions test.

Returning to the researcher in Delaney County, to obtain a known parameter on poverty rate, she examines county population figures from the U.S. Bureau of the Census and finds a poverty rate of 22 percent, which is a proportion of .22. If her sample is representative of Delaney County households, the poverty rate of the survey sample households should also be .22—give or take a little sampling error. After completing all survey phone calls, she finds that 66 of the 387 households are below the poverty threshold for a sample proportion of .17:

$$P_s = \frac{66}{387} = .17$$

The test effect of the sampling procedure for poverty rate is the difference between the observed sample proportion, P_s, and the true county proportion, P_u, which is .22. Thus:

Effect of sampling procedure on gauging poverty rate $= P_s - P_u = .17 - .22 = -.05$

A large single-sample proportions test is used to determine if this test effect is (a) due to random sampling error, or (b) due to a failure to adequately sample and represent poorer households. From her experience with repeated sampling, the researcher knows that sample statistics vary slightly from known population parameters. Is the effect of $-.05$ so slight as to be sampling error? The large single-sample proportions test determines this. If the $-.05$ is not statistically significant but is simply due to sampling error, she may say that the sample is representative. This means that the population group she sampled is the one she meant to sample—the targeted population of adults from all Delaney County households including poorer ones. It means that she tapped into all segments of the population in their correct proportions.

What is the significance of finding representativeness with regard to demographic variables? If the sample is representative of the demographic makeup of the county, she can safely *assume* that it is representative of other variables, such as support for the tax increase. Simply put, if her sample procedure correctly samples poverty rate, chances are that it correctly samples positive, negative, and neutral opinions on a tax increase. A correct balance of demographics suggests that the entire sampling procedure is correctly balanced. By contrast, if the demographic profile of the sample does not fit that of the population, the sample will be "biased" toward one segment of the population or another. Such response bias introduces errors into computations and leads to incorrect conclusions.

A challenge in testing sample representativeness is to properly conceive of the population. To test a hypothesis, of course, we must state it statistically—in such a way that we will know the shape of the sampling distribution *assuming that the hypothesis about the population is true*. Step 1 of the six steps of hypothesis testing is as follows:

$$H_0: P_{u(sampled\ population)} = .22 \ \text{(the known parameter, } P_u \text{, of the}$$
$$\text{targeted Delaney County population)}$$

That is, the sample *is* representative of Delaney County households.

$$H_A: P_{u(sampled\ population)} \neq .22$$

That is, the sample *is not* representative of Delaney County households. Two-tailed.

Picturing the notion of representativeness is a bit tricky. Notice that we *do not* state the hypothesis with reference to the sample value (an often used but misleading device in some textbooks). That is, we do *not* hypothesize that the sample proportion is equal to the population proportion (i.e., that $P_s = P_u$). *Hypotheses statements always pertain to a population.* Observed sample statistics should never appear in step 1 of a hypothesis test. Samples and their statistics are merely tools to address questions about a population.

For the Delaney County example, it is absurd for at least two reasons to state the hypothesis as "The sample poverty rate is equal to the population poverty rate." First, we can see that it is not; clearly, $.17 \neq .22$. Second, experience with sampling distributions tells us that if we draw another sample, its poverty rate probably will differ from the .17 of the current sample.

The real question of sample representativeness is: Did we actually sample the target population, or did we inadvertently obtain too many (overrepresent) or too few (underrepresent) sample subjects from some segment of this population? For example, with a telephone poll we may actually sample the population of "primarily nonpoor households in Delaney County."

Notice that for this hypothesis test, we wish to *fail to reject* the null hypothesis (H_0). When this occurs, we assert that the targeted population and the sampled population are the same—Delaney County households. We further assert that our study results on opinions toward tax increases may be applied, or *generalized,* to all county residents. This conclusion is graphically conceived as follows:

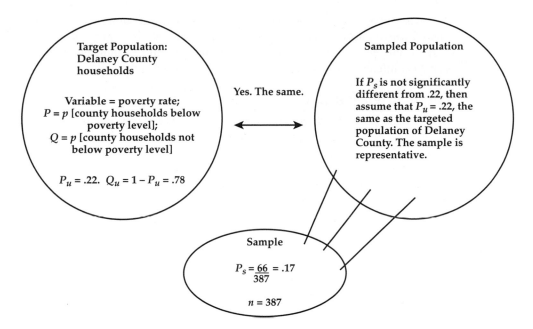

On the other hand, if we reject the H_0 and accept the H_A, we are asserting that the sample is not representative and that a bias in our sampling procedure caused us to miss the targeted population. When this occurs, our study results on opinions toward tax increases cannot be generalized to all county residents. Rejecting the H_0 and accepting the H_A that the sample is not representative may be conceived like this:

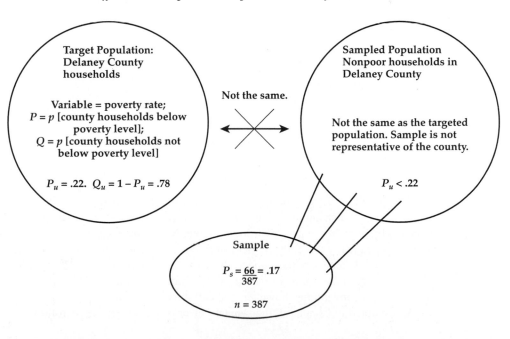

In summary, sample representativeness is not really about the sample. It is a question of what population does the sample represent and, thus, to what population the study results may be generalized. Let us use this example to illustrate the six steps of statistical inference for a large single-sample proportions test.

Large Single-Sample Proportions Test

A "large single-sample proportions test," as the word *proportion* implies, is used with one nominal/ordinal level variable, where $P = p$ [of the success category] of the variable and $Q = p$ [of the failure category(ies)]. This test is used when the smaller of P_u and Q_u times n is greater than or equal to 5 (i.e., $[(p_{smaller}) (n)] \geq 5$). If $[(p_{smaller}) (n)]$ < 5, the appropriate statistical test is called the binomial distribution, which is covered in Chapter 13.

When to Use a Large Single-Sample Proportions Test (t-distribution, $df = \infty$)

In general: With a sufficiently large sample that is useful for testing a hypothesis that the proportion of a category of a nominal/ordinal variable in a population is equal to a target value. Especially useful for testing the representativeness of a sample.

1. There is only one variable.
2. The variable is of nominal/ordinal level of measurement with $P = p$ [of the success category].
3. There is a single sample and population.
4. The sample size is sufficiently large that $[(p_{smaller}) (n)] \geq 5$, where $p_{smaller} =$ the smaller of P_u and Q_u.
5. There is a target value of the variable to which we may compare the sample proportion.

The sampling distribution of proportions when $[(p_{smaller}) (n)] \geq 5$ is the approximately normal t-distribution. Thus, the test statistic is a t-score, and the p-value is estimated by referring to the t-distribution table. Note, however, that if the sample size passes as sufficiently large, the degrees of freedom are equal to infinity (∞) and, therefore, the critical values are the same as those of the normal curve. In fact, we could use the normal curve table for this test and call it a Z-distribution test. We will follow computer software conventions, however, and call it a t-test.

As we noted in Chapter 7, the standard error of proportions is as follows:

Computing the Standard Error of a Sampling Distribution of Proportions When P_u and Q_u Are Known (for a nominal variable)

$$\sigma_{P_s} = \sqrt{\frac{P_u Q_u}{n}}$$

where

σ_{P_s} = standard error of proportions for a nominal/ordinal variable with
$\quad P = p$ [of the success category], $Q = p$ [of the failure category]
P_u = hypothesized p [of the success category in the population]
Q_u = hypothesized p [of the failure category in the population]
n = sample size

Note that the symbols in the numerator of this equation indicate population parameters (P_u and Q_u). This differs from the calculation of the standard error for confidence intervals, where sample statistics (P_s and Q_s) are used as estimates. Although P_u and Q_u often are not truly known, in this hypothesis test the standard error is always computed in this manner. This is done because the sampling distribution describes sample outcomes assuming that the population parameters are equal to the *hypothesized* values. P_u and Q_u are known in the sense that we know what to expect in repeated sampling when their hypothesized values are true.

The test statistic is calculated as follows:

Calculating the Test Statistic for a Large Single-Sample Proportions Test

$$t_{P_s} = \frac{P_s - P_u}{\sigma_{P_s}}$$

$$= \frac{\text{the effect}}{\text{standard error}} = \begin{array}{l} \text{number of standard errors (SE)} \\ \text{difference between what was} \\ \text{observed and what was hypothesized} \end{array}$$

where

t_{P_s} = number of standard errors a sample proportion (P_s) deviates from the
$\quad$ hypothesized population proportion (P_u)
P_s = p [of the success category in the sample]
P_u = p [of the success category hypothesized for the population]
σ_{P_s} = standard error of the sampling distribution of proportions

The formula for t_{P_s} is derived from the dimensions of the approximately normal t-distribution curve as follows. Notice the similarity to other t- and Z-score calculations.

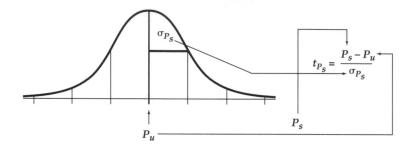

$$t_{P_s} = \frac{P_s - P_u}{\sigma_{P_s}}$$

This test statistic, like the one we calculated for the means test, tells us how many standard errors (SE) an observed sample proportion falls from the hypothesized population proportion. Now let us apply the six steps of statistical inference and discuss the particulars of this hypothesis test for our Delaney County example.

The Six Steps of Statistical Inference for a Large Single-Sample Proportions Test

Problem: A researcher in fictional Delaney County conducts a telephone poll on citizens' support for a property tax increase. Aware of the potential for underrepresenting poor households, she wishes to determine whether her sample is representative of county households with respect to poverty level—the percentage of households with incomes below the U.S. government poverty threshold. U.S. Census data reveal 22 percent (.22) of Delaney County households are below the poverty threshold. For her sample of 387 households, 66 are below the poverty threshold.

This problem meets the criteria of a large single-sample proportions test. First, we have one variable. Second, the variable is of nominal level of measurement. Third, there is a single sample from one population. Fourth, the sample size, n, is shown below to be sufficiently large such that $[(p_{smaller})\,(n)] \geq 5$. Fifth, there is a known parameter that provides a target value; that is, census data reveal the poverty rate of the county to be .22.

Solution for a Large Single-Sample Proportions Test (t-distribution, when $[(p_{smaller})(n)] \geq 5$)

TEST PREPARATION
Research Question: Is the sample of 387 surveyed Delaney County households representative of county households with respect to poverty rate? Statistical procedure: Large single-sample proportions test. $[(p_{smaller})\,(n)] \geq 5$; $(.22)\,(387) = 85.14$; $85.14 > 5$.

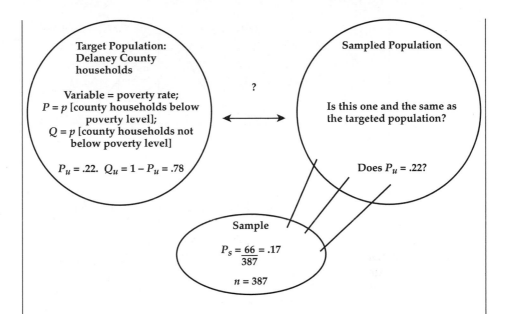

1: H_0: $P_{u(sampled\ population)} = .22$ (the known poverty rate, P_u, in targeted Delaney County)

That is, the sample *is* representative of Delaney County households with regard to poverty rate.

H_A: $P_{u(sampled\ population)} \neq .22$. Two-tailed

That is, there is a bias in our sampling procedure resulting in the sample *not being* representative with regard to poverty rate.

2. Sampling Distribution: If H_0 is true and samples of size 387 are repeatedly drawn from Delaney County households, sample proportions (P_s) will center around .22 as an approximately normal t-distribution and $df = \infty$, with a standard error:

$$\sigma_{P_s} = \sqrt{\frac{P_u Q_u}{n}} = \sqrt{\frac{(.22)(.78)}{387}} = .02$$

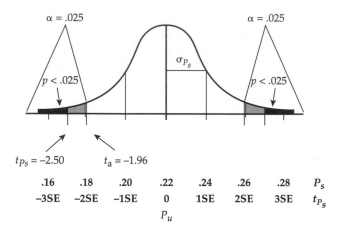

(Shading of the curve is done with steps 3 and 4.)

3. *Level of significance:* $\alpha = .05$. Two-tailed. Critical test score $t_\alpha = \pm 1.96$ SE. (Shade and mark the critical region on the curve in step 2.)

4. *Observation:*

$$\text{Test effect: } P_s - P_u = .17 - .22 = -.05$$

$$\text{Test statistic: } t_{Ps} = \frac{P_s - P_u}{\sigma_{Ps}} = \frac{.17 - .22}{.02} = -2.50 \text{ SE}$$

p-value: p [observing a sample proportion, P_s, as unusual as or more unusual than .17 when the true population proportion, P_u, is .22] < .05. (Shade and mark the area of the *p*-value on the curve in step 2.)

5. *Rejection decision:* $|t_{Ps}| > |t_\alpha|$ (i.e., $2.50 > 1.96$); thus, $p < \alpha$ (i.e., $p < .05$); Reject H_0 and accept H_A at the 95 percent level of confidence.

6. *Interpretation:* There appears to be a bias in our sampling procedure resulting in the sample not being representative of Delaney County households with regard to poverty rate. *Best estimate:* Whereas 22 percent of Delaney County households are below the poverty threshold, only 17 percent of our sample is so. Poor households are underrepresented and nonpoor households are overrepresented. *Answer:* The sample is not representative of Delaney County households. Our sampled population has too many nonpoor respondents.

Some things to note about this hypothesis test:

• In step 1, we state the alternative hypothesis as a two-tailed test. It would not be appropriate to examine the sample statistic, P_s, to determine the direction of the test. In general, tests of sample representativeness are done as two-tailed tests.

- In step 2, as with any hypothesis test, the test depends on describing the sampling distribution, which tells us what happens with repeated sampling. With this example, we are making a prediction for any nominal/ordinal variable having a population proportion (i.e., parameter) of .22 when samples of size 387 are repeatedly drawn: About 68 percent of the time the sample proportion, P_s, will compute to between .20 and .24, and about 95 percent of the time between .18 and .26. Although the variable itself is nominal and, therefore, we compute proportions, the calculated sample proportions, P_s, constitute a ratio level score and these scores are plotted on the horizontal axis. The distribution curve has a *mean* proportion, which in this case is .22. In other words, if you drew, say, 10,000 samples, summed the sample proportions, P_s, and divided by 10,000, the result would be .22.

- In step 4, the difference between the observed sample proportion and hypothesized proportion of poor households (i.e., $P_s - P_u = .05$, or 5 percent) is "the effect" of the test. Essentially, the purpose of the hypothesis test is to determine whether this test effect is due to random sampling error (as asserted by the null hypothesis) or due to a bias in our sampling procedure (as asserted by the alternative hypothesis).

- In step 4, we determined that the observed sample proportion, $P_s - .17$, has a low probability of occurrence with repeated sampling. This led us to conclude in step 5 that the observed P_s of .17 was not due to normal, random sampling error but instead was due to the fact that the population from which our sample came was not one and the same as the population of households in Delaney County. In other words, the sample is not representative of the population.

- In step 4, in computing the *p*-value, we are stating "how unusual" the observed sample outcome is "if the null hypothesis is true." Thus, if the population proportion, P_u, is indeed .22, and we have no reason beforehand to predict a direction, then it would be just as unusual to draw a sample proportion 2.50 SE above the mean proportion of .22 as a sample proportion 2.50 SE below it. This is why we identify areas in *both tails* of the curve of step 2 for a two-tailed test.

- In step 6, we focus on the alternative hypothesis and disregard the null hypothesis because it was rejected in step 5. With a public audience, the concept of representativeness may not resonate. Therefore, to bring substance to the answer, we provide a best estimate—some concrete numbers—that a public audience can relate to. We note that poor households are undersampled by 5 percent [i.e., $(.17 - .22)(100) = 5\%$].

What to Do If a Sample Is Found Not to Be Representative

With our sample of 387 Delaney County households, we have now concluded that this sample is not representative with respect to poverty rate. When this situation occurs, three issues must be addressed. First, what defect in sampling design led to undersampling of poor households? The researcher suspects that a telephone survey excluded many poor households who could not afford telephones.

Our second question is: In what ways will this biased sample change our conclusions? Clearly, a "middle-class" bias—an oversampling of them—can lead to the wrong conclusions about opinions related to economic issues such as tax hikes. For example, persons in wealthier households in suburban municipalities are more likely to own homes, and property tax increases affect them directly. They may support a local municipality tax increase that directs revenues to the local schools attended by their children. They may oppose, however, a county-wide tax increase since these revenues are dispersed widely to include large inner-city and poorer rural parts of the county. Because wealthier households were oversampled, their opinions are overrepresented. This could lead to the wrong conclusion that there is widespread opposition to a tax increase. If the correct proportion of poorer households had an opportunity to respond to the poll on this issue, their opinions might have tipped the balance and revealed that a majority of county residents actually support the tax increase. The obtained sample estimate may be lower than the real proportion of support for the tax increase (i.e., the parameter). A nonrepresentative sample can be a dangerous tool.

Our third question is: What adjustments are in order when a sample is not representative? Several things can be done to compensate for sample bias. First, additional subjects can be selected from the underrepresented categories. For instance, to avoid underrepresentation of poor households without telephones, telephone surveys often are supplemented with door-to-door interviews in poor neighborhoods. In fact, to assist in this endeavor, the U.S. Bureau of the Census provides neighborhood-based data on the percentages of households without telephones. Second, we can proceed with data analysis but stipulate that the population over- or underrepresents some groups. For example, with a telephone survey we may simply note that those without telephones—the poor—are underrepresented in the study. This, of course, opens the door to criticism. Finally, a nonrepresentative sample can be artificially adjusted mathematically by "weighting" sample categories to bring them up to their correct population proportions. Such sample weighting is complicated, must be done with great care, and is beyond the scope of this text. Suffice it to say that every effort should be made to design a sampling procedure that obtains correct proportions of meaningful segments of the population.

Presentation of Data from Single-Sample Hypothesis Tests

It is in the area of sample representativeness that single-sample hypothesis tests are most frequently used. Table 10–2 comes from a scientific research journal article in which the author addressed the issue of sample representativeness. The sample consisted of 206 physicians in Jefferson County, Alabama, and the study was conducted from a local academic health science center. The table assesses whether the sample is representative of Jefferson County physicians and physicians in U.S. metropolitan areas. The percentages reported for these two *populations* are known parameters taken from medical directories. These known parameters were used as the target values in single-sample proportions tests. The probabilities reported under "p" are the p-values of each test, with "NS" indicating that there was not a significant difference between the population and the sample proportions at the .05 level of significance.

TABLE 10–2 I Comparison of physician specialty categories for the sample with the population of physicians in Jefferson County, Alabama, and in metropolitan areas of the United States

	Percentage of Physicians in				
Specialty Category	Sample (%)	Jefferson County (%)	p	U.S. Metro-politan Areas (%)	p
General practice	7.77	7.95	NS*	10.81	NS
Medical specialties	31.07	32.83	NS	28.46	NS
Surgical specialties	28.64	35.45	$p < .05$	24.35	NS
Other specialties	32.52	23.77	$p < .01$	36.38	NS

* NS = not significant at the .05 level of significance, two-tailed test.
Source: Clair et al., 1993. Population data from *Physicians Characteristics and Distribution in the U.S.* Copyright 1982, American Medical Association. Reprinted with permission.

The table shows that for all four specialty categories the sampled physicians were representative of physicians in U.S. metropolitan areas. However, the sample was not representative of physicians in Jefferson County. Surgical specialties were underrepresented, and "other specialties" (such as nuclear medicine) were overrepresented. With additional analysis, it was determined that academic health science center physicians, many of whom were in the "Other Specialties" category, were more likely to respond, perhaps because they felt compelled to cooperate with their campus colleagues who were conducting the study. To address the consequences of this sample bias, the authors stated that their results were more applicable to cities with academic health science centers. In other words, they acknowledged that the population to which their results were generalizable consisted not of all physicians but of those who reflected the makeup of their sample.

A Confidence Interval of the Population Mean When *n* Is Small

Recall that in Chapter 8 we presented the calculation of a confidence interval of a population mean for a large sample, one where $n > 121$. In calculating the error term, we used critical scores from the normal curve table, such as $Z_\alpha = 1.96$ for a 95 percent confidence interval. When $n \leq 121$ the critical score comes from the *t*-distribution table. The following sample problem is the same one illustrated in Chapter 8 for calculating the confidence interval of a population mean, except the sample size is smaller.

Solution for a Confidence Interval of the Mean When *n* ≤ 121 (using *t*-scores in calculating the error term)

Problem: We are conducting a study of the wage structure of an industrial plant employing several thousand computer assemblers. We need to get a rough idea of the mean hourly wage of this population of assemblers. We randomly select

15 personnel files and record the hourly wages. In this sample, we find a mean of $8.00 and a standard deviation of $1.70. Compute the 95 percent confidence interval for the mean hourly wage of the plant's assemblers.

Step 1   Research question: Within a specified span of dollar amounts, what is the parameter, μ_X, the mean hourly wage of the population of computer assemblers? *Givens:*

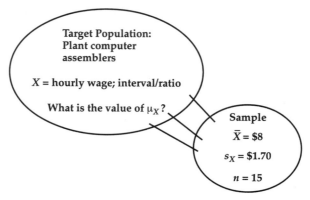

Step 2   (standard error, critical *t*-score and error term)

$$(s_{\overline{X}}) = \frac{s_X}{\sqrt{n}} = \frac{1.70}{\sqrt{15}} = \$0.44$$

$df = n - 1 = 15 - 1 = 14$. For 95 percent confidence, $t_\alpha = 2.145$

Error term $= (t_\alpha)(s_{\overline{X}}) = (2.145)(\$0.44) = \$0.94$

Step 3   (the LCL and UCL)

$$95\% \ CI \ of \ \mu_X = \overline{X} \pm (2.145)(s_{\overline{X}})$$

$$= \text{sample mean} \pm \text{error term}$$

$$= \$8.00 \pm (2.145)(\$0.44) = \$8.00 \pm \$0.94$$

$$LCL = \$8.00 - \$0.94 = \$7.06$$

$$UCL = \$8.00 + \$0.94 = \$8.94$$

Step 4   (interpretation in everyday language)

"I am 95 percent sure that the mean hourly wage of the plant's computer assemblers is between $7.06 and $8.94."

Step 5   (statistical interpretation illustrating the notion of "confidence in the procedure")

"If the same sampling and statistical procedures are conducted 100 times, 95 times the true population parameter, μ_X, will be encompassed in the computed intervals and 5 times it will not. Thus, I have 95 percent confidence that this single confidence interval I computed includes the true parameter."

Let us compare the results of this small sample calculation of a confidence interval of a population mean to the results we obtained in Chapter 8.

From Chapter 8 with $n > 121$	Problem above with $n \leq 121$
$\bar{X} = \$8.00$	$\bar{X} = \$8.00$
$s_X = \$1.70$	$s_X = \$1.70$
$n = 129$	$n = 15$
$s_{\bar{X}} = \$.15$	$s_{\bar{X}} = \$.44$
Critical score: $Z_\alpha = 1.96$	Critical score: $t_\alpha = 2.145$
Error term $= (1.96)(\$0.15) = \$0.29$	Error term $= (2.145)(\$0.44) = \$0.94$
Confidence interval: \$7.71 to \$8.29	Confidence interval: \$7.06 to \$8.94
Precision (width) of confidence interval $= \$8.29 - \$7.71 = \$0.58$	Precision (width) of confidence interval $= \$8.94 - \$7.06 = \$1.88$

Consistent with the law of large numbers (Chapter 7), the error for the smaller sample is much larger than that of the larger one. The smaller sample size influences the calculation of the confidence interval in two ways. First, the smaller n results in a larger standard error of the mean, $s_{\bar{x}}$. Second, the critical score for the error term is larger (i.e., 2.145 compared to 1.96). Suffice it to say that a larger sample allows greater precision in estimating population parameters.

Statistical Follies and Fallacies: Issues of Sample Size and Sample Representativeness

The issue of sample representativeness concerns whether all segments of a population are fairly represented in a sample. Because a test of representativeness requires a target value, we must rely on known parameters to state null hypotheses. It is *assumed* that if a sample is representative with respect to known parameters, that sample is representative with respect to the variety of opinions held by the members of a population. For instance, in our example of Delaney County residents we assume that if the researcher's sample procedure correctly samples poverty rate, chances are that it correctly samples residents holding positive, negative, and neutral opinions on a tax increase. Such assumptions are not always realized. For one, if a sample is rather small, it may not have room for the variety of opinions that exists within the population. For example, if the researcher randomly selected only 10 households, even if they accurately represent proportions at each income level, with so few cases there is a good chance that not all opinions are represented. Suppose, for instance, that the poverty rate of Delaney county's households is 22 percent and the researcher's sample is size 10, with 8 households above the poverty threshold and 2 below it. Mathematically, this constitutes a representative sample. But can only 2 poor households represent the opinions of all poor people? Establishing sample representativeness for a small sample is a shaky endeavor at best.

The analogy of tasting a pot of chili comes to mind here, where the pot represents a population with a variety of ingredients and nuances of flavors (or opinions). If we taste a large sample—an entire cup from a stirred pot—chances are that we will get a taste of every ingredient. If, however, we use a one-fourth-teaspoon measure—which lacks room for the beans and slices of rattlesnake meat—we are likely to sample only the broth.

In a small sample there may not be room for the expanse of opinions. Imagine that you have been charged with a misdemeanor and are to appear before a three-judge panel. On a given day, even a randomly selected panel may load up with two or three especially tough or especially forgiving judges. The disposition of your case may hinge on the luck of the draw. Small samples are inherently error-prone in terms of representativeness.

Another consideration about sample size and testing for sample representativeness has to do with the fact that sample representativeness is established by *failing to reject* the null hypothesis (H_0). Rejecting the H_0 is more difficult when the sample size is small, because small samples produce a large range of error in the sampling distribution. With a very small sample the sampling error is so great that it would take an especially large test effect to reject the H_0. If we fail to reject a false H_0 and this occurred because we simply used a small sample, there is great potential for a type II error. Recall that a type II error occurs when a statistical test fails to reject a false null hypothesis (H_0). In this case, a type II error would be to conclude that the sample is representative of the population when, in fact, it is not. To avoid this potential error, sample sizes must be large enough to reduce the chances of a type II error. We use the term *statistical power* to refer to *a test statistic's probability of not incurring a type II error for a given level of significance.* Establishing statistical power is a rather complicated task. It is addressed on *The Statistical Imagination* Web site under Chapter Extensions for Chapter 10. As a rule of thumb, however, if you have a small sample with a considerable range of error, say, greater than ±3.0 percent, you may wish to simply make a 3 percent effect a cutoff point for establishing the representativeness of a sample. For example, suppose our Delaney County sample size was 50. Substituting this sample size in our solution box above would result in a standard error of .06. It would take about twice this size effect, an effect of .12, to reject the H_0. So we could have a sample proportion, P_s, as low as .11, which is an effect of .11 (i.e., .11 − .22 = .11) and fail to reject the H_0. We would conclude that our sample is representative. But is it reasonable to believe that you could have half the proportion of poor households in your sample as there are in the county and consider this sample representative? Chances are, the small sample with its large range of error has led to a type II error.

What to do about small samples? One, simply choose an effect size, such as .03 (3 percent), as a cutoff for establishing representativeness. In other words, if the test effect, the difference between the sample proportion and the known population parameter is more than .03, assume that the sample may have a bias. Two, look for other ways to detect bias. For example, if data are available, compare characteristics of respondents and nonrespondents on some known parameters. Three, simply do not pretend to generalize the data to a known population. Assert that the data are exploratory and caution readers not to put too much faith in the results. There are many methodological issues related to the integrity of samples. It is unwise to blindly conduct statistical tests following a textbook.

SUMMARY

1. A single-sample hypothesis test is used to answer the question: For a population of interest, is a parameter equal to some chosen target value?

2. Target values may come from: (*a*) a known population parameter from a comparison group; (*b*) known parameters from a past time period; (*c*) a statistical ideal; (*d*) comparing the sample statistics from a sampled population to known population parameters to determine whether the sample is representative of the population.

3. A single-sample means test is useful for testing a hypothesis that the mean of X for a population is equal to a target value. The sampling distribution is the t-distribution, which may be used for means tests of all sample sizes but must be used when $n \leq 121$. Computer programs refer to all single-sample means tests, regardless of sample sizes, as t-tests.

4. The t-distribution is an approximately normal distribution. The t-distribution table is organized differently from the normal curve table and requires calculation of degrees of freedom.

5. Degrees of freedom are a way to adjust for limitations in statistical calculations. For means tests, the degrees of freedom are based on sample size because the calculation of sample means with small samples can be distorted by extreme scores.

6. Understanding the relationships among hypothesized parameters, observed sample statistics, computed test statistics, p-values, and alpha levels enhances competence in hypothesis testing. Rule 1: The null hypothesis is rejected when the test effect is large enough that the test statistic value is greater than the critical test score. Rule 2: The larger the test effect and the test statistic, the smaller the p-value. Rule 3: It is easier to reject the null hypothesis with a one-tailed test than with a two-tailed test. Rule 4: The lower the level of significance, the harder it is to reject the null hypothesis. Rule 5: When an observed sample outcome is in the opposite direction of that predicted by the alternative hypothesis, immediately fail to reject the null hypothesis.

7. The large single-sample proportions test is useful for testing a hypothesis that the proportion of a success category of a nominal/ordinal variable in a population is equal to a target value. The sample size must be sufficiently large that the smaller P_u and Q_u times n is greater than or equal to 5.

8. The large single-sample proportions test is especially useful for testing the representativeness of a sample. Government agencies, such as the U.S. Bureau of the Census, have many known parameters for nominal/ordinal variables, such as age and gender.

9. For calculating the error term of a confidence interval when $n \leq 121$, t-scores are used in place of Z-scores in the error term. Everything else being equal, compared to a large sample, a small sample results in a larger standard error, a larger error term, and a less precise confidence interval.

CHAPTER EXTENSIONS ON *THE STATISTICAL IMAGINATION* WEB SITE

Chapter 10 Extensions of text material available on *The Statistical Imagination* Web site at www.mhhe.com/ritchey2 include a discussion of statistical power and the importance of having a sufficiently large sample to conduct a hypothesis test of sample representativeness. The *SPSS* command sequences for procedures in this chapter appear in Appendix D of this text.

STATISTICAL PROCEDURES COVERED TO THIS POINT

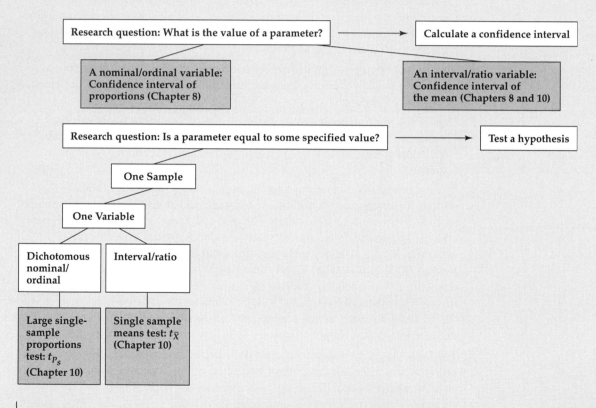

FORMULAS FOR CHAPTER 10

Single-sample means test (*t*-test):

Given: An interval/ratio variable X and a single sample and population.

Research question: Is μ_X (i.e., the mean of X in the population) equal to a target value?

H_0: μ_X = a target value

Sampling distribution: *t*-distribution with $df = n - 1$ standard error estimated using the sample standard deviation.

Standard error =

$$s_{\overline{X}} = \frac{s_X}{\sqrt{n}}$$

Test effect $= \overline{X} - \mu_X$

Test statistic [for use with the approximately normal *t*-distribution table (Statistical Table C in Appendix B)]:

$$t_{\overline{X}} = \frac{\overline{X} - \mu_X}{s_{\overline{X}}}$$

$$df = n - 1$$

Large single-sample proportions test:

Given: A nominal/ordinal variable with $P = p$ [of the success category].

Use when: $[(p_{smaller})(n)] \geq 5$. (If $[(p_{smaller})(n)] < 5$, see Chapter 13.)

Research question: Is P_u (i.e., the p [of the success category in the population]) equal to a target value?

H_0: P_u = a target value.

Sampling distribution: t-distribution with $df = \infty$.

Standard error

$$\sigma_{P_s} = \sqrt{\frac{P_u Q_u}{n}}$$

Test effect $= P_s - P_u$

Test statistic [for use with the approximately normal *t*-distribution table (Statistical Table C in Appendix B)]:

$$t_{P_s} = \frac{P_s - P_u}{\sigma_{P_s}}$$

QUESTIONS FOR CHAPTER 10

1. What is the purpose of a single-sample hypothesis test? What type of question does it answer with regard to a population?

2. For single-sample hypotheses tests, target parameter values come from four sources. Name each source and provide an example hypothesis for each one.

3. Describe the situation (i.e., the selection criteria) for using a "small single-sample means test."

4. Describe the situation (i.e., the selection criteria) for using a "large single-sample proportions test."

5. Match the following:
   a. σ_{P_s} _____ The observed sample proportion
   b. P_u _____ The standard error of sample proportions
   c. t_{P_s} _____ The hypothesized population proportion
   d. P_s _____ The test statistic (i.e., the number of standard errors distance from the observed sample proportion to the hypothesized population proportion)

6. Match the following:
   a. $\bar{X}$ _____ The estimated standard error of sample means
   b. $t_{\bar{X}}$ _____ The hypothesized population mean
   c. $s_{\bar{X}}$ _____ The observed sample mean
   d. μ_X _____ The test statistic (i.e., the number of standard errors distance from the observed sample mean to the hypothesized population mean)

7. The statistics observed and calculated in step 4 of the six steps of hypothesis testing should never appear in steps 1 through 3. Why?

8. What is the relationship between the effect of a hypothesis test and the test statistic? Specifically, in what manner does the test statistic measure the test effect?

9. Is the null hypothesis more likely to be rejected when the test effect is large or small? Illustrate your answer by drawing an approximately normal t-distribution curve for a single-sample means test.

10. Is the null hypothesis likely to be rejected when the test statistic is large or small? Illustrate your answer by drawing an approximately normal t-distribution curve for a single-sample means test.

11. What is the relationship between the sizes of calculated values of test statistics and their p-values?

12. Is it easier to reject the null hypothesis with a one-tailed or a two-tailed test? Illustrate your answer by using an approximately normal t-distribution curve for a single-sample means test.

13. What does the word *critical* mean in the terms *critical region* and *critical test score?*

14. Provide an example of how a nonrepresentative sample can lead to faulty conclusions.

15. For a hypothesis test of sample representativeness, distinguish the sampled population from the targeted population. Are these populations the same or different when the sample is indeed representative of the target population?

16. In general, with a "single-sample means test," when the null hypothesis is true, the scores (i.e., sample means) in the sampling distribution will center on what value of X?

17. For a single-sample means test, when $t_{\bar{X}} > t_\alpha$, is the p-value greater than or less than α? Will we reject the null hypothesis or fail to reject it?

18. For a large single-sample proportions test, when $t_{P_s} < t_\alpha$ is the p-value greater than or less than α? Will we reject the null hypothesis or fail to reject it?

19. Like the normal curve, a t-distribution is symmetrical and its mean, median, and mode are equal. Why do we say, however, that a t-distribution is only *approximately* normal?

20. What underlying feature of the mean causes a loss of degrees of freedom when the mean is used in a statistical test?

21. What effect does an increase in sample size have on the size of the standard error of a sampling distribution?

EXERCISES FOR CHAPTER 10

Problem Set 10A

On all hypotheses tests, follow the six steps of statistical inference, including test preparation, a conceptual diagram, and probability curves. For consistency, round standard errors to two decimal places. Use $\alpha = .05$ unless otherwise stipulated.

10A-1. For the following hypothesized target parameter values and observed sample statistics, compute the effect of the test. Show formulas.

	Hypothesized Target Parameter Value (from step 1 of the six steps)	Observed Sample Statistic (from step 4 of the six steps)	Effect of Test
a.	$\mu_X = 32$ years	$\bar{X} = 28.6$ years	
b.	$P_u = .79$	$P_s = .65$	
c.	$\mu_X = 216$ pounds	$\bar{X} = 176.4$ pounds	
d.	$P_u = .44$	$P_s = .69$	

10A-2. Test your ability to correctly use the t-distribution table (Statistical Table C in Appendix B). Complete the following table, which presents the results of a series of t-tests of various sample sizes and levels of significance. For each test, stipulate: (*a*) the "critical score" (t_α); (*b*) an estimate of the p-value; and (*c*) whether you would reject or fail to reject the null hypothesis.

	Sample Size (n)	Level of Significance (α)	Tails (direction of test)	Obtained Score ($t_{\bar{x}}$)	Critical Score (t_α)	Estimated p-Value (p)	Reject or Fail to Reject H_0?
a.	25	.05	Nondirectional	2.068			
b.	17	.05	One-tailed	2.550			
c.	32	.001	Two-tailed	2.122			
d.	7	.01	Two-tailed	−3.219			
e.	14	.05	Directional	2.398			

10A-3. Suppose that at a university in 1985 a proportion of .47 of sociology majors were women. You assess the gender composition of a random sample of 187 sociology majors at the same university today and discover 105 females. Test a hypothesis to see if this proportion has changed since 1985.

10A-4. As the quality control supervisor of a water bottler, Mountain Geyser, Inc., you wish to test a hypothesis to determine whether there is a loss in the volume of the 16-ounce water bottle during the bottling and delivery processes. To sample, you randomly remove 5 bottles from each of seven retail outlets from the previous delivery. Your findings:

$$\bar{X} = 15.6 \text{ ounces} \qquad s_X = .7 \text{ ounces} \qquad n = 35 \text{ bottles}$$

10A-5. Loureiro and Nayga (2006) examined the relationship between physician advice, obesity, and patient weight loss. Assume that the mean weight loss of patients in a study of physician-recommended diets is 7.9 pounds. You decide to conduct a similar research project. Test the hypothesis that patients in your study lost similar weight when adhering to physician-recommended diet plans. Your sample data:

$$n = 27 \qquad \bar{X} = 6.7 \text{ pounds} \qquad s_X = 2.3 \text{ pounds}$$

10A-6. In step 3 of the six steps of a hypothesis test we decide on a level of significance (α), which is the amount of p-value below which we will define the sampling outcome as unusual and reject the H_0. On the sampling distribution curve, this is the critical region with a critical score expressed as a number of standard errors.

   a. For exercise 10A-4, what is its critical score expressed in the raw score units of ounces?

   b. For exercise 10A-5, what is its critical score expressed in the raw score units of pounds?

10A-7. Using a random sampling technique, you conduct a political survey of 462 adults in the Johnsonville metropolitan area. The following table provides known parameters about Johnsonville's population from U.S. Census data as well as data from your sample.

   a. Is this sample representative of Johnsonville's population with respect to gender?

   b. Is this sample representative of Johnsonville's population with respect to race?

Comparison of Johnsonville Population and Sample Data ($n = 462$)

Characteristic	Johnsonville Parameters from U.S. Census Data	Sample Statistics
Gender (% female)	53.2	53.0
Race (% White)	66.9	65.5

10A-8. You wish to compute an interval estimate of the mean incomes of city planners in 150 Metropolitan Statistical Areas (MSAs) in the Sun Belt. You obtain a random sample of 21 city planners and find a mean income of $43,571 with a standard deviation of $4,792.

    a. Following the five steps of computing a confidence interval, construct the 99 percent confidence interval of the mean income of city planners.

    b. Except for the smaller sample size, this exercise is the same as exercise 8A-3 in Chapter 8. Complete that exercise and compare the results to this exercise. Comment on how a small sample size affects the precision of a confidence interval.

Problem Set 10B

On all hypotheses tests, follow the six steps of statistical inference, including test preparation, a conceptual diagram, and probability curves. For consistency, round standard errors to two decimal places. Use $\alpha = .05$ unless otherwise stipulated.

10B-1. For the following hypothesized target parameter values and observed sample statistics, compute the effect of the test. Show formulas.

	Hypothesized Target Parameter Value (from step 1 of the six steps)	Observed Sample Statistic (from step 4 of the six steps)	Effect of Test
a.	$\mu_X = 100$ ears per bushel	$\bar{X} = 113$ ears per bushel	
b.	$P_u = .50$	$P_s = .39$	
c.	$\mu_X = 572$ stolen cars	$\bar{X} = 591$ stolen cars	
d.	$P_u = .29$	$P_s = .34$	

10B-2. Test your ability to correctly use the *t*-distribution table (Statistical Table C in Appendix B). Complete the following table, which presents the results of a series of *t*-tests of various sample sizes and levels of significance. For each test, stipulate: (*a*) the "critical score" (t_α); (*b*) an estimate of the *p*-value; and (*c*) whether you would reject or fail to reject the null hypothesis.

	Sample Size (n)	Level of Significance (α)	Tails (direction of test)	Obtained Score ($t_{\bar{x}}$)	Critical Score (t_α)	Estimated p-Value (p)	Reject or Fail to Reject H_0?
a.	23	.05	Nondirectional	1.720			
b.	9	.01	Directional	−3.081			
c.	13	.05	Directional	−1.133			
d.	22	.001	Two-tailed	3.141			
e.	11	.001	Two-tailed	13.462			

10B-3. Suppose that the proportion of ethnic Russians in a 1996 sample of post-Soviet Russian citizens was .63. You ask a random sample of 139 Russian citizens today about their ethnic identity, and 91 claim that they are ethnic Russians. Test a hypothesis to see if the proportion of ethnic Russians has changed since 1996.

10B-4. The mean number of physician visits for persons in the United States over age 55 years is 5.2 per year, and the mean number of disability days (full days when unable to perform normal functions) is 7.5 days per year (fictional data). Test the hypothesis that those over age 55 in your city have the national mean for physician visits. Your sample data:

$$n = 65 \qquad \bar{X} = 5.8 \text{ visits} \qquad s_X = 1.8 \text{ visits}$$

10B-5. Matthews, Jagger, and Hancock (2006) examined the relationship between socioeconomic status (SES) and life expectancy. In an attempt to replicate these results in a different population, you choose a sample of 29 participant records. Given the level of SES of this group, its mean life expectancy should be 75.0 years. Test a hypothesis to establish whether this is true. Your sample data:

$$n = 29 \qquad \bar{X} = 71.8 \text{ years} \qquad s_X = 9.2 \text{ years}$$

10B-6. In step 3 of the six steps of a hypothesis test we decide on a level of significance (α), which is the amount of p-value below which we will define the sampling outcome as unusual and reject the H_0. On the sampling distribution curve, this is the critical region with a critical score expressed as a number of standard errors.
a. For exercise 10B-4, what is its critical score expressed in the raw score units of physician visits?
b. For exercise 10B-5, what is its critical score expressed in the raw score units of years?

10B-7. Using a random sampling technique, you conduct a health survey of 485 adults in the Commonwealth metropolitan area. The following table provides known parameters about Commonwealth's population from U.S. Census data as well as data from your sample.
a. Is this sample representative of Commonwealth's population with respect to percent living below the poverty level?
b. Is this sample representative of Commonwealth's population with respect to gender?

Comparison of Commonwealth Population and Sample Data ($n = 485$)

Characteristic	Commonwealth Parameters from U.S. Census Data	Sample Statistics
Gender (% female)	52.1	54.0
% living below poverty level	29.0	33.1

10B-8. Dr. Latisia Latham, a marriage counselor, administers the Global Distress Scale (GDS), which measures overall marital discord. It consists of 43 true/false questions with a total score combined for the two partners (Snyder, Willis, and Grady-Fletcher 1991). She asks you to provide a rough estimate of the average score of her clientele. You obtain a random sample of 25 couples and find a mean GDS score of 59 with a standard deviation of 5.2.

  a. Following the five steps of computing a confidence interval, construct the 95 percent confidence interval of the mean GDS score of Dr. Latham's clients.

  b. Except for the smaller sample size, this exercise is the same as exercise 8B-3 in Chapter 8. Complete that exercise and compare the results to this exercise. Comment on how a small sample size affects the precision of a confidence interval.

Problem Set 10C

On all hypotheses tests, follow the six steps of statistical inference, including test preparation, a conceptual diagram, and probability curves. For consistency, round standard errors to two decimal places. Use $\alpha = .05$ unless otherwise stipulated.

10C-1. For the following hypothesized target parameter values and observed sample statistics, compute the effect of the test. Show formulas.

	Hypothesized Target Parameter Value (from step 1 of the six steps)	Observed Sample Statistic (from step 4 of the six steps)	Effect of Test
a.	$\mu_X = 22$ years	$\bar{X} = 21.4$ years	
b.	$P_u = .75$	$P_s = .69$	
c.	$\mu_X = 146$ pounds	$\bar{X} = 138.8$ pounds	
d.	$P_u = .56$	$P_s = .74$	

10C-2. Test your ability to correctly use the *t*-distribution table (Statistical Table C in Appendix B). Complete the following table, which presents the results of a series of *t*-tests of various sample sizes and levels of significance. For each test, stipulate: (*a*) the "critical score" (t_α); (*b*) an estimate of the *p*-value; and (*c*) whether you would reject or fail to reject the null hypothesis.

	Sample Size (n)	Level of Significance (α)	Tails (direction of test)	Obtained *Score* ($t_{\bar{x}}$)	Critical *Score* (t_α)	Estimated *p*-value (p)	Reject or Fail to Reject H_0?
a.	15	.05	Directional	2.421			
b.	9	.01	Two-tailed	−3.081			
c.	37	.001	Two-tailed	1.986			
d.	19	.05	One-tailed	2.470			
e.	30	.05	Nondirectional	2.049			

10C-3. A researcher found that two decades ago 53 percent of the population favored some form of handgun control. Test the hypothesis that the same proportion favors it today. Your sample data: 105 randomly selected adults among whom 66 favor control, 32 do not favor control, and 7 are undecided or have no opinion.

10C-4. As the quality control supervisor of a snack packaging company, Snak Trak, Inc., you wish to test a hypothesis to determine whether there is a loss in the volume of 12-ounce snack packages during the packaging and delivery processes. To sample, you randomly remove 4 packages from each of six retail distributors from last week's delivery. Your findings:

$$\overline{X} = 11.8 \text{ ounces} \qquad s_X = .7 \text{ ounces} \qquad n = 24 \text{ snack packages}$$

10C-5. Kahn and Pearlin (2006) studied the impact of financial strain on health over the life course among older adults in the United States. In their population, they found an average of 5.6 physical symptoms. You undertake a similar study on 29 older Americans who have always struggled financially and, therefore, fit a *high-strain* financial category. Test the hypothesis that subjects in your high-strain sample report higher numbers of physical symptoms than the subjects in the other study. Your sample data:

$$n = 29 \qquad \overline{X} = 6.3 \text{ symptoms} \qquad s_X = 1.1 \text{ symptoms}$$

10C-6. In step 3 of the six steps of a hypothesis test we decide on a level of significance (α), which is the amount of p-value below which we will define the sampling outcome as unusual and reject the H_0. On the sampling distribution curve, this is the critical region with a critical score expressed as a number of standard errors.

    a. For exercise 10C-4, what is its critical score expressed in the raw score units of ounces?

    b. For exercise 10C-5, what is its critical score expressed in the raw score units of symptoms?

10C-7. Using a random sampling technique, you conduct a sociological survey of 511 adults in the Smithville metropolitan area. The following table provides known parameters about Smithville's population from U.S. Census data as well as data from your sample.

    a. Is this sample representative of Smithville's population with respect to gender?

    b. Is this sample representative of Smithville's population with respect to the percentage of the population with a college education?

Comparison of Smithville Population and Sample Data ($n = 511$)

Characteristic	Smithville Parameters from U.S. Census Data	Sample Statistics
Gender (% male)	46.3	48.0
% with college education	37.0	36.1

10C-8. You need to compute an interval estimate of the mean ages of voting-age adults in a congressional district. You obtain a random sample of 29 voting-age adults and find a mean age of 36.3 years with a standard deviation of 9.7 years.

    a.   Following the five steps of computing a confidence interval, construct the 99 percent confidence interval of the mean age of voting-age adults.

    b.   Except for the smaller sample size, this exercise is the same as exercise 8C-3 in Chapter 8. Complete that exercise and compare the results to this exercise. Comment on how a small sample size affects the precision of a confidence interval.

Problem Set 10D

On all hypotheses tests, follow the six steps of statistical inference, including test preparation, a conceptual diagram, and probability curves. For consistency, round standard errors to two decimal places. Use $\alpha = .05$ unless otherwise stipulated.

10D-1. For the following hypothesized target parameter values and observed sample statistics, compute the effect of the test. Show formulas.

	Hypothesized Target Parameter Value (from step 1 of the six steps)	Observed Sample Statistic (from step 4 of the six steps)	Effect of Test
a.	$\mu_X = 220$ chips per bag	$\overline{X} = 242$ chips per bag	
b.	$P_u = .72$	$P_s = .48$	
c.	$\mu_X = 483$ occupied buildings	$\overline{X} = 612$ occupied buildings	
d.	$P_u = .21$	$P_s = .52$	

10D-2. Test your ability to correctly use the *t*-distribution table (Statistical Table C in Appendix B). Complete the following table, which presents the results of a series of *t*-tests of various sample sizes and levels of significance. For each test, stipulate: (*a*) the "critical score" (t_α); (*b*) an estimate of the *p*-value, and (*c*) whether you would reject or fail to reject the null hypothesis.

	Sample Size (*n*)	Level of Significance (α)	Tails (direction of test)	Obtained *Score* $(t_{\overline{x}})$	Critical *Score* (t_α)	Estimated *p*-value (*p*)	Reject or Fail to Reject H_0?
a.	13	.001	Two-tailed	15.651			
b.	27	.001	Two-tailed	4.249			
c.	16	.05	Directional	−1.741			
d.	21	.05	Nondirectional	2.115			
e.	7	.01	Directional	−3.994			

10D-3. The proportion of nonwhites (African-Americans, Asians, Hispanics, and other non-Anglo persons) in a state's population is .18. A random sample of 95 students at the state's major university reveals that 12 are nonwhite. Is the student population representative of the state population with respect to race?

10D-4. Suppose that you want to determine the efficiency of the packing and distribution systems at a major paper manufacturer, so you decide to test a hypothesis to determine whether 200-count filler paper packages come up short because of the packaging process. To sample, you randomly remove 5 packages of paper from each of seven cases of packages from the next delivery to leave the factory. Your findings:

$$\bar{X} = 194 \text{ sheets} \qquad s_X = 12 \text{ sheets} \qquad n = 35 \text{ packages}$$

10D-5. Gaughan (2006) examined peer influence on adolescent drinking behavior. Data from these types of studies reveal that adolescents consume an average of 8.8 alcoholic beverages per month. You live in a socially conservative area and suspect that adolescents there consume fewer alcoholic beverages. Test a hypothesis with the following data to see if this is true.

$$n = 28 \qquad \bar{X} = 8.5 \text{ drinks} \qquad s_X = 1.8 \text{ drinks}$$

10D-6. In step 3 of the six steps of a hypothesis test we decide on a level of significance (α), which is the amount of p-value below which we will define the sampling outcome as unusual and reject the H_0. On the sampling distribution curve, this is the critical region with a critical score expressed as a number of standard errors.

    a. For exercise 10D-4, what is its critical score expressed in the raw score units of sheets of paper?

    b. For exercise 10D-5, what is its critical score expressed in the raw score units of drinks?

10D-7. Using random sampling procedures, you conduct a major demographic survey of 512 adults in the city of Galway. The following table provides known parameters about Galway's population from U.S. Census data as well as data from your sample.

    a. Is this sample representative of Galway's population with respect to percent of respondents with children?

    b. Is this sample representative of Galway's population with respect to gender?

Comparison of Galway Population and Sample Data ($n = 512$)

Characteristic	Galway Parameters from U.S. Census Data	Sample Statistics
Gender (% female)	54.9	56.6
% respondents with children	42.0	39.9

10D-8.   You wish to calculate an interval estimate of the mean Graduate Record
Examination (GRE) scores among incoming graduate students at a large urban
university. You have collected a random sample of 19 students and find a
mean GRE score of 1,200 points with a standard deviation of 60 points.

a.   Following the five steps of computing a confidence interval, construct
the 99 percent confidence interval of the mean GRE score of the
incoming graduate students.

b.   Except for the smaller sample size, this exercise is the same as exercise
8D-3 in Chapter 8. Complete that exercise and compare the results to
this exercise. Comment on how a small sample size affects the precision
of a confidence interval.

OPTIONAL COMPUTER APPLICATIONS
FOR CHAPTER 10

If your class uses the optional computer applications that accompany this text, open the
Chapter 10 exercises on *The Statistical Imagination* Web site at www.mhhe.com/ritchey2.
The exercises focus on (1) running single-sample hypothesis tests in *SPSS for Windows*,
(2) using single-sample hypothesis tests to test target parameters, and (3) using single-
sample hypothesis tests to examine the representativeness of samples. In addition,
Appendix D of this text provides a brief overview of the *SPSS* command sequences for
procedures covered in this chapter.

11

Bivariate Relationships: *t*-Test for Comparing the Means of Two Groups

CHAPTER OUTLINE

Introduction: Bivariate Analysis

As we noted in Chapter 6, prediction provides the connection between statistical analysis and probability theory. The ability to predict sampling outcomes and other future events is a valuable skill. Making predictions is an important part of science, marketing, finance, manufacturing, medical and social services, gambling, and every other endeavor that uses statistics.

The statistical imagination goes beyond predicting merely for the sake of anticipating what will happen: Prediction also assists in understanding. Scientific predictions depend on measuring several phenomena and tying those measurements together in a meaningful way. With the assistance of well-organized ideas (i.e., theory), prediction enhances understanding and vice versa. For example, in studying psychological depression, if we can determine what triggers depression, we can identify the "populations at risk" and institute preventive measures. For instance, research shows that people who experience multiple life crises—several "stressful life events" in a short period—are at greater risk of experiencing depression. The knowledge that such crises foster depressive symptoms has fueled a movement toward organizing crisis clinics and self-help groups. Simply put, there is a relationship between stressful life events and becoming depressed.

Bivariate (or two-variable) analysis involves searching for statistical relationships between two variables. A **statistical relationship** between two variables asserts that *the measurements of one variable tend to consistently fluctuate with the measurements of the other, making one variable a good predictor of the other*. In scientific research we call the *predictor* variable the independent variable and the *predicted* variable the dependent variable. How a relationship is measured depends on the levels of measurement of the two variables. There are three common approaches to measuring statistical relationships:

1. *Difference of means testing:* comparing means of an interval/ratio variable among the categories or groups of a nominal/ordinal variable

2. *Counting the frequencies of joint occurrences* of attributes of two nominal variables

3. *Measuring the correlation* between two interval/ratio variables

These approaches are summarized in Table 11–1. This chapter focuses on the difference of means approach, but let us begin by exploring all three approaches briefly.

---

a statistical relationship   The measurements of one variable tend to consistently fluctuate with the measurements of another, making one variable a good predictor of the other.

Difference of Means Tests

In hypothesizing a relationship between a dependent interval/ratio variable and an independent dichotomous (i.e., two-group) nominal/ordinal variable, we use the difference of means approach. The hypothesis test for this relationship is called a two-group difference of means test, the topic of this chapter. For example, advertisers may wish to see if there is a relationship between the nominal variable *gender* and the interval/ratio variable *time spent watching sports programs on television*. To hypothesize this relationship is to assert that the mean of hours spent watching is higher for men than for

TABLE 11–1 | Common approaches to measuring the statistical relationship between two variables

Levels of Measurement of the Two Variables		Approach to Measuring the Statistical Relationship Between the Two Variables
Independent Variable	Dependent Variable	
Nominal or ordinal	Interval or ratio	Compare differences of means of the interval/ratio variable among the categories of a nominal or ordinal variable (Chapters 11 and 12).
Nominal or ordinal	Nominal or ordinal	Count the frequencies of the joint occurrence of category attributes of two nominal/ordinal variables (Chapter 13).
Interval or ratio	Interval or ratio	Measure the correlation between the two variables (Chapters 14 and 15).

women. If this is found to be true, advertisements for male products such as mustache trimmers may be placed in sports programs.

To test for a difference among three or more means, we use a procedure called analysis of variance (ANOVA). See Chapter 12. With ANOVA, group means are compared indirectly by determining how much of the variance in the interval/ratio variable is explained by group membership. Suppose, for example, we have an interval/ratio variable called "favorableness to team concept" for hospital care, a measurement scale that consists of 40 questionnaire items. It discerns whether a hospital's medical professionals believe in sharing authority for patient care. A theory about interprofessional relationships might raise the question: Do physicians treat nurses, pharmacists, and physical therapists as coprofessionals, part of a team of relative equals, or as subordinates, underlings who are to be bossed around? The ANOVA test would compare the mean favorableness to team concept scores for these four groups to see whether physicians are less favorable. In terms of establishing a relationship between two variables, ANOVA is similar to the two-group difference of means test; both involve comparing means (of an interval/ratio) among the groups or categories of a nominal/ordinal variable.

Joint Occurrences of Attributes

A second way to view the relationship between two variables pertains to two nominal variables with a focus on the *joint occurrence* of attributes. An attribute is some quality or characteristic of a subject that is conveyed in the category names of a nominal/ordinal variable. For gender, there are the attributes male and female; for race, there are the attributes of white, African-American, and Hispanic; and so on. A joint occurrence of attributes involves two variables *for a single individual,* with pairings of attributes of the two variables. For instance, Mary Smith is a "white female"; she has the joint occurrence of the attributes white and female. Similarly, John Jones is an "African-American male."

An example of a research question about the relationship between two nominal/ordinal variables is: Are women more likely than men to support government-subsidized child care services? Stated as a testable alternative hypothesis: There is a relationship between gender (male versus female) and support for government-subsidized child care services (yes versus no). If this alternative hypothesis is accepted, it will be because the joint occurrences of the attributes female–yes and male–no occur significantly more than expected. Identifying these types of relationships is important for public policy. For example, knowing the gender makeup of a community allows better predictions of whether it will support tax-subsidized child care services. We use a chi-square test (Chapter 13) to determine relationships between two nominal variables.

Correlation

A relationship between two interval/ratio variables indicates that scores on one variable tend to change consistently, or *correlate,* with scores on the other. For example, there is a correlation between the variables frequent experience of stressful life events (such as death of a loved one, a divorce, or the loss of a job) and psychological depression. To say that these two variables are correlated is to say that individuals who experience very few stressful life events are likely to score low on measures of psychological depression, while those who experience a large number of these events are likely to score high on depression measures. Correlation statistics are discussed in Chapters 14 and 15.

For two ordinal level variables, we use a "rank-order correlation" test. This involves seeing whether those study subjects who rank high on one measure also tend to rank high on another. For example, in comparing the 50 states, is there a correlation between a state's ranking on poverty level and its ranking on crime rates? Put simply, among the 50 states, if a state ranks in the top 10 in poverty, does it also rank in the top 10 in crime rates? This test is covered on the Web site.

In all research questions on the relationship between two variables, we hypothesize a relationship between an independent variable and a dependent variable (review Chapter 1). The dependent variable is the one of main interest—the variable we are attempting to explain—and the independent variable is the one used to predict scores of the dependent variable. For example, do stressful life circumstances (independent variable) cause psychological depression (dependent variable)? Do poverty conditions (independent variable) contribute to the incidence of criminal acts (dependent variable)? This text deals only with two-variable cases, or bivariate statistical tests. The relationships among three or more variables are the topics of advanced *multivariate* statistics texts. Let us focus on the difference of means approach for the two-group case.

Two-Group Difference of Means Test (*t*-Test) for Independent Samples

A two-group difference of means test simply compares the means of an interval/ratio variable for two groups or categories of a nominal/ordinal variable. For example, we may be interested in whether mean college admissions test scores are higher for students at City University than for students at State University. Or we may want to prove that there is no difference in the mean energy levels of subjects in an experimental group taking a multi-vitamin pill and control group subjects who are given placebos (fake pills).

Of course, the variable on which the mean is computed must be an interval/ratio variable. Moreover, in this two-group means test, this variable is typically the dependent variable.

The two comparison groups of the independent variable may come from separate populations, such as City University and State University. The same test can be used, however, if the two groups are categories of a dichotomous nominal/ordinal variable from a single population (such as the variable gender, with the categories male and female). In such a situation we compare the separate populations of men and women within the total population.

To illustrate a two-group difference of means test, suppose we have gotten into an argument with a friend over whether men or women get better grades at Faroff University, a campus with approximately 9,000 students. We argue that there is no difference in the mean grade point averages (GPAs) of these two categories of students. Our friend, who has been influenced by traditional myths that women are intellectually inferior to men, bets us $10 that men do better than women. We feel that he is unaware of how markedly gender roles have changed. For example, the college campus was once a bastion of male dominance, but today women outnumber men in U.S. colleges. Thus, we take his bet.

To resolve the issue of GPAs, we randomly select the records of 208 students, 102 males and 106 females. We find that the mean GPA for males is 2.70 GPA points with a standard deviation of .65; for females the mean is 2.63 GPA points with a standard deviation of .71. Our friend says: "See. I told you. Pay up, sucker!" We respond: "Wait a minute. Sample differences do not always imply population differences." We then attempt to explain to our friend that it is necessary to test the hypothesis that there is a significant difference between the GPAs of men and women students *in the total population* of Faroff University students. We must convince our friend that the .07 difference between GPAs found in the samples may be due to sampling error.

In this hypothesis test, GPA is the dependent variable and gender is the independent variable because we are interested in whether gender predicts GPA. Our concern, of course, is with the population of Faroff University students. To keep our focus on the population, in doing a two-group means test it is good to view the subgroups in the context of their separate populations. In other words, imagine males and females as two distinct populations on the campus, as depicted in Figure 11–1.

The research question deals with the two groups' populations and inquires whether their parameters for mean GPA (i.e., μ_X) are different. The null hypothesis, however, is that the two μ_X's are the same, because it is this hypothesis that provides us with fixed, expected outcomes in sampling. Specifically, if the parameters of the two populations are equal, we should expect the two sample means to have a difference of zero—give or take a little sampling error. That is, if $\mu_{X_1} = \mu_{X_2}$, then by subtracting μ_{X_2} from both sides of this equation, we obtain $\mu_{X_1} - \mu_{X_2} = 0$.

Figure 11–1 shows that "$\mu_X = ?$" for each population, meaning that we do not know the actual mean GPA for either males or females. This highlights an interesting point: Unlike the single-sample means test in Chapter 10, with a two-group difference

FIGURE 11–1

Testing the equality of two population means (μ_X)

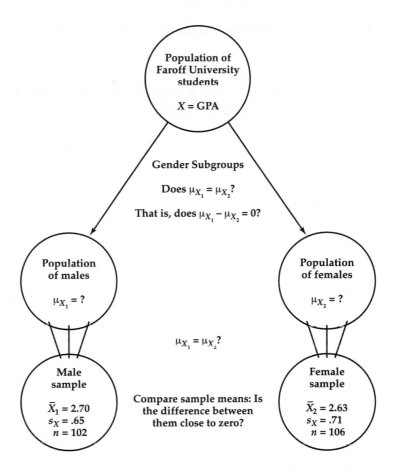

of means test it is *not* necessary to have a target value for a parameter of X for the entire population or its subgroups. For all hypothesis tests, however, we must be able to predict a parameter and describe the sampling distribution around it. The known parameter required for the two-group difference of means test is zero. Regardless of the actual values of the mean GPAs of male and female students, if these values are equal, their difference is zero. It is zero, the "difference of means," not the means themselves, that is the target value of this hypothesis test.

The two-group difference of means is a *t*-test. It focuses on the computed difference between two sample means, $\bar{X}_1 - \bar{X}_2$, where $\bar{X}_1$ and $\bar{X}_2$ are the means of groups 1 and 2, respectively. In describing the sampling distribution, we can predict that the difference between any two randomly drawn sample means is zero, give or take expected sampling error. The test addresses the question of whether the observed difference between these sample means for our single observation of data reflects a real difference in the population means of the subgroups or simply is due to sampling error. In other words, we determine whether the effect of the test is statistically significant. For example, if we find a significant difference in GPAs between male and female college students, we will conclude that that difference is an effect of gender.

The *t*-test of differences between two means is used when the following criteria are met:

When to Use a Two-Group Difference of Means Test (*t*-Test) for Independent Groups (*t*-Distribution)

In general: Testing a hypothesis between a dichotomous nominal/ordinal independent variable and an interval/ratio dependent variable.

1. There are two variables from one population and sample, where one variable is of interval/ratio level of measurement and the other is a dichotomous nominal/ordinal variable, *or* there are two populations and samples and one interval/ratio variable; the samples are representative of their populations.

2. The interval/ratio variable is the dependent variable.

3. The two groups are independent of one another; that is, they do not consist of the same subjects.

4. For the interval/ratio variable, the variances (or standard deviations) in the *populations* from which the two groups come must be assumed to be equal to one another and must appear so in the sample variances. If *in the samples* the variance of one group is more than twice the size of the variance of the other, adjustments are required in the calculation of the standard error of the sampling distribution.

The third criterion—the independence of groups—distinguishes this statistical test from one in which the same group of subjects is being compared on two variables or at two different times on one variable. Later in this chapter we will learn about the *t*-test for a difference in means of "nonindependent" groups.

In statistics texts, the fourth criterion is called the assumption of equal variances (or equal standard deviations, keeping in mind that the variance is the standard deviation squared). If population variances are not equal, adjustments must be made to the statistical test. That is, slightly different *t*-test statistical formulas are used depending on whether the variances (or standard deviations) in the *populations* from which the two groups came are equal to one another. We will begin by illustrating the statistical test when the variances are equal. Later we will discuss why the test must be adjusted when the variances of the two groups are not equal.

The Standard Error and Sampling Distribution for the t-Test of the Difference Between Two Means

To grasp how the sampling distribution for a two-group difference of means test is shaped, let us imagine that we are to do bean counting, repeatedly sampling from two populations with the same means for some interval/ratio variable *X*. For each sample we will compute the mean of *X* and subtract these two sample means to get the difference of means: $\overline{X}_1 - \overline{X}_2$. With the subscripts 1 and 2 representing the two groups, computations will fall in the positive or negative directions as follows:

- When $\overline{X}_1 > \overline{X}_2$, the difference will be positive.
- When $\overline{X}_1 < \overline{X}_2$, the difference will be negative.
- When $\overline{X}_1 = \overline{X}_2$, the difference will be zero.

If the null hypothesis that the two populations' means are equal is true, in repeated sampling we expect to miss on the high (positive) side just as often as we miss on the low (negative) side. Thus, the sampling distribution of a large number of sample mean differences is symmetrical and centers on zero. The shape is an approximately normal *t*-distribution, and the *t*-distribution table (Table C in Appendix B) is used to obtain the *p*-value: the probability of the sampling outcome assuming that the two population means are equal.

The sampling distribution centers on a difference of zero between the two population means (i.e., the difference between parameters: $\mu_{X_1} - \mu_{X_2}$). The standard error of the sampling distribution is estimated by using the variances (i.e., the squared standard deviations) and sample sizes of the two samples. When one sample variance is no larger than twice the size of the other, this suggests that the two population variances are equal and we "assume equality of variances." (Equality of variances also is referred to as *homogeneity of variances* or *homoscedasticity*. When variances are found to be unequal, the respective terms are *heterogeneity of variances* and *heteroscedasticity*.)

In this situation where equal variances are assumed, the standard error of the difference of means is computed by averaging the two variances. This is called a pooled variance estimate of the standard error, and it has the following formula.

Calculating the Standard Error of the Differences Between Two Means (pooled variance estimate, used when the two population variances appear equal)

$$s_{\overline{X}_1 - \overline{X}_2} = \sqrt{\frac{(n_1 - 1)s_{X_1}^2 + (n_2 - 1)s_{X_2}^2}{n_1 + n_2 - 2}} \sqrt{\frac{n_1 + n_2}{n_1 n_2}}$$

with $df = n_1 + n_2 - 2$

where

$s_{\overline{X}_1 - \overline{X}_2}$ = pooled variance estimate of the standard error of the difference between two means

n_1 = sample size of group 1

n_2 = sample size of group 2

$s_{X_1}^2$ = variance of group 1

$s_{X_2}^2$ = variance of group 2

Note that the *subscript* of the symbol for this standard error formula is $\overline{X}_1 = \overline{X}_2$. This standard error is the standard deviation of the distribution of *differences* between two sample means.

The *t*-test statistic is computed as follows:

Calculating a *t*-Test of the Difference Between Two Population Means

$$t_{\overline{X}_1 - \overline{X}_2} = \frac{\overline{X}_1 - \overline{X}_2}{s_{\overline{X}_1 - \overline{X}_2}}$$

where

$t_{\overline{X}_1 - \overline{X}_2}$ = number of standard errors that the difference between two sample means deviates from the hypothesized difference of zero

$\overline{X}_1$ = sample mean of group 1

$\overline{X}_2$ = sample mean of group 2

$s_{\overline{X}_1 - \overline{X}_2}$ = standard error of the differences between two means

This test statistic, like all statistical tests, is designed to answer questions about parameters. The null hypothesis for this test will always be that the two population means are equal; that is,

$$H_0: \mu_{X_1} = \mu_{X_2}$$

That is, there is no difference between the two population means.

Note, however, that the parameters μ_{X_1} and μ_{X_2} do not appear in the *t*-test formula. This is the case because when the two population means are equal, the difference between them is zero, which cancels out of the formula. In fact, the complete formula for the test statistic $t_{\overline{X}_1} - t_{\overline{X}_2}$ is reduced to the preceding formula as follows:

$$t_{\overline{X}_1 - \overline{X}_2} = \frac{(\overline{X}_1 - \overline{X}_2) - (\mu_{X_1} - \mu_{X_2})}{s_{\overline{X}_1 - \overline{X}_2}}$$

$$= \frac{(\overline{X}_1 - \overline{X}_2)}{s_{\overline{X}_1 - \overline{X}_2}} - 0 = \frac{\overline{X}_1 - \overline{X}_2}{s_{\overline{X}_1 - \overline{X}_2}}$$

This is consistent with all our test statistics. The numerator is a computation of the effect of the test, the difference between what we observe in the sample and what is expected when the null hypothesis is true. Here we observe $\overline{X}_1 - \overline{X}_2$ and expect zero because $\mu_{X_1} - \mu_{X_2} = 0$ when the population means are equal. When computed, the test statistic simply leaves off the zero because it is redundant.

A look at the terms of this formula in relation to the distribution curve reveals that it is yet another distribution that measures how far off from an expected statistic the observed sample statistic falls. Any *Z*-distribution or *t*-distribution curve has a mean and a standard deviation (SD), and an interval/ratio score is measured across its horizontal axis as follows:

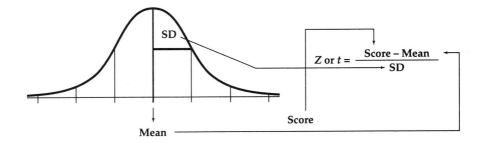

When the interval/ratio measurement is a raw score *X*, then Z_X is computed, as in Chapter 6.

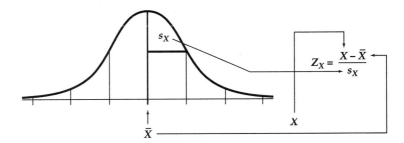

In the case of the sampling distribution for the difference of means, the formula takes shape in the same way, but with the standard deviation being the standard error (SE) of the difference between two means, as follows:

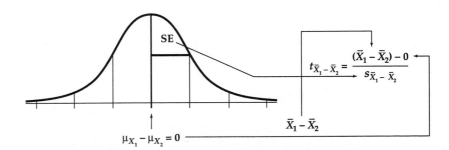

Now let us proceed with the six steps of statistical inference for the two-group difference of means test.

The Six Steps of Statistical Inference for the Two-Group Difference of Means Test

---

Brief Checklist for the Six Steps of Statistical Inference

TEST PREPARATION

State the research question. Draw conceptual diagrams depicting givens, including the population(s) and sample(s) under study, variables (e.g., $X = \ldots$, $Y = \ldots$,) and their levels of measurement, and given or calculated statistics and parameters. State the proper statistical test procedure.

SIX STEPS

Using the symbol H for *hypothesis:*

1. State the H_0 and the H_A and stipulate test direction.
2. Describe the sampling distribution.
3. State the level of significance (α) and test direction and specify the critical test score.
4. Observe the actual sample outcomes and compute the test effects, the test statistic, and p-value.
5. Make the rejection decision.
6. Interpret and apply the results and provide best estimates in everyday terms.

Solution for the Two-group Difference of Means Test (*t*-test) for Independent Groups

TEST PREPARATION

Research question: The $10 bet with our friend hinges on the question: Is the average GPA of male students at Faroff University higher than that of female students? *Givens:*

Statistical procedure: *t*-test of difference between two population means; *t*-distribution; assume equal variances of GPA in the populations of men and women. *Givens:*

(Provide givens here as graphically depicted in Figure 11–1.)

SIX STEPS

1. H_0: $\mu_{X_1(male\ students)} = \mu_{X_2(female\ students)}$ (or $\mu_{X_1} - \mu_{X_2} = 0$)

   That is, there is no difference in the average GPAs of male and female students.

   H_A: $\mu_{X_1(male\ students)} > \mu_{X_2(female\ students)}$ (or $\mu_{X_1} - \mu_{X_2} > 0$). One-tailed.

   That is, male students have a higher average GPA than do female students.

2. *Sampling distribution.* If H_0 is true and samples of 102 male and 106 female students are drawn repeatedly from their separate populations at Faroff University, differences between sample means, $\bar{X}_1 - \bar{X}_2$, will center on zero as an approximately normal *t*-distribution $df = n_1 + n_2 - 2 = 206$ with a standard error as follows. (This equation assumes that the population variances are equal.)

$$s_{\bar{X}_1-\bar{X}_2} = \sqrt{\frac{(n_1-1)s_{X_1}^2 + (n_2-1)s_{X_2}^2}{n_1 + n_2 - 2}}\sqrt{\frac{n_1 + n_2}{n_1 n_2}}$$

$$= \sqrt{\frac{(101).65^2 + (105).71^2}{102 + 106 - 2}}\sqrt{\frac{102 + 106}{(102)(106)}} = .09$$

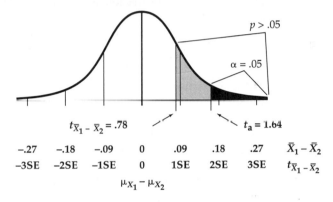

3. *Level of significance:* $\alpha = .05$. One-tailed. Critical test score $= t_\alpha = 1.64$. (Mark on curve.)

4. *Observation:* Test effect $= \bar{X}_1 - \bar{X}_2 = 0.7$ GPA point

   Test statistic:

$$t_{\bar{X}_1-\bar{X}_2} = \frac{\bar{X}_1 - \bar{X}_2}{s_{\bar{X}_1-\bar{X}_2}} = \frac{2.70 - 2.63}{.09} = \frac{.07}{.09} = .78 \text{ SE}$$

   p-value: *p* [drawing sample means ($\bar{X}$) with a difference as unusual as or more unusual than .07 when the difference in the population means (μ_X's) is zero] $> .05$. (This *p*-value is shaded on the curve in step 2.)

5. *Rejection decision:* $[|t_{\bar{X}_1-\bar{X}_2}| < |t_\alpha|$ (i.e., $.78 < 1.64$); thus, $p > \alpha$ (i.e., $p > .05$). Fail to reject H_0.

6. *Interpretation:* There is not a real difference in the average GPAs of male and female students at Faroff University. *Best estimate:* The mean GPAs are the same. The difference of .07 GPA point observed in the samples resulted from normal, expected sampling error. *Answer:* The GPA of the men is not higher than that of the women. Our friend must pay up!

Some comments about the two-group difference of means test are in order.

- In step 1 we stated the H_0 as "the means are equal." As indicated, we could have stated it as "the difference between the means is zero." It is zero that centers the curve of step 2.

- In test preparation and step 1, we defined group 1 as males because they have a higher group mean. This results in a positive t-score and avoids confusion caused by negative critical scores and t-scores.

- In step 2, in calculating the standard error, take care to distinguish the standard deviation from the variance. If a problem provides the standard deviation, the standard deviation must be squared to obtain the variance. If, however, a problem provides the variance, no squaring is necessary.

- In step 2, the degrees of freedom are computed as $df = n_1 + n_2 - 2$. One degree of freedom "is lost" in the calculation of each sample mean. (Recall that in the calculation of a single-sample t-test, $df = n - 1$. See Chapter 10.)

- In step 3, notice that we observed the t-distribution table to obtain the critical t-value (i.e., t_α), the value of t past which the critical region falls. Given the sample sizes and standard deviations for the two groups, t_α is the number of standard errors from zero that the calculated difference of sample means must be before we begin to suspect that the two populations' means are not equal. In other words, with repeated sampling, a difference between means that is 1.64 standard errors away from the hypothesized value of zero occurs less than five times out of 100 samples drawn. An observed, computed t-value (i.e., $t_{\bar{X}_1 - \bar{x}_2}$) equal to or larger than 1.64 would be unusual in populations with equal means. In this example, our observed t-value ($t_{\bar{X}_1 - \bar{x}_2}$) of .78 is not that large; it is less than 1.64, falling short of the critical region. Thus, the .07 difference between sample means is not significantly different from the hypothesized value of zero. We conclude that this test effect is not unusual and simply is due to sampling error; therefore, we allow the null hypothesis to stand. Remember that there is an inverse relationship between the value of a test statistic and the likelihood of rejecting the null hypothesis. The larger the calculated t-value is, the more likely we are to reject the hypothesis of equal means.

- In step 5, we *fail to reject* the statistical hypothesis of equal means in the populations of the two groups. We demonstrate that the difference observed in the samples, given sample sizes of 102 and 106, is very slight and can be expected to occur quite frequently in estimating the difference using sample data.

When the Population Variances (or Standard Deviations) Appear Radically Different

As we noted above, the t-test of differences of means uses the preceding formulas only if the variances in the populations are equal. Adjustments to the t-test formula are necessary if these variances are radically different. A rule of thumb is that we may assume that the *population* variances are equal if the *sample* variance of one group is no more than twice the size of that of the other group. If this limit is exceeded, a different standard error formula may be needed, as is described below. The use of this modified formula, however, depends on several other factors, such as how large the samples are, whether they are of similar sizes, the sizes of the standard deviations relative to their means, and whether either of their distributions is skewed. These complications can be avoided by using the computer to do the calculations. Computer programs run the *t*-test both ways and provide guidelines for choosing the appropriate output. Given the complexities involved, we infrequently hand-calculate *t*-tests for populations with unequal variances. Still, to enhance proportional and linear thinking, it is worthwhile to discuss the meaning of the assumption of equal variances and the consequences that arise when this assumption cannot be made.

Why must we know that the variances (or standard deviations) of the two populations are equal? With the standard error of any test we are estimating sampling error. As it turns out, if the population variances are *not* equal, the outcomes of repeated sampling will be more spread out. Sampling error will be larger. The calculation of the standard error for unequal variances takes this into account. If we ignore this extra error, we may incorrectly conclude that there is a difference of means between the two populations when in fact a large *observed* difference in the sample means is due to the large difference in variances.

To illustrate this, suppose we have two populations with equal mean intelligence quotient (IQ) test scores. One population is an upper-middle-class preparatory high school whose students have a mean IQ of 120 IQ score points with a standard deviation of 6; thus, the variance is $6^2 = 36$. IQ scores are normally distributed, and so we can expect almost all these students to fall within 3 standard deviations of 120; thus, the raw scores range from about 102 to 138. Repeated sampling from this population will result in a sampling distribution of means with a relatively small standard error, and most sample means will fall rather close to 120. Suppose a researcher named Carl samples this population once to test the hypothesis that the mean is equal to 120 IQ points. He obtains a sample mean of 120.4. This group 1 mean is very close to 120. It is within expected sampling error, and so he correctly concludes that the population mean is 120.

The second sample is a special program "magnet" high school that also has a mean IQ of 120, but this population has more diversity—its scores are more spread out. It has a standard deviation of 15 IQ score points with a range from about 75 to 165; thus, its variance is $15^2 = 225$—a variance over six times the size of that of the other high school (that is, the ratio of 225 to 36 is 6.25). If we *repeatedly sample* this population, the means in this sampling distribution also will center on 120 but the observations will have a larger spread. Sample means, being sensitive to extreme scores, frequently will calculate farther from 120. The standard error of this sampling distribution will be large. Suppose another researcher, Carolyn, samples this population once to test the hypothesis that the mean IQ of this school is 120. She obtains a sample mean of 118 IQ points. Since the variance and the standard error in her group 2 population are so large, it turns out that this sample mean, although a full

2 points from 120, is not unusual in repeated sampling, given the broad spread in the scores. Thus, Carolyn correctly concludes that her population, like Carl's, has a mean of 120 IQ ponts.

Suppose now that Carl hears about Carolyn's exercise and inquires about her results. She simply says that she found a mean of 118. Carl fails to ask about the size of the variance and falsely assumes that it is equal to that of his population. He compares their results and finds a difference between means of 2.4 IQ points:

$$\bar{X}_1 - \bar{X}_2 = 120.4 - 118 = 2.4 \text{ IQ points}$$

This difference appears very large to Carl because Carolyn's result appears quite far removed from 120 using Carl's small standard error. He concludes that Carolyn's population mean is different from 120 and therefore significantly different from his single-sample mean of 120.4. Unfortunately, Carl is drawing the wrong conclusion. The two separate tests each found correctly that the population means were no different from 120 and therefore were no different from one another. But in comparing the two means, Carl misread the large spread in Carolyn's population and sampling distribution to reveal a significant difference in means. In actuality, it was the large difference in variances that produced the spread of 2.4 IQ points between the two sample means. If Carl conducted a difference of means test using the pooled variance estimate of the standard error and incorrectly assumed that the variances were equal, he would incorrectly conclude that his sample mean was significantly different from Carolyn's. Even when two populations have the same means, when group variances differ, large differences *in observed sample means* can be due to a large difference in variances. Mistaken interpretations can result.

Being aware of this potential pitfall when one population variance is much larger than the other, we make adjustments in the calculation of both the standard error and the degrees of freedom of the *t*-test. The standard error for unequal variances is called a *separate variance estimate* of the standard error of the differences between means. We subscript the symbol for this formula with *separate* to indicate that we are aware that the assumption of equal variances does not hold. Except for the notation that a separate variance estimate is used, the *t*-test formula *will appear* the same as that using the pooled variance estimate of the standard error.

Calculating the Standard Error of the Differences Between Two Means (separate estimate, used when the two population variances appear unequal)

$$s_{\bar{X}_1 - \bar{X}_2 \, (separate)} = \sqrt{\frac{s_{X_1}^2}{n_1 - 1} + \frac{s_{X_2}^2}{n_2 - 1}}$$

with

$$df_{(separate)} = \frac{\left(\dfrac{s_{X_1}^2}{n_1 - 1} + \dfrac{s_{X_2}^2}{n_2 - 1}\right)^2}{\left(\dfrac{s_{X_1}^2}{n_1 - 1}\right)^2\left(\dfrac{1}{n_1 + 1}\right) + \left(\dfrac{s_{X_2}^2}{n_2 - 1}\right)^2\left(\dfrac{1}{n_2 + 1}\right)} - 2$$

where

$s_{\overline{X}_1 - \overline{X}_{2(separate)}}$ = separate variance estimate of the standard error of the difference between two means

n_1 = sample size of group 1

n_2 = sample size of group 2

$s_{X_1}^2$ = variance of group 1

$s_{X_2}^2$ = variance of group 2

A true determination of whether the population variances are equal requires testing a separate hypothesis before we even calculate the *t*-test of the differences between the means. This extra test, along with the complicated calculation of degrees of freedom just shown, complicates things to a point where it is more sensible to rely on a computer. The *t*-test procedure in the software that accompanies this text is designed to test the assumption of equality of variances before the *t*-test is run for differences of means. It is advisable to use a computer when variances appear unequal. Nonetheless, gaining an understanding of the principles behind the assumption of equality of variances is an important exercise in proportional thinking.

The Two-Group Difference of Means Test for Nonindependent or Matched-Pair Samples

Sometimes there is a need to compare the statistics of two sets of scores from the same individuals. For example, we may wish to compare a sample of subjects who have completed two measurement scales that are scored the same way. Suppose we have questionnaire scales measuring marital happiness and overall life satisfaction for a sample of recently married women. The two scales are scored between 1 and 100, with high scores indicating high marital happiness or high life satisfaction. We might wish to determine whether there is a significant difference between the two scale scores matched for each individual in the sample. We have two "groups" or sets of scores, but we do not have two groups of individuals. Furthermore, the scores on the two scales are not independent of one another. How a subject scores on marital happiness is likely to be a good predictor of how that subject scores on overall life satisfaction. Thus, we refer to these sets of scores as *nonindependent* of one another. We call the sample a noninde-pendent, matched-pair sample.

A common matched-pair sample design is a "before-after" or "test-retest" experi-mental design in which a variable is measured twice for the same individuals, with some type of intervention employed between tests. Suppose, for example, a corporation is concerned with whether its workplaces are "hostile environments" for female work-ers because of sexual innuendo, obscene remarks, and "dirty" jokes on the part of the male employees. To make the place more comfortable for female employees and to avoid sexual harassment lawsuits, the company institutes a worker sensitivity program aimed at teaching the men about this problem. The program runs six months and requires all male employees to attend periodic discussion sessions at which female employees relate some of their negative experiences with gender discrimination. The overall objective of the training is to teach both men and women that sexual harassment has more to do with power and male dominance than with sexuality per se. If the pro-gram is effective, the gender sensitivity training should affect the attitudes of the men in a positive way by sensitizing them to the harm that sexual remarks can inflict on their female coworkers.

To evaluate the effectiveness of the training program, we select a random sample of 15 male employees. We use a gender sensitivity scale that consists of 20 question-naire items, with the respondents being asked to score each item from strongly disagree to strongly agree. The scale has an interval level of measurement, and scores range from 0 to 100, with higher scores indicating high sensitivity. The scale is administered to the 15 employees on "day 1" of the training program—before any sensitivity sessions are held. These "before-treatment" scores provide baseline data. A month after the comple-tion of training sessions the gender sensitivity scale is administered to these 15 men again. This retest measurement constitutes the "after-treatment" score. We then subtract the before-treatment from the after-treatment scores to measure improvement from baseline. If there is significant improvement, this suggests that sensitivity training has a positive effect on male attitudes.

Since we observe only 15 employees out of the larger population, any difference we obtain between the before and after measurements may simply be due to sampling error. If in fact the training did nothing to improve attitudes, the second measurement will be equivalent to drawing a second sample from the population. The difference between before-treatment and after-treatment scores will be zero. But slightly different scores can be expected in repeated sampling. Thus, we must test a hypothesis to determine whether any difference between measurements is simply due to sampling error.

We might be tempted to compute an *independent* groups *t*-test of the difference between mean gender sensitivity scores before and after training. But we do not have 30 subjects, only 15, and therefore we do not have 28 degrees of freedom. The sub-jects of the two groups are not independent of one another—they are the same indi-viduals. How they score the second time is likely to depend on how they scored the first time. That is, if a man scored high the first time, he is likely to do so the second time. What we are truly interested in is whether each score has changed and whether the difference between before and after scores is in the positive direction (i.e., the subjects have become more, not less, sensitive). Thus, we will acknowledge that the true sample size is 15 and treat each subject as a single case with a matched pair of test scores.

To state a null hypothesis—one that allows us to predict sampling outcomes when it is true—we focus on the difference between the before- and after-training sensitivity scores. Our null hypothesis is that the gender sensitivity training has *no* effect. If the null hypothesis is true, we can predict no change in scores and expect the mean of the differences between before and after scores to be zero. Where *D* represents the difference between the before and after scores, our null hypothesis is that the mean of differences is zero:

$$H_0: \mu_D = 0$$

That is, in the population of male workers there is no difference in mean sensitivity training scores in the before and after measurements. The training has no effect.

Note that this statement is like a single-sample means test in that it has a target value of zero. In actuality, then, this is a single-sample means test, but it involves two "groups" of scores. It is a test of whether *the mean of the differences* between matched scores is significantly different from zero.

Table 11–2 presents the computational spreadsheet for computing the mean of the differences between matched-pair scores. For this example of 15 cases, the test is essentially a single-sample means test (as illustrated in Chapter 10).

The criteria for using this test are as follows.

When to Use a Two-Group Difference of Means Test (*t*-Test) for Nonindependent or Matched-Pair Samples (*t*-distribution, *df* = *n* − 1)

In general: Testing the hypothesis that the scores of an interval/ratio variable differ at two points in time for the same subjects.

1. There is one population with a representative sample from it.

2. There are two interval/ratio variables with the same score design or a single variable measured twice for the same sample subjects.

3. There is a target value of the variable to which we may compare the mean of the differences between the two sets of scores. (This target value usually will be zero for a test of no difference between the two scores.)

TABLE 11–2 | Computational spreadsheet for calculating the mean and standard deviation of the differences between matched-pair scores

X = Gender Sensitivity Scale Score

	Givens		Calculations		
Subject Number	(A) Before-Training Score	(B) After-Training Score	D (difference = B − A)	(D − D̄)	(D − D̄)²
1	47	53	6	.73	.53
2	39	38	−1	−6.27	39.31
3	52	54	2	−3.27	10.69
4	48	56	8	2.73	7.45
5	45	49	4	−1.27	1.61
6	42	51	9	3.73	13.91
7	48	54	6	.73	.53
8	50	56	6	.73	.53
9	45	54	9	3.73	13.91
10	44	51	7	1.73	2.99
11	46	44	−2	−7.27	52.85
12	45	54	9	3.73	13.91
13	43	53	10	4.73	22.37
14	47	55	8	2.73	7.45
15	41	39	−2	−7.27	52.85

$n = 15$ $\Sigma(D - \bar{D}) = .05^*$

$\Sigma D = 79$ $\Sigma(D - \bar{D})^2 = 240.89$

*Not equal to zero due to rounding error.

Computation of the mean and the standard deviation of the differences between scores proceeds as follows:

$$\bar{D} = \frac{\Sigma D}{n} = \frac{79}{15} = 5.27 \text{ sensitivity scale points}$$

$$s_D = \sqrt{\frac{\Sigma(D - \bar{D})^2}{n - 1}} = \sqrt{\frac{240.89}{14}} = 4.15 \text{ sensitivity scale points}$$

The test statistic is the same as that for a one-sample t-test except that the symbols correspond to the calculation of differences (D). In the following box, note that the calculation of the standard error and t-test statistic parallel the formulas used for a single-sample means test (Chapter 10).

Calculating the Standard Error of Differences Between Matched-Pair Scores

$$s_{\bar{D}} = \frac{s_D}{\sqrt{n}}$$

where

$s_{\bar{D}}$ = standard error of differences between matched-pair scores

s_D = standard deviation of differences between matched-pair scores

n = sample size

The effect of this test, like that of any hypothesis test, is the difference between the observed sample observation and the hypothesized parameter, in this case $\bar{D} - \mu_D$. Since the hypothesized parameter difference is zero, this test effect reduces to $\bar{D}$, and this is the way the effect appears in the numerator of the test statistic.

Calculating the *t*-Test of Differences Between Matched-Pair Scores

$$t_{\bar{D}} = \frac{\bar{D}}{s_{\bar{D}}}$$

$$df = n - 1$$

where

$t_{\bar{D}}$ = number of standard errors that a sample mean difference between matched-pair scores deviates from the hypothesized mean difference of zero

$\bar{D}$ = mean of differences between matched-pair scores of the sample

$s_{\bar{D}}$ = standard error of differences between matched-pair scores

df = degrees of freedom

n = sample size = number of matched-pair scores

Let us use the data and calculations in Table 11–2 and follow the six steps of statistical inference.

The Six Steps of Statistical Inference for the Two-Group Difference of Means Test for Nonindependent or Matched-Pair Samples

Solution for the Two-Group Difference of Means Test (*t*-test) for Nonindependent or Matched-Pair Samples

TEST PREPARATION

Research question: Did gender sensitivity scores improve significantly after sensitivity training sessions? Were the sessions effective? Should the program be instituted for all male employees? *Statistical procedure:* *t*-test of differences between matched-pair scores. *Givens:*

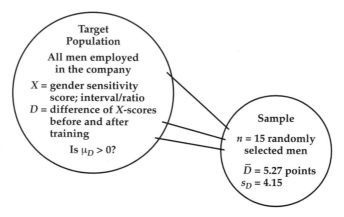

SIX STEPS

1. H_0: $\mu_{D(all\ male\ employees\ taking\ training)} = 0$ (i.e., the difference in scores if training is ineffective)

   That is, the gender sensitivity training is ineffective; there is no improvement in gender sensitivity scores after training.

   H_A: $\mu_{0(all\ male\ employees\ taking\ training)} > 0$. One-tailed

   That is, the gender sensitivity training is effective; gender training results in an improvement in gender sensitivity scores.

2. *Sampling distribution:* If H_0 is true and samples of size 15 are drawn repeatedly from the population of all male employees who are undergoing training, the sample means of the differences between matched-pair scores ($\bar{D}$'s) will center on zero as an approximately normal *t*-distribution, $df = n - 1 = 14$, with a standard error:

$$s_{\bar{D}} = \frac{s_D}{\sqrt{n}} = \frac{4.15}{\sqrt{15}} = 1.07 \text{ sensitivity scale points}$$

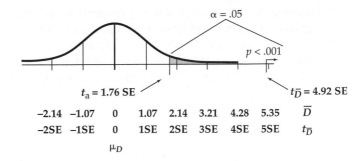

−2.14	−1.07	0	1.07	2.14	3.21	4.28	5.35	$\overline{D}$
−2SE	−1SE	0	1SE	2SE	3SE	4SE	5SE	$t_{\overline{D}}$
		μ_D					

3. *Level of significance:* $\alpha = .05$. One-tailed. Critical test score $= t_\alpha = 1.76$. (Mark critical region on curve.)

4. *Observation:*

   Test effect: $\overline{D} - \mu_D = 5.27 - 0 = 5.27$ sensitivity scale points

   Test statistic $= t_{\overline{D}} = \dfrac{\overline{D}}{s_{\overline{D}}} = \dfrac{5.27}{1.07} = 4.92$ SE

   p-value: *p* [drawing a sample with a mean difference between scores ($\overline{D}$) as unusual as or more unusual than 5.27 points when the true population mean of differences (μ_D) is 0] $< .001$. (This *p*-value is noted in the curve in step 2.)

5. *Rejection decision:* $|t_{\overline{D}}| > |t_\alpha|$ (i.e., 4.92 > 1.76); thus, $p < \alpha$ (i.e., $p < 05$). Reject the H_0 and accept the H_A at the 95 percent level of confidence.

6. *Interpretation:* The gender sensitivity training does appear to be effective. *Best estimate of the effect:* Gender sensitivity training sessions result in an average improvement of 5.27 points on the gender sensitivity scores. *Answer:* The program should be instituted for all male employees.

Practical versus Statistical Significance

The problem involving gender sensitivity training that was just described highlights an important point about statistical hypothesis testing. This hypothesis test focuses on whether to attribute a difference in sample data to sampling error or to a true effect of training on the population. In this example we did conclude—with 95 percent confidence—that the difference of 5.27 gender sensitivity scale points between before- and after-treatment measurements was so great that it probably was not due to expected sampling error. But is this difference of 5.27 points meaningful in practical terms? The gender sensitivity scale had a possible score range of 100 points. At baseline— before sensitivity training—the mean scale score was 45.47 points. The men appeared to be only moderately sensitive at that time. After the training the mean score was 50.73 points. The men were still only moderately sensitive. Moreover, with a 20-item questionnaire, a subject could pick up the average 5-point difference by moving up one level of agreement on only 5 of the 20 items. Is this enough to make a difference in behavior of men in the office? Perhaps not. This 5-point increase in sensitivity may have no influence on behavior. Additional research would be required, perhaps analyzing reports of harassment and data on female perceptions of it. *A hypothesis test determines significance in terms of likely sampling error. It simply tells us whether a sample difference is so large that there probably is a difference in the populations.* It does not guarantee that the difference is meaningful or significant in practical terms. Any statistical results must be weighed against well-thought-out theoretical ideas and practical circumstances. Practical significance, theoretical significance (i.e., whether the results support a theory), and statistical significance are separate issues.

The Four Aspects of Statistical Relationships

The ultimate goal of scientific research is to produce empirically tested statements that explain a phenomenon by giving us an understanding of how it relates to other phenomena. These statements take the form of a theory that describes the interrelationships among measured variables. A theory, along with its list of hypotheses, is tested by making predictions that assert that the measurements made on one variable are somehow related to the measurements made on others. As we have noted, these relationships can take the form of higher means being statistically related to one group or another, a high frequency of joint occurrences for two nominal variables, or a correlation between two interval/ratio variables. Once we conclude that two variables are related, we can say more about the relationship between them. An exhaustive analysis of statistical findings addresses four "aspects of a relationship" between variables. We address these four aspects in step 6 of the six steps of statistical inference.

Existence of a Relationship

The first aspect of a statistical relationship is *existence.* The existence of a relationship answers the question: On the basis of the statistical analysis of a sample, can we conclude that a relationship exists between two variables among all subjects *in the population?* For instance, among Americans, does a relationship exist between religious preference and amount of time spent in prayer? Is there a relationship between poverty levels and crime rates in American cities? Is there a relationship between the amount of time spent watching television and grade point average among college students? The existence of a relationship pertains to the *population* of study subjects. Keep in mind that sample data and the statistics computed from them provide only estimates of population parameters. Basically, determining whether a relationship exists establishes that sample statistical findings are not simply due to sampling error. In other words, the existence of a relationship is established by rejecting the null hypothesis. The first thing we say in step 6 is whether a relationship exists.

Direction of the Relationship

The second aspect of a relationship between two variables is *direction,* although this aspect does not apply to all bivariate analyses. The direction of a relationship addresses the question: When the independent variable increases, does the dependent variable increase or decrease? We use the terms *positive* and *negative* here. A positive relationship is one in which an increase in one variable is related to an increase in the other. For instance, there is a positive relationship between family income and the receipt of preventive dental care: *The higher* the family income, *the more* preventive dental care is received by the family members. A negative relationship is one in which an increase in one variable is related to a decrease in the other. For example, there is a negative relationship between the income levels of neighborhoods and their crime rates: *The higher* the income, *the lower* the crime rate. Direction is specified in the alternative hypothesis as a one-tailed test. Direction is a very straightforward issue for the relationship between two interval/ratio variables, a topic thoroughly examined in Chapter 15.

Strength of the Relationship, Predictive Power, and Proportional Reduction in Error

The third aspect of a statistical relationship is *strength*. The strength of a relationship between two variables establishes the extent to which errors are reduced in predicting the scores of a dependent variable. A measurement of the strength of a relationship gives us an indication of **predictive power**, how well the independent variable predicts the outcomes of a dependent variable. Does the related variable explain a lot or very little about the dependent variable? For example, how good is high school GPA at predicting college GPA? Is it a strong indicator, say, accurate 50 percent of the time, or a weak one, accurate only 10 percent of the time? Do other variables, such as reading comprehension level, predict college GPA better? A focus on the strength of a relationship is useful for comparing the relative effects of several independent variables on a dependent variable.

Another way to view the predictive power of an independent variable on the scores of a dependent variable is to inquire: To what extent is error in the scores of the dependent variable reduced by knowledge of scores in the independent variable? This approach is referred to as proportional reduction in error (PRE). It is most useful with an interval/ratio dependent variable on which the mean has been calculated. Recall that the difference between the mean and any individual score in a distribution of scores is the deviation score. For example, let X = salary of middle-level managers in a company. The mean is $50,000. If someone challenged us to guess Jacob Smith's salary, our best estimate would be the mean of $50,000. But suppose we find out that he makes $60,000. We erred by $10,000, which is Jacob's deviation from the overall company mean. How can we explain this deviation score of $10,000? Can we find variables that allow us to reduce the error in making a best estimate of salary? Perhaps Jacob's "high-side" salary is related to his being with the company longer than other middle-level managers have been employed there. We test a hypothesis that length of service with the company is related to salary level. Using a difference of means test, we compare the mean salaries of "long-timers" to those more recently hired. Suppose the long-timers average $58,000—$8,000 more than the overall company average. Since Jacob is a long-timer, we can now make a better estimate of his salary—$58,000—the company mean of $50,000 plus $8,000 for length of service. By estimating his salary at $58,000 we deviate from his true salary of $60,000 by only $2,000. We have explained $8,000 of Jacob's $10,000 deviation from the mean of $50,000. Knowledge of the relationship between length of service (an independent variable) and salary (the dependent variable) allowed us to reduce error in prediction by 80 percent (i.e., $8,000/$10,000).

For an entire sample, PRE depends on finding relationships that explain the variance in the sample—the average of the sum of squared deviation scores (review Chapter 5). In Chapter 12 we will show how we can explain parts of the dependent variable's variance by identifying related independent variables. We ask: What proportion of the variance is explained by knowing about the relationship? The explained amount of variance constitutes a proportional reduction in error. As we will see in Chapter 15, when both the independent variable and the dependent variable are of interval/ratio levels of measurement, PRE can be calculated very precisely.

Practical Applications of the Relationship

The fourth aspect of a relationship between two variables is its practical applications. This involves describing how knowledge of a relationship between two variables helps us both understand a phenomenon and apply the results to practical circumstances. In describing this aspect of a relationship, we avoid statistical jargon by presenting research findings in everyday language, especially when we present them to a public audience. We bring our findings to life by revealing their worth for improving society or the lives of individuals. We answer the questions: So what? and Now that a statistical relationship has been found, what is this knowledge good for?

A scientific finding is especially worthwhile if it can change the lives of people. Practical applications involve focusing on exactly how scientific knowledge can be applied in such a way that one variable predicts the other. Under the best circumstances, the relationship is shown to be "causal." That is, altering an independent variable can be shown to result directly in a change in the dependent variable. Where a causal relationship exists, we describe exactly how much change in the score of an independent variable causes how much change in the score of the dependent variable. For example, for the relationship between taking aspirin and reducing joint swelling, how much aspirin brings about how much reduction in swelling? Causation is best established with longitudinal data—data collected over time. This is the case because logically, X can cause Y only if it occurs before Y. Our nonindependent two-group test of the effectiveness of sensitivity training on gender attitudes is a situation where we could make a case for causation. Most social science research, however, relies on cross-sectional survey data—data collected at one point in time. Although causal relationships often are asserted for findings from cross-sectional data, such interpretations must be made carefully.

In circumstances where a statistical relationship is found to exist but causation is not clear, in describing the practical applications of the relationship we simply present the substance of the findings by providing specific empirical information. For example, if we find a relationship between gender and a preference for R-rated movies, what does this say in everyday terms? Is it males or females who are more interested in these movies? (You can guess the answer.) We report precisely those percentages of men and women in a sample expressing great interest in R-rated movies. In doing so, we are providing the best estimates available of how a dependent variable may be adjusted for the effects of an independent variable. The effect of the test (i.e., the difference between what is observed and what is statistically hypothesized) is typically the most meaningful component in describing how findings may be applied to real-world situations. To remind us of this important practical side of testing a hypothesis, in the sixth step of statistical inference we not only make a general statement that the relationship exists but also provide best estimates based on computations of statistical test effects.

The Four Aspects of a Relationship Between Two Variables

Existence: On the basis of statistical analysis of a sample, can we conclude that a relationship exists between two variables among all subjects in the population?

Direction: Can the dependent variable be expected to increase or decrease as the independent variable increases?

Strength: To what extent are errors reduced in predicting the scores of a dependent variable when an independent variable is used as a predictor?

Practical Applications: In practical, everyday terms, how does knowledge of a relationship between two variables help us understand and predict outcomes of the dependent variable?

When to Apply the Various Aspects of Relationships

Testing a hypothesis to establish the existence of a relationship is the first step in any analysis. If a relationship is found *not* to exist between two variables, the other three aspects of a relationship are irrelevant; obviously, if no relationship exists, then the relationship has no direction, strength, or practical applications. Moreover, even when a relationship is found between two variables, the strength and direction may not be meaningful or useful. As we proceed through the remaining chapters, we will point out which aspects of a relationship are useful for each bivariate test.

Relevant Aspects of a Relationship for Two-Group Difference of Means Tests

With either the independent or the nonindependent two-group difference of means test, only two aspects of a relationship apply: existence and practical applications. The *existence* of a relationship between a dichotomous independent variable and an interval/ratio dependent variable is established by using one of the *t*-tests described in this chapter. When the null hypothesis of no difference in means is rejected, we may conclude that a relationship exists.

Existence of a Relationship Using Two-Group Differences of Means Tests

Test the null hypothesis that $\mu_{X_1} = \mu_{X_2}$ (where X is an interval/ratio variable and 1 and 2 designate groups 1 and 2, respectively). That is, there is no difference between the means in the two populations. Use the test statistic:

Independent groups

$$t_{\overline{X}_1 - \overline{X}_2} = \frac{\overline{X}_1 - \overline{X}_2}{s_{\overline{X}_1 - \overline{X}_2}}$$

Matched pairs

$$t_{\overline{D}} = \frac{\overline{D}}{s_{\overline{D}}}$$

When the H_0 is rejected, we assert that a relationship exists.

With the t-test of independent groups, the *direction* of the relationship is not relevant. For example, if a difference is found between the mean incomes of men and women in a corporation, we would *not* say that an increase in maleness is related to an increase in income, because a person is either male or female, not more or less of one or the other. (Having said this, we should point out that some researchers use the phrasing "in the direction of males" to indicate that males have the higher income.) In a nonindependent groups matched-pair test, however, we may assert that we observed an effect of treatment that was positive—in the direction of improvement. This is what we did in the gender sensitivity example, using a one-tailed test.

The *strength* of the relationship for the t-test does not apply either. It can be computed, but the simplicity of the two-group difference of means test is such that typically we do not bother.

Direction and Strength of a Relationship Using Two-Group Differences of Means Tests

Not applicable.

For any statistical test the practical applications of the relationship depend on our describing the effect of the test. Typically, the effect of a test is found in the numerator of the test statistic. For a two-group difference of means test, the effect is the difference between sample means. That is, the effect of the independent variable on the dependent variable $= \overline{X}_1 - \overline{X}_2$. When a relationship is found to exist, this difference between the sample means is treated as an estimate of the difference between population means. This amount is often called the effect of group membership. For example, suppose we test the null hypothesis that the mean weights of men and women are equal. We find a 25-pound difference in the mean weights and reject the null hypothesis. We may then conclude that the effect on bodily weight of being male is 25 pounds: On average, men tend to weigh 25 pounds more than women.

Practical Applications of a Relationship Using Two-Group Differences of Means Tests

Describe the effect of the test in everyday terms, where the effect of the independent variable on the dependent variable is as follows:

Independent groups	Matched pairs
$\overline{X}_1 - \overline{X}_2$	$\overline{D}$

To summarize, only two aspects of a relationship are typically reported for the two-group difference of means test: existence and practical applications. Remember that if we fail to reject the null hypothesis of no difference between means, then no relationship exists between the two variables. When this is the case, practical applications are irrelevant. By letting the null hypothesis stand, we are asserting that the effect of the test is not real in the populations and that the observed difference between sample means is simply due to sampling error.

Statistical Follies and Fallacies: Fixating on Differences of Means While Ignoring Differences in Variances

Differences of means tests are used very frequently. Even in multivariate analysis, bivariate tests such as the ones presented in this chapter constitute the first step in getting a good grasp of the nature of data. Unfortunately, an emphasis on searching for differences between means can override a concern with differences in the spreads of scores between two groups. As we have seen in this chapter, it is important to look for differences in spread because unequal variances in comparison groups create additional sampling error and require adjustments in describing the sampling distribution. However, aside from this statistical necessity, much can be learned about the nature of two groups when their variances are found to be different.

Suppose we compare the educational levels of homeless men and homeless women and find no difference in the mean years of education. Suppose, however, we do find a significant difference in the variances, with women tending to have a greater spread in their education levels. Like the men, many of the women have about 6 to 14 years of schooling, but among the women there are more with meager educations (less than 6 years) but also more with college educations (16-plus years). This difference in spreads of the distributions is very informative. Why are there more meagerly educated individuals among the homeless women? Because many of them come from families that relied on family assistance from the government. In their struggle for economic survival, they left school early for low-paying jobs or because of pregnancy or other circumstances. This puts women at great risk of becoming homeless. Men growing up in these circumstances have other opportunities (such as construction work) that are more economically lucrative and steer them away from becoming homeless. But why are there more highly educated homeless women than men? Because many of these women are victims of spousal abuse, and this phenomenon is not uncommon even among college-educated women. There may be other reasons for differing variances in the educational levels of homeless men and women. If a researcher fixates on observing and interpreting only differences between means, he or she may miss an opportunity to better understand the true nature of the relationship between two variables. Paying close attention to differences in variances as well as differences in means is an important guide to the next level of research.

SUMMARY

1. Bivariate (two-variable) analysis involves searching for statistical relationships between two variables.

2. A statistical relationship between two variables asserts that the measurements of one variable tend to consistently fluctuate with the measurements of the other, making one variable a good predictor of the other. The predictor variable is the independent variable and the predicted variable is the dependent variable.

3. There are three common approaches to measuring statistical relationships: (a) difference of means testing (comparing means of an interval/ratio variable among the categories or groups of a nominal/ordinal variable), (b) counting the frequencies of joint occurrences of attributes of two nominal variables, and (c) measuring the correlation between two interval/ratio variables.

4. A two-group difference of means test for independent samples (t-test) is used to test the hypothesis that the means of a variable differ between two populations or between two categories of a nominal/ordinal variable. The two groups are independent of one another; that is, they do not consist of the same subjects.

5. The sampling distribution for a two-group difference of means test is the approximately normal t-distribution. The calculation of the standard error depends on

whether it can be assumed that the population variances are equal. This is called the assumption of equality of variances.

6. When one sample variance is not larger than twice the size of the other, this suggests that the two population variances are equal, and we assume equality of variances. Equality of variances is also termed *homogeneity of variances* or *homoscedasticity*. When equal variances are assumed, a pooled variance estimate of the standard error is used.

7. Heterogeneity of variances, or heteroscedasticity, occurs when variances appear to be unequal. When this is the case, adjustments to the standard error and its degrees of freedom are needed. This is called a separate variance estimate of the standard error.

8. The two-group difference of means test for nonindependent or matched-pair samples is used to test a difference of means between two sets of scores of the same research subjects, such as two questionnaire items or scores measured at two points in time. The sampling distribution is the approximately normal *t*-distribution.

9. It is important to distinguish between practical and statistical significance. A hypothesis test determines statistical significance in terms of likely sampling error. Practical significance has to do with whether a statistically significant finding truly means anything in real-world applications of results.

10. There are four aspects of statistical relationships: (*a*) *Existence:* On the basis of statistical analysis of a sample, can we conclude that a relationship exists between two variables among all subjects in the population? (*b*) *Direction:* Can the dependent variable be expected to increase or decrease as the independent variable increases? (*c*) *Strength:* To what extent are errors reduced in predicting the scores of a dependent variable when an independent variable is used as a predictor? (*d*) *Practical Applications* (of results): In practical, everyday terms, how does knowledge of a relationship between the two variables help us understand and predict outcomes of the dependent variable?

11. Only two aspects of a relationship apply to a two-group difference of means test, existence and practical applications.

CHAPTER EXTENSIONS ON *THE STATISTICAL IMAGINATION* WEB SITE

Chapter 11 Extensions of text material available on *The Statistical Imagination* Web site at www.mhhe.com/ritchey2 include further discussion of why modifications in a *t*-test are required when the variances of the two groups are unequal.

STATISTICAL PROCEDURES COVERED TO THIS POINT

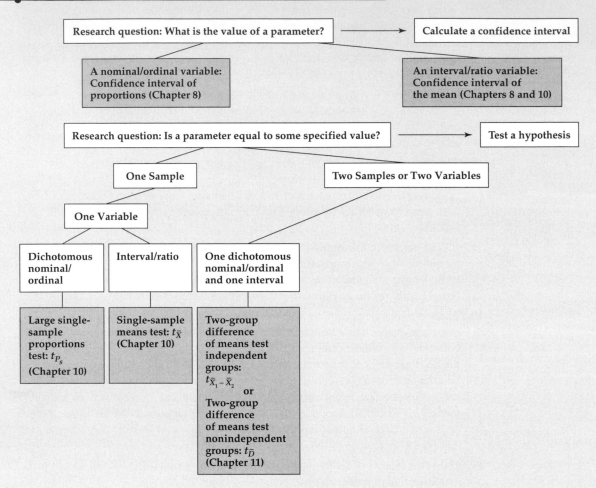

FORMULAS FOR CHAPTER 11

Two-group difference of means test (*t*-test) for independent groups:

Given: An interval/ratio dependent variable *X* compared for two groups that consist of different subjects (i.e., independent groups) obtained from either (1) a dichotomous nominal/ordinal variable from one sample and population or (2) two populations and samples.

Research question: Are the means of *X* in populations of the two groups different?

$$H_0: \mu_{X_1} = \mu_{X_2} \text{ (i.e., } \mu_{X_1} - \mu_{X_2} = 0)$$

Sampling distribution: *t*-distribution; standard error estimated one of two ways depending on whether variances of the two populations appear equal.

Standard error: If variances of the two populations appear equal, use the pooled variance estimate of the standard error:

$$s_{\overline{X}_1 - \overline{X}_2} = \sqrt{\frac{(n_1 - 1)s_{X_1}^2 + (n_2 - 1)s_{X_2}^2}{n_1 + n_2 - 2}} \sqrt{\frac{n_1 + n_2}{n_1 n_2}}$$

with

$$df = n_1 + n_2 - 2$$

If variances of the two populations appear unequal (i.e., the variance of one group is twice as large as that of the other), use the separate variance estimate of the standard error:

$$s_{\overline{X}_1 - \overline{X}_2 \, (separate)} = \sqrt{\frac{s_{X_1}^2}{n_1 - 1} + \frac{s_{X_2}^2}{n_2 - 1}}$$

$$df_{(separate)} = \frac{\left(\dfrac{s_{X_1}^2}{n_1 - 1} + \dfrac{s_{X_2}^2}{n_2 - 1}\right)^2}{\left(\dfrac{s_{X_1}^2}{n_1 - 1}\right)^2 \left(\dfrac{1}{n_1 + 1}\right) + \left(\dfrac{s_{X_2}^2}{n_2 - 1}\right)^2 \left(\dfrac{1}{n_2 + 1}\right)} - 2$$

Test effect: $\overline{X}_1 - \overline{X}_2$

Test statistic [for use with the approximately normal *t*-distribution table (Statistical Table C in Appendix B)] determines whether a relationship exists:

$$t_{\overline{X}_1 - \overline{X}_2} = \frac{\overline{X}_1 - \overline{X}_2}{s_{\overline{X}_1 - \overline{X}_2}}$$

Addressing the aspects of a relationship:
Direction: Usually not applicable
Strength: Not applicable
Practical applications: Specify the difference between group means:

$$\overline{X}_1 - \overline{X}_2$$

Two-group difference of means test (*t*-test) for nonindependent or matched-pair samples:

Given: (1) Two interval/ratio variables with the same score design measured on the same subjects or (2) a single interval/ratio variable measured twice for the same sample subjects (i.e., nonindependent groups).

Research question: Are the means of X different for the two variables or two measurements?

H_0: $\mu_D = 0$

Sampling distribution: t-distribution of the distribution of mean differences ($\overline{D}$, with $df = n - 1$)
Standard error:

$$s_{\overline{D}} = \frac{s_D}{\sqrt{n}}$$

Test effect: $\overline{D}$ (i.e., $\overline{D} - \mu_D = \overline{D} - 0 = \overline{D}$)
Test statistic [for use with the approximately normal t-distribution table (Statistical Table C in Appendix B)]: determines whether a relationship exists):

$$t_{\overline{D}} = \frac{\overline{D}}{s_{\overline{D}}}$$
$$df = n - 1$$

Addressing the aspects of a relationship:
Direction: Usually not applicable
Strength: Not applicable
Practical applications: Report the mean difference $\overline{D}$

QUESTIONS FOR CHAPTER 11

1. Study Table 11–1 until you are able to reproduce it.

2. Describe the situation where we use a "two-group difference of means test" for independent groups.

3. With a two-group difference of means test, we must assume equality of variances. Why must this be considered?

4. Explain the distinction between independent and nonindependent groups two-group difference of means tests.

5. How is the null hypothesis stated for a two-group difference of means test? Why must it be stated this way?

6. Statistical test effects involve both sample statistics and population parameters. The effect of the test is found in the numerator of the test statistic. For two-group difference of means tests, why do parameters *not* appear in the formulas for the test statistics?

7. With a two-group difference of means test for independent groups where equal population variances are assumed, why are degrees of freedom calculated as follows?

$$df = n_1 + n_2 - 2$$

8. The existence of a relationship between two variables determines the following: On the basis of the statistical analysis of a _____, can we conclude that a relationship exists between two variables among all subjects in the _____?

9. The existence of a relationship is determined by hypothesis testing, which establishes whether sample statistical findings are due to _____ error.

10. Regarding the direction of a relationship, a positive relationship is one in which an increase in one variable is related to an _____ in the other. A negative relationship is one in which an increase in one variable is related to a _____ in the other.

11. The _____ of a relationship between two variables establishes the extent to which errors are reduced in predicting the scores of a dependent variable. This measurement gives us an indication of _____, how well the independent variable predicts outcomes of a dependent variable.

12. The _____ of the relationship involves describing how knowledge of a relationship between two variables helps us understand a phenomenon and apply the results to practical circumstances.

13. In describing the _____ of a relationship, we avoid statistical jargon by presenting research findings in everyday language, especially when we present the results to a public audience.

14. A _____ statistical test is useful for "before-after" or "test-retest" experimental design, where a variable is measured twice for the same individuals with some type of intervention between the tests.

15. Distinguish statistical significance from practical significance. Give examples.

16. For the two-group difference of means test, which aspects of a relationship are relevant? How are these aspects addressed?

17. Match the following:

   a. $s_{\bar{X}_1 - \bar{X}_2}$ _____ The number of standard errors that independent sample mean differences deviate from the hypothesized mean difference of zero

   b. $t_{\bar{D}}$ _____ The standard error of differences between matched-pair scores

   c. $t_{\bar{X}_1 - \bar{X}_2}$ _____ The number of standard errors that a sample mean difference between matched-pair scores deviates from the hypothesized mean difference of zero

   d. $s_{\bar{D}}$ _____ The pooled variance estimate of the standard error of the difference between two means

EXERCISES FOR CHAPTER 11

Problem Set 11A

On all hypotheses tests, follow the six steps of statistical inference, including test preparation, a conceptual diagram, probability curves, and appropriate aspects of a relationship. For consistency, round standard errors to two decimal places. Use $\alpha = .05$ unless otherwise stipulated.

11A-1. A restaurant conducts a random survey of two groups of women: those working inside the home and those working elsewhere. The survey inquires about how many times in the past two weeks they prepared meals at home. Using the following (fictional) responses, determine whether women who work outside the home prepare meals less often than do those who work at home. Assume equality of population variances.

Work Situation	Number of At-Home Meals Past Two Weeks
At home	9
At home	10
At home	11
At home	8
At home	9
At home	12
At home	14
At home	10
At home	12
At home	13
At home	9
At home	10
At home	12
At home	14
At home	10
Outside home	8
Outside home	10
Outside home	8
Outside home	7
Outside home	9
Outside home	9
Outside home	12
Outside home	8
Outside home	10
Outside home	10
Outside home	7
Outside home	12
Outside home	6
Outside home	10
Outside home	9
Outside home	8
Outside home	10
Outside home	9

11A-2. Suppose two random samples of 40 companies each were selected to compare the mean hourly incomes of union workers and nonunion workers. The 40 nonunion companies offered a mean wage of $10.80 with a variance of $2.50, while the 40 unionized companies offered a mean wage of $11.90 with a variance of $2.50. Do these data present sufficient evidence to indicate that a worker is better off with a unionized company? Assume equality of population variances.

11A-3. For a random survey of 641 adults, determine if there is a gender difference in degree of support for gun control. Support is measured with an "attitude toward gun control" scale (X) that has an interval level of measurement (fictional data). A high score indicates a more favorable attitude toward gun control. Assume equality of population variances.

Men	Women
$\bar{X} = 6.2$	$\bar{X} = 6.5$
$s_X = 1.3$	$s_X = 1.4$
$n = 324$	$n = 317$

11A-4. A comparison of life expectancy in random samples of 40 less-developed countries and 31 industrialized countries reveals the following (fictional) data. The standard deviations are significantly different from one another. Is there a significant difference in mean life expectancy between countries with these two levels of economic development? $X = $ life expectancy of a resident at birth.

Less-Developed Countries	Industrialized Countries
$\bar{X} = 66.1$ years	$\bar{X} = 76.7$ years
$s_X = 28.9$ years	$s_X = 4.2$ years
$n = 40$	$n = 31$

11A-5. Rotator cuff injuries to the arm and shoulder are common among athletes. A sports medicine institute is testing the effectiveness of a new therapy for improving arm range of motion (ROM). The new therapy is administered to an experimental treatment group and traditional treatments are given to a control group. Subjects are randomly assigned to each group and ROM is measured on a device scaled in centimeters. The experimental treatment regimen involved sessions three times per week for six weeks with measurements at time 1 (i.e., start of treatment) and time 2 (i.e., end of treatment). The (fictional) results are in the following table. Test hypotheses to answer questions (a) through (c) and then answer (d). Take care to use matched-pair tests when appropriate. Use $\alpha = .01$ and assume that the population variances are equal. Y = range of motion (ROM) of arm.

a. If the members of the two groups were truly randomly assigned, then there should be no significant difference in ROM at time 1. Was this the case?

b. Was there a significant difference between the experimental and control groups at time 2?

c. Was there a significant difference in ROM at times 1 and 2 for the experimental subjects?

d. Considering the results of (a) through (c), does the new treatment appear an improvement over traditional treatment?

	Control Group (n = 35)	Experimental Treatment Group (n = 35)
Time 1	$\bar{Y} = 16.9$ cm	$\bar{Y} = 17.1$ cm
	$s_Y = 3.6$ cm	$s_Y = 3.7$ cm
Time 2	$\bar{Y} = 32.1$ cm	$\bar{Y} = 35.5$ cm
	$s_Y = 3.4$ cm	$s_Y = 3.4$ cm
Mean difference per subject	$\bar{D} = 14.7$ cm	$\bar{D} = 18.2$ cm
	$s_D = 3.1$ cm	$s_D = 3.0$ cm

Problem Set 11B

On all hypotheses tests, follow the six steps of statistical inference, including test preparation, a conceptual diagram, probability curves, and appropriate aspects of a relationship. For consistency, round standard errors to two decimal places. Use $\alpha = .05$ unless otherwise stipulated.

11B-1. In the upcoming National Football League (NFL) draft of new players, the team that finished last a season ago seeks to fill skill positions, those that are productive in scoring. They sample records of college football players and tabulate the number of touchdowns scored in their last year by position (fictional data). Which position is more productive, running back or wide receiver? Assume equality of population variances.

Position	Touchdowns
Running Back	10
Running Back	15
Running Back	12
Running Back	13
Running Back	16
Running Back	11
Running Back	13
Running Back	13
Running Back	14
Running Back	12
Running Back	12
Running Back	15
Running Back	11
Running Back	13
Wide Receiver	8
Wide Receiver	12
Wide Receiver	10
Wide Receiver	10
Wide Receiver	9
Wide Receiver	13
Wide Receiver	11
Wide Receiver	8
Wide Receiver	8
Wide Receiver	10
Wide Receiver	12
Wide Receiver	15
Wide Receiver	10
Wide Receiver	12
Wide Receiver	9

11B-2. Shallowstone Pictures is the leading motion picture company in the United States. Company executives wish to know to which population movies should be targeted, younger people or older people. They sample populations of college students and retired people. The sample of 61 college students saw an average of 23.45 movies per year with a variance of 6.86 movies, and the sample of 61 retirees saw an average of 21.79 movies per year with a variance of 6.86 movies. Do these data indicate that college students see more movies than retirees? Assume equality of population variances.

11B-3. You wish to research whether psychological depression is higher among first-year than sophomore college students. Your theory is that first-year students must adapt to new life circumstances and the stress causes more instances of depression. Depression is an interval level measure, the Center for Epidemiological Studies Depression Scale (CESD), which ranges from 0 to 60. High scores (in CESD scale points) indicate higher levels of depression. Do your statistics below support the theory? Assume equality of population variances.

First-year	Sophomores
$\bar{X} = 9.42$	$\bar{X} = 9.13$
$s_X = 2.18$	$s_X = 2.29$
$n = 169$	$n = 174$

11B-4. Research shows that even for married couples in two-income households, women perform significantly more housework than men (see Hersch and Stratton 2000). You wish to replicate this study and sample populations of married men and women, all of whom work 40 hours per week outside the home. Housework (X) is measured in hours and the standard deviations *are* significantly different from one another. Do your data below support these previous findings?

Men	Women
$\bar{X} = 23.24$	$\bar{X} = 29.15$
$s_X = 11.05$	$s_X = 4.12$
$n = 57$	$n = 52$

11B-5. A psychologist treats patients with high levels of anxiety. He is curious to know whether reading a self-help book decreases the level of anxiety beyond the standard therapy he gives his patients. He samples his patient population and randomly assigns experimental group subjects to read the book, and control group subjects do not. He measures anxiety at time 1 (before) and time 2 (after) the experimental group has read the book. The fictional results are in the following table. Test the hypotheses to answer questions (*a*) through (*c*) and then answer (*d*). Take care to use matched-pair tests when appropriate. Use $\alpha = .01$ and assume that the population variances are equal. Y = level of anxiety.

   a.   If the members of the two groups were truly randomly assigned, then there should be no significant difference between their levels of anxiety at time 1. Was this the case?

   b.   Was there a significant difference in mean levels of anxiety between the experimental and control groups at time 2?

   c.   Was there a significant difference in mean levels of anxiety at times 1 and 2 for the experimental subjects?

d. Considering the results of (*a*) through (*c*), is reading the book better than just the standard treatment?

	Control Group (n = 40)	Experimental Group (n = 40)
Time 1	$\bar{Y}$ = 26.61 points s_Y = 4.33 points	$\bar{Y}$ = 25.95 points s_Y = 4.87 points
Time 2	$\bar{Y}$ = 19.12 points s_Y = 3.76 points	$\bar{Y}$ = 15.57 points s_Y = 2.64 points
Mean difference per subject	$\bar{D}$ = 7.49 points s_D = 2.81 points	$\bar{D}$ = 10.38 points s_D = 3.63 points

Problem Set 11C

On all hypotheses tests, follow the six steps of statistical inference, including test preparation, a conceptual diagram, probability curves, and appropriate aspects of a relationship. For consistency, round standard errors to two decimal places. Use α − .05 unless otherwise stipulated.

11C-1. Two social movement organizations that arose in the 1980s to increase public awareness of the dangers of drinking before driving were Mothers Against Drunk Driving (MADD) and Remove Intoxicated Drivers (RID) (McCarthy and Wolfson 1996). Suppose the following are survey data of a random sample of chapter presidents of the two organizations. *X* = the number of public appearances in the past year. Is there a significant difference in the means of *X*? Assume equality of population variances.

President's Organization	X
MADD	41
MADD	29
RID	10
MADD	33
RID	24
RID	26
MADD	45
MADD	39
MADD	33
RID	26
MADD	28
RID	23

MADD	45
RID	10
MADD	26
RID	19
MADD	37
RID	15
MADD	32
MADD	32
RID	20
RID	14
MADD	36
MADD	38
RID	24

11C-2. Random samples of 100 adults selected from two ethnic groups in a large city were questioned concerning the number of years they attended public schools. See if there is a significant difference in the two population means. Assume equality of population variances.

	Ethnic Group 1	Ethnic Group 2
Mean	7.4 years	8.2 years
Standard Deviation	2.1 years	2.4 years
n	100	100

11C-3. Orbuch and Eyster (1997) asked the wives of black couples and white couples to rate the husband's participation in traditionally feminine tasks such as preparing meals, dishwashing, house cleaning, laundry, and child care. They used a six-item scale with a high score indicating that the husband is perceived to do more. Previous studies showed that black husbands do more. Is this borne out in the Orbuch and Eyster data? Assume equality of population variances. X = husband participation score.

Blacks	Whites
$\bar{X} = 1.54$	$\bar{X} = 1.47$
$s_X = .36$	$s_X = .37$
$n = 199$	$n = 174$

11C-4. An upstart electronics company has been test marketing two models of compact disc (CD) players, one with a rotary disc changer and the other with a stacked changer. Random samples of recent purchasers returned questionnaires with a multi-item satisfaction scale that is of an interval level of measurement. The standard deviations are significantly different from one another. Is there a significant difference in mean purchaser satisfaction for the two models? Y = score on product satisfaction scale.

Purchasers of Rotary Model	Purchasers of Stack Model
$\overline{Y} = 31.1$	$\overline{Y} = 28.1$
$s_Y = 2.4$	$s_Y = 4.2$
$n = 149$	$n = 167$

11C-5. At the start of a weight-loss program, participants were asked to identify on a checklist foods that are high in saturated fat (i.e., HSF foods). After the nutritional education program, the same participants were administered the checklist again. Was the educational program effective in increasing the participants' knowledge of HSF foods? Assume that the population variances are equal. X = number of HSF foods correctly identified on a checklist (fictional data).

	Number of HSF Foods Identified	
Subject	Before Program	After Program
1	7	11
2	4	9
3	8	14
4	7	12
5	5	11
6	2	7
7	6	15
8	5	12
9	7	10
10	8	13
11	5	11
12	4	10
13	7	13
14	6	10
15	8	12
16	4	8
17	7	14
18	6	11
19	6	10
20	8	13

Problem Set 11D

On all hypotheses tests, follow the six steps of statistical inference, including test preparation, a conceptual diagram, probability curves, and appropriate aspects of a relationship. For consistency, round standard errors to two decimal places. Use $\alpha = .05$ unless otherwise stipulated.

11D-1.   The ABC Cab Company is competing with XYZ Cabs in New York City. ABC figures that the best way to make more money is to pick up more passengers. It surveys the population of XYZ Cab drivers and its own cab drivers to see how many passengers they each pick up on a given day. Use the following (fictional) data to determine if there is a significant difference in the mean number of passengers picked up between the two cab companies. $X =$ the number of passengers. Assume equality of the population variances.

Cab Company	X
XYZ	19
XYZ	15
ABC	25
XYZ	22
ABC	26
XYZ	23
ABC	28
ABC	27
ABC	31
XYZ	15
ABC	26
XYZ	16
XYZ	23
ABC	21
XYZ	18
XYZ	26
ABC	30
XYZ	24
ABC	22
XYZ	25
ABC	31
ABC	27
XYZ	19
XYZ	21
XYZ	23
ABC	27
XYZ	16
ABC	24
ABC	26
XYZ	21
ABC	24

11D-2. The BodyMax Fitness Company holds a publicity stunt where it accuses the HeavyLift Company of making dumbbells that are lighter than they are supposed to be. The BodyMax Fitness Company weighs a 25-pound HeavyLift dumbbell and one of its own. The HeavyLift dumbbell weighs 23.6 pounds, and the BodyMax dumbbell weighs exactly 25 pounds. As an independent researcher, you want to know if this accusation is accurate. You take samples of dumbbells from both companies that are marked as weighing 25 pounds and, indeed, the mean weight of BodyMax dumbbells is slightly greater than that of HeavyLift dumbbells. Using the following data, determine if the HeavyLift dumbbells are really lighter than the BodyMax dumbbells. In other words, is there a significant difference between the weight of the dumbbells?

	BodyMax Dumbbells (group 1)	HeavyLift Dumbbells (group 2)
Mean	25.00 pounds	24.70 pounds
Standard Deviation	1.27 pounds	1.13 pounds
n	35 weights	35 weights

11D-3. DuBois and Silverthorn (2005) reported that having a mentor was associated with increased self-esteem in adolescents. You wish to replicate their study, so you sample a population of adolescents ages 12 to 17 and obtain the following statistics. Self-esteem (X) is measured using a self-esteem scale. Do adolescents with mentors have higher self-esteem than those without them? Assume equality of population variances.

With Mentor	Without Mentor
$\bar{X} = 13.35$	$\bar{X} = 10.02$
$s_X = 1.39$	$s_X = 1.45$
$n = 104$	$n = 110$

11D-4. You wish to determine whether women in the United States earn less than men for the same amount and type of work. You sample data-entry workers from 100 companies and obtain the following data. Determine if there is a statistically significant difference in the mean income between men and women. The standard deviations are significantly different. $Y =$ hourly pay in dollars.

Men	Women
$\bar{X} = 12.50$	$\bar{X} = 10.75$
$s_X = 1.25$	$s_X = 2.50$
$n = 50$	$n = 50$

11D-5. Research has shown that movement such as running, walking, or lifting weights increases levels of MGF protein in the muscles (Deschenes 2004). To replicate this study, you sample the population of adults ages 35 to 45 and measure MGF protein levels in their leg muscles. The subjects are then put on a 10-week weight-training regimen focusing on the lower body. At the end of the 10 weeks, you again measure MGF protein levels. Was there an increase in MGF protein among the subjects? X = units of MGF protein.

	MGF Protein Levels	
Subject	Before Program	After Program
1	11	17
2	9	16
3	15	20
4	13	16
5	11	21
6	9	16
7	10	15
8	14	17
9	11	19
10	10	16
11	15	21
12	14	19
13	9	16
14	10	16
15	13	21
16	12	15
17	14	18
18	11	17
19	11	19
20	8	16
21	16	19
22	11	20
23	14	18
24	9	14
25	11	16

OPTIONAL COMPUTER APPLICATIONS
FOR CHAPTER 11

If your class uses the optional computer applications that accompany this text, open the Chapter 11 exercises on *The Statistical Imagination* Web site at www.mhhe.com/ritchey2. The exercises for the two-group difference of means test in *SPSS for Windows* focus on choosing the appropriate test command sequences and correctly interpreting the output. Of particular interest is distinguishing output from equal and unequal variance tests. In addition, Appendix D of this text provides a brief overview of the *SPSS* command sequences for procedures covered in this chapter.

12

Analysis of Variance: Differences Among Means of Three or More Groups

Introduction

Just before the turn of the millennium, a nationwide movement began in the United States to reduce government assistance to poor single mothers and encourage them to seek employment. In most states, family assistance has never been sufficient to push all families out of poverty; it is a stopgap measure used by most recipients for a short time. Yet in the heat of political rhetoric, some politicians and citizens have come to believe that living "on welfare" is a paid long-term vacation of sorts.

Social researchers and social workers familiar with state assistance programs are skeptical of this public stereotype. In fact, a close look at the everyday lives of recipients of family assistance reveals a lifestyle characterized by a struggle for economic survival. For example, using a sample of 214 welfare-reliant mothers in four cities, Edin and Lein (1997) measured "monthly entertainment expenses" (MEES) to see how "lavishly" these mothers live. They found a mean MEES of only $22. This low average expenditure challenged the stereotype that welfare recipients are on an extended holiday.

The main purpose of Edin and Lein's study, however, was to see whether the average MEES differed from city to city. The cost of living varied among the cities, suggesting that entertainment costs also would vary. In theoretical terms, the research question was: Is there a relationship between the city in which a welfare-reliant mother resides and her MEES? City of residence is one variable, X, with a nominal level of measurement. MEES is the second variable, Y, and it is of ratio level. It is also the dependent variable, and the focus is on its mean.

The statistical design for comparing three or more group means is one-way analysis of variance (ANOVA). ANOVA is an extension of the two-group difference of means test (t-test) covered in Chapter 11, but with ANOVA we take a slightly different approach. To illustrate how ANOVA works, let us use data similar to those of Edin and Lein. To simplify, we will examine a sample of only 15 mothers from three cities. Our interest, of course, is in whether the mean MEES (μ_Y's) differ *in the populations* of welfare-reliant mothers in the three cities. That is, do their parameters, μ_Y, differ, where Y = MEES? This research question is graphically illustrated in Figure 12–1.

The data are presented in Table 12–1, where Y = MEES and X is the city of residence. In the lower right-hand corner of Table 12–1, we find that the mean MEES of all 15 mothers is $22. This overall, total sample mean is called the grand mean. Above the grand mean are the means for the three cities: Boston ($28), Chicago ($24), and Charleston ($14); these are called group means.

To test for differences among the means of the three cities, we could use t-tests (Chapter 11), but the process would require three tests, one for each of the following pairs of cities: Boston–Chicago, Boston–Charleston, and Chicago–Charleston. Comparing the means of, say, six cities would be even messier, requiring 15 t-tests. The cumbersome nature of calculating large sets of t-tests challenged statisticians to develop ANOVA, an extension of the t-test.

Like the t-test, with ANOVA the null hypothesis is stated as: There are no differences among group means. For our welfare-reliant mothers, we state the null hypothesis as follows:

$$H_0: \mu_{Y(Boston)} = \mu_{Y(Chicago)} = \mu_{Y(Charleston)}$$

where Y = MEES. This statement meets the requirements of a null hypothesis. When it is true, the differences among the three means will be zero, give or take some predictable sampling error.

Calculating Main Effects

Although the statement of the null hypothesis is essentially the same as it is with the t-test, with ANOVA we take a slightly different approach. Instead of comparing each group mean to the others, ANOVA compares each group mean to the grand mean. This makes sense. If the population means are equal for the three groups, the mean of all cases combined will be the same. Thus, the null hypothesis can be restated as

$$H_0: \mu_{Y(Boston)} = \mu_{Y(Chicago)} = \mu_{Y(Charleston)} = \mu_{Y(grand)}$$

FIGURE 12–1

Are the mean monthly entertainment expenses the same in the populations of welfare-reliant mothers in three cities?

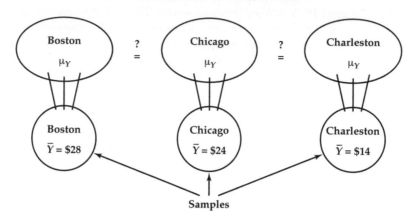

Populations: welfare-reliant mothers in three cities

Y = monthly entertainment expenses (MEES)

TABLE 12–1 I Computational spreadsheet of monthly entertainment expenses (MEES) for 15 welfare-reliant mothers from three cities

	Givens		Calculations		
Case	City (X)	MEES (Y)	$(Y_{(each\ case)} - \bar{Y}_{(grand)})$ (deviation score)	$(Y_{(each\ case)} - \bar{Y}_{(grand)})^2$	Group Means
1	Boston	$33	$ 11	$121	
2	Boston	30	8	64	
3	Boston	28	6	36	$\bar{Y}_{(Bos.)} = \dfrac{\Sigma Y}{n} = \dfrac{140}{5} = \$28$
4	Boston	26	4	16	
5	Boston	23	1	1	
6	Chicago	26	4	16	
7	Chicago	19	−3	9	
8	Chicago	24	2	4	$\bar{Y}_{(Chic.)} = \dfrac{\Sigma Y}{n} = \dfrac{120}{5} = \$24$
9	Chicago	22	0	0	
10	Chicago	29	7	49	
11	Charleston	14	−8	64	
12	Charleston	19	−3	9	
13	Charleston	16	−6	36	$\bar{Y}_{(Char.)} = \dfrac{\Sigma Y}{n} = \dfrac{70}{5} = \$14$
14	Charleston	12	−10	100	
15	Charleston	9	−13	169	
	$\Sigma Y_{(grand)} = \$330$		$\Sigma(Y_{(each\ case)} - \bar{Y}_{(grand)})^2 = \$694$		

$n = 15$

$\Sigma(Y_{(each\ case)} - \bar{Y}_{(grand)}) = \$0$

$\bar{Y}_{(grand)} = \dfrac{\Sigma Y_{(grand)}}{n} = \dfrac{330}{15} = \$22$

Moreover, if the three means each equal the grand mean, the difference between any group mean and the grand mean is zero. In ANOVA, these *differences between each group mean and the grand mean* are the test effects, which for ANOVA are called **main effects**.

Calculating the Main Effect of a Group Mean

Main effect of a group mean $= \overline{Y}_{(group)} - \overline{Y}_{(grand)}$

$\qquad\qquad\qquad\qquad = $ difference between a group's mean and mean of all scores in the sample

where

$\qquad\qquad\qquad\qquad Y = $ an interval/ratio level variable

$\qquad\qquad\qquad \overline{Y}_{(group)} = $ mean of Y for a group (i.e., category of the nominal level variable)

$\qquad\qquad\qquad \overline{Y}_{(grand)} = $ mean of all scores in the sample

---

Recall that the test effect of a variable is the difference between what is observed in the sample (in step 4 of the six steps of statistical inference) and what is statistically hypothesized (in step 1 of the six steps). When the null hypothesis is true, there is no difference between the means of the three cities and the grand mean. The mean MEES of each city would be \$22, and *all main effects would be zero*. Thus, the null hypothesis can be viewed in yet another way:

$$H_0: \overline{Y}_{(any\ group)} - \overline{Y}_{(grand)} = 0$$

We can see, however, in Table 12–1 that the *sample* means from the three cities are not the same. Indeed, for the populations of welfare-reliant mothers of the three cities, the alternative hypothesis is that the mean MEES are not the same (i.e., the main effects are not zero). For our welfare-reliant mothers, the main effects are as follows:

Main effect on MEES of living in Boston $= \overline{Y}_{(Boston)} - \overline{Y}_{(grand)} = \$28 - \$22 = \$6$

Main effect on MEES of living in Chicago $= \overline{Y}_{(Chicago)} - \overline{Y}_{(grand)} = \$24 - \$22 = \$2$

Main effect on MEES of living in Charleston $= \overline{Y}_{(Charleston)} - \overline{Y}_{(grand)} = \$14 - \$22 = -\$8$

Focusing on the grand mean and comparing each city's mean to it is a roundabout way of testing the difference among any number of group means. Using ANOVA, we can determine whether the main effects are significantly different from zero. This test hinges on whether the observed main effects are so great that they are unlikely to be due to sampling error.

In mathematical terms, then, with ANOVA the null hypothesis can be stated in any of several ways that convey the same meaning: There is no difference among group means, all means are equal, all means are equal to the grand mean, and all main effects are zero. If we reject the null hypothesis and accept the alternative hypothesis, we are asserting that some or all of the main effects are significantly different from zero. This in turn indicates that *at least two* of the population means differ. Moreover, accepting the alternative hypothesis asserts that there is a relationship between the nominal/ordinal level independent variable and the interval/ratio level dependent variable.

The General Linear Model: Testing the Statistical Significance of Main Effects

As it turns out, Edin and Lein found that there was indeed a relationship between city of residence and MEES. The effects of city of residence on MEES were significantly different from zero. They concluded that on average, *the populations* of welfare-reliant mothers in Boston had entertainment expenses that were $6 greater than the grand mean of $22; in Chicago, the expenses were $2 greater; and in Charleston, they were $8 less.

How are these effects used to come to this conclusion? The answer to this question lies in showing that the individual MEES scores in the sample are determined partly by the main effect of a subject's city of residence. This is done by focusing on individual deviations from the grand mean and seeing how much of this deviation is due to the effect of city of residence. Recall from Chapter 5 that a deviation score is the difference between an individual's score and the grand mean.

Calculating a Deviation Score

Deviation score for a case $= Y_{(each\ case)} - \overline{Y}_{(grand)}$

$\qquad\qquad\qquad$ = difference between the score of a case and the mean of all scores in the sample

where

$$Y = \text{an interval/ratio level variable}$$

$$Y_{(each\ case)} = Y\text{-score of an individual case}$$

$$\overline{Y}_{(grand)} = \text{mean of all scores in the sample}$$

Let us examine the deviation score of case 1 in Table 12–1, a Ms. Jones. With Y = monthly entertainment expenses (MEES), her MEES or Y-score is $33. Therefore, her deviation score is

$$\text{Ms. Jones's deviation score} = Y_{(Ms.\ Jones)} - \overline{Y}_{(grand)} = \$33 - \$22 = \$11$$

Why does Ms. Jones spend $11 more than the average on entertainment? If MEES is related to city of residence, we can argue that $6 of this $11 deviation is "explained" by the differences in mean MEES among city of residence groups. Ms. Jones's group membership is Boston. The difference between the mean MEES in Boston and the grand mean is $6. This is the main effect for Boston, the "extra cost" of MEES of living in Boston. For Ms. Jones, $6 is the part of her $11 deviation that is explained by differences between group means. This is Ms. Jones's "between-group deviation." It is the same for all mothers in the Boston group and is equal to the main effect for Boston:

$$\text{Ms. Jones's between-group deviation} = \text{main effect on MEES of living in Boston}$$

$$= \overline{Y}_{(Boston)} - \overline{Y}_{(grand)} = \$28 - \$22 = \$6$$

Although living in Boston explains $6 of Ms. Jones's $11 deviation score, this leaves an additional $5 that cannot be explained by city of residence. This is the difference between Ms. Jones's Y-score and the mean for Boston. This amount is called the within-group deviation because even within her Boston group Ms. Jones spends $5 more than the average. The within-group deviation accounts for why an individual does not score the mean within his or her group. It is the difference between an individual's Y-score and the mean of that individual's group. Whereas the *between*-group deviation is the same for all cases in a group, the *within*-group deviation varies among group members:

Calculating the Within-Group Deviation Score of a Case

$$\text{Within-group deviation} = Y_{(a\ group's\ case)} - \overline{Y}_{(group)}$$

$$= \text{difference between the score of a}$$
$$\text{case and the mean of all scores}$$
$$\text{in its group}$$

where

$$Y = \text{an interval/ratio level variable}$$

$$Y_{(a\ group's\ case)} = Y\text{-score of an individual case in a group}$$

$$\overline{Y}_{(group)} = \text{mean of all scores in that case's group}$$

Thus,

$$\text{Within group deviation}_{(Ms.\ Jones)} = Y_{(Ms.\ Jones)} - \overline{Y}_{(Boston)} = \$33 - \$28 = \$5$$

The within-group deviation is also referred to as the "unexplained" deviation. While we can explain that $6 of Ms. Jones's $11 above-average MEES is due to her Boston residence, we do not know why she spends an extra $5 beyond the Boston average. It could be due to transportation costs, having kids who are big eaters, or some other reason. For the time being, these other variables are unmeasured, and therefore, Ms. Jones's within-group deviation is left unexplained.

When all is said and done, we cannot explain every dollar of Ms. Jones's $33 expenditure for entertainment. We can, however, *account for it* by focusing on her

$11 deviation score and isolating the parts explained and unexplained by her Boston residence:

$$Y_{(Ms.\ Jones)} = \$33 = \overline{Y}_{(grand)} + \text{her deviation score}$$

$$= \overline{Y}_{(grand)} + [Y_{(Ms.\ Jones)} - \overline{Y}_{(grand)}]$$

$$= \overline{Y}_{(grand)} + [\overline{Y}_{(Boston)} - \overline{Y}_{(grand)}] + [Y_{(Ms.\ Jones)} - \overline{Y}_{(Boston)}]$$

$$= \$22 + \$6 + \$5$$

Explained between-group deviation (that part of deviation score explained by Boston residence)

Unexplained within-group deviation (that part of deviation score explained by other unmeasured variables)

In this fashion, we can account for the Y-scores (i.e., MEES) of all cases in a sample. For instance, for case 15, a welfare-reliant mother from Charleston:

$$Y_{(case\ 15)} = \$9 = \overline{Y}_{(grand)} + [\overline{Y}_{(Charleston)} - \overline{Y}_{(grand)}] + [Y_{(case\ 15)} - \overline{Y}_{(Charleston)}]$$

$$= \$22 + (-\$8) + (-\$5)$$

Explained deviation (effect of Charleston)

Unexplained deviation (effect of other variables)

This approach to analysis, which focuses on deviations from the mean of a dependent variable Y and explains its deviation scores $Y - \overline{Y}$, is called the general linear model, a type of additive-effects model. It simply states that the best prediction of any dependent variable Y is its mean plus the effects of an independent variable X. Whether for ANOVA or for any other statistical procedure, the general linear model is mathematically represented as follows:

The General Linear Model

$$Y_{(each\ case)} = \overline{Y}_{(grand)} + \text{explained effect of } X + \text{unexplained error}$$

where

$$Y = \text{an interval/ratio dependent variable}$$
$$X = \text{an independent variable related to } Y$$
$$Y_{(each\ case)} = \text{a } Y\text{-score in the sample}$$
$$\overline{Y}_{(grand)} = \text{mean of all } Y\text{-scores in the sample}$$

The general linear model breaks apart (or "decomposes") each Y-score into three parts:

1. The "amount of the Y-score explained by the grand mean" (i.e., the mean of all Y-scores)
2. The "amount of its deviation score explained by X" (i.e., the main effect for the category of X)
3. The "amount of its deviation score unexplained by X" (i.e., error)

Table 12–2 provides a breakdown of each of the 15 cases of our sample of welfare-reliant mothers in terms of these three parts. This type of table is called a decomposition table. For each city of residence, column (A) is the part of a Y-score explained by the grand mean. Column (B) is the main effect of the group: that part of the deviation score explained by city of residence (X). Column (C) lists that part of each individual's Y-score that is not explained by city of residence—unexplained error.

Determining the Statistical Significance of Main Effects Using ANOVA

How do we determine that the \$6 difference between the mean MEES of Boston residents and the grand mean is not simply due to sampling error? Is it not possible that in

TABLE 12–2 | Decomposition of effects of city of residence (X) on total monthly entertainment expenses [MEES (Y)] of welfare-reliant mothers, $n = 15$

All Columns (A): Grand Mean $= \bar{Y}_{(grand)} = \dfrac{\Sigma Y}{n} = \dfrac{330}{15} = \$22$

Boston			Chicago			Charleston		
(A)	(B) Main Effect	(C)	(A)	(B) Main Effect	(C)	(A)	(B) Main Effect	(C)
$Y = \bar{Y}_{(grand)} +$	of X	$+$ Error	$Y = \bar{Y}_{(grand)} +$	of X	$+$ Error	$Y = \bar{Y}_{(grand)} +$	of X	$+$ Error
\$33 = 22 +	6	+ 5	\$26 = 22 +	2	+ 2	\$14 = 22 +	(−8)	+ 0
\$30 = 22 +	6	+ 2	\$19 = 22 +	2	+ (−5)	\$19 = 22 +	(−8)	+ 5
\$28 = 22 +	6	+ 0	\$24 = 22 +	2	+ 0	\$16 = 22 +	(−8)	+ 2
\$26 = 22 +	6	+ (−2)	\$22 = 22 +	2	+ (−2)	\$12 = 22 +	(−8)	+ (−2)
\$23 = 22 +	6	+ (−5)	\$29 = 22 +	2	+ 5	\$ 9 = 22 +	(−8)	+ (−5)

$$\bar{Y}_{(Bos.)} = \frac{\Sigma Y}{n} = \frac{140}{5} = \$28 \qquad \bar{Y}_{(Chic.)} = \frac{\Sigma Y}{n} = \frac{120}{5} = \$24 \qquad \bar{Y}_{(Char.)} = \frac{\Sigma Y}{n} = \frac{70}{5} = \$14$$

Column (B): | Column (B): | Column (B):
Between-group deviation = | Boston-group deviation = | Between-group deviation =
main effect for Boston | main effect for Chicago | main effect for Charleston

$$\bar{Y}_{(Bos.)} - \bar{Y}_{(grand)} = \$28 - \$22 = \$6 \qquad \bar{Y}_{(Chic)} - \bar{Y}_{(grand)} = \$24 - \$22 = \$2 \qquad \bar{Y}_{(Char.)} - \bar{Y}_{(grand)} = \$14 - \$22 = -\$8$$

Column (C): | Column (C): | Column (C):
Within-group deviation = error | Within-group deviation = error | Within-group deviation = error

$$= Y - \bar{Y}_{(Bos.)} \qquad\qquad = Y - \bar{Y}_{(Chic.)} \qquad\qquad = Y - \bar{Y}_{(Char.)}$$

repeated sampling the mean of another Boston sample would be different? In other words, how do we determine that main effects, and therefore the differences among group means, are statistically significant? Is there truly a relationship between city of residence and MEES in the populations under study, or would a second sample produce radically different main effects?

To test whether the effects of city of residence are real in these populations, we must provide a summary measure—a statistic—that accounts for variation in all cases. If there are real differences between group means, as a general rule, welfare-reliant

FIGURE 12–2

Comparison of the spread of score distributions when main effects of groups are large (*A*) and small (*B*)

(A) When means are significantly different: Main effects are relatively large; scores cluster around group means.

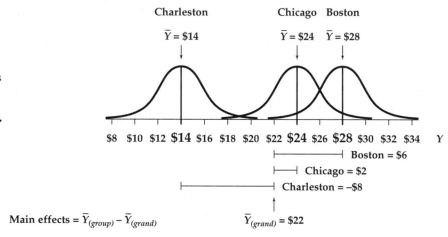

Main effects = $\bar{Y}_{(group)} - \bar{Y}_{(grand)}$

(B) When means are not significantly different: Main effects are relatively small; scores cluster around the grand mean.

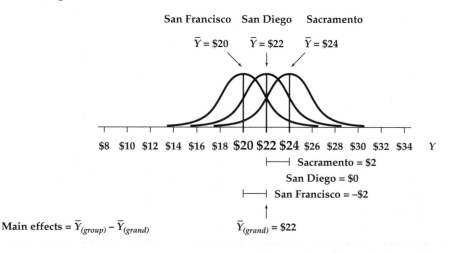

Main effects = $\bar{Y}_{(group)} - \bar{Y}_{(grand)}$

Boston mothers should have MEES about $6 above the grand mean. Similarly, the effects of Chicago and Charleston should be reflected in the pattern of MEES scores for subjects from those cities. With ANOVA, we are asserting that *the spread of scores*—Boston on the high end and Charleston on the low end—is due to the effects of residing in those different cities. The overall pattern of spread of scores should show a clustering of cases based on city of residence. This is depicted in Figure 12–2A, where the MEES scores of Charleston residents cluster $8 below the grand mean of $22 and those of Chicago and Boston residents cluster $2 above and $6 above, respectively.

When clustering does occur among cases from each city, as in Figure 12–2A, this indicates that the deviations of individual scores in a group (i.e., city) are due mostly to group membership. A group's cases vary about its group mean.

When clustering does not occur in a pattern related to group membership, as in Figure 12–2B, then scores simply vary around the grand mean. For example, suppose we are researching Sacramento, San Francisco, and San Diego, California, cities with similar economies and family assistance programs (fictional data). Deviations from the grand mean are random—occurring in either direction—uninfluenced by group membership. This is the pattern that occurs when the null hypothesis of no differences among these means is true. ANOVA is the statistical test that establishes whether the pattern of clustering is more like Figure 12–2A, with group scores bunched around different means, or Figure 12–2B, where all scores regardless of city of residence tend to cluster around the grand mean.

As the name implies, ANOVA focuses on the variances of scores. Recall once again (see Chapter 5) that a deviation score for an individual case is the difference between its score and the grand mean. To obtain a summary measure for the entire sample, however, we must square the deviation scores. This is the case because the sum of (nonsquared) deviations is always zero, as is the case in Table 12–1. The sum of squared deviation scores is the *variation,* or "sum of squares." Finally, recall that the *variance* is the variation divided by sample size to produce an average of the variation. Deviation scores, the variation, and the variance all gauge how scores are spread about the mean. ANOVA focuses on the variation and then the variance of the sample as a whole. It then establishes whether those measures of spread are explained by differences in mean MEES among the three cities or simply result from random sampling error.

Just as we decomposed Ms. Jones's deviation score, ANOVA summarizes the decomposition for the entire sample. Let us compare the individual decomposition to the summary decomposition:

Explaining the individual case as an effect of group membership:

$$\text{Ms. Jones's deviation score} = Y_{(Ms. Jones)} - \overline{Y}_{(grand)}$$
$$= (\overline{Y}_{(Boston)} - \overline{Y}_{(grand)}) + (Y_{(Ms. Jones)} - \overline{Y}_{(Boston)})$$

$$\uparrow \qquad\qquad\qquad\qquad \uparrow$$

Explained deviation   Unexplained deviation

Explaining the deviations of all cases taken together:

Total variation = total sum of squares

$$= \Sigma\,(Y_{(each\ case)} - \bar{Y}_{(grand)})^2$$

$$= \Sigma\,(\bar{Y}_{(group)} - \bar{Y}_{(grand)})^2 + \Sigma\,(Y_{(each\ case)} - \bar{Y}_{(group)})^2$$

$$\uparrow \qquad\qquad\qquad\qquad \uparrow$$

Explained variation   Unexplained variation

Note that in these summary measurements we calculate three types of sums of squares: the total sum of squares (SS_T), the between-group or "explained" sum of squares (SS_B), and the within-group or "unexplained" sum of squares (SS_W).

Types of Variation or "Sums of Squares"

SS_T = total variation = total sum of squares

$$= \Sigma(Y_{(each\ case)} - \bar{Y}_{(grand)})^2$$

SS_B = between-group sum of squares

$$= \Sigma(\bar{Y}_{(group)} - \bar{Y}_{(grand)})^2$$

= explained variation (i.e., that explained by group effects)

SS_W = within-group sum of squares

$$= \Sigma(Y_{(each\ case\ of\ group)} - \bar{Y}_{(group)})^2$$

= unexplained variation or error (i.e., variation not explained by group membership but by other unmeasured variables)

The calculations of the explained variation and the unexplained variation are made with the data in Tables 12–1 and 12–2. The *total variation,* or "total sum of squares" (SS_T), is the same calculation we made in Chapter 5 in calculating the standard deviation. For the data in Table 12–1, we see that SS_T is $694. For purposes of illustration, let us examine how this total accumulated:

$$SS_T = \Sigma\,(Y_{(each\ case)} - \bar{Y}_{grand})^2$$

```
            Boston                        Chicago
|---------------------------|    |------------------------------------|
```

$$= 11^2 + 8^2 + 6^2 + 4^2 + 1^2 + 4^2 + (-3)^2 + 2^2 + 0^2 + 7^2$$
$$+ (-8^2) + (-3^2) + (-6^2) + (-10^2) + (-13^2) = 694$$

```
      |-----------------------------------------------------|
                        Charleston
```

Note that Boston residents tend to deviate in the positive direction and that Charleston residents deviate in the negative direction.

The part of the SS_T explained by group effects (i.e., city of residence) is called the explained sum of squares. This is calculated as the sum of squared group effects. The explained sum of squares also is called the between-group sum of squares (SS_B), because it is due to differences between group means.

Because every individual within a group (i.e., city) has the same effect score, calculating the SS_B is rather straightforward. These are the test effects listed under column (B) for each city in Table 12–2. Thus, for all welfare-reliant mothers in Boston, the squared effect is $\$6^2$; for those in Chicago, it is $\$2^2$; and for those in Charleston, it is $-\$8^2$. Thus, for the whole sample, the computation of the explained sum of squares is

$$SS_B = \Sigma\,(\overline{Y}_{(group)} - \overline{Y}_{grand})^2$$

$$
\begin{array}{cc}
\text{Boston} & \text{Chicago} \\
|\text{---------------------------}| & |\text{---------------------------}|
\end{array}
$$

$$= 6^2 + 6^2 + 6^2 + 6^2 + 6^2 + 2^2 + 2^2 + 2^2 + 2^2 + 2^2$$
$$+ (-8)^2 + (-8^2) + (-8^2) + (-8^2) + (-8^2) = 520$$

$$|\text{--}|$$

$$\text{Charleston}$$

These calculations can be abbreviated since every case in a group has the same effect.

Calculating the Between-Group (or Explained) Sum of Squares (SS_B)

$$SS_B = \Sigma\,(\overline{Y}_{(group)} - \overline{Y}_{(grand)})^2 = \Sigma\,[(n_{(group)})\,(\text{effect of group}^2)]$$

where

SS_B = between-group (or explained) sum of squares

$\overline{Y}_{(group)}$ = mean of Y for a group or category of X

$\overline{Y}_{(grand)}$ = mean of Y for all scores in the sample

$n_{(group)}$ = number of cases in a group or category of X

Effect of group = $(\overline{Y}_{(group)} - \overline{Y}_{(grand)})$

Thus, for the sample of welfare-reliant mothers:

$$SS_B = \Sigma\,(\overline{Y}_{(group)} - \overline{Y}_{(grand)})^2 = \Sigma\,[(n_{(group)})\,(\text{effect of group}^2)]$$
$$= (5)\,(6^2) + (5)\,(2^2) + (5)\,(-8^2) = 180 + 20 + 320 = 520$$

In column (C) of Table 12–2, we list the part of each individual's Y-score that is not explained by city of residence. This is the within-group deviation, the difference between an individual's Y-score and the mean of that individual's group. These within-group deviations are also squared and summed to obtain the "within-group sum of squares," or SS_W. For the welfare-reliant mothers' MEES scores in Table 12–2,

Boston

$$SS_w = \Sigma(Y_{(each\ case\ of\ group)} - \overline{Y}_{(group)})^2 = 5^2 + 2^2 + 0^2 + (-2^2) + (-5^2)$$
$$+ 2^2 + (-5^2) + 0^2 + (-2^2) + 5^2 + 0^2 + 5^2 + 2^2 + (-2^2) + (-5^2) = 174$$

Chicago   Charleston

As we can see, calculation of the SS_W is somewhat cumbersome. However, there is a less complicated way to obtain this sum. Note that the between-group sum of squares and the within-group sum of squares are equal to the total sum of squares:

$$SS_T = SS_B + SS_W$$

That is, $694 = 520 + 174$. Therefore, once we have calculated the SS_T and SS_B, we can quickly compute the SS_W.

Calculation of the Within-Group (or Unexplained) Sum of Squares (SS$_W$)

$$SS_W = SS_T - SS_B$$

where

SS_W = within-group (or unexplained) sum of squares of Y
SS_T = total sum of squares (or variation) of Y
SS_B = between-group (or explained) sum of squares of Y

Thus, for the sample of welfare-reliant mothers,

$$SS_W = SS_T - SS_B = 694 - 520 = 174$$

What do the relative sizes of these sums tell us? If the group means differ, the effects of city of residence, and therefore the SS_B, will be large. How large is a statistically significant SS_B? In testing a null hypothesis of equal group means, it is not enough to simply observe the size of the SS_B, because that size depends greatly on the total number of cases in a sample (n). That is, regardless of whether group means differ, the more cases that are used in calculations, the greater will be all three types of sums of squares. Similarly, the number of groups (K) affects computations of the sums of squares; that is, the more groups being hypothesized, the more test effects to be computed, squared, and summed. Thus, we must account for sample size and the number of groups; therefore, variances are computed by dividing these sums of squares by their respective degrees of freedom. In ANOVA the resulting variances are called mean square variances. The between-group degrees of freedom (df_B) are $K - 1$; the within-group degrees of freedom (df_W) are $n - K$. The df_B is $K - 1$, because once the means and effects are calculated for all but one group, the last group's mean and effect are fixed. (Note in Table 12–2 that the effects sum to zero; if two effects are known, the other is mathematically fixed.) The df_W reflects the fact that when all but one case is known *within a group,* the last case is mathematically fixed. Thus, 1 degree of freedom is lost for each group. For the between-group sum of squares, the mean square variance is as follows:

Calculating the Mean Square Variance Between Groups (i.e., the Explained Variance)

$$MSV_B = \frac{SS_B}{df_B} = \frac{SS_B}{K - 1}$$

where

MSV_B = mean square variance between groups, or "explained variance"

SS_B = between-group sums of squares (i.e., the explained variation)

df_B = degrees of freedom between groups

K = number of groups being compared

For the sample of welfare-reliant mothers,

$$MSV_B = \frac{SS_B}{df_B} = \frac{SS_B}{K - 1} = \frac{520}{2} = 260$$

For the within-group sum of squares, the mean square variance within groups is as follows:

Calculating the Mean Square Variance Within Groups (i.e., the Unexplained Variance)

$$MSV_W = \frac{SS_W}{df_W} = \frac{SS_W}{n - K}$$

where

MSV_W = mean square variance within groups, or the "unexplained variance"

SS_W = within-group sums of squares (i.e., the explained variation)

df_W = degrees of freedom within groups

n = total sample size

K = number of groups being compared

For the sample of welfare-reliant mothers,

$$MSV_W = \frac{SS_W}{df_W} = \frac{SS_W}{n - K} = \frac{174}{12} = 14.50$$

The F-Ratio Test Statistic

In ANOVA, the test formula for computing the probability of sample outcomes involves taking the ratio of explained *mean square variance* to unexplained *mean square variance*. This is called the **F-ratio statistic**, and its formula is as follows:

Calculating the *F*-Ratio Statistic

$$F = \frac{MSV_B}{MSV_W}$$

where

$F = F$-ratio statistic

MSV_B = mean square variance between groups (or explained variance)

MSV_W = mean square variance within groups (or unexplained variance)

For the sample of welfare-reliant mothers,

$$F = \frac{MSV_B}{MSV_W} = \frac{260}{14.50} = 17.93$$

A computed F-ratio will always be positive because squaring the numerator and denominator eliminates negative signs. To organize these calculations, the F-ratio is commonly presented in a "source table" that distinguishes the between-group, within-group, and total sums of squares. Table 12–3 is the source table for the MEES of welfare-reliant mothers.

TABLE 12–3 | Analysis of variance source table for data in table 12–2

Source of Variation	SS	df	Mean Square Variance: MSV = SS/df	$F = \frac{MSV_B}{MSV_W}$
Between groups (SS_B)	520	$K - 1 = 2$	260	17.93
Within groups (SS_W)	174	$n - K = 12$	14.50	
Total (SS_T)	694	$n - 1 = 14$	49.57	

Just as *t*-tests measure the significance of test effects, the *F*-ratio gauges whether observed main effects of sampled group means are significantly different from zero, the hypothesized effects. When the main effects are large, the SS_B and the MSV_B are large. Since MSV_B is in the numerator, when it is large, the *F*-ratio statistic will be large. The larger the *F*-ratio, the greater the chance that the null hypothesis will be rejected. As we will demonstrate when we do ANOVA with the six steps of statistical inference, an *F*-ratio of 17.93 is quite large. We will conclude that there is a significant difference in the mean MEES of at least two cities.

How the F-Ratio Turns Out When Group Means Are Not Significantly Different

Before completing the hypothesis test for the sample of welfare-reliant mothers, let us get a better sense of proportion about ANOVA and the *F*-ratio. Let us examine the case where group means are found *not* to be significantly different. In other words, what is the value of *F* when the null hypothesis of equal population means is not rejected?

TABLE 12–4 I   Decomposition of effects of city of residence (*X*) on total monthly entertainment expenses [MEES (*Y*)] for the hypothetical example of insignificant group differences (welfare-reliant mothers, *n* = 15)

All Columns (A): Grand Mean $= \bar{Y}_{(grand)} = \dfrac{\Sigma Y}{n} = \dfrac{330}{15} = \$22$								

Sacramento			San Diego			San Francisco		
(A)	**(B)** Main Effect	**(C)**	**(A)**	**(B)** Main Effect	**(C)**	**(A)**	**(B)** Main Effect	**(C)**
$Y = \bar{Y}_{(grand)} +$	of *X*	+ error	$Y = \bar{Y}_{(grand)} +$	of *X*	+ error	$Y = \bar{Y}_{(grand)} +$	of *X*	+ error
$\$22 = 22 \ +$	2	$+ \ (-2)$	$\$27 = 22 \ +$	0	$+ \ 5$	$\$25 = 22 \ +$	(-2)	$+ \ 5$
$\$26 = 22 \ +$	2	$+ \ 2$	$\$24 = 22 \ +$	0	$+ \ 2$	$\$22 = 22 \ +$	(-2)	$+ \ 2$
$\$24 = 22 \ +$	2	$+ \ 0$	$\$22 = 22 \ +$	0	$+ \ 0$	$\$20 = 22 \ +$	(-2)	$+ \ 0$
$\$19 = 22 \ +$	2	$+ \ (-5)$	$\$20 = 22 \ +$	0	$+ \ (-2)$	$\$18 = 22 \ +$	(-2)	$+ \ (-2)$
$\$29 = 22 \ +$	2	$+ \ 5$	$\$17 = 22 \ +$	0	$+ \ (-5)$	$\$15 = 22 \ +$	(-2)	$+ \ (-5)$

$$\bar{Y}_{(Sacra.)} = \frac{\Sigma Y}{n} = \frac{120}{5} = \$24 \qquad \bar{Y}_{(Diego)} = \frac{\Sigma Y}{n} = \frac{110}{5} = \$22 \qquad \bar{Y}_{(Fran.)} = \frac{\Sigma Y}{n} = \frac{100}{5} = \$20$$

Column (B):	Column (B):	Column (B):
Between-group deviation = main effect for Sacramento	Between-group deviation = main effect for San Diego	Between-group deviation = main effect for San Francisco

$$\bar{Y}_{(Sacra.)} - \bar{Y}_{(grand)} = \$24 - \$22 = \$2 \qquad \bar{Y}_{(Diego)} - \bar{Y}_{(grand)} = \$22 - \$22 = \$0 \qquad \bar{Y}_{(Fran.)} - \bar{Y}_{(grand)} = \$20 - \$22 = -\$2$$

Column (C):	Column (C):	Column (C):
Within-group deviation = error	Within-group deviation = error	Within-group deviation = error
$= Y - \bar{Y}_{(Sacra.)}$	$= Y - \bar{Y}_{(Diego)}$	$= Y - \bar{Y}_{(Fran.)}$

TABLE 12–5 | Analysis of variance source table for data in table 12–4 where differences among means are not significant

Source of Variation	SS	df	Mean Square Variance: $MSV = SS/df$	$F = \dfrac{MSV_B}{MSV_W}$
Between groups (SS_B)	40	$K - 1 = 2$	20	1.38
Within groups (SS_W)	174	$n - K = 12$	14.50	
Total (SS_T)	214	$n - 1 = 14$	15.29	

Table 12–4 presents such a scenario for the fictional data from three California cities. For illustration purposes, the grand mean of MEES is still $22 but the group means are not significantly different from $22. Note in the distributions of MEES of the three groups that all scores are in a similar range, from the upper teens to upper twenties. The means are quite close, and this suggests that the scores may have come from the same population (e.g., a statewide sample of welfare-reliant mothers whose average MEES is $22). With these new data, the main effects of city of residence [columns (B)] are small compared to the within-group effects [columns (C)]. Table 12–5 presents the source table for the data in Table 12–4. With the small main effects, the F-ratio is only 1.38 compared to an F-ratio of 17.93 with the original data in Table 12–2.

The source table reveals that when the means are not significantly different, the between-group sum of squares (SS_B) is relatively small. This in turn results in a small F-ratio score. Note also that since all 15 scores are closely bunched together around the grand mean of $22, the total sum of squares is relatively small.

Return to Figure 12–2 above. Figure 12–2B provides a graphical illustration of the data in Table 12–4. The small main effects *in the sample* suggest that in fact the group *population means* are the same and are equal to the grand mean of $22. There is no clear clustering of scores. The minor differences in the California cities' mean MEES is due to sampling error.

The F-Ratio as a Sampling Distribution

As we have noted, the F-ratio is used to determine statistical significance with ANOVA. The F-ratio is a sampling distribution and can be depicted with a curve such as the one in Figure 12–3. With repeated sampling, the F-ratio can be calculated for all possible sampling outcomes *when the null hypothesis is true*. These outcomes are represented by the area under the curve, which, like the normal and t-distribution curves, totals to 1.00, or 100 percent. Note that the F-distribution curve is skewed and that all scores are positive. This is due to the squaring in the F-ratio equation.

With ANOVA, the null hypothesis is that group population means are equal. When the null hypothesis is indeed true and we sample repeatedly, sample group means will differ little and the computed main effects will be small. These small main effects—which are due to random sampling error—result in a small F-ratio calculation. In the F-distribution curve, this high frequency of small F-scores is apparent in the lumping

FIGURE 12–3

Critical values of the *F*-distribution for 2 and 12 degrees of freedom at the .05 and .01 levels of significance

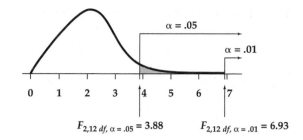

of sampling outcomes toward the low end of the curve (resulting in the right skew in Figure 12–3).

For our samples of welfare-reliant mothers, the null hypothesis is that mothers in Charleston, Chicago, and Boston all average the same MEES. If this is true, repeated sampling will provide a description of the sizes of sample means and differences of means that occur, say, 95 percent of the time. With repeated sampling, sometimes Boston will come out slightly on top as we frame our illustrations. Other times, Charleston or Chicago will have slightly larger *sample* means. If the null hypothesis of no difference in means is true, most of the time all three group means will be close to the grand mean (as was the case of the three California cities). As we repeatedly calculate main effects, sums of squares, and *F*-ratios, the results will show that the distribution of *F*-ratios has a lower limit of zero and no upper limit.

We have noted, however, that the size of the *F*-ratio is influenced by degrees of freedom—sample size and the number of groups. Thus, a sampling distribution of *F*-ratios is shaped in accordance with its degrees of freedom. Statistical Tables D and E in Appendix B present *F*-ratio values for specified degrees of freedom for the .05 and .01 levels of significance, respectively. The bodies of the tables provide critical values of the *F*-ratio. Across the top are degrees of freedom for the MSV_B, the numerator of the *F*-ratio. Down the left side are degrees of freedom for the MSV_W, the denominator of the *F*-ratio. The *F*-ratio values in the table are like *t*-scores; they are critical values of *F* for the .05 and .01 levels of significance. For example, for our data in Tables 12–2 and 12–4, we have $(K - 1) = 2$ degrees of freedom between groups and $(n - K) = 12$ degrees of freedom within groups. From Statistical Table D, the critical *F*-ratio value for 2 and 12 degrees of freedom at the .05 level is

$$\text{Critical } F_{2,\ 12\ df,\ \alpha\ =\ .05} = 3.88$$

This means that when the null hypothesis of equal group means is true, with repeated sampling, calculations of the *F*-ratio will equal or exceed 3.88 only 5 percent of the time. From Statistical Table E in Appendix B, the corresponding critical value of the *F*-ratio at the .01 level of significance is 6.93. Figure 12–3 identifies the critical regions and illustrates the shape of the *F*-ratio distribution for 2 and 12 degrees of freedom.

For our original data in Table 12–2, we obtained an *F*-ratio of 17.93. This is larger than the critical value of the *F*-ratio at the .01 level, a value of 6.93. Thus, for step 4 of the six steps of statistical inference, the calculated *p*-value would be $p < .01$. And if we are testing at the .05 level of significance, the statistical hypothesis is rejected because

$$|F_{observed}| > |F_{\alpha}| \text{ (i.e., } 17.93 > 3.88)$$

Thus, $p < \alpha$ (i.e., $p < .05$).

However, for our hypothetical example of no significant differences (Tables 12–4 and 12–5), we would fail to reject the null hypothesis because

$$|F_{observed}| < |F_{\alpha}| \text{ (i.e., } 1.39 < 3.88)$$

Thus, $p > \alpha$ (i.e., $p > .05$).

These "nonsignificant" data illustrate that it is not unusual in repeated sampling to get main effects of $2, $0, and −$2 when there are indeed no differences among three population means.

Relevant Aspects of a Relationship for ANOVA

Existence of the Relationship

The existence of the relationship for ANOVA is determined by using the F-ratio to test the null hypothesis of equal group means, as was just described. (The complete six steps of statistical inference are presented later.) The alternative hypothesis is that the group means are not equal. If the null hypothesis is rejected and the alternative hypothesis is accepted, there is a relationship between city of residence and MEES.

Existence of a Relationship using ANOVA

Test the null hypothesis:

$$H_0: \overline{Y}_{(group\ 1)} = \overline{Y}_{(group\ 2)} = \overline{Y}_{(group\ 3)} = \cdots = \overline{Y}_{(grand)}$$

and therefore main effects = 0. That is, there is no relationship between X and Y. Use the F-ratio test statistic:

$$F = \frac{MSV_B}{MSV_W}$$

Direction of the Relationship

Keep in mind that we address the direction, strength, and nature of a relationship between variables only when that relationship exists. Since the independent variable in ANOVA is typically of the nominal level of measurement, direction is meaningless. For example, it is meaningless to say that Ms. Jones is more in the direction of Boston than in that of Chicago or Charleston. Either she is from Boston or she is not. This absence of meaning for direction also is implied by the fact that the F-ratio statistic is always one-tailed yet nondirectional, because its calculations involve squaring away negative signs. Thus, a correct way to report the direction of an ANOVA test is to say that it is not applicable.

> **direction of a relationship using ANOVA**   Not applicable.

Strength of the Relationship

With ANOVA, if a relationship is found in a sample, this simply indicates that the main effects are significantly different from zero in the population. The strength of the relationship lies in the separate question: How large are these main effects in practical terms? Do the group means in the population differ only a little or a lot? For example, if city of residence is related to MEES, does this improve our understanding and prediction of MEES a little or a lot?

A strong relationship is one in which knowing group main effects allows us to make very precise predictions of the dependent variable. For example, suppose all welfare-reliant mothers in Boston spend exactly \$28 on MEES, all in Chicago spend exactly \$24, and all in Charleston spend exactly \$14. The variances or spreads of scores around group means (i.e., the within-group variances) would be zero. Knowing city of residence would be a perfect predictor of MEES, and there would be no error in predictions of an individual welfare-reliant mother's MEES. In such an unlikely case, if we are given a mother's city of residence, we can perfectly predict her MEES: The main effects will explain all the total variance in MEES. A strong relationship is one in which a high proportion of the total variance in the dependent, interval/ratio variable is accounted for by the group variable.

There are several measures of the strength of the relationship for ANOVA, but often none is reported because each one must be used with caution. Any single measure may be biased by sample size and other issues related to sampling error. One conservative measure, however, is the *correlation ratio,* ε^2 (pronounced "epsilon squared") (Blalock 1979: 373–74). Keeping in mind that we are using sample data, ε^2 is conservative in that it is unlikely to overinflate the strength of the relationship in the population. The correlation ratio is a proportional reduction in error (PRE) measure. It provides a sense of how much more accurately the dependent variable (in this case MEES) can be predicted by using knowledge of the independent variable (in this case city of residence). Its formula is as follows:

Calculating the Correlation Ratio ε^2 to Measure the Strength of a Relationship Using ANOVA

$$\varepsilon^2 = 1 - \frac{MSV_W}{MSV_T}$$

where

ε^2 = correlation ratio of the strength of the relationship

MSV_T = total mean square variance

MSV_W = mean square variance within groups (or unexplained variance)

Note that this formula does not measure the proportion of explained variance (i.e., MSV_B) directly because the MSV_B depends heavily on the number of groups used in its calculation. Instead, it treats a proportion of 1 (or 100 percent) as the total variance to be explained and subtracts from it the proportion that is unexplained (i.e., MSV_W/MSV_T). Moreover, with this formula, the correlation ratio ε^2 has defined limits; it ranges from 0 to 1.00 and thus is always positive. When the main effects of city of residence completely explain variance in MEES, within-group effects will be 0, leaving MSV_W at 0 and producing an ε^2 of 1:

$$\varepsilon^2 = 1 - \frac{MSV_W}{MSV_T} = 1 - \frac{0}{MSV_T} = 1 - 0 = 1$$

At the other extreme, when group effects are 0, the unlikely case in which all the subjects score the grand mean of $22 on MEES, the MSV_B will be 0. This will leave the MSV_W equal to the MSV_T. Thus,

$$\varepsilon^2 = 1 - \frac{MSV_W}{MSV_T} = 1 - 1 = 0$$

In real situations, we seldom have perfect relationships between variables. An ε^2 will fall between 0 and 1.00, and the larger it is, the stronger the relationship is. For instance, using data from Table 12–3, the source table for our sample of welfare-reliant mothers,

$$\varepsilon^2 = 1 - \frac{MSV_W}{MSV_T} = 1 - \frac{14.50}{49.57} = 1 - .2935 = .7065$$

As a percentage, this is $(.7065)(100) = 70.65$ percent. We conclude that 70.65 percent of the variance in MEES is explained by city of residence. Unfortunately, the interpretation of ε^2 must be made with caution. *In fact, it should not be computed and reported unless all groups have about the same number of cases and the variances within each group are about the same.*

Strength of a Relationship Using ANOVA

Calculate the percent of the variance in Y explained by knowledge of X by using the correlation ratio:

$$\varepsilon^2 = 1 - \frac{MSV_W}{MSV_T}$$

Practical Applications of the Relationship

If a relationship between variables is found to exist, we may describe its practical applications. We focus on substance—welfare-reliant mothers, their cities of residence, and

TABLE 12–6 I Tree diagram of differences between means for range test comparisons

Group Means		Differences
$\bar{Y}_{(Charleston)} = \$14$		
	$\$10$	$\$14$
$\bar{Y}_{(Chicago)} = \$24$		
	$\$4$	
$\bar{Y}_{(Boston)} = \$28$		

their MEES—and provide best estimates of the dependent variable. Simply put, how does knowledge of a relationship between city of residence and MEES lead to improved predictions of the MEES of welfare-reliant mothers?

First, we make best estimates at the group level by reporting the grand mean, group means, and main effects. Second, we provide examples of best estimates for individuals. Finally, we specify which group means are significantly different from others. This requires the additional computation of what is called a range test.

Range Tests   Range tests are a necessary additional step with ANOVA because with ANOVA the rejection of the null hypothesis merely indicates that *at least two* of the group means are significantly different from each other. Especially in dealing with a large number of groups, range tests provide a quicker way than do a series of *t*-tests to identify which group means are significantly different from others.

A range test determines how much of a difference between means (i.e., a range of differences) is statistically significant. If the sample sizes and standard deviations of group means are not very different, we can start by assuming that the smallest and largest group means are significantly different—for the MEES example, those of Charleston and Boston. But perhaps other differences are also significant, such as that between Charleston and Chicago. A range test tells us how far apart two group means must be before we can assume that they are different in the populations. Range tests are also called multiple comparison tests.

There are several range tests. A conservative one is Tukey's highly significant difference formula, the HSD (Tukey 1953). The HSD formula is conservative because it is unlikely to mistakenly tell us that a difference exists when in fact it does not.

Since range tests compare each group to the others, we start by constructing a tree diagram that orders the means from lowest to highest and indicates the differences between group means (Table 12–6). In Table 12–6 we see that the difference between Charleston and Chicago is $10, that between Charleston and Boston is $14, and that between Chicago and Boston is $4. The HSD tells us exactly how large the difference between two sample means must be for us to assume that a difference truly exists between the means of the two populations. For instance, is a $4 difference statistically significant? The HSD formula is as follows:

Calculating Tukey's Highly Significant Difference (HSD) Range Test

$$HSD = q\sqrt{\frac{MSV_W}{n_{(per\ group)}}}$$

where

HSD = highly significant difference range test value: how large the difference between two sample means must be for us to assume that the difference truly exists between the population means

q = a critical value of the range test from Statistical Table F in Appendix B for a specified level of significance and degrees of freedom

MSV_W = mean square variance within groups

$n_{(per\ group)}$ = sample size of the groups (assuming sample n's are equal); if the sample sizes are not the same for all groups, complicated calculations must be made to arrive at an average group size

Degrees of Freedom (for Use with Statistical Table F in Appendix B)

df for the $MSV_W = n_{(total)} - K$ (listed down the left side of Statistical Table F)

where

$n_{(total)}$ = total sample size

K = number of groups

df for $n_{(per\ group)} = K$ (listed across the top of the Statistical Table F as "number of groups")

where

K = number of groups

Statistical Table F in Appendix B provides the values of q—critical values for the .05 and .01 levels of significance. To obtain q for the problem at hand, let us choose the .05 level of significance. We calculated degrees of freedom for the MSV_W when we did the F-ratio test, and in this case there are 12. There are 3 degrees of freedom for $n_{(per\ group)}$. Observing the table, for 12 and 3 degrees of freedom, the q-value is 3.77. The calculation of HSD then is

$$HSD = q\sqrt{\frac{MSV_W}{n_{(per\ group)}}} = 3.77\sqrt{\frac{14.50}{5}} = 6.42$$

Thus, a difference of at least $6.42 between any two means is statistically significant. From Table 12–6 we see that the mean MEES is significantly different between Charleston and Chicago (i.e., $10 > $6.42) and between Charleston and Boston (i.e., $14 > $6.42). The mean MEES of Chicago and Boston are not significantly different (i.e., $4 < $6.42). With the calculation of the range test, we have everything we need to address the practical applications of the relationship between city of residence and MEES. Now let us follow the six steps of statistical inference.

Practical Applications of a Relationship Using ANOVA

1. Provide best estimates of the grand mean, group means, and main effects.

2. Provide examples of best estimates of Y for individual cases in the population:

$$Y'_{(each\ case)} = \bar{Y}_{(grand)} + \text{(explained) effect of } X$$

$$= \bar{Y}_{(grand)} + \text{main effect of the } X\text{-group}$$

3. Use range tests to determine which group means are significantly different from one another.

The Six Steps of Statistical Inference for One-Way ANOVA

Now that we have acquired a sense of the logic of one-way ANOVA, let us follow the six steps of statistical inference. First we review the criteria for selecting ANOVA.

When to Use One-Way Analysis of Variance (ANOVA) to Test Differences of Means Among Three or More Groups (F-distribution)

In general: Testing a hypothesis between a nominal/ordinal independent variable with three or more categories and an interval/ratio dependent variable.

1. Number of variables, samples, and populations: (*a*) One population with a single interval/ratio dependent variable, comparing means for three or more

groups of a single nominal/ordinal independent variable. Each group's sample must be representative of its subpopulation. Or, (*b*) a single interval/ratio dependent variable whose mean is compared for three or more populations using representative samples.

2. Sample size. Generally no requirements. However, the dependent interval/ratio variable should not be highly skewed within any group sample. Moreover, range tests are unreliable unless the sample sizes of groups are about equal. These restrictions are less important when group sample sizes are large.

3. Variances (and standard deviations) of the groups are equal. This is the same constraint used for the *t*-test (see the material on equality of variances in Chapter 11).

The requirement of equality of variances is necessary in any difference of means test, including the *t*-test and the *F*-ratio test. A large spread of scores in one group may mislead us into believing that a difference of means exists when in fact this is not the case. Recall from Chapter 11 that when there is a large difference between group variances (and therefore between the standard deviations), degrees of freedom must be adjusted. With ANOVA this is a difficult chore that is best left to a computer. Fortunately, however, with ANOVA and the *F*-ratio test, if the samples are large (each group > 30), unequal variances are less likely to affect the results of the test.

Brief Checklist for the Six Steps of Statistical Inference

TEST PREPARATION
State the research question. Draw conceptual diagrams depicting givens, including the population(s) and sample(s) under study, variables (e.g., $X = \ldots , Y = \ldots ,$) and their levels of measurement, and given or calculated statistics and parameters. State the proper statistical test procedure.

SIX STEPS
Using the symbol *H* for *hypothesis:*

1. State the H_0 and the H_A and stipulate test direction.
2. Describe the sampling distribution.
3. State the level of significance (α) and test direction and specify the critical test score.
4. Observe the actual sample outcomes and compute the test effects, the test statistic, and *p*-value.
5. Make the rejection decision.
6. Interpret and apply the results and provide best estimates in everyday terms.

Solution for One-Way Analysis of Variance (ANOVA; *F*-distribution)

TEST PREPARATION

Research question: Is there a relationship between city of residence and monthly entertainment expenses (MEES)? That is, are there significant differences among the mean MEES of welfare-reliant mothers in Boston, Chicago, and Charleston? *Givens:* Variables: Y = MEES, the dependent variable, ratio level; X = city of residence, a nominal variable with three categories. *Population:* welfare-reliant mothers in three cities. *Sample:* n = 15 welfare-reliant mothers in Boston (n = 5), Chicago (n = 5), and Charleston (n = 5). *Statistical procedure:* One-way ANOVA, *F*-test of difference among three or more sample means; assumes equal variances of MEES in the subpopulations of the cities. *Observation:* Data in Table 12–1. The research question is depicted in Figure 12–1.

SIX STEPS

1. H_0: $\mu_{Y(Boston)} = \mu_{Y(Chicago)} = \mu_{Y(Charleston)} = \mu_{Y(grand)}$
   Therefore, main effects = 0.
   That is, there is no relationship between city of residence and MEES.

   H_A: $\mu_{Y(Boston)} \neq \mu_{Y(Chicago)} \neq \mu_{Y(Charleston)} \neq \mu_{Y(grand)}$
   Therefore, main effects $\neq$ 0.
   That is, there is a relationship between city of residence and MEES. Nondirectional.

2. *Sampling distribution:* If the H_0 is true and samples of size 5 are drawn repeatedly from the populations of welfare-reliant mothers in the three cities, the sampling distribution will take the shape of the *F*-distribution with

$$df_B = K - 1 = 3 - 1 = 2$$

and

$$df_W = n - K = 15 - 3 = 12$$

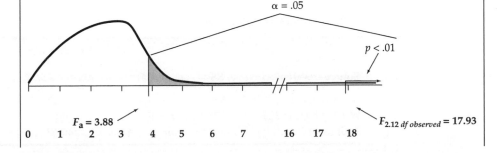

3. *Level of significance:* $\alpha = .05$ (nondirectional). Critical $F_\alpha = 3.88$ (for 2 and 12 df, from Statistical Table D in Appendix B). (Mark area on curve.)

4. *Observations:* From spreadsheet in Table 12–1.

Test effects: First, calculate means and the total variation:

$$\text{Grand mean} = \overline{Y}_{(grand)} = \$22$$

Group means:

$$\overline{Y}_{(Boston)} = \$28 \quad \overline{Y}_{(Chicago)} = \$24 \quad \overline{Y}_{(Charleston)} = \$14$$

$$\text{Total variation} = SS_T = \Sigma\,(Y_{(each\ case)} - \overline{Y}_{(grand)})^2 = 694$$

Second, calculate main effects:

$$\text{Main effect for Boston} = \overline{Y}_{(Boston)} - \overline{Y}_{(grand)} = \$28 - \$22 = \$6$$

$$\text{Main effect for Chicago} = \overline{Y}_{(Chicago)} - \overline{Y}_{(grand)} = \$24 - \$22 = \$2$$

$$\text{Main effect for Charleston} = \overline{Y}_{(Charleston)} - \overline{Y}_{(grand)} = \$14 - \$22 = -\$8$$

Third, calculate between-group and within-group sums of squares:

$$\text{Between-group sum of squares} = SS_B = \Sigma\,(\overline{Y}_{(group)} - \overline{Y}_{(grand)})^2$$
$$= \Sigma\,[(n_{(group)})\,(\text{effect of group}^2)]$$
$$= (5)(6)^2 + (5)(2^2) + (5)(-8^2)$$
$$= 180 + 20 + 320 = 520$$

$$\text{Within-group sum of squares} = SS_W = SS_T - SS_B = 694 - 520 = 174$$

Fourth, calculate mean square variances (using degrees of freedom from step 2):

$$\text{Mean square variance between groups} = MSV_B = \frac{SS_B}{K-1} = \frac{520}{2} = 260$$

$$\text{Mean square variance within groups} = MSV_W = \frac{SS_W}{n-K} = \frac{174}{12} = 14.5$$

Fifth, calculate the test statistic:

$$\text{Test statistic} = F = \frac{MSV_B}{MSV_W} = \frac{260}{14.50} = 17.93$$

Sixth, summarize in a source table:

Source of Variation	SS	df	Mean Square Variance: $MSV = SS/df$	$F = \dfrac{MSV_B}{MSV_W}$
Between groups (SS_B)	520	$K - 1 = 2$	260	17.93
Within groups (SS_W)	174	$n - K = 12$	14.50	
Total (SS_T)	694	$n - 1 = 14$	49.57	

Seventh, compute the *p*-value (using Statistical Tables D and E in Appendix B): *p-value: p* [main effects as unusual as or more unusual than those observed when in fact there are no differences among group means] $< .01$. (This *p*-value is noted on the curve in step 2.)

5. *Rejection decision:* $|F_{observed}| > |F_\alpha|$ (i.e., $17.93 > 3.88$)

   Thus, $p < \alpha$ (i.e., $p < .05$). Reject the H_0 and accept the H_A at the 95 percent level of confidence.

6. *Interpretation:* Aspects of relationship and best estimates.

   Existence: There is a relationship between city of residence and MEES; *F*-ratio $= 17.93$; $p < .01$.
   Direction: Not applicable.
   Strength:

   $$\varepsilon^2 = 1 - \frac{MSV_W}{MSV_T} = 1 - \frac{14.50}{49.57} = 1 - .2935 = .7065$$

   $(.7065)(100) = 70.65$ percent.
   Thus, 70.65 percent of the variance in MEES is explained by knowledge of city of residence.

   Practical Applications:

   a. Means and main effects: grand mean $= \$22$; group means: Boston $= \$28$, Chicago $= \$24$, and Charleston $= \$14$. Main effects: Boston $= \$6$, Chicago $= \$2$, Charleston $= -\$8$.

   b. Best estimate of the MEES of a welfare-reliant mother is

   $$Y'_{(each\ case)} = \overline{Y}_{(grand)} + (\text{explained}) \text{ effect of } X$$
   $$= \$22 + \text{main effect of the } X\text{-group}$$

   (where Y' is a calculated estimate of Y).

   For example, the best estimate of MEES for Ms. Jones of Boston is $\$22$ + effect of Boston $= \$22 + \$6 = \$28$.

   c. Range test: The mean MEES of welfare-reliant mothers in Charleston is significantly different from those of mothers in Boston and Chicago (based on Tukey's HSD and Table 12–6).

   Answer to research question: There is a relationship between city of residence and monthly entertainment expenses among welfare-reliant mothers. Welfare-reliant mothers in Boston and Chicago have higher average monthly entertainment expenses than do those in Charleston.

TABLE 12–7 | Monthly welfare incomes, selected monthly expenses, and budget deficits of welfare-reliant mothers in three cities

Average Monthly Expenses/Income	Boston n = 75	Chicago n = 75	Charleston n = 75	Significance
Mean monthly welfare income	$696	$599	$493	†
Mean total expenses	$927	$1,003	$891	†
Housing	239	289	224	†
Food	217	288	249	†
Other essential expenses	372	365	372	*
Entertainment	28	24	14	†
Other nonessential expenses	70	37	31	†
Mean monthly budget deficit	−$231	−$404	−$398	†

Note: Expenses are in 1991 dollars. Subcategories may not sum to total because of rounding error.

* $p < .05$

† $p < .01$

Nondirectional F-tests of differences between means.

Source: Modified from Edin and Lein (1997). Reprinted with permission from the American Sociological Association.

Tabular Presentation of Results

In a real-life study such as that of Edin and Lein (1997), the results of ANOVA can be presented to public or professional audiences in a format like that of Table 12–7. This format highlights a comparison of groups, and the table includes several dependent variables. Groups are listed across the top, and variables are listed down the left column. Although some of the figures correspond to those of Edin and Lein, Table 12–7 uses fictitious data.

Multivariate Applications of the General Linear Model

Although the calculations are beyond the scope of this text, it is worthwhile to point out how useful the general linear model is for proportional reduction in error when several independent variables are used to explain a dependent interval/ratio variable. Each additional independent variable increases the precision of best estimates of the dependent variable and reduces predictive error. Suppose, for example, we have additional data on Ms. Jones, the welfare-reliant mother in Boston. We find that she has no personal transportation and that her children are big eaters, two variables known to affect a household's MEES. She has an especially high MEES. With the additional data, we explain this high Y-score as follows:

$$Y_{(Ms. Jones)} = \overline{Y}_{(grand)} + [Y_{Ms. Jones} - \overline{Y}_{(grand)}]$$
$$= \overline{Y}_{(grand)} + \text{effect of } X_1 + \text{effect of } X_2 + \text{effect of } X_3 + \text{error}$$

That is,

$$\$33 = \$22 + \$6 + \$2 + \$1 + \$2$$
$$= \$22 + \$9 + \$2$$

where Y = MEES; X_1 = city of residence, main effect of Boston = $6; X_2 = personal transportation, main effect of having none = $2; and X_3 = children are big eaters, main effect of yes = $1. These effects combined account for $9 of her $11 deviation above the grand mean. Only $2 of Ms. Jones's MEES of $33 is left unexplained. Ideally, if all the variables that affect MEES are identified, we can perfectly explain and predict every welfare-reliant mother's MEES, thereby reducing predictive error to zero.

When we have more than one predictor variable to consider, the strength of a relationship becomes especially important. By comparing the strengths of various relationships, we establish which predictor variables are better. We found that city of residence improves predictions of MEES, but there may be other variables that characterize welfare-reliant mother's lives that are better at improving predictions. For example, MEES may be related to income, amount of assistance received from the state, health insurance coverage, and other benefits. As we have noted, the calculation of strength of relationship for city of residence in predicting MEES is not especially valuable by itself. The correlation ratio, ε^2 is most useful when it is computed and compared for several independent variables.

Multivariate analysis also takes into account interrelationships among independent variables. Suppose, for instance, that not only Ms. Jones but nearly all the Boston mothers lack transportation. This effect is already combined in the $6 effect of Boston. Multivariate analysis helps separate out the test effects of various independent variables even when some are related to others.

Similarities Between the *t*-Test and the *F*-Ratio Test

Both the *t*-test and the *F*-ratio test compare group means. In fact, even a two-group comparison of means can be tested with the *F*-ratio statistic instead of a *t*-test. As we have emphasized in this chapter, the *F*-ratio test weighs explained variance against unexplained variance:

$$F = \frac{\text{explained variance}}{\text{unexplained variance}}$$

When the null hypothesis is true (i.e., there is no significant difference between means), the unexplained variance in the denominator is essentially a standard error. It describes the variance in sampling error that can be expected when the independent variable has no effect. Similarly, in the *t*-test, the denominator of the test statistic is a standard error that describes variation in error when the null hypothesis is true. Moreover, variation in differences between means are calculated in the numerator of both tests, although in slightly different ways. These mathematical similarities are such that an *F*-ratio test *for a two-group comparison* is equal to the square of *t*-test results, and therefore, *t* is equal to the square root of the *F*-ratio. Thus,

$$F = t^2 \qquad t = \sqrt{F}$$

This consistency between measures also reveals that the F-ratio distribution is another approximately normal one, reflecting the natural tendency for sampling outcomes to take a predictable shape.

Statistical Follies and Fallacies: Individualizing Group Findings

Comparing means from several groups is very informative. Care must be taken, however, to remember that the results are statistical generalizations—statements that apply to populations and subgroups, not to individuals (see Chapter 2). Our analysis focuses on averages between groups. We should avoid treating the results in a stereotypical fashion by assuming, for instance, that every welfare-reliant mother in Boston spends more than does every mother in the other cities. In fact, for the individual scores in Table 12–1, one of the mothers in Charleston had the same MEES as did one in Chicago. Although the means are significantly different, there is some overlap in the score distributions of the three cities. Statistical analysis is more aptly applied to groups than to individuals.

The statistical imagination emphasizes seeing the broad picture—seeing the forest (the group) as well as the trees (individuals). Analyzing a single hypothesis, alone and outside the context of a broader theory, is only a preliminary step toward understanding. Multivariate analysis, the next stage of study beyond this course, is essential to gaining a complete understanding. When other variables are considered and controlled, the focus shifts from individuals to larger social systems. For instance, the results of our ANOVA of MEES, when coupled with other results, tell us as much about the cities as they do about the welfare-reliant residents. Note, for example, that in Table 12–7, in addition to expenses, we included monthly incomes and budget deficits (the shortfall between expenses and incomes). The total expenses are low for Charleston, but so is total welfare income. We could hypothesize that the low MEES of Charleston mothers is a combination of lower-cost entertainment and less income to spend on it. How much a mother spends on entertainment may have little to do with her attitudes toward having fun or her frugality in managing the family's meager budget. Instead, the differences we found among the three cities may have to do with the characteristics of the cities, not those of the mothers.

Another issue related to correct interpretation is avoiding the "ecological fallacy." This is the mistake of drawing conclusions about individual behavior on the basis of an analysis of groups such as families, communities, states, and nations. Ecology is the study of the environment, the reality outside individual human beings. Ecological analysis produces conclusions about these large entities, not necessarily about the individuals who compose them. Emile Durkheim, one of the first scientifically oriented sociologists, did an excellent ecological study of suicide rates over a hundred years ago (Durkheim 1951 [1897]). He found that predominantly Catholic counties in Europe had lower suicide rates than did predominantly Protestant counties. A first look at these data suggests that (1) Catholics commit suicide at a lower rate and (2) religious prohibitions against suicide in Catholic theology discourage this action. These conclusions, however, focus on individual choice, and they may be fallacious or wrong. In fact, it could be that Catholics actually commit suicide at a higher rate. Perhaps Catholics in predominantly Protestant counties commit suicide to escape oppression. The low suicide rates in the Catholic counties may simply indicate lack of oppression.

To avoid the ecological fallacy, Durkheim carefully interpreted his findings and focused on the social systems of the counties, not the individual characteristics of suicide victims. Through careful control of many variables, Durkheim's study avoids the ecological fallacy. He made a convincing argument that suicide rates are influenced not so much by the perspective of individuals but by the social systems in which individuals reside. He argued that Catholic religion, with its emphasis on community interests over those of individuals, encouraged social solidarity and provided a social support network that assisted individuals in hard times. His main point was that suicide is not an individual act but a social phenomenon.

The statistical imagination requires that conclusions always take into account the bigger picture. Stereotypical conclusions must be avoided. Statistical generalizations must be interpreted for what they are: averages, summary statements about a group or category of people. ANOVA, with its emphasis on variance both between and within groups, clearly reveals that an average is only one aspect of basic statistical work. Individuals vary around averages, and to ignore this variation is to be statistically unimaginative.

SUMMARY

1. Analysis of variance (ANOVA) is used to compare three or more group means. Instead of comparing each group mean to the others (as you would in a t-test), ANOVA compares each group mean to the grand mean, which is the mean for all cases in the sample.

2. In ANOVA, the differences between each group mean and the grand mean are the test effects, which are called main effects. When the main effects are zero, there are no differences among the means. In the hypothesis test, the null hypothesis states that the means are equal, which is to say that main effects are equal to zero.

3. ANOVA hypothesizes about differences among means but its calculation is based on explaining variance around the grand mean. Recall that the difference between an individual score and the grand mean is a deviation score. ANOVA determines whether it is feasible to say that part of an individual's deviation score can be explained by the individual's membership in a category (group) of the independent variable. Thus, the focus with ANOVA is on explaining deviation scores. Recall that deviation scores are squared and averaged to obtain the variance. Hence the name "analysis of variance."

4. The general linear model states that the best prediction of any dependent variable, Y, is its overall mean plus an adjustment for the effects of an

independent variable, X. An individual's score is decomposed as follows: $Y =$ the grand mean plus the explained effect of a category of X plus unexplained error. These individual parts of a score are squared, summed, and averaged by degrees of freedom to obtain variances for all cases. The ratio of the explained to the unexplained variance comprises the F-ratio, which is the test statistic for ANOVA. The calculations for ANOVA are conveniently summarized in a "source table."

5. The p-value is determined using F-distribution curves, Appendix B, Tables D and E.

6. Relevant aspects of the relationship for ANOVA: (a) Existence is determined by using the F-ratio to test the null hypothesis of equal group means. When the H_0 is rejected, a relationship exists. (b) Direction is not applicable (because the independent variable is nominal). (c) Strength is established with the correlation ratio, ε^2 (epsilon squared). A strong relationship is one in which a high proportion of the total variance in the dependent interval/ratio variable is accounted for by the group variable. (d) Practical applications are described with (i) best estimates at the group level by reporting the grand mean, group means, and main effects; (ii) providing examples of best estimates for individuals; and (iii) using range tests to specify which group means are significantly different from others.

7. With ANOVA, rejection of the null hypothesis merely indicates that at least two of the group means are significantly different. Range tests determine specifically which two or more means differ. Range tests establish how much of a difference between means is statistically significant. Of several available range tests, a conservative one is Tukey's Highly Significant Difference (HSD).

8. The ecological fallacy is the mistake of drawing conclusions about individual behavior on the basis of an analysis of groups. Because an individual belongs to a group with a certain mean, this does not mean that every individual fits this score. Sample statistics apply to the group and to apply them to an individual is to stereotype.

CHAPTER EXTENSIONS ON *THE STATISTICAL IMAGINATION* WEB SITE

Chapter 12 Extensions of text material available on *The Statistical Imagination* Web site at www.mhhe.com/ritchey2 include a brief introduction to multivariate ANOVA, which is called *N*-way ANOVA.

STATISTICAL PROCEDURES COVERED
TO THIS POINT

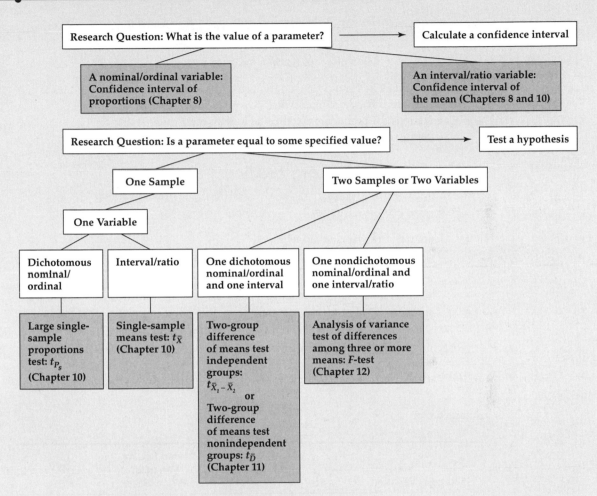

FORMULAS FOR CHAPTER 12

One-way analysis of variance (ANOVA), F-test of difference of means among three or more groups:

Given: An interval/ratio dependent variable Y compared for three or more groups obtained from either (1) the categories of a nominal/ordinal variable X from one sample and population or (2) three or more populations and samples.

Research question: Are the means of Y in the populations of the groups different?

$$H_0: \mu_{Y_1} = \mu_{Y_2} = \mu_{Y_3} = \ldots = \mu_{Y(grand)}$$

Sampling distribution: F-distribution with $df_B = K - 1$ and $df_W = n - K$
Test effects: Calculate main effects:

$$\text{Main effect of a group mean} = \overline{Y}_{(group)} - \overline{Y}_{(grand)}$$

Test statistic: The F-ratio statistic [for use with the F-table (Statistical Tables D and E in Appendix B); determines whether a relationship exists]:
Calculations for producing a source table with the F-ratio statistic:
Calculating sums of squares:

$$SS_T = \Sigma\, [Y_{(each\ case)} - \overline{Y}_{grand}]^2$$
$$SS_B = \Sigma\, (\overline{Y}_{(group)} - \overline{Y}_{(grand)})^2 = \Sigma\, [(n_{(group)})\, (\text{effect of group}^2)]$$
$$SS_W = SS_T - SS_B$$

Calculating mean square variances:

$$MSV_B = \frac{SS_B}{df_B} = \frac{SS_B}{K - 1}$$

$$MSV_W = \frac{SS_W}{df_W} = \frac{SS_W}{n - K}$$

The F-ratio statistic itself:

$$F = \frac{MSV_B}{MSV_W}$$

Source table:

Source of Variation	SS	df	Mean Square Variance: $MSV = SS/df$	$F = \dfrac{MSV_B}{MSV_W}$
Between groups	SS_B	$K - 1$	MSV_B	
Within groups	SS_W	$n - K$	MSV_W	$F = \dfrac{MSV_B}{MSV_W}$
Total	SS_T	$n - 1$	MSV_T	

Addressing the aspects of a relationship:
Existence: the F-ratio test
Direction: usually not applicable
Strength: the correlation ratio ε^2:

$$\varepsilon^2 = 1 - \frac{MSV_W}{MSV_T}$$

Practical Applications:

1. Report group means and main effects

2. Best estimate of *Y*:

$$Y'_{(each\ case)} = \overline{Y}_{(grand)} + \text{the (explained) effect of } X$$

3. Tukey's HSD range tests to determine which group means are different from one another:

$$HSD = q\sqrt{\frac{MSV_W}{n_{(per\ group)}}}$$

QUESTIONS FOR CHAPTER 12

1. Both the *t*-test (Chapter 11) and the analysis of variance (ANOVA) test are used to establish differences among means. Explain the difference in approach between these two statistical tests.

2. Specify the formula for the general linear model. Explain what each part of this model means.

3. Describe at least three ways in which the null hypothesis may be stated for an ANOVA test.

4. What are main effects in an ANOVA test? For what aspect of a relationship are they important?

5. In plain language, explain what within-group and between-group variations are.

6. Suppose we test a hypothesis that the means of a variable differ among four populations and then reject the null hypothesis. Does this assure us that each of the four means is significantly different from the other three? Explain.

7. What is the ecological fallacy? Give an example.

EXERCISES FOR CHAPTER 12

Problem Set 12A

On all hypotheses tests, follow the six steps of statistical inference, including test preparation, a conceptual diagram, probability curves, and appropriate aspects of a relationship. For consistency, round calculations to two decimal places. Use $\alpha = .05$ unless otherwise stipulated.

12A-1. With the following data, calculate the main effects of academic school on grade point average (GPA). Show symbols and formulas.

Academic School of Students	Mean GPA
Arts & Sciences	2.74
Engineering	2.54
Business	2.62
Overall	2.63

12A-2. The general linear model arranges the individual scores of an interval/ratio dependent variable (Y) into parts that are and parts that are not explained by an independent variable (X). With the following statistics, use this model to explain the Y-scores listed. Y = months served in prison; X = type of crime.

$$\overline{Y}_{(grand)} = 55 \text{ months} \qquad \overline{Y}_{(armed\ robbery)} = 71 \text{ months}$$
$$\overline{Y}_{(felony\ theft)} = 27 \text{ months} \qquad \overline{Y}_{(homicide)} = 133 \text{ months}$$

Inmate ID Number	X	Y
1	Felony theft	22
2	Homicide	156
3	Armed robbery	79
4	Homicide	131
5	Armed robbery	67
6	Felony theft	37

12A-3. Political ideology often is measured with a conservative–liberal scale. Suppose you have an interval level ideology scale with scores ranging from 0 (extremely conservative) to 15 (extremely liberal). With the following survey data, test the hypothesis that various racial/ethnic categories differ in political ideology. Assume equality of population variances.

Race/Ethnic Category	Conservative–Liberal Ideology Score
Anglo-American	7
Anglo-American	8
Anglo-American	7
Anglo-American	5
Anglo-American	4
Anglo-American	8
Anglo-American	4
African-American	10
African-American	10

African-American	7
African-American	8
African-American	9
African-American	8
African-American	10
Hispanic	8
Hispanic	7
Hispanic	10
Hispanic	9
Hispanic	8
Hispanic	12
Hispanic	11

12A-4. In the United States about one in four people is obese—seriously overweight to the extent that a person is at risk of adverse physical health effects, such as diabetes and heart disease. Obesity also has adverse psychological effects, such as causing its victims to feel bad about how their body appears to others (Freidman and Brownell 1995). Suppose we compare three weight groups on a Body Dissatisfaction Scale, an interval/ratio level survey instrument with scores ranging from 0 to 30. Taking into account height, gender, and body build, subjects are classified as normal, borderline obese (20 to 30 percent over normal weight), and obese (greater than 30 percent over normal weight). Does obesity affect one's satisfaction with one's bodily appearance? Assume equality of population variances.

Weight Group	Body Dissatisfaction Scale Score
Normal range	11
Borderline obese	15
Borderline obese	13
Obese	16
Normal range	9
Borderline obese	14
Obese	19
Obese	17
Normal range	13
Borderline obese	16
Obese	15
Normal range	12
Borderline obese	11
Obese	15
Normal range	10

12A-5. In most prisons there are a variety of treatment and rehabilitation programs, such as substance abuse, psychological, and spiritual counseling, as well as academic and vocational education programs. An interesting question is whether corrections officers of various races are more likely to oppose such inmate programs and take a punitive attitude toward doing time (Jackson and Ammen 1996). Using the following statistics, test the hypothesis that there are differences on a punitive attitude scale among whites, African-American, and Hispanic corrections officers. Assume equality of population variances.

Race	Mean	Standard Deviation	n
White	27.90	3.09	30
African-American	21.77	3.39	30
Hispanic	25.58	3.03	30
Total	25.08	4.03	90

Source of Variation	SS	df	Mean Square Variance: $MSV = SS/df$	$F = \dfrac{MSV_B}{MSV_W}$
Between groups (SS_B)	567.12	$K - 1 = 2$	283.56	28.19
Within groups (SS_W)	875.60	$n - K = 87$	10.06	
Total (SS_T)	1,442.72	$n - 1 = 89$	16.21	

Tukey's HSD at the .05 level of significance = 1.95 punitive attitude scale points.

12A-6. Haijar and Kotchen (2003) studied systolic blood pressure readings in the United States and found them to be significantly higher for adults in certain geographic regions. Suppose you wish to replicate their findings and sample adults from three regions. Using the following (fictional) statistics, test the hypothesis that there are regional differences in systolic blood pressure units in the South, West, and Northeast. Assume equality of population variances.

Region	Mean	Standard Deviation	n
South	126.04 units	.65 units	20
West	123.09 units	.77 units	20
Northeast	125.22 units	.61 units	20
Total	124.79 units	1.42 units	60

Source of Variation	SS	df	Mean Square Variance: $MSV = SS/df$	$F = \dfrac{MSV_B}{MSV_W}$
Between groups (SS_B)	92.76	$K - 1 = 2$	46.38	98.68
Within groups (SS_W)	26.54	$n - K = 57$	.47	
Total (SS_T)	119.30	$n - 1 = 59$	2.02	

Tukey's HSD at the .05 level of significance $= .438$.

Problem Set 12B

On all hypotheses tests, follow the six steps of statistical inference, including test preparation, a conceptual diagram, probability curves, and appropriate aspects of a relationship. For consistency, round calculations to two decimal places. Use $\alpha = .05$ unless otherwise stipulated.

12B-1. Arthur and Graziano (1996) examined personality predictors of vehicle crash involvement. One interval level measure was overall conscientiousness: the dependability and feeling of an obligation to follow social norms in all aspects of life. With the following modified data, calculate the main effects of vehicle crash involvement on conscientiousness. Show symbols and formulas.

Vehicle Crash Involvement	Mean Conscientiousness
Crash, but not at fault	122.70
Crash and at fault	109.41
No crash	134.63
Overall	123.11

12B-2. The general linear model arranges the individual scores of an interval/ratio dependent variable (Y) into parts that are and parts that are not explained by an independent variable (X). With the following statistics, use this model to explain the Y-scores listed. Y = frequent flyer miles accumulated by employees of ACME, Inc.; X = employee job classification.

$$\overline{Y}_{(grand)} = 16,489 \text{ miles}$$

$$\overline{Y}_{(vice\ presidents)} = 9,737 \text{ miles}$$

$$\overline{Y}_{(sales\ representatives)} = 26,391 \text{ miles}$$

$$\overline{Y}_{(engineers)} = 13,655 \text{ miles}$$

Case	X	Y
John Callahan	Vice president of finance	3,248
Michael Windom	Vice president of manufacturing	11,522
Antonio Williams	Materials engineer	21,467
Arlene Slater	Chemical engineer	2,487
Kathy Schaefer	East coast sales representative	24,829
Charles Brown	Southwest sales representative	35,663

12B-3. Searching for the dangers of caffeine, a researcher adds two types of caffeine (those found in coffee and chocolate) to the water supply of groups of laboratory-bred rats. This species ordinarily survives about 13 months. The water supply of a control group of rats was not fortified. Does caffeine affect the life span of rats? Test a hypothesis with the following data. Assume equality of population variances.

Treatment Group	Days Rat Lived
Coffee caffeine	398
Coffee caffeine	372
Coffee caffeine	413
Coffee caffeine	419
Coffee caffeine	408
Coffee caffeine	393
Coffee caffeine	387
Coffee caffeine	414
Chocolate caffeine	401
Chocolate caffeine	389
Chocolate caffeine	413
Chocolate caffeine	396
Chocolate caffeine	406
Chocolate caffeine	378
Chocolate caffeine	382
Chocolate caffeine	417
Control (no caffeine)	412
Control (no caffeine)	386
Control (no caffeine)	394
Control (no caffeine)	409
Control (no caffeine)	415
Control (no caffeine)	401
Control (no caffeine)	384
Control (no caffeine)	398

12B-4. Like Guth et al. (1995), we are to examine whether religious ideas affect a person's views on the environment. We compare clergy of three types—Evangelical, mainline Protestant, and Catholic—with the assumption that religious leaders of a particular denomination have similar religious beliefs. Our dependent variable is an interval/ratio scale that measures positive attitudes toward environmentalism—support of government efforts to control pollution. (A high score indicates high support.) Is there a relationship between religious beliefs and environmentalism? Assume equality of population variances.

Clergy	Environmentalism Scale
Mainline Protestant minister	26
Catholic priest	30
Mainline Protestant minister	24
Evangelical minister	14
Catholic priest	25
Evangelical minister	12
Mainline Protestant minister	31
Catholic priest	34
Mainline Protestant minister	22
Evangelical minister	23
Mainline Protestant minister	28
Catholic priest	28
Catholic priest	24
Evangelical minister	17
Mainline Protestant minister	32
Catholic priest	25
Evangelical minister	22
Evangelical minister	19

12B-5. The Environmental Protection Agency monitors the toxic risk of counties by keeping records on the number of times chemicals are released into the air or streams by industries (Rogge 1996). Suppose we have the following data on the number of toxic releases last year for 60 counties with low, moderate, and high median incomes. Is the income level of a county related to the toxic risk experienced by its population? Assume equality of population variances.

Income Level of County	Mean Number of Toxic Releases in 1996	Standard Deviation	n
Low	252.65	19.68	20
Moderate	159.10	17.87	20
High	129.95	27.49	20
Total	180.57	57.07	60

Source of Variation	SS	df	Mean Square Variance: MSV = SS/df	$F = \dfrac{MSV_B}{MSV_W}$
Between groups (SS_B)	164,377.43	$K - 1 = 2$	82,188.72	168.63
Within groups (SS_W)	27,781.30	$n - K = 57$	487.39	
Total (SS_T)	192,158.73	$n - 1 = 59$		

Tukey's HSD at the .05 level of significance = 17.67 toxic releases.

12B-6. Pinquart and Sorensen (2005) report that African-American caregivers exhibit lower levels of caregiver burden than their white or Hispanic counterparts. Do the (fictional) data shown here confirm or disconfirm their findings? In other words, test the hypothesis that there are ethnic differences in self-reported caregiver burden (measured with a "Caregiver Burden scale").

Ethnicity	Mean Score on Caregiver Burden Scale	Standard Deviation	n
African-American	22.35	1.97	17
White	26.06	1.64	17
Hispanic	28.65	1.69	17
Total	25.69	3.13	51

Source of Variation	SS	df	Mean Square Variance: MSV = SS/df	$F = \dfrac{MSV_B}{MSV_W}$
Between groups (SS_B)	340.28	$K - 1 = 2$	170.14	54.18
Within groups (SS_W)	150.71	$n - K = 48$	3.14	
Total (SS_T)	490.98	$n - 1 = 50$	9.82	

Tukey's HSD at the .05 level of significance = 1.15 points.

Problem Set 12C

On all hypotheses tests, follow the six steps of statistical inference, including test preparation, a conceptual diagram, probability curves, and appropriate aspects of a relationship. For consistency, round calculations to two decimal places. Use $\alpha = .05$ unless otherwise stipulated.

12C-1. With the following data, calculate the main effects of income level on number of doctor visits per year (fictional data). Show symbols and formulas.

Income Level	Mean Doctor Visits per Year
High income	5.12
Moderate income	4.75
Low income	1.87
Overall	3.91

12C-2. The general linear model arranges the individual scores of an interval/ratio dependent variable (Y) into parts that are and parts that are not explained by an independent variable (X). With the following statistics, use this model to explain the Y-scores listed. Y = number of hours spent on the Internet per week; X = age category.

$$\overline{Y}_{(grand)} = 18.56 \text{ hours} \qquad \overline{Y}_{(adolescents)} = 26.67 \text{ hours}$$
$$\overline{Y}_{(middle\text{-}aged)} = 18.67 \text{ hours} \qquad \overline{Y}_{(elderly)} = 10.00 \text{ hours}$$

Subject Number	X	Y
1	Adolescent	27
2	Elderly	10
3	Elderly	12
4	Middle-aged	16
5	Adolescent	24
6	Middle-aged	21
7	Elderly	8
8	Middle-aged	19
9	Adolescent	30

12C-3. You are studying the relationship between occupation and level of depression as measured by the Center for Epidemiological Studies Depression Scale (CES-D). With the following (fictional) survey data, test the hypothesis that depression varies across different occupations. Assume equality of population variances.

Occupation	CES-D Score
Bank teller	6
Bank teller	9
Bank teller	11
Bank teller	6
Bank teller	4
Bank teller	5
Bank teller	3

Paramedic	14
Paramedic	18
Paramedic	15
Paramedic	13
Paramedic	19
Paramedic	14
Paramedic	13
College professor	8
College Professor	13
College professor	9
College professor	9
College professor	12
College professor	7
College professor	14

12C-4. Researchers have found less-affluent neighborhoods to have fewer places to buy healthy types of foods (Lewis, Sloane, Nascimento, Diamant, et al. 2005). Suppose you wish to replicate this finding in your own region. You sample various neighborhoods classified into three neighborhood income levels (X). You measure the number of places in each neighborhood to buy healthy foods (Y). Does neighborhood income level affect the number of healthy food options? Assume equality of population variances.

X Neighborhood Income Level	Y Number of Places Selling Healthy Foods
Lower-income	7
Upper-income	14
Lower-income	4
Middle-income	9
Middle-income	10
Upper-income	12
Lower-income	6
Upper-income	15
Middle-income	13
Lower-income	8
Upper-income	10
Lower-income	10
Middle-income	11
Upper-income	13
Lower-income	5
Upper-income	10
Middle-income	8
Middle-income	10

12C-5. Researchers have found that African-Americans tend to have higher levels of religious involvement than whites (Hunt and Hunt 2001). Suppose you wish to replicate this study and include Hispanics. You measure religious involvement by the number of times a person attended church per month. Using the (fictional) statistics shown here, test the hypothesis that there are racial differences in religious involvement among whites, Hispanics, and African-Americans. Assume equality of population variances.

Race	Mean	Standard Deviation	n
White	4.08	2.08	24
Hispanic	5.21	2.47	24
African-American	6.88	2.87	24
Total	5.39	2.50	72

Source of Variation	SS	df	Mean Square Variance: $MSV = SS/df$	$F = \dfrac{MSV_B}{MSV_W}$
Between groups (SS_B)	94.70	$K - 1 = 2$	47.35	7.59
Within groups (SS_W)	430.42	$n - K = 69$	6.24	
Total (SS_T)	525.11	$n - 1 = 71$	7.40	

Tukey's HSD at the .05 level of significance = 1.44 times per month.

12C-6. A local Rugby organization recently asserted that Rugby players are in better physical condition than other professional athletes. You wish to test this assertion, so you sample professional athletes who play rugby, basketball, and football. You measure athletic ability with a series of physical tests and sum scores to obtain a General Athletic Ability Scale. Test the hypothesis that rugby players have greater general athletic ability. Assume equality of variances in athletic ability among the three subpopulations.

Sport	General Athletic Ability Scale	Standard Deviation	n
Rugby	66.72	3.91	25
Basketball	65.92	3.20	25
Football	65.72	3.52	25
Total	66.12	3.55	75

Source of Variation	SS	df	Mean Square Variance: MSV = SS/df	$F = \dfrac{MSV_B}{MSV_W}$
Between groups (SS_B)	14.00	$K - 1 = 2$	7.00	.55
Within groups (SS_W)	909.92	$n - K = 72$	12.64	
Total (SS_T)	923.92	$n - 1 = 74$	12.49	

Tukey's HSD at the .05 level of significance = 2.42 General Athletic Ability Scale Points

Problem Set 12D

On all hypotheses tests, follow the six steps of statistical inference, including test preparation, a conceptual diagram, probability curves, and appropriate aspects of a relationship. For consistency, round calculations to two decimal places. Use $\alpha = .05$ unless otherwise stipulated.

12D-1. The type of car one owns likely has a lot to do with how much is spent on gasoline every month, since some cars get better gas mileage than others. Using the following (fictional) statistics, calculate the main effects of type of car owned on monthly gasoline expenditure. Show symbols and formulas.

Type of Car Owned	Monthly Gas Costs (in dollars)
SUV	188.21
Economy	107.87
Mid-size	131.26
Overall	142.45

12D-2. The general linear model arranges the individual scores of an interval/ratio dependent variable (Y) into parts that are and parts that are not explained by an independent variable (X). With the following statistics, use this model to explain the Y-scores listed. Y = income per year; X = level of education.

$$\overline{Y}_{(grand)} = 49{,}257 \text{ dollars}$$
$$\overline{Y}_{(college)} = 47{,}352 \text{ dollars}$$
$$\overline{Y}_{(high\ school)} = 25{,}167 \text{ dollars}$$
$$\overline{Y}_{(post-graduate)} = 78{,}492 \text{ dollars}$$

Case	X	Y
George Youngblood	College graduate	46,725
Amber Moore	High school graduate	27,316
Geoff Thomas	Post-graduate	67,256
Chris Kyden	High school graduate	35,951
Nicole Owens	Post-graduate	81,247
Elise Palmer	College graduate	57,124

12D-3. Antioxidant vitamins have been reported to bolster immunity levels in the human body. You wish to test the hypothesis and give subjects two types of antioxidant supplements: manufactured antioxidants (such as a pill) or natural antioxidants (such as fruit). For comparison, you include a control group not given antioxidants. Test the hypothesis with the following (fictional) data. Assume equality of population variances.

Treatment Group	Immunity Level
Manufactured	21
Manufactured	23
Manufactured	19
Manufactured	17
Manufactured	26
Manufactured	28
Manufactured	16
Manufactured	23
Natural	27
Natural	19
Natural	18
Natural	28
Natural	21
Natural	23
Natural	24
Natural	20
Control (no antioxidants)	15
Control (no antioxidants)	17
Control (no antioxidants)	19
Control (no antioxidants)	14
Control (no antioxidants)	15
Control (no antioxidants)	13
Control (no antioxidants)	20
Control (no antioxidants)	15

12D-4. In an effort to boost membership, a local group of nondenominational churches reported that their members have greater life satisfaction than members of local Protestant and Catholic churches. You wish to test this assertion, so you sample the populations of nondenominational, Protestant, and Catholic church members. Using the (fictional) data shown, test the hypothesis that there is a difference in life satisfaction among Protestant, Catholic, and nondenominational church members. Assume equality of population variances.

Religious Affiliation	Life-Satisfaction Score
Protestant	20
Catholic	27
Nondenominational	22
Catholic	16
Protestant	15
Catholic	28
Nondenominational	24
Nondenominational	23
Protestant	14
Catholic	13
Nondenominational	27
Protestant	23
Nondenominational	21
Catholic	15
Nondenominational	15
Catholic	19
Protestant	16
Protestant	22

12D-5. The contact hypothesis states that increased interaction between groups results in more positive intergroup attitudes. For example, studies show that adolescents who have more contact with elderly persons tend to have more positive attitudes toward them (Meshel and McGlynn 2004). Suppose that you wish to verify this theory. You sample adolescents with varying categories of contact. You measure their attitudes toward elderly persons with a "Positive Aging Perceptions (PAP)" scale, where a high score indicates a more positive attitude. Test the hypothesis that contact makes adolescents' attitudes toward elderly persons more positive.

Contact with Elderly Persons	Positive Aging Perceptions Scale	Standard Deviation	n
Low	10.00	2.42	15
Moderate	17.60	2.47	15
High	22.27	3.01	15
Total	16.62	2.65	45

Source of Variation	SS	df	Mean Square Variance: $MSV = SS/df$	$F = \dfrac{MSV_B}{MSV_W}$
Between groups (SS_B)	1150.04	$K - 1 = 2$	575.02	82.02
Within groups (SS_W)	294.53	$n - K = 42$	7.01	
Total (SS_T)	1444.58	$n - 1 = 44$	32.83	

Tukey's HSD at the .05 level of significance = 1.96.

12D-6. A sizeable amount of research has shown racial disparities in judicial sentencing. One study shows that African-Americans and Hispanics are more likely to be classified as habitual offenders and serve more time in prison (Crawford 2000; Crawford, Chiricos, and Kleck 1998). Suppose you wish to study the effect of race on sentence length. You sample criminal offenders who have committed the same crime and measure their sentences in years. Using the following (fictional) statistics, test the hypothesis that African-Americans and Hispanics are more likely to get longer sentences than whites. Assume equality of population variances.

Race	Mean	Standard Deviation	n
White	4.50	1.07	30
Hispanic	5.63	.96	30
African-American	6.13	1.20	30
Total	5.42	1.27	90

Source of Variation	SS	df	Mean Square Variance: $MSV = SS/df$	$F = \dfrac{MSV_B}{MSV_W}$
Between groups (SS_B)	42.02	$K - 1 = 2$	21.01	17.96
Within groups (SS_W)	101.93	$n - K = 87$	1.17	
Total (SS_T)	143.96	$n - 1 = 89$	1.62	

Tukey's HSD at the .05 level of significance = .56 years.

OPTIONAL COMPUTER APPLICATIONS FOR CHAPTER 12

If your class uses the optional computer applications that accompany this text, open the Chapter 12 exercises on *The Statistical Imagination* Web site at www.mhhe.com/ritchey2 to learn about one-way ANOVA in *SPSS for Windows*. The exercises emphasize proper interpretation of output for ANOVA and ways to address the aspects of the relationship. In addition, Appendix D of this text provides a brief overview of the *SPSS* command sequences for procedures covered in this chapter.

13

Nominal Variables: The Chi-Square and Binomial Distributions

CHAPTER OUTLINE

Introduction: Proportional Thinking About Social Status

In social and behavioral science research, variables with nominal and ordinal levels of measurement are used frequently. In particular, much research is done on how individuals' social status in groups and societies affects their opportunities in everyday life. Social positions have *status,* a Greek word meaning "rank or position within a group." Social status defines the relative amounts of privilege and authority awarded to any person occupying a social position within a group, community, or society. A person occupying a high-status position, such as a corporation president, is afforded more rights, rewards, and privileges than are given to individuals in lower-ranking positions, such as computer programmers.

Every individual occupies an assortment of statuses, such as student, spouse, parent, club treasurer, and office worker. Some social statuses are open for the choosing and can be earned, although competition for them may be stiff. These are called achieved statuses, and they include positions such as husband, doctor, and bank vice president. Other status positions are ascribed—assigned or "stamped onto" individuals at birth. For example, being male and white has its privileges in American society, but (short of undergoing a sex or color change) these statuses are fixed and not chosen. Ascribed statuses are easily identifiable because of physical markers such as skin color and the distinctive biological traits of sex or ethnic heritage. Biological research is unclear about the effects of ascribed statuses on behavior. For example, it is not clear whether women are truly more emotional than men. But it is important to understand the effects of ascribed statuses because they are consequential for individuals. Whether men or women are more emotional is beside the point if the myth that it is women who are is widely believed. Ascribed statuses are social markers that affect how, for instance, women and minority group members are treated. Statuses limit opportunities for those occupying minority positions, as is evident in light of racism and sexism. On a positive note, since ascribed statuses often are visible, they are convenient for targeting products and focusing social interventions. For instance, golf clubs are advertised in male-oriented magazines, and breast cancer screening in female-oriented magazines.

Because of the importance of status, social research often begins by determining the effects of status variables on the dependent variables of a study. For example, in studies of criminal behavior, the first hypotheses to be tested probably will pertain to demographic relationships. (Demography is the study of a society's population.) Are criminal acts more likely to be committed by men or women, young or old, in rural areas or urban areas, and so on? Once statistics are computed, it is vital that they be interpreted statistically—as percentages of a group of observations—rather than individualistically. For instance, U.S. Department of Justice statistics consistently reveal that men are arrested for nearly 90 percent of violent crimes. However, this does not mean that every man is a potential criminal or that women do not commit crimes. A proper interpretation is that men have a higher probability of committing a violent crime. To interpret the data otherwise is to stereotype—to apply a statistical generalization to an individual. Stereotypes are common within every society and lead to prejudice and injustice. For instance, if a police officer apprehended a man and a woman alleged to have robbed a bank, could the woman perhaps have been the mastermind and the leader of the plot? The tendency is to assume that the man is.

Research on status has the potential of reinforcing stereotypes, and therefore, care must be taken to avoid this pitfall. When statistics are reported as characterizations of individuals rather than as probabilistic generalizations, misunderstanding of data abounds. For example, in a demographic profile of homeless persons in Midcity, U.S.A., data may reveal that 70 percent of homeless persons in the community are male, 60 percent are African-American, and 50 percent are substance abusers. It would be wrong to report that the typical homeless person in Midcity is an African-American male who is addicted to drugs or alcohol. In fact, it may be that the homeless women are more likely to be substance abusers because women who are destitute but not addicted are more likely to be taken in by relatives. Scientific researchers must take care not to reinforce stereotypes. The key feature of the statistical imagination is to view isolated observations in relation to a larger whole.

This chapter focuses heavily on nominal variables, many of which are status markers. We start with the chi-square test of a relationship between two nominal variables. We will carefully interpret findings by using the language of proportions and percentages of the whole group. Conclusions will be about the category (i.e., the group), not the individual. Moreover, the findings will accurately portray the complex relationships among variables. These precautions are in order because in the popular press so much is made of relationships between status markers such as gender, race, and ethnic identity and other consequential phenomena such as crime rates. The failure to present results in a proportional manner adds to the disadvantages of minority statuses such as African-American, Arab-American, and female. In other words, popular reports often lack the statistical imagination. This chapter also covers the binomial distribution test, which is a small-sample proportions test.

Crosstab Tables: Comparing the Frequencies of Two Nominal/Ordinal Variables

A common device for presenting data is a **cross-tabulation** (or cross-classification) **table** that *compares two nominal/ordinal variables at once.* Such "crosstab" tables are essential for testing a hypothesis about the relationship between these variables. For example: Is there a relationship between gender (X) and church attendance (Y) among college students. The (fictional) results of a campus study are presented in Table 13–1.

For the data in Table 13–1, Table 13–2 presents the conventional language used to describe parts of a crosstab table. In the heart of the table lie *cells*. The number in a cell represents the frequency of joint occurrence (or simply "joint frequency") of the categories of the two variables. A joint occurrence is the combination of categories *for a single individual*. For example, say Charles attended church; then he is counted as part of the joint frequency of the "men-attended" cell, in which there are 66 subjects. The joint frequency of men who did not attend is 134; of women who attended, 94; and of women who did not attend, 146. The sums in the table margins are called marginal totals. The column total for men tells us that altogether there are 200 men in the sample; similarly, there are 240 women. The row totals for attended and did not attend are 160 and 280, respectively. The grand total is the sample size (n), which is presented in the bottom right corner. Note that both column and row totals add to the grand total.

---

joint frequency (or joint occurrence of categories)   For a single individual, the joint occurrence of the categories of two nominal/ordinal variables, such as Male–Attended church or Female–Did not attend church.

TABLE 13–1 | Church attendance in the past month by gender among college students, $n = 440$ (fictional data)

	Givens		
	Gender (X)		
Church Attendance (Y)	Men	Women	Total
Attended	66	94	160
Did not attend	134	146	280
Total	200	240	440

TABLE 13–2 | Crosstab table language: church attendance in the past month by gender among college students, $n = 440$

	Gender (X)		
Church Attendance (Y)	Men	Women	Totals
Attended	66	94	160

Cells (Contain Joint Frequencies)   Row (Marginal) Totals

| Did not attend | 134 | 146 | 280 |
| Total | 200 | 240 | 440 |

Column (Marginal) Totals   Grand Total (n)

If there is a relationship between gender and church attendance, one or the other gender has a much higher frequency of church attendance. The raw numbers in the table can be confusing, however, because there are more women than men in the sample. We must ask, Out of how many? Thus, we use marginal totals to compute *percentages* of men and women who attended church:

$$p\,[\text{of men attending church in past month}] = \frac{\#\text{ men attending}}{\text{total }\#\text{ of men}} = \frac{66}{200} = .3300$$

$\%\,[\text{of men attending church in past month}] = (p)\,(100) = (.3300)\,(100) = 33.00\%$

Similarly, the percentage of women attending church in the past month is 94/240 (100) = 39.17 percent. After calculating these percentages, we clearly see that a higher percentage of women attended church in the past month. These percentages, incidentally, are called column percentages because they are based on column marginal totals. That is, a **column percentage** is *a cell's frequency as a percentage of the column marginal total.* Similarly, a **row percentage** is *a cell's frequency as a percentage of the row marginal total.* For example, the row percentage of church attenders who are men is 66/160 (100) = 41.25 percent. These simple crosstab tables provide important descriptive statistics and help determine whether a relationship exists between two nominal/ordinal variables.

Calculating Column and Row Percentages of Cells in a Crosstab Table

$$\text{Column \% [of joint occurrence]} = \frac{\text{\# in a cell}}{\text{total \# in column}}(100)$$

$$\text{Row \% [of joint occurrence]} = \frac{\text{\# in a cell}}{\text{total \# in row}}(100)$$

The Chi-Square Test: Focusing on the Frequencies of Joint Occurrences

The existence of a relationship between two nominal variables is established with a hypothesis test called the chi-square test. Suppose that we wish to examine the relationship between race and political party preference using the fictional data in the crosstab table of Table 13–3. Let us review the elements of the table. In the crosstab table we put the categories of the independent variable (race) in the columns and those of the dependent variable (political party preference) in the rows. We call this a 2 × 3 (stated, "two by three") table to indicate the number of categories of each variable. The number of rows times the number of columns is the number of joint frequency cells, with six in a 2 × 3 table. The six possible pairings of categories for the variables race and political party preference are white–Democrat, African-American–Democrat, white–Republican, African-American–Republican, white–Independent/Other/None, and African-American–Independent/Other/None. The total sample size, or *grand total,* is 400, which is reported in the bottom right corner. The marginal totals on the right indicate row totals, with 150 cases in each of the Democratic and Republican parties and 100 in the Independent/Other/None category, for a grand total of 400 respondents. The marginal totals at the bottom indicate column totals, with 300 of the sample subjects being white and 100 being African-American, again summing to the grand total of 400. Focusing on the joint frequencies, we find that 96 sample subjects are both

TABLE 13-3 | Political party preference by race (expected cell frequencies in parentheses)

Political Party (Y)	Race (X) → White	African- American	Row Totals
Democrat	96 (112.5)	54 (37.5)	150
Republican	123 (112.5)	27 (37.5)	150
Independent/Other/None	81 (75.0)	19 (25.0)	100
Column totals	300 (300)	100 (100)	400

white and Democrat, 123 are both white and Republican, 54 are both African-American and Democrat, and so forth. Finally, the numbers in parenthesis to the right of each joint frequency is the expected frequency, which we will address shortly.

If there is a relationship between race and political party preference, we expect to find that a higher percentage of one race prefers one party to another. We might hypothesize that a higher percentage of African-Americans identify themselves as Democrats. If this is true, in a random sample of American adults we expect to find especially high frequencies of the joint occurrence African-American Democrat.

As with any hypothesis test, the hypothesis must be stated in a way that allows us to know what sampling outcomes to expect when the hypothesis is true. With the chi-square test, we state our null hypothesis as one of "no relationship" between the two variables. As we will see in a moment, when this is the case, the chi-square statistic will compute to zero within sampling error. Thus, we state step 1 of the test as follows:

$$H_0: \chi^2 = 0$$

That is, there is no relationship between race and political party preference.

$$H_A: \chi^2 > 0$$

That is, there is a relationship between race and political party preference. One-tailed but nondirectional.

As with any null hypothesis, this statement allows predictions of outcomes with repeated sampling. In this case, assuming no relationship, we can use the marginal frequencies to predict the *expected frequencies* of each cell. We then compare these expected frequencies to our *observed frequencies,* the joint frequencies actually found in the sample data and presented in the crosstab table. If the observed frequencies are about equal to the expected ones, give or take a little sampling error, we allow the hypothesis of "no relationship" to stand and conclude that race has nothing to do with political party preference. If, however, there is a large difference between observed and expected frequencies, we begin to suspect that there is a relationship between the variables. The chi-square hypothesis test tells us whether the summed differences between the observed and expected cell frequencies are so great that they are not simply the result of sampling error. As we will discuss in detail later, the test is nondirectional. Any chi-square test, however, is one-tailed because this statistic is based on squared numbers, which are always positive.

Calculating Expected Frequencies

How are expected frequencies computed? In Table 13–3 we can see that three-fourths (300 of 400) of the sample subjects are white. We can predict that *if race has nothing to do with political party preference, that is, if there is no relationship between race and political party preference,* we can expect three-fourths of Democrats, three-fourths of Republicans, and three-fourths of Independent/Other/None to be white. In other words, whites will be represented among the political parties in proportion to their numbers in the general population. Similarly, given that one-fourth of the sample is African-American, we can expect one-fourth of each of the political party categories to be African-American. The expected cell frequencies tell us how many cases should fall in a cell if each cell is proportional to the marginal frequencies—the situation where the two variables are unrelated and thus the cells are filled randomly.

The expected cell frequency, E, for each cell is computed precisely with the following formula:

Calculating the Expected Cell Frequencies of a Crosstab Table

$$E_{cell} = \frac{(\text{column marginal total for cell})\,(\text{row marginal total for cell})}{\text{grand total}}$$

where

$$E_{cell} = \text{expected frequency of a cell}$$
$$\text{Column marginal total for cell} = \text{total cases for the column category of the cell}$$
$$\text{Row marginal total for cell} = \text{total cases for the row category of the cell}$$
$$\text{Grand total} = \text{total sample size}$$

For example, the expected frequency of white Democrats is

$$E_{(white\text{-}Dem)} = \frac{(\text{total number of whites})\,(\text{total number of democrats})}{\text{grand total}}$$

$$= \frac{(300)\,(150)}{(400)} = 112.5 \text{ cases}$$

Differences Between Observed and Expected Cell Frequencies

With all hypothesis tests, the difference between what is observed in the actual sample data and what is hypothesized for the null hypothesis constitutes the "effect" of the test.

The calculation of the chi-square statistic is based on measuring the differences between the observed frequencies and the expected frequencies, with the expected frequencies being the joint frequencies that will occur in repeated sampling when there is *no* relationship between the two variables. As in many statistical formulas, these differences are in the numerator of the test statistic. Similarly, the denominator of most test statistics is a measure of normal sampling error when the null hypothesis is true. Thus, the expected frequencies are used in the denominator.

Calculation of the Chi-Square Test Statistic

$$\chi^2 = \sum \frac{(O - E)^2}{E}$$

where

χ^2 = a measure of the likelihood of differences between observed and expected cell frequencies

O = observed frequency of a cell

E = expected frequency of a cell

Table 13–4 presents a computational spreadsheet for computing the chi-square statistic. The data come from Table 13–3.

A close look at this formula provides a sense of proportion on how its values relate to real statistical outcomes. When the effects (i.e., the differences between observed and expected frequencies) are large, this suggests that the cases are not

TABLE 13–4 | Computational spreadsheet for calculating the chi-square statistic using the data from table 13–3

Givens			Calculations		
Cell (*X, Y*)	*O*	*E*	(*O* − *E*)	[(*O* − *E*)^2/E]	(*O* − *E*)^2
White Democrat	96	112.5	−16.5	272.25	2.42
African-American Democrat	54	37.5	16.5	272.25	7.26
White Republican	123	112.5	10.5	110.25	.98
African-American Republican	27	37.5	−10.5	110.25	2.94
White Independent	81	75.0	6.0	36.0	.48
African-American Independent	19	25.0	−6.0	36.0	1.44
Totals	400	400.0	0.0		χ^2 = 15.52

randomly distributed among the cells and that the null hypothesis should be rejected. Large differences appear when some of the cells (often the cells in opposite diagonal corners) "load up" because of a relationship between the two variables. Let us examine one of the cell differences more closely. The actual "observed frequency" of white Democrats is 96 cases. The difference between this observed frequency of 96 and the expected frequency of 112.5 is −16.5 cases (i.e., about 17 fewer than expected given the overall numbers of Democrats and whites). It appears that whites are underrepresented among Democrats in proportion to their numbers in the general population. As we shall see, similar effects of race on political party preference appear in other cells.

We must consider, however, the possibility that differences for this cell and the others result from chance sampling error. Even if there is no relationship between race and political party preference, in repeated sampling we will obtain a variety of cell distributions. A first sample might pick up slightly fewer white Democrats than expected, but the next sample might pick up slightly more. These fluctuations from one sample to the next would result from normal, expected sampling error. Our hypothesis test of the relationship between race and political party preference depends on the single sample we actually draw. The chi-square test answers the question: In repeated sampling, how unusual is it to see gaps between observed and expected frequencies when race has nothing to do with political party preference? In other words, are the effects of race on political party preference significant? A random distribution of cell frequencies—in proportion to marginal totals—is what occurs in sampling when there is no relationship between the two variables. The alternative hypothesis is likely to be accepted when the effects of the test are large (i.e., when there are large differences between the observed and expected frequencies).

The chi-square statistic and the chi-square table (Statistical Table G in Appendix B) allow us to compute the exact probability (the p-value) of the differences between observed and expected cell frequencies when the null hypothesis of "no relationship" is true. Comparing this probability to our alpha level, we either reject the null hypothesis or fail to reject it. If we fail to reject it, we conclude that there is no reason to believe that race and political party preference are related, that the differences between observed and expected cell frequencies result from sampling error. If we reject the null hypothesis, however, we conclude that there is a relationship between race and political party preference. We would also describe the practical applications of this relationship, pointing out strong effects—cells where large discrepancies exist between observed and expected frequencies. For example, we would point out that a disproportionately low percentage of whites identify themselves as Democrats in contrast to a disproportionately high percentage of African-Americans.

Degrees of Freedom for the Chi-Square Test

To read the chi-square distribution table (Statistical Table G in Appendix B), we must compute the chi-square test statistic and the appropriate degrees of freedom. For the chi-square test, degrees of freedom are determined by the number of columns and rows in the crosstab table.

Calculating the Degrees of Freedom for the Chi-Square Test

$$df = (r - 1)(c - 1)$$

where

df = degrees of freedom for the chi-square test

r = number of rows in the crosstab table

c = number of columns in the crosstab table

For a 2×3 crosstab table such as Table 13–3 on race and party preference,

$$df = (r - 1)(c - 1) = (3 - 1)(2 - 1) = 2$$

Recall that degrees of freedom are the number of opportunities in sampling to compensate for limitations in a statistic or a statistical test. For example, in Chapter 10 we noted that with means tests, extreme scores tend to pull the mean of a sample away from the true parameter. For the chi-square test, as its df formula suggests, the number of cells in a crosstab table influences the size of the calculated statistic. A crosstab table can be distorted if, just by chance in this particular sampling, one cell is over- or underloaded in frequency compared to its true occurrence in the population. For example, suppose that in the population there are many white Democrats but this sample just happened to miss them. Just as an extreme score "distorts" a mean, one or more randomly over- or underloaded cells in a crosstab table can distort the computation of the chi-square test statistic. Calculation of degrees of freedom compensates for this tendency. Close examination of the df formula for the chi-square statistic reveals that the more categories the two variables of the crosstab table have, the higher the degrees of freedom are. Conversely, tables with few cells, such as 2×2 and 2×3 tables, have few degrees of freedom. With these small tables, if by chance the sample incurs an inaccurately over- or underloaded cell, there are few opportunities (i.e., other cells) to balance out this unlucky sampling event. Repeated sampling tells us that over time, when a large number of samples is drawn, we sometimes oversample one cell and at other times oversample another. With only four cells, an oversampling in only one cell can distort the outcomes. In fact, if we know the expected frequency of one cell in a 2×2 crosstab table, we can use the marginal totals to compute the other three. In other words, only one cell is free to vary independently of the way the statistic is calculated; hence, there is only 1 degree of freedom.

Minimum Cell Frequency Requirement   With chi-square, an increase in degrees of freedom is not always a blessing, however. This test statistic has a shortcoming that restricts the number of categories used. The expected frequency of each cell in a crosstab table must equal at least 5, or adjustments must be made in the calculation of the chi-square statistic. Small cells introduce additional sampling error that can lead to an incorrect rejection decision and a wrong conclusion. When cell sizes come up short, we call this cell depletion. The practical experience of the author suggests that to avoid cell depletion, the overall sample size should be equal to the number of cells times 12. Thus, for a simple 2×2 table, we need about 48 cases; for a 2×3 table, 72 cases; and so on. Even with a large overall sample size, however, cell depletion can be a problem for some variables. For instance, with the variable religious preference we may have a sample of 100 but only 6 Muslims. If we attempt to break out this variable by, say, gender, there is no possibility that the joint frequencies of male–Muslim and female–Muslim will both have the required minimum of 5 cases.

When there is a shortage of cases in a cell, several corrections can be made. First, the number of cells can be reduced by eliminating sparse categories. For instance, for religious preference, the Muslim category might be dropped or folded into an "other" category with other religions with low frequencies, such as Hindu. This, of course, requires that the results be reported as having these modifications. A second alternative to dealing with cell depletion is to absorb the small-frequency category into another category that is theoretically meaningful. For example, for the variable race, the "other" category could be combined with African-American to create a new category called "nonwhite." This is appropriate if the race variable is essentially a proxy (or substitute) for majority-minority status. A third alternative is to make a correction in the computation of chi-square by subtracting 0.5 from each calculation of the difference between the observed and the expected frequencies. This is called Yates's correction for continuity; it adjusts for inconsistency in the sizes of cells. A fourth alternative is to use another statistical test called Fisher's exact test (Blalock 1979: 292). This is useful in situations where there are many cell frequencies less than 5 but none can be justifiably eliminated or combined.

Yates's correction and Fisher's exact test complicate calculations to the point where the time spent learning them would be better used learning how to calculate crosstab statistics on a computer. Computer crosstab programs typically provide a count of cells with small frequencies. Then the programs present a Yates's corrected chi-square and a Fisher's exact test along with the chi-square statistic so that they may be substituted when appropriate. A comparison of these statistics in the computer output will reveal that when the sample size is quite large, a few small-frequency cells have little impact on the resulting chi-square statistic. In other words, with large samples the corrected chi-square value will be about the same as the uncorrected value and both statistics will have the same p-values.

The Chi-Square Sampling Distribution and Its Critical Regions

The chi-square formula was derived by an early twentieth-century statistician named Karl Pearson, who also is noted for developing the statistics in Chapters 14 and 15. Most likely, he figured out this formula mathematically, but let us imagine how he might have determined the formula empirically—through repeated sampling, as was done by the bean counters of old. He takes a large box full of equal numbers of assorted beans— a population of beans. He treats white beans as white Democrats, red beans as African-American Democrats, spotted beans as white independents, and so on. He draws a random

FIGURE 13–1

The shape of the chi-square probability distribution curve with the critical region for $\alpha = .05$ and 2 degrees of freedom

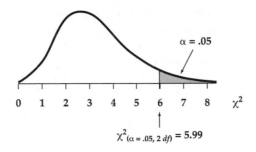

$$\chi^2_{(\alpha = .05,\, 2\, df)} = 5.99$$

sample of 400 beans and counts each type to obtain the observed frequencies of the crosstab table. After calculating the expected frequencies, for each cell he subtracts the observed and expected frequencies, squares the result, and divides it by the expected frequency. Then he sums these quotients to obtain the χ^2 statistic. He does this, say, 10,000 times and plots the resulting calculations as a probability curve—a smoothed-out histogram. The shape of this probability distribution is presented in Figure 13–1. Note that it is one-tailed. This will always be the case, because squaring removes any negative signs. The test, however, is nondirectional, as we will discuss later.

As we noted earlier, the particular shape of the chi-square distribution for a given problem depends on the number of degrees of freedom, which is determined by the number of cells in the crosstab table. Figure 13–1 presents the critical values of chi-square for a level of significance of .05 with 2 degrees of freedom. This critical value means that if there is no relationship between the two variables, with repeated sampling the chi-square statistic will compute as high as or higher than 5.99 only 5 percent of the time. The other 95 percent of the time chi-square will compute below 5.99, with most outcomes falling just above zero; this is just what we expect when the observed and expected frequencies are the same within sampling error.

The chi-square test is used in the following circumstances:

When to Use the Chi-Square Test of a Relationship Between Two Nominal Variables

In general: Testing a hypothesis of a relationship between two nominal variables.

1. There is one population with a representative sample from it.
2. There are two variables, both of a nominal/ordinal level of measurement.
3. The expected frequency of each cell in the crosstab table is at least 5.

The Six Steps of Statistical Inference for the Chi-Square Test

Let us use the data in Table 13–3 and its spreadsheet (Table 13–4) to answer the research question of whether there is a relationship between race and political party preference. The null hypothesis is that there is no relationship. Since both variables are nominal and the expected frequencies are all above 5, we may use the chi-square test.

Brief Checklist for the Six Steps of Statistical Inference

TEST PREPARATION

State the research question. Draw conceptual diagrams depicting givens, including the population(s) and sample(s) under study, variables (e.g., $X = \ldots$, $Y = \ldots$,) and their levels of measurement, and given or calculated statistics and parameters. State the proper statistical test procedure.

SIX STEPS

Using the symbol H for *hypothesis:*

1. State the H_0 and the H_A and stipulate test direction.
2. Describe the sampling distribution.
3. State the level of significance (α) and test direction and specify the critical test score.
4. Observe the actual sample outcomes and compute the test effects, the test statistic, and p-value.
5. Make the rejection decision.
6. Interpret and apply the results and provide best estimates in everyday terms.

Solution for the Chi-Square Test for a Relationship Between Two Nominal/Ordinal Variables

TEST PREPARATION

Research question: Are certain races more likely to favor certain political parties? That is, is there a relationship between race and political party preference? *Givens:* Variables: X = race, nominal level; Y = political party preference, nominal level. *Population:* The American adult population. *Sample:* $n = 400$ adults. *Statistical procedure:* Chi-square test of a relationship between two nominal variables. *Observation:* Observed frequencies and computed expected frequencies (E_{cell}), where

$$E_{cell} = \frac{(\text{column marginal total for cell})\,(\text{row marginal total for cell})}{\text{grand total}}$$

(*Note:* For some chi-square problems, we forgo diagramming the populations and instead focus on the crosstab table.)

Political Party (Y)	Race (X) → White	African-American	Row Totals
Democrat	96 (112.5)	54 (37.5)	150
Republican	123 (112.5)	27 (37.5)	150
Independent/Other/None	81 (75.0)	19 (25.0)	100
Column totals	300 (300)	100 (100)	400

SIX STEPS

1. H_0: $\chi^2 = 0$

That is, there is no relationship between race and political party preference.

H_A: $\chi^2 > 0$

That is, there is a relationship between race and political party preference. One-tailed test but nondirectional.

2. *Sampling distribution:*

$$\chi^2 = \sum \frac{(O - E)^2}{E}$$
$$df = (r - 1)(c - 1) = (3 - 1)(2 - 1) = 2$$

If the H_0 is true and samples of size 400 are drawn repeatedly from the population and cross-tabulated for race and political preference, the calculations of the chi-square statistic will produce the following chi-square distribution:

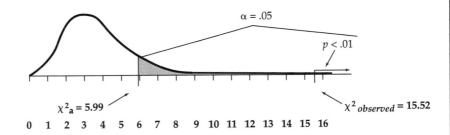

3. *Level of significance:* $\alpha = .05$ (nondirectional). One-tailed $df = 2$. Critical test score = $\chi^2_\alpha = 5.99$ (from Statistical Table G in Appendix B). (Shaded area on curve.)

4. *Observations:*

Test effects and test statistic:

Givens	Calculations				
Cell (*X, Y*)	*O*	*E*	(*O* − *E*)	(*O* − *E*)²	[(*O* − *E*)²/*E*]
White Democrat	96	112.5	−16.5	272.25	2.42
African-American Democrat	54	37.5	16.5	272.25	7.26
White Republican	123	112.5	10.5	110.25	.98
African-American Republican	27	37.5	−10.5	110.25	2.94
White Independent	81	75.0	6.0	36.0	.48
African-American Independent	19	25.0	−6.0	36.0	1.44
Totals	400	400.0	0.0		$\chi^2 = 15.52$

p-value: *p* [drawing a sample with differences between observed and expected frequencies as unusual as or more unusual than those observed when in fact there is no relationship between the variables] < .001 (area noted on curve in step 2).

5. *Rejection decision:* $|\chi^2_{observed}| > |\chi^2_{\alpha}|$ (i.e., 15.52 > 5.99); $p < \alpha$; .001 < .05. Reject H_0 and accept the H_A at the 95 percent level of confidence.

6. *Interpretation:* Aspects of relationship and best estimates.
Existence: There is a relationship between race and political party preference; $\chi^2 = 15.52$, $p < .001$.

Practical Applications: A disproportionately high number of African-Americans prefer the Democratic party. *Best estimates:* Fifty-four percent of African-Americans are Democrats compared with 32 percent of whites. Only 27 percent of African-Americans are Republicans compared with 41 percent of whites.

Relevant Aspects of a Relationship for the Chi-Square Test

Note that in the last step of the hypothesis test only two of the four aspects of a relationship are readily addressed: existence and practical applications. The existence of a relationship is established with the chi-square test formula, testing the hypothesis of no relationship between the two nominal variables. If a relationship is found, we describe its practical applications by reporting the "effects" (i.e., the differences between the observed and expected cell frequencies) of noteworthy cells in the crosstab table. In everyday terms, we report best estimates by calculating column percentages for selected cells. Recall that a column percentage is *a cell's frequency as a percentage of the column marginal total:*

$$\text{Column \% [of joint frequency]} = \frac{\text{\# in a cell}}{\text{total \# in column}} \times 100$$

To calculate the percentage of African-Americans who are Democrats:

$$\% \begin{bmatrix} \text{of African-Americans} \\ \text{who are Democrats} \end{bmatrix} = \frac{\text{\# of African-American Democrats}}{\text{total \# of African-Americans}} \times 100$$

$$= \frac{54}{100} \times 100 = 54\%$$

Similar calculations of column percentages are made for the white–Democrat, African-American–Republican, and white–Republican. We report the column percentages that make relevant points, in this case that one major political party is disproportionately African-American and the other is disproportionately white.

The direction of a test is meaningless for nominal variables. For example, with the variable gender, it is meaningless to say that males are more "positive" or "negative"; one is either male or female. (Chi-square can be used with ordinal variables, and in that situation direction sometimes does make sense.)

Measures of the strength of a relationship for the chi-square test statistic exist. Those measures are seldom reported, however, because such reports are fraught with potential error. Each measure requires very careful use and applies only in very specific circumstances (see Lee and Maykovich 1995: 129).

Aspects of a Relationship Using the Chi-Square Statistic

Existence: Test the null hypothesis that $\chi^2 = 0$; that is, there is no relationship between X and Y.

Use the chi-square test statistic:

$$\chi^2 = \sum \frac{(O-E)^2}{E}$$

$$df = (r-1)(c-1)$$

Direction: not applicable.

Strength: Usually not reported.

Practical Applications: Report column percentages for selected cells that accurately convey the substance of findings.

Using Chi-Square as a Difference of Proportions Test

When the joint frequencies of two nominal variables are presented in a crosstab table, it is very easy to calculate their percentages. For example, suppose we have the data in Table 13–5. The data come from a study of elderly patients seeing physicians at clinics

TABLE 13–5 | Type of clinic by whether caregiver is referred to a support group (expected cell frequencies in parentheses)

Referred to Support Group	Type of Clinic →	Primary Care	Geriatric	Row Totals
Yes		7 (15.83)	23 (14.17)	30
No		50 (41.17)	28 (36.83)	78
Column totals		57 (57.00)	51 (51.00)	108

for the first time. Each patient is accompanied by a caregiver, usually a family member, particularly a wife or daughter. Some of the patients and caregivers attend a regular primary care clinic that provides services to people of all ages. The others go to a geriatric clinic that specializes in providing care to elderly patients. Because caregivers often are stressed out, the geriatric clinic claims to include them in the treatment process and to provide assistance, such as referrals to caregiver support groups.

To evaluate this claim, we interview random samples of caregivers at both clinics. The data in Table 13–5 compare the numbers of caregivers at each clinic who are referred to support groups. One nominal variable, then, is clinic type, and the other is referral to support groups. We can investigate the research question that there is a relationship between type of clinic and likelihood of referral to a support group. If a geriatric clinic's patients are referred at a significantly higher rate, that clinic's claims are justified.

In Table 13–5 let us focus on the percentage of geriatric clinic caregivers referred to support groups by calculating the column percentage:

$$\% \text{ [of geriatric clinic caregivers referred to support group]} = \frac{\text{\# in geriatric-yes cell}}{\text{total \# for geriatric clinic}} \times 100$$

$$= \frac{23}{51}(100) = 45.10\%$$

Similarly, the column percentage of primary care clinic caregivers being referred to support groups is 12.28 percent [i.e., (7/57) (100)]. On the face of it, there is a large difference in these two percentages. We must remember, however, that these are sample data. Any difference between the two percentages may be due to sampling error. Thus, we must test a hypothesis to determine whether these percentages are significantly different for the caregiver populations of the two clinics. Conceptually, this research problem may be conceived as it is in Figure 13–2. Although we multiplied the fractions by 100 to get column percentages, for consistency we call this a proportions test and use the symbol P_u in Figure 13–2.

Using a chi-square test, we may then investigate the research question of whether there is a significant difference in the percentage of caregivers referred to support groups by type of clinic.

For practice, follow the previous solution box and resolve this issue. The null hypothesis (H_0) is that there is no difference between the clinics in referrals to support

FIGURE 13–2

Testing the
difference of
proportions or
percentages
between groups
using the
chi-square test

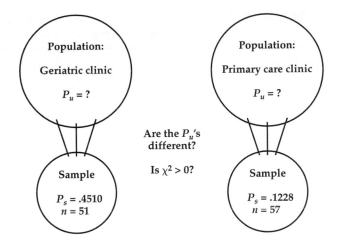

groups, which is to say that chi-square equals zero. The alternative hypothesis is that chi-square is greater than zero. But with $P = p$ [referred to support groups], the H_0 may also be stated as

$$H_0: P_{u_{(caregivers\ at\ geriatric\ clinic)}} = P_{u_{(caregivers\ at\ primary\ care\ clinic)}}$$

In step 4, we observe a chi-square value of 14.43 with 1 degree of freedom. The p-value is less than .001; therefore, in step 5 we reject the H_0 at the .05 level of significance. Step 6 of the six steps of statistical inference will read:

6. *Interpretation:* Aspects of relationship and best estimates.

   Existence: There is a significant difference in the percentage of caregivers referred to support groups by type of clinic; $\chi^2 = 14.43$; $p < .001$.

   Practical applications: Caregivers at geriatric clinics are more likely to be referred to support groups. *Best estimates:* 45.10 percent of caregivers accompanying patients to the geriatric clinic are referred to support groups compared to only 12.28 percent of caregivers accompanying patients to the primary care clinic.

   Answer: Caregivers assisting patients to the geriatric clinic are more likely to be referred to support groups. The clinic's claims are justified.

   In the early stages of data analysis, after each variable is scrutinized for peculiarities such as skews, the next stage is to run bivariate tests. When comparing two or more groups, the t-test for two-group difference of means (Chapter 11), the analysis of variance test (ANOVA, Chapter 12), and the chi-square test provide a concise way to present results in tabular form, as shown in the next section.

Tabular Presentation of Data

As has been noted in several chapters, the main goal of research usually is to explain variation in an outcome variable—a single dependent variable. Sometimes, however, the focus is on a single independent nominal/ordinal variable—two or more groups—and

TABLE 13–6 I A comparison of primary care and geriatric clinic caregivers on services received, demographic variables, and stress outcomes (*n* = 108)

Variables		Primary Care Clinic (*n* = 57)	Geriatric Clinic (*n* = 51)	Significance
Services received				
Percent referred to support groups		12.28%	45.10%	‡
Percent told of counseling services		5.26	43.14	‡
Percent told of community agencies that assist caregivers		14.04	45.10	‡
Percent referred to legal counsel		1.75	23.53	†
Percent advised on home safety		10.53	52.94	‡
Demographics				
Caregiver age	Mean	55.1 years	61.2 years	*
	Standard deviation	12.5	12.1	
Years of education	Mean	10.6 years	11.1 years	NS
	Standard deviation	3.1	3.2	
Stress outcomes				
Caregiver burden	Mean	17.2	21.2	‡
	Standard deviation	4.7	6.5	‡
Psychological depression	Mean	17.0	18.7	NS
	Standard deviation	11.2	11.5	

NS = not significant.
* $p < .05$.
† $p < .01$.
‡ $p < .001$.
Source: Clair, Ritchey, and Allman 1993.

the groups are compared for several dependent variables. For example, in the illustration of the chi-square test of differences of proportions, we compared two groups of caregivers. Table 13–6 presents additional data comparing these two groups. The statistical significance of differences between percentages was determined with chi-square tests. This table also compares these two groups on some interval/ratio variables (i.e., differences of means) by using independent sample *t*-tests (Chapter 11).

A table such as Table 13–6 packs a lot of information on one page. First, it appears that the geriatric clinic is much more involved with its patients' caregivers. Nearly half the caregivers there indicate that they are referred to support groups, counseling services, and community agencies, and about half are advised on home safety, an important concern among elderly persons. In the primary care clinic very small percentages are advised on these things. Second, the data in the lower part of the table—based on *t*-tests—is important for guiding additional multivariate analysis. The caregivers of the geriatric clinic patients have a higher mean age of about six years. Although the rate of psychological depression is not statistically different between the groups, the geriatric clinic caregivers are found to experience a greater burden in the caregiver role. These findings may help explain why more of the geriatric clinic caregivers are being sent to counseling and support groups. Perhaps their patients are sicker, creating greater burdens for the caregivers. And perhaps the lack of caregiver services at the primary care clinic results from the fact that especially ill patients are referred to the geriatric clinic. Clearly, additional analysis is in order with controls for severity of patient condition, age of caregiver, and other variables. One of the main functions of bivariate analysis—such as that reported in Table 13–6—is to guide the research process into the next stage.

A couple of technical comments are in order in regard to how Table 13–6 was designed. Note that at the primary care clinic, only about 2 percent of caregivers were referred to legal counsel and only 5 percent were told about other counseling services. These small percentages required Yates's correction in the calculation of the chi-square statistic. Finally, note that for the variable caregiver burden, not only the group means but also the group standard deviations were significantly different. There was a significantly wider distributional spread in the burden scores of caregivers at the geriatric clinic. The t-test of the differences in means for the burden variable required the separate variance estimate of the standard error because of the inequality of variances (or standard deviations). Some scientific journals require table footnotes to specify these fine statistical points, whereas others presume that their readers will assume that such corrections were made. For a public audience there is no point discussing statistical procedures. The data are accepted on the authority of the presenter. Moreover, pictorial presentations, especially bar graphs, are a more appropriate device for communicating a sense of proportion to a public audience.

Small Single-Sample Proportions Test: The Binomial Distribution

A "small single-sample proportions test," as the word *proportion* implies, is used with one nominal level variable, where $P = p$ [of the success category] of the variable and $Q = p$ [of the failure category(ies)]. This test is used when the smaller of P_u and Q_u times n is less than 5 (i.e., $[(p_{smaller})\ (n) < 5]$). Recall from Chapter 10 that when $[(p_{smaller})\ (n) \geq 5]$, we use the large single-sample proportions test.

The test statistic for the small single-sample proportions test is called the binomial distribution test. The term *binomial* means "two-number," and this test is used with very common dichotomous variables—those with only two categories. Examples of dichotomous variables are gender (male/female), majority-minority race classification (white/nonwhite), a coin toss (heads/tails), attitude toward an issue (for/against), existence of a trait (present/absent), outcome of an experiment (effect/no effect), effectiveness of treatment (effective/not effective), and outcomes for at-risk groups such as heart attack victims (survived/died). It also should be noted that with variables of any level of measurement, we often "dichotomize" by collapsing scores into two groups. For example, in a study of retirees it may be useful to compare those who retired before and after age 65 years (the age at which full Social Security benefits are attainable).

The binomial distribution is especially useful in laboratory experiments with few subjects. For example, suppose previous research reveals that one-half (a proportion of .5000) of all patients receiving chemotherapy can be expected to experience nausea. We have a sample of eight patients and expect four to experience nausea. We administer a new nausea-reducing drug. If it is effective, *significantly fewer* than four patients should experience nausea. Suppose only one of the eight (12.50 percent) experiences nausea with the new drug. This is three fewer nausea cases than expected with no drug, suggesting that the drug is effective. But does it truly mean that the drug is effective? Could this apparently favorable outcome have resulted from random sampling error? In other words, in a second group of eight patients receiving the new drug seven could experience nausea. In a third group some other random number may experience nausea. A hypothesis test would resolve the question of how unusual the outcome is in repeated sampling. The binomial distribution provides a quick way to determine this *p*-value and establish whether the observed reduction in the number of nauseated patients is statistically significant. This hypothesis test would lead to one of the following conclusions:

1. The drug is effective and reduces nausea in an additional three of eight cases.
2. The drug is not effective. The reduction in nausea cases is due to sampling error.

When to Use a Small Single-Sample Proportions Test (the Binomial Distribution)

In general: One dichotomous nominal/ordinal variable and one sample.

1. There is only one nominal variable that is dichotomous (i.e., it has *only two* categories, where $P = p$ [of the success category] and $Q = p$ [of the failure category]).
2. There is a single, representative sample from one population.
3. The sample size is such that $[(p_{smaller})(n)] < 5$, where $p_{smaller}$ = the smaller of P_u and Q_u.
4. There is a target value of the variable to which we may compare the sample proportion.

The Binomial Distribution Equation

To illustrate how sampling outcomes are predicted for dichotomous variables, let us take the example of flipping two coins. In Chapter 6, when we discussed probabilities, we noted that with repeated tossing, the outcomes of two flipped coins are predictable, as is shown in Figure 13–3.

Early mathematician bean counters, or in this case coin flippers, surely used coin tosses to discover the predictability of sampling events. They probably tossed two coins

FIGURE 13–3

Possible
outcomes of two
flipped coins

First Coin   Second Coin

over and over while recording the frequency of outcomes of heads and tails. Then they did the same for three coins, four coins, and so on. After noting a pattern or "law of nature," these mathematicians proceeded to develop a formula that readily calculates outcomes. For dichotomous outcomes such as heads and tails, yes and no, present and absent, and the like, the binomial equation quickly describes all possible outcomes and the probability of each one. This equation, then, can be used as a sampling distribution.

A binomial distribution is an expansion of the following general binomial equation:

The Binomial Distribution Equation

$$(P + Q)^n$$

where

$$P = p \text{ [of the success category]}$$
$$Q = p \text{ [of the failure category]}$$
$$n = \text{sample size}$$

Recall that $P + Q = 1$; therefore, $Q = 1 - P$ and $P = 1 - Q$. To expand the equation is to raise it to the designated power of n. For example, if n is 2, then $(P + Q)$ is raised to the power of 2 (or simply squared):

$$(P + Q)^2 = (P + Q)(P + Q) = (P)(P) + (P)(Q) + (Q)(P) + (Q)(Q)$$
$$= P^2 + 2PQ + Q^2$$

For tossing two coins, let us define heads as success and tails as failure: $P = p$ [of heads] and $Q = p$ [of tails]. The sample size is $n = 2$, since only two coins are tossed. The expanded equation gives all possible outcomes and the probability of each one by delineating all possible heads-tails combinations that match Figure 13–3:

$$(P + Q) = \quad P \quad + \quad 2PQ \quad + \quad Q^2$$
$$= \text{heads, heads} + (2) \text{ heads, tails} + \text{tails, tails}$$

The coefficients of the equation (1, 2, and 1) represent how often each combination occurs in a large number of trials or samples. (Note that we did not write the coefficient 1, as this is redundant and unnecessary.) Since p [of heads] $= .5$ and p [of tails] $= .5$, both P and $Q = .5$. Thus, the sampling distribution of the tossing of two coins is

$$(P + Q)^2 = P^2 \quad + \quad 2PQ \quad + \quad Q^2$$
$$= (.5)^2 + 2(.5)(.5) + (.5)^2$$
$$= .25 \quad + \quad .5 \quad + .25$$
$$= \frac{1}{4} \quad + \quad \frac{2}{4} \quad + \quad \frac{1}{4}$$

In other words, as is evident in Figure 13–3, when two coins are tossed, "double heads" occurs 1 in 4 times; the combination "heads-tails" occurs 2 in 4 times, or half the time; and "double tails" occurs 1 in 4 times.

Shortcut Formula for Expanding the Binomial Equation

Expanding the binomial equation is a difficult task. For example, to describe the sampling distribution for the tossing of four coins, we confront this:

$$(P + Q)^4 = (P + Q)(P + Q)(P + Q)(P + Q), \text{etc.}$$

Fortunately, mathematicians value parsimony, *the preference for economy and simplicity over complexity.* This attitude is exemplified in the statement "The simplest solution is the best," and mathematicians spend lots of time simplifying calculations. Blaise Pascal (1623–1662) developed a shortcut method for expanding the binomial equation. First, he noted that once it is expanded, any binomial equation has $n + 1$ terms, where each term represents a combination of P and Q outcomes. For instance, in the tossing of three coins, we have four terms or combinations: (1) all three heads, (2) one heads and two tails, (3) one tails and two heads, and (4) all three tails. Second, Pascal discovered that the equation's coefficients—the numbers that tell us how often a combination occurs—follow a predictable pattern. This discovery is called Pascal's triangle (Table 13–7). For dichotomous variables, Pascal's triangle allows a quick computation of the probabilities of all possible outcomes. For any sample size n, by adding coefficients as we move down, the triangle provides the coefficients of the outcomes. Moreover, in the very common instance when P and Q are equal—in other words, when $P = .5$ and $Q = .5$—the sum of the coefficients provides the total number of outcome combinations and therefore the denominator for computing probabilities.

TABLE 13–7 I Pascal's triangle of coefficients of binomial equations for sample sizes 1 to 10

n	Coefficients											Sum of Coefficients (= 2 to the nth power)*
					1							
1					1	1						2
2				1	2	1						4
3			1	3	3	1						8
4		1	4	6	4	1						16
5	1	5	10	10	5	1						32
6	1	6	15	20	15	6	1					64
7	1	7	21	35	35	21	7	1				128
8	1	8	28	56	70	56	28	8	1			256
9	1	9	36	84	126	126	84	36	9	1		512
10	1	10	45	120	210	252	210	120	45	10	1	1,024
Etc.												

* Use this sum of coefficients as a denominator of probabilities only when $P = Q = .5$.

Again, let us illustrate with two coins, using the coefficients for $n = 2$ from Table 13–7:

$$(P + Q)^2 = P^2 + 2PQ + Q^2$$

From Pascal's triangle: 1 (heads, heads) + 2 (heads, tails) + 1 (tails, tails). Since P and Q are equal for coins, the probability of an outcome is quickly computed by dividing the coefficient for any combination by the sum of coefficients for the equation. Thus,

$$p \text{ [of heads and heads]} = P^2 = \frac{1}{4}$$

With a few steps, we can use Pascal's triangle to quickly compute the probabilities of outcomes. Let us illustrate for the tossing of five coins, $(P + Q)^5$, where $P = p$ [of heads] and $Q = p$ [of tails] and $n = 5$ (for five coins).

1. Since $n + 1 = 6$, write out the term "$PQ +$" six times to obtain the following partially completed equation:

$$(P + Q)^5 = PQ + PQ + PQ + PQ + PQ + PQ$$

2. Specify the exponent for each term, which will represent possible outcomes (possible combinations of heads and tails). At most, we can obtain five heads, and this occurs with no tails. Thus, the exponents for P's begin with 5 (i.e., the value

of n) and then decrease to zero as we move across. The exponents for Q's begin with zero and increase to the value of n as we move across. Therefore, start with the P's, putting the exponents 5, then 4, and so on, from left to right. Similarly, insert zero for the first Q, and so on, to obtain the following partially completed equation:

$$(P + Q)^5 = P^5Q^0 + P^4Q^1 + P^3Q^2 + P^2Q^3 + P^1Q^4 + P^0Q^5$$

Since any number raised to the power of zero $= 1$, this equation can be simplified by removing such terms to obtain the following partially completed equation:

$$(P + Q)^5 = P^5 + P^4Q^1 + P^3Q^2 + P^2Q^3 + P^1Q^4 + Q^5$$

This provides all combinations: P^5 represents the combination five heads and no tails, P^4Q^1 represents four heads and one tails, and so on, over to Q^5, which represents no heads and five tails.

3. Use Pascal's triangle (Table 13–7) to obtain coefficients for each term. Once these coefficients are inserted, we have the complete expanded binomial equation for $n = 5$:

$$(P + Q)^5 = P^5 + 5P^4Q^1 + 10P^3Q^2 + 10P^2Q^3 + 5P^1Q^4 + Q^5$$

4. Finally, since P and Q are equal, from the right column of Pascal's triangle (Table 13–7) obtain the sum of coefficients for a sample of $n = 5$ and divide this into each coefficient to obtain the probabilities of each outcome:

$$(P + Q)^5 = P^5 + 5P^4Q^1 + 10P^3Q^2 + 10P^2Q^3 + 5P^1Q^4 + Q^5$$

$$= \frac{1}{32} + \frac{5}{32} + \frac{10}{32} + \frac{10}{32} + \frac{5}{32} + \frac{1}{32}$$

Thus, the probability of tossing five coins and getting all heads is 1 in 32; four heads and one tails, 5 in 32; three heads and two tails, 10 in 32, and so forth.

With a little experience, Pascal's triangle is very efficient, especially when P and Q are equal. To illustrate, the following answers may be quickly taken from Table 13–7 without the need to construct the equations:

1. p [of flipping a coin 7 times and getting all heads] $= \dfrac{1}{128} = .0078$

2. p [of flipping 9 coins and getting 7 heads and 2 tails] $= \dfrac{36}{512} = .0703$

In instances where P and Q are *not* equal, Pascal's triangle still can be used to obtain coefficients. The sums on the right side of the table, however, do not apply, and the terms of the equation must be multiplied out. For example, suppose a room full of people is 70 percent male ($P = .7$) and 30 percent female ($Q = .3$). If three persons are randomly selected from the room, what possible male-female combinations will occur and with what probabilities? We observe Pascal's triangle to construct the equation and then insert values of .7 and .3 to solve for the probabilities of each combination:

$$(P + Q)^3 = \quad P^3 \quad + \quad 3P^2Q^1 \quad + \quad 3P^1Q^2 \quad + \quad Q^3$$
$$= (.7^3) + 3(.7^2)(.3) + 3(.7)(.3^2) + (.3^3)$$
$$= .343 \quad + \quad .441 \quad + \quad .189 \quad + .027$$

Note that the four probabilities sum to 1.0. Note also that the two predominantly male combinations on the left side of the equation occur much more frequently than do the two predominantly female combinations. This makes sense because the proportion of men in the room is much larger than the proportion of women. Indeed, Pascal's triangle is a handy device!

The Six Steps of Statistical Inference for a Small Single-Sample Proportions Test: The Binomial Distribution Test

Now let us use the binomial equation as a sampling distribution for hypothesis tests. Suppose that at the fictional Overlord College the issue of date rape has become a hot topic. In response to pressure from students and parents, Overlord's president announces that he will convene a focus group to begin discussing date rape and what can be done to eliminate it. Some outspoken students suspect that to minimize negative publicity about the college, the president wants a focus group to say that date rape is not a problem. They eagerly watch to see who the president selects for the focus group. They anticipate that he will load it with males, who are assumed to be less sympathetic to the problem than are females.

The proportion of males and females on campus is equal. The president announces his selection, and it is a group of eight students, six of whom are male. The outspoken students accuse him of loading the group with males. The president has stated publicly that he simply made a random selection of students by using a computer program and student records. Is the president of the college lying?

How can the binomial distribution be used here? Since the proportion of males and females is equal on the campus, each sex has an equal chance of being selected, just as a coin has an equal chance of coming up heads or tails. Thus, making a truly random selection of students is like tossing eight coins with, say, male as heads and female as tails. This does not mean, however, that a random selection of eight persons will always result in four males and four females. In tossing eight coins, there are nine possible outcomes, ranging from all heads to all tails. We would expect nevertheless to obtain balanced combinations—such as four heads and four tails, five and three, or three and five—because these combinations occur more frequently in repeated tossing. Used along with Pascal's triangle (Table 13–7), the binomial distribution provides a description of all possible combinations of males and females for a group of eight and the probability of each combination *if the selection is indeed a random one.*

As with any hypothesis test, we must state a hypothesis so that it predicts sampling outcomes. The binomial distribution provides predictable outcomes for a random selection, one in which males and females have an equal chance of selection and "the coins" are not weighted in either's favor. Therefore, we can state the null hypothesis as: The president is not a liar; the focus group was chosen randomly. This *null* hypothesis tests *no* bias. If we find that the president's outcome is common with a random or "blindfold" selection, we will stick with this null hypothesis of no bias. The alternative hypothesis is that the president intentionally loaded the focus group with males and lied when he said he made a random selection. The effect of the test is the difference between the observed number in the category, P, and the expected number, assuming no bias (i.e., assuming that P_u is true). This is a one-tailed test because it states that males had a *greater* chance of selection. Our rejection decision hinges on whether a combination as unusual as or more unusual than six males and two females is unlikely to happen by chance. Is the effect of having two more males than predicted by a 50–50 split due to random sampling error or to bias on the part of the university president? Put another way, in repeatedly tossing eight coins, is it unusual to get six heads or more? Does this occur quite frequently, say, more than .05 of the time, or is this an unlikely event? Let us frame this problem by using the six steps of statistical inference.

Solution for a Small Single-Sample Proportions Test (the Binomial Distribution)

TEST PREPARATION

Research question: Is the president of Overlord College truthful in saying that his focus group was randomly selected (i.e., males and females had an equal chance of selection)? *Statistical procedure:* small single-sample proportions test, binomial distribution; target value: $P_u = .50$ (the known, true proportion of male students in the Overlord College student population). *Observation:* $n = 8$. Six males and two females were selected for focus group (which is the binomial formula term P^6Q^2). As a proportion

$$P_s = \frac{\#\text{ males}}{n} = \frac{6}{8} = .75$$

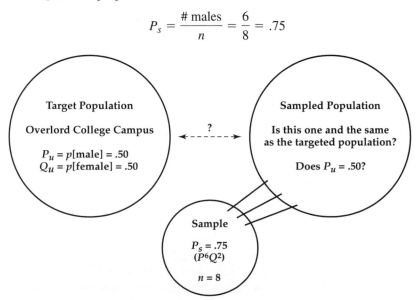

SIX STEPS

1. H_0: $P_{u(sampled\ population)} = .50$ (the known proportion of males (P_u) in the targeted Overlord College population).

   That is, the president is not a liar; the focus group was chosen randomly.

   H_A: $P_{u(sampled\ population)} > .50$ (the known proportion of males (P_u) in the targeted Overlord College population).
   One-tailed.

   That is, the president is a liar. Males are overrepresented, suggesting that the focus group was loaded with males.

2. *Sampling distribution:* If H_0 is true and samples of size 8 are drawn repeatedly from the Overlord College student population, combinations of males and females will fit the binomial distribution with $P = .5$, $Q = .5$, $n = 8$, and coefficients from Pascal's triangle (Table 13–7):

   $$(P + Q)^8 = P^8 + 8P^7Q^1 + 28P^6Q^2 + 56P^5Q^3 + 70P^4Q^4 + 56P^3Q^5$$
   $$+ 28P^2Q^6 + 8P^1Q^7 + Q^8$$

3. *Level of significance:* $\alpha = .05$. One-tailed.

4. *Observation:* $n = 8$

   Test effect: Six males and two females; two more males than expected.

   Test statistic

   $$= (P + Q)^8 = P^8 + 8P^7Q^1 + 28P^6Q^2 + 56P^5Q^3 + 70P^4Q^4 + 56P^3Q^5$$
   $$+ 28P^2Q^6 + 8P^1Q^7 + Q^8$$

   $$= \frac{1}{256} + \frac{8}{256} + \frac{28}{256} + \frac{56}{256} + \frac{70}{256} + \frac{56}{256} + \frac{28}{256} + \frac{8}{256} + \frac{1}{256}$$

   $$37/256 = .1445$$

   p-value: *p* [observing a sample outcome as unusual as or more unusual than six males and two females when the true population proportion P_u is .50] = .1445.

5. *Rejection decision:* $p > \alpha$, $.1445 > .05$. Fail to reject the H_0.

6. *Interpretation*
   Existence: The president appears not to be a liar; the focus group could have been chosen randomly. *Best estimates:* The apparent overrepresentation of males in the focus group could easily have resulted from random sampling error. A combination as extreme as or more extreme than six males and two females occurs over 14 percent of the time in such random selections. *Answer:* We have no reason to believe that the president is a liar.

Some things of note about this hypothesis test:

- In step 2, note the efficiency of the binomial equation. Unlike the Z-test, t-test, and F-ratio test, this sampling distribution is not described with a frequency curve. This means that a frequency curve table (such as the t-distribution table) is not required. This concise equation alone meets the requirements of describing the sampling distribution. It describes all possible combinations of males and females for a group of eight and the probability of each combination occurring in repeated sampling.

- In step 4, in the binomial equation the term P^6Q^2 represents the combination of six males and two females, our sampling outcome. When "honest" sampling occurs, it would be more unusual to have drawn seven males and one female or eight males and no females. Thus, the p-value for the sampling outcome includes the probabilities of P^7Q^1 and P^8. We added the probabilities of all terms in the "tail" of the equation—those as unusual as or more unusual than P^6Q^2.

- In step 4, *if we had done a two-tailed test*, we also would have included the probabilities of P^2Q^6, P^1Q^7, and Q^8, because it would have been just as unusual to randomly select these female-biased combinations as to select the male-biased combinations. The p-value would have been computed by adding the probabilities of both "tails" of the equation as follows:

$$(P + Q)^8 = P^8 + 8P^7Q^1 + 28P^6Q^2 + 56P^5Q^3 + 70P^4Q^4 + 56P^3Q^5 + 28P^2Q^6$$
$$+ 8P^1Q^7 + Q^8$$
$$= \frac{1}{256} + \frac{8}{256} + \frac{28}{256} + \frac{56}{256} + \frac{70}{256} + \frac{56}{256} + \frac{28}{256} + \frac{8}{256} + \frac{1}{256}$$

$$37/256 = .1445 \qquad\qquad 37/256 = .1445$$

In other words, since the equation is symmetrical when P and Q are equal (i.e., combinations are balanced on both sides), the p-value is doubled and computes to $(2) (.1445) = .2890$.

- In steps 5 and 6 in this example, we failed to reject the null hypothesis. In situations in which the null hypothesis is rejected, provide best estimates of P_u and/or Q_u by reporting which category is overrepresented; for instance, "men are overrepresented."

Statistical Follies and Fallacies: Low Statistical Power when the Sample Size Is Small

In our illustration of the binomial equation we found that even though his focus group appeared to be weighted in favor of males, we "have no reason to believe" that the president of Overlord College lied when he said the group was randomly selected. Although we gave him the benefit of the doubt, it is still possible that he loaded the focus group with males.

For one thing, in testing the null hypothesis that he was *not* a liar, we used the .05 level of significance. This kept the chance of a type I error (i.e., rejecting the null hypothesis when in fact it is true) at a moderately low level. In other words, we took only a 5 percent chance of calling him a liar if in fact he was not. The outspoken students who accuse him of bias might prefer a higher level of significance (say, .20) because they are viewing things politically, not scientifically. They might argue that we made it almost impossible to reject the null hypothesis because a *p*-value less than .05 could be obtained only if the president had selected seven males and one female or eight males:

$$(P + Q)^8 = P^8 + 8P^7Q^1 + 28P^6Q^2 + 56P^5Q^3 + 70P^4Q^4 + 56P^3Q^5 + 28P^2Q^6$$
$$+ 8P^1Q^7 + Q^8$$

$$= \frac{1}{256} + \frac{8}{256} + \frac{28}{256} + \frac{56}{256} + \frac{70}{256} + \frac{56}{256} + \frac{28}{256} + \frac{8}{256} + \frac{1}{256}$$

$$\downarrow$$

9/256 = .0352 (which is less than α = .05, one-tailed)

These students would protest that the president would have had to select not one, not two, but three too many males to be called a liar with such a low alpha level.

What these students are actually expressing is their suspicion that a type II error occurred (see Chapter 9). Recall that a type II error occurs when a statistical test fails to reject a false null hypothesis. Recall also that β is the probability of making a type II error and that it is inversely related to α; as α increases, β decreases, and vice versa. In this case, a type II error would have occurred if the president actually had lied, but we concluded the opposite.

By setting the level of significance (α) higher, we could reduce β—the chance of making a type II error. For instance, if we had used α = .20, we would have rejected the president's honesty when he selected six males and two females because the *p*-value that we had for the test was .1445, which is less than .20. If we had done this, however, the president could have accused us of bias in favor of the outspoken students. What this conundrum illustrates is that a small sample size is a rather weak device for determining whether observed facts are due to sampling error. Because the binomial equation is used with small samples, its results are rather tenuous. In statistical language, we say that such a limited statistic has low statistical power. **Statistical power** refers to *a test statistic's probability of not incurring a type II error for a given level of significance.* Mathematically,

$$\text{Power of a test} = 1 - \beta = 1 - p \text{ [of a type II error]}$$

As we noted in Chapter 10, calculating the power of a statistical test is quite complicated and is beyond the scope of this text. Nevertheless, with the binomial equation it is easy to see that small sample test statistics are limited.

A simpler case may help us remember this limitation. Suppose the college president had chosen only three students for the focus group. At the .05 level of significance, would it even be possible to reject the null hypothesis that he lied? The answer is no. Even in the worst-case scenario that all three selected students turned out to be male, there would be no way to reject the null hypothesis. Using Pascal's triangle, with three persons randomly chosen, the probability of selecting all males is 1 in 8, or .1250. That is, this worst-case scenario with its p-value of .1250 is greater than .05. There would be no way to reject the null hypothesis using such a small, low-power sample and the binomial equation. Even an all-male result would not be unusual in an honest random selection of three students.

There is a second reason to be skeptical of the conclusion we drew that the president was not lying. As we discussed in Chapter 1, statistical work occurs within a larger political and cultural context. It is subject to distortion by dishonest users. Our hypothesis test simply determined that this president was in a position to assert that his selection was random. In fact, he could have placed six males on the focus group intentionally. Perhaps he knew that that was the maximum number of males that could be in the group without having a null hypothesis rejected at the .05 level of significance. Statistical conclusions based on small samples are not absolutely certain even when statistical test conclusions support a position. This is why the ethics of science is an important part of statistical work. An honest statistician would not support the president's position without noting that it is hard to draw a firm conclusion with a small sample.

Assuming that indeed the president of Overlord College is honest, he could have prevented student protest by using gender quotas in forming the focus group. That is, he could have randomly selected exactly four males and four females—the correct proportions of gender representation in the student population. This would have saved him a lot of headaches.

SUMMARY

1. In social science research, many status variables, such as gender and race, are of a nominal level of measurement. The chi-square test, based on calculations made from a crosstab table, examines the relationship between two nominal variables.

2. Calculations for the chi-square test are made using a cross-tabulation (or "crosstab") table, which reports frequencies of joint occurrences of categories of two nominal/ordinal variables. The categories of the independent variable (X) go in the columns of the crosstab table, and those of the dependent variable (Y) in the rows.

3. For a single individual, a joint-occurrence of categories involves pairings of categories of the two nominal/ordinal variables, such as white–Democrat or African-American–Republican.

4. Using the crosstab table, expected frequencies are computed and compared to the actual observed frequencies in the cells. Expected frequencies are the cell

frequencies that would occur if there is no relationship between the two nominal variables. When the observed and expected frequencies are the same, give or take some sampling error, there is no relationship and the chi-square equation calculates to zero. Therefore, the null hypothesis is that chi-square equals zero.

5. The sampling distribution is the chi-square distribution, with degrees of freedom determined by the number of columns and rows in the crosstab table: $df = (r - 1)(c - 1)$.

6. The p-value is obtained by comparing the calculated chi-square value to the critical values of the chi-square statistic in Statistical Table G in Appendix B.

7. Relevant aspects of a relationship for the chi-square test: (*a*) Existence: Test the H_0 that $\chi^2 = 0$; that is, there is no relationship between X and Y. If the H_0 is rejected, a relationship exists. (*b*) Direction is not applicable because the variables are nominal level. (*c*) Strength is usually not reported because those measures that exist are inadequate and fraught with potential error. (*d*) Practical applications are described by reporting the differences between the observed and expected cell frequencies for a couple of outstanding cells and by calculating column percentages for selected cells.

8. The chi-square test is commonly used as a difference of proportions test.

9. The binomial distribution test is a small single-sample proportions test, used when the sample size is such that $[(p_{smaller})(n)] < 5$, where $p_{smaller} =$ the smaller of P_u and Q_u. Contrast this hypothesis test to the large single-sample proportions test of Chapter 10.

10. For the binomial distribution hypothesis test, the null hypothesis is stated as H_0: $P_u =$ a target value. Expansion of the binomial distribution equation, $(P + Q)^n$, provides the sampling distribution for dichotomous events. The p-value is calculated directly from this equation. Pascal's triangle provides a shortcut method for expanding the binomial equation. It allows a quick computation of the probabilities of all possible outcomes, when P and Q are equal to .5. It takes the place of a statistical table.

11. Statistical power is a test statistic's probability of not incurring a type II error for a given level of significance. Small samples have low statistical power. The binomial distribution test is a good device for illustrating low statistical power.

CHAPTER EXTENSIONS ON *THE STATISTICAL IMAGINATION* WEB SITE

Chapter 13 Extensions of text material available on *The Statistical Imagination* Web site at www.mhhe.com/ritchey2 include extensive materials on the test statistic *gamma*, which is used for categorical variables that are of ordinal level of measurement.

STATISTICAL PROCEDURES COVERED TO THIS POINT

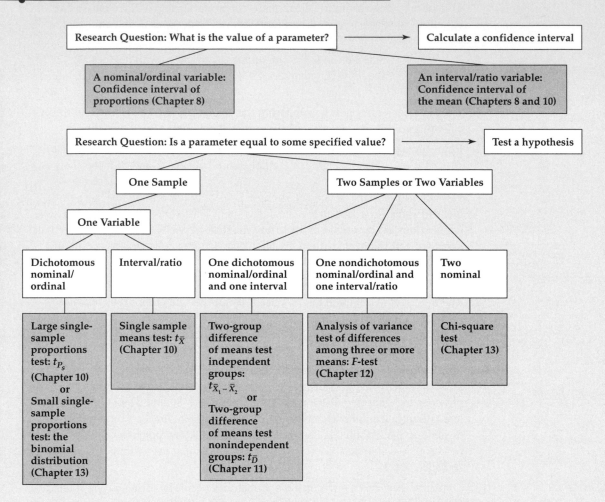

FORMULAS FOR CHAPTER 13

Chi-square test of a relationship between two nominal variables:

Given: two nominal/ordinal variables *X* and *Y* or a nominal/ordinal variable for two groups. A crosstab table of the variables reveals at least five cases per cell.

Research question: Is there a relationship between the two nominal/ordinal variables? Or is there a difference between two groups in the proportions of a category of a nominal/ordinal variable?

$H_0: \chi^2 = 0$

Sampling distribution: The chi-square distribution with

$$df = (r - 1)(c - 1)$$

Test effects: Differences between observed and expected frequencies, $O - E$, best illustrated with column percentages.

Test statistic: Chi-square [for use with the chi-square table (Statistical Table G in Appendix B); determines if a relationship exists]:

Calculations for producing the chi-square test statistic:

1. Organize data in a crosstab table and calculate the expected cell frequencies:

$$E_{cell} = \frac{(\text{column marginal total for cell})\,(\text{row marginal total for cell})}{\text{grand total}}$$

2. Insert observed and expected cell frequencies into this spreadsheet:

Givens		Calculations			
Cell (*X*, *Y*)	*O*	*E*	(*O* – *E*)	(*O* – *E*)^2	[(*O* – *E*)^2/*E*]
X–*Y* cell	...	...	...	...	...
X–*Y* coll	...	...	...	...	...
X–*Y* cell	...	...	...	...	...
X–*Y* cell	...	...	...	...	...
Totals	*n*	*n*	0.0		$\chi^2 = ...$

3. Calculate the chi-square statistic (from the right lower corner of the spreadsheet):

$$\chi^2 = \sum \frac{(O - E)^2}{E}$$

Addressing the aspects of a relationship:

Direction: Usually not applicable

Strength: Not applicable

Practical Applications: Calculate column percentages of interesting cells:

$$\text{Column \% [of joint frequency]} = \frac{\text{\# in a cell}}{\text{total \# in column}} \times 100$$

Small single-sample proportions test (the binomial distribution):

Given: one nominal dichotomous variable where $P = p$ [of the success category] and $Q = p$ [of the failure category]; a single representative sample from one population; the sample size is such that $[(p_{smaller})(n)] < 5$, where $p_{smaller} =$ the smaller of P_u and Q_u, and there is a target value of the variable to which we may compare the sample proportion.

Research question: Is P_u, the proportion of cases in the success category, significantly different from a target value?

H_0: $P_{u \ (sampled \ population)}$ = known target value

Sampling distribution: The binomial distribution

Test effect: The difference between the observed number in the category, P, and the expected number, assuming P_u is true

Test statistic: The binomial distribution equation, $(P + Q)^n$
Calculations for getting a p-value using the binomial equation:

1. Determine whether the binomial equation is appropriate by seeing that

$$[(p_{smaller}) \, (n)] < 5$$

   (If $[(p_{smaller}) \, (n)] \geq 5$, then use the large single-sample proportions test in Chapter 10.)
2. Expand the formula $(P + Q)^n$ by:
   a. Listing the term "PQ" $n + 1$ times.
   b. Specifying exponents for each term (to represent possible outcomes).
   c. Using Pascal's triangle (Table 13–7) to obtain coefficients for each term and inserting these coefficients to complete the expanded binomial equation.
   d. Calculate the p-value = p [combinations as unusual as or more unusual than the combination observed] by adding probabilities in the appropriate tail(s) of the equation.

QUESTIONS FOR CHAPTER 13

1. A quality or characteristic of a subject is conveyed in the names of categories of a nominal/ordinal variable. To the best of your knowledge, identify the categories of the following variables:
   a. College grade level
   b. Hair color
   c. Religious preference
   d. Physician's medical specialty
2. For a single individual, the pairing of categories from two variables is called a joint occurrence. The joint occurrence female-surgeon represents which two variables?
3. Choose two nominal variables, create some fictional data, and set up a crosstab table to depict joint frequencies. Label the parts of the table (cells, totals, etc.) to illustrate that you know how to read such tables.
4. Variables of what level of measurement are appropriate for using the chi-square test?
5. In a chi-square test, what does it indicate when the observed and expected frequencies are equal?
6. Variables of what level of measurement are appropriate for using the small single-sample proportions test, and what is this test called?

7. What does the term *binomial* mean? Must a variable necessarily be dichotomous in order to use the binomial distribution? Explain.

8. What is statistical power? Provide an example of an incorrect conclusion based on a sample with low statistical power.

EXERCISES FOR CHAPTER 13

Problem Set 13A

On all hypotheses tests, follow the six steps of statistical inference, including test preparation, a conceptual diagram and/or crosstab table, probability curves, and appropriate aspects of a relationship. Use $\alpha = .05$ unless otherwise stipulated.

13A-1. The following crosstab table is from a random sample of physicians. The row variable distinguishes whether a physician is a member of a medical specialty with a high risk of being sued for medical malpractice (e.g., obstetrics or neurosurgery). The column variable, practice location, indicates rural (i.e., a county not adjacent to a metropolitan area), urban community (i.e., a metropolitan area but not affiliated with a medical school), or academic health science center (i.e., medical center attached to a medical school). Compute column percentages for all joint frequency cells.

Risk of Suit ↓	Practice Location → Rural County	Urban Community	Academic Health Science Center	Totals
High-risk specialty	100	462	77	
Low-risk specialty	42	279	23	
Totals				

13A-2. Among 43 professors and 55 students surveyed, 25 professors and 18 students preferred the quarter system to the semester system. Present these data in a crosstab table. Test the hypothesis that there is a relationship between organizational status and preferred type of academic system.

13A-3. Use the following data from the General Social Survey to test the hypothesis that those who marry at a young age are more likely to divorce.

	Married When Under 20	Married When 20 or Older
Divorced	27	52
Never divorced	59	244

13A-4. Organize the following spreadsheet data into a crosstab table. Test the hypothesis that there is a significant difference between city-center residents and suburban residents in terms of support of a tax increase for expanding the size of the police department.

Residence Location	Supports Tax Increase
Suburban	No
City center	Yes
Suburban	No
Suburban	Yes
City center	No
City center	Yes
Suburban	No
City center	Yes
City center	Yes
Suburban	Yes
City center	Yes
City center	No
Suburban	No
City center	Yes
City center	Yes
Suburban	Yes
City center	Yes
Suburban	No
Suburban	No
City center	No
City center	Yes
Suburban	Yes
City center	Yes
City center	No
Suburban	No
City center	Yes
Suburban	No
City center	Yes
City center	Yes
Suburban	Yes
City center	Yes
Suburban	Yes
City center	Yes
Suburban	No
City center	No

13A-5. Use Pascal's triangle to quickly report the following probabilities for the tosses of coins. For this exercise, it is not necessary to write out the equations.
   a. p [of tossing nine coins and getting all heads] =
   b. p [of tossing four coins and getting one heads and three tails] =
   c. p [of tossing six coins and getting three heads and three tails] =

13A-6. Micro-Medication Corporation is testing a new cancer drug on genetically infected mice. Previous research in its laboratories shows that 50 percent of these mice survive six months without any treatment. Eight mice are administered the drug. Six survive for six months. Test the hypothesis that the drug treatment results in a better survival rate than does no drug at all. Use $\alpha = .001$.

13A-7. A fertility clinic claims to have a procedure for selecting the gender of a child. Among nine randomly selected couples who wished to have girls, seven got the intended result. Test a hypothesis to determine if the procedure does better than chance.

13A-8. Suppose you intend to use the binomial distribution to test a hypothesis at the .01 level of significance with a two-tailed test. What minimum sample size would be required for you to possibly reject the null hypothesis? Show calculations.

Problem Set 13B

On all hypotheses tests, follow the six steps of statistical inference, including test preparation, a conceptual diagram and/or crosstab table, probability curves, and appropriate aspects of a relationship. Use $\alpha = .05$ unless otherwise stipulated.

13B-1. The following crosstab table is from a random sample of social science professors. The row variable, teaching environment, distinguishes whether a professor teaches at a public or a private university. The column variable, job location, indicates the region of the United States where the professors are employed. Compute column percentages for all joint frequency cells.

Teaching Environment	Job Location →	Northeast	West/ Southwest	South	Totals
Public university		192	155	188	
Private university		173	231	55	
Totals					

13B-2. Among 64 physicians and 89 patients surveyed, 36 physicians and 52 patients claimed to favor universal health care coverage over the current diversified medical system. Present these data in a crosstab table. Test the hypothesis that there is a relationship between doctor-patient status and preferred type of medical care system.

13B-3. Use the following data to test the hypothesis that older students are more likely to excel in sophomore-level sociology classes at a large, public university.

	Enrolled and Under 25	Enrolled and 25 or Older
Final grade C or below	33	63
Final grade A or B	72	296

13B-4. Organize the following spreadsheet data into a crosstab table. Test the hypothesis that there is a significant difference between Democrats and Republicans in terms of support for increased protection of marine environments that are home to endangered species.

Political Party Affiliation	Supports Protection
Democrat	No
Republican	No
Democrat	Yes
Democrat	No
Democrat	Yes
Republican	Yes
Democrat	Yes
Republican	No
Republican	Yes
Democrat	Yes
Democrat	No
Republican	No
Republican	Yes
Republican	No
Democrat	Yes
Democrat	Yes
Republican	Yes
Democrat	Yes
Republican	No
Democrat	Yes
Democrat	No

Republican	Yes
Republican	No
Democrat	Yes
Democrat	Yes
Democrat	Yes
Republican	Yes
Democrat	Yes
Democrat	No
Democrat	Yes
Republican	No
Democrat	Yes
Republican	No

13B-5. Use Pascal's triangle to quickly report the following probabilities for the tosses of coins. For this exercise, it is not necessary to write out the equations.

a. p [of tossing eight coins and getting all tails] =

b. p [of tossing five coins and getting two heads and three tails] =

c. p [of tossing four coins and getting two heads and two tails] =

13B-6. Medic-8 Corporation is testing a new cardiovascular drug on genetically infected mice. Previous research in its laboratories shows that 50 percent of these mice survive six months without any treatment. Ten mice are administered the drug. Seven survive for six months. Test the hypothesis that the drug treatment results in a better survival rate than does no drug at all. Use $\alpha = .001$.

13B-7. A fertility clinic claims to have a procedure for selecting the gender of a child. Among eight randomly selected couples who wished to have girls, five got the intended result. Test a hypothesis to determine if the procedure does better than chance.

13B-8. Suppose you intend to use the binomial distribution to test a hypothesis at the .01 level of significance with a two-tailed test. What minimum sample size would be required for you to possibly reject the null hypothesis? Show calculations.

Problem Set 13C

On all hypotheses tests, follow the six steps of statistical inference, including test preparation, a conceptual diagram and/or crosstab table, probability curves, and appropriate aspects of a relationship. Use $\alpha = .05$ unless otherwise stipulated.

13C-1. The following crosstab table is from a random sample of employees of a city government. The column variable is job sector classification, and the row variable is *has earned a college degree*. Compute column percentages for all joint frequency cells.

College Degree	Job Sector →	Service	Staff Support	Managerial/ Administrative	Totals
Yes		6	57	29	
No		41	29	5	
Totals					

13C-2. In a local taste test between vanilla ice cream and vanilla yogurt, 41 of 69 men surveyed preferred ice cream. Among 75 women surveyed, 62 preferred ice cream. Construct a crosstab table. Is there a relationship between gender and dessert choice?

13C-3. A campus student art council proposes to exhibit the work of a controversial artist known for his violent and sexual depictions of religious figures. The council surveys both students and alumni to assess opposition to the exhibit. Using the following fictional data, determine if there is a significant difference in the proportions of students and alumni opposing the exhibit.

	Students	Alumni
Supports the exhibit	172	278
Opposes the exhibit	60	170

13C-4. Organize the following spreadsheet data into a crosstab table. Test the hypothesis that there is a significant difference in support for privatizing public schools between those who voted for Republicans and those who voted for Democrats in the last election (fictional data).

How Voted in Last Presidential Election	Supports Privatizing Schools?
Republican	Yes
Republican	No
Democrat	No
Democrat	No
Republican	No
Republican	Yes
Democrat	No
Republican	Yes
Republican	Yes
Democrat	Yes
Republican	Yes
Republican	No
Democrat	No

Republican	Yes
Republican	Yes
Democrat	No
Republican	Yes
Democrat	No
Democrat	Yes
Republican	No
Republican	Yes
Democrat	Yes
Republican	Yes
Republican	No
Democrat	No
Republican	Yes
Democrat	No
Republican	Yes
Democrat	No
Republican	Yes
Democrat	Yes
Democrat	No
Republican	Yes
Democrat	Yes
Republican	Yes
Democrat	Yes
Democrat	No
Republican	Yes

13C-5. As parents of the baby boom generation, Phillip and Kitty had seven children—all boys. Assuming that for a single birth the probability of having a boy and that of having a girl are the same, what is the probability of a seven-child family being all male? Use Pascal's triangle. For this exercise, it is not necessary to write out the equations.

13C-6. Micro-Medication Corporation is testing another new cancer drug on genetically infected mice. Previous research in its labs shows that 50 percent of these mice survive six months without any treatment. Ten mice are administered this drug treatment. Nine survive for six months. Test the hypothesis that the drug treatment results in a better survival rate than does no drug at all. Use $\alpha = .05$ since this drug is known to be safe.

13C-7. A consumer watch group claims that most charity organizations spend over half their contributions on fund-raising activities. You examine the public disclosure forms of ten randomly selected charity organizations and find that six fit the watch group's criticism. Test a hypothesis to determine whether the watch group's conclusion is correct.

13C-8. Suppose you intend to use the binomial distribution to test a hypothesis at the .05 level of significance with a one-tailed test. What minimum sample size would be required for you to possibly reject the null hypothesis? Show calculations.

Problem Set 13D

On all hypotheses tests, follow the six steps of statistical inference, including test preparation, a conceptual diagram and/or crosstab table, probability curves, and appropriate aspects of a relationship. Use $\alpha = .05$ unless otherwise stipulated.

13D-1. The following crosstab table is from a random sample of adults in a large, southern city. The column variable is *educational attainment,* and the row variable is *gender*. Compute column percentages for all joint frequency cells.

Gender	Highest Educational Attainment →	High School Diploma	College Degree	Graduate Degree	Totals
Female		14	58	24	
Male		17	68	19	
Totals					

13D-2. In a taste test between regular soda and diet soda, 52 of 88 men surveyed preferred regular soda. Among 83 women surveyed, 62 preferred regular soda. Construct a crosstab table. Is there a relationship between gender and soda preference?

13D-3. You survey both students and professors at a university to assess support for changing the format of classroom interaction from lecture-style to discussion-style. Using the following data, determine if there is a significant difference in the proportions of students and professors supporting the change in classroom format.

	Professors	Students
Supports discussion-style	90	602
Supports lecture-style	55	210

13D-4. Organize the following spreadsheet data into a crosstab table. Test the hypothesis that there is a significant difference in support for privatizing the Social Security System between registered Republicans and registered Democrats (fictional data).

Political Party Affiliation	Supports Privatizing the Social Security System?
Democrat	Yes
Democrat	No
Republican	No

Republican	Yes
Republican	Yes
Democrat	Yes
Democrat	No
Republican	Yes
Republican	No
Republican	Yes
Republican	Yes
Democrat	No
Republican	Yes
Democrat	No
Republican	Yes
Democrat	No
Democrat	Yes
Republican	No
Republican	Yes
Republican	No
Democrat	No
Republican	Yes
Republican	Yes
Democrat	Yes
Democrat	No
Republican	Yes
Republican	No
Republican	Yes
Democrat	No
Republican	Yes
Democrat	No
Republican	Yes
Democrat	No
Democrat	No
Republican	No
Republican	Yes
Democrat	No
Republican	Yes
Democrat	Yes
Republican	Yes

13D-5. As parents of the baby boom generation, Sam and Edna had six children—all girls. Assuming that for a single birth the probability of having a boy and that of having a girl are the same, what is the probability of a six-child family being all girls? Use Pascal's triangle. For this exercise, it is not necessary to write out the equations.

13D-6. A pharmaceutical company is testing a new cancer drug on genetically infected mice. Previous research in its labs shows that 50 percent of these mice survive six months without any treatment. Seven mice are administered this drug treatment. Five survive for six months. Test the hypothesis that the drug treatment results in a better survival rate than does no drug at all. Use $\alpha = .05$ since this drug is known to be safe.

13D-7. Someone comments to you that many churches spend over half their contributions on salary for their employees. You examine the public disclosure forms of eight randomly selected churches and find that five fit the watch group's criticism. Test a hypothesis to determine whether the watch group's conclusion is correct.

13D-8. Suppose you intend to use the binomial distribution to test a hypothesis at the .05 level of significance with a one-tailed test. What minimum sample size would be required for you to possibly reject the null hypothesis? Show calculations.

OPTIONAL COMPUTER APPLICATIONS FOR CHAPTER 13

If your class uses the optional computer applications that accompany this text, open the Chapter 13 exercises on *The Statistical Imagination* Web site at www.mhhe.com/ritchey2. The exercises focus on running crosstabs and binomial procedures in *SPSS for Windows* and properly interpreting the output. In addition, appendix D of this text provides a brief overview of the *SPSS* command sequences for procedures covered in this chapter.

Bivariate Correlation and Regression
Part 1: Concepts and Calculations

CHAPTER OUTLINE

Introduction: Improving Best Estimates of a Dependent Variable

Statisticians often are criticized for using jargon and being concerned with theory rather than practical results. A good researcher, whether testing theory or not, places much value on the practical aspects of analysis—making predictions about how the things around us work. In testing hypotheses about relationships between variables, describing practical applications is the final step of analysis, where we answer the questions: So what? What does all this gobbledygook about statistical hypotheses, levels of significance and confidence, and *p*-values mean in the real world? Our responses to these questions should be phrased in down-to-earth language and provide the nitty-gritty details of how findings can be applied to everyday situations. Putting our efforts into practice allows us to contribute to the welfare of society (e.g., improving the delivery of services) or its individuals (e.g., giving advice on stock investments).

The simple idea of making best estimates is a valuable one in applying the findings of statistical work. Especially valuable is the use of predictor (i.e., independent) variables to improve best estimates of a dependent variable of particular interest. Best estimates are directed toward the future. They are based on probabilities that establish confidence in what we are doing. Throughout this textbook we have emphasized that a key ingredient of the statistical imagination is the analysis of causes and consequences with the goal of predicting future events. Making a best estimate focuses our analysis on the practical side. Best estimates allow us to produce results that matter.

Let us retrace our experiences with making best estimates. Suppose, for example, we wish to estimate the mean weight of a population of seventh-graders. In dealing with this single variable, the best estimate of its parameter is a confidence interval—a point estimate such as the mean weight of a sample plus or minus a span of predictable error. If we find a sample mean of, say, 90 pounds, a 95 percent confidence interval may allow us to conclude that the mean weight is between 85 and 95 pounds. But what if we wish to make an estimate of the weight of an *unseen* individual in this population? Here we are left with a very gross estimate—the sample mean weight of 90 pounds—a point estimate. We make this estimate grudgingly because we know that not every seventh-grader weighs exactly 90 pounds. *Without any other information about the individual*, this is the best we can do.

From our experience with two variables, however, we know that the best estimate of a dependent variable can be improved if we can identify independent variables—predictor variables—and extend the analysis to the bivariate level. Suppose, for example, Doug is a seventh-grade boy and we know that boys tend to weigh on average 10 pounds more than the mean weight of seventh-graders as a whole. As we learned in Chapter 11, given this effect of male gender, we can now improve our best estimate of Doug's weight by adding 10 pounds to the mean of 90 to get a best estimate of 100 pounds—the mean weight of seventh-grade boys. By introducing a predictor or independent variable, X = gender, we improve estimates of the dependent variable, Y = weight. Knowledge about X is used to adjust the precision of best estimates of Y.

A Correlation Between Two Interval/Ratio Variables

With a nominal independent variable such as gender, estimates of Y can be adjusted for only two "scores"—the "X-categories" of male and female. In examining the relationship between two interval/ratio variables, however, we must deal with a large number of scores. For a sample of adults, with an independent variable X such as height, there are as many as 25 "height membership categories"—scores ranging from about 56 inches (4 feet, 8 inches tall) to about 80 inches (6 feet, 8 inches tall). We could test for differences of means among 25 height categories, but this would be cumbersome and would require a very large sample.

Fortunately, it is not necessary to think of each inch as a separate height category or X-category. Instead we treat each inch of height as an X-score, an increment along its interval/ratio unit of measure. If we are attempting to estimate weight (Y), we can seek to improve our estimates *for each additional inch* of height (X) from a low of 56 inches to a high of 80 inches. Because we know that taller people tend to be heavier, we search for a way to determine how much weight should be added *for each additional inch of height*. The statistical imagination beckons us to ask: What is the effect on weight of a 1-inch increase in height? Informed by such knowledge, we can quickly make very fine, 1-inch height adjustments to best estimates of weight.

How are these fine adjustments made? Interval/ratio variables, with their set units of measurement, offer many mathematical and geometric advantages. Whereas with earlier statistical tests we were unable to address all four aspects of a relationship, with two interval/ratio variables we are able to do that quite precisely by using the mathematical qualities of a straight line to estimate Y for given quantities of X. This straight-line, or "linear," geometry can be used when two variables are correlated. A **correlation** is *a systematic change in the scores of two interval/ratio variables*.

---

a correlation   A systematic change in the scores of two interval/ratio variables.

Two interval/ratio variables correlate (or "co-relate") when the measurements of one variable change in tandem with the measurements of the other. For example, there is a correlation between height (X) and weight (Y). Measurements of lots of inches (tallness) tend to coincide with measurements of lots of pounds (heaviness). Thus, to estimate weight, if someone is tall, add some pounds, or if that person is short, subtract some. Correlations between two interval/ratio variables are very common, and therefore, the idea of correlation is intuitively appealing. For example, in a population of adults, a correlation exists between age and the number of times a doctor is seen in a year; that is, older adults tend to go to the doctor more. Among college students, time spent reading is correlated with grade point average (GPA); the more time spent reading, the better the grades. Using slightly different terminology, we can say that educational level is "a correlate of" income; the higher the educational level, the higher the income. Two variables are correlated if their measurements consistently change together from case to case. We say that the measurements are ordered together or coordinated—or, simply, correlated.

Identifying a Linear Relationship

With two interval/ratio variables, the procedure for improving best estimates of a dependent variable (Y) by accounting for its relationship with an independent variable (X) is called *simple or bivariate linear correlation and regression analysis. (Simple* refers to the two-variable case. With three or more variables, we say *multiple correlation and regression analysis.)* The central idea behind simple linear correlation and regression is to use the formula for a straight line to obtain a best estimate of Y (e.g., weight in pounds) for any given value of X (e.g., any height in inches). We use the symbol $\hat{Y}$ (Y-cap) to refer to this estimated value of Y.

Central Idea Behind Simple, Bivariate Linear Correlation and Regression Analysis

To use the formula for a straight line to improve best estimates of an interval/ratio dependent variable (Y) for all values of an interval/ratio independent variable (X).

The formula for a straight line to estimate Y is

$$\hat{Y} = a + bX$$

(You may have seen different symbols in geometry texts, where the straight-line formula is often presented as $\hat{Y} = mx + b$.) Before describing what each of the symbols in the formula signifies, we must grasp the circumstances in which this formula can be used accurately. First of all, this formula applies only when both variables are of interval/ratio levels of measurement. Second, the formula can be used appropriately only when there is a linear relationship between X and Y on a scatterplot, a graphical representation of data. A **scatterplot** is *a two-dimensional grid* (like the lines on graph paper) *of the coordinates of two interval/ratio variables, X and Y*. A **coordinate** is *a point on a scatterplot where the values of X and Y are plotted for a case*. The statistics that accompany scatterplots apply only to situations in which the coordinates fall into a **linear pattern**—*one where the coordinates of the scatterplot fall into a cigar-shaped pattern that approximates the shape of a straight line*. The consequence of failing to properly identify a linear relationship are further discussed in the *Statistical Follies and Fallacies* section of this chapter.

Graphical Representation of the Relationship Between Two Interval/Ratio Variables

Scatterplot: A two-dimensional grid of the coordinates of two interval/ratio variables, X and Y.

Coordinate: A point on a scatterplot where the values of X and Y are plotted for a case.

Linear pattern: One where the coordinates of the scatterplot fall into a cigar-shaped pattern that approximates the shape of a straight line.

Drawing the Scatterplot

Table 14–1 presents data on the heights (X) and weights (Y) of 16 male high school seniors. Figure 14–1 presents the scatterplot of height (X) as a predictor of weight (Y). (For clarity, we do not draw the grid lines on the scatterplot; we simply imagine that they are there.) The coordinates of students 2 and 16 are highlighted in the table and the figure. A scatterplot is similar to a histogram; on both, the horizontal axis provides values of the interval/ratio variable X, and we call this the X-axis. The vertical axes of the two graphs are different, however. Recall that on a histogram, the vertical axis represents the frequency of occurrence (f) for a given value of X. But on a scatterplot the vertical axis represents values of a second interval/ratio variable Y, and we call this the Y-axis. Traditionally, X symbolizes the predictor (or independent) variable and Y symbolizes the dependent variable, the one we desire to explain.

Coordinates are plotted by finding an X-score on the X-axis and a Y-score on the Y-axis and then locating the coordinate in the grid. For instance, student 16's X, Y-coordinate is $X = 72$ inches, $Y = 176$ pounds, or simply (72, 176). It is plotted by moving over to 72 inches on the X-axis and then moving upward to 176 pounds on the Y-axis.

Identifying a Linear Pattern

On a scatterplot, a linear relationship is present if the coordinates fall into an elongated, cigar-shaped pattern that slopes up or down. The data in Figure 14–1 appear to fit an upward-sloping pattern. To get a sense of proportion about linear relationships, observe the actual numbers in Table 14–1, where the values of X and Y are rank-ordered

TABLE 14–1 | Heights and weights for 16 male high school seniors

Student	Height (in inches) (X)	Weight (in pounds) (Y)
1	65	140
2	66	144
3	66	150
4	67	145
5	67	155
6	68	149
7	68	154
8	68	160
9	69	155
10	69	164
11	70	159
12	70	164
13	70	170
14	71	164
15	71	170
16	72	176

FIGURE 14–1

Scatterplot of height (X) as a predictor of weight (Y)

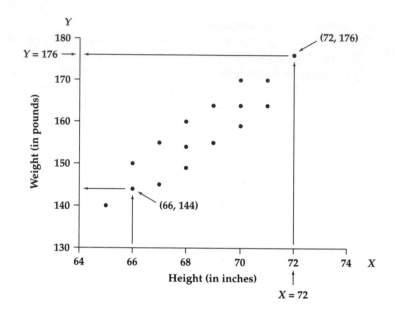

from the shortest to the tallest heights. Note that as we move down the table column for heights, weights also tend to increase. This is an indication that the sizes of X and Y systematically change; that is, they shift upward together. In the scatterplot of Figure 14–1 this shift is apparent in the steady upward rise of the coordinates from left to right. The coordinates fit rather well into a cigar-shaped, linear pattern. As we increase height by moving over on the X-axis, the scores of Y (weight) also increase upward along the Y-axis. When both variables increase in tandem, we call this a positive relationship.

> **a positive correlation**   An increase in X is related to an increase in Y. (As X increases, Y has a tendency to increase.)

The scatterplot in Figure 14–2 presents a negative relationship between two interval/ratio variables. The coordinates fit a cigar-shaped, linear pattern, but with a steady downward drop in the positions of the coordinates from left to right. An increase in caregiver role strain is related to a decrease in caregiver satisfaction with physician communication. As the X-scores go up, the Y-scores go down.

> **a negative correlation**   An increase in X is related to a decrease in Y. (As X increases, Y has a tendency to decrease.)

Finally, what can we expect of a scatterplot if two variables are unrelated; that is, what if X is not a good predictor of Y? This is illustrated in Figure 14–3, where X is a caregiver's education and Y is the degree to which a patient can function without the caregiver's help. This scatterplot reveals no relationship between X and Y. The pattern

FIGURE 14-2

Scatterplot of the negative relationship of caregiver satisfaction with physician communication regressed on caregiving role strain: As caregiving role strain increases, caregiver satisfaction with physician communication decreases

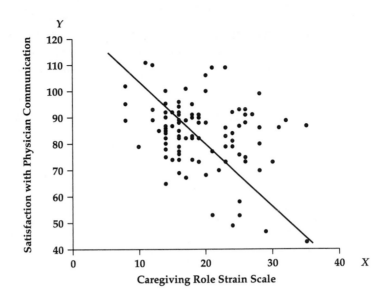

FIGURE 14-3

Scatterplot of patient's ability to function without help regressed on caregiver education (shows no relationship between the two variables): Caregiver's educational level does not predict patient's ability to function

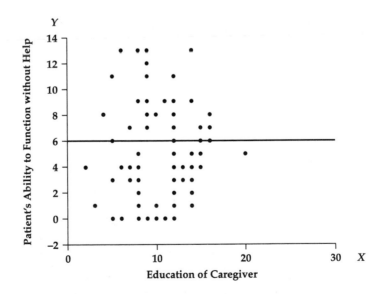

of coordinates lacks an elongated, sloped cigar shape. When no correlation exists between X and Y, the mean of Y remains the best estimate of Y for all values of X. In other words, knowing a caregiver's education does not give us any information on how to improve a best estimate of a patient's ability to function without help. The medical condition of the patient has nothing to do with the educational level of the caregiver.

> **no correlation**   An increase in *X* is unrelated to the scores of *Y*. (As *X* increases, *Y*-scores vary randomly.)

Using the Linear Regression Equation to Measure the Effects of *X* on *Y*

When we find a distinctive linear pattern in the coordinates of a scatterplot, this tells us that the scores of a dependent variable *Y* follow those of an independent variable *X* either upward or downward. With knowledge of this predictable pattern, we are equipped to adjust estimates of *Y*. For example, in Figure 14–1 we appear to have a positive relationship between height (*X*) and weight (*Y*). Thus, we know to provide a high estimate of weight if height is high (i.e., tall) and provide a low estimate of weight if height is low (i.e, on the shorter side). In fact, linear correlation and regression analysis allows us to make very fine mathematical adjustments in these estimates.

How can we make highly precise adjustments? If the scatterplot reveals a cigar-shaped, linear pattern of coordinates, a straight line can be drawn to "fit" the pattern of coordinates. This line is the *one that falls as close to every coordinate as possible* and is called the "best-fitting" line or, technically, the **regression line**. *Regression* means falling back or "gravitating" toward a point or having a tendency to move in a direction. For instance, we would predict that taller people tend to move in the heavy direction on weight. It is customary to say that the dependent variable (*Y*) "is regressed on" the independent variable (*X*). In this example we would say that weight is regressed on height.

> **the regression line**   The best-fitting straight line plotted through the *X, Y*-coordinates of a scatterplot of two interval/ratio variables.

Figure 14–4 shows Figure 14–1 with the regression line drawn in. (We will discuss how to determine the precise location of this line below.) Once we have located this line, we can use coordinates on it to identify *the best estimate* of weight ($\acute{Y}$) for any amount of height (*X*). In Figure 14–4, two coordinates on the regression line, (67, 150.23) and (72, 173.33), are highlighted to show how *X* (height) is used to estimate *Y* (weight). The best estimate of the weight of a 67-inch-tall senior is 150.23 pounds; that of a 72-inch-tall senior, 173.33 pounds. In fact, we can use this line to estimate the weight of individuals of any height. We move over to a value of *X* on the *X*-axis and draw a perpendicular line up to the regression line. Then we draw a line from there over to the *Y*-axis; our best estimate of weight is the point where this line crosses the *Y*-axis. These values of *X* and *Y* will be coordinates that sit on the regression line. Note carefully that we call this estimate of weight the predicted *Y* and use the symbol $\acute{Y}$ to distinguish it from the actual observed weight of *Y* = 176 pounds.

FIGURE 14–4

Illustration of
the regression
line for height
as a predictor of
weight, that is,
weight
regressed on
height

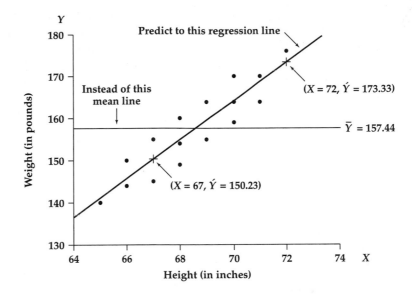

The $\acute{Y}$ is a "knowledgeable" estimate—*one based on knowing the precise relationship between height and weight.*

The key benefit of bivariate regression analysis is the ability to improve estimates of Y in a population by using the regression line instead of merely reporting the sample mean of Y. Remember that if we know nothing but the mean of Y, this mean is the best we can do in predicting weight. In Figure 14–4 note that we also drew the line representing the mean of Y. When we do not know a person's height, we always predict to this mean line for weight. Once we add the knowledge of a relationship with height, however, we can predict to a value of Y on the regression line—the $\acute{Y}$ that corresponds to a subject's X-score. Essentially, what linear regression analysis does is allow us to predict to the regression line rather than to the flat line that represents the mean of Y. When we do this, the resulting estimates are closer to the true values of Y. This can be observed in the scatterplot (Figure 14–4). The regression line is intentionally designed to get as close to the actual coordinates as possible. This line is the best fit.

Benefit of Bivariate Regression Analysis for Improving Best Estimates of a Dependent Variable Y

Allows us to use an X, $\acute{Y}$-coordinate point on the regression line as a prediction of Y (in place of simply reporting the mean of Y).

$\acute{Y}$ = value of Y predicted by the regression line ($\acute{Y}$ is a knowledgeable estimate of Y based on knowing that Y is related to X).

For instance, if we are asked to estimate the weight of a high school senior *without* knowing his or her height, our best estimate would be 157.44 pounds—the total sample mean of Y computed from the data in Table 14–1. But if we know that height and weight are "linearly" related, we can place a straight line through the coordinates on the scatterplot and estimate a weight (Y) by finding its $X, \hat{Y}$-coordinate on this regression line. For instance, if this senior is rather tall at 72 inches, we will estimate his weight to be 173.33 pounds. In so doing, we are adding 15.89 pounds to the mean of 157.44 pounds to account for his above-average height.

Another way to look at the improvement in prediction is to view it in terms of proportional reduction in the error (PRE) of prediction. Suppose our 72-inch-tall student is named Christopher. Without knowledge of his height we would have had to predict his weight to be the mean of 157.44 pounds. Later, we find that he is case 16 in Table 14–1 with an actual weight of 176 pounds. The estimate "to the mean" misses his true weight by 18.56 pounds on the low side. (Recall from Chapter 5 that this amount is his deviation score.)

Christopher's deviation score $=$ error in estimating to the mean
$$= Y_{(Christopher)} - \bar{Y} = 176 - 157.44 = 18.56 \text{ pounds}$$

Suppose that we have the opportunity to predict his weight again, but with knowledge of the relationship of height to weight. Instead of predicting to the mean, we predict "to the regression line" (Figure 14–4). The best estimate of a 72-inch-tall student is the $\hat{Y}$-score of 173.33. Using this as a knowledgeable estimate of Christopher's weight results in considerably less error—only 2.67 pounds compared to the error of 18.56 pounds when we predict to the mean:

Error in estimating Christopher's weight to the regression line
$$= Y_{(Christopher)} - \hat{Y}_{(X = 72)} = 176 - 173.33 = 2.67 \text{ pounds}$$

We have improved this estimate of weight (Y) by a considerable amount by taking into account the fact that weight is correlated with height (X). As we can see by observing the scatterplot in Figure 14–4, error in predictions for the whole sample (and population) is reduced greatly if predictions are made to the regression line instead of the mean line.

In summary, when a relationship is found to exist between two interval/ratio variables, make best estimates by using the regression line rather than the mean. Knowledgeable estimates of Y—those taking into account X—reduce errors in predictions. This is the essence of bivariate correlation and regression analysis.

Pearson's *r* Bivariate Correlation Coefficient

On a scatterplot, the tighter the fit of data coordinates around the regression line is, the stronger the correlation between X and Y is and the more precisely Y is estimated for any value of X. Pearson's r is a widely used bivariate correlation coefficient that measures tightness of fit of X, Y-coordinates around the regression line. The formula for Pearson's r is as follows:

Calculating Pearson's *r* Bivariate Correlation Coefficient

$$r = \frac{\Sigma (X - \overline{X}) (Y - \overline{Y})}{\sqrt{\Sigma (X - \overline{X})^2 \, \Sigma (Y - \overline{Y})^2}}$$

where

 r = Pearson's bivariate correlation coefficient

 X = an interval/ratio independent variable

 Y = an interval/ratio dependent variable

 $\overline{X}$ = the mean of the independent variable, X

 $\overline{Y}$ = the mean of the dependent variable, Y

What Pearson's *r* Measures

Tightness of fit of X, Y-coordinates around the regression line.

The extent to which deviations of scores from the means of X and Y tend to fluctuate in tandem.

Computational Spreadsheet for Calculating Bivariate Correlation and Regression Statistics

To compute the statistics in this chapter, the following statistics and sums are needed. (Review Chapter 5, Table 5–1, where some of these statistics were used in calculating the standard deviation.)

$$n, \Sigma X, \Sigma Y, \overline{X}, \overline{Y}, \Sigma (X - \overline{X}), \Sigma (Y - \overline{Y}), \Sigma (X - \overline{X}) (Y - \overline{Y}),$$
$$\Sigma (X - \overline{X})^2, \Sigma (Y - \overline{Y})^2$$

Using the data on heights and weights in Table 14–1, we can quickly compute these elements of the equations with the computational spreadsheet in Table 14–2. First, compute the means of X and Y:

$$\overline{X} = \frac{\Sigma X}{n} = \frac{1,097}{16} = 68.56 \text{ inches}$$

$$\overline{Y} = \frac{\Sigma Y}{n} = \frac{2,519}{16} = 157.44 \text{ pounds}$$

These means are then used to compute the sums of deviations scores for X and Y (i.e., $\Sigma(X - \bar{X})$ and $\Sigma(Y - \bar{Y})$, columns A and B in Table 14–2). Recall that the deviation scores for a variable must sum to zero within rounding error. Therefore, these deviation scores are squared and summed to obtain the sums of squares (or *variation*) for X and Y (columns D and E in Table 14–2). The sum for column C in Table 14–2 is called the *covariation*. For each case, the deviation score for X is multiplied by the deviation score for Y and the results are summed.

---

covariation of *X* and *Y*

$$\Sigma\,(X - \bar{X})(Y - \bar{Y})$$

The sum of the deviation scores of X multiplied by the deviation scores of Y.

TABLE 14–2 | Spreadsheet for computing correlation and regression statistics: heights and weights for 16 male high school seniors

Student	Givens Height (inches) X	Givens Weight (pounds) Y	A $X - \bar{X}$	B $Y - \bar{Y}$	C $(X - \bar{X})(Y - \bar{Y})$	D $(X - \bar{X})^2$	E $(Y - \bar{Y})^2$
1	65	140	−3.56	−17.44	62.09	12.67	304.15
2	66	144	−2.56	−13.44	34.41	6.55	180.63
3	66	150	−2.56	−7.44	19.05	6.55	55.35
4	67	145	−1.56	−12.44	19.41	2.43	154.75
5	67	155	−1.56	−2.44	3.81	2.43	5.95
6	68	149	−.56	−8.44	4.73	.31	71.23
7	68	154	−.56	−3.44	1.93	.31	11.83
8	68	160	−.56	2.56	−1.43	.31	6.55
9	69	155	.44	−2.44	−1.07	.19	5.95
10	69	164	.44	6.56	2.89	.19	43.03
11	70	159	1.44	1.56	2.25	2.07	2.43
12	70	164	1.44	6.56	9.45	2.07	43.03
13	70	170	1.44	12.56	18.09	2.07	157.75
14	71	164	2.44	6.56	16.01	5.95	43.03
15	71	170	2.44	12.56	30.65	5.95	157.75
16	72	176	3.44	18.56	63.85	11.83	344.47

$n = 16$ $\Sigma Y = 2{,}519$ $\Sigma(Y - \bar{Y}) = -.04^*$ $\Sigma(X - \bar{X})^2 = 61.88$

$\Sigma X = 1{,}097$ $\Sigma\,(X - \bar{X}) = .04^*$ $\Sigma\,(X - \bar{X})(Y - \bar{Y}) = 286.12$ $\Sigma(Y - \bar{Y})^2 = 1{,}587.88$

* Deviations did not sum to zero due to rounding error.

The calculations and sums in the spreadsheet in Table 14–2 provide what is needed to calculate Pearson's r for our data on the heights and weights of male high school seniors:

$$r = \frac{\Sigma (X - \overline{X})(Y - \overline{Y})}{\sqrt{\Sigma (X - \overline{X})^2 \Sigma (Y - \overline{Y})^2}} = \frac{286.12}{\sqrt{(61.88)(1,587.88)}} = \frac{286.12}{313.46} = .91$$

Characteristics of the Pearson's r *Bivariate Correlation Coefficient*

Computed values of Pearson's r can range from -1.0 to $+1.0$. The sign ($+$ or $-$) of r indicates the direction of a relationship. For the example in Figure 14–4 on the relationship between height and weight, we can see that the regression line slopes upward: Low values of X correspond with low values of Y, and high values of X correspond with high values of Y. The upward slope indicates that the direction of the relationship is positive, and the Pearson's r calculates to a positive value. When $r = +1.0$, this is a (very unusual) perfect positive correlation, meaning that X is a perfect predictor of Y and that as X increases, Y increases. With a perfect positive correlation, every coordinate of the scatterplot rests on the regression line itself, and the line slopes upward.

When X and Y are correlated in the negative direction, the regression line of the scatterplot slopes downward so that as X increases, Y decreases. Pearson's r will calculate to a negative value. For example, the greater the number of poor people living in a community (X), the lower the rate of home ownership (Y). When $r = -1.0$, we have a (very unusual) perfect negative correlation, meaning that X is a perfect predictor of Y and that as X increases, Y decreases. With a perfect negative correlation, every coordinate of the scatterplot rests on the downward-sloping regression line. Perfect correlations in either the positive or the negative direction are unusual, especially in the social sciences.

The absolute value of Pearson's r (its size, ignoring its sign) indicates the tightness of fit of coordinates around the regression line of a scatterplot. The larger the absolute value of Pearson's r is, the closer coordinates cling to the line. For the plot of Figure 14–4 the coordinates fit rather tightly around the regression line, as reflected in the rather large Pearson's r of .91.

As we noted above, when we have *no correlation* between X and Y, knowing the values of X does not improve estimates of Y. This is the case in Figure 14–3. With no correlation, $r = 0$. Another example of no correlation is weight as a predictor of GPA; knowing how much people weigh tells us nothing about their GPAs.

The characteristics of bivariate Pearson's r can be summarized as follows:

Characteristics of the Pearson's *r* Correlation Coefficient

1. Computed values of Pearson's r can range from -1.0 to $+1.0$.
2. The larger the absolute value of Pearson's r, the tighter the fit of X,Y-coordinates around the regression line.

3. When the regression line slopes upward, we have a positive correlation: An *increase* in the level of X-scores is related to an *increase* in the level of Y-scores. Pearson's r will be positive up to a value of +1.00.

4. When the regression line slopes downward, we have a negative correlation: An *increase* in the level of X-scores is related to a *decrease* in the level of Y-scores. Pearson's r will be negative down to a value of −1.00.

5. When the regression line is flat (i.e., has no slope), we have no correlation and Pearson's r = 0. An *increase* in the level of X-scores is *not* related to a change in the level of Y-scores. That is, knowing an X-score does not improve an estimate of Y-scores.

Understanding the Pearson's r Formulation

Let us examine the equation for Pearson's r and relate it to the scatterplot to gain a sense of proportion about what this statistic gauges. Figure 14–5 presents the scatterplot broken into squares or *quadrants* marked in circled numbers 1 through 4. The quadrants identify areas above and below the means of X and Y. Quadrant 1 holds coordinates for male high school seniors who score below the mean of X (below average height) but above the mean of Y (above average weight). Quadrant 2 presents coordinates for those students with scores above both the means of X and Y. Quadrant 3 holds coordinates for those with scores below both the means of X and Y. Quadrant 4 presents coordinates for students above the mean of X but below the mean of Y. Notice that for this positive linear relationship quadrants 2 and 3 load up with coordinates. Those students who score high on height (X) tend also to score high on weight (Y) and they fall in quadrant 2.

FIGURE 14–5

How coordinates of height and weight load in diagonal quadrants when there is a linear relationship

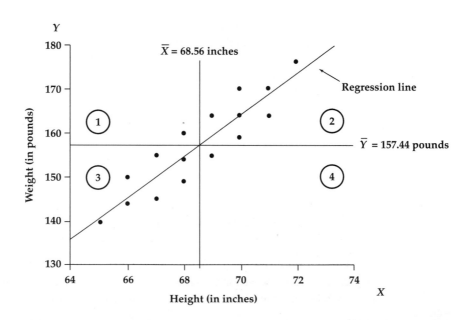

Those students who score low on height tend also to score low on weight and they fall in quadrant 3.

When a student falls above the mean of X, we can say that he deviates in the positive direction; that is, his deviation score is positive. For example, if a senior is 72 inches tall, his deviation score is

$$(X - \overline{X}) = 72 - 68.56 = 3.44 \text{ inches}$$

A focus on deviation scores is apparent in the equation for Pearson's r and in the calculation spreadsheet in Table 14–2. All elements of the Pearson's r equation involve deviation scores and squared deviation scores (i.e., sums of squares or variation).

So how does the Pearson's r equation measure bivariate correlation? In its calculation, Pearson's r gauges how deviation scores of X and Y fluctuate together, or *covary*. If there is a positive relationship between X and Y, then we would expect that students who deviate on the positive side of height also deviate on the positive side of weight. To measure deviations for an entire sample, we must square them and sum them to obtain the variation or sum of squares. The denominator of the Pearson's r equation multiplies the total sum of squares for X times the total sum of squares for Y. (Taking the square root is necessary to deal with the fact that the scores were squared because the sum of deviation scores for any variable is zero.) The total sums of squares or total variation for a variable gauges *error*, how much the scores miss the mean. The denominator of the Pearson's r equation gauges how much total error X and Y have relative to one another. However, by simply multiplying these variations of X and Y this calculation assumes that scores of X and Y are randomly distributed around their means. The sum of these multiples is essentially a standard error. The denominator provides total error assuming no relationship between X and Y. It does not take into account that the X, Y-coordinates may fluctuate together in a linear pattern. For our example of weight regressed on height, the result in the denominator is 313.46.

The numerator of the Pearson's r equation, however, gauges how well X and Y fluctuate in a pattern. It involves multiplying, for each case, the deviation scores of X by the deviation scores of Y to obtain the covariation. Notice columns A, B, and C in spreadsheet Table 14–2. Negative deviation scores for X (column A) tend to occur with negative deviation scores for Y (column B). These are the coordinates that fall in quadrant 3 of Figure 14–5. When two negatives are multiplied, the result is positive (column C). Similarly, the positive deviation scores for X tend to cluster with positive deviation scores for Y (quadrant 2 in Figure 14–5). The multiple of these scores is also positive. Thus, when quadrants 2 and 3 load up because of a linear relationship, the results for column C include lots of positive numbers that sum to a considerably large covariation, in this case 286.12. The numerator takes into account how the scores of X and Y are linked and, thus, measures the correlation effect of the relationship. When this number is large relative to the total error of the denominator, a considerable value of r results. When there is a perfect positive relationship, the numerator will equal the denominator, resulting in a Pearson's r of 1.00.

What the equation does then is calculate in the denominator the total error—deviations from the means of X and Y—disregarding any connection between X and Y. The numerator gauges how deviations from X and Y fluctuate together due to their correlation effect. This effect happens when there is a relationship between the variables.

The ratio of the correlation effect in the numerator to the total error in the denominator is Pearson's r. It essentially determines how much of the deviation scores for X and Y can be explained by their covariance, their tendency to fluctuate in a linear pattern. In Chapter 15, we will discuss the strength of a relationship for bivariate correlation and regression statistics. We will show how Pearson's r can be used to very precisely establish how much error in predictions of Y can be reduced by knowledge of its relationship with X. Fundamentally, Pearson's r establishes whether deviations of X and Y are patterned.

As noted, Pearson's r can calculate to a negative score. When the relationship is negative with a downward slope in the regression line, quadrants 1 and 4 will load up with cases. In these quadrants, one variable has positive deviation scores and the other has negative deviation scores. When they are multiplied to obtain the covariation, the result is a high but negative sum in the numerator of the equation. This produces a negative r.

When there is no relationship between X and Y, deviation scores will be randomly positive and negative. All four quadrants will have randomly scattered coordinates. The positive and negative multiples for the covariation (column C in Table 14–2) will wash out, resulting in a zero or small numerator. The calculation of r will fall close to zero.

Regression Statistics

Now that we have a general idea of how a straight line in a scatterplot can be used to make better estimates of Y if we know X, let us discuss how to make precise mathematical calculations of these estimates. For instance, let us continue to examine the correlation between height and weight by using the spreadsheet in Table 14–2 and the scatterplot of Figure 14–4. Now that we know that height and weight are related, we can adjust estimates of weight by taking into account the fact that taller boys are heavier than shorter boys. We can answer the question: In general, how many extra pounds should be added or subtracted to any estimate of weight for a particular height? Specifically, what are the best estimates of weight for male high school seniors of various heights? Answers are established with the following formula for a straight line:

Linear Equation Formula (or Regression Line Formula) for the Relationship Between Two Interval/Ratio Variables

$$\acute{Y} = a + bX$$

where

$\acute{Y} =$ "the predicted Y" (an estimate of the dependent variable Y computed for a given value of the independent variable X)

$a =$ Y-intercept, the point at which the regression line intersects the Y-axis when $X = 0$

$b =$ slope of the regression line (called the regression coefficient)

To use this formula, we start by calculating the values of a and b. Once a and b are plugged into the formula, any number of inches of height, or X-scores, can be substituted for X in the formula. Then we solve for $\acute{Y}$—the best estimate of weight for that number of inches of height. The resulting X, $\acute{Y}$-coordinates will fit onto a straight line that best fits the pattern of coordinates on the scatterplot. Before calculating the elements of this formula, let us examine each term.

The Regression Coefficient or Slope, b

In the regression equation $\acute{Y} = a + bX$, b is the *slope* of the regression line and is called the *regression coefficient*. The regression coefficient tells us how many pounds to add to an estimate of weight for each additional 1-inch increase in height.

The Regression Coefficient, b

$$b = \text{slope of the regression line of the scatterplot}$$
$$= \text{effect on } Y \text{ of a 1-}unit \text{ change in } X$$
$$= \text{"rise divided by run"}$$

where

$Y = $ an interval/ratio level dependent variable

$X = $ an interval/ratio level independent variable

What does the slope convey? For our data on the heights and weights of high school senior boys, $b = 4.62$ pounds per inch. A 1-unit change in X would be 1 inch. To interpret this slope we would say that "a 1-inch increase in the level of height is related to a 4.62-pound increase in the level of weight."

As with jogging up or down a hill, the slope tells us how much rise (a vertical gain of b on Y) we accomplish when we run 1 mile (a horizontal gain or "run" of 1 unit on X). For example, if the slope of a mountainside road is 300 feet per mile, for every mile we jog, we rise 300 feet in elevation. The larger the value of b, the steeper the slope. If a jogger elsewhere is rising 600 feet per mile, he or she is running up a much steeper hill. Figure 14–6 illustrates how the size of b conveys the steepness of the slope.

The Y-intercept, a

The Y-intercept, a, in the regression equation $\acute{Y} = a + bX$ is the value of Y when $X = 0$. The Y-intercept is called the *constant* of the equation. Whereas the equation multiplies the slope b by different X-scores, we add the same (a constant) amount of a to each calculation. As we will calculate below, for our data on heights and weights, $a = -159.31$ pounds. We may view this quantity as a starting point from which to add or subtract amounts of bX.

What does a do? It anchors the regression line to the Y-axis. This is necessary because there can be any number of independent variables (X's) that correlate with Y *and* have the same slope but different magnitudes of Y. Or there can be different populations with the same slopes but different Y-intercepts. Having the same slopes, b, these regression lines

FIGURE 14–6

Illustration of the slope as the ratio of a vertical change in Y to a horizontal change of one unit in X

X = distance run in miles Y = elevation in feet

A. Slope of rise in elevation regressed on a distance run: b = 600 feet of "rise" per mile

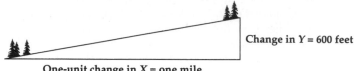

Change in Y = 600 feet

One-unit change in X = one mile

$$b = \text{slope} = \frac{\text{rise}}{\text{run}} = \frac{\text{change in } Y}{\text{one-unit change in } X} = \frac{600 \text{ feet}}{1 \text{ mile}} = 600 \text{ feet per mile}$$

B. Slope of rise in elevation regressed on a distance run: b = 300 feet of "rise" per mile)

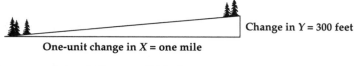

Change in Y = 300 feet

One-unit change in X = one mile

$$b = \text{slope} = \frac{\text{rise}}{\text{run}} = \frac{\text{change in } Y}{\text{one-unit change in } X} = \frac{300 \text{ feet}}{1 \text{ mile}} = 300 \text{ feet per mile}$$

C. Slope of rise in elevation regressed on distance run on flat land (i.e., b = 0 feet "rise" per mile)

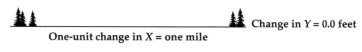

Change in Y = 0.0 feet

One-unit change in X = one mile

$$b = \text{slope} = \frac{\text{rise}}{\text{run}} = \frac{\text{change in } Y}{\text{one-unit change in } X} = \frac{0 \text{ feet}}{1 \text{ mile}} = 0 \text{ feet per mile}$$

would be parallel to one another on a scatterplot and would be distinguishable only by their constants, a. Finally, note that the Y-intercept is often a hypothetical point because there may be no case where $X = 0$. For example, no one in a population can have a height of zero. Thus, it is not unusual for a to calculate to an impractical value such as *minus* 159.31 pounds.

The *Y*-intercept, *a* (the constant of the regression equation)

a = Y-intercept of the regression line of a scatterplot

= the point where the regression line intersects the Y-axis when $X = 0$

= the predicted value of Y when $X = 0$ (i.e., $\acute{Y}_{(X = 0)}$)

where

Y = an interval/ratio level dependent variable

X = an interval/ratio level independent variable

Calculating the Terms of the Regression Line Formula

To compile the linear equation formula $\acute{Y} = a + bX$, we first compute b as follows:

Calculating the Bivariate Regression Coefficient *b*, the Slope of the Regression Line

$$b = \frac{\Sigma (X - \overline{X})(Y - \overline{Y})}{\Sigma (X - \overline{X})^2}$$

where

> b = the regression coefficient (the slope of the regression line)
>
> X = an interval/ratio level independent variable
>
> Y = an interval/ratio level dependent variable
>
> $\overline{X}$ = the mean of the independent variable, X
>
> $\overline{Y}$ = the mean of the dependent variable, Y

We then compute a by substituting the calculated value of b into the equation $\acute{Y} = a + bX$. But in order to solve for a, we must stipulate known values of X and Y. As it turns out, on any regression line, the coordinate of the means of X and Y will fall on the line. Thus, we can substitute the means of X and Y, along with b, and solve for a.

Calculating the Y-intercept, *a*

$$a = \overline{Y} - b\overline{X}$$

where

> a = Y-intercept
>
> $\overline{Y}$ = mean of the dependent variable
>
> b = regression coefficient (the slope of the regression line)
>
> $\overline{X}$ = mean of the independent variable

Finally, we insert a and b into the regression line formula:

$$\acute{Y} = a + bX$$

Let us now compute the regression line statistics for weight regressed on height (Figure 14–4). Taking sums from the computational spreadsheet in Table 14–2, we first compute b:

$$b = \frac{\Sigma (X - \overline{X})(Y - \overline{Y})}{\Sigma (X - \overline{X})^2} = \frac{286.12}{61.88} = 4.62 \text{ pounds per inch}$$

Next we use $\overline{X}$, $\overline{Y}$ and b to compute a:

$$a = \overline{Y} - b\overline{X} = 157.44 - (4.62)(68.56) = -159.31 \text{ pounds}$$

Finally, we specify the precise equation for the regression line that fits the scatterplot of weight regressed on height by substituting the computed values of a and b (Figure 14–4):

$$\acute{Y} = a + bX = -159.31 + (4.62)X$$

This regression equation now may be used to calculate $\acute{Y}$, the "best estimate" of Y (weight) for any value of X (height). We insert a few X-scores into the equation and solve for $\acute{Y}$ to get the results in Table 14–3.

We plot the regression line by marking two or more of these $X, \acute{Y}$-coordinates on the scatterplot and drawing a straight line between them. This is shown above in Figure 14–4, where the coordinates (67, 150.23) and (72, 173.33) are used as reference points for the line. Double-check the accuracy of the line by finding on Figure 14–4 the other $X, \acute{Y}$-coordinates computed in Table 14–3. These coordinates will fall in a straight line. Note also that although the Y-intercept is *minus* 159.31 pounds, the regression line crosses the Y-axis at about a positive 140 pounds. This discrepancy is due to the fact that the values of X and Y where their axes intersect are not zeros. Instead, the X- and Y-axes, as drawn, start at about 65 inches and 130 pounds,

TABLE 14–3 I X, $\acute{Y}$-Coordinates: Best estimates of weights ($\acute{Y}$) of the population of male high school seniors based on heights (X)

Givens	Calculations		Important Points about the Characteristics of the Linear Equation $\acute{Y} = a + bX$
X (height in inches)	$\acute{Y}(= a + bX)$ (best estimate of weight in pounds)		
0	−159.31	←	The Y-intercept is sometimes a computational
65	140.99		abstraction; it may not exist in reality.
66	145.61		
67	150.23		
68	154.85		
68.56	157.44	←	The coordinate ($\overline{X}$, $\overline{Y}$) will always be on the
69	159.47		regression line.
70	164.09		
		> ←	The difference in weight (Y) between any two
71	168.71		heights (X) that are 1 inch apart is the slope,
		> ←	b = 4.62 pounds.
72	173.33		
73	177.95		

respectively. This is not a mistake. The axes of the plot have been "truncated" (or shortened) for clarity of presentation.

Why Truncate the Axes of the Scatterplot?   Sometimes the interval/ratio variables of a scatterplot have many values that are impractical. For our illustration using the variables height and weight, no high school seniors are, say, 19 inches tall or weigh only 30 pounds. In the scatterplots of weight regressed on height we truncated, or shortened, the axes for each variable to make the scatterplot appear balanced on the page. Figure 14–7 presents the scatterplot for the data in Figure 14–4 without truncating the axes. The value of truncating should be obvious when Figures 14–4 and 14–7 are compared.

For the Especially Inquisitive: The Mathematical Relationship Between Pearson's r Correlation Coefficient and the Regression Coefficient, b

Notice that there are similarities in the formulas for r and b. In particular, the numerators are the same. This means that the signs of r and b will always be the same. Notice also that both equations include sums of squares, the same calculations that go into computing standard deviations (Chapter 5). As it turns out, Pearson's r, like b, is a slope of a regression line. Pearson's r is a standardized slope and it goes with the plot of standardized scores for X and Y (Z-scores, Chapter 5). Recall that a Z-score is a deviation score divided by the standard deviation and its unit of measure *is* a standard deviation. If we plotted coordinates for the standardized scores of X and Y (i.e., Z_X, Z_Y-coordinates), r would be the slope of this line. The regression coefficient, b, is an unstandardized slope, meaning that the scatterplot and regression line are constructed around the raw score units of measure of the variables. In the case of our high school seniors, these units of measure are *inches* for height (X) and *pounds* for weight (Y). Pearson's r is a standardized slope in that it presents the slope in standard deviation

FIGURE 14–7

A scatterplot lacking truncated axes: Height as a predictor of weight

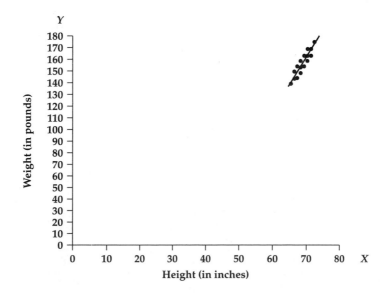

units of measure. Let us contrast the interpretations of these unstandardized and standardized slopes for our height-weight example:

Unstandardized slope, $b = 4.62$ pounds per inch: On the regression line of the scatterplot of heights and weights, a 1-inch increase in height is related to a 4.62 pounds increase in weight.

Standardized slope, $r = .91$ standard deviation of pounds of weight per 1 standard deviation of inches of height: On the regression line of the scatterplot of the Z-scores of heights (Z_X) and weights (Z_Y), a 1 *standard deviation* increase in height is related to a .91 *standard deviation* increase in weight.

Standardized slopes are important for multiple regression, the situation where there are two or more independent variables predicting Y. These independent variables will likely have different raw score units of measure. In order to compare their slopes, we often must standardize the units of measure of all variables. Additional information on standardized slopes and multiple regression is available in the Chapters 14–15 Extensions on *The Statistical Imagination* Web site at www.mhhe.com/ritchey2.

Step-by-Step Calculations of Bivariate Correlation and Regression Statistics

Using our example of whether there is a correlation between the heights and weights of high school seniors (data from Table 14–1):

1. Decide which variable is independent and which is dependent and draw the scatterplot (Figure 14–1).

2. Observe the scatterplot for a linear, cigar-shaped pattern in the coordinates. There appears to be a linear pattern.

3. Organize the calculation spreadsheet (Table 14–2).

4. Calculate the means of X and Y:

$$\bar{X} = \frac{\Sigma X}{n} = \frac{1,097}{16} = 68.56 \text{ inches}$$

$$\bar{Y} = \frac{\Sigma Y}{n} = \frac{2,519}{16} = 157.44 \text{ pounds}$$

5. Complete columns A through E of the calculation spreadsheet by:
(*a*) computing deviation scores for X and Y (columns A and B) and confirming that their sums are equal to zero within rounding error;
(*b*) computing the covariation of X and Y (column C); and (*c*) computing the sums of squares for X and Y (columns D and E).

---

6. Calculate Pearson's r correlation coefficient:

$$r = \frac{\Sigma(X - \bar{X})(Y - \bar{Y})}{\sqrt{\Sigma(X - \bar{X})^2 \, \Sigma(Y - \bar{Y})^2}} = \frac{286.12}{\sqrt{(61.88)\,(1{,}587.88)}} = \frac{286.12}{313.46} = .91$$

7. Calculate the regression coefficient (slope), b:

$$b = \frac{\Sigma(X - \bar{X})(Y - \bar{Y})}{\Sigma(X - \bar{X})^2} = \frac{286.12}{61.88} = 4.62 \text{ pounds per inch}$$

8. Calculate the Y-intercept, a:

$$a = \bar{Y} - b\bar{X} = 157.44 - (4.62)(68.56) = -159.31 \text{ pounds}$$

9. Specify the regression equation:

$$\acute{Y} = a + bX = -159.31 + (4.62)X$$

10. Calculate best estimates of Y by plugging some values of X into the regression equation and solving for $\acute{Y}$. For example, for $X = 67$ inches and $X = 72$ inches:

$$\acute{Y} = a + bX = -159.31 + (4.62)(67) = 150.23 \text{ pounds}$$

$$\acute{Y} = a + bX = -159.31 + (4.62)(72) = 173.33 \text{ pounds}$$

11. Use these estimates (the $X, \acute{Y}$-coordinates) to plot the regression line on the scatterplot as in Figure 14–4.

Statistical Follies and Fallacies: The Failure to Observe a Scatterplot Before Calculating Pearson's *r*

Linear Equations Work Only with a Linear Pattern in the Scatterplot

Eager to see his or her results, a researcher may be tempted to skip the tedious task of drawing and observing scatterplots. Even with computers, this task is somewhat time-consuming. It is a mistake, however, to proceed without observing a scatterplot. Bivariate linear regression statistics are based on predicting from the straight line produced by the formula $\acute{Y} = a + bX$. If the coordinates do not fit around a straight line, the predictions of Y based on X (i.e., the $\acute{Y}$'s) will not be close to the observed values of Y. Simply put, the line will not fit the pattern of coordinates; therefore, predictions made by using such a misplaced line will be erroneous. Linear regression statistics are not appropriate for nonlinear (or curvilinear) relationships such as the one shown in Figure 14–8. In Figure 14–8, each dot (coordinate) represents a neighborhood (using fictional data). The position on the X-axis indicates the percentage of the neighborhood's population that is of minority status (i.e., African-American,

FIGURE 14–8

Scatterplot of incidence of hate crimes against minority members of neighborhoods regressed on percentage of minority population in neighborhood (shows nonlinear relationship)

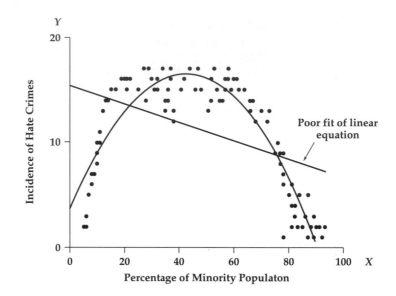

Asian-American, Native-American, and Hispanic racial/ethnic classifications). The position on the Y-axis represents the number of hate crimes occurring in the neighborhood over a period of time. This curvilinear plot tells us that hate crimes occur *in*frequently when the size of the minority population is either very low or very high. When the minority population is very low, it poses no threat to the majority white population. When the minority population is very high, hate-filled whites feel outnumbered and are afraid to act on their feelings. Hate crimes are highest when minority and white populations are roughly equal and are "contesting for control" of the neighborhood. The shape of this curve is an inverted parabola, and its equation— not the equation for a straight line—would be used to estimate the number of hate crimes based on the size of the minority population. [The equation for an inverted parabola is $\acute{Y} = [-c_1(X = c_2)^2] + c_3$, where the c's symbolize constants that establish the width of the parabola and the location of its vortex (i.e., its peak).] If the linear equation is used mistakenly, the resulting linear regression line (indicated in Figure 14–8) is a poor fit to the pattern of coordinates. Estimates made from this line will be erroneous.

Analysis of curvilinear relationships is beyond the scope of this text. If the coordinates in a scatterplot do not fit the cigar-shaped, linear pattern, the statistics in this chapter do not apply. Fortunately, a linear pattern between interval/ratio variables is extremely common. It is important, however, to observe a scatterplot for nonlinear patterns such as that in Figure 14–8.

Outlier Coordinates and the Attenuation and Inflation of Correlation Coefficients

Note that we used the means of X and Y to calculate the correlation coefficient r and the regression line equation. All these statistics are "mean-based." As we discussed in

Chapter 4, the mean is susceptible to distortion by extreme scores, or "outliers," in a variable's score distribution. Similarly, in the coordinates of a scatterplot, a few extreme or **outlier coordinates**—*ones that fall way outside the overall pattern of the scatterplot*—may distort correlation and regression coefficients. If they are significant, these distortions can cause the regression line to misfit the data on the scatterplot. Outlier coordinates may weaken or "attenuate" the correlation and regression coefficients computed with them.

Attenuation of correlation is *the weakening or reduction of correlation and regression coefficients.* An attenuated correlation will produce a small Pearson's *r* and therefore may cause us to conclude that a relationship between two interval/ratio variables does not exist when in fact it does.

---

attenuation of correlation   The weakening or reduction of correlation and regression coefficients (often as a result of the presence of outlier coordinates).

The following scatterplot illustrates attenuation resulting from an outlier coordinate for the weights and heights of male high school seniors. Suppose that unintentionally a member of the basketball team is included in our sample. This player is a tall, skinny guy with a height of 73 inches but a weight of only 146 pounds. Figure 14–9 shows the scatterplot of the new data. The basketball player's *X,Y*-coordinate (73, 146) is an outlier coordinate, and regression lines are presented with and without it. The different locations of the regression lines reveal that the addition of this single outlier shifts the regression line away from the linear pattern

FIGURE 14–9

Illustration of attenuation resulting from outlier coordinates: weight (*Y*) regressed on height (*X*)

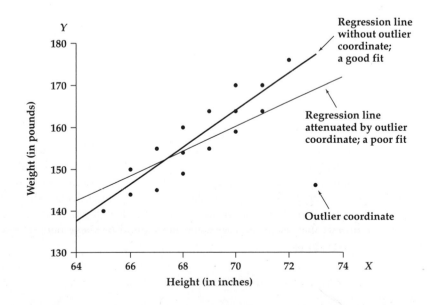

FIGURE 14–10

Illustration of inflation of Pearson's *r* as a result of outlier coordinates: patient's ability to function independently (*Y*) regressed on caregiver's education (*X*) (compare to Figure 14–3)

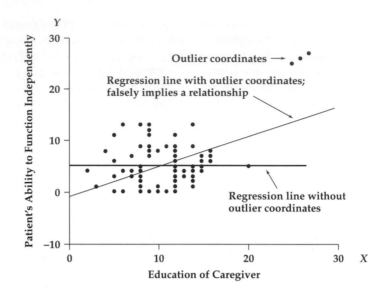

found in the remaining cases. This attenuated regression line is not useful in predicting weights from heights. Moreover, the addition of this single outlier coordinate reduces or "attenuates" the correlation coefficient from our original value of .91 to a mere .64 (calculations not shown). The potential for attenuation of correlation is another important reason for observing the scatterplot before proceeding with correlational analysis.

Just as an outlier coordinate may weaken coefficients, they also may inflate them. We found in Figure 14–3 that there was no relationship between a caregiver's education and a patient's ability to function without help. Suppose now that the sample included the three outlier coordinates in Figure 14–10. These outliers pull the calculated regression line upward, giving it a positive slope. Moreover, the Pearson's *r* increases from zero (i.e., no relationship) to .46 (i.e., a positive relationship; calculations not shown). Outlier coordinates that inflate correlation and regression coefficients lead to the false conclusion that a relationship exists when in fact it does not.

How can we avoid attenuation or inflation of coefficients? Often one or two outlier coordinates can be explained by circumstances and can be justifiably excluded from the analysis. In the attenuation case in Figure 14–9, we could eliminate the basketball player and report the stronger correlation of *r* = .91. Our report would say that except for especially tall, thin seniors such as basketball players, height is a moderately strong predictor of weight for male high school seniors. Similarly, for the inflated coefficients of the caregiver example (Figure 14–10) we might declare that the outlier coordinates are random cases that do not fit the overall pattern. In either figure, the scatterplot reveals that using the regression lines based on these outlier data would not provide good estimates.

In everyday research circumstances, much potential exists for attenuation or inflation of correlation, especially if the researcher is not savvy about the makeup of the data and its population of origin. For example, in a study of factory workers and the relationship of time employed (X) to pay scale (Y), it would be a mistake to mix managers (who are highly paid) and assembly-line workers in the same sample. Managers who have been employed for even a short time may have very high salaries, and their coordinates will land high up in the left-hand side of a scatterplot.

A second example would be a study of states and the relationship of population size (X) to divorce rates (Y). The inclusion of Nevada with its exorbitantly high divorce rates would greatly distort the results. Most divorces in Nevada are for people from other states. In recognition of this commonly known fact, Nevada could be excluded and the results could be reported as "with the exception of Nevada."

Finally, the potential for attenuation or inflation of correlation and regression coefficients highlights the desirability of a large sample. As with any mean-based statistics, the more opportunities in sampling to compensate for the effect of outlier coordinates, the weaker their effects on predictions of Y based on knowing X. In other words, it is desirable to have many degrees of freedom.

SUMMARY

1. A bivariate correlation is a systematic change in the scores of two interval/ratio variables.

2. Simple bivariate linear correlation and regression analysis is the name of the procedure for improving best estimates of a dependent variable (Y) by accounting for its relationship with a single independent variable (X). This procedure uses the formula for a straight line to improve best estimates of Y for all values of X.

3. A scatterplot is a two-dimensional grid of the coordinates of two interval/ratio variables, X and Y. A coordinate is a point on a scatterplot where the values of X and Y are plotted for a case.

4. Bivariate linear correlation and regression statistics apply only to scatterplots with coordinates that fit a linear pattern—a cigar-shaped pattern that approximates the shape of a straight line.

5. The regression line is the best-fitting straight line plotted through the X, Y-coordinates of a scatterplot of two interval/ratio variables. The formula for a straight line to estimate Y is $\hat{Y} = a + bX$.

6. The benefit of regression analysis is the ability to improve estimates of Y in a population by using the regression line and reporting a $\hat{Y}$ instead of merely reporting the sample mean of Y.

7. Sometimes it is advisable to truncate when labeling the axes of a scatterplot.

8. Pearson's r is a widely used bivariate correlation coefficient that measures the tightness of fit of X, Y-coordinates around the regression line. It gauges how well deviation scores for X and Y change in tandem. Its formulation involves deviation scores and sums of squares.

9. The characteristics of Pearson's r are as follows: (*a*) Computed values of Pearson's r can range from -1 to $+1$. (*b*) The larger the absolute value of Pearson's r, the tighter the fit of X,Y-coordinates around the regression line. (*c*) When the regression line slopes upward, we have a positive correlation. Pearson's r will be positive up to a value of $+1.00$. (*d*) When the regression line slopes downward, we have a negative correlation. Pearson's r will be negative down to a value of -1.00. (*e*) When the regression line is flat, we have no correlation and Pearson's $r = 0$.

10. The coefficients and symbols of the regression line formula, $\hat{Y} = a + bX$, are as follows: (*a*) $\hat{Y} =$ the predicted Y (an estimate of the dependent variable Y computed for a given value of the independent variable X). (*b*) $b =$ slope of the regression line (called the regression coefficient). It conveys slope in the sense of going up or down a hill. It answers the question: How far does the line rise for every 1-unit run of X? (*c*) $a = Y$-intercept, the point at which the regression line intersects the Y-axis when $X = 0$.

11. The unstandardized slope, b, is expressed in raw score units of measure. Pearson's r can be interpreted as a standardized slope expressed in standard deviation units of measure.

12. Observe scatterplots closely to determine if a linear relationship is apparent in the pattern of coordinates. Look for nonlinear or curvilinear relationships and outlier coordinates.

13. Attenuation of correlation is the weakening or reduction of correlation and regression coefficients due to outlier coordinates or other peculiarities in the data.

CHAPTER EXTENSIONS ON *THE STATISTICAL IMAGINATION* WEB SITE

Chapters 14–15 Extensions of text material available on *The Statistical Imagination* Web site at www.mhhe.com/ritchey2 include an introduction to multiple correlation and regression, the situation where a dependent variable is regressed on two or more independent variables.

STATISTICAL PROCEDURES COVERED TO THIS POINT

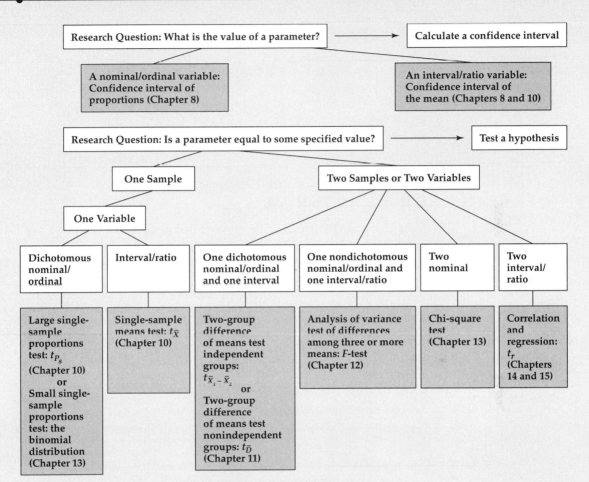

FORMULAS FOR CHAPTER 14

To complete the calculation spreadsheet (Table 14–2):

$$\overline{X} = \frac{\Sigma X}{n} \qquad \overline{Y} = \frac{\Sigma Y}{n}$$

Pearson's r correlation coefficient:

$$r = \frac{\Sigma (X - \overline{X})(Y - \overline{Y})}{\sqrt{\Sigma (X - \overline{X})^2 \, \Sigma (Y - \overline{Y})^2}}$$

The regression coefficient or slope, b:

$$b = \frac{\Sigma (X - \overline{X})(Y - \overline{Y})}{\Sigma (X - \overline{X})^2}$$

The Y-intercept, a:

$$a = \overline{Y} - b\overline{X}$$

The regression equation:

$$\acute{Y} = a + bX$$

QUESTIONS FOR CHAPTER 14

1. With the help of a hand-sketched scatterplot and the regression equation $\acute{Y} = a + bX$, explain the central idea behind regression analysis.

2. With the help of hand-sketched scatterplots, illustrate why linear correlation and regression analysis apply only when there is a cigar-shaped, linear pattern of coordinates.

3. With the help of hand-sketched scatterplots, illustrate the pattern of coordinates for positive, negative, and no relationships between X and Y.

4. With the help of hand-sketched scatterplots, illustrate why it sometimes is necessary to truncate the axis of a scatterplot.

5. What does Pearson's r correlation coefficient measure?

6. What does the regression coefficient b measure?

7. On the regression line, the Y-intercept, a, is the value of $\acute{Y}$ where $X =$ _____.

8. With a linear relationship between two interval/ratio variables, what is the X,Y-coordinate that will always fall on the regression line?

9. Match the following regarding the direction of correlations:
   a. A positive correlation _____ The regression line has no slope; $r = 0$ and $b = 0$.
   b. No correlation _____ The regression line slopes downward; r and b have a negative sign; an increase in X is related to a decrease in Y.
   c. A negative correlation _____ The regression line slopes upward; r and b have a positive sign; an increase in X is related to an increase in Y.

10. Attenuation or inflation of the calculation of correlation and regression coefficients can result from the presence of _____ in the scatterplot.

EXERCISES FOR CHAPTER 14

Problem Set 14A

Show all sums and formulas.

14A-1. An instructor with 16 students gives midterm and final examinations. She is interested in whether the midterm score is a good predictor of the final exam score. Her data are listed in the table.
  a. Decide which variable is independent and which is dependent and draw the scatterplot.
  b. Calculate the regression line statistics and plot the line.
  c. Calculate the Pearson's r bivariate correlation coefficient.
  d. Does there appear to be a linear relationship in the pattern of test score coordinates?

Midterm Exam Score	Final Exam Score
78	83
91	82
95	91
74	81
87	85
83	87
89	83
92	97
94	98
58	66
71	79
76	84
87	91
91	92
77	75
85	89

14A-2. The following are data from a sample of 23 underclass students (first year students and sophomores) at Tuffstuff University.
  a. Draw the scatterplot for GPA (Y) regressed on reading comprehension score (X).
  b. *Without making any computations,* draw what appears to be the best-fitting straight line through the plot of the coordinates.
  c. *Without making any calculations,* estimate a and b in the regression equation: $\acute{Y} = a + bX$.
  d. Now compute the regression statistics for the relationship of reading comprehension to GPA and plot the regression line.
  e. Compare your computed statistics to those you estimated in part (c) to make sure you understand what each statistic means.

Student	GPA	Reading Comprehension Score	Hours of Study per Class Session
1	0.90	2	2.00
2	1.12	3	1.25
3	1.46	2	2.50
4	1.93	4	5.00
5	2.00	3	3.00
6	2.16	3	4.15
7	2.18	2	4.72
8	2.21	3	5.75
9	2.33	4	6.13
10	2.39	6	4.75
11	2.46	5	4.25
12	2.54	6	4.84
13	2.68	5	5.75
14	2.73	4	6.00
15	2.85	7	5.89
16	2.87	6	6.37
17	2.93	8	6.50
18	2.99	7	7.00
19	3.04	9	6.00
20	3.14	8	6.93
21	3.22	9	7.16
22	3.27	9	6.94
23	3.28	8	8.10

14A-3. As an employee of a health consumer watchdog agency, you track the activities of health maintenance organizations (HMOs). HMOs have been criticized for pushing people too quickly out of hospitals to cut costs and increase profits. You examine angioplasty procedures done at hospitals owned by 12 HMOs. The fictional data shown here are the average reductions in the length of stay for these patients in days and the percentage increase in profits for the HMOs over the past year.

a. Draw the scatterplot for percentage increase in profits (Y) regressed on reduction in length of stay (X).

b. Compute the regression statistics and plot the regression line.

c. Calculate Pearson's r bivariate correlation coefficient.

d. Does there appear to be a linear relationship in the pattern of coordinates?

Average Reduction in Length of Stay (days)	Percentage Increase in Profits
1.3	2.9
2.2	15.3
2.3	13.9
1.7	6.3
1.9	10.4
1.0	0.8
2.1	15.3
1.6	13.1
2.2	8.9
1.4	6.8
1.3	11.5
1.9	11.4

14A-4. One measure of the poverty level of a county is the percentage of children who qualify for free lunches at school. The following spreadsheet includes this "% pupils with free lunch" variable (X) as well as a composite measure of how well the county's pupils scored on the SAT college entrance examination (average system SAT, Y).

    a. Draw the scatterplot for Y regressed on X.

    b. Calculate Pearson's r bivariate correlation coefficient.

    c. Note the outlier coordinates in the scatterplot. Identify them in the spreadsheet.

    d. Recalculate Pearson's r without these outlier coordinates.

    e. Comment on the effect of the outlier coordinates on the calculation of Pearson's r correlation coefficient.

Average System SAT	% Pupils with Free Lunch
68	34
71	15
56	37
61	33
39	75
65	73
47	59
57	40
43	79
69	69
54	59
55	38
70	17
63	36

Problem Set 14B

Show all sums and formulas.

14B-1. The ACT is a standardized test used to evaluate whether a student is qualified to enter college. An admissions counselor at your university is interested in whether the ACT score is a good predictor of grade point average (GPA) in college. She collects a sample of 14 junior-level college students. Her data are listed in the table.

    a. Decide which variable is independent and which is dependent and draw the scatterplot.

    b. Calculate the regression line statistics and plot the line.

    c. Calculate the Pearson's *r* bivariate correlation coefficient.

    d. Does there appear to be a linear relationship in the pattern of ACT scores and GPA points?

ACT Score	GPA
24	3.10
29	3.68
31	3.82
21	3.00
17	2.78
21	3.23
24	2.86
23	3.07
25	3.15
21	2.87
28	3.65
27	3.41
23	2.96
21	3.10
18	2.75

14B-2. You have an interest in intergenerational uses of types of sound recording technology. The following are (fictional) data from a sample of 20 adults.

    a. Draw the scatterplot for compact discs owned (Y) regressed on age (X).

    b. *Without making any computations,* draw what appears to be the best-fitting straight line through the plot of the coordinates.

    c. *Without making any calculations,* estimate *a* and *b* in the regression equation: $\acute{Y} = a + bX$.

d.   Now compute the regression statistics for the relationship of reading comprehension to GPA and plot the regression line.

e.   Compare your computed statistics to those you estimated in part (c) to make sure you understand what each statistic means.

Adult	Age (X)	Compact Discs Owned (Y)	Vinyl Records Owned
1	36	12	16
2	51	6	25
3	32	15	18
4	34	10	20
5	28	15	16
6	27	18	15
7	44	10	19
8	45	8	24
9	29	18	23
10	50	7	27
11	49	9	26
12	37	10	20
13	47	9	23
14	44	12	20
15	41	9	22
16	32	15	21
17	51	6	25
18	33	18	23
19	28	16	18
20	44	12	23

14B-3.   Social capital is a measure of social ties that people use as beneficial resources. As a researcher, you examine whether individuals with higher social capital have more people to "lean on" and, therefore, tend to have greater life satisfaction. You use a social capital scale that ranges from 10 to 25 and a life satisfaction scale that ranges from 20 to 40.

a.   Draw the scatterplot for life satisfaction (Y) regressed on social capital (X).

b.   Compute the regression statistics and plot the regression line.

c.   Calculate Pearson's r bivariate correlation coefficient.

d.   Does there appear to be a linear relationship in the pattern of coordinates?

Social Capital	Life Satisfaction
15	25
12	24
23	31
24	34
19	28
21	31
17	25
14	21
21	35
19	26
20	28
15	23
12	20
17	27
16	24
22	31

14B-4. Studies show that within school districts there is a correlation between binge drinking in high schools and binge drinking in middle schools (Guilamo-Ramos, Jaccard, Turrisi, and Johansson 2005). To replicate this study, you survey students in schools in 18 districts about alcohol consumption behaviors. You measure a school's binge drinking as the percentage of students that report consuming five or more drinks in one outing at least once in the last 12 months. Then you compute the percentage of students in the school who did so.

a. Decide which variable is independent (X) and which is dependent (Y) and draw the scatterplot for Y regressed on X.

b. Calculate Pearson's r bivariate correlation coefficient.

c. Note the outlier coordinates in the scatterplot. Identify them in the spreadsheet.

d. Recalculate Pearson's r without these outlier coordinates.

e. Comment on the effect of the outlier coordinates on the calculation of Pearson's r correlation coefficient.

School District	% Binge Drinking in High School	% Binge Drinking in Middle School
1	16	13
2	15	11
3	19	7
4	18	15
5	15	8
6	18	12
7	14	9
8	12	7

9	10	6
10	19	16
11	12	14
12	16	12
13	15	9
14	13	7
15	14	11
16	20	16
17	14	10
18	10	16

Problem Set 14C

Show all sums and formulas.

14C-1.   As the personnel director of a company, it is your responsibility to assure merit-based equity in salary levels. In other words, salary level should roughly parallel educational qualifications. The following are the salary levels and years of education of 15 employees who have been with the company for five years. Use the figures where salaries are rounded to thousands of dollars.

a.   Decide which variable is independent and which is dependent and draw the scatterplot.

b.   Calculate the regression line statistics and plot the line. For ease of computation, calculate salary in thousands of dollars (e.g., $22,500 = 22.5 thousand dollars).

c.   Calculate the Pearson's r bivariate correlation coefficient.

d.   Does there appear to be a linear relationship in the pattern of coordinates?

Years of Education	Salary	Salary in $1,000's
12	$22,500	22.5
12	17,900	17.9
11	16,500	16.5
16	29,600	29.6
16	34,500	34.5
18	42,600	42.6
17	45,800	45.8
16	24,000	24.0
12	22,300	22.3
10	14,000	14.0
12	13,700	13.7
19	54,000	54.0
18	34,000	34.0
14	25,000	25.0
13	21,400	21.4

14C-2. Suppose that you study college grade performance as measured by grade point average (GPA). You use an innovative measure of hours of study per class session by equipping students with an electronic time counter that is turned on and off as a student studies. Your data are listed in the following table.

a.   Draw the scatterplot for GPA (Y) regressed on hours of study per class session (X).

b.   *Without making any computations,* draw what appears to be the best-fitting straight line through the plot of the coordinates.

c.   *Without making any calculations,* estimate a and b in the regression equation: $\hat{Y} = a + bX$.

d.   Now compute the regression statistics for the relationship of hours of study to GPA and plot the regression line.

e.   Compare your computed statistics to those you estimated in part (c) to make sure you understand what each statistic means.

Student	GPA	Reading Comprehension Score	Hours of Study per Class Session
1	0.90	2	2.00
2	1.12	3	1.25
3	1.46	2	2.50
4	1.93	4	5.00
5	2.00	3	3.00
6	2.16	3	4.15
7	2.18	2	4.72
8	2.21	3	5.75
9	2.33	4	6.13
10	2.39	6	4.75
11	2.46	5	4.25
12	2.54	6	4.84
13	2.68	5	5.75
14	2.73	4	6.00
15	2.85	7	5.89
16	2.87	6	6.37
17	2.93	8	6.50
18	2.99	7	7.00
19	3.04	9	6.00
20	3.14	8	6.93
21	3.22	9	7.16
22	3.27	9	6.94
23	3.28	8	8.10

14C-3. Disability days are the number of days individuals are unable to engage in their regular activities because of illness or injury. For workers without adequate health and disability insurance coverage, disability days can cause a loss in income. The following data are indicative of the pattern of disability days per year as they relate to total family income (in thousands of dollars).
   a.   Draw the scatterplot for total family income (Y) regressed on disability days (X).
   b.   Compute the regression statistics and plot the regression line.
   c.   Calculate Pearson's r bivariate correlation coefficient.
   d.   Does there appear to be a linear relationship in the pattern of coordinates?

Family Income	Disability Days
5	27
15	19
28	14
40	10
6	29
14	21
26	13
37	6

14C-4. Suppose you are studying skill development among 14-year-old pianists in a city music club and wonder if time of membership in the club (X) is related to the number of awards and trophies won (Y) in recital competitions.
   a.   Draw the scatterplot for Y regressed on X.
   b.   Calculate Pearson's r bivariate correlation coefficient.
   c.   Note the outlier coordinate in the scatterplot. Identify it in the spreadsheet.
   d.   Recalculate Pearson's r without this outlier coordinate.
   e.   Comment on the effect of an outlier coordinate on the calculation of Pearson's r correlation coefficient.

Years in Music Club	Merit Awards and Trophies
4	5
6	6
2	1
3	4
2	7
1	2
3	3
5	4
4	4

Problem Set 14D

Show all sums and formulas.

14D-1. Educational attainment has long been noted as beneficial for increasing one's job opportunities and income. For the following data, examine the relationship of years of schooling to income.
  a. Decide which variable is independent and which is dependent and draw the scatterplot.
  b. Calculate the regression line statistics and plot the line.
  c. Calculate the Pearson's r bivariate correlation coefficient.
  d. Does there appear to be a linear relationship in the pattern of education and income?

Years of Schooling	Income (in thousands)
12	29
16	45
15	37
16	39
18	51
15	35
12	31
12	33
11	27
15	40
14	36
16	45
15	38
20	55
12	31
16	45
10	27

14D-2. Having a curiosity about old vinyl sound recordings and whether persons in your parents' generation are still listening to them, you gather the following data from a sample of 20 adults.
  a. Draw the scatterplot for vinyl records owned (Y) regressed on age (X).
  b. *Without making any computations,* draw what appears to be the best-fitting straight line through the plot of the coordinates.
  c. *Without making any calculations,* estimate a and b in the regression equation: $\acute{Y} = a + bX$.

d. Now compute the regression statistics for the relationship and plot the regression line.
e. Compare your computed statistics to those you estimated in part (*c*) to make sure you understand what each statistic means.

Adult	Age	Compact Discs Owned	Vinyl Records Owned
1	36	12	16
2	51	6	25
3	32	15	18
4	34	10	20
5	28	15	16
6	27	18	15
7	44	10	19
8	45	8	24
9	29	18	23
10	50	7	27
11	49	9	26
12	37	10	20
13	47	9	23
14	44	12	20
15	41	9	22
16	32	15	21
17	51	6	25
18	33	18	23
19	28	16	18
20	44	12	23

14D-3. Research has found that one's self-perceived health status is often a good predictor of actual health status. Using the fictional data in the following table, determine whether this is the case. For both variables, health status is measured using a scale that ranges from 10 (very poor health) to 45 (very good health).
a. Draw the scatterplot for actual health status (Y) regressed on perceived health status (X).
b. Compute the regression statistics and plot the regression line.
c. Calculate Pearson's r bivariate correlation coefficient.
d. Does there appear to be a linear relationship in the pattern of coordinates?

Self-perceived Health Status	Actual Health Status
12	10
15	13
17	21
19	22
23	22
25	28
27	32
29	33
31	30
33	29
35	31
37	38
39	39
41	40
43	41
45	44

14D-4. A recent study concluded that exposure to an antismoking ad campaign did predict lower rates of smoking among youth (Farrelly, Davis, Haviland, Messeri, and Healton 2005). You replicate this study with data from 20 randomly selected counties. Exposure to antismoking ads (X) is measured in hours broadcast per month. Smoking prevalence (Y) is measured as the percent of youth ages 13 to 17 who report smoking in the last month.
  a. Draw the scatterplot for Y regressed on X.
  b. Calculate Pearson's r bivariate correlation coefficient.
  c. Note the outlier coordinates in the scatterplot. Identify them in the spreadsheet.
  d. Recalculate Pearson's r without these outlier coordinates.
  e. Comment on the effect of the outlier coordinates on the calculation of Pearson's r correlation coefficient.

% Youth in County Who Smoke	Hours of Ad Broadcast
14	4
12	16
13	18
15	13
20	10
14	16
24	8
26	19
19	9
17	11
15	13
14	17
19	12
18	11
21	9
14	16
23	8
20	10
17	16
13	18

OPTIONAL COMPUTER APPLICATIONS FOR CHAPTER 14

If your class uses the optional computer applications that accompany this text, open the Chapter 14 exercises on *The Statistical Imagination* Web site at www.mhhe.com/ritchey2. With instructions on producing scatterplots and correlation-regression statistics, these exercises emphasize understanding the relationship between the shape of a scatterplot and the size of Pearson's *r*. In addition, Appendix D of this text provides a brief overview of the *SPSS* command sequences for procedures covered in this chapter.

15

Bivariate Correlation and Regression

Part 2: Hypothesis Testing and Aspects of a Relationship

CHAPTER OUTLINE

Introduction: Hypothesis Test and Aspects of a Relationship Between Two Interval/Ratio Variables

In Chapter 14 we introduced the basic ideas behind bivariate correlation and regression analysis and the computation of coefficients. In this chapter we will use those statistics to test hypotheses about the relationship between two interval/ratio variables.

  To illustrate the hypothesis test, let us examine the relationship between level of education and acceptance of "lowbrow" music—styles associated with political protest, the lower classes, and ethnic and racial minorities (Bryson 1996; Peterson and Kern 1996). This type of music stands in contrast to "highbrow" music such as classical symphonic, chamber, and opera music; swing; show tunes; easy listening; "soft rock"; and popular music that is light on sexuality. The styles of music favored by a society are viewed by some individuals as symbolic of that society's moral character. A small but vocal minority points to lowbrow music as a form of deviance and a clear sign of moral decline. Even the middle class in American society takes issue with musical forms that have countercultural elements that challenge the dominant social, moral, and political systems. Some parents fear that heavy metal and politically charged rap music will corrupt the morals of their children. Other popular musical styles—those associated with the lower classes and ethnic minorities—evoke class prejudices and racist sentiments among some people. Such styles include rap, reggae, blues, rhythm and blues, rock and roll, alternative rock, heavy metal, country and western, Latin, contemporary jazz, and nontraditional contemporary Christian music.

What accounts for differences in how people evaluate and accept various forms of music? Among the predictor variables typically examined are age, race, gender, marital status, political opinions, religious affiliation, and education (Bryson 1996; Peterson and Kern 1996). One research hypothesis is that better-educated persons are more accepting—more tolerant—of lowbrow musical styles.

Organizing Data for the Hypothesis Test

Suppose we investigate this hypothesis by using questionnaire data from a sample of 12 mothers of high school students. These parents are asked to rate assorted musical styles. We then sum up the number of lowbrow styles each mother tolerates (i.e., considers acceptable for her teenage children) and call this variable lowbrow tolerance. The higher the score, the more favorable a mother is toward lowbrow styles. The educational level of the mothers is operationalized as the number of years of formal schooling completed.

Let us follow the step-by-step calculation box toward the end of Chapter 14. We start by establishing which is the independent variable and which is the dependent variable. In this case we are interested in explaining lowbrow tolerance by mothers; thus, this is the dependent variable, to be designated as Y. We are hypothesizing that educational level is a predictor of lowbrow tolerance. Thus, education level is the independent variable X.

Next we organize the data into a computational spreadsheet. Table 15–1 presents the data on educational level and lowbrow tolerance along with the sums required for computing bivariate correlation and regression statistics.

Before we compute linear regression statistics, we must make sure they apply to these data; that is, we must observe a scatterplot to determine whether the data appear to fit the cigar-shaped pattern approximating a straight line. Figure 15–1 presents the scatterplot for the data in Table 15–1. Indeed, the data appear linear. Moreover, the slope is positive; that is, the coordinates of the scatterplot extend upward from left to right. Thus, we may proceed to calculate correlation and regression statistics.

First we compute $\overline{X}$ and $\overline{Y}$:

$$\overline{X} = \frac{\Sigma X}{n} = \frac{150}{12} = 12.50 \text{ years}$$

$$\overline{Y} = \frac{\Sigma Y}{n} = \frac{66}{12} = 5.50 \text{ styles}$$

TABLE 15–1 I Spreadsheet for computing correlation and regression statistics: education levels and lowbrow tolerance of 12 mothers of high school students (X = education level in years of education; Y = number of lowbrow styles tolerated)

	Givens		Calculations				
Mother	X	Y	$X - \bar{X}$	$Y - \bar{Y}$	$(X - \bar{X})(Y - \bar{Y})$	$(X - \bar{X})^2$	$(Y - \bar{Y})^2$
1	9	3	−3.5	−2.5	8.75	12.25	6.25
2	10	4	−2.5	−1.5	3.75	6.25	2.25
3	10	5	−2.5	−0.5	1.25	6.25	.25
4	11	4	−1.5	−1.5	2.25	2.25	2.25
5	12	4	−0.5	−1.5	.75	.25	2.25
6	12	6	−0.5	0.5	−.25	.25	.25
7	12	7	−0.5	1.5	−.75	.25	2.25
8	13	6	0.5	0.5	.25	.25	.25
9	14	6	1.5	0.5	.75	2.25	.25
10	15	6	2.5	0.5	1.25	6.25	.25
11	16	7	3.5	1.5	5.25	12.25	2.25
12	16	8	3.5	2.5	8.75	12.25	6.25

$n = 12$ $\Sigma Y = 66$ $\Sigma(Y - \bar{Y}) = 0$ $\Sigma(X - \bar{X})^2 = 61$

     $\Sigma X = 150$ $\Sigma(X - \bar{X}) = 0$ $\Sigma(X - \bar{X})(Y - \bar{Y}) = 32$ $\Sigma(Y - \bar{Y})^2 = 25$

FIGURE 15–1

Scatterplot of educational level as a predictor of lowbrow tolerance among 12 mothers of high school students

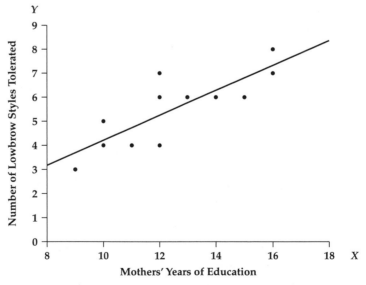

Next we use the means of X and Y to compute deviation scores and sums of squares to complete the calculations in Table 15–1. Using the sums of squares in Table 15–1, we then calculate Pearson's r correlation coefficient:

$$r = \frac{\Sigma(X - \bar{X})(Y - \bar{Y})}{\sqrt{\Sigma(X - \bar{X})^2 \Sigma(Y - \bar{Y})^2}} = \frac{32}{\sqrt{(61)(25)}} = \frac{32}{39.05} = .82$$

Next we compute the regression coefficient, b:

$$b = \frac{\Sigma (X - \overline{X})(Y - \overline{Y})}{\Sigma (X - \overline{X})^2} = \frac{32}{61} = .52 \text{ style tolerated per year of education}$$

Next we use $\overline{X}$, $\overline{Y}$, and b to compute a:

$$a = \overline{Y} - b\overline{X} = 5.50 - (.52)(12.50) = -1.00 \text{ styles}$$

Next we specify the precise regression line equation for calculating $\acute{Y}$'s (i.e., predicted values of Y) by substituting the computed values of a and b:

$$\acute{Y} = a + bX = -1.00 + (.52)X$$

Finally, we insert a few values of X into the regression equation and solve for $\acute{Y}$. It is best to use low, medium, and high values of X.

X	$\acute{Y}$
9	3.68
12	5.24
16	7.32

Thus, the best estimate of lowbrow tolerance for a mother with 9 years of education is acceptance of 3.68 music styles; for a mother with 12 years of education, 5.24 music styles; and so on. Using the resulting $X, \acute{Y}$-coordinates, we plot the regression line on the scatterplot (Figure 15–1).

The Six Steps of Statistical Inference and the Four Aspects of a Relationship

Pearson's r correlation coefficient is the statistic we use to test the hypothesis of the existence of a relationship between two interval/ratio variables, an independent variable X and a dependent variable Y. The following criteria must be met for us to be able to use bivariate linear correlation and regression statistics:

When to Test a Hypothesis Using Bivariate Correlation and Regression Analysis (t-distribution, $df = n - 2$)

In general: Testing a hypothesis that a relationship exists between two interval/ratio variables.

1. There is one representative sample from a single population.
2. There are two interval/ratio variables.
3. There are no restrictions on sample size, but generally, the larger the n, the better.
4. A scatterplot of the coordinates of the two variables fits a linear pattern.

Existence of a Relationship

In our example of mothers of high school students, we used a sample of 12. Of course, with sample data the results may be due to sampling error. Although the data in the scatterplot of Figure 15–1 appear to be linear, it is possible that these sample coordinates poorly represent the coordinates *for the population* of all mothers of high school students. The linear pattern of the sample may simply be the result of sampling error. Especially with such a small sample size, drawing second, third, fourth, fifth, and sixth samples will produce different scatterplots each time. Some may appear linear, while others may not.

When we use sample data, then, we must address this question: Does a linear relationship between X and Y truly exist *in the population,* or is the linear pattern in this sample the result of sampling error? In practical terms, we are interested in the question: For *all* mothers, is there a relationship between educational level and lowbrow tolerance, or is the apparent linear pattern a chance occurrence in our sample? As with any hypothesis test, the real interest lies in the parameter, the summary measurement that applies to the entire population.

The Pearson's r correlation coefficient allows us to test a hypothesis to answer this question. Pearson's r is a statistic, a measure of the tightness of fit of coordinates around the regression line *for the sample. For the population* the corresponding parameter is symbolized by the Greek letter *rho* (ρ). *Rho* is the correlation coefficient that would be obtained if Pearson's correlation coefficient were computed for the entire population. It would measure the tightness of fit of X,Y-coordinates if they were plotted for all mothers, not just those in the sample.

As we noted in Chapter 14, Pearson's correlation coefficient computes to zero when there is no relationship between X and Y. Knowing this, we can state a null hypothesis—one that tells us what to expect of statistical calculations in repeated sampling when this statement is true. If there is no relationship between educational level and lowbrow tolerance *in the population of mothers,* then *rho* equals zero and sample Pearson's r's will compute to zero, give or take a little sampling error. The alternative hypothesis is that rho is *not* zero. The hypothesis test hinges on whether the observed sample Pearson's r is "significantly different" from zero.

As with any hypothesis test, the *effect* of the test is the difference between an observed sample statistic and the expected parameter when the null hypothesis is true. For a correlation hypothesis, the effect is the difference between the observed sample Pearson's r and the expected *rho* of zero. This difference calculates to the value of r:

$$\text{Test effect for a Pearson's correlation} = r - \rho = r - 0 = r$$

The hypothesis test determines whether this effect found in a sample is real for the population. Is the absolute value of the sample r so large that we are led to believe that ρ is not zero and that this effect is not simply the result of sampling error?

In general, for any hypothesis about the relationship between two interval/ratio variables, the null hypothesis is stated as

$$H_0: \rho = 0$$

That is, there is no relationship between X and Y.

The statement of the alternative hypothesis can be two-tailed, nondirectional (i.e., $\rho \neq 0$; there *is* a relationship), one-tailed in the negative direction (i.e., $\rho < 0$; there *is* a negative relationship), or one-tailed in the positive direction (i.e., $\rho > 0$; there *is* a positive relationship).

---

existence of a relationship between two interval/ratio variables

Test the null hypothesis that there is no relationship between X and Y:

$$H_0: \rho = 0$$

That is, there is *no* relationship between X and Y.

In step 2 of the six steps of statistical inference we project the size of the sampling error by describing the sampling distribution. In this case, if rho is indeed equal to zero and we repeatedly draw samples of size 12 from the population of mothers, what sample correlations (r's) will we obtain? Pearson's r's will center on zero as an approximately normal t-distribution. Calculation of the standard error for this test is very cumbersome. Fortunately, the test statistic is designed so that calculation of the standard error is unnecessary. We can say, however, that the standard error is inversely related to sample size. That is, the larger the sample size, the smaller the standard error. The test statistic for this hypothesis test is as follows:

The *t*-Test Formula for Testing the Significance of Pearson's *r* Bivariate Correlation Coefficient

$$t_r = r\sqrt{\frac{n-2}{1-r^2}}$$

with $df = n - 2$

where

t_r = the t-test for Pearson's r correlation coefficient
r = Pearson's r correlation coefficient calculated on a sample
n = sample size
df = degrees of freedom

Let us proceed to test the null hypothesis of no relationship between X (educational level) and Y (lowbrow tolerance). We will go ahead and complete all four aspects of a relationship; then we will discuss the details of each step and each aspect.

Brief Checklist for the Six Steps of Statistical Inference

TEST PREPARATION

State the research question. Draw conceptual diagrams depicting givens, including the population(s) and sample(s) under study, variables (e.g., $X = \ldots$, $Y = \ldots$,) and their levels of measurement, and given or calculated statistics and parameters. State the proper statistical test procedure.

SIX STEPS

Using the symbol H for *hypothesis:*

1. State the H_0 and the H_A and stipulate test direction.
2. Describe the sampling distribution.
3. State the level of significance (α) and test direction and specify the critical test score.
4. Observe the actual sample outcomes and compute the test effects, the test statistic, and *p*-value.
5. Make the rejection decision.
6. Interpret and apply the results and provide best estimates in everyday terms.

Solution for Hypothesis Test of a Relationship between Two Interval/Ratio Variables (*t*-test of Pearson's *r*)

TEST PREPARATION

Research question: Is there a relationship between educational level and lowbrow tolerance among mothers of high school students? *Statistical procedure:* *t*-test for the significance of Pearson's *r* correlation coefficient; *t*-distribution. Scatterplot (Figure 15–1) suggests a linear relationship; data and computations from the spreadsheet in Table 15–1.

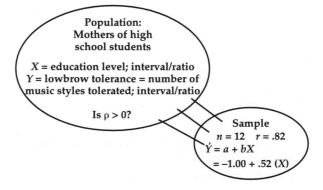

SIX STEPS

1. H_0: $\rho_{(mothers\ of\ high\ school\ students)} = 0$

   That is, there is *no* relationship between educational level and lowbrow tolerance.

   H_A: $\rho_{(mothers\ of\ high\ school\ students)} > 0$

   That is, there *is* a positive relationship between educational level and lowbrow tolerance. One-tailed.

2. *Sampling distribution:* Approximately normal, *t*-distribution, $df = n - 2 = 10$. If the H_0 is true and samples of size 12 are drawn repeatedly from the population of high school mothers, sample *r*'s will center on zero with a standard error inversely related to sample size (i.e., the larger the sample size, the smaller the standard error).

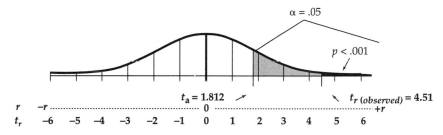

3. *Level of significance:* $\alpha = .05$, one-tailed; critical value $t_\alpha = 1.812$ [from the *t*-distribution table (Statistical Table C in Appendix B)]. (Shade area on curve).

4. *Observation:*

   Test effect: $r = .82$ (i.e., effect $= r - \rho = r - 0 = .82 - 0 = .82$).

   Test statistic:

   $$t_r = r\sqrt{\frac{n-2}{1-r^2}} = .82\sqrt{\frac{10}{1-.67}} = 4.51\ \text{SE}$$

   From the *t*-table (Statistical Table C in Appendix B):

   p-value: *p* [observing an *r* as unusual as or more unusual than .82 when $\rho = 0$] $< .001$ (area noted on curve in step 2).

5. *Rejection decision:* $|t_r| > |t_\alpha|$ (i.e., $4.51 > 1.812$); thus, $p < \alpha$, (i.e., $p < .05$). Reject H_0 and accept H_A at the 95 percent level of confidence.

6. *Interpret results:* (addressing the four aspects of a relationship) and make best estimates (details to be discussed below).

   Existence: There is a relationship between educational level and tolerance of lowbrow music among mothers of high school students; $r = .82$, $p < .001$.

Direction: Positive. As the level of education increases, the number of music styles tolerated tends to increase.

Strength: $r^2 = .82^2 = .6724;(100)(.6724) = 67.24$ percent; thus, 67.24 percent of the variation in the number of lowbrow music styles tolerated is explained by knowledge of educational level.

Practical Applications: (Interpret the slope of the regression line): $b = .52$ styles per year of education; a one-year increase in educational level is related to a .52 increase in the number of music styles tolerated.

Best estimates (use $X, \acute{Y}$-coordinates to illustrate the usefulness of knowing about the relationship between educational level and number of music styles tolerated):

$$\acute{Y} = a + bX = -1.00 + (.52)X$$

Thus, for example, the best estimate of the number of music styles tolerated by mothers with a high school education (12 years) is 5.24 styles, and with a college education (16 years) it is 7.32 styles.

We will comment further on the strength, direction, and practical applications of the relationship below. First, let us note some things about this hypothesis test:

- In step 1 we used a one-tailed test, but *not* because we saw a positive relationship in the scatterplot. This pattern could have occurred by chance. We did this because even before the sample was drawn, we posed the research question of whether *better*-educated mothers are more tolerant of diverse musical styles.

- In step 2, as we noted earlier, for the sake of computational simplicity, we use the test statistic t_r. This saves us from having to compute a very complicated standard error. Once t_r is computed, however, the standard error can be calculated quite easily. We now know that the Pearson's r quantity of .82 is 4.51 standard errors from a rho of zero. Thus, the width of one standard error is

$$s_{t_r} = \frac{.82}{4.51} = .18$$

where s_{t_r} is the estimated standard error of the t-distribution for Pearson's r (estimated because it is based on the sample r). Insert this value on the curve, and its fit will become apparent. Of further note, because regression statistics are based on deviations from the mean of Y, just as analysis of variance (ANOVA) statistics are, we could have used an F-ratio test. This, however, would require many more computations.

- In step 2, note that on the t-distribution curve, sample r's near zero occur frequently when the null hypothesis is true and large sample r's occur infrequently. That is, if rho is indeed zero, large absolute values of r are unusual in repeated sampling. Thus, when a significantly large r does occur, we reject the assumption that ρ is zero.

- In step 2, 2 degrees of freedom are lost because Pearson's r is computed from the sample means and variances of X and Y. The computation of each mean results in a loss of 1 degree of freedom (see Chapter 10).

- This hypothesis test, through "Existence" in step 6, simply establishes whether a correlation exists between X and Y. If this is found to be true (i.e., *if we reject the null hypothesis that* $\rho = 0$), we can address the other aspects of the relationship. However, *if we fail to reject the null hypothesis, these other aspects are irrelevant.* We simply conclude that there is no relationship and do not mention direction, strength, and practical applications. Since we did reject the null hypothesis, we will now discuss direction, strength, and practical applications of a relationship for two interval/ratio variables.

Direction of the Relationship

The direction of a relationship between two interval/ratio is ascertained by the sign of r and b, the slope of the regression line. An upward slope is positive, and a downward slope is negative. The direction of the slope for a truly linear, moderately strong relationship will be apparent in the scatterplot. The direction of the relationship can be observed directly in the signs ($+$ or $-$) of b and Pearson's r, which will always be the same. As part of our interpretation in step 6 of the hypothesis test, the direction of the relationship for educational level and lowbrow tolerance is revealed in the sign of r, with $r = +.82$. Therefore, the direction of the relationship is positive and is described as follows:

> Positive: As education level increases, the number of music styles tolerated tends to increase.

---

direction of a relationship between two interval/ratio variables
Observe the sign ($+$ or $-$) of b and Pearson's r. Also observe the slope (or lean) of the pattern of coordinates in a scatterplot.

Strength of the Relationship

The correlation of educational level with lowbrow tolerance asserts that some part of the differences in the number of music styles tolerated (Y) by mothers is due to differences in their education levels—the effects of X. In Chapter 14 we observed that when these differences are systematic and X,Y-coordinates on a scatterplot have a linear pattern, we can improve best estimates of Y by estimating to the regression line rather than to the "mean line." The regression line is the one that is as close as possible to all X,Y-coordinates. By predicting to the regression line, we reduce error in predictions.

Let us apply these ideas to the population of mothers of high school students. From the data in Table 15–1 we found that the mean number of lowbrow music styles tolerated by these mothers is 5.50 styles. If we were asked to estimate the number for any mother *without any other knowledge* about her, 5.50 would be our best estimate—a prediction to the mean line of the scatterplot. How good is this *un*knowledgeable estimate? Mother 12 tolerates 8 lowbrow musical styles. If we had estimated her Y-score to the mean of 5.50, we would have erred by 2.50 styles. Recall from Chapter 5 that this amount—the difference between a score and the mean of scores—is her deviation score:

Mother 12's deviation score = error in estimating to the mean

$$= Y_{(mother\ 12)} - \overline{Y} = 8 - 5.50 = 2.50 \text{ music styles}$$

Suppose we now follow a different course of action. In this scenario we are given the opportunity to predict her music tolerance level with the knowledge that educational level and lowbrow tolerance are correlated. Instead of predicting to the mean, we predict "to the regression line" (Figure 15–1), which we know is close to the observed X,Y-coordinates. The best estimate of styles tolerated for mother 12 with her 16 years of education is now more accurately estimated by the regression line equation. Based on her 16 years of education, her predicted $\hat{Y}$-score of 7.32 styles is

$$\hat{Y}_{(X\ =\ 16\ years)} = a + bX = -1.00 + (.52)16 = 7.32 \text{ music styles}$$

Using this as *a knowledgeable estimate*—a coordinate point on the regression line—we now estimate mother 12's tolerance level as being much closer to her true tolerance level. The error in this knowledgeable estimate is only .68 styles:

Error in estimating mother 12's music tolerance level when predicting to the regression line $= Y_{(mother\ 12)} - \hat{Y}_{(X\ =\ 16\ years)} = 8 - 7.32 = .68 \text{ music style}$

This estimate is a considerable improvement over the one made to the mean. Error is reduced from 2.50 styles to .68 style. To determine how much of an improvement this is, we take the difference between the knowledgeable estimate ($\hat{Y}$ predicted for 16 years of education) and the unknowledgeable estimate (i.e., $\overline{Y}$, the mean of Y):

Improvement in estimating Y using knowledge that it is related to X
$$= \hat{Y}_{(X\ =\ 16\ years)} - \overline{Y} = 7.32 - 5.50 = 1.82 \text{ music styles}$$

This reduction in error of 1.82 styles is the part of the error "explained" by level of education. In predicting to the regression line, we explain 1.82 of mother 12's 2.50 deviation score. We attribute the 1.82 styles above the mean of 5.50 to her higher educational level.

The strength of a relationship between two interval/ratio variables is a measure of just how much improvement occurs in making these estimates for the sample (and population) as a whole. For a summary statistic that applies to the entire sample, we must calculate the best estimates of every case and compare these knowledgeable estimates to the unknowledgeable estimates based on the mean. A measure of the total strength for the sample must assess how much of the total error—the sum of deviation scores—can be eliminated by using the regression line instead of the mean line as a basis for predicting lowbrow tolerance.

There is, however, an additional step required in making these summary calculations. We cannot simply sum deviation scores, because they always sum to zero. Thus, the deviation scores must be squared. Recall that the sum of squared deviation scores for an entire sample is called the total variation:

$$\text{Total variation in } Y = \Sigma\,(Y_{(each\ case)} - \overline{Y})^2$$

The variation is the total amount of squared deviations from the mean *that is in need of being explained.* Why is one mother two styles tolerant over the mean while another mother is one style under it? If the relationship between educational level and tolerance of lowbrow musical styles is strong, educational level will explain a large *proportion of the total variation* in lowbrow tolerance. A large amount of each subject's lowbrow tolerance deviation score could be attributed to her educational level. Thus, we must determine *what proportion of the total variation in Y can be explained by X.*

Let us make the extra calculation of squaring for mother 12. Again, we find that her deviation score is 2.50 styles. Her squared deviation is $(2.50)^2 = 6.25$. What proportion of this *squared* deviation is explained by her education?

Amount of mother 12's squared deviation explained by her educational level

$$= \frac{\text{squared improvement using knowledgeable estimate}}{\text{squared deviation score}}$$

$$= \frac{(Y'_{(X=16\ years)} - \overline{Y})^2}{(Y_{(mother\ 12)} - \overline{Y})^2} = \frac{1.82^2}{2.50^2} = .5296$$

Thus, the proportion of mother 12's *squared* deviation in lowbrow tolerance (Y) explained by her 16 years of education (X) is .5296, or 52.96 percent.

To obtain the total amount of variation in Y explained by X for the whole sample, we make these calculations for every individual in the sample and sum the calculations. This is a cumbersome process. Fortunately, there is a shortcut method for obtaining the proportion of the total variation in Y explained by X.

Shortcut Method for Computing the Strength of the Relationship   Mathematically, the proportion of the total variation in Y explained by X can be obtained quickly by squaring Pearson's r correlation coefficient. That is, the statistic r^2 readily provides this proportion, and it is a measure of the strength of the relationship between X and Y.

$$r^2 = \text{proportion of variation in } Y \text{ explained by } X$$

$$= \frac{\Sigma\,(Y'_{(each\ case)} - \overline{Y})^2}{\Sigma\,(Y_{(each\ case)} - \overline{Y})^2}$$

---

strength of a relationship between two interval/ratio variables
r^2 = proportion of the variation in Y explained by knowing that it is related to X.

For the hypothesis on educational level and lowbrow tolerance, $r^2 = (.82)^2 = .6724$; $(100)(.6724) = 67.24$ percent. Thus, 67.24 percent of the variation in the number of musical styles tolerated is explained by knowing educational levels.

When there is a strong relationship between two interval/ratio variables, the X,Y-coordinates on the scatterplot will fit tightly around the regression line. The tighter the fit, the larger the value of Pearson's r and therefore the larger the value of r^2. And when the fit is tight, best estimates to the regression line are close to the actual observed Y-scores, just as in the case of mother 12. Error in predictions of Y taking into account its relationship with X will be small, and the proportional reduction in error (PRE) will be great. This means that X-scores are good, strong predictors of Y-scores. In other words, the relationship is strong.

Focus on r^2, Not r   In interpreting the strength of a relationship, we focus on r^2 rather than r because both the sign of r and its size can be misleading. The sign of r has nothing to do with the strength of relationship; it merely indicates the direction of the relationship. Moreover, whether the relationship is positive or negative, squaring the r always results in a positive "proportion of variation explained" because squaring removes any negative signs. With respect to the size of r, squaring reveals the true strength of a relationship—the amount of PRE in predicting the dependent variable Y that is due to its correlation with the independent variable X.

Observing r directly (i.e., without squaring) encourages an overestimation of the strength of the relationship. This is revealed in Table 15–2. For instance, directly observing, say, $r = .50$, could lead to the incorrect conclusion that we are "halfway there" in reducing errors in prediction. In fact, we are only a quarter of the way there because $r^2 = (.50)^2 = .25$; that is, only 25 percent of the variation in Y is explained by X. Remember, it is r^2, not r, that establishes the strength of a relationship between two interval/ratio variables.

The General Linear Model Applied to Correlation and Regression Analysis
Examining the amount of variation explained should be familiar to those who have covered the material in Chapter 12 on ANOVA. There we used the general linear model by decomposing the Y-scores of a sample into their parts explained by the mean of Y, the effects of X, and the effects of other unmeasured variables (i.e., remaining error). The same approach may be applied to regression analysis. For instance, we can decompose mother 12's lowbrow music tolerance score into those parts explained and those parts unexplained by educational level:

$$Y_{(mother\ 12)} = \text{mean of } Y + \text{mother 12's deviation score}$$
$$= Y' + (Y_{(mother\ 12)} - \overline{Y})$$
$$= Y' + (Y'_{(X=16\ years)} - \overline{Y}) + (Y_{(mother\ 12)} - Y'_{(X=16\ years)})$$

Thus:

$$8 \text{ styles} = 5.50 \text{ styles} + 2.5 \text{ styles}$$
$$= 5.50 \text{ styles} + 1.82 \text{ styles} \qquad + .68 \text{ styles}$$

$$= \text{the mean} + \begin{array}{c}\text{amount explained}\\ \text{by 16 years of}\\ \text{education}\end{array} + \begin{array}{c}\text{error—the amount}\\ \text{explained by other}\\ \text{variables}\end{array}$$

TABLE 15–2 | Comparing r to r^2: the importance of focusing on r^2 to assess the strength of a relationship

r	r^2	Proportion and Percentage of Variation in Y Explained by X		Strength of the Relationship
		p	%	
1.00	1.00	1.00	100	Perfect positive relationship
.90	.81	.81	81	Very strong positive
.80	.64	.64	64	
.70	.49	.49	49	Moderately strong positive
.60	.36	.36	36	
.50	.25	.25	25	
.40	.16	.16	16	Moderately weak positive
.30	.09	.09	9	
.20	.04	.04	4	
.10	.01	.01	1	Very weak positive
.00	**.00**	**.00**	**0**	**No relationship**
−.10	.01	.01	1	Very weak negative
−.20	.04	.04	4	
−.30	.09	.09	9	
−.40	.16	.16	16	Moderately weak negative
.50	.25	.25	25	
−.60	.36	.36	36	
−.70	.49	.49	49	Moderately strong negative
−.80	.64	.64	64	
−.90	.81	.81	81	Very strong negative
−1.00	1.00	1.00	100	Perfect negative relationship

This illustrates that the general linear model works whenever we have an interval/ratio dependent variable (Y) on which we are computing its mean. Measures of the strength of a relationship in both ANOVA and regression analysis simply sum up the amount of explained variation in Y and calculate the proportion of the total variation that this amount constitutes.

Practical Applications of the Relationship

Keep in mind that the practical applications of the relationship provide a down-to-earth description of the results—in everyday terms to the extent possible. For two interval/ratio variables, we start with a general description of how to estimate the number of musical styles tolerated when we know the educational level. This general description is simply an interpretation of the regression coefficient b, the slope of the regression line. Recall from Chapter 14 that in general

$$b = \text{slope of the regression line of the scatterplot}$$
$$= \text{effect on } Y \text{ of a } \textit{one-unit} \text{ change in } X$$

The slope of the regression line in the scatterplot tells us how much vertical rise occurs with a one-unit horizontal run (see Figure 14–6 in the previous chapter). In Chapter 14 we stated that Pearson's r is a measure of the effect of X on Y. In fact, r and b are both measures of slope, but in different ways. (Pearson's r is a standardized slope, the slope as a number of standard deviations. It tells us how many standard deviations rise in Y can be expected with a 1 standard deviation run on X.) This connection between the two statistics also means that b is a measure of the effect of X on Y.

For our sample of mothers, a general description of the nature of the relationship between educational level and number of musical styles tolerated would be stated as follows:

$$b = .52 \text{ styles per year of education}$$

A one-year increase in education level is related to a .52 increase in number of lowbrow musical styles tolerated. Put another way, add .52 to the estimates of musical styles tolerated with the addition of each year of education. If Ms. Franklin has one year of education more than Ms. Curry, estimate Ms. Franklin's lowbrow tolerance as .52 style higher.

After reporting the slope, we provide examples of "best estimates" (i.e., $\acute{Y}$'s) of the number of musical styles tolerated for a few selected educational levels (X). Specific examples are especially meaningful to a public audience. These best estimates are calculated from the regression equation $\acute{Y} = a + bX$. We insert chosen values of X and compute $\acute{Y}$'s. It is useful to choose a low value and a high value of X or a number of years of education that is especially meaningful, such as 12 years (i.e., high school graduate) or 16 years (i.e., college graduate). Thus, we make the following calculations:

$$\acute{Y} = a + bX = -1.00 + (.52)X$$
$$\acute{Y}_{(X = 12)} = -1.00 + (.52)12 = 5.24 \text{ styles}$$
$$\acute{Y}_{(X = 16)} = -1.00 + (.52)16 = 7.32 \text{ styles}$$

In reporting these best estimates we state that

$$\acute{Y} = a + bX = -1.00 + (.52)X$$

Thus, for example, the best estimate of the number of musical styles tolerated by mothers with a high school education (12 years) is 5.24 styles, and among mothers with a college education (16 years) it is 7.32 styles.

---

practical applications of a relationship between two interval/ratio variables   In general, describe the slope of the regression line of the scatterplot:

$$b = \text{effect on } Y \text{ of a one-unit change in } X$$

Provide best estimates using the regression line equation:

$$\acute{Y} = a + bX$$

Insert chosen values of X, compute $\acute{Y}$'s and interpret them in everyday language.

Careful Interpretation of Correlation and Regression Statistics

Correlations Apply to a Population, Not to an Individual

A key facet of the statistical imagination is interpreting data in relation to a whole—a population—rather than with respect to a single individual or case. Statements about an individual case are weak estimates because individuals are highly complex. Statements about a population based on a sample are also estimates. Proper interpretation of data requires a clear understanding of the application of estimates. Does an estimate apply to an individual or to the group to which that individual belongs?

This distinction between an individual and a group is important in the interpretation of correlation statistics. The interpretation is limited by the fact that for most studies, data on subjects are collected only once. *Data collected at one point in time for each person in a sample* are called **cross-sectional data**, and the sample is called a cross-sectional sample. For example, every data set mentioned in this text is cross-sectional. *Data collected over a period of time with multiple contacts with subjects* are called **longitudinal data**, and the sample is called a longitudinal sample. For example, we might study the effects of a new prescription drug for high blood pressure for a one-year period by examining the same sample of patients every two months.

Interpretation of regression statistics differs for these two types of data. For the cross-sectional data in this text, estimates cannot be made about changes over time. Interpretation of the slope applies to a single point in time. For example, when we say that a one-year change in educational level is related to a .52 increase in lowbrow musical styles tolerated, we do not mean that a mother will necessarily become more tolerant by picking up an additional year of education. Instead, we are saying that within the sample and as an estimate for the population, .52 style is the difference *in the mean number of musical styles tolerated* between two categories that are one year apart in education level. We are comparing levels of education among sampled individuals at one point in time.

This distinction is illustrated by the *negative* correlation between age and educational level. In a cross-sectional sample of adults who have *already finished* their schooling (say, people age 25 and older) an increase in age is related to a *decrease* in education; that is, the correlation is in the negative direction. Does this mean that people lose education as they age? Of course not. The data are cross-sectional; we did not track people over time. We are comparing distinct individuals at different age levels, say, 30, 40, 50, and 60 years, at one point in time. The negative correlation simply indicates that people in older age groups have fewer years of education. For instance, members of your grandparents' generation typically acquired only a high school diploma. A correct interpretation would be that an increase in *the level of age within the population* is related to a decrease in *the level of* education. Furthermore, suppose we use a regression equation to calculate a best estimate of Grandfather Parker's educational level. We determine that his age is 76 years and predict an educational level of 10.5 years of schooling. This does not mean that he quit school in the middle of his junior year of high school. Rather, this estimate is the mean education level of all 76-year-olds. The best estimate is based on an

X-score. It applies to the X-score of all 76-year-olds. Short of a multivariate analysis that takes into account a large number of predictor variables, this estimate must do. But not too much should be made of estimates of Y based on X unless the correlation is very strong, say, .9 or higher. Unless the correlation is perfect, there will still be error in estimates of Y based on knowing X.

Careful Interpretation of the Slope, b

Correlation and regression analysis has much in common with analysis of variance (see Chapter 12). In both procedures we examine the variation around the mean of an interval/ratio dependent variable Y. With ANOVA, we examine differences in means among three or more *groups or categories*. For example, is there a difference in the mean incomes of Catholic, Protestant, and Jewish households, and if so, what are the best estimates of the dollar amount differences in income? Similarly, with correlation and regression analysis we indirectly focus on the mean because deviation scores are distances from the mean. This is an important point: Correlation and regression statistics are based on the means of X and Y, and it is the mean of Y about which we are making estimates. When we estimate that a mother with 12 years of education tolerates 5.24 lowbrow styles of music, we are not asserting that every mother at this educational level scores 5.24 styles. What we are saying is that the best estimate *of the mean* number of musical styles tolerated by *all mothers with 12 years of education* is 5.24 styles. Just as with ANOVA, we are basing best estimates of an individual on the mean of his or her group. In the case of these mothers, the group is an X-score on an interval/ratio measure.

Distinguishing Statistical Significance from Practical Significance

Statistical significance demonstrates that a measured test effect for a sample is so large that it indicates a real effect in the population and is not merely the result of random sampling error. As we noted in Chapters 11 and 12 in discussing difference of means tests, with a large sample a small difference may be found to be statistically significant. For example, with a very large sample we may find a $10 difference in mean annual salaries of men and women in a corporation. Using a t-test, we conclude that the $10 difference between the sample means reflects a real $10 difference in the populations of men and women.

But does $10 suggest rampant gender discrimination? For 250 working days in a year, a $10 difference comes out to 4 cents per day, or less than a penny per hour. In practical terms the difference is meaningless. Statistical significance and practical significance are separate issues.

In all hypotheses tests, a large sample size reduces the standard error of the sampling distribution. This makes the test more sensitive in detecting statistical significance even if the effect of the test is small. With simple bivariate correlation and regression analysis, Pearson's r is the measure of the effect of the test. With large samples, even a small r will produce a large t-test statistic. This in turn may result in a small p-value and lead to a rejection of the null hypothesis. The size of the standard error—and therefore the size of the p-value—is greatly influenced by sample size. All else being equal, the larger the sample size, the smaller the p-value is and the more likely it is that the null hypothesis will be rejected. This is illustrated with t-tests for two samples, one quite small and the other quite large, where Pearson's r came out the same:

Illustration 1: Sample size, $n = 16$; $r = .10$; one-tailed test, $\alpha = .05$, $df = n - 2 = 14$.

$$t_r = r\sqrt{\frac{n-2}{1-r^2}} = .10\sqrt{\frac{14}{1-.01}} = .38 \text{ SE}$$

From the t-distribution table (Statistical Table C in Appendix B): p-value: p [observing an r as unusual as or more unusual than .10 when $\rho = 0$] $> .05$.

Conclusion: Not statistically significant.

Illustration 2: Sample size, $n = 2002$; $r = .10$; one-tailed test, $\alpha = .05$. $df = n - 2 = 2,000$.

$$t_r = r\sqrt{\frac{n-2}{1-r^2}} = .10\sqrt{\frac{2000}{1-.01}} = 4.49 \text{ SE}$$

From the t-distribution table (Statistical Table C in Appendix B): p-value: p [observing an r as unusual as or more unusual than .10 when $\rho = 0$] $< .001$.

Conclusion: Statistically significant at the .05 level of significance.

Even though the r's are the same in both illustrations, different conclusions are drawn. In Illustration 2 we conclude that the sample correlation r indicates a real correlation in the population.

But is an r of .10 meaningful? The strength of the relationship is measured with r^2. For Illustration 2: $r^2 = (.10)^2 = .01$ (or 1 percent). Thus, 1 percent of the variation in the dependent variable Y is explained by knowledge of the independent variable X.

The effect is real in the population, as we established with 95 percent confidence when we rejected the null hypothesis of no relationship. The effect, however, is so weak as perhaps to be meaningless. In a sense, a large sample can be overly sensitive to small test effects. The determination of statistical significance is not the only consideration. Strength also must be considered.

Of course, because they are insensitive to even large test effects, small samples present a different problem. With a small sample, we may conclude that a large Pearson's r is not statistically different from zero. If it turns out that there truly is a relationship in the population but we simply missed it, then we have made a type II error: failing to reject a false null hypothesis (see Chapter 9). Another illustration reveals that even a moderately strong relationship can be missed when we use a small sample.

Illustration 3: Sample size, $n = 5$; $r = .70$; one-tailed test, $\alpha = .05$. $df = n - 2 = 3$.

$$t_r = r\sqrt{\frac{n-2}{1-r^2}} = .70\sqrt{\frac{3}{1-.49}} = 1.69 \text{ SE}$$

From the t-distribution table (Statistical Table C in Appendix B): p-value: p [observing an r as unusual as or more unusual than .70 when $\rho = 0$] $> .05$.

Conclusion: Not statistically significant.

In this illustration, the strength of the relationship would be $r^2 = (.70)^2 = .49$ (or 49 percent). Thus, it appears that 49 percent of the variation in the dependent variable Y is explained by knowledge of the independent variable X. We must conclude, however, that there is no relationship between the variables, and given the small sample size, this is all we can do. This raises the suspicion, however, that we have made a type II error. The relationship may or may not exist, but with such a small sample we may never know. This illustration highlights the importance of having a large enough sample to avoid type II errors. In "Statistical Follies and Fallacies" in Chapter 13 we addressed this issue as one of statistical power. Small samples have low statistical power.

These illustrations of the influence of sample size on statistical testing also highlight the importance of not treating the p-value of a statistical test as a measure of the strength of the relationship. If one correlation is found significant at the .001 level of significance and a second at the .05 level, this does not mean that the first correlation is necessarily stronger than the second. The p-values of Illustrations 1 and 2 above are radically different, yet the strength of the relationship is the same. The existence and strength of the relationship are separate issues.

Tabular Presentation: Correlation Tables

Bivariate correlations often are presented in tables as matrices with a diagonal shape. Table 15–3 is an example. It presents aggregate data—data based on groups—for students in 76 randomly selected school districts. The mean Stanford Admissions Test (SAT) score for the district is correlated with the percentage of families in the district with only one parent and the percentage of students in the district who receive free school lunches. The last variable is a common measure of poverty in a residential area.

The table is designed so that quick comparisons can be made among correlations. First, note that the correlation of a variable with itself is perfect (i.e., $r = 1.00$). Of course, a variable is a perfect predictor of itself. Second, correlations are presented on only one cornered side, or "diagonal," of the table because it is redundant to repeat them on the other side. Third, the p-values for significant r's are presented by footnoted

TABLE 15–3 | Bivariate correlations among mean Stanford Admissions Test (SAT) scores, percentage of one-parent families, and percentage of students receiving free lunches for 76 school districts (fictional data)

	1	2	3
1 Mean SAT score	1.00		
2 Percent one-parent families	−.61***	1.00	
3 Percent students receiving free school lunches	−.91***	.63***	1.00

* $p < .05$. ** $p < .01$. *** $p < .001$. One-tailed tests.

asterisks. The signs of the correlation coefficients provide information on the direction of the relationship, and by squaring a coefficient we can estimate the proportion and percentage of variation explained by a chosen independent variable.

The statistics in the table reveal that average test performance in a school district is moderately related to the percentage of one-parent families (Pearson's $r = -.61$; $p < .001$). This moderate strength is determined by squaring $-.61$ and seeing that about 36 percent of the variance is explained by this family structure variable. The negative sign tells us that the higher the percentage of one-parent families in a district, the lower the mean SAT score.

The mean SAT score in a district also has a strong negative correlation with the percentage of students receiving free lunches: $r = -.91; p < .001; r^2$ equals about 82 percent. The higher the percentage of students in a district relying on the school for free lunches, the lower the mean SAT score in the district.

We also can see that the percentage of one-parent families is related to poverty; that is, the correlation between one-parent families and free lunches is a moderate, positive one: $r = .63; p < .001; r^2$ equals about 40 percent. As one can imagine, a correlation table with a large number of variables packs a lot of information onto one page.

Statistical Follies and Fallacies: Correlation Does Not Always Indicate Causation

In attempting to explain a phenomenon of interest (i.e., our dependent variable Y), we search for a correlated variable X. Finding a correlation, however, does not necessarily mean that X causes Y. The existence of a correlation simply denotes that the scores of the two variables systematically change together in a predictable pattern. This discovery by itself does not establish causation between the variables. Many correlations are spurious.

A **spurious correlation** is *one that is conceptually false, nonsensical, or theoretically meaningless.* This is illustrated by the correlation between ice cream consumption (X) and the rape rate (Y) over time. As ice cream consumption goes up, the rape rate increases. Many spurious correlations are like this one. The simultaneous increases and decreases in the rates of these two variables are explained by a third variable—seasonal change. As it turns out, people eat more ice cream in warm weather, and for reasons related to victim availability, more rapes occur during the warm summer months. Thus, although changes in the rates of one have nothing to do with changes in the rates of the other, ice cream consumption and rape rates go up and down together as the seasons change. To imply a meaningful connection between the two behaviors, however, is nonsensical.

> **spurious correlation**   A correlation between two variables that is conceptually false, nonsensical, or theoretically meaningless.

Another spurious correlation concerns the relationship between crime rates in city neighborhoods and the racial makeup of a community. There is a positive correlation between the percentage of the minority population (e.g., African-Americans) living in neighborhoods and crime rates. That is, for a sample of communities, those with a high percentage of African-Americans tend to have high rates of crime. On the face of it, this suggests that African-Americans are more prone to criminal behavior, and indeed, racists often quote this statistic. This correlation, however, is spurious. Crime rates are high in *poor* neighborhoods regardless of their racial makeup, and a disproportionate share of minority neighborhoods are poor. Moreover, the relationship between poverty and racial makeup is due to racism, not biological race. That is, being poor has nothing to do with genetics. It is the racist heritage of the United States that contributes to the fact that a disproportionate share of African-Americans live in poverty, which in turn is a good predictor of crime rates.

How do we prove this point to a racist? Examine only wealthy neighborhoods, some that are predominantly white and some that are predominantly African-American. Regardless of racial predominance, these neighborhoods will have low crime rates. Moreover, *within* a sample of wealthy neighborhoods, the correlation between percentage minority and crime rate will be zero. Similarly, in poor neighborhoods—regardless of racial makeup—crime rates are relatively high and a zero correlation is found between poverty and racial makeup. This approach of focusing on a constant level for a third variable, such as the socioeconomic status of a neighborhood, is called *holding that variable constant*. When we hold socioeconomic status constant, its effects on the crime rate are eliminated, and thus this variable no longer produces the spurious relationship between X (percentage minority population) and Y (crime rate). Calculating correlation and regression statistics to control for additional variables is called *multiple correlation and regression,* a topic covered on *The Statistical Imagination* Web site at www.mhhe.com/ritchey2. These illustrations of spurious effects underscore the importance of interpreting statistical findings with a great deal of caution.

Spurious correlations are not unusual. This is due partly to the fact that many things, such as the size of the earth's population, continually increase. Any other thing that continually increases (such as the growth of gargantuan underground mushrooms) will be positively correlated with population size. Similarly, any other variable that continually decreases (such as the size of ice shelves on the continent of Antarctica or the percentage of American adults smoking cigarettes) will be negatively correlated with population size. Recall from Chapter 1 that a good scientific theory has two elements: a sense of understanding and the ability to provide empirical predictions. Spurious correlations allow for predictions but fail to provide a sense of understanding. In fact, they often confuse a situation.

SUMMARY

1. The hypothesis test for a relationship between two interval/ratio variables is a t-test of Pearson's r bivariate correlation coefficient.

2. Use this t-test when (a) there is one representative sample from a single population; (b) there are two interval/ratio variables; (c) there are no restrictions on sample size, but generally, the larger the n, the better; (d) observation of the scatterplot of the coordinates of the two variables reveals a linear pattern.

3. Test the H_0 that $\rho = 0$; that is, that there is no relationship between X and Y. The Greek letter rho (ρ) is the correlation coefficient obtained if Pearson's r were computed for the entire population.

4. The sampling distribution is a t-distribution for Pearson's r bivariate correlation coefficient with $df = n - 2$. If rho is indeed zero, then with repeated sampling Pearson's r's would calculate to a value of zero, give or take some sampling error. It is not necessary to calculate a standard error.

5. The test effect is the value of Pearson's r bivariate correlation coefficient, which is the observed sample r minus the hypothesized rho of zero.

6. The test statistic is t_r and the p-value is estimated using the t-distribution table, Appendix B, Statistical Table C.

7. Existence of a relationship is established by testing the H_0 that $\rho = 0$; that is, there is no relationship between X and Y. If the H_0 is rejected, then a relationship exists.

8. Direction is indicated by the sign of r and b and by observing the slope of the regression line on the scatterplot. A positive relationship is revealed with an upward slope, and r and b will be positive. A negative relationship is revealed with a downward slope, and r and b will be negative.

9. Strength of the relationship is determined by the proportion of the total variation in Y explained by X. It is quickly obtained by squaring Pearson's r bivariate correlation coefficient.

10. Practical applications of results are presented as follows: (*a*) Interpret the regression coefficient, *b*, the slope of the regression line. State the effect on Y of a one-unit change in X. (*b*) Provide best estimates using the regression line equation. Insert chosen values of X, compute $\acute{Y}$s, and interpret them in everyday language.

11. Care must be taken when interpreting correlation coefficients: (*a*) A correlation applies to a population, not an individual. A $\acute{Y}$ is an estimate of the mean of Y for all population subjects with the given value of X. (*b*) Especially with large samples, a statistically significant correlation coefficient can have a small value and, therefore, represent a very weak or practically insignificant relationship. (*c*) A correlation between X and Y does not always mean that X causes Y. A correlation can be spurious; it may be mathematically sound, but is conceptually false, nonsensical, or theoretically meaningless.

CHAPTER EXTENSIONS ON *THE STATISTICAL IMAGINATION* WEB SITE

Chapters 14–15 Extensions of text material available on *The Statistical Imagination* Web site at www.mhhe.com/ritchey2 include an introduction to multiple correlation and regression, the situation where a dependent variable is regressed on two or more independent variables.

STATISTICAL PROCEDURES COVERED TO THIS POINT

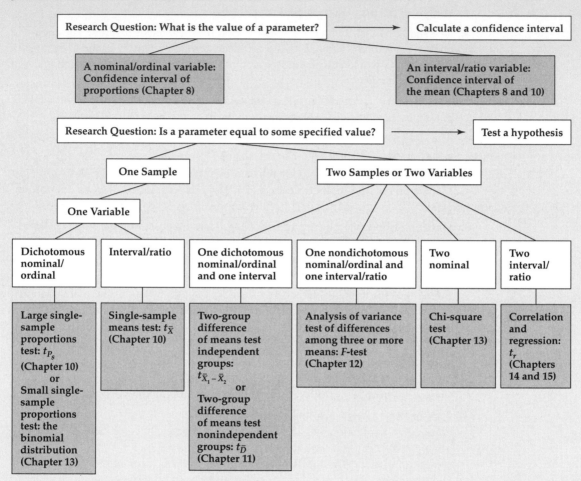

FORMULAS IN CHAPTER 15

For calculation of correlation and regression coefficients and the regression line equation (see Chapter 14):

To complete the calculation spreadsheet (Table 15–1):

$$\overline{X} = \frac{\Sigma X}{n} \qquad \overline{Y} = \frac{\Sigma Y}{n}$$

Pearson's correlation coefficient:

$$r = \frac{\Sigma (X - \overline{X})(Y - \overline{Y})}{\sqrt{\Sigma (X - \overline{X})^2 \, \Sigma (Y - \overline{Y})^2}}$$

The regression coefficient or slope, b:

$$b = \frac{\Sigma(X - \overline{X})(Y - \overline{Y})}{\Sigma(X - \overline{X})^2}$$

The Y-intercept, a:

$$a = \overline{Y} - b\overline{X}$$

The regression equation:

$$\acute{Y} = a + bX$$

The test statistic:

$$t_r = r\sqrt{\frac{n - 2}{1 - r^2}}$$

For describing the strength of a relationship between two interval/ratio variables:

$$r^2$$

QUESTIONS FOR CHAPTER 15

1. For Pearson's r correlation coefficient, draw a conceptual diagram depicting a population and a sample and insert the appropriate statistics and parameters. Stipulate how the null hypothesis is stated for the hypothesis test.

2. For a hypothesis test of the relationship between two interval/ratio variables, what is the shape of the sampling distribution and what test statistic is used?

3. In testing a hypothesis between two interval/ratio variables, the direction of the test is stated in the alternative hypothesis. For the general case of Y regressed on X, show how the alternative hypothesis is stated when the direction is hypothesized to be positive. Indicate the shape of the pattern of coordinates of a scatterplot when this is the case. Do the same for a negative relationship.

4. Observe the formulas for the Pearson's r correlation coefficient and the regression coefficient b and explain why these two coefficients always have the same directional sign (+ or −).

5. Explain what r^2 tells us.

6. In ascertaining the strength of a relationship between two interval/ratio variables, what is the danger in relying solely on an interpretation of the absolute value of Pearson's r? Explain.

7. Provide a one-word answer to this question: When no relationship is found between X and Y, what do we say about the other aspects of a relationship?

8. Match the following with regard to the relationship between two interval/ratio variables:

a. Pearson's r _____ The Y-intercept; the value of Y when $X = 0$

b. a _____ The proportion of variation in Y explained by knowledge of X; a measure of the strength of the relationship

c. r^2 _____ Slope of the regression line; the effect on Y of a one-unit change in X; a measure of the practical applications of the relationship

d. b _____ Predicted value of Y; best estimate of Y for a given value of X; used to describe the practical applications of the relationship

e. $\acute{Y}$ _____ Measures how tightly X,Y-coordinates fit around the regression line; used to describe the existence and direction of a relationship

9. Explain the difference between cross-sectional data and longitudinal data.

10. Using cross-sectional data, a researcher finds a negative relationship between age and knowledge about personal computers. Does this mean that as people age, they lose this knowledge? Explain.

11. Mathematically, there is a positive correlation between shoe size and the ability to do complicated mathematical problems. Is this really meaningful? Explain.

12. Mathematically, there is a negative correlation between the number of movies being produced in Hollywood each year and the size of the Amazon rain forests. Is this really meaningful? Explain.

EXERCISES FOR CHAPTER 15

Problem Set 15A

On all hypotheses tests, follow the six steps of statistical inference, including test preparation, a conceptual diagram, probability curves, and appropriate aspects of a relationship. For consistency, round calculations to two decimal places. Use $\alpha = .05$ unless otherwise stipulated.

15A-1. Interpret the following Pearson's r bivariate correlation coefficients with regard to the direction of the relationship (fictional data).

X	Y	r
a. Yearly income	Dollar value of long-term investments	.69
b. Literacy rate of the population	Extent to which a government is democratic	.73
c. Age	Number of movies seen in past six months	−.45
d. Traffic citations and accidents in the past three years	Cost of automobile insurance premiums	.87

15A-2. You are conducting a "Couch Potato" study of young teenagers at risk of developing obesity. You gather the following data from a sample of adolescent males in one of 14 experimental groups from seven cities. The variables include the number of hours a subject watches television per week, weight, age, and height.

a. Draw a scatterplot of weight regressed on TV hours per week.

b. For these two variables, compute Pearson's *r* bivariate correlation coefficient and the regression equation: $\acute{Y} = a + bX$.

c. Test the hypothesis that there is a relationship between these two variables and address appropriate aspects of the relationship.

d. Age and height are roughly equal among the subjects. In fact, these variables were intentionally "held constant." Why is it wise to do this in testing for a relationship between the amount of time subjects watch TV and their weights?

Subject	TV Hours per Week	Weight (pounds)	Age	Height (inches)
1	9	112	13	62
2	14	131	14	65
3	20	171	14	64
4	18	160	13	63
5	16	182	14	64
6	14	165	15	67
7	19	149	14	64
8	12	137	13	65

15A-3. Imagine that you are an admissions officer of a university. For a random sample of 114 sophomores, you compare current college grade point average (GPA) to high school GPA (raw data not shown). A computer-generated scatterplot reveals a linear relationship between the variables. Computer output gives you the following: Pearson's $r = .47$, $b = .73$, and the *Y*-intercept $a = .80$. Test the hypothesis that students who did well in high school also do well in college.

15A-4. The following are interval/ratio level variables with appropriate statistics computed for a sample of adult males (fictional data). All of the coefficients are statistically significant at the .05 level.

X = Age	*Y* = Occupational Prestige Score	*Z* = Educational Level
$r_{yx} = .24$	$r_{zx} = -.32$	$r_{zy} = .31$
$b_{yx} = 2$	$b_{zx} = -.3$ years	$b_{zy} = 6$

a. Which is the stronger relationship, that between age and occupational prestige score or that between age and educational level? Why?
b. Interpret b_{zx}.
c. Interpret the direction of r_{zx}.
d. Organize the bivariate correlation coefficients into a correlation table.

15A-5. The following are fictional data from 12 randomly selected cities. Is there a relationship between the level of education of a city (i.e., median years of education of adult household heads) and fire and burn fatalities per 100,000 population?

Fire/Burn Deaths per 100,000	Median Level of Education
2.3	11.7
1.5	12.2
2.1	11.3
2.3	11.1
1.4	12.2
1.9	12.0
1.6	12.3
1.7	12.4
1.5	12.5
1.7	11.6
2.2	10.9
2.1	12.1

15-A6. From Chapter 14, use the data in exercise 14A-3 about Health Maintenance Organizations (HMOs). Complete that exercise to obtain a scatterplot and bivariate correlation and regression statistics. Test the hypothesis that the average reduction in length of stay is correlated with the percentage increase in profits for the HMOs over the past year.

Problem Set 15B

On all hypotheses tests, follow the six steps of statistical inference, including test preparation, a conceptual diagram, probability curves, and appropriate aspects of a relationship. For consistency, round calculations to two decimal places. Use $\alpha = .05$ unless otherwise stipulated.

15B-1. Interpret the following Pearson's r bivariate correlation coefficients with regard to the direction of the relationship (fictional data).

X	Y	r
a. Level of education	Occupational prestige	.75
b. Amount spent on promoting seat belts	Traffic accident deaths (in a state)	−.58
c. Age	Health status	−.51
d. Amount spent on an automobile	Amount spent on house	.81

15B-2. The following fictional data are for a study of 10-year-old girls and their mothers. Determine if there is a relationship between mother's weight and child's weight. For these data, do the following:

   a. Draw a scatterplot of child's weight regressed on mother's weight.

   b. Compute Pearson's *r* bivariate correlation coefficient for these two variables as well as the regression equation: $\acute{Y} = a + bX$.

   c. Test the hypothesis that there is a relationship between these two variables and address appropriate aspects of the relationship.

   d. Age is held constant through sampling. Daily calories consumed and daily exercise were also intentionally "held constant." Why is it wise to do this in testing for a relationship between mother's weight and child's weight?

Subject	Daily Calories	Mother's Weight	Child's Weight	Daily Exercise (in minutes)
1	2,206	150	80	24
2	2,246	185	91	23
3	2,211	134	68	23
4	2,203	215	93	22
5	2,229	287	91	22
6	2,223	147	71	23
7	2,241	175	81	24
8	2,233	195	92	24
9	2,219	167	75	22

15B-3. Suppose you wish to test the hypothesis that younger people are more computer literate than older people. You collect a random sample of 150 adults and gather data on their age and computer literacy using the computer literacy scale (CLS). A computer-generated scatterplot reveals a linear relationship between the variables. Computer output gives you the following: Pearson's $r = -.72$, $b = -.08$, and the Y-intercept $a = 25.31$. Test the hypothesis that younger people are more computer literate than older people.

15B-4. The following are interval/ratio level variables with appropriate statistics computed for a sample of adult males (fictional data). All of the coefficients are statistically significant at the .05 level.

X = One's Own Income (in $1,000s)	Y = Parents' Income (in $1,000s)	Z = Number of Extended Relatives in Household
$r_{yx} = .51$	$r_{zx} = -.47$	$r_{zy} = -.39$
$b_{yx} = 1.7$	$b_{zx} = -.11$	$b_{zy} = -.08$

    a. Which is the stronger relationship, that between one's own income and parents' income or that between one's own income and the number of extended relatives in the household? Why?

    b. Interpret b_{zx}.

    c. Interpret the direction of r_{yx}.

    d. Organize the bivariate correlation coefficients into a correlation table.

15B-5. The following are fictional data from 10 randomly selected middle schools. Is there a relationship between the healthy food choices in their school cafeterias and the number of obese students in the school? Healthy food choices were measured by a ratio of healthy foods (i.e., fruit, vegetables, whole grains, etc.) to nonhealthy foods (i.e., foods high in fat, sugar, sodium, etc).

Healthy Food Choices	Number of Obese Students per 100
2.01	22
.82	25
.67	27
1.50	25
1.90	21
2.14	23
1.01	26
.87	25
.91	24
1.75	23

15-B6. From Chapter 14, use the data in exercise 14B-3 about social capital and life satisfaction. Complete that exercise to obtain a scatterplot and bivariate correlation and regression statistics. Test the hypothesis that individuals with higher social capital tend to have greater life satisfaction.

Problem Set 15C

On all hypotheses tests, follow the six steps of statistical inference, including test preparation, a conceptual diagram, probability curves, and appropriate aspects of a relationship. For consistency, round calculations to two decimal places. Use $\alpha = .05$ unless otherwise stipulated.

15C-1. Interpret the following Pearson's *r* bivariate correlation coefficients with regard to the direction of the relationship (fictional data).

X	Y	r
a. High school grade point average	College grade point average	.57
b. Number of previous convictions	Length of prison sentence	.38
c. Socioeconomic status of convicted felon	Length of prison sentence	−.71
d. Socioeconomic status of neighborhood	Percentage of high school graduates attending college	.68

15C-2. Suppose that the following table presents data for a study of young teenagers at risk of developing obesity. Do the following:

   a. Draw a scatterplot of weight regressed on the number of fast-food meals consumed in the past week.
   b. For these two variables, compute Pearson's *r* bivariate correlation coefficient and the regression equation: $\hat{Y} = a + bX$.
   c. Test the hypothesis that there is a relationship between these two variables and address appropriate aspects of the relationship.
   d. Age and height are roughly equal among the subjects. In fact, these variables were intentionally "held constant." Why is it wise to do this in testing for a relationship between the number of fast-food meals consumed in the past week and weight?

Subject	TV Hours per Week	Age (years)	Weight (pounds)	Height (inches)	Number of Fast-Food Meals in Past Week
1	9	12	112	65	2
2	14	13	131	66	2
3	20	12	171	66	5
4	18	14	160	66	2
5	16	13	182	67	4
6	14	14	165	66	3
7	19	13	149	67	3
8	12	13	137	66	2

15C-3. Survey measures of religiosity gauge the extent to which an individual believes, prays, attends church, and follows the moral codes set down by a religion. The variable life satisfaction is a perception of how well things are going in a person's life at present. A computer-generated scatterplot reveals a linear relationship between these variables. Computer output gives you the following (fictional) results: $n = 14$ adults, Pearson's $r = .48$, $b = .78$, and the Y-intercept $a = 6.24$. Test the hypothesis that religious persons tend to have greater life satisfaction.

15C-4. The following are interval/ratio level variables with appropriate statistics computed for a sample of 100 Internet users (fictional data). All of the coefficients are statistically significant at the .05 level.
   a. Which is the stronger relationship, that between age and hours connected or that between political conservatism and hours connected? Why?
   b. Interpret b_{zx}.
   c. Interpret the direction of r_{zx}.
   d. Organize the bivariate correlation coefficients into a correlation table.

X = Age	Y = Political Conservatism	Z = Hours Connected (to the Internet—World Wide Web—per month)
$r_{yx} = .19$	$r_{zx} = -.26$	$r_{zy} = .25$
$b_{yx} = .35$ conservatism scale points	$b_{zx} = -1.1$ hours	$b_{zy} = .79$ hours

15C-5. An interesting psychological trait is openness to experience: a willingness to try new things and keep an open mind (McCrae 1996). Another often-researched trait is authoritarianism: a general belief that society is better off with strongly enforced laws and punitive parents and bosses to keep people in line. Is there a relationship between these two traits for a group of randomly selected adults?

Openness to Experience Scale	Authoritarianism Scale
9	31
12	20
17	15
16	14
15	12
13	26
10	28
7	34
11	27
9	24
10	22
6	33
7	27
13	22
15	17

15-C6. From Chapter 14, use the data in exercise 14C-3 about disability days and loss of income. Complete that exercise to obtain a scatterplot and bivariate correlation and regression statistics. Test the hypothesis that disability days per year predict total family income (in thousands of dollars).

Problem Set 15D

On all hypotheses tests, follow the six steps of statistical inference, including test preparation, a conceptual diagram, probability curves, and appropriate aspects of a relationship. For consistency, round calculations to two decimal places. Use $\alpha = .05$ unless otherwise stipulated.

15D-1. Interpret the following Pearson's r bivariate correlation coefficients with regard to the direction of the relationship (fictional data).

X	Y	r
a. Height	Weight	.68
b. Age	Concerts attended last year	−.72
c. Media coverage of crime	Fear of crime	.56
d. Neighborhood poverty rate	Neighborhood crime rate	.79

15D-2. You are conducting a study to find out if class attendance predicts grade point average (GPA). You collect a sample of college students and gather the following data on their GPAs and the number of classes missed in the last year. Determine if students who miss a lot of class tend to have lower GPAs.

   a.   Draw a scatterplot of GPA regressed on classes missed.

   b.   For these two variables, compute Pearson's r bivariate correlation coefficient and the regression equation: $\hat{Y} = a + bX$.

   c.   Test the hypothesis that there is a relationship between these two variables and address appropriate aspects of the relationship.

   d.   IQ and SAT score are roughly equal among the subjects. In fact, these variables were intentionally "held constant." Why is it wise to do this in testing for a relationship between the number of classes missed and GPA?

Subject	GPA	Classes Missed	IQ	SAT
1	3.12	5	114	1,014
2	2.42	9	110	996
3	1.95	16	101	1,012
4	3.89	4	112	978
5	2.56	7	108	994
6	2.34	9	119	1,025
7	1.84	14	114	1,017
8	3.64	4	106	980
9	3.91	3	116	1,020
10	2.49	8	115	989

15D-3. A nurse's patient load is related to job satisfaction (Aiken, Clarke, Sloane, Sochalski, and Silber 2002). In other words, the fewer patients under a nurse's care, the higher the job satisfaction. You wish to confirm this finding with a study of your own. You measure patient load as nurse-to-patient ratio, the number of nurses per 100 patients. Job satisfaction is gauged with an "I Like Nursing" (ILN) scale. A computer-generated scatterplot reveals a linear relationship between these variables. Computer output gives you the following (fictional) results: $n = 210$ nurses, Pearson's $r = .79$, $b = .44$, and the Y-intercept $a = 11.53$. Test the hypothesis that the nurse-to-patient ratio is related to job satisfaction.

15D-4. The following are interval/ratio level variables with appropriate statistics computed for a sample of 442 working mothers (fictional data). All of the coefficients are statistically significant at the .05 level.
   a. Which is the stronger relationship, that between stressful life events and depression, or that between stressful life events and life satisfaction? Why?
   b. Interpret b_{zx}.
   c. Interpret the direction of r_{zx}.
   d. Organize the bivariate correlation coefficients into a correlation table.

X = Stressful Life Events (in the past year)	Y = Depression	Z = Life Satisfaction
$r_{yx} = .46$	$r_{zx} = -.51$	$r_{zy} = -.39$
$b_{yx} = -1.3$ scale points	$b_{zx} = -1.9$ scale points	$b_{zy} = .81$ scale points

15D-5. You are researching assorted relationships with psychological mastery, the amount of control individuals believe they have over their lives and the things that happen to them. Using survey measurement scales, you obtain the following data for a group of randomly selected adults. Determine if there is a relationship between mastery and the belief that voting is important.

Mastery Scale	Voting Is Important Scale
10	12
25	30
33	34
31	41
15	13
19	28
22	27
29	24
24	21
25	23

13	15
17	14
21	20
28	23
30	29

15D-6. From Chapter 14, use the data in exercise 14D-1. Complete that exercise to obtain a scatterplot and bivariate correlation and regression statistics. Test the hypothesis that there is a relationship between years of schooling and income.

OPTIONAL COMPUTER APPLICATIONS FOR CHAPTER 15

If your class uses the optional computer applications that accompany this text, open the Chapter 15 exercises on *The Statistical Imagination* Web site at www.mhhe.com/ritchey 3. The exercises involve using *SPSS for Windows* to obtain statistics to test hypotheses and address the four aspects of relationship for two interval/ratio variables. In addition, Appendix D of this text provides a brief overview of the *SPSS* command sequences for procedures covered in this chapter.

APPENDIX

A

Review of Basic Mathematical Operations

This appendix does not provide a thorough lesson in mathematical computations. It merely provides review examples to assist students in recalling the basic mathematical operations typically encountered in statistical calculations. After each review section, problems are provided; the answers appear at the end of this appendix.

BASIC MATHEMATICAL SYMBOLS AND TERMS

$\pm$ Plus or minus	$\div$ or /	Divided by
$<$ Less than	$\times$ or $\cdot$ or $(\cdot\,\cdot)$	Multiplied by
$>$ Greater than	$\leq$	Less than or equal to
$\geq$ Greater than or equal to	∞	Infinity
$\approx$ Approximately equal	$\neq$	Not equal
$|\ |$ Absolute value of	$\sqrt{}$	Square root (reviewed below)
(e.g., $|-15| = 15$)		

A *sum* is the answer to an addition or subtraction problem.

A *product* is the answer to a multiplication problem.

A *quotient* is the answer to a division problem.

ORDER OF MATHEMATICAL OPERATIONS

In calculating the parts of a formula, follow these rules:

1. Work inside each set of parentheses before moving outside them. If sets of parentheses are bracketed, work inside each set of brackets before moving outside them.

2. Terms are parts of an equation separated by addition and subtraction signs. Before adding and subtracting terms, complete any multiplications and divisions within each term.

3. With division problems, complete all calculations above and below the division sign before dividing.

4. Treat a radical sign (i.e., the square root sign) as a large set of brackets; that is, complete all calculations under the radical sign before taking the square root.

EXPONENTS: SQUARING AND SQUARE ROOTS

Exponents: Raising to a Power An exponent is the number of times a base number is multiplied by itself. When we make such calculations, we say that we "raise the base number to a power." To "square" a base number is to raise it to the power of 2. For example, 4 to the power of 2 is 4^2 (i.e., 4 squared), or 4 multiplied by itself:

$$4^2 = (4)(4) = 16$$

A base number raised to the first power is the base number itself, and we do not bother to place the exponent 1 in the notation: $4^1 = 4$. In general, for any number a: $a^1 = a$.

Any number raised to the exponent of zero equals 1: $4^0 = 1$, $7^0 = 1$. In general, $a^0 = 1$.

A base number raised to the power of 3 is "cubed." Thus, 4 cubed is

$$4^3 = (4)(4)(4) = 64$$

Similarly, 5 raised to the fifth power is

$$5^5 = (5)(5)(5)(5)(5) = 3,125$$

Note that 5^5 is equal to 5 squared times 5 cubed, or 5 to the fourth power times 5. That is, when a base number raised to a power is multiplied by the same base number raised to a power, the result is equal to the base number raised to the sum of the exponents:

$$5^5 = (5^2)(5^3) = (25)(125) = 3,125 \text{ or } 5^5 = (5^1)(5^4) = (5)(625) = 3,125$$

This is called the product rule for exponents. In general, it states that for any positive integers m and n,

$$(a^m)(a^n) = a^{m+n}$$

There are several general *power rules for exponents*. For any positive integers m and n,

$$(a^m)^n = a^{mn}; \text{ for example, } (6^2)^3 = 6^6 = 46,656$$
$$(ab)^m = a^m b^m; \text{ for example, } (2 \cdot 3)^2 = (2^2)(3^2) = 4 \cdot 9 = 36$$
$$(a/b)^m = \frac{a^m}{b^m}; \text{ for example, } (4/2)^3 = \frac{4^3}{2^3} = \frac{64}{8} = 8$$

The quotient rule for exponents states that

$$\frac{a^m}{a^n} = a^{m-n}; \text{ for example, } \frac{3^4}{3^2} = 3^{(4-2)} = 3^2 = 9$$

REVIEW PROBLEMS

1. $7^2 =$ 2. $21^2 =$ 3. $21^3 =$ 4. $19^2 =$ 5. $9^4 =$

6. $10^3 =$ 7. $(2^2)(2^5) =$ 8. $(3^2)^4$ 9. $100^2 \div 10^2 =$

10. $10^4 \div 10^3 =$

Square Roots Taking the square root is the inverse of squaring. Thus, the square root of 16 is 4:

$$\sqrt{16} = 4$$

To check the accuracy of taking a square root, square the result to see if the number under the radical reappears. Similarly, when a number is squared, take the square root of the result to see if the base number reappears. This means that the square root of a number squared is equal to the number:

$$\sqrt{16} = \sqrt{4^2} = 4$$

In general, $\sqrt{a^2} = a$, where a is some base number.

REVIEW PROBLEMS

Note the pattern of answers for items 11 through 16.

11. $\sqrt{8.1} =$ 12. $\sqrt{81} =$

13. $\sqrt{810} =$ 14. $\sqrt{8,100} =$

15. $\sqrt{81,000} =$ 16. $\sqrt{810,000} =$

17. $\sqrt{7.568} =$ 18. $\sqrt{100} =$

19. $\sqrt{10^2} =$ 20. $\sqrt{41^2}$

SUMMATION NOTATION

The Greek letter sigma (Σ) is used to mean "sum of." Care must be taken to sum the proper terms of an equation.

Illustration: The variable X = age. John is 32, Kirk is 40, and Jim is 24.

Example 1: Their average or "mean" age is "the sum of X" divided by 3:

$$\bar{X} = \frac{\Sigma X}{3} = \frac{(32 + 40 + 24)}{3} = 32 \text{ years}$$

where the symbol $\bar{X}$ is read "mean" (see Chapter 4).

Example 2: To calculate the *sum of ages squared,* first square each X-score and then sum:

$$\Sigma X^2 = (32^2 + 40^2 + 24^2) = 1,024 + 1,600 + 576 = 3,200 \text{ squared years}$$

Example 3: To calculate the *sum of ages* squared, first sum the ages and then square the result:

$$(\Sigma X)^2 = 96^2 = 9,216 \text{ squared years}$$

Summations are facilitated when the data are organized into spreadsheets with variables in columns and cases in rows. The following spreadsheet provides ages (X) and weights (Y) for four cases or subjects. Use this spreadsheet for review problems 21 through 26.

Case/Subject	X (age)	X^2	Y (weight)	Y^2
John	32	1,024	169	28,561
Kirk	40	1,600	191	36,481
Jim	24	576	157	24,649
Carl	44	1,936	212	44,944

REVIEW PROBLEMS

21. $\Sigma X =$ **22.** $\Sigma X^2 =$ **23.** $(\Sigma X)^2 =$ **24.** $\Sigma Y =$

25. $\Sigma Y^2 =$ **26.** $(\Sigma Y)^2 =$

FRACTIONS AND COMMON DENOMINATORS

Before fractions can be added or divided, they must have common denominators. An easy way to determine a common denominator is to multiply the denominators. (This method works, although it does not always result in the "lowest common denominator.") Once a common denominator is found, the numerators are added or subtracted.

Example:

$$\frac{1}{2} + \frac{1}{3} = \frac{3}{6} + \frac{2}{6} = \frac{5}{6}$$

Example:

$$\frac{1}{2} - \frac{1}{3} = \frac{3}{6} - \frac{2}{6} = \frac{1}{6}$$

Multiplication of fractions is straightforward: We simply multiply numerators and denominators. Again, the answer to a multiplication problem is called the *product*.

Example 1: The product of one-half of one-third is one-sixth.

$$\frac{1}{2} \cdot \frac{1}{3} = \frac{1}{6}$$

Example 2:

$$\frac{3}{52} \cdot \frac{4}{51} = \frac{12}{2,652}$$

In general, to multiply fractions,

$$\frac{a}{b} \cdot \frac{c}{d} = \frac{a \cdot c}{b \cdot d}$$

In dividing fractions, we refer to the answer as a *quotient*. In general,

$$\frac{a}{b} \div \frac{c}{d} = \frac{a \cdot d}{b \cdot c}$$

For example, the quotient of three-fourths divided by two-thirds is one and one-eighth:

$$\frac{3}{4} \div \frac{2}{3} = \frac{3 \cdot 3}{4 \cdot 2} = \frac{9}{8} = 1\frac{1}{8}$$

An easier way to deal with fractions is to transform them into decimal numbers. This is illustrated below.

REVIEW PROBLEMS

27. $\dfrac{5}{8} + \dfrac{3}{12} =$

28. $\dfrac{13}{22} - \dfrac{7}{49} =$

29. $\dfrac{6}{11} + \dfrac{2}{3} - \dfrac{1}{8} =$

30. $\dfrac{10}{12} \cdot \dfrac{4}{5} =$

31. $\dfrac{13}{25} \cdot \dfrac{6}{14} \cdot \dfrac{2}{5} =$

32. $\dfrac{16}{18} \div \dfrac{5}{6} =$

DECIMALS AND DECIMAL PLACE LOCATIONS

Deci- means 10, and the decimal system of numbers is based on multiples of 10. Figure A–1 stipulates decimal place locations. When a number is multiplied by a multiple of 10, the decimal point is simply moved the appropriate number of places to the right. When a number is divided by a multiple of 10, the decimal point is moved to the left. Decimal place location also may be conceived in terms of raising 10 to a power or whole-number exponent. For instance,

$$10^1 = 10, \ 10^2 = 100, \ 10^3 = 1{,}000, \ 10^4 = 10{,}000, \text{ etc.}$$

In multiplying by 10, move the decimal point one place to the right; by 100, two places; and so on:

$$(98.49)(1{,}000) = 98{,}490 \quad (.3587)(100) = 35.87$$

Negative exponents imply division. Thus, $10^{-1} = .1$, $10^{-2} = .01$, $10^{-3} = .001$, $10^{-4} = .0001$, and so on. In dividing by 10, move the decimal point one place to the left; by 100, two places; and so on:

$$(45.91)/100 = .4591$$
$$(.0083)/1{,}000 = .0000083$$

FIGURE A–1

Decimal place locations

Decimal Places														
X	X	X	X	X	X	X	•	X	X	X	X	X	X	X
Millions	Hundred thousands	Ten thousands	Thousands	Hundreds	Tens	Ones (integer)	Decimal point	Tenths	Hundredths	Thousandths	Ten-thousandths	Hundred-thousandths	Millionths	Ten-millionths

REVIEW PROBLEMS

Round answers to four decimal places.

33. $29.869/1{,}000 =$ **34.** $(.0388)(10{,}000) =$ **35.** $4/1{,}000 =$

36. $(1.957)(100) =$ **37.** $(3.503)(10^{-3}) =$ **38.** $(3.503)(10^{3}) =$

As we discussed in Chapter 1, fractions are easier to deal with in decimal form. A fraction is "decimalized" simply by dividing the numerator by the denominator. To transform this quotient into a percentage, move the decimal point two places to the right, which is simply a matter of multiplying by 100.

Care must be taken in using various decimal places in a single problem. Test your ability to keep track of decimal places with the following review problems.

REVIEW PROBLEMS

39. $(.15)(4) =$ **40.** $(2.0)(.3) =$ **41.** $(.024 - .03) =$

42. $(.05 + 235.44) =$ **43.** $(34.076 - 6.3) =$ **44.** $(4.141 - .09) =$

THE RELATIONSHIP OF THE NUMERATOR TO THE DENOMINATOR

Having a feel for the relative size of fractions, percentages, and proportions is important in statistics, because every statistical procedure uses fractions. *Percent* means "per hundred." If the term *percent* does not convey a sense of proportion for you, take 100 pennies and toss them on the bed. Then compute the percentage of heads by simply counting the number of heads.

Mathematical proportions are derived from fractions, and understanding the dynamics of fractions goes a long way toward helping one get a feel for statistics. Let us study these dynamics by comparing the relative sizes of the numerator and denominator of fractions and see how these sizes affect quotients. Such a study reveals the following:

1. When the numerator is small in comparison to the denominator, the quotient will be small. As an example, compare 1/567 to 439/567 by dividing each of these fractions to obtain their proportions in decimal form.

2. When the numerator is at least half the size of the denominator, the quotient will be above 50 percent, and this constitutes a simple majority. For example, in a runoff election for sorority president, if Nancy gets 51 of the 100 votes, she wins.

3. When the numerator is almost as large as the denominator, the quotient will be close to a proportion of 1.0 and a percentage of 100 percent. For example, if 222 out of 236 students pass a course,

$$p \text{ [of students in a course who passed]} = \frac{\text{\# passed}}{\text{total class size}} = \frac{222}{236} = .9407$$

$$\% \text{ [of students in a course who passed]} = (p)(100) = 94.07\%$$

That is, for every 100 students, about 94 pass.

4. When the numerator is larger than the denominator, the quotient will be greater than 1.

5. In summary, the larger the numerator in relation to the denominator, the larger the quotient.

BASIC ALGEBRAIC SOLUTIONS

Algebra involves the use of symbols, such as letters, to represent a general mathematical case. Specific numbers then may be substituted for symbols to arrive at a specific answer. For example, we might define X as height and Y as weight and understand that weight is a function of height: The taller a person is, the more that person tends to weigh. To estimate weight for a given height, we may substitute values of X into an appropriate equation and solve for Y. For instance,

$$Y = -159.31 + (4.62)X$$

If X is 68 inches, the best estimate of that person's weight is 154.85 pounds:

$$Y = -159.31 + (4.62)(68) = 154.85 \text{ pounds}$$

BASIC RULES OF ARITHMETIC AND ALGEBRA

In multiplying or dividing two numbers, the product, or quotient, is positive if both numbers have the same sign but negative if the two numbers have different signs:

$$(4)(3) = 12 \qquad (-4)(3) = -12$$

$$(-4)(-3) = 12 \qquad (4)(-3) = -12$$

$$\frac{4}{3} = 1.25 \qquad \frac{-4}{3} = -1.25 \qquad \frac{4}{-3} = -1.25$$

In general, any number times zero is zero. Any number times 1 is that number. Zero divided by any number is zero. Division by zero is not permitted (because it results in an undefined quotient). Thus,

$$0 \cdot a = 0; \text{ for example, } 0 \cdot 25 = 0 \text{ and } (0)(4{,}500) = 0$$
$$1 \cdot a = a; \text{ for example, } 1 \cdot 25 = 25 \text{ and } (1)(4{,}500) = 4{,}500$$
$$0 \div a = 0; \text{ for example, } 0 \div 25 = 0 \text{ and } (0/4{,}500) = 0$$
$$a \div 0 = \text{undefined (because something cannot be divided by nothing)}$$

Any number divided by itself equals 1. In general,

$$\frac{a}{a} = 1; \text{ for example } \frac{34}{34} = 1 \text{ and } \frac{3}{3} = 1$$

The *multiplicative inverse* of a number is equal to 1 divided by that number. A number times its multiplicative inverse equals 1:

$$a \cdot \frac{1}{a} = 1; \text{ for example, } 3 \cdot \frac{1}{3} = 1$$

Terms may be simplified by using *commutative and distributive properties*. In general,

$$(a + b) = (b + a); \text{ for example, } (2 + 3) = (3 + 2) = 5$$
$$(ab) = (ba); \text{ for example, } (2 \cdot 3) = (3 \cdot 2) = 6$$
$$a(b + c) = ab + ac; \text{ for example, } 6(2 + 3) = 6(2) + 6(3) = 30$$
$$a(b - c) = ab - ac; \text{ for example, } 6(3 - 2) = 6(3) - 6(2) = 6$$

Consistent with algebraic properties and rules, exponential equations may be "expanded" into a set of terms. For example,

$$(a + b)^3 = (a + b)(a + b)(a + b) = a^3 + 3a^2b + 3ab^2 + b^3$$

There is a simple method of expanding such equations when they have only two base numbers, *a* and *b* (see "The Binomial Distribution Equation" in Chapter 13).

SOLVING FOR AN UNKNOWN QUANTITY

A common mathematical problem involves solving an equation for an unknown variable or function. For example, we might be told that some quantity X is such that 3 times that quantity plus 30 is equal to 100, minus 6 times the quantity, plus 2 times the quantity. In symbolic form,

$$3X + 30 = 100 - 6X + 2X$$

We are asked to determine the quantity; that is, we are asked to "solve for X." These types of solutions depend on *mathematical equivalency*. That is, the equals sign must be respected so that quantities on both sides of the equals sign remain the same. Any mathematical operation performed on one side of the equation must be performed on the other side to maintain mathematical equivalency. Solutions are arrived at by combining like terms and performing mathematical operations on each side of the equation. To solve for X, we select mathematical operations that "isolate" X to one side of the equation. Thus,

We start with:	$3X + 30 = 100 - 6X + 2X$
Simplify by combining like terms to obtain:	$3X + 30 = 100 - 4X$
Add $4X$ to both sides of the equation:	$3X + 30 + 4X = 100 - 4X + 4X$
To obtain:	$7X + 30 = 100$
Subtract 30 from both sides:	$7X + 30 - 30 = 100 - 30$
To obtain:	$7X = 70$
Divide both sides by 7:	$\dfrac{7X}{7} = \dfrac{70}{7}$
To obtain:	$X = 10$

Check the accuracy of the answer by substituting 10 for X in the original equation:

$$3X + 30 = 100 - 6X + 2X$$

Substituting 10 for X: $3(10) + 30 = 100 - 6(10) + 2(10)$
Solve: $60 = 60$

Thus, we know that 10 is a correct solution because its substitution for X maintains mathematical equivalency.

REVIEW PROBLEMS

45. *Given: $Y = a + bX$, $a = 17$, $b = 5$, and $X = -2$. Solve for Y.*

46. If $a = 3$, solve the equation $(4a^2)(6a^3) =$

47. Given: $8 - 3X = 4X - 6$. Solve for X.

48. Given: $7X - 5X - 4 = 4X - 10$. Solve for X.

49. $a = \dfrac{b}{c} \cdot$ Solve for c.

50. Expand the equation $(a + b)^2 =$

ANSWERS

1. 49   **2.** 441   **3.** 9,261   **4.** 361   **5.** 6,561   **6.** 1,000   **7.** 128   **8.** 6,561
9. 100   **10.** 10   **11.** 2.85   **12.** 9   **13.** 28.46   **14.** 90   **15.** 284.60   **16.** 900
17. 2.75   **18.** 10   **19.** 10   **20.** 41   **21.** 140 years   **22.** 5,136 squared years
23. 19,600 squared years   **24.** 729 pounds   **25.** 134,635 squared pounds
26. 531,441 squared pounds   **27.** 21/24 = .8750   **28.** 483/1,078 = .4480
29. 287/264 = 1.0871   **30.** 2/3 = .6667   **31.** 156/1,750 = .0891   **32.** 96/90 = 1.0667   **33.** .0299   **34.** 388   **35.** .0040   **36.** 195.7   **37.** .0035   **38.** 3,503   **39.** .60
40. .6   **41.** −.006   **42.** 235.49   **43.** 27.776   **44.** 4.051   **45.** $Y = 7$ **46.** 5,832
47. $X = 2$ **48.** $X = 3$ **49.** $c = b/a$ **50.** $a^2 + 2ab + b^2$

Statistical Probability Tables

STATISTICAL TABLE A Random Number Table

```
9 5 7 3 4 3 9 3 1 1 1 5 6 7 8 2 9 3 5 3 2 5 0 1 4 8 2 4 3 7 3 2 4 2 8
5 7 9 4 6 5 7 5 9 3 6 5 8 5 3 7 2 4 9 3 7 7 5 2 6 1 5 1 6 5 2 6 0 9 4
3 9 9 2 6 8 1 4 8 1 8 7 1 8 3 5 0 7 9 6 0 8 2 2 5 1 8 7 7 3 7 3 1 3 7
3 6 1 4 3 4 8 4 9 7 0 3 1 8 3 6 8 0 9 2 4 9 5 3 8 9 2 9 6 7 3 7 5 1 1
3 2 7 6 1 8 7 3 2 2 2 9 8 4 0 5 4 0 5 7 3 3 2 7 2 8 4 7 0 5 9 3 8 1 1
5 8 3 7 5 7 2 0 1 9 4 9 4 1 8 7 0 4 4 9 1 3 5 9 3 1 1 8 5 0 1 7 8 2 8
6 6 7 9 7 5 5 9 0 8 7 4 1 1 1 6 4 9 3 5 1 0 0 6 0 2 7 9 6 2 5 9 8 3 7
1 0 9 6 5 4 0 7 6 1 2 1 6 0 2 1 5 8 4 1 3 5 0 7 6 9 0 8 1 6 0 8 2 5 9
2 0 8 5 1 0 4 4 0 7 6 2 2 5 5 9 4 6 6 7 4 0 2 5 9 3 5 8 3 9 5 7 6 7 0
0 4 2 5 8 3 4 3 3 5 3 6 3 1 8 7 9 1 1 7 5 6 8 5 9 3 9 3 8 7 7 9 5 2 6
0 5 7 5 5 2 6 0 4 5 0 9 8 6 2 2 3 2 0 8 5 6 4 8 9 7 9 7 6 5 6 2 0 9 5
2 3 8 8 4 9 4 2 2 0 0 8 2 0 4 1 8 6 3 9 6 0 7 2 4 7 7 9 5 9 9 6 9 2 8
1 4 0 2 8 2 5 7 0 2 2 5 6 9 6 5 9 3 2 9 8 1 1 7 8 5 1 2 1 8 9 0 6 5 4
1 6 8 2 3 7 6 4 0 5 9 3 4 7 8 9 0 4 9 0 8 3 4 3 6 6 1 1 4 7 0 8 7 9 6
3 6 9 5 8 1 1 5 3 1 1 3 0 8 4 7 8 5 7 7 0 2 2 4 0 2 1 8 2 1 9 3 1 8 2
1 2 2 3 9 4 2 4 0 1 8 1 0 2 1 1 7 3 6 8 9 8 3 8 7 8 0 2 4 9 0 4 8 8 4
9 3 4 4 9 2 2 5 9 3 3 4 8 0 9 0 6 2 2 4 5 7 6 2 8 0 7 9 2 4 1 5 0 4 7
9 4 5 9 6 9 2 4 1 8 1 3 2 9 7 6 3 0 0 5 6 8 9 1 4 4 2 6 0 8 1 5 3 1 5
1 4 6 4 5 4 2 4 3 6 7 1 4 3 9 4 4 0 5 7 4 0 3 9 0 7 9 5 3 6 6 0 1 6 7
6 8 0 5 5 2 3 5 8 6 4 4 1 0 7 5 5 7 0 3 1 9 6 9 8 6 1 3 4 4 6 9 5 7 9
2 1 7 4 7 0 5 3 6 7 8 6 5 0 6 4 7 6 0 6 2 5 2 7 1 8 3 6 1 8 7 1 2 1 5
3 9 1 8 7 0 5 6 6 7 3 3 0 4 0 2 4 3 5 7 7 3 7 7 1 8 4 2 4 0 9 4 8 3 0
4 8 2 8 4 0 2 7 9 8 6 7 1 0 4 6 1 6 9 7 0 9 1 7 6 6 4 3 8 6 5 9 6 0 9
5 1 9 8 4 8 4 6 4 1 4 0 1 8 2 3 7 5 3 0 7 9 5 1 3 8 0 1 6 8 9 2 0 6 5
3 7 4 9 7 9 4 4 7 2 3 9 3 8 4 9 2 2 1 8 5 9 7 7 1 0 6 0 2 0 7 8 0 5 6
5 9 1 1 0 6 5 5 0 4 7 8 6 8 7 8 8 6 3 1 3 1 4 6 0 8 5 5 2 8 9 7 4 6 0
2 2 6 4 9 7 8 8 4 3 6 9 6 3 7 6 3 1 2 5 4 3 0 5 1 1 5 6 6 6 1 2 9 4 1
6 5 2 2 5 3 4 3 3 9 1 3 4 2 2 0 7 5 1 9 2 7 9 5 6 0 9 4 9 4 6 0 3 3 3
1 7 1 4 3 3 3 4 8 7 8 2 2 8 3 9 3 2 4 1 6 5 1 6 5 7 5 5 9 9 5 6 1 4 5
9 6 7 5 3 4 9 2 2 8 1 5 0 1 9 3 8 4 5 4 6 3 4 3 4 4 5 8 4 2 9 3 3 7 3
5 0 4 1 9 6 3 9 2 3 2 5 7 8 9 2 8 0 6 3 6 0 6 7 4 6 3 8 0 8 9 4 2 9 5
9 5 6 8 8 4 0 2 8 9 3 9 7 5 3 9 1 7 3 9 3 2 7 8 3 4 7 3 0 8 0 5 1 4 2
1 9 4 6 0 7 1 9 6 6 2 9 8 0 4 8 7 4 6 4 7 4 8 2 9 6 1 5 0 8 0 8 3 6 7
9 3 0 9 9 7 0 5 5 7 3 4 5 5 0 3 0 2 8 4 7 4 6 2 1 9 4 1 9 6 2 8 3 3 4
6 7 6 6 1 2 7 5 4 5 6 7 5 9 5 3 4 2 4 0 1 0 3 8 7 5 9 5 2 3 7 1 0 0 0
3 8 7 5 1 2 2 0 1 3 5 2 2 5 5 0 4 8 0 8 9 7 6 4 3 7 9 5 0 2 9 6 7 2 1
3 9 3 2 4 1 1 1 6 5 7 4 2 6 5 0 0 2 2 0 0 1 5 0 2 1 6 8 6 7 9 7 3 2 5
```

STATISTICAL TABLE B Normal Distribution Table

Specified areas under the normal curve (columns B and C) for stipulated Z-scores (column A)

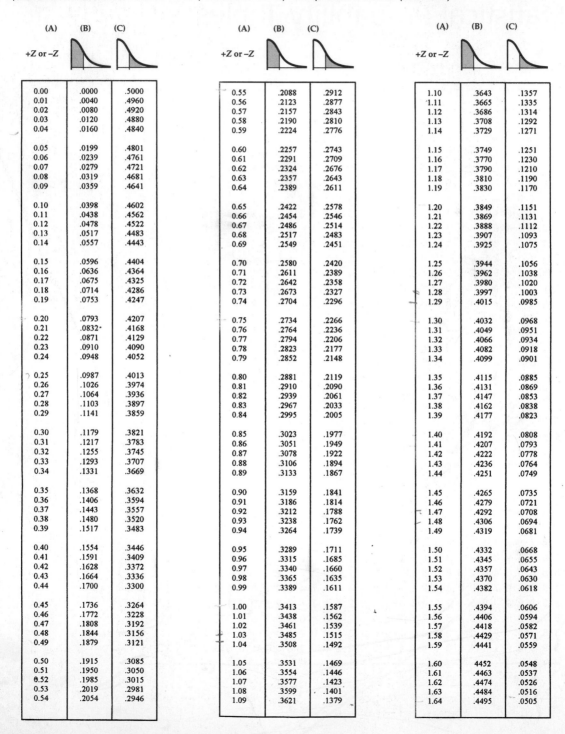

(A) +Z or –Z	(B)	(C)	(A) +Z or –Z	(B)	(C)	(A) +Z or –Z	(B)	(C)
0.00	.0000	.5000	0.55	.2088	.2912	1.10	.3643	.1357
0.01	.0040	.4960	0.56	.2123	.2877	1.11	.3665	.1335
0.02	.0080	.4920	0.57	.2157	.2843	1.12	.3686	.1314
0.03	.0120	.4880	0.58	.2190	.2810	1.13	.3708	.1292
0.04	.0160	.4840	0.59	.2224	.2776	1.14	.3729	.1271
0.05	.0199	.4801	0.60	.2257	.2743	1.15	.3749	.1251
0.06	.0239	.4761	0.61	.2291	.2709	1.16	.3770	.1230
0.07	.0279	.4721	0.62	.2324	.2676	1.17	.3790	.1210
0.08	.0319	.4681	0.63	.2357	.2643	1.18	.3810	.1190
0.09	.0359	.4641	0.64	.2389	.2611	1.19	.3830	.1170
0.10	.0398	.4602	0.65	.2422	.2578	1.20	.3849	.1151
0.11	.0438	.4562	0.66	.2454	.2546	1.21	.3869	.1131
0.12	.0478	.4522	0.67	.2486	.2514	1.22	.3888	.1112
0.13	.0517	.4483	0.68	.2517	.2483	1.23	.3907	.1093
0.14	.0557	.4443	0.69	.2549	.2451	1.24	.3925	.1075
0.15	.0596	.4404	0.70	.2580	.2420	1.25	.3944	.1056
0.16	.0636	.4364	0.71	.2611	.2389	1.26	.3962	.1038
0.17	.0675	.4325	0.72	.2642	.2358	1.27	.3980	.1020
0.18	.0714	.4286	0.73	.2673	.2327	1.28	.3997	.1003
0.19	.0753	.4247	0.74	.2704	.2296	1.29	.4015	.0985
0.20	.0793	.4207	0.75	.2734	.2266	1.30	.4032	.0968
0.21	.0832	.4168	0.76	.2764	.2236	1.31	.4049	.0951
0.22	.0871	.4129	0.77	.2794	.2206	1.32	.4066	.0934
0.23	.0910	.4090	0.78	.2823	.2177	1.33	.4082	.0918
0.24	.0948	.4052	0.79	.2852	.2148	1.34	.4099	.0901
0.25	.0987	.4013	0.80	.2881	.2119	1.35	.4115	.0885
0.26	.1026	.3974	0.81	.2910	.2090	1.36	.4131	.0869
0.27	.1064	.3936	0.82	.2939	.2061	1.37	.4147	.0853
0.28	.1103	.3897	0.83	.2967	.2033	1.38	.4162	.0838
0.29	.1141	.3859	0.84	.2995	.2005	1.39	.4177	.0823
0.30	.1179	.3821	0.85	.3023	.1977	1.40	.4192	.0808
0.31	.1217	.3783	0.86	.3051	.1949	1.41	.4207	.0793
0.32	.1255	.3745	0.87	.3078	.1922	1.42	.4222	.0778
0.33	.1293	.3707	0.88	.3106	.1894	1.43	.4236	.0764
0.34	.1331	.3669	0.89	.3133	.1867	1.44	.4251	.0749
0.35	.1368	.3632	0.90	.3159	.1841	1.45	.4265	.0735
0.36	.1406	.3594	0.91	.3186	.1814	1.46	.4279	.0721
0.37	.1443	.3557	0.92	.3212	.1788	1.47	.4292	.0708
0.38	.1480	.3520	0.93	.3238	.1762	1.48	.4306	.0694
0.39	.1517	.3483	0.94	.3264	.1739	1.49	.4319	.0681
0.40	.1554	.3446	0.95	.3289	.1711	1.50	.4332	.0668
0.41	.1591	.3409	0.96	.3315	.1685	1.51	.4345	.0655
0.42	.1628	.3372	0.97	.3340	.1660	1.52	.4357	.0643
0.43	.1664	.3336	0.98	.3365	.1635	1.53	.4370	.0630
0.44	.1700	.3300	0.99	.3389	.1611	1.54	.4382	.0618
0.45	.1736	.3264	1.00	.3413	.1587	1.55	.4394	.0606
0.46	.1772	.3228	1.01	.3438	.1562	1.56	.4406	.0594
0.47	.1808	.3192	1.02	.3461	.1539	1.57	.4418	.0582
0.48	.1844	.3156	1.03	.3485	.1515	1.58	.4429	.0571
0.49	.1879	.3121	1.04	.3508	.1492	1.59	.4441	.0559
0.50	.1915	.3085	1.05	.3531	.1469	1.60	4452	.0548
0.51	.1950	.3050	1.06	.3554	.1446	1.61	.4463	.0537
0.52	.1985	.3015	1.07	.3577	.1423	1.62	.4474	.0526
0.53	.2019	.2981	1.08	.3599	.1401	1.63	.4484	.0516
0.54	.2054	.2946	1.09	.3621	.1379	1.64	.4495	.0505

(A) +Z or −Z	(B)	(C)		(A) +Z or −Z	(B)	(C)		(A) +Z or −Z	(B)	(C)
1.65	.4505	.0495		2.22	.4868	.0132		2.79	.4974	.0026
1.66	.4515	.0485		2.23	.4871	.0129		2.80	.4974	.0026
1.67	.4525	.0475		2.24	.4875	.0125		2.81	.4975	.0025
1.68	.4535	.0465		2.25	.4878	.0122		2.82	.4976	.0024
1.69	.4545	.0455		2.26	.4881	.0119		2.83	.4977	.0023
1.70	.4554	.0446		2.27	.4884	.0116		2.84	.4977	.0023
1.71	.4564	.0436		2.28	.4887	.0113		2.85	.4978	.0022
1.72	.4573	.0427		2.29	.4890	.0110		2.86	.4979	.0021
1.73	.4582	.0418		2.30	.4893	.0107		2.87	.4979	.0021
1.74	.4591	.0409		2.31	.4896	.0104		2.88	.4980	.0020
1.75	.4599	.0401		2.32	.4898	.0102		2.89	.4981	.0019
1.76	.4608	.0392		2.33	.4901	.0099		2.90	.4981	.0019
1.77	.4616	.0384		2.34	.4904	.0096		2.91	.4982	.0018
1.78	.4625	.0375		2.35	.4906	.0094		2.92	.4982	.0018
1.79	.4633	.0367		2.36	.4909	.0091		2.93	.4983	.0017
1.80	.4641	.0359		2.37	.4911	.0089		2.94	.4984	.0016
1.81	.4649	.0351		2.38	.4913	.0087		2.95	.4984	.0016
1.82	.4656	.0344		2.39	.4916	.0084		2.96	.4985	.0015
1.83	.4664	.0336		2.40	.4918	.0082		2.97	.4985	.0015
1.84	.4671	.0329		2.41	.4920	.0080		2.98	.4986	.0014
1.85	.4678	.0322		2.42	.4922	.0078		2.99	.4986	.0014
1.86	.4686	.0314		2.43	.4925	.0075		3.00	.4987	.0013
1.87	.4693	.0307		2.44	.4927	.0073		3.01	.4987	.0013
1.88	.4699	.0301		2.45	.4929	.0071		3.02	.4987	.0013
1.89	.4706	.0294		2.46	.4931	.0069		3.03	.4988	.0012
1.90	.4713	.0287		2.47	.4932	.0068		3.04	.4988	.0012
1.91	.4719	.0281		2.48	.4934	.0066		3.05	.4989	.0011
1.92	.4726	.0274		2.49	.4936	.0064		3.06	.4989	.0011
1.93	.4732	.0268		2.50	.4938	.0062		3.07	.4989	.0011
1.94	.4738	.0262		2.51	.4940	.0060		3.08	.4990	.0010
1.95	.4744	.0256		2.52	.4941	.0059		3.09	.4990	.0010
1.96	.4750	.0250		2.53	.4943	.0057		3.10	.4990	.0010
1.97	.4756	.0244		2.54	.4945	.0055		3.11	.4991	.0009
1.98	.4761	.0239		2.55	.4946	.0054		3.12	.4991	.0009
1.99	.4767	.0233		2.56	.4948	.0052		3.13	.4991	.0009
2.00	.4772	.0228		2.57	.4949	.0051		3.14	.4992	.0008
2.01	.4778	.0222		2.58	.4951	.0049		3.15	.4992	.0008
2.02	.4783	.0217		2.59	.4952	.0048		3.16	.4992	.0008
2.03	.4788	.0212		2.60	.4953	.0047		3.17	.4992	.0008
2.04	.4793	.0207		2.61	.4955	.0045		3.18	.4993	.0007
2.05	.4798	.0202		2.62	.4956	.0044		3.19	.4993	.0007
2.06	.4803	.0197		2.63	.4957	.0043		3.20	.4993	.0007
2.07	.4808	.0192		2.64	.4959	.0041		3.21	.4993	.0007
2.08	.4812	.0188		2.65	.4960	.0040		3.22	.4994	.0006
2.09	.4817	.0183		2.66	.4961	.0039		3.23	.4994	.0006
2.10	.4821	.0179		2.67	.4962	.0038		3.24	.4994	.0006
2.11	.4826	.0174		2.68	.4963	.0037		3.25	.4994	.0006
2.12	.4830	.0170		2.69	.4964	.0036		3.30	.4995	.0005
2.13	.4834	.0166		2.70	.4965	.0035		3.35	.4996	.0004
2.14	.4838	.0162		2.71	.4966	.0034		3.40	.4997	.0003
2.15	.4842	.0158		2.72	.4967	.0033		3.45	.4997	.0003
2.16	.4846	.0154		2.73	.4968	.0032		3.50	.4998	.0002
2.17	.4850	.0150		2.74	.4969	.0031		3.60	.4998	.0002
2.18	.4854	.0146		2.75	.4970	.0030		3.70	.4999	.0001
2.19	.4857	.0143		2.76	.4971	.0029		3.50	.4999	.0001
2.20	.4861	.0139		2.77	.4972	.0028		3.90	.49995	.00005
2.21	.4864	.0136		2.78	.4973	.0027		4.0	.49997	.00003

Source: Table III, page 45 of *Statistical Tables for Biological, Agricultural and Medical Research*. Copyright 1963. R.A. Fisher and S. Yates. Reprinted by permission of Pearson Education Limited.

STATISTICAL TABLE C *t*-Distribution Table

Critical values of $t\,(t_\alpha)$ for specified levels of significance and degrees of freedom

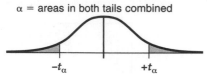

α = areas in both tails combined

Two-tailed or nondirectional test
Level of Significance

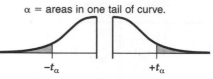

α = areas in one tail of curve.

One-tailed or directional test
Level of Significance

df	α = .05	α = .01	α = .001	*df*	α = .05	α = .01	α = .001
1	12.706	63.657	636.62	1	6.314	31.821	318.31
2	4.303	9.925	31.598	2	2.920	6.965	22.326
3	3.182	5.841	12.924	3	2.353	4.541	10.213
4	2.776	4.604	8.610	4	2.132	3.747	7.173
5	2.571	4.032	6.869	5	2.015	3.365	5.893
6	2.447	3.707	5.959	6	1.943	3.143	5.208
7	2.365	3.499	5.408	7	1.895	2.998	4.785
8	2.306	3.335	5.041	8	1.860	2.896	4.501
9	2.262	3.250	4.781	9	1.833	2.821	4.297
10	2.228	3.169	4.587	10	1.812	2.764	4.144
11	2.201	3.105	4.437	11	1.796	2.718	4.025
12	2.179	3.055	4.318	12	1.782	2.681	3.930
13	2.160	3.012	4.221	13	1.771	2.650	3.852
14	2.145	2.977	4.140	14	1.761	2.624	3.787
15	2.131	2.947	4.073	15	1.753	2.602	3.733
16	2.120	2.921	4.015	16	1.746	2.583	3.686
17	2.110	2.898	3.965	17	1.740	2.567	3.646
18	2.101	2.878	3.922	18	1.734	2.552	3.610
19	2.093	2.861	3.883	19	1.729	2.539	3.579
20	2.086	2.845	3.850	20	1.725	2.528	3.552
21	2.080	2.831	3.819	21	1.721	2.518	3.527
22	2.074	2.819	3.792	22	1.717	2.508	3.505
23	2.069	2.807	3.767	23	1.714	2.500	3.485
24	2.064	2.797	3.745	24	1.711	2.492	3.467
25	2.060	2.787	3.725	25	1.706	2.485	3.450
26	2.056	2.779	3.707	26	1.705	2.479	3.435
27	2.052	2.771	3.690	27	1.703	2.473	3.421
28	2.048	2.763	3.674	28	1.701	2.467	3.408
29	2.045	2.756	3.659	29	1.699	2.462	3.396
30	2.042	2.750	3.646	30	1.697	2.457	3.385
40	2.021	2.704	3.551	40	1.684	2.423	3.307
60	2.000	2.660	3.460	60	1.671	2.390	3.232
120	1.980	2.617	3.373	120	1.658	2.358	3.160
∞	1.96	2.58	3.30	∞	1.64	2.33	3.096

Source: Table III, page 46 of *Statistical Tables for Biological, Agricultural and Medical Research*. Copyright 1963. R.A. Fisher and S. Yates. Reprinted by permission of Pearson Education Limited.

STATISTICAL TABLE D

Critical Values of the F-Ratio Distribution at the .05 Level of Significance

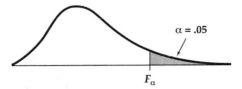

$\alpha = .05$

F_α

df for the Denominator

df for the numerator $\alpha = .05$ (df_B)

(df_ω)

	1	2	3	4	5	6	8	12
1	161.4	199.5	215.7	224.6	230.2	234.0	238.9	243.9
2	18.51	19.00	19.16	19.25	19.30	19.33	19.37	19.41
3	10.13	9.55	9.28	9.12	9.01	8.94	8.84	8.74
4	7.71	6.94	6.59	6.39	6.26	6.16	6.04	5.91
5	6.61	5.79	5.41	5.19	5.05	4.95	4.82	4.68
6	5.99	5.14	4.76	4.53	4.39	4.28	4.15	4.00
7	5.59	4.74	4.35	4.12	3.97	3.87	3.73	3.57
8	5.32	4.46	4.07	3.84	3.69	3.58	3.44	3.28
9	5.12	4.26	3.86	3.63	3.48	3.37	3.23	3.07
10	4.96	4.10	3.71	3.48	3.33	3.22	3.07	2.91
11	4.84	3.98	3.59	3.36	3.20	3.09	2.95	2.79
12	4.75	3.88	3.49	3.26	3.11	3.00	2.85	2.69
13	4.67	3.80	3.41	3.18	3.02	2.92	2.77	2.60
14	4.60	3.74	3.34	3.11	2.96	2.85	2.70	2.53
15	4.54	3.68	3.29	3.06	2.90	2.79	2.64	2.48
16	4.49	3.63	3.24	3.01	2.85	2.74	2.59	2.42
17	4.45	3.59	3.20	2.96	2.81	2.70	2.55	2.38
18	4.41	3.55	3.16	2.93	2.77	2.66	2.51	2.34
19	4.38	3.52	3.13	2.90	2.74	2.63	2.48	2.31
20	4.35	3.49	3.10	2.87	2.71	2.60	2.45	2.28
21	4.32	3.47	3.07	2.84	2.68	2.57	2.42	2.25
22	4.30	3.44	3.05	2.82	2.66	2.55	2.40	2.23
23	4.28	3.42	3.03	2.80	2.64	2.53	2.38	2.20
24	4.26	3.40	3.01	2.78	2.62	2.51	2.36	2.18
25	4.24	3.38	2.99	2.76	2.60	2.49	2.34	2.16
26	4.22	3.37	2.98	2.74	2.59	2.47	2.32	2.15
27	4.21	3.35	2.96	2.73	2.57	2.46	2.30	2.13
28	4.20	3.34	2.95	2.71	2.56	2.44	2.29	2.12
29	4.18	3.33	2.93	2.70	2.54	2.43	2.28	2.10
30	4.17	3.32	2.92	2.69	2.53	2.42	2.27	2.09
40	4.08	3.23	2.84	2.61	2.45	2.34	2.18	2.00
60	4.00	3.15	2.76	2.52	2.37	2.25	2.10	1.92
120	3.92	3.07	2.68	2.45	2.29	2.17	2.02	1.83
∞	3.84	3.00	2.60	2.37	2.21	2.10	1.94	1.75

Source: From Table 18 of Pearson and Hartley (1976: 171), Biometrika Tables for Statisticians, volume 1. London: Biometrika Trust. By permission of Oxford University Press.

STATISTICAL TABLE E

Critical Values of the *F*-Ratio Distribution at the .01 Level of Significance

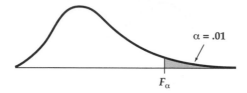

$\alpha = .01$

F_α

df for the Denominator

df for the numerator $\alpha = .01$

	1	2	3	4	5	6	8	12
1	4052	4999.5	5403	5625	5764	5859	5981	6106
2	98.49	90.01	99.17	99.25	99.30	99.33	99.36	99.42
3	34.12	30.81	29.46	28.71	28.24	27.91	27.49	27.05
4	21.20	18.00	16.69	15.98	15.52	15.21	14.80	14.37
5	16.26	13.27	12.06	11.39	10.97	10.67	10.27	9.89
6	13.74	10.92	9.78	9.15	8.75	8.47	8.10	7.72
7	12.25	9.55	8.45	7.85	7.46	7.19	6.84	6.47
8	11.26	8.65	7.59	7.01	6.63	6.37	6.03	5.67
9	10.56	8.02	6.99	6.42	6.06	5.80	5.47	5.11
10	10.04	7.56	6.55	5.99	5.64	5.39	5.06	4.71
11	9.65	7.20	6.22	5.67	5.32	5.07	4.74	4.40
12	9.33	6.93	5.95	5.41	5.06	4.82	4.50	4.16
13	9.07	6.70	5.74	5.20	4.86	4.62	4.30	3.96
14	8.86	6.51	5.56	5.03	4.69	4.46	4.14	3.80
15	8.68	6.36	5.42	4.89	4.56	4.32	4.00	3.67
16	8.53	6.23	5.29	4.77	4.44	4.20	3.89	3.55
17	8.40	6.11	5.18	4.67	4.34	4.10	3.79	3.45
18	8.28	6.01	5.09	4.58	4.25	4.01	3.71	3.37
19	8.18	5.93	5.01	4.50	4.17	3.94	3.63	3.30
20	8.10	5.85	4.94	4.43	4.10	3.87	3.56	3.23
21	8.02	5.78	4.87	4.37	4.04	3.81	3.51	3.17
22	7.94	5.72	4.82	4.31	3.99	3.76	3.45	3.12
23	7.88	5.66	4.76	4.26	3.94	3.71	3.41	3.07
24	7.82	5.61	4.72	4.22	3.90	3.67	3.36	3.03
25	7.77	5.57	4.68	4.18	3.86	3.63	3.32	2.99
26	7.72	5.53	4.64	4.14	3.82	3.59	3.29	2.96
27	7.68	5.49	4.60	4.11	3.78	3.56	3.26	2.93
28	7.64	5.45	4.57	4.01	3.75	3.53	3.23	2.90
29	7.60	5.42	4.54	4.04	3.73	3.50	3.20	2.87
30	7.56	5.39	4.51	4.02	3.70	3.47	3.17	2.84
40	7.31	5.18	4.31	3.83	3.51	3.29	2.99	2.66
60	7.08	4.98	4.13	3.65	3.34	3.12	2.82	2.50
120	6.85	4.79	3.95	6.48	3.17	2.96	2.66	2.34
∞	6.63	4.61	3.78	3.32	3.02	2.80	2.51	2.18

Source: From Table 18 of Pearson and Hartley (1976: 173), *Biometrika Tables for Statisticians*, volume 1. London: Biometrika Trust. By permission of Oxford University Press.

STATISTICAL TABLE F

q-Values of Range Tests at the .05 and .01 Levels of Significance

k = Number of Group Means Compared

df for
MSV_W Level of
$(n-k)$ Significance

	α	2	3	4	5	6	7	8	9	10	11
5	.05	3.64	4.60	5.22	5.67	6.03	6.33	6.58	6.80	6.99	7.17
	.01	5.70	6.98	7.80	8.42	8.91	9.32	9.67	9.97	10.24	10.48
6	.05	3.46	4.34	4.90	5.30	5.63	5.90	6.12	6.32	6.49	6.65
	.01	5.24	6.33	7.03	7.56	7.97	8.32	8.61	8.87	9.10	9.30
7	.05	3.34	4.16	4.68	5.06	5.36	5.61	5.82	6.00	6.16	6.30
	.01	4.95	5.92	6.54	7.01	7.37	7.68	7.94	8.17	8.37	8.55
8	.05	3.26	4.04	4.53	4.89	5.17	5.40	5.60	5.77	5.92	6.05
	.01	4.75	5.64	6.20	6.62	6.96	7.24	7.47	7.68	7.86	8.03
9	.05	3.20	3.95	4.41	4.76	5.02	5.24	5.43	5.59	5.74	5.87
	.01	4.60	5.43	5.96	6.35	6.66	6.91	7.13	7.33	7.49	7.65
10	.05	3.15	3.88	4.33	4.65	4.91	5.12	5.30	5.46	5.60	5.72
	.01	4.48	5.27	5.77	6.14	6.43	6.67	6.87	7.05	7.21	7.36
11	.05	3.11	3.82	4.26	4.57	4.82	5.03	5.20	5.35	5.49	5.61
	.01	4.36	5.15	5.62	5.97	6.25	6.48	6.67	6.84	6.99	7.13
12	.05	3.08	3.77	4.20	4.51	4.75	4.95	5.12	5.27	5.39	5.51
	.01	4.32	5.05	5.50	5.84	6.10	6.32	6.51	6.67	6.81	6.94
13	.05	3.06	3.73	4.15	4.45	4.69	4.88	5.05	5.19	5.32	5.43
	.01	4.26	4.96	5.40	5.73	5.98	6.19	6.37	6.53	6.67	6.79
14	.05	3.03	3.70	4.11	4.41	4.64	4.83	4.99	5.13	5.25	5.36
	.01	4.21	4.89	5.32	5.63	5.88	6.08	6.26	6.41	6.54	6.66
15	.05	3.01	3.67	4.08	4.37	4.59	4.78	4.94	5.08	5.20	5.31
	.01	4.17	4.84	5.25	5.56	5.80	5.99	6.16	6.31	6.44	6.55
16	.05	3.00	3.65	4.05	4.33	4.56	4.74	4.90	5.03	5.15	5.26
	.01	4.13	4.79	5.19	5.49	5.72	5.92	6.08	6.22	6.35	6.46
17	.05	2.98	3.63	4.02	4.30	4.52	4.70	4.86	4.99	5.11	5.21
	.01	4.10	4.74	5.14	5.43	5.66	5.85	6.01	6.15	6.27	6.38
18	.05	2.97	3.61	4.00	4.28	4.49	4.67	4.82	4.96	5.07	5.17
	.01	4.07	4.70	5.09	5.38	5.60	5.79	5.94	6.08	6.20	6.31
19	.05	2.96	3.59	3.98	4.25	4.47	4.65	4.79	4.92	5.04	5.14
	.01	4.05	4.67	5.05	5.33	5.55	5.73	5.89	6.02	6.14	6.25
20	.05	2.95	3.58	3.96	4.23	4.45	4.62	4.77	4.90	5.01	5.11
	.01	4.02	4.64	5.02	5.29	5.51	5.69	5.84	5.97	6.09	6.19
24	.05	2.92	3.53	3.90	4.17	4.37	4.54	4.68	4.81	4.92	5.01
	.01	3.96	4.55	4.91	5.17	5.37	5.54	5.69	5.81	5.92	6.02
30	.05	2.89	3.49	9.85	4.10	4.30	4.46	4.60	4.72	4.82	4.92
	.01	3.89	4.45	4.80	5.05	5.24	5.40	5.54	5.65	5.76	5.85
40	.05	2.86	3.44	3.79	4.04	4.23	4.39	4.52	4.63	4.73	4.82
	.01	3.82	4.37	4.70	4.93	5.11	5.26	5.39	5.50	5.60	5.69
60	.05	2.83	3.40	3.74	3.98	4.16	4.31	4.44	4.55	4.65	4.73
	.01	3.76	4.28	4.59	4.82	4.99	5.13	5.25	5.36	5.45	5.53
120	.05	2.80	3.36	3.68	3.92	4.10	4.24	4.36	4.47	4.56	4.64
	.01	3.70	4.20	4.50	4.71	4.87	5.01	5.12	5.21	5.30	5.37
∞	.05	2.77	3.31	3.63	3.86	4.03	4.17	4.29	4.39	4.47	4.55
	.01	3.64	4.12	4.40	4.60	4.76	4.88	4.99	5.08	5.16	5.23

Source: From Table 29 of Pearson and Hartley (1976: 192–3), *Biometrika Tables for Statisticians,* volume 1. London: Biometrika Trust. By permission of Oxford University Press.

STATISTICAL TABLE G

Critical Values of the Chi-Square Distribution

	Level of Significance			
df	Critical χ^2, $\alpha = .10$	Critical χ^2, $\alpha = .05$	Critical χ^2, $\alpha = .01$	Critical χ^2, $\alpha = .001$
1	2.71	3.84	6.64	10.83
2	4.50	5.99	9.21	13.82
3	6.25	7.81	11.34	16.27
4	7.78	9.49	13.28	18.47
5	9.24	11.07	15.09	20.52
6	10.64	12.59	16.81	22.46
7	12.02	14.07	18.48	24.32
8	13.36	15.51	20.09	26.12
9	14.68	16.92	21.67	27.88
10	15.99	18.31	23.21	29.59
11	17.28	19.68	24.72	31.26
12	18.55	21.03	26.22	32.91
13	19.81	22.36	27.69	34.53
14	21.06	23.68	29.14	36.12
15	22.31	25.00	30.58	37.70
16	23.54	26.30	32.00	39.25
17	24.77	27.59	33.41	40.79
18	25.99	28.87	34.80	42.31
19	27.20	30.14	36.19	43.82
20	28.41	31.41	37.57	45.32
21	29.62	32.67	38.93	46.80
22	30.81	33.92	40.29	48.27
23	32.01	35.17	41.64	49.73
24	33.20	36.42	42.98	51.18
25	34.38	37.65	44.31	52.62
26	35.56	38.88	45.64	54.05
27	36.74	40.11	45.96	55.48
28	37.92	41.34	48.28	56.89
29	39.09	42.56	49.59	58.30
30	40.25	43.77	50.89	59.70
40	51.80	55.76	63.69	73.40
50	63.17	67.50	75.15	86.66
60	74.40	79.08	88.38	99.61
70	85.53	90.53	100.42	112.32

Source: From Table 8 of Pearson and Hartley (1976: 137), *Biometrika Tables for Statisticians*, volume 1. London: Biometrika Trust. By permission of Oxford University Press.

Answers to Selected Chapter Exercises

These are partial answers. Be sure to show all work, including formulas and curves. Look to the answers of other problem sets for a chapter for additional guidance.

CHAPTER 1

Problem Set 1A

1A-1. *a.* 13.64% *e.* $\dfrac{2,321}{10,000}$

1A-3. 56,227 low-security inmates; 15,691 high-security inmates

1A-5. .8947, 89.47% 1A-7. 30,081 per 100,000 never married; 2,464 per 100,000 separated; 9,490 per 100,000 divorced

Problem Set 1B

1B-2. Byron will start; he has a throw-out percentage of 43.75% compared to David's 35.42% 1B-4. .0621 ages 15–24 years; .2219 aged 35–44 years; .1381 aged 55–64 years 1B-6. Males: ages 21–30, $p = .0992$, 5 to attend Olympics; ages 41–50, $p = .3421$, 17 to attend Olympics; Females: ages 21–30, $p = .1307$, 7 to attend Olympics; ages 41–50, $p = .2876$, 14 to attend Olympics 1B-8. $p = .2441$, 24.41% with no professional courses; $p = .2142$, 21.42% with technical school

Problem Set 1C

1C-1. *a.* $\dfrac{6,046}{10,000}$, $p = .6046$ *d.* $p = .2136$, 21.36%

1C-3. *a.* 7,764 crimes against persons *c.* 4,340 acts of intimidation

1C-5. $p = .7859$, 78.59% 1C-7. Anderson, Indiana: 3,047 per 100,000 population; Duluth, Minnesota: 1,921 per 100,000 population

Problem Set 1D

1D-2. Alabama ($p = .1304$). 1D-4. Anne. 1D-6. p[Los Angeles Personnel Department to attend] $= .1558$; number to attend $= 6$. 1D-8. *a.* Females ($p = .1423$); *b.* Women; .7297 returned to work.

CHAPTER 2

Problem Set 2A

2A-1.   *a.* Ratio level   *c.* Interval level   *g.* Nominal level
2A-3.   *a.* Not inclusive. No place to score a response of General Surgery, Pediatrics, etc. To improve: add an "other" category   *c.* Not inclusive; no place to score income from \$41,000 to \$55,000. To improve, change the category \$26,000–\$40,000 to \$26,000–\$50,000. Not exclusive; income of \$100,000 could be included in two categories. To improve, change the category \$100,000–\$150,000 to \$101,000–\$150,000   2A-5.   *a.* .0585–.0595   *d.* 5,350–5,450   *f.* 3 years to 3 years, 364 days   2A-7.   *a.*

Number of Vehicles Registered	f	Proportional f	Percentage (%) f	Cumulative Percentage (%) f
0	1	.0500	5.00	5.00
1	3	.1500	15.00	20.00
2	8	.4000	40.00	60.00
3	3	.1500	15.00	75.00
4	5	.2500	25.00	100.00
Totals	20	1.0000	100.00	

b. The 75th percentile. This household has as many or more vehicles than 75% of all households.

Problem Set 2B

2B-2.   *a.* Ratio level   *c.* Ordinal level   *f.* Interval level
2B-4.   *a.* 28.3   *d.* 25.638   *g.* 30   2B-6. 1.46:1
2B-8.   *a.* $p = .7857$, 79%. Therefore, Jennifer's percentile rank is 79. She scored equal to or higher than 79% of her classmates.

Problem Set 2C

2C-1.   *a.* Ratio level   *c.* Nominal level   *d.* Interval level

2C-3.   *a.* Not inclusive; there are no responses for individuals less than age 25. To improve, add this response category. Not exclusive; individuals age 74 may fit into either of the last two response categories. To improve, create response categories that do not overlap (i.e., 65–74, 75 or above, etc.).

c. Not exclusive; individuals with 9 or 15 years of education may fall into more than one response category. To improve, create response categories that do not overlap (i.e., less than 9 years, more than 15 years, etc.)

2C-5.   *b.* .023805–.023815   *e.* 6.5–7.5 years   *g.* 7.5–8.5

2C-7.   *a.*

Scores on CES-D Scale	*f*	Proportional *f*	Percentage (%) *f*	Cumulative Percentage (%) *f*
2	3	.1500	15.00	15.00
3	3	.1500	15.00	30.00
4	5	.2500	25.00	55.00
5	4	.2000	20.00	75.00
6	3	.1500	15.00	90.00
7	2	.1000	10.00	100.00
Totals	20	1.0000	100.00	

b. The 90th percentile. This worker scored as high or higher than 90% of workers involved in this study.

Problem Set 2D

2D-2.   *a.* Ordinal level   *c.* Nominal level   *e.* Interval level

2D-4.   *a.* 5.5   *d.* 400   *f.* 500,000   2D-6. 2.82:1

2D-8. $p = .8500$, 85%. Therefore, Jeff's percentile rank is 85. He scored equal to or higher than 85% of his classmates.

CHAPTER 3

Problem Set 3A

3A-1.

Security Level	Percent (%)	*p*	*p* × 360
Minimum	19.4	.194	70
Low	38.9	.389	140
Medium	24.8	.248	89
High	10.7	.107	39
No security level	6.1	.061	22
Totals	99.9*	.999*	360°

* Totals may not sum to 100% or 1.000 due to rounding error.

CHART 3A–1

United States
prison inmates
by security
level, 2003

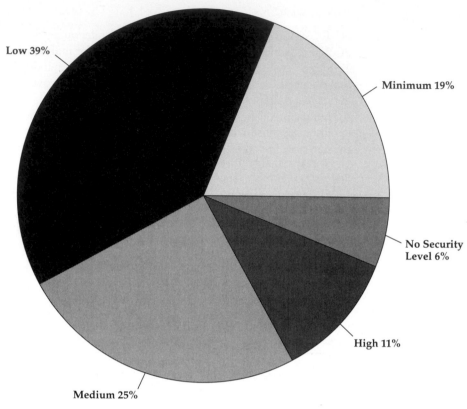

Note: Percentages were rounded to simplify for presentation.

3A-2. Bar chart:

CHART 3A–2

Percentage of
gross domestic
product spent
on health care
in selected
European
countries

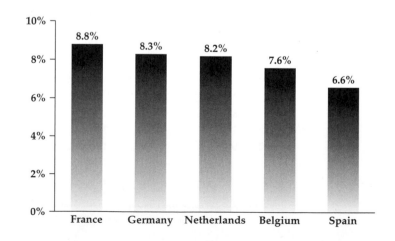

3A-3.   Clustered bar chart: See Chart 3C-3 below for the basic layout. Comment: It appears that females in the United States possess more high school diplomas and college degrees, while males appear to possess more graduate and professional degrees.

3A-4.   *a.* Pie charts:

CHART 3A–4a

Makeup of white ethnic neighborhoods in New York City, 1980 and 1990

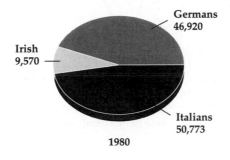

1980

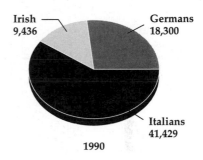

1990

3A-5.   *a.* Frequency histogram:

CHART 3A–5a

Ages of students on a college debating team

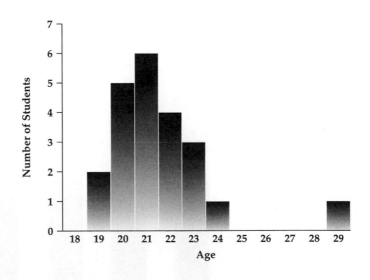

b. See exercise 3B-6 for hints.   *c.* Probably the histogram. With a small sample size, it is easier on the histogram to match frequency (number of students) with each age. *d.* The student aged 29 years is an outlier.

3A-6.   *a.* Overlying frequency polygons (line graphs):

CHART 3A–6a

A comparison of distances traveled to school by suburban and rural students

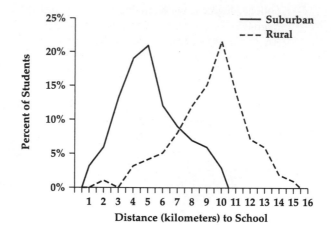

Problem Set 3B

3B-1.   Pie chart: See the pie chart of 3A-1 on 606 for the basic layout.

3B-2.   Bar chart:

CHART 3B–2

Liters of alcohol consumed by adults over 24 in 1990 for selected European countries

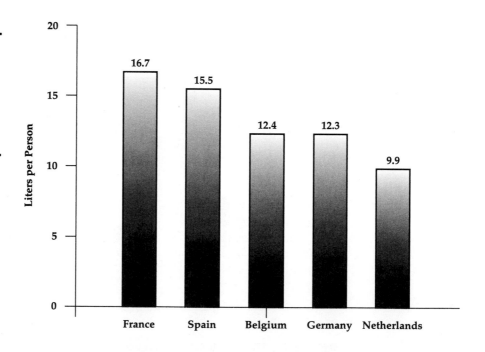

Comment: The average consumption of alcohol is quite a bit higher in France and Spain.

3B-4.   *a.* Pie charts: See Chart 3A–4a on page 607 for the basic layout.   *b.* See Chart 3C-3a on page 610 for the basic layout.   *c.* While employer and smuggling investigations generally declined between 1992 and 2002 within the INS Investigations Program, the total number of criminal investigations significantly increased. The clustered bar chart is better than the pie charts at depicting these changes. The bar chart not only conveys a comparison of years but also the over-all, proportional changes among different types of INS investigations. To similar-ly depict these changes, the pie charts would have to be of different sizes based on the proportion of total investigations undertaken in a given year. Two pie charts of different sizes would appear awkward.

3B-5.   *b.* Frequency polygon (line graph):

CHART 3B–5b

Participation in campus events

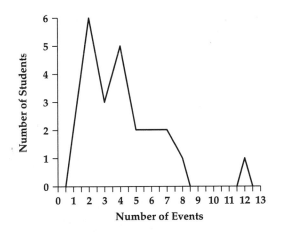

3B-6.   *a.* Overlying frequency polygons (line graphs); see Chart 3A–6a on page 608 for the basic layout. Since the sample sizes differ, plot the percentage frequencies. *b.* Cocaine addicts tend to be younger than alcohol addicts.

Problem Set 3C

3C-1.   *a.* Pie chart; see Chart 3A–1 on page 606 for the basic layout.

3C-3.   *a.* Clustered bar chart:

**CHART
3C–3a**

Age distribu-
tions of males
and females in
the United
States, 2000

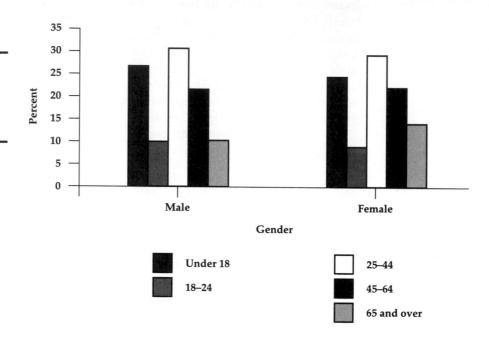

b. Comment: There are similar percentages of males and females except in the 65 and over age group where there are more females (reflecting the fact that women tend to live longer than men).

3C-5.   *a.* Frequency histogram: See Chart 3A–5a on page 607 for the basic layout. *b.* See the partial answer for exercise 3B-5b on page 609 for hints.   *c.* Probably the histogram. With a small sample size such as this and the small range of scores, it is easier on the histogram to match frequency (number of students) with each age. *d.* The student aged 28 years is an outlier.

3C-6.   *a.* Overlying frequency polygons (line graphs): See Chart 3A–6a on page 108 for the basic layout. Since the sample sizes differ, plot the percentage frequencies.

Problem Set 3D

3D-2.   *a.* Bar chart:

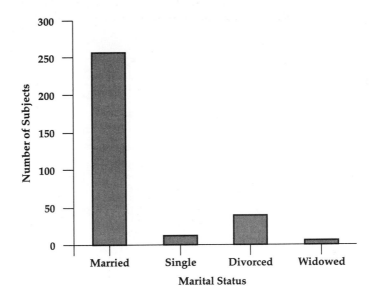

CHART 3D–2a

Marital status of Czech Republic adults

Comment: The overwhelming majority of study participants in the Czech Republic are married.

3D-3.   *a.* Clustered bar chart: See Chart 3C–3a on page 610 for the basic layout.

3D-4.   *a.* Pie charts: See Chart 3A–4a on page 607 for the basic layout.   *b.* See Chart 3C-3a on page 610 for the basic layout.   c. In general, both types of charts indicate a substantial growth of the upper middle class as well as a marked decline in the working class. However, the clustered bar chart is more appropriate in depicting this phenomenon, as it is capable of showing more subtle changes in social class composition over the two selected years.

3D-6.   *a.* Overlying frequency polygon; see Chart 3A-6a on page 608 for the basic layout.

b. Center I appears to be comprised of younger senior citizens, while Center II appears to be made up of senior citizens that are somewhat older.

CHAPTER 4

Problem Set 4A

4A-1.   Calculation spreadsheet:

X	X (cont.)	X (ranked)	X (ranked, cont.)
. . .	. . .	. . .	. . .

Mo = 19 years; Mdn = 19 years; Mean = 18.9 years

4A-3.   *a.* Frequency curves:

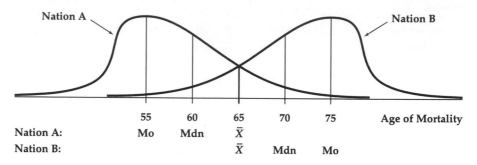

Nation A: Mo   Mdn $\overline{X}$
Nation B: $\overline{X}$ Mdn   Mo

b. Nation B appears better off. Its left skew reveals fewer people dying at earlier ages.

4A-5.   *a.* Mdn = $11,300; Mean = $14,160   *d.* Adjusted mean = $10,450

4A-7.   Spreadsheet:

X = Chicken reaction times

X (ranked)
.88
. . .
. . .
1.45

b. Mdn = .96 seconds; Mo = .93 seconds   *c.* Right skew

Problem Set 4B

4B-2.   *a.* Mdn = 625 points; Mean = 631 points   4B-4.   *b.* Mdn = 2.2 GPA points; Mean = 2.39 GPA points   *e.* Adjusted mean = 2.13 GPA points

4B-6.   Mean = 34.82 years   4B-8.   Height: right skew; Grocery budget: right skew

Problem Set 4C

4C-1.   Mo = 70 inches; Mdn = 69.5 inches; Mean = 68.7 years

4C-3.   *a.* Frequency curves: See the partial answer to exercise 4A-3 above for the basic layout.   *b.* Class B appears to have scored better on this exam. It's left skew reveals more students scoring higher on the exam.

4C-5. Y = employee rating, spreadsheet:

Y	Y (ranked)
8	3
. . .	. . .
. . .	. . .
7	9

b. Mean = 7.2 points; Mdn = 8 points   *e.* Adjusted mean = 7.75 points
4C-7. *b.* Mean = 4.98 seconds; Mdn = 4.9 seconds; Mo = 4.8 seconds
c. Approaches normality, with a slight right skew

Problem Set 4D

4D-2.   Mdn = 3.6 inches; Mean = 3.86 inches   4D-4.   *a.* Mean = 82.9 students; Mdn = 79 students   *e.* Adjusted mean = 77.5 students   4D-6.   The mean GRE score for all 93 applicants is 1181.   4D-8.   Cholesterol levels: Mean = 182; Mdn = 207; Mo = 219; left skew

CHAPTER 5

Problem Set 5A

5A-1. Partial answer:

Sum of Squares	n	Variance	Standard Deviation
893.49	30	30.81	5.55
43,128.90	347	124.65	11.16

5A-3.   *b.* $\overline{X}$ = 7.86 patients   *d.* s_X = 3.18 visits   5A-5.   *b.* $\overline{X}$ = 20.40 years   *c.* s_x = 1.42 years   5A-7. For X = 128, Z_x = −2.28 SD

Problem Set 5B

5B-2.   *b.* $\overline{X}$ = $2,198.43   *d.* s_x = $356.53   5B-4.   *b.* $\overline{X}$ = 3.59 Richter Scale points; s_X = 1.73 Richter Scale points   5B-6. Texas. (In fact, the high rate for Texas skews the distribution.)

Problem Set 5C

5C-1.   Partial answer:

Sum of Squares	n	Variance	Standard Deviation
975.46	29	34.82	5.90
74,828.25	526	142.53	11.94

5C-3.   *b.* $\overline{X}$ = 9.29 case contacts   *d.* s_X = 3.54 case contacts   5C-5.   *b.* $\overline{X}$ = 74.50 years   *c.* s_X = 2.98 years   5C-7.   For X = 42, Z_x = 1.22 SD

Problem Set 5D

5D-2.   *b.* $\overline{X}$ = 60.14 years   *d.* s_X = 3.29 years   5D-4.   *d.* $\overline{X}$ = 170 pounds; s_X = 19.36 pounds   5D-6.   *b.* Area 2 stands out as having a relatively high rate of homicides.

CHAPTER 6

Problem Set 6A

6A-1.   *a.* .1667   *b.* .3333   *c.* .0046   6A-3.   *a.* .5000   *b.* .2500   *c.* .1250
6A-5.   *a.* .0228   *b.* 26,759   *c.* .6687   6A-7.   95% of scores range from 20.93
to 33.47 CESD scale points

Problem Set 6B

6B-2.   *a.* .0628   *b.* .0625   *c.* .0316   6B-4.   *a.* .0769   *b.* .1538   *c.* .3077
d. .0090   6B-6.   *a.* .8413   *b.* .0359   *c.* 31.3 CESD points
6B-8.   *a.* .9878; Jennifer scored better than 98% of test takers. (If the percentile is
rounded, it must be rounded down. It would be incorrect to say that she scored better than 99%.)

Problem Set 6C

6C-1.   *a.* .1667   *b.* .3333   *c.* .0046   6C-3.   *a.* .5000   *b.* .2500   *c.* .1250
6C-5.   *a.* .0228   *b.* 135,786   *c.* .6687   6C-7.   *b.* The least satisfied social
workers were the 2.5% that scored about 19 and below. The most satisfied social
workers were the 2.5% that scored about 28 and above.

Problem Set 6D

6D-2.   *a.* .0333   *b.* .0460   *c.* .0657   6D-4.   *a.* .0769   *b.* .1538   *c.* .3077
d. .0090   6D-6.   *a.* 168 workers   *b.* .0294   *c.* 23.2 or above
6D-8.   .9925; Caroline's percentile rank on the GRE is 99. That is, Caroline
scored better than 99% of test takers in this sample.

CHAPTER 7

Problem Set 7A

7A-1.   .22   7A-3.   *c.* The histogram should appear as one peaked in the middle,
centering around the outcome of 5 heads.   *d.* $p[5 \text{ heads}] = .25$
7A-7.   *b.* 50

Problem Set 7B

7B-2.   *a.* .25   *b.* .08   *c.* .02   *d.* .10   *e.* .02   7B-6.   *a.* $P_u = .5$ *b.* Estimate of
σ_{P_s} should fall between .06 and .08, depending on the size of the spoon and its samples.

Problem Set 7C

7C-1.   .19   7C-3.   *c.* The histogram should appear as one peaked in the middle,
centering around the outcome of 5 heads.   *d.* $p[8] = .05$
7C-7.   *b.* 13

Problem Set 7D

7D-2. *a.* .11   *b.* .09   *c.* .03   *d.* .10   *e.* .03   7D-6. P_u = .5 *b*. Estimate of σ_{P_s} should fall between .06 and .08, depending on the size of the spoon and its samples.

CHAPTER 8
Problem Set 8A

8A-1.   55.73 to 58.27 years   8A-3. $42,725.87 to $44,416.13
8A-5.   46.67% to 63.33% The bill cannot be guaranteed to pass.
8A-7.   99%: 2.58; .0158; .0408; .4592; .5408; .0816   *a.* The width of the confidence interval increases as the level of confidence increases. A higher level of confidence requires a lower level of precision.   *b.* The lower confidence level is subtracted from the upper confidence level.

Problem Set 8B

8B-2.   172.74 to 175.26 pounds   8B-4.   No. His support could be as low as 40.67%.   8B-6.   You will need a sample of 1,508 persons.

Problem Set 8C

8C-1.   14.8 to 15.2 years   8C-3. 34.78 to 37.82 years
8C-5.   30.38% to 41.62%   8C-7. 99%: 2.58; .0209; .0539; .3461; .4539;
.1078   *a.* The width of the confidence interval increases as the level of confidence increases. A higher level of confidence requires a lower level of precision.   *b.* The lower confidence level is subtracted from the upper confidence level.

Problem Set 8D

8D-2.   2.86 to 2.94 points   8D-4. Yes. His support is likely from at least 56% of registered voters.   8D-6. You would need a sample of 3,393 investors.

CHAPTER 9
Problem Set 9A

9A-1.   *a.* If H_0 is true, that the mean age of students on campus is 21 years, and if we repeatedly sampled the campus population, sample means for age will center on 21 years.   *b.* If H_0 is true, that the percentage of female corporate board members is 20%, and if we repeatedly sampled Fortune 500 companies, sample proportions of female corporate board members will center on .20.
9A-3.   *a.* One-tailed, positive direction. Use the greater than sign (>) to indicate *over* 50%   9A-5.   *a.* Reject   *e.* Fail to reject   9A-7. Yes. The average age of Clarksdale homes appears to be over 15 years.

Problem Set 9B

9B-2.   *a.* Alternative hypothesis. The research question asks if the speed is *greater than* 70. The null hypothesis is stated as *equal to* 70 miles per hour.   *b.* Null hypothesis. The research question asks if the average weight is *equal to* 224 pounds. The alternative hypothesis is stated as *not equal to* 224 pounds.

9B-4.   *a.* The null hypothesis is stated as equal, so that we can establish a sampling distribution. The issue of lower income for women is addressed in the alternative hypothesis.   *b.* She will use a one-tailed test because she is hypothesizing that the income of women is *below that* of men.   9B-6.   The average body mass index (BMI) among Jackson Middle School students appears to be greater than 25.   9B-8.   *a.* 25.25 kg per meters squared

Problem Set 9C

9C-1.   *a.* If H_0 is true, that the mean age of employees is 32 years, and if we repeatedly sampled the employee population, sample means for age will center on 32 years.   *b.* If H_0 is true, that the mean weight of the team's players is 207 pounds, and if we repeatedly sampled the population of players, sample means for weight will center on 207 pounds.   9C-3.   *a.* One-tailed, positive direction. Use the greater than sign ($>$) to indicate *over* 60 percent.   9C-5.   *a.* Fail to reject   *d.* Reject   9C-7.   The grade point average (GPA) of State University students appears to be less than a B average.

Problem Set 9D

9D-2.   *a.* Alternative hypothesis. The research question asks if the dice are *not* fair (i.e., are they loaded). The null hypothesis is stated as: The dice are fair, because we can predict how dice will roll in the long run and, therefore, predict a sampling distribution.   *b.* Alternative hypothesis. The research question asks if the dropout rate among freshmen chemistry majors is *greater than* the rate of dropouts among other disciplines. The null hypothesis is stated as the rates are *equal*.   9D-4.   *a.* The null hypothesis is stated as equal, so that we can establish a sampling distribution. The issue of occupational esteem for women is addressed in the alternative hypothesis.   *b.* The researcher will use a one-tailed test because (s)he is hypothesizing that levels of occupational esteem among women are *less than* those among men.   9D-6.   Yes. The average age of homeless persons now appears to be under 40 years.   9D-8.   *a.* 38.71 years

CHAPTER 10

Problem Set 10A

10A-1.   *a.* -3.4 years   *b.* $-.14$ 10A-3.   The proportion of female sociology majors at a university today is significantly different from .47.

10A-5.   Patients in the new study lost significantly less weight than participants in the earlier study.   10A-7.   *a.* We have no reason to believe that the proportion of females in our sampled population is any different from that in the target population of Johnsonville.

Problem Set 10B

10B-2.   *a.* 2.074; $p > .05$; fail to reject   *b.* -2.896; $.01 > p > .001$; reject
10B-4.   Those over age 55 in this city do not visit physicians an average of 5.2 visits per year. For those persons in the city over age 55, we estimate the average number of physician visits per year to be 5.8, .6 visits more than the national average.   10B-6.   *a.* 5.64 physician visits   10B-8. *a.* 56.85 to 61.15

Problem Set 10C

10C-1.   *a.* $-.6$ years   *b.* $-.06$ 10C-3. The proportion of adults favoring handgun control appears no longer to be .53 (or 53%). Today, approximately 63% of adults favor handgun control.   10C-5. Subjects in the high-strain sample appear to report more physical symptoms than subjects in the previous study. 10C-7.   *b.* There is no reason to believe that the proportion of college-educated adults in our sampled population is any different from that in the target population of Smithville.

Problem Set 10D

10D-2.   *a.* 4.318; $p < .001$; reject   *c.* -1.753; $p > .05$; fail to reject
10D-4.   200-count filler paper packages do not appear to average 200 sheets each when leaving the factory. We estimate that the average volume of the 200-count packages of paper is 194 sheets.   10D-6.   *a.* 196.56 sheets   10D-8.   *a.* 1160.40 to 1239.60 points

CHAPTER 11

Problem Set 11A

11A-1. $t_{\bar{X}_1 - \bar{X}_2} = -3.07$ SE; $p < .01$; yes   11A-3. $t_{\bar{X}_1 - \bar{X}_2} = -2.73$ SE; $p < .01$; yes   11A-5.   *a.* $t_{\bar{X}_1 - \bar{X}_2} = -.23$ SE; $p > .05$; were randomly assigned *b.* $t_{\bar{X}_1 - \bar{X}_2} = 4.20$ SE; $p < .001$; yes   *c.* $t_{\bar{D}} = 35.68$ SE; $p < .001$; yes

Problem Set 11B

11B-2. $t_{\bar{X}_1 - \bar{X}_2} = 3.53$ SE; $p < .001$; yes   11B-4. $t_{\bar{X}_1 - \bar{X}_2} = -3.72$ SE; $p < .001$; yes

Problem Set 11C

11C-1. $t_{\bar{X}_1 - \bar{X}_2} = 6.68$ SE; $p < .001$; yes   11C-3. $t_{\bar{X}_1 - \bar{X}_2} = 1.75$ SE; $p < .05$; yes   11C-5.   *a.* $t_{\bar{D}} = 16.56$ SE; $p < .001$; yes

Problem Set 11D

11D-2. $t_{\bar{X}_1 - \bar{X}_2} = 1.55$ SE; $p > .05$; no   11D-4. $t_{\bar{X}_1 - \bar{X}_2} = 4.38$ SE; $p < .001$; yes

CHAPTER 12

Problem Set 12A

12A-1.   Main effect for arts and sciences = .11   12A-3. $F = 7.76; p < .01$
12A-5.   Main effect for African-Americans = $-3.31; F = 28.19; p < .01$; Yes, white correction officers have the most punitive attitudes and African-American the least.

Problem Set 12B

12B-2. $Y_{(Kathy\ Schaefer)} = 24,829 = 16,489 + (9,902) + (-1,562)$
12B-4. $F = 11.27; p < .01$; yes   12B-6.   Main effect for whites = .37; $F = 54.18; p < .01$; Yes, there is a relationship between ethnicity and caregiver burden.

Problem Set 12C

12C-1.   Main effect for moderate income = .84   12C-3. $F = 19.73; p < .01$; Yes
12C-5.   Main effect for Hispanics = $-.18; F = 7.59; p < .01$ yes, there is a relationship between race and religious involvement.

Problem Set 12D

12D-2. $Y_{(Nicole\ Owens)} = 81,247 = 49,257 + (29,235) + (2,755)$
12D-4. $F = .87; p > .05$; no   12D-6.   Main effect for African-Americans = .71; $F = 17.96; p < .01$; Yes, there is a relationship between race and sentencing.

CHAPTER 13

Problem Set 13A

13A-1.   % [of rural county physicians employed in high-risk specialty] = 70.42%
13A-3. $\chi^2 = 7.77; p < .01$; reject   13A-5. p [of tossing four coins and getting one heads and three tails] = .25   13A-7. $p = .0898; p > .05$; the procedure is not any better.

Problem Set 13B

13B-2. $\chi^2 = 0.072; p > .05$; fail to reject.   13B-4. $\chi^2 = 3.18; p > .05$; fail to reject
13B-6. $p = .172; p > .001$; fail to reject.   13B-8.   Minimum size: $n = 8$

Problem Set 13C

13C-1.   %[of service employees with college degree] = 12.77%
13C-3. $\chi^2 = 9.97; p < .01$; reject   13C-5. $p = .0078$ 13C-7. $p = .3769; p > .05$; fail to reject

Problem Set 13D

13D-2. $\chi^2 = 4.69; p < .05$; reject   13D-4. $X^2 = 7.82; p < .01$; reject
13D-6. $p = .2266; p > .05$; fail to reject   13D-8.   Minimum size: $n = 5$

CHAPTER 14

Problem Set 14A

14A-1. *b.* $\acute{Y} = 27.92 + .69(X)$ *c.* $r = .85$ 14A-3. *b.* $\acute{Y} = -4.64 + 8.24(X)$
c. $r = .74$

Problem Set 14B

14B-2. *d.* $\acute{Y} = 27.78 + (-.41)X$ 14B-4. *b.* $r = .36$ *d.* $r = .93$

Problem Set 14C

14C-1. *b.* $\acute{Y} = (-\$26,413.60) + (3,768.54)\,X$ *c.* $r = .90$
14C-3. *b.* $\acute{Y} = \$49,190 + (-1,600)X$

Problem Set 14D

14D-2. *d.* $\acute{Y} = 9.20 + .307(X)$ 14D-4. *b.* $r = -.36$ *d.* $r = -.91$

CHAPTER 15

Problem Set 15A

15A-1. *c.* Negative relationship. As age increases, the number of movies seen in the past six months decreases.   15A-3. $t_r = 5.63$ SE; $p < .001$
15A-5. $t_r = -3.61$ SE; $p < .01$

Problem Set 15B

15B-2. *b.* $\acute{Y} = 57.43 + .136(X)$; *c.* $t_r = 2.15$ SE; $p < .01$
15B-4. *a.* The relationship between one's own income and parent's income is stronger, because its r^2 is larger.   15B-6. $t_r = 7.73$ SE; $p < .001$

Problem Set 15C

15C-1. *b.* Positive relationship. The greater the number of previous convictions, the longer the prison sentence.   15C-3. $t_r = 1.89$ SE; $p < .05$
15C-5. $t_r = -6.68$ SE; $p < .001$

Problem Set 15D

15D-2. $\acute{Y} = 4.09 + (-.162)\,X$; $t_r = 6.21$; $p < .001$. 15D-4. The relationship between life satisfaction and stressful life events is stronger, because its r^2 is larger.
15D-6. $t_r = 13.14$ SE; $p < .001$

D | Guide to *SPSS for Windows*

This guide to *Statistical Package for the Social Sciences, SPSS for Windows,* provides basic information on setting up, running, and interpreting the findings from *SPSS. SPSS* comes in a full version, which is available on many college campuses. *The Statistical Imagination* comes with *SPSS for Windows Student Version,* which includes all procedures used in this text. The student version has limitations. For those familiar with *SPSS*, the greatest limitation is the absence of a *Syntax* window that allows commands to be pasted into a file and saved for later use. Therefore, each time a user wishes to execute an *SPSS* procedure, the user must complete a series of point-and-click commands with the mouse. For the statistical procedures covered in this text, this limitation is not serious.

Another limitation of the *SPSS for Windows Student Version* is that it has a time-of-use limit. Thirteen months after the date and time in which the user loads the software, it will no longer open on that computer. In summary, the *SPSS for Windows Student Version* software is a learning tool. For research purposes, the user is advised to use the full version of *SPSS*.

BASIC INPUT AND OUTPUT SETUP

In computer lingo, there are *input* and *output*. Input is what the user provides to the computer, such as data entries. In addition, instructional input is entered according to the design of a software package such as *SPSS*. Instructional or "command" input tells the computer what procedures to execute or "run." For *SPSS for Windows Student Version,* these instructions are made by simply pointing-and-clicking the mouse cursor over icons and menu items in the computer screen windows. Herein, this type of input is called a *command sequence*, a series of point-and-click instructions. These command sequences are presented in easy-to-follow tree diagrams. Input in *SPSS* is initiated through a window called the *SPSS* Data Editor. Output is the results of the computations. It appears in an Output-*SPSS* Viewer window as a series of boxes called pivot tables.

This appendix is framed according to the *SPSS* procedures required of each chapter. Additional information on applying the results of *SPSS* procedures to a chapter's Computer Applications Exercises is provided with the exercises on *The Statistical Imagination* Web site at www.mhhe.com/ritchey2.

SPSS FOR CHAPTER 1 OF *THE STATISTICAL IMAGINATION:* "*INTRODUCTION*"

Installing SPSS for Windows Student Version

On most computers, to install *SPSS for Windows Student Version*, insert the *SPSS* disk into the CD/DVD drive. An installation window should appear automatically. In this window, click "Install SPSS Student Version x.x" (where x.x represents the latest version, such as 15.0). Follow the Setup instructions.

Opening SPSS for Windows

Command Sequence to Open *SPSS for Windows*:

From Computer Desktop
    └ Start
        └ All Programs
            └ SPSS for Windows
                └ double-click SPSS (version#) for Windows Integrated
                    Student Version

An *SPSS* (version #) for Windows Integrated Student Version window will appear. Use this window after you become familiar with *SPSS*. For now, click cancel and this will leave an Untitled [data set0]-SPSS Data Editor window, which you may view as a home base for operating *SPSS*.

To Create a Shortcut Icon on Your Desktop

From Computer Desktop
    └ Start
        └ All Programs
            └ SPSS for Windows
                └ place cursor over SPSS (version #) for Windows
                    Integrated Student Version; press right button on mouse;
                    click Create Shortcut

"SPSS (version #) for Windows (2)" will appear. Drag it onto the desktop and an *SPSS* icon will appear. Once that is accomplished, open *SPSS* by double-clicking the Desktop icon.

Downloading and Printing Data Files, Codebooks, and Chapter Exercises from The Statistical Imagination Web Site

Computer applications exercises, data sets, and codebooks describing the variables in data sets are available for downloading on *The Statistical Imagination* Web site at www.mhhe.com/ritchey2. These files are found under Student Resources, Computer Application Exercises. The data sets have file names such as FEAR981. The name is a reference to the content of the data set and the number indicates the number of cases in the file. For example, FEAR981 is a sample of 981 physicians who were surveyed about their fears of being sued for medical malpractice.

Downloading from the Web Site   Follow instructions on the Web site to download data sets, codebooks, and chapter computer applications exercises. If you are working from your own computer, you may download these files to your hard drive. If working on a community computer (e.g., in a campus lab), save the files to your personal floppy disk,

CD/DVD disk, or memory stick. Store files in an easily identifiable directory so that you will remember their locations.

Printing from the Web Site   Chapter exercises may also be printed directly from *The Statistical Imagination* Web site. Under "DOWNLOAD OF COMPUTER APPLICA-TIONS EXERCISE FILES," double-click a chapter number to open it. In the Web browser, click File then Print.

Answers to Selected Exercises   A file titled "Answers to Selected Exercises" may also be downloaded or printed. This file supplies partial answers to some of the exercises in each chapter.

Command Sequence to Open an Existing *SPSS* Data (*.sav) File   After the data sets are downloaded from the Web site to your computer, open *SPSS for Windows Student Version* and follow this sequence:

SPSS Data Editor window
    ⌐File
        ⌐Open
            ⌐Data → Open File window
                       ├"Look in:" to locate *.sav file on computer drive
                       └Double-click file name

    The Data Editor Window

When a data set is opened, the actual data codes will appear in the Data Editor window as a matrix of scores. Variable names are situated in columns, and cases in rows. Point to a variable name to observe its label. In the menu across the top of the *SPSS* Data Editor window, click Utilities then Variables to obtain an overview of variables in the data set. If the meaning of a variable is not apparent, refer to the data set's codebook (from the Web site) for a full description of the variable.

Data View and Variable View   At the bottom left corner of the *SPSS* Data Editor window you will see two tabs marked Data View and Variable View. *SPSS for Windows* is defaulted to open in the Data View, which lists the actual scores for each variable.

Click the Variable View tab. This presents a matrix in which the variable names are listed down the left column and characteristics of the variables are listed across the top. The meaning of each characteristic will become apparent with Chapter 2 exercises.

SPSS FOR CHAPTER 2 OF *THE STATISTICAL IMAGINATION:* "ORGANIZING DATA"

Chapter 2 Computer Applications Exercises on *The Statistical Imagination* Web site have the following objectives: (1) to create and save data (*.sav) files using *SPSS for Windows;* (2) to learn the importance of quality control in data coding and entry; (3) to produce frequency distributions, and calculate quartiles and percentiles; and (4) to manage and save output and data files.

Creating an SPSS for Windows Data File (*.sav File)

Command Sequence for Opening a New (Empty) Data File:

SPSS Data Editor window
  └File
    └New
      └Data

An empty data matrix will appear as "Untitled-SPSS Data Editor."

Table D-1 is a spreadsheet of fictional data from a sample of college students and Table D-2 is a codebook describing the variables and their codes. Use this small, manageable data set to learn the basics of data entry. Insert the codes and define the variables according to the instructions below. Save the data set as stu7.sav.

Defining the Characteristics of Each Variable in the Variable View Window

Before entering the data, inform the computer of the variables you are to create and define. Follow your codebook, such as Table D–2 below. Provide a name for each variable, a label describing the variable, and labels for the category names of nominal/ordinal variables. This process is called "Data Definition," which is accomplished in the Variable View of the *SPSS* Data Editor window. The figures in the boxes of this window are default values, which may need changing.

TABLE D–1 | Spreadsheet of Student Data with *SPSS* Variable Names

CASENO1	GENDER2	AGE3	ICECRM4
1	0	18	1
2	1	21	3
3	9	20	1
4	1	22	2
5	1	999	1
6	0	19	9
7	1	20	2

TABLE D–2 | Codebook of Student Data

Variable Name	Variable Labels and Description of Variable Codes	Missing Values
CASENO1	Case Identification Number	NA
GENDER2	Gender: 0 = Male, 1 = Female	9
AGE3	Student Age: Self-reported	999
ICECRM4	Favorite Flavor of Ice Cream. 1 = Chocolate, 2 = Vanilla, 3 = Other or no preference	9

Command Sequence for Data Definition:

SPSS Data Editor window
    └Variable View tab
       ├Name: insert variable name in Name column
       ├Type: click for variable then click tab → Variable Type window
            ├choose variable type
            ├for numeric variables, insert number of decimal places
            ├for string variables, increase number of characters
            └OK
       ├Label: insert variable label in Label column
       ├Values: click for variable then click tab → Value Labels window
            ├specify value labels
            └OK
       ├Missing: click for variable then click tab → Missing Values window
            ├specify codes for missing values
            └OK
       └Measure: click for variable then click tab → a menu
            └Specify level of measure of the variable, whether
             nominal, ordinal, or *scale* (the *SPSS* term for an
             interval/ratio level variable).

Note: Although decimal places and width may be set in the Variable Type window, these items may also be changed directly in their columns of the Variable View of the *SPSS* Data Editor window.

Variable Name   In the Variable View of the *SPSS* Data Editor window, variables are listed under the Name column and their characteristics under remaining columns. Using Tables D–1 and D–2 as a guide, for variable 1 insert CASENO1 under the name column (which is limited to 8 characters). Start the name with a letter. Do not end with a period. Do not include special characters such as commas, apostrophes, ?, !, or *. Insert GENDER2 as the name of the second variable, etc.

Variable Type and Decimal Places   In the Variable View window of the *SPSS* Data editor, in the Type column, go to the box for a particular variable and click it. Click the tab that appears to the right. A small window called Variable Type will open. Specify whether the variable is *numeric* (i.e., comprised of numerical—or number—codes and perhaps decimal places) or *string* (i.e., comprised of letters and words). For numeric variables, field width is the number of spaces assigned for codes. The default of 8 spaces will usually suffice. Also enter the number of Decimal Places. For instance, for the variable CASENO1, stipulate Numeric and zero decimal places. For GENDER2, also click Numeric with zero decimal places, because we will use numbers for male and female. For string variables, a wider field width may be required and entered in the "Characters" box. Click Continue and the small window will close.

Variable Labels   A Variable Label is a descriptive label that will print with output. For instance, for the variable CASENO1, we will use the label "Case Identification Number" from the codebook in Table D–2 above. In the Variable View window of the *SPSS* Data editor, move the cursor under the Label column to the empty box for variable 1. Type the variable label. When you return to the Data View of the Data Editor window, if the entire variable name does not appear in its column heading, the mouse pointer can be used to stretch the column's width.

Value Labels   For nominal and ordinal variables, Value Labels assigns each numeric (number) code its respective name. Most researchers use numeric codes to represent a category name for nominal/ordinal variables (e.g., for GENDER4, "Male" = "0" and "Female" = "1", as in the codebook in Table D–2 above). Insert each code and its name in their respective boxes and click Add. Highlight a label to Change or Remove it. (For the variable CASENO1, value labels are unnecessary.) When finished assigning labels for a variable, click Continue. It is not necessary to assign value labels to interval/ratio variables, although selected labels may be useful. For instance, in coding ages, we might assign the code 60 to all who are 60 years of age and older. To remember this, for a code of 60, we assign the value label "60 and older."

Missing Values   Some variables may have "missing data" due to a respondent's inability or refusal to answer a survey question. For instance, in Table D–1 for the variable age (AGE3), case number 5 failed to report age. Thus, we coded her response as 999 and must define this score as a "missing value" code. This instructs the computer to ignore this value when making calculations. Traditionally, missing values are assigned combinations of 9 (9, 99, 999, etc.). The missing values for variables in Table D–1 are specified in the codebook of Table D–2.

    To define missing values: In the Variable View of the *SPSS* Data Editor window under the Missing column, go to the box for a particular variable and click it. Click the tab that appears to the right and a Missing Values window will open. Assign specific Discrete missing values or a Range of missing values. For instance, for the variable AGE3, we specify the discrete missing value of 999.

Level of Measurement of a Variable   In the Define Variable window, in the Measure box, check Nominal, Ordinal, or Scale (interval/ratio).

Making Data Definition Changes Later   To make data definition changes at any time, go to the Variable View window and click the location of the change.

Double-Checking the Data Definition of Variables   After defining the characteristics of variables, to quickly view them, at the top of the *SPSS* Data Editor window click Utilities, Variables.

Rearranging the Order and Adding Variables to the Data Set   In the Data Editor window, variables can be moved within the data matrix and new variables and cases can be inserted using the Edit and Data menus and Help.

Data Entry

In the *SPSS* Data Editor window, enter data by highlighting a square within the data matrix by clicking over it. Type the code (score) for that case and variable and hit the Enter key. Use the mouse and direction keys to move around in the matrix. For repetitive codes, use the Copy and Paste commands under Edit. A shortcut method of copying and pasting is to block off a selected entry with the mouse. Hit the Control button and the letter C simultaneously (Ctrl-C) to copy and Ctrl-V to paste.

Saving the Data File

For practice, create a data file using the entries in Table D–1 and the codebook in Table D–2.

Command Sequence for Saving a Data File:

SPSS Data Editor window
    └File
        └Save as. . . → Save Data As window
                    ├choose file location in "Save in. . ." panel
                    ├type chosen file name in File Name panel
                    └Save

Data files in *SPSS* are saved with the suffix, ".sav". For example, the data of Table D–1 might be saved under the file name stu7.sav.

Resaving Altered Files   Once you have used a data set for an exercise, it is advisable that you resave it. This is because some exercises require modification of the data. If you made slight modifications and wish not to save the original file, simply click the Save File icon in the shape of a floppy disk at the top of the *SPSS* Data Editor window. If you make substantial changes and wish to save them in a separate file from the original data set, follow the command sequence above for saving a data file but provide a new file name, such as stu7b.sav.

Choosing Optional Display Styles

When a data set is opened, *SPSS* will use default (preset) styles for its display of variables lists, screen views, output, charts, and so on. You may wish to change some defaults to suit your tastes and purposes. For example, you may prefer that variable lists appear using variable names rather than variable labels or that variables be listed in their order in the data file rather than in alphabetical order. Or you may wish to change the font style of output tables to match other documents for a report you are compiling. To change these default settings, in the *SPSS* Data Editor window use the command sequence Edit, Options. These changes will take effect next time the data set is opened. The following command sequence illustrates how to navigate the Options window.

Command Sequence for Optional Styles:

SPSS Data Editor window
└ Edit (to change default settings)
    └ Options → Options window
        ├ General: Choose to Display (variable) labels or Display (variable)
        | names, and other options
        ├ Viewer: Set font style and font size for output
        ├ Output Labels: Choose how value labels are to appear (e.g., for the variable
        | GENDER2 in Table D–2, the code "female" may be printed as the value "1" or
        | the label "female" or both)
        ├ Pivot Table: Choose style of output tables.
        └ OK

Quality Control: Printing Output and Sight Checking a List of Cases

To check the accuracy of data entries, obtain a list of data entries and sight check them by using the command sequence that follows. The output will be a ready-to-print data matrix in the Output-*SPSS* Viewer window.

Command Sequence for Printing Data Lists of Data Entries:

SPSS Data Editor window
└ Analyze
    └ Reports
        └ Case Summaries → Summarize Cases box
            ├ insert variables into Variable(s): box
            ├ check Display cases button
            ├ perhaps uncheck Limit cases to first 100 button
            └ OK

Editing and Printing Output Files in the Output-SPSS Viewer Window

When a procedure is executed, the results appear in an Output-*SPSS* Viewer window. Various parts of output appear in bordered tables called pivot tables. A pivot table or an entire output file may be edited, printed, and/or saved with the suffix "*.spo."

Editing Output   To avoid wasting paper, delete unneeded material from output tables and files before printing. To edit a pivot table, in the Output-*SPSS* Viewer window, double-click over the table. Edit by blocking things off with the mouse. Column widths may be adjusted by locating the cursor over a table border. An arrow will appear. Drag the arrow to broaden or narrow a column. When editing is complete, click outside the table to return to the Output-*SPSS* Viewer window. Experiment with editing tools until you become familiar with them.

Printing Output   To print the output, click over a single pivot table, or click the output tree on the left side of the screen to highlight selected parts of the output. Click File, Print Preview (or the Print Preview icon) to observe how the output will appear. To make adjustments to page size, margins, or layout, in the Output Viewer Window click File, Page Setup. When ready, click File, Print (or the Print icon).

Correcting Data Entries   If an entry error (or "stray code") is found, correct it by moving to its location in the data file in the Data View of the *SPSS* Data Editor window. Click on the location, type the correct data entry, and hit Enter. If multiple corrections are needed for the same code, use the Recode procedure described below under the section "Recoding Variables."

Moving between *SPSS* Data Editor and Output Windows   In an *SPSS* Data Editor window or in an Output-*SPSS* Viewer window, use the Window menu item to move from one to the other.

Saving an Output File and Printing from Other Software Packages:

SPSS Data Editor window
    └ File
        └ Save as → Save Data As window
            ├ choose file location in "Save in. . ." panel; type chosen file name in File
            │ Name panel in place of default "output".
            └ Save

The file will be saved with the suffix "*.spo" (for *SPSS* output). For example, the output file for the case summary of data in Table D–1 might be saved as A:Stu7list.spo. The file may be retrieved later in *SPSS for Windows*.

Copying Output Tables to Word Processing Software

To copy a pivot table from an output file into a word processing package, place the mouse pointer over the table and click; click Edit, Copy (or Ctrl-C). Minimize *SPSS* and maximize the word processing package and click Edit, Paste (or Ctrl-V). Use the word processing program's table editor to modify the output. In general, however, it is more efficient to edit output in *SPSS* prior to moving it to a word processing package.

Producing Frequency Distributions, Quartiles, and Percentiles

Command Sequence for Frequency Distributions, Quartiles, and Percentiles:

SPSS Data Editor window
    └ Analyze
        └ Descriptive Statistics
            └ Frequencies → Frequencies window
                ├ insert variables into Variable(s): box
                ├ check Display frequency tables
                ├ Statistics button
                    ├Quartiles (check if desired)
                    ├Percentiles; specify values and Add
                     them (if desired)
                    └Continue
              └ OK

Output   The output for a Frequencies run will produce a Statistics pivot table. For each variable, a Frequencies distribution table appears with five columns. The headings of the columns from left to right are: Valid (score values of the variable, such as an age of 19 years), Frequency (the number or "frequency" of cases for each score), Percent (the percentage frequencies of the scores), Valid Percent (the percentage frequencies of the scores excluding missing values), and Cumulative Percent (the cumulative percentage frequency of scores).

Recoding Variables

There are situations where we may wish to change a code in the data set. This is called recoding. For example, in Table D–1, only case 2 responded with "other flavor" of ice cream. Since there are a lot of chocolate choices, we may choose to throw the "other flavor" case in with the "vanillas" and compare chocolate to other flavors. To be on the safe side, we will recode to a new variable name ICECRM42, so that the "other flavor" code will be retained under the current variable name ICECRM4. To recode with a new variable name: click Transform, Recode into Different Variables; insert ICECRM4 into "Input Variable->Output Variable" box; type the new variable name, ICECRM42, in the "Name" box; click Change. Click Old and New Values buttons and use options for recoding, all of which are designed to "Add" recodes in the "Old->New" box of this window. To recode ICECRM4, under Old Values, type 3; under New Values, type 2; click Add to enter this recode into the "Old->New" box; click Continue. Notice that in the Old and New Values window there are shortcut ways of entering a series of recodes by specifying a range of values to be recoded. Here are the command sequence and description of output for recoding.

Command Sequence for Recoding Variables:

SPSS Data Editor window
    └Transform
        └Recode
            └ Into Different Variables → Recode into Different
            Variables window
                  ├ insert variable name of variable to be recoded into
                  "Numeric Variable- > Output Variable" box
                  ├ type the new variable name in the Output Variable
                  "Name" box; click Change.
                  ├ Click Old and New Values → Recode into Different
                  Variables: Old and New Values window
                        ├ use options for recoding and "Add" them
                        └Continue
              └ OK

Output   After recoding to create a new variable, return to the *SPSS* Data Editor window. You will find the new variable in the rightmost column of the data matrix. Now click Variable View. You will find the new variable name as the last variable listed at the bottom. Edit value labels, define missing values, and so on, as needed. You may wish to move this variable next to its original.

Recoding Into Same Variables   You may choose to recode a variable and not change its variable name. To do this, after clicking Transform-Recode, select Into Same Variables in place of Into Different Variables. Your recodes will be made retaining the current variable name. Note, however, that once a variable is recoded with the same name, you cannot retrieve the old codes and connect them to case numbers. If you think there might be a reason to later identify cases with the old codes, recode the variable to a new name.

Saving Changes to the Data Set   To retain changes to the data set, such as recodes and new variables, remember to save the file. If many changes are made and you are unsure about them, save the file under a new name to retain the old file in its original form.

SPSS FOR CHAPTER 3 OF *THE STATISTICAL IMAGINATION:* "CHARTS AND GRAPHS"

Chapter 3 Computer Application Exercises on *The Statistical Imagination* Web site have the following objectives: (1) to produce graphs and charts using *SPSS for Windows;* and (2) to learn to edit graphs and charts in *SPSS.*

SPSS Graphs and Charts

Graphs and charts are drawn from the Graphs menu of the *SPSS for Windows* Data Editor menu.

Pie Charts

Command Sequence for Pie Charts:

SPSS Data Editor window
    └Graphs
        └Pie → Pie Charts window
            └Check Summaries for group of cases and click Define
                └ In Define Pie: Summaries of Groups of Cases window
                  ├click "% of cases"
                  ├insert variable name in "Define Slices by" box
                  ├Titles button on lower right → Titles window
                      ├type in title
                      └Continue
                  ├Options button on lower right → Options window
                      └unmark "Display groups defined by missing values"
                       └Continue
                └OK

Output The pie chart will appear in the Output-*SPSS* Viewer window. Examine it carefully because it may require editing. See the section on 633 titled "Editing Chart Output."

Bar Charts

Command Sequence for Bar Charts:

SPSS Data Editor window
    └Graphs
        └Bar → Bar Charts window
        ├click Simple
        └check Summaries for group of cases and click Define
            └ In Define Simple Bar: Summaries of Groups of Cases window
              ├click "% of cases"
              ├insert variable name in "Category Axis" panel
              ├Titles button on lower right → Titles window
                  ├type in title
                  └Continue
              ├Options button on lower right → Options window
                  ├unmark "Display groups defined by missing values"
                  └Continue
            └OK

Output   The bar chart will appear in the Output-*SPSS* Viewer window. Examine it carefully because it may require editing. See the section on next page titled "Editing Chart Output."

Histograms

Command Sequence for Histograms:

SPSS Data Editor window
 └Graphs
    └Histogram → Histogram window
        ├ insert variable name into "Variable" panel
        ├ if desired, check Display normal curve
        ├ Titles button on lower right → Titles window
        │   ├ type in title
        │   └ Continue
        └ OK

Output   The histogram will appear in the Output-*SPSS* Viewer window. Examine it carefully because it may require editing. See the section on next page titled "Editing Chart Output."

Polygons (Line Charts in SPSS)

Command Sequence for Line Charts:

SPSS Data Editor window
 └Graphs
    └Line → Line Charts window
        ├click Simple
        └check Summaries for group of cases and click Define
              └In Define Simple Line: Summaries of Groups of Cases
               window
                   ├click "% of cases"
                   ├insert variable name in "Category Axis" panel
                   ├Titles button on lower right → Titles window
                   │   ├type in title
                   │   └Continue
                   ├Options button on lower right → Options window
                   │   ├unmark "Display groups defined by missing
                   │   values"
                   │   └Continue
                   └OK

Output   The polygon (line chart) will appear in the Output-*SPSS* Viewer window. Examine it carefully because it may require editing. See the section on next page titled "Editing Chart Output."

Editing Chart Output

In the Output-*SPSS* Viewer window, double-click over the chart to access the *SPSS* Chart Editor. Highlight selected parts of the chart or graph, such as a single slice of a pie chart, by clicking over it. Click Edit then Properties. A Properties window will open with assorted options. Experiment with them until you become familiar with the options that are pertinent to each type of chart. The Chart menu item in the Chart Editor window also provides options. When done, click the close box (the X-box in the upper right corner) of the Chart Editor window to return to the Output-*SPSS* Viewer window.

Copying Charts for Insertion into Word Processing Documents

An *SPSS* chart may be copied and inserted in the text of a word processing document, such as a report prepared in *MSWord* or *WordPerfect*. In the Output-*SPSS* Viewer window, click over the chart and a border will appear around it. Hit Ctrl-C to copy. Move to the word processing package and hit Ctrl-V to paste the chart. Once in the word processing package, the chart may be edited, but there will be limitations on what can be changed. Therefore, as a general rule, it is best to complete editing of a chart in *SPSS* prior to insertion in a word processing package.

SPSS FOR CHAPTER 4 OF *THE STATISTICAL IMAGINATION:* "MEASURING AVERAGES"

Chapter 4 Computer Application Exercises on *The Statistical Imagination* Web site have the following objectives: (1) to generate central tendency statistics using *SPSS for Windows;* and (2) to use central tendency statistics to gain a sense of proportion about the shapes of score distributions.

Central Tendency Statistics: The Mean, Median, and Mode

Central tendency statistics may be calculated in several ways in *SPSS for Windows*. First, they are accessible with Frequency Distributions. Second, they are accessible as "Descriptives." Finally, they are options with other statistical procedures.

Command Sequence for Central Tendency Statistics Using "Frequencies":

SPSS Data Editor window
  └Analyze
    └Descriptive Statistics
      └Frequencies → Frequencies window
          ├ insert variables into Variable(s): box
          ├ check Display frequency tables (if desired)
          ├ Statistics button → Frequencies: Statistics window
          │   ├check Mean, Median, and Mode
          │   ├check Skewness (if desired)
          │   └Continue
          └ OK

Output   Output will consist of a pivot table with the requested statistics and frequency tables if they are requested.

Command Sequence for Central Tendency Statistics Using "Descriptives":

SPSS Data Editor window
    └ Analyze
        └ Descriptive Statistics
            └ Descriptives → Descriptives window
                ├ insert variables into Variable(s): box
                ├ Options button → Descriptives: Options window
                │   ├ check Mean
                │   ├ check other desired statistics
                │   └ Continue
                └ OK

Output   Output will consist of a Descriptive Statistics pivot table with the requested statistics.

SPSS FOR CHAPTER 5 OF *THE STATISTICAL IMAGINATION:* "MEASURING SPREAD"

Chapter 5 Computer Application Exercises on *The Statistical Imagination* Web site have the following objectives: (1) to use *SPSS for Windows* to compute the range, the standard deviation, and Z-scores; (2) to use central tendency and dispersion statistics to discern the shapes of score distributions; and (3) to use Z-scores to identify extreme scores in a distribution.

Like central tendency statistics, dispersion statistics are found in both the Frequencies and Descriptives sections of the Descriptive Statistics menu item. Typically, we obtain central tendency and dispersion statistics together.

Command Sequence for Dispersion Statistics Using "Frequencies":

SPSS Data Editor window
    └ Analyze
        └ Descriptive Statistics
            └ Frequencies → Frequencies window
                ├ insert variables into Variable(s): box
                ├ check Display frequency tables (if desired)
                ├ Statistics button → Frequencies: Statistics window
                │   ├ check Std. deviation and Range
                │   ├ check other desired statistics
                │   └ Continue
                └ OK

Output   Output will consist of a pivot table with the requested statistics and frequency tables if they are requested.

Command Sequence for Dispersion Statistics Using "Descriptives":

SPSS Data Editor window
    └ Analyze
        └ Descriptive Statistics
            └ Descriptives → Descriptives window
                ├ insert variables into Variable(s): box
                ├ Options button → Descriptives: Options window
                      ├ check Std. Deviation and Range
                      ├ check other desired statistics
                      └ Continue
              └ OK

Output   Output will consist of a Descriptive Statistics pivot table with the requested statistics.

Computing Standardized Scores (Z-Scores)

For interval/ratio level variables, standardized scores (Z-scores) are an expression of a raw score (*X*-score) in standard deviation units of measure.

Command Sequence for Standardized Scores (Z-Scores):

SPSS Data Editor window
    └ Analyze
        └ Descriptive Statistics
            └ Descriptives → Descriptives window
                ├ insert variables into Variable(s): box
                ├ check "Save standardized values as variables"
                ├ Options button → Descriptives: Options window
                      ├ check desired statistics
                      └ Continue
              └ OK

Output   New variables comprised of Z-scores are created and assigned names with the letter Z preceding the original variable names (e.g., ZAGE3). These new variables are found in the data matrix of the Data Editor-Data View window in the rightmost column. Click the tab for the Variable View window and the new variables will be found at the bottom. Specify their properties, such as labels. You may wish to move these variables next to their original variables. If you desire to save these new variables, save the data file before exiting *SPSS for Windows*.

It is useful to generate a listing of case identification numbers, raw scores, and standardized scores (Z-scores) for interval/ratio variables. The list of Z-scores helps to identify the highest and lowest values of a variable in terms of how far these scores differ from the mean. Large differences (i.e., 3 standard deviations or more in either direction) may indicate an outlier. To obtain a listing of variables, see "Command Sequence for Printing Data Lists of Data Entries" for Chapter 2 of this appendix.

SPSS FOR CHAPTER 6 OF *THE STATISTICAL IMAGINATION:* "PROBABILITY"

Chapter 6 Computer Application Exercises on *The Statistical Imagination* Web site have the following objectives: (1) to learn to use score frequency distributions as probability distributions; and (2) to use Z-scores to compute probabilities with normally distributed interval/ratio variables.

Chapter 6 Computer Application Exercises utilize frequency distributions and standardized scores (Z-scores). For frequency distributions, review from this appendix, Chapter 2 above: "Command Sequence for Frequency Distributions, Quartiles, and Percentiles." For Z-scores, review from this appendix, Chapter 5 above: "Command Sequence for Standardized Scores (Z-Scores)."

SPSS FOR CHAPTER 7 OF *THE STATISTICAL IMAGINATION:* "SAMPLING DISTRIBUTIONS"

Chapter 7 Computer Application Exercises on *The Statistical Imagination* Web site have the following objectives: (1) to reinforce understanding of the concept of sampling distributions; and (2) to gain a sense of proportion about the relationship between sample size and sampling error.

Chapter 7 Computer Application Exercises utilize frequency histograms and descriptive statistics. For histograms, review from this appendix, Chapter 3 above: "Command Sequence for Histograms." For descriptive statistics, review from this appendix, Chapter 5 above: "Command Sequence for Dispersion Statistics Using Frequencies," and request both central tendency and dispersion statistics.

SPSS FOR CHAPTER 8 OF *THE STATISTICAL IMAGINATION*: "CONFIDENCE INTERVALS"

Chapter 8 Computer Application Exercises on *The Statistical Imagination* Web site have the following objectives: (1) to compute confidence intervals using *SPSS;* and (2) to understand the importance of examining the effects of skewness on the computation of a confidence interval.

Computing Confidence Intervals

In addition to the following command sequence, confidence intervals may be computed as an option with other procedures in *SPSS for Windows*. These options will be noted in later chapters.

Confidence Interval of a Population Mean

Command Sequence for Computing Confidence Intervals of the Mean:

SPSS Data Editor window
 └ Analyze
    └ Descriptive Statistics
       └ Explore → Explore window
                ├ insert variable into Dependent List: box
                ├ in Display: box, check Statistics
                ├ Statistics button → Explore: Statistics window
                         ├ check Descriptives
                         ├ stipulate level of confidence
                         └ Continue
                └ OK

Output In a pivot table of the Output-*SPSS* Viewer window, the confidence interval is provided with the lower confidence limit (LCL), stipulated as Lower Bound, and the upper confidence limit (UCL), stipulated as Upper Bound.

Confidence Interval of a Population Proportion

To compute a confidence interval of a proportion, it is necessary to "dummy code" the variable by recoding the success category of the nominal/ordinal variable to a value of 1 and all remaining categories to zero. For some variables, such as GENDER2 in Tables D–1 and D–2 above, recoding is unnecessary. Also note in the command sequence that Descriptives are not requested. For a nominal/ordinal variable, interval/ratio descriptive statistics are open to misinterpretation.

Command Sequence for Computing Confidence Intervals of a Proportion: To Recode a Nominal/Ordinal Variable as a Dummy Variable:

SPSS Data Editor window
 └ Transform
    └ Recode
       └ Into Different Variables → Recode into Different
       Variables: box
                ├ insert variable name of variable to be recoded into "Numeric
                │ Variable->Output Variable" box
                ├ type a new variable name in the Output Variable "Name" box;
                │ click Change
                ├ Click Old and New Values → Recode into Different Variables:
                │ Old and New Values window
                         ├ recode success category as "1" and all other values
                         │ (except missing values) as "0" and
                         │ "Add" them
                         └ Continue
                └ OK

Output   After recoding to create the new dummy variable, return to the *SPSS* Data Editor window. You will find the new variable in the rightmost column of the data matrix. Click the Variable View tab. Find the new dummy variable at the bottom of the variable names column. Edit variable and value labels, define missing values, and so on, as needed. You may wish to move this variable next to its original.

To Compute the Confidence Interval of a Population Proportion:

SPSS Data Editor window
 └ Analyze
   └ Descriptive Statistics
     └ Explore → Explore window
         ├ insert dummy variable into Dependent List: box
         ├ in Display box, check Statistics
         ├ Statistics button → Explore: Statistics window
         │   ├ stipulate level of confidence
         │   └ Continue
         └ OK

Output   In a pivot table of the Output-*SPSS* Viewer window, the confidence interval is provided with the lower confidence limit (LCL), stipulated as Lower Bound, and the upper confidence limit (UCL), stipulated as Upper Bound. (If either of these values is greater than 1.00, you forgot to dummy code the variable.) Note in the output that the reported "mean" of this dummy-coded nominal/ordinal variable is the proportion of cases in the success category.

SPSS FOR CHAPTER 9 OF *THE STATISTICAL IMAGINATION:* "HYPOTHESIS TESTING 1: LARGE SINGLE-SAMPLE MEANS TEST"

Chapter 9 Computer Application Exercises on *The Statistical Imagination* Web site have the following objectives: (1) to run single-sample means tests; and (2) to focus on locating and interpreting *p*-values in statistical output.

The Large Single-Sample Means Test

Even though the large single-sample means test utilizes the normal curve, computer software packages, including *SPSS,* refer to the test as a *t*-test. The same statistical procedure is used regardless of sample size. The reasons for this become apparent in Chapter 10.

Command Sequence for the Large Single-Sample Means Test:

SPSS Data Editor window
 └ Analyze
   └ Compare Means
     └ One-Sample T Test → One-Sample T Test window
         ├ insert interval/ratio variable into Test Variable(s): box
         ├ enter the value of the targeted hypothesized parameter into Test
         │ Value: box
         └ OK

Output   The output provides descriptive statistics in a pivot box titled "One-Sample Statistics." These statistics include the mean, standard deviation, and standard error. In a second pivot box titled "One-Sample Test," the output provides test procedure statistics. These statistics include: (1) The test statistic, t (which may be viewed as a Z-score if $n > 121$), (2) The p-value assuming a two-tailed test listed as "Sig" (for *significance*). If the test is one-tailed, divide the two-tailed p-value ("Sig") by 2, (3) The test effect stipulated as "mean difference" and (4) The upper and lower real limits of a 95 percent confidence interval of the mean difference. *Note:* This 95 percent confidence interval is of this mean *difference* (not to be confused with a confidence interval of the mean itself). The box also provides degrees of freedom (df), which are explained in Chapter 10.

SPSS FOR CHAPTER 10 OF *THE STATISTICAL IMAGINATION:* "HYPOTHESIS TESTING II: SMALL SINGLE-SAMPLE MEANS TEST (*t*-TEST) AND LARGE SINGLE-SAMPLE PROPORTIONS TEST"

Chapter 10 Computer Application Exercises on *The Statistical Imagination* Web site have the following objectives: (1) to learn how to run single-sample means tests (*t*-test) for any sample size; and (2) to learn how to run the large single-sample proportions test (*t*-test).

The Small Single-Sample Means Test (t-test)

The small single-sample means test uses the same command sequence as the large single-sample means test. When $n < 121$, degrees of freedom (df) are meaningful because the distribution is only approximately normal.

Command Sequence for the Small Single-Sample Means Test:

SPSS Data Editor window
    └ Analyze
        └ Compare Means
            └ One-Sample T Test → One-Sample T Test window
                ├ insert interval/ratio variable into Test Variable(s): box
                ├ enter the value of the targeted hypothesized parameter into
                │ Test Value: box
                └ OK

Output   The output provides descriptive statistics in a pivot box titled "One-Sample Statistics." These statistics include the mean, standard deviation, and standard error. In a second pivot box titled "One-Sample Test," the output provides test procedure statistics. These statistics include: (1) The test statistic, t. (2) The p-value assuming a two-tailed test listed as "Sig" (for *significance*). If the test is one-tailed, divide the two-tailed p-value ("Sig") by 2. (3) The test effect stipulated as "mean difference." and (4) The upper and lower real limits of a 95 percent confidence interval of the mean difference. *Note:* This 95 percent confidence interval is of this mean *difference* (not to be confused with a confidence interval of the mean itself).

Large Single-Sample Proportions Test

For a nominal/ordinal variable, a large single-sample proportions test uses the same command sequence as that of interval/ratio variables. However, the nominal/ordinal variable must be dummy coded such that the success category (the category we are testing) is coded "1" and all other categories, "0". Unless a variable is already dummy coded, this requires recoding.

To Recode a Nominal/Ordinal Variable into a Dummy Variable:
See Chapter 8, "Command Sequence for Computing Confidence Intervals of a Proportion: To Recode Nominal/Ordinal Variable as a Dummy Variable."

Command Sequence for the Large Single-Sample Proportions Test:

SPSS Data Editor window
└ Analyze
  └ Compare Means
    └ One-Sample T Test → One-Sample T Test window
      ├ insert dummy variable into Test Variable(s): box
      ├ enter the value of the targeted hypothesized parameter into Test
      │ Value: box
      └ OK

Output   Output is the same as for a Single-Sample Means Test. Note, however, that the reported "mean" of this dummy-coded nominal/ordinal variable is the proportion of cases in the success category.

SPSS FOR CHAPTER 11 OF *THE STATISTICAL IMAGINATION:* "TWO-GROUP DIFFERENCE OF MEANS TEST"

Chapter 11 Computer Application Exercises on *The Statistical Imagination* Web site have the following objectives: (1) to learn two-group difference of means tests; and (2) to identify the appropriate computer output for addressing the aspects of relationships for these tests

The Two-Group Difference of Means Test for Independent Groups

The independent groups test is for separate groups of subjects.

Command Sequence for the Two-Group Difference of Means Test:

SPSS Data Editor window
    └ Analyze
        └ Compare Means
            └ Independent-Samples T Test → Independent Samples T Test window
                ├ insert dependent interval/ratio variable into the Test Variables(s): box
                ├ insert independent dichotomous nominal variable into the Grouping
                │ Variable: box
                ├ Define Groups button → Define Groups window
                │   ├ insert the codes for groups 1 and 2
                │   └ Continue
            └ OK

After clicking the Define Groups button, if you fail to recall the codes for the Grouping Variable, close the Define Groups window. Click Utilities at the top of the *SPSS* Data Editor window, then Variables. Click the name of the grouping variable and its codes will appear; take note of the codes. (This may be done while the Independent-Samples T Test window is open.) Hit the Define Groups button and continue with the command sequence.

Output This procedure produces two pivot tables. The first is a Group Statistics pivot table that provides descriptive statistics for the interval/ratio variable for both groups of the nominal variable. The second table is the Independent Samples Test and it has two parts. One part, on the right, is the "t-test for Equality of Means." These statistics address the hypothesis of a difference of means. This part of the table presents the following results for a hypothesis test of a difference between means: (1) The test statistic, t, (2) The degrees of freedom under df, (3) the p-value for a two-tailed test under "Sig. (2-tailed)." If the test is one-tailed, divide this p-value by 2, (4) The effect of the test (i.e., the difference between means) under "Mean Difference," (5) The standard error, and (6) The upper and lower confidence limit of the mean *difference*.

Note that two sets of t-test output are presented. The top line is results for "Equal variances assumed." These results use a pooled variance estimate for the standard error. The second line of statistics is for "Equal variances not assumed," where the standard error is the separate variance estimate. (See Formulas in Chapter 11 in the text.) Under the t-test for Equality of Means part of the table, only one of these sets of statistics is used in a given hypothesis test, depending on whether we can assume equal variances.

Determining Which *t*-test of Equality of Means Output to Report The left part of the Independent Samples Test pivot table, under "Levine's Test for Equality of Variances," determines which t-test results to report. The Levine's Test tests the hypothesis that the *variances* are equal. It uses a sampling distribution called an F-test, and this test statistic is reported under "F". Under "Sig. (significance), the *p*-value for the Levine's test is reported. If this *p*-value is less than .05, then the hypothesis of equal *variances* is rejected. When this occurs, the "Equal variances *not* assumed" statistics apply under "t-test for Equality of Means." If the Levine's *p*-value (Sig.) is greater than .05, then the hypothesis of equal variances is not rejected. When this occurs, the "Equal variances assumed" statistics apply under "t-test for Equality of Means." Once you have determined which line of output to report from the "*t*-test for Equality of Means" part of the table, disregard the statistics in the other line of this table.

The Two-Groups Difference of Means Test for Nonindependent or Matched-Pairs Groups

The two-group difference of means for nonindependent groups or matched-pair samples test makes comparisons on variables for the same group of subjects. This *t*-test may be used to compare the same subjects at two times on the same variable, or to compare the same subjects on two variables that are coded the same.

Command Sequence for the Two-Groups Difference of Means Test for Nonindependent or Matched-Pairs Groups

SPSS Data Editor window
└ Analyze
   └ Compare Means
      └ Paired-Samples T Test → Paired-Samples T Test window
         ├ From the variable list, click variable1 to insert it in the Current Selections: box
         ├ From the variable list, click variable2 to insert it in the Current Selections: box
         ├ Use arrow button to move the pair of variables into the Paired Variables: box
         ├ Follow the same procedure to select additional pairs of variables (if desired)
         └ OK

Output Output will include: (1) a "Paired Samples Statistics" pivot table with descriptive statistics for both variables; (2) a "Paired Samples Correlations" table with Pearson's correlation coefficient (see Chapters 14 and 15); and (3) a "Paired Samples Test" table with the *t*-test statistics to test the null hypothesis of no difference between means. Under Paired Differences, this table provides the mean, standard deviation, standard error, and confidence limits of the *differences* between the scores. The remainder of the table provides the test statistic (*t*-test), degrees of freedom (*df*), and the two-tailed *p*-value under "Sig (2-tailed)." If the test is one-tailed, divide this *p*-value by 2.

SPSS FOR CHAPTER 12 OF *THE STATISTICAL IMAGINATION:* "ANALYSIS OF VARIANCE (ANOVA)"

Chapter 12 Computer Application Exercises on *The Statistical Imagination* Web site have the following objectives: (1) to learn one-way analysis of variance (ANOVA); and (2) to learn the aspects of the relationship for ANOVA tests.

One-Way Analysis of Variance (ANOVA) in SPSS for Windows

Command Sequence for One-Way ANOVA:

SPSS Data Editor window
    └ Analyze
        └ Compare Means
            └ One-way ANOVA → One-way ANOVA window
              ├ insert dependent interval/ratio variable into the
               Dependent List: box
              ├ insert independent nominal/ordinal variable into the
               Factor: box
              ├ For range tests, click Post Hoc button → One-Way
               ANOVA: Post Hoc Multiple Comparisons window
                        ├ check Tukey under Equal Variances
                        Assumed box
                        ├ check Tamhane's T2 under Equal Variances
                        Not Assumed box
                        └ Continue
              ├ Options → One-Way ANOVA: Options window
                 ├ check Descriptives
                 ├ check Homogeneity of variance test
                 └ Continue
             └ OK

Output A Descriptives pivot table provides descriptive statistics for each group as well as confidence intervals. A second pivot table entitled "Test of Homogeneity of Variances" establishes whether there are significant differences in the variances or spreads of the dependent variable between the groups. Recall that a difference of means test assumes equal variances in the population of the groups. Similar to the options presented in Chapter 11, the assumption of equal variances is tested with the Levine statistic. The results determine which set of range tests apply. When the Levine statistic's *p*-value under "Sig." is greater than .05, this indicates that it is safe to assume equal variances; therefore, report range tests from the Tukey HSD output of the Multiple Comparisons pivot table described below. When the Levine statistic's *p*-value under "Sig." is less than or equal to .05, this indicates significant differences among group variances; therefore, report range tests from the Tamhane output of the Multiple Comparisons pivot table described below.

The third pivot table, titled "ANOVA," is the source table for the *F*-test. Range tests are presented in a Post Hoc Tests-Multiple Comparisons pivot table. (Report results from either the Tukey or Tamhane boxes but not both, depending on the Test of Homogeneity of Variances described above.) These multiple comparisons tables compare the differences between means of each group to the others and use asterisks to highlight significant differences. Finally, a "Homogeneous Subsets" pivot table provides a rough guide to which groups cluster (i.e., are about the same) in terms of their means for the dependent variable.

SPSS FOR CHAPTER 13 OF *THE STATISTICAL IMAGINATION:* "CHI-SQUARE AND BINOMIAL TESTS"

Chapter 13 Computer Application Exercises on *The Statistical Imagination* Web site have the following objectives: (1) to learn the Crosstabs and Binomial procedures in *SPSS for Windows;* and (2) to learn how to interpret these statistical tests and their aspects of a relationship.

The Chi-Square Test

Command Sequence for the Chi-Square Test:

SPSS Data Editor window
 └ Analyze
   └ Descriptive Statistics
     └ Crosstabs → Crosstabs window
      ├ insert dependent, nominal variable into Row(s): box
      ├ insert independent, nominal variable into Column(s): box
      ├ Statistics → Crosstabs: Statistics window
        ├ check Chi-Square
        └ Continue
      ├ Cells → Crosstabs: Cell Display window
        ├ check Observed, Expected, and Column
        └ Continue
      ├ Format → Crosstabs: Table Format window
        ├ check Ascending
        └ Continue
      └ OK

Output   Crosstabs output will consist of three pivot tables: (1) a Case Processing Summary table that reports total sample size, missing, and valid cases; (2) a crosstabulation table; and (3) a Chi-Square Tests table with several optional Chi-Square statistics, with the pertinent one being the "Pearson Chi-Square." The value of the computed Chi-Square statistic is listed under "Value," degrees of freedom under "df," and the *p*-value under "Asymp. Sig. (2-sided)," the two-sided meaning nondirectional. If there is a cell frequency less than 5, either Fisher's exact test or Yates's "Continuity Correction" will appear in the output.

The Binomial Test

Command Sequence for the Binomial Test:

SPSS Data Editor window
 └ Analyze
   └ Nonparametric Tests
     └ Binomial → Binomial Test window
       ├ insert dichotomous variable into Test Variable List: box
       ├ stipulate the hypothesized value of P_u in the Test
       │ Proportion: box
       └ OK

Output   Output appears in a Binomial Test pivot table. The table reports: the category names and their frequencies (N); the observed sample proportion, P_s, as "Observed Prop."; the hypothesized test proportion, P_u, under "Test Prop."; and a two-tailed *p*-value under "Asymp. Sig. (2-tailed)." To obtain the *p*-value for a one-tailed test, divide the two-tailed value by 2.

SPSS FOR CHAPTERS 14 AND 15 OF *THE STATISTICAL IMAGINATION*: "SIMPLE CORRELATION AND REGRESSION ANALYSIS"

Chapters 14 and 15 Computer Application Exercises on *The Statistical Imagination* Web site have the following objectives: (1) to learn to produce scatterplots and correlation-regression statistics; (2) to learn the relationship between the shape of a scatterplot and the size of Pearson's *r* correlation coefficient; and (3) to obtain correlation and regression statistics to test hypotheses and address the four aspects of a relationship between two interval/ratio variables.

Scatterplots

A scatterplot is used to verify that a linear relationship exists between the two interval/ratio variables. The scatterplot also reveals outlier coordinates.

Command Sequence for Producing Scatterplots:

SPSS Data Editor window
 └ Graphs
   └ Scatter/Dot → Scatter/Dot window
     ├ Simple Scatter
     └ Define → Simple Scatterplot window
       ├ insert dependent variable into the Y Axis: box
       ├ insert independent variable into the X Axis: box
       ├ Titles button on lower right → Titles window
       │   ├ type in title
       │   └ Continue
       └ OK

Output The scatterplot will appear in the Output-*SPSS* Viewer window. The scatterplot may be edited by double-clicking over it to open the *SPSS* Chart Editor window. Try various buttons and options to become acquainted with editing capabilities. The following command sequences utilize some of the options.

Plotting the Regression Line and Mean Line on the Scatterplot

The regression and mean of Y reference line may be drawn on the scatterplot. This is done in the Chart Editor after the scatterplot appears in the output.

Command Sequence for Plotting Regression Line and Mean Line:

In Output-*SPSS* Viewer window
└ Double-click over scatterplot → Chart Editor window
    ├ For regression line, select (highlight)) data coordinates by
    right-clicking over a single data coordinate → Properties menu
    window appears
        └ click Add Fit Line at Total → Properties window
            └ Close (unless you wish to alter chart style)
    ├ Regression line appears with value of r^2. If you wish to
    remove the value of r^2, click over it to reveal its text box and
    delete the box.
    ├ For mean of Y reference line, select (highlight)) data coordinates
    by right-clicking over a single data coordinate.
    → Properties menu window appears
        └ click Add Y Axis Reference Line → Properties window
           └ Close (unless you wish to alter chart style)
    └ Click close box (the X-box in upper right corner) of the Chart Editor
    window to return to the Output-*SPSS* Viewer window.

The plot will reappear with the stipulated modifications.

Adding Titles and Truncating Axes on the Scatterplot

On the scatterplot, you may add titles, reshape or truncate the axes, modify an axis title, add or remove grid lines, and so on. While in the *SPSS* Chart Editor window, click Options or Elements to obtain menus. You may also double-click parts of the chart, such as an axis label, to automatically open an edit facility. Experiment with the options available. When editing is complete, click the close box (the X-box in upper right corner) of the Chart Editor window to return to the Output-*SPSS* Viewer window.

Copying a Scatterplot to a Word Processing Package

To copy a scatterplot to a word processing program, in the Output-*SPSS* Viewer window, scroll to bring the scatterplot into view. Click once over the plot to box it off, then hit Ctrl-C. In the word processing package, hit Ctrl-V to insert the chart into the text. In some word processing packages, additional editing may be done to the chart, unless it requires calculations or plotting. In general, it is best to complete editing while in *SPSS* prior to copying the chart to other software.

Pearson's Correlation Coefficient

Correlation statistics are found in a variety of menus in *SPSS for Windows*. To quickly obtain them use the following command sequence. However, Pearson's *r* is also reported with the regression statistics. (See the section "Regression Coefficients" below.)

Command Sequence for Pearson's *r* Correlation Coefficient:

SPSS Data Editor window
    └Analyze
        └Correlate
            └ Bivariate → Bivariate Correlations window
                ├ insert two or more desired interval/ratio variables into
                │ Variables: box
                ├ check Pearson in the Correlations Coefficients box
                ├ check Two-tailed or One-Tailed in the Test of
                │ Significance box
                ├ Options → Bivariate Correlations: Options window
                │   ├ check desired statistics
                │   └ Continue
                └ OK

Output   If optional statistics are requested, their output appears in a Descriptive Statistics pivot table. A Correlations table provides correlation coefficients, the *p*-value on the "Sig." line, an indication of whether the *p*-value is one- or two-tailed, and the number of cases used (N).

Regression Coefficients

In *SPSS for Windows,* use the following command sequence to obtain regression coefficients in the linear equation, $\acute{Y} = a + bX$. This output also provides Pearson's *r* correlation coefficient.

Command Sequence for Regression Coefficients, *a* and *b* (as well as Pearson's r):

SPSS Data Editor window
    └ Analyze
        └ Regression
            └ Linear → Linear Regression window
                ├ insert the dependent variable (*Y*) into the Dependent: box
                ├ insert the independent variable(s) (*X*) into the Independent(s):
                │ box
                ├ Statistics → Linear Regression: Statistics window
                │   ├ check Estimates, Model Fit, Descriptives
                │   └ Continue
                └ OK

Output   The output for Linear Regression supplies six pivot tables. This extensive output is designed for *multiple* correlation and regression, the situation of several independent variables. For simple, bivariate correlation and regression, the situation of only one independent variable, focus on pivot tables 1, 2, and 6 as described as follows: (1) a Descriptive Statistics pivot table with means, standard deviations, and sample size (N); (2) a Correlations table (which is especially valuable for multiple regression where there is more than one independent variable); (3) a Variables Entered/Removed table which also applies for multiple regression; (4) a Model Summary table which provides Pearson's r and r-squared (but reports these statistics as R and R Square, which is applicable to multiple regression); (5) an ANOVA table, which applies to multiple regression; and (6) a Coefficients table that contains the regression coefficients. In pivot table 6, the Y-intercept, a, is next to "(Constant)" under the "B" column situated under "Unstandardized coefficients." The slope, b, is in the same column next to the variable label (name) of the independent variable. The name of the dependent variable is noted in a footnote to this box. The p-value for the slope is listed under "Sig." Compare this p-value to the one obtained for Pearson's r using the Analyze-Correlate-Bivariate sequence under "Command Sequence for Pearson's r Correlation Coefficient," and you will find it is the same. Recall from Chapter 14 of the text that for bivariate correlation and regression, Pearson's r is a standardized form of the unstandardized slope, b.

Abbotts, Joanne E., Rory G.A. Williams, Helen N. Sweeting, and Patrick B. West. 2004. "Is Going to Church Good or Bad for You? Denomination, Attendance, and Mental Health of Children in West Scotland." *Social Science and Medicine* 58:645–56.

Aiken, L.H., S.P. Clarke, D.M. Sloane, J. Sochalski, and J.H. Silber. 2002. "Hospital Nurse Staffing and Patient Mortality, Nurse Burnout, and Job Dissatisfaction." *Journal of the American Medical Association* 288:1987–93.

Alabama Center for Health Statistics, 2004. http://ph.state.al.us/csc/vs/Query/Mortality/MortalityQrySLT.htm.

Alba, Richard D., John R. Logan, and Kyle Crowder. 1997. "White Ethnic Neighborhoods and Assimilation: The Greater New York Region, 1980–1990." *Social Forces* 75:883–909.

American Medical Association. 1997. *Physician Characteristics and Distribution in the U.S., 1996–97*. Chicago: The American Medical Association.

Arthur, Winfred, Jr., and William G. Graziano. 1996. "The Five-Factor Model, Conscientiousness, and Driving Accident Involvement." *Journal of Personality* 64(3):593–615.

Babbie, Earl. 1992. *The Practice of Social Research*, 6th ed. New York: Wadsworth.

Bailey, Kenneth D. 1978. *Methods of Social Research*. New York: Free Press.

Bastiaens, Leo. 2004. "Response to Antidepressant Treatment in a Community Mental Health Center." *Community Mental Health Journal* 40:561–67.

Betts, Julian R., and Darlene Morell. 1999. "The Determinants of Undergraduate Grade Point Average: The Relative Importance of Family Background, High School Resources, and Peer Group Effects." *The Journal of Human Resources* 34:268–93.

Blalock, Hubert M. 1979. *Social Statistics*, 3rd ed. New York: McGraw-Hill.

Boardman, Jason D. 2004. "Stress and Physical Health: The Role of Neighborhoods as Mediating and Moderating Mechanisms." *Social Science and Medicine* 58:2473–83.

Browning, Christopher R., Tama Leventhal, and Jeanne Brooks-Gunn. 2004. "Neighborhood Context and Racial Differences in Early Adolescent Sexual Activity." *Demography* 41: 697–720.

Bryant, Richard A., Michelle L. Moulds, and Rachel M. Guthrie. 2000. "Acute Stress Disorder Scale: A Self-Report Measure of Acute Stress Disorder." *Psychological Assessment* 12:61–68.

Bryson, Bethany. 1996. "'Anything But Heavy Metal': Symbolic Exclusion and Musical Dislikes." *American Sociological Review* 61:884–99.

Cardano, Mario, Giuseppe Costa, and Moreno Demaria. 2004. "Social Mobility and Health in the Turin Longitudinal Study." *Social Science and Medicine* 58:1563–74.

Central Bank of the Russian Federation. 2000. *Bulletin of Banking Statistics*. Moscow, Russia: Prime-TASS.

_____ 2002. *Bulletin of Banking Statistics*. Moscow, Russia: Prime-TASS.

_____ 2003. *Bulletin of Banking Statistics*. Moscow, Russia: Prime-TASS.

Clair, Jeffrey M., Ferris J. Ritchey, and Richard M. Allman. 1993. "Satisfaction with Medical Encounters Among Caregivers of Geriatric Outpatients." *Sociological Practice* 11:139–57.

Cockerham, William C., M. Christine Snead, and Derek F. DeWaal. 2002. "Health Lifestyles in Russia and the Socialist Heritage." *Journal of Health and Social Behavior* 43:42–55.

Crawford, Charles. 2000. "Gender, Race, and Habitual Offender Sentencing in Florida." *Criminology* 38:263–80.

Crawford, Charles, Ted Chiricos, and Gary Kleck. 1998. "Race, Racial Threat, and Sentencing of Habitual Offenders." *Criminology* 36:481–510.

David, F.N. 1962. *Games, Gods and Gambling*. London: Charles Griffen and Company.

Deschenes, M.R. 2004. "Effects of Aging on Muscle Fibre Type and Size." *Sports Medicine* 34:809–24.

DuBois, David L., and Naida Silverthorn. 2005. "Natural Mentoring Relationships and Adolescent Health: Evidence from a National Study." *American Journal of Public Health* 95:518–25.

Durkheim, Emile. 1951 [1897]. *Suicide: A Study in Sociology*. Translated by John A. Spaulding, and George Simpson. Glencoe, Ill.: The Free Press.

Ebrahim, Shah, Olia Papacosta, Goya Wannamethee, and Joy Adamson. 2004. "Social Inequalities and Disability in Older Men: Prospective Findings from the British Regional Heart Study." *Social Science and Medicine* 59:2109–20.

Edin, Kathryn, and Laura Lein. 1997. "Work, Welfare, and Single Mothers' Economic Survival Strategies." *American Sociological Review* 61:253–66.

Egan, Marcia, and Goldie Kadushin. 2004. "Job Satisfaction of Home Health Social Workers in the Environment of Cost Containment." *Health and Social Work* 29:287–96.

Elder, Randy W., Ruth A. Shults, Monica H. Swahn, Brian J. Strife, and George W. Ryan. 2004. "Alcohol-Related Emergency Department Visits Among Young People Ages 13 to 25 Years." *Journal of Studies on Alcohol* 65:297–300.

Ellickson, Phyllis L., Chloe E. Bird, Maria Orlando, David J. Klein, and Daniel F. McCaffrey. 2003. "Social Context and Adolescent Health Behavior: Does School-Level Smoking Prevalence Affect Students' Subsequent Smoking Behavior?" *Journal of Health and Social Behavior* 44:525–35.

Ensminger, Margaret E. 1995. "Welfare and Psychological Distress: A Longitudinal Study of African American Urban Mothers." *Journal of Health and Social Behavior* 36:346–59.

Farrelly, Matthew C., Kevin C. Davis, M. Lyndon Haviland, Peter Messeri, and Cheryl G. Healton. 2005. "Evidence of Dose-Response Relationship Between "Truth" Antismoking Ads and Youth Smoking Prevalence." *American Journal of Public Health* 95:425–31.

Federal Bureau of Investigation. 2002a. *Crime in the United States, 2002: Uniform Crime Reports.* Washington, D.C.: U.S. Government Printing Office.

_____ 2002b. "Hate Crime Statistics Press Release." November 25, 2002. Washington, D.C.: FBI National Press Office.

Ferraro, Kenneth F., and Yan Yu. 1995. "Body Weight and Self-Ratings of Health." *Journal of Health and Social Behavior* 36:274–84.

Fischer, Hans. 2000. *The Central Limit Theorem from Laplace to Cauchy: Changes in Stochastic Objectives and in Analytical Methods.* Aachen, Netherlands: Shaker Publishing.

Fisher, Ronald A., and Frank Yates. 1963. *Statistical Tables for Biological, Agricultural and Medical Research.* New York: Hafner Publishing Company. (Previously published by Longman Group Ltd., London, and Oliver and Boyd, Edinburgh.)

Franks, Peter, Marthe R. Gold, and Kevin Fiscella. 2003. "Sociodemographics, Self-Rated Health, and Mortality in the U.S." *Social Science and Medicine* 56:2505–14.

Freedle, Roy O. 2003. "Correcting the SAT's Ethnic and Social-Class Bias: A Method for Reestimating SAT Scores." *Harvard Educational Review* 73:1–43.

Freund, John E., and Gary A. Simon. 1991. *Statistics: A First Course*, 5th ed. Englewood Cliffs, N.J.: Prentice-Hall.

Friedman, Michael A., and Kelly D. Brownell. 1995. "Psychological Correlates of Obesity: Moving to the Next Research Generation." *Psychological Bulletin* 117:3–20.

Funk, Jeanne B., Debra D. Buchman, Jennifer Jenks, and Heidi Bechtoldt. 2003. "Playing Violent Video Games, Densensitization, and Moral Evaluation in Children." *Applied Developmental Psychology* 24:413–36.

Gardner, Donald G., Linn Van Dyne, and Jon L. Pierce. 2004. "The Effects of Pay Level on Organization-Based Self-Esteem and Performance: A Field Study." *Journal of Occupational and Organizational Psychology* 77:307–22.

Garroutte, Eva M., Robert M. Kunovich, Clemma Jacobsen, and Jack Goldberg. 2004. "Patient Satisfaction and Ethnic Identity Among American Indian Older Adults." *Social Science and Medicine* 59:2233–44.

Gaughan, Monica. 2006. "The Gender Structure of Adolescent Peer Influence on Drinking." *Journal of Health and Social Behavior* 47:47–61.

Gillings, Richard J. 1972. *Mathematics in the Time of the Pharaohs.* Cambridge, Mass.: MIT Press.

Goesling, Brian. 2001. "Changing Income Inequalities Within and Between Nations: New Evidence." *American Sociological Review* 66:745–61.

Goldberg, Amie, and Joseph Pedulla. 2002. "Performance Differences According to Test Mode and Computer Familiarity on a Practice Graduate Record Exam." *Educational and Psychological Measurement* 62:1053–67.

Green, Donald P., Laurence H. McFalls, and Jennifer K. Smith. 2001. "Hate Crime: An Emergent Research Agenda." *Annual Review of Sociology* 27:479–504.

Greiner, Birgit A., Niklas Krause, David Ragland, and June M. Fisher. 2004. "Occupational Stressors and Hypertension: A Multi-Method Study Using Observer-Based Job Analysis and Self-Reports in Urban Transit Operators." *Social Science and Medicine* 59:1081–94.

Groome, David, and Anastasia Soureti. 2004. "Post-Traumatic Stress Disorder and Anxiety Symptoms in Children Exposed to the 1999 Greek Earthquake." *British Journal of Psychology* 95:387–97.

Grove, Wayne A., and Tim Wasserman. 2004. "The Life-Cycle Pattern of Collegiate GPA: Longitudinal Cohort Analysis and Grade Inflation." *Journal of Economic Education* 35:162–74.

Guilamo-Ramos, Vincent, James Jaccard, Robert Turrisi, and Margaret Johansson. 2005. "Parental and School Correlates of Binge Drinking Among Middle School Students." *American Journal of Public Health* 95:894–99.

Guo, Chiquan. 2004. "Marketing Research: Cui Bono?" *Business Horizons* 47:33–38.

Guth, James L., John C. Green, Lyman A. Kellstedt, and Corwin E. Smidt. 1995. "Faith and the Environment: Religious Beliefs and Attitudes on Environmental Policy." *American Journal of Political Science* 39:364–82.

Hajjar, Ihab, and Theodore Kotchen. 2003. "Regional Variations of Blood Pressure in the United States Are Associated with Regional Variations in Dietary Intakes: The NHANES-III Data." *The Journal of Nutrition* 133:211–14.

Harmelink, Philip J., and William M. VanDenburgh. 2003. "On the CPA's Role in Guarding Clients' Investments." *The CPA Journal* 73:6–10.

He, Meizi, and Judy Sutton. 2004. "Using Routine Growth Monitoring Data in Tracking Overweight Prevalence in Young Children." *Canadian Journal of Public Health* 95:419–23.

Henning, Kris, and Lynette Feder. 2004. "A Comparison of Men and Women Arrested for Domestic Violence: Who Presents the Greater Threat?" *Journal of Family Violence* 19:69–80.

Hersch, Joni, and Leslie S. Stratton. 2002. "Housework and Wages." *The Journal of Human Resources* 37:217–29.

Hoff, Timothy J. 2003. "How Physician-Employees Experience Their Work Lives in a Changing HMO." *Journal of Health and Social Behavior* 44:75–96.

Hollinger, Constance, and Carla Baldwin. 1990. "The Stanford-Binet, 4th ed.: A Small Study of Concurrent Validity." *Psychological Reports* 66:1331–36.

Hughes, Mary Elizabeth, and Linda J. Waite. 2002. "Health in Household Context: Living Arrangements and Health in Late Middle Age." *Journal of Health and Social Behavior* 43:1–21.

Hunt, Larry L., and Matthew O. Hunt. 2001. "Race, Region, and Religious Involvement: A Comparative Study of Whites and African Americans." *Social Forces* 80:605–31.

Jackson, Jerome E., and Sue Ammen. 1996. "Race and Correctional Officers' Punitive Attitudes Toward Treatment Programs for Inmates." *Journal of Criminal Justice* 24:153–66.

Jewkes, Rachel, Jonathan Levin, and Loveday Penn-Kekana. 2002. "Risk Factors for Domestic Violence: Findings from a South African Cross-Sectional Study." *Social Science and Medicine* 55:1603–17.

Johnson, Elmer H. 1973. *Social Problems of Urban Man*. Homewood, Ill.: Dorsey Press.

Kahn, Joan R., and Leonard I. Pearlin. 2006. "Financial Strain Over the Life Course and Health Among Older Adults." *Journal of Health and Social Behavior* 47:17–31.

Kim, Sung Soo, Stan Kaplowitz, and Mark V. Johnston. 2004. "The Effects of Physician Empathy on Patient Satisfaction and Compliance. *Evaluation & Health Professions* 27:237–51.

Klem, Adena M., and James P. Connell. 2004. "Relationships Matter: Linking Teacher Support to Student Engagement and Achievement." *The Journal of School Health* 74:262–73.

Laplace, Pierre S. 1951 (origin. 1820). *A Philosophical Essay on Probabilities*. Translated from the sixth French edition by F.W. Truscott and F.L. Emory. New York: Dover.

Lee, Ivy, and Minako Maykovich. 1995. *Statistics: A Tool for Understanding Society*. Needham Heights, Mass.: Allyn and Bacon.

Lewis, LaVonna B., David C. Sloane, Lori M. Nascimento, Allison L. Diament, et al. 2005. "African Americans' Access to Healthy Food Options in South Los Angeles Restaurants." *American Journal of Public Health* 95:668–74.

Likert, Rensis. 1932. "A Technique for the Measurement of Attitudes." *Archives of Psychology* 21 (140).

Loureiro, Maria L., and Rodolfo M. Nayga, Jr. 2006. "Obesity, Weight Loss, and Physician's Advice." *Social Science and Medicine* 62:2458–68.

Lueschen, Guenther, William Cockerham, Jouke van der Zee, Fred Stevens, Jos Diederiks, Manuel Garcia Ferrando, Alphonse d'Houtaud, Ruud Peeters, Thomas Abel, and Steffen Niemann. 1995. *Health Systems in the European Union: Diversity, Convergence, and Integration*. Munich: Oldenbourg.

Lynch, Wendy L., Paul K. Maciejewski, and Mark N. Potenza. 2004. "Psychiatric Correlates of Gambling in Adolescents and Young Adults Grouped by Age at Gambling Onset." *Archives of General Psychiatry* 61:1116–22.

Macassa, Gloria, Gebrenegus Ghilagaber, Eva Bernhardt, Finn Diderichsen, and Bo Burström. 2003. "Inequalities in Child Mortality in Mozambique: Differentials by Parental Socio-Economic Position." *Social Science and Medicine* 57:2255–64.

Madriz, Esther. 1996. "The Perception of Risk in the Workplace: A Test of Routine Activity Theory." *Journal of Criminal Justice* 24:407–18.

Marshall, Grant N., M. Audrey Burnam, Paul Koegel, Greer Sullivan, and Bernadette Benjamin. 1996. "Objective Life Circumstances and Life Satisfaction: Results from the Course of Homelessness Study." *Journal of Health and Social Behavior* 37:44–58.

Martin, Paul. 2003. "Voting Rewards: Voter Turnout, Attentive Publics, and Congressional Allocation of Federal Money." *American Journal of Political Science* 47:110–27.

Matthews, Ruth J., Carol Jagger, and Ruth M. Hancock. 2006. "Does Socioeconomic Advantage Lead to a Longer, Healthier Old Age?" *Social Science and Medicine* 62:2489–99.

McCarthy, John D., and Mark Wolfson. 1996. "Resource Mobilization by Local Social Movement Organizations: Agency, Strategy, and Organization in the Movement Against Drinking and Driving." *American Sociological Review* 61:1070–88.

McCrae, Robert R. 1996. "Social Consequences of Experiential Openness." *Psychological Bulletin* 120:323–37.

Meshel, David S., and Richard P. McGlynn. 2004. "Intergenerational Contact, Attitudes, and Stereotypes of Adolescents and Older People." *Educational Gerontology* 30:457–79.

Mills, C. Wright. 1959. *The Sociological Imagination*. New York: Oxford University Press.

Molyneux, C.S., N. Peshu, and K. Marsh. 2004. "Understanding of Informed Consent in a Low-Income Setting: Three Case Studies from the Kenyan Coast." *Social Science and Medicine* 59:2547–59.

National Advisory Commission on Civil Disorders. 1968. *Report of the National Advisory Commission on Civil Disorders*. Washington, D.C.: U.S. Government Printing Office.

National Oceanic and Atmospheric Administration. 2003. National Weather Service. http://www.nws.noaa.gov/om/severe_weather/63yrstat.pdf.

Neugebauer, O. 1962. *The Exact Sciences in Antiquity*. New York: Harper.

Nishi, Nobuo, Kae Makino, Hideki Fukuda, and Kozo Tatara. 2004. "Effects of Socioeconomic Indicators on Coronary Risk Factors, Self-Rated Health and Psychological Well-Being Among Urban Japanese Civil Servants." *Social Science and Medicine* 58:1159–70.

Orbuch, Terri L., and Sandra L. Eyster. 1997. "Division of Household Labor among Black Couples and White Couples." *Social Forces* 76:301–32.

Pearson, E.S., and H.O. Hartley. 1976. *Biometrika Tables for Statisticians, Volume I*. London: Biometrika Trust.

Pearson, Jane L., Andrea G. Hunter, Margaret E. Ensminger, and Sheppard G. Kellam. 1990. "Black Grandmothers in Multigenerational Households: Diversity in Family Structure and Parenting Involvement in the Woodlawn Community." *Child Development* 61:434–42.

Peterson, Richard A., and Roger M. Kern. 1996. "Changing Highbrow Taste: From Snob to Omnivore." *American Sociological Review* 61:900–7.

Pikhart, Hynek, Martin Bobak, Andrzej Pajak, Sofia Malyutina, Ruzena Kubinova, Roman Topor, Helena Sebakova, Yuri Nikitin, and Michael Marmot. 2004. "Psychosocial Factors at Work and Depression in Three Countries of Central and Eastern Europe." *Social Science and Medicine* 58:1475–82.

Pinquart, Martin, and Silvia Sorenson. 2005. "Ethnic Differences in Stressors, Resources, and Psychological Outcomes of Family Caregiving: A Meta-analysis." *The Gerontologist* 45:90–106.

Prosser, Helen, and Tom Walley. 2005. "A Qualitative Study of GP's and PCO Stakeholders' Views on the Importance and Influence of Cost on Prescribing." *Social Science and Medicine* 60:1335–46.

Ram, Rati. 2004. "School Expenditures and Student Achievement: Evidence from the United States."*Education Economics* 12:169–76.

Ramstedt, Mats. 2004. "Alcohol Consumption and Alcohol-Related Mortality in Canada, 1950–2000." *Canadian Journal of Public Health* 95:121–26.

Reynolds, John R. 1997. "The Effects of Industrial Employment Conditions on Job-Related Distress." *Journal of Health and Social Behavior* 38:105–16.

Riebschleger, Joanne. 2004. "Good Days and Bad Days: The Experiences of Children of a Parent with a Psychiatric Disability." *Psychiatric Rehabilitation Journal* 28:25–31.

Rogge, Mary E. 1996. "Social Vulnerability to Toxic Risk." *Journal of Social Service Research* 22:109–29.

Roose, Steven P., Harold A. Sackeim, K. Ranga Rama Krishnan, Bruce G. Pollock, George Alexopoulos, Helen Lavretsky, Ira R. Katz, and Heikki Hakkarainen. 2004. "Antidepressant Pharmacotherapy in the Treatment of Depression in the Very Old: A Randomized, Placebo-Controlled Trial." *The American Journal of Psychiatry* 161:2050–59.

Sagan, Carl. 1995a. "Crop Circles and Aliens: What's the Evidence?" *Parade Magazine*, December 3:10–13.

_____. 1995b. *The Demon-Haunted World*. New York: Random House.

Sheynin, O.B. 1970. "On the Early History of the Law of Large Numbers." In E.S. Pearson amd M.G. Kendall, *Studies in the History of Statistics and Probability*, pp. 231–39. London: Griffin.

Sibicky, Mark E., David A. Schroeder, and John F. Dovidio. 1995. "Empathy and Helping: Considering the Consequences of Intervention." *Basic and Applied Psychology* 16:435–53.

Siebert, Darcy C. 2004. "Depression in North Carolina Social Workers: Implications for Practice and Research." *Social Work Research* 28:30–40.

Slater, Michael D., Kimberly L. Henry, Randall C. Swaim, and Lori L. Anderson. 2003. "Violent Media Content and Aggressiveness in Adolescents." *Communication Research* 30:713–36.

Snyder, Douglas K., Robert M. Willis, and Averta Grady-Fletcher. 1991. "Long-term Effectiveness of Behavioral Versus Insight-Oriented Marital Therapy: A 4-Year Follow-up Study." *Journal of Consulting and Clinical Psychology* 59:138–41.

Spoge, Liga, and Janet Trewin. 2003. "The Basics of E-File." *Strategic Finance* 85:13–14.

Steelman, Lala Carr, Brian Powell, and Robert M. Carini. 2000. "Do Teacher Unions Hinder Educational Performance? Lessons Learned from State SAT and ACT Scores." *Harvard Educational Review* 70:437–66.

Struik, Dirk J. 1948. *A Concise History of Mathematics*. New York: Dover.

Takao, Soshi, Norito Kawakami, Tadahiro Ohtsu, and the Japan Work Stress and Health Cohort Study Group. 2003. "Occupational Class and Physical Activity Among Japanese Employees." *Social Science and Medicine* 57:2281–89.

Tohill, Beth C., Jennifer Seymour, Mary Serdula, Laura Kettel-Khan, and Barbara J. Rolls. 2004. "What Epidemiologic Studies Tell Us About the Relationship Between Fruit and Vegetable Consumption and Body Weight." *Nutrition Reviews* 62:365–74.

Tompkins, Peter. 1971. *Secrets of the Great Pyramid*. New York: Harper and Row.

Tukey, J.W. 1953. *The Problem of Multiple Comparisons*. Princeton, N.J.: Princeton University, mimeographed monograph.

Turner, Jonathon B. 1995. "Economic Context and the Effects of Unemployment." *Journal of Health and Social Behavior* 36:213–29.

U.S. Bureau of the Census. 2000. *Census of the Population: General Population Characteristics*. Washington, D.C.: U.S. Government Printing Office. http://eire.census.gov/popest/ national_dataset.csv.

_____. 2003. Population Division. *Children's Living Arrangements and Characteristics: March 2002*. http://www.census.gov/population/socdemo/ hh-fam/cps2002/tabA1-all.pdf.

U.S. Department of Energy. 2004. *U.S. Environmental Protection Agency Fuel Economy Guide: Model Year 2004*. Pub. No. DOE/EE-0283. Washington, D.C.: U.S. Government Printing Office. http://www.fueleconomy.gov/feg/ FEG2004_GasolineVehicles.pdf.

U.S. Department of Health and Human Services. 1999. *Mental Health: A Report of the Surgeon General—Executive Summary*. Rockville, Md.: U.S. Department of Health and Human Services, Substance Abuse and Mental Health Services Administration, Center for Mental Health Services, National Institutes of Health, National Institute of Mental Health. 1999.

U.S. Department of Homeland Security. 2003. *Yearbook of Immigration Statistics, 2002*. Washington, D.C.: U.S. Government Printing Office.

U.S. Federal Bureau of Prisons. "Federal Bureau of Prisons Quick Facts," August 2003. www.bop.gov/fact0598.html.

Varano, Sean P., John D. McCluskey, Justin W. Patchin, and Timothy S. Bynum. 2004. "Exploring the Drugs–Homicide Connection." *Journal of Contemporary Criminal Justice* 20:369–92.

Wee, Christina C., Russell S. Phillips, Anna T.R. Legedza, Roger B. Davis, Jane R. Soukup, Graham A. Colditz, and Mary Beth Hamel. 2005. "Health Care Expenditures Associated with Overweight and Obesity Among U.S. Adults: Importance of Age and Race." *American Journal of Public Health* 95:159–65.

Wiesner, Margit. 2003. "A Longitudinal Latent Variable Analysis of Reciprocal Relations Between Depressive Symptoms and Delinquency During Adolescence." *Journal of Abnormal Psychology* 112:633–45.

Williams, Robin M., Jr. 1970. *American Society,* 3rd ed. New York: Knopf.

Wong, Yin-Ling Irene, and Irving Piliavin. 2001. "Stressors, Resources, and Distress Among Homeless Persons: A Longitudinal Analysis." *Social Science & Medicine* 52:1029–42.

Xiaoxing, Z. He, and David W. Baker. 2004. "Body Mass Index, Physical Activity, and the Risk of Decline in Overall Health and Physical Functioning in Late Middle Age." *American Journal of Public Health* 94:1567–73.

INDEX